HANDBOOK OF MIDDLE AMERICAN INDIANS, VOLUME 16
Sources Cited and Artifacts Illustrated

HANDBOOK OF MIDDLE AMERICAN INDIANS

EDITED AT MIDDLE AMERICAN RESEARCH INSTITUTE, TULANE UNIVERSITY, BY

ROBERT WAUCHOPE, *General Editor*
MARGARET A. L. HARRISON, *Associate Editor*
GERTRUDE P. BROWN, *Administrative Assistant*

ASSEMBLED WITH THE AID OF A GRANT FROM THE NATIONAL SCIENCE FOUNDATION, AND UNDER THE SPONSORSHIP OF THE NATIONAL RESEARCH COUNCIL COMMITTEE ON LATIN AMERICAN ANTHROPOLOGY

Editorial Advisory Board

HANDBOOK OF MIDDLE AMERICAN INDIANS

ROBERT WAUCHOPE, General Editor

VOLUME SIXTEEN

Sources Cited and Artifacts Illustrated

MARGARET A. L. HARRISON, Volume Editor

UNIVERSITY OF TEXAS PRESS   AUSTIN

International Standard Book Number 0-292-73004-7
Library of Congress Catalog Card Number 64-10316
Copyright © 1976 by the University of Texas Press

The preparation and publication of the
Handbook of Middle American Indians
has been assisted by grants from
the National Science Foundation.

Printed in the United States of America

CONTENTS

Part I
SOURCES CITED

Sources Cited

MARGARET A. L. HARRISON

ISTED BELOW are the bibliographical entries, reassembled into one alphabet, of all the works cited in volumes 1–11 of the *Handbook of Middle American Indians*. The cutting and pasting of copy onto some 3500 cards was the work of Gertrude P. Brown.

This composite bibliography does not include citations in volumes 12–15, the four parts of the Guide to Ethnohistorical Sources, because those volumes stand somewhat apart in subject matter and their articles contain or constitute independent bibliographical material. Bibliographies, mostly annotated, form the major part of Article 9 (vol. 12, pp. 370–95), Article 12 (vol. 13, pp. 107–37), and Article 13 (vol. 13, pp. 167–85). In volume 13, Articles 14–21 are biobibliographies, to which are appended a selection of writings by the subject that relate to ethnohistory, as well as publications about him. The whole of Article 32 (vol. 15, pp. 537–724) is an annotated list of works cited in Articles 22–32. It was not thought warranted to repeat in the compilation below the bibliographical information given in fuller form in the eth-nohistory volumes of the series.

The letter following the date of two or more titles published in one year has been removed from the present listings because the same title can be, for example, 1925a in one volume, 1925b or later in another; this differentiation could not, obviously, be matched in the bibliography at hand. Further, such a method of distinguishing these entries has no advantage here, for no text refers to them. The volume References supply this detail wherever the article citation requires it.

Five categories of titles are grouped under their respective headings: Anales, Codices, Documentos, Homenajes, or Relaciones.

Effort has been made to correct previous errors and omissions, and "in press" items have been brought up to date as of January 1975.

Certain titles may be entered more than once and may differ slightly between entries. In a series of eleven volumes, to which some 200 authors contributed 296 pages of bibliography in 197 articles (again, omitting vols. 12–15), the bulk of reference material made it almost impossible to achieve total internal consistency in ordering the variations in which authors cited their sources.

The bibliography in each volume (and therefore in this integration of eleven) was not intended to be a precise compilation based on principles of bibliographic scholarship. It was essentially a list of all the references combined into a single sequence and adjusted to all the articles in an individual volume, which could number as many as forty-three. To produce even such a list took much time for the repair of conflicts, inaccuracies, and omissions thrown up in the merging of the bibliographic cards. In the working out of a scheme that best fitted all the forms submitted on the cards, duplications and inconsistencies inevitably resulted but they were not, it is believed, of great importance. The risk of error made it essential to change an author's citations as little as could be helped. He was asked to bend only to a reasonable consistency in a generally acceptable form. And since a volume's bibliography was not made up until after all articles were edited and sent to the printer, the turning of citations into complete uniformity was not practicable.

If these limitations are understood, the amalgamated bibliography that follows will provide, it is hoped, a useful adjunct to the anthropology, geography, history, and linguistics of Middle America.

ABARCA ALARCÓN, R.
1934 Contribución al estudio de los grupos sanguíneos en México. Mexico.

ABBOTT, E.
1960 An analysis of Mercado Red-on-Cream: a diagnostic ceramic grouping of the Ayala phase of the Chalchihuites culture. Master's thesis, Southern Illinois Univ.

ABEL, T. M., and R. A. CALABRESI
1951 The people as seen from their Rorschach tests. In O. Lewis, 1951, pp. 306–18, 463–90.

ABEL, W.
1934 Hand- und Fingerabdrucke von Feuerlandern. Zeitschr. für Morph. und Anthr., 34: 15–20.

ABOGADO, E. L.
1911 Cuadro estadístico manifestando los resultados de la medición del diámetro bi-isquiático, hecha en 569 enfermas de las atendidas en la sección de ginecología del consultorio no. 2 de la beneficencia pública. Crónica Méd. Mex., 16: 1–224. Mexico.

ABREGO, F.
n.d. Una aplicación de la antropometría en el ejército. Gaceta Médico-Militar, 6: 173–76. Mexico.

ACOSTA, J. DE
1590 Historia natural y moral de las Indias. Seville.

ACOSTA, J. R.
1939 Exploraciones arqueológicas realizadas en el estado de Michoacán durante los años de 1937 y 1938. Rev. Mex. Estud. Antr., 3: 85–98.

1940 Exploraciones en Tula, Hidalgo, 1940. Ibid., 4: 172–94.

1941 Los últimos descubrimientos arqueológicos en Tula, Hidalgo, 1941. Ibid., 5: 239–48.

1944 La tercera temporada en exploraciones arqueológicas en Tula, Hidalgo, 1942. Ibid., vol. 6, no. 3.

1945 Las cuarta y quinta temporadas de exploraciones arqueológicas en Tula, Hidalgo, 1943–1944. Ibid., 7: 23–64.

1949 El pectoral de jade de Monte Alban. An. Inst. Nac. Antr. Hist., 3: 17–26.

1956 El enigma de los chacmooles de Tula.

In Estudios antropológicos, pp. 159–70.

1956 Resumen de los informes de las exploraciones arqueológicas en Tula, Hidalgo, durante las VI, VII y VIII temporadas, 1946–1950. An. Inst. Nac. Antr. Hist., 8: 37–115.

1956–57 Interpretación de algunos de los datos obtenidos en Tula relativos a la época tolteca. Rev. Mex. Estud. Antr., 14: 75–110.

1957 Exploraciones arqueológicas en Tula, Hgo. An. Inst. Nac. Antr. Hist., vol. 9.

1957 Resumen de los informes de las exploraciones arqueológicas en Tula, Hidalgo, durante las IX y X temporadas, 1953–54. Ibid., 9: 119–69.

1958–59 Exploraciones arqueológicas en Monte Alban, XVIII temporada. Rev. Mex. Estud. Antr., 15: 7–50.

1959 Técnicas de la construcción. In Esplendor del México antiguo, 2: 501–18.

1960 La doceava temporada de exploraciones en Tula, Hidalgo. An. Inst. Nac. Antr. Hist., 13: 29–58.

1960 Las exploraciones en Tula, Hidalgo, durante la XI temporada, 1955. Ibid., 11: 39–72.

1961 La doceava temporada de exploraciones en Tula, Hidalgo. Ibid., 13: 29–58.

1961 La indumentaria de las cariátides de Tula. In Homenaje Martínez del Río, pp. 221–28.

1962 El Palacio de las Mariposas de Teotihuacán. Bol. Inst. Nac. Antr. Hist., 9: 5–7.

1964 El Palacio del Quetzalpapalotl. Mem. Inst. Nac. Antr. Hist., no. 10.

1964 La decimotercera temporada de exploraciones en Tula, Hgo. An. Inst. Nac. Antr. Hist., 16: 45–76.

1965 Guía oficial de Teotihuacán. Inst. Nac. Antr. Hist. Mexico.

1966 Una clasificación tentativa de los monumentos arqueológicos de Teotihuacán. In Teotihuacán, pp. 45–56.

—— AND H. MOEDANO KOER
1946 Los juegos de pelota. In México prehispánico, 1946, pp. 365–84.

ACOSTA SAIGNES, M.
1945 Los Pochteca. *Acta Anthr.*, vol. 1, no. 1.
1946 Los Teopixque: organización sacerdotal entre los Mexica. *Rev. Mex. Estud. Antr.*, 8: 147–205.

ADAMS, E. B.
n.d. Tabulation of the encomiendas, encomenderos, and principal items of the tribute in the 1549 tax list. MS. Archivo General de Indias, Guatemala 128.

ADAMS, R. E. W.
1963 The ceramic sequence at Altar de Sacrificios, Guatemala. Doctoral dissertation, Harvard Univ.
1964 The ceramic sequence at Altar de Sacrificios and its implications. *35th Int. Cong. Amer.* (Mexico, 1962).
—— AND A. S. TRIK
1961 Temple I: post-constructional activities. *Mus. Monogr., Univ. Pennsylvania,* Tikal Reports, no. 7.

ADAMS, R. M., JR.
1953 Some small ceremonial structures of Mayapan. *Carnegie Inst. Wash., Current Reports,* no. 9.
1961 Changing patterns of territorial organization in the central highlands of Chiapas, Mexico. *Amer. Antiquity,* 26: 341–60. [Issued in mimeographed form 1960.]
—— AND N. A. McQUOWN
1959 Pre-history, proto-history, and post-conquest developments. *In* McQuown, 1959, Man-in-Nature.

ADAMS, R. N.
1952 Un análisis de las creencias y prácticas médicas en un pueblo indígena de Guatemala. *Inst. Nac. Indig.,* Pub. Especiales, no. 17. Guatemala.
1955 A nutritional research program in Guatemala. *In* B. D. Paul, 1955, pp. 435–58.
1956 La ladinoización en Guatemala. *In* Arriola, 1956, pp. 213–44.
1956 Cultural components of Central America. *Amer. Anthr.,* 58: 881–907.
1956 Encuesta sobre la cultura de los Ladinos en Guatemala. *Seminario de Integración Social Guatemalteca,* Pub. 2.
1957 Cultural surveys of Panama–Nicaragua–Guatemala–El Salvador–Honduras. *Pan Amer. Sanitary Bur., Sci. Pub.* 33.
1957 [comp.] Political changes in Guatemalan Indian communities: a symposium. *Tulane Univ., Middle Amer. Research Inst.,* Pub. 24, pp. 1–54.
1958 The problem of national culture in Central America. *In* Misc. Paul Rivet 1: 341–59.
1959 Freedom and reform in rural Latin America. *In* F. B. Pike, 1959, pp. 203–30.
1960 Exploración de la madera en el municipio de Totonicapan. *Bol. Inst. Indig. Nac.,* vol. 2. Guatemala.
1961 Social change in Guatemala and U.S. policy. *In* Council on Foreign Relations, 1961, pp. 231–84.

ADÁN, E.
1922 La organización actual de los zapotecos. *An. Mus. Nac. Arqueol. Hist. Etnog.,* 1: 53–64.
1927 Nota acerca de unas piedras talladas de aspecto prehistórico, procedentes de Mitla, estado de Oaxaca. *An. Mus. Nac. Mex.,* 5: 157–67.

AGRINIER, P.
1960 The carved human femurs from Tomb 1, Chiapa de Corzo, Chiapas, Mexico. *New World Archaeol. Found.,* Pub. 5, no. 6.

AGÜERO, C. DE
1893 Vocabulario castellano-zapoteco. Sec. Fomento. Mexico.

AGUILAR, F. DE
1579 Historia de la Nueva España. *An. Mus. Nac. Mex.,* ep. 1–7, pp. 3–25 (1903). (Another ed. 1954.)

AGUILAR, F. J.
1941 Parásitos que existen: la tenia equinococo en estado larvario infesta en considerable proporción al cerdo. *Guatemala Méd.,* 6 (11): 4–6.
1944 La equinococosis en Guatemala. Tesis de médico y cirujano, Facultad Cien. Méd., Univ. Nac. Guatemala.
1955 Estado actual del paludismo en Guatemala: epidemiología, análisis de los

índices parasitarios y esplénicos. *Rev. Colegio Méd. Guatemala*, 6: 170–172.

1958 Consideraciones sobre parasitismo intestinal en Guatemala: importancia médico-social. *Ibid.*, 9: 294–301.

1960 Consideraciones sobre toxoplasmosis en Guatemala. Tesis de médico y cirujano, Facultad Cien. Méd., Univ. San Carlos de Guatemala.

—— AND C. VIZCAÍNO GÁMEZ

1954 Cisticercosis en Guatemala. *Rev. Colegio Méd. Guatemala*, 5: 92–98.

AGUILAR P., C. H.

1946 La orfebrería en el México precortesiano. *Acta Anthr.*, vol. 2, no. 2.

1953 Retes, un depósito arqueológico en las faldas del Irazu. San Jose.

AGUILAR Y SANTILLÁN, R.

1908 Bibliografía geológica y minera de la República Mexicana, completada hasta el año de 1904. *Bol. Inst. Geol. de Mex.*, no. 17.

1918 Bibliografía geológica y minera de la República Mexicana, 1905–1918.

1930 Bibliografía geológica y minera de la República Mexicana, correspondiente a los años de 1919 a 1930.

AGUILERA, J. G.

1907 Les volcans du Mexique dans leur relations avec le relief et la tectonique du pays. *10th Int. Cong. Geol., Compte Rendu*, 2: 1155–68.

—— AND E. ORDÓÑEZ

1895 Excursión científica al Popocatépetl.

AGUILERA HERRERA, N.

1955 Los suelos tropicales de Mexico. Inst. Mex. Recursos Naturales Renovables, mesas redondas sobre problemas del trópico mexicano, pp. 3–24.

1959 Suelos. *In* Beltrán, 1959, pp. 177–212.

AGUIRRE, F., O. B. TANDON, AND N. S. SCRIMSHAW

1953 Distribution of blood groups in Guatemalan Indians. *Rec. Genetic Soc. Amer.*, 22: 63 (abstr. in *Genetics*, 38: 653).

AGUIRRE BELTRÁN, G.

1940 El señorío de Cuautochco. Mexico.

1946 La problación negra de México: 1519–1810. Mexico.

1950 Pobladores del Papaloapan. MS.

1952 Problemas de la población indígena de la cuenca del Tepalcatepec. *Inst. Nac. Indig.*, Mem. 3. Mexico.

1953 Formas del gobierno indígena. *Cultura Mex.*, Pub. 5.

1954 *Introduction to* Tlaxiaco, una ciudad mercado, by A. Marroquín. *Inst. Nac. Indig.*, Ed. Mimeográficas, no. 4.

1955 A theory of regional integration: the coordinating centers. *Amer. Indig.*, 15: 29–42. Same in Spanish entitled Teoría de los centros coordinadores, *Ciencias Sociales*, 6 (32): 66–77. Washington.

1957 El proceso de aculturación. Univ. Nac. Autónoma Mex.

1958 Cuijla: esbozo etnográfico de un pueblo negro. Fondo de Cultura Económica. Mexico.

—— AND R. POZAS A.

1954 Instituciones indígenas en el México actual. *In* Caso, 1954, Métodos, pp. 171–272.

AGUIRRE PEQUEÑO, F.

1942 Mal de pinto (autoobservación), empeines o jiotes, lesiones principio, ensayo crítico. *Rev. Méd. Méx.*, 22: 542.

AHLMANN, H. W.

1953 Glacier variations and climatic fluctuations. *Amer. Geog. Soc., Bowman Memorial Lectures*, 3d ser.

ALADRO AZUETA, F.

1944 Informe sobre la exploración sanitaria del municipio de Tlacotepec, Puebla. Mexico.

ALANIZ PATIÑO, E.

1946 La población indígena en México. *In* M. O. Mendizabal, Obras completas, 1: 29–98.

ALBA, C. H.

1949 Las industrias zapotecas. *In* Mendieta y Núñez, 1949, pp. 493–600.

—— AND J. CRISTERNA

1949 La agricultura entre los zapotecos. *Ibid.*, pp. 449–89.

ALBERT, E. M.

1956 The classification of values: a method and illustration. *Amer. Anthr.*, 58: 221–48.

ALBORNOZ, J. DE
1691 Arte de la lengua chiapaneca. MS in Bibliothèque Nationale.

ALBRITTON, C. C.
1958 Quaternary stratigraphy of the Guadiana Valley, Durango, Mexico. *Bull. Geol. Soc. Amer.*, 69: 1197–1216.

ALCALÁ, M.
1906 Sondeos en las lagunas o ciénegas de Almoloya y Lerma. *Bol. Soc. Geol. Mex.*, 2: 15–34.

ALCALÁ DONDÉ, R.
1954 Una vieja tradición campechana. *Yikal Maya Than,* 15 (175): 30, 40–42.

ALCAREZ, A.
1930 Las canacuas. *Mex. Folkways,* 6: 117–28.

ALCOCER, G.
1905 Breves consideraciones acerca de la asistencia al parto. Mexico.

ALCOCER, I.
1935 Apuntes sobre la antigua México-Tenochtitlan. *Inst. Panamer. Geog. Hist.,* Pub. 14.

ALDAMA, F. R.
1945 Geografía del estado de Chihuahua. Chihuahua.

ALDAMA Y GUEVARA, J. A. DE
1754 Arte de la lengua mexicana. (Mexico, 1892.)

ALDRETE, E.
1958 Baja California heroica: episodios de la invasión filibustera-magonista de 1911 por el Sr. Enrique Aldrete, testigo presencial. Mexico.

ALEGRE, F. J.
1841 Historia de la compañía de Jesús en Nueva España al tiempo de su expulsión. C. M. de Bustamante, ed. 3 vols. Mexico.

ALEGRÍA, R. E.
1951 The ball game played by the aborigines of the Antilles. *Amer. Antiquity,* 16: 348–52.

ALEJANDRE, M.
See Alexandre, M.

ALEMÁN, L.
1884 Grammaire élémentaire de la langue Quiché. Suppl. to Compte-rendu, 5th Int. Cong. Amer., 1883. Copenhagen.

ALESSIO ROBLES, V.
1927 Bibliografía de Coahuila. Mexico.
1938 Coahuila y Texas en la época colonial. Mexico.

ALEXANDER, H. B.
1920 Mexico. *In* The mythology of all races, L. H. Gray, ed., 10 (Latin American): 41–123. (2d ed. 1964.)

ALEXANDRE, M.
1890 Cartilla huasteca con su gramática, diccionario y varias reglas para aprender el idioma. Mexico.

ALLBROOK, D.
1961 The estimation of stature in British and East African males. *Jour. Forensic Med.,* 8: 15–29.

ALLEN, C. R., L. T. SILVER, AND F. G. STEHLI
1960 Agua Blanca fault: a major transverse structure of northern Baja California, Mexico. *Bull. Geol. Soc. Amer.,* 71: 457–82.

ALLEN, F. H., JR., L. K. DIAMOND, AND B. NIEDZIELA
1951 A new blood-group antigen. *Nature,* 167: 482. London.

ALLEN, H.
1890 A clinical study of the skull. *Smithsonian Misc. Coll.* Washington.
1896 Crania from the mounds of the Saint John's river, Florida. *Jour. Acad. Natural Sci.,* 10: 367–488.

ALLEN, P. H.
1956 The rain forests of Golfo Dulce. Univ. Florida.

ALLEN, W. E.
1939 Surface distribution of marine plankton diatoms in the Panama region in 1933. *Bull. Scripps Inst. Oceanogr., Univ. Calif., Tech. Ser.,* 4: 181–95.

ALLISON, A. C., O. HARTMANN, O. J. BRENDEMOEN, AND A. E. MOURANT
1952 The blood groups of the Norwegian Lapps. *Acta Pathol. Microbiol. Scand.,* 31: 334–38.

ALMADA, F. R.
1945 Geografía del estado de Chihuahua. Chihuahua.

ALMARAZ, R.
1865 Apuntes sobre las pirámides de San Juan Teotihuacán. *In* Memorias y Trabajos ejecutados por la Comisión

Científica de Pachuca en el año de 1864, pp. 349–58. Mexico.

ALMEIDA, R. DE
1957 Mutilaçoes dentárias nos Negros da Lunda: memoria descritiva de dois casos raros de anomalias dentárias. Companhia de diamantes de Angola (Diamang). *Pub. Culturais*, no. 33. Lisbon.

ALOJA, A. D'
1939 Informe sobre la investigación antropológica-demográfica realizada en Centroamérica. *Inst. Panamer. Geog. Hist.*, Pub. 39. Mexico.
1939 Sobre la variabilidad de algunos caracteres antropométricos observados en grupos de indígenas centroamericanos. *Ibid.*, Pub. 43.
1943 Estudio somatométrico de los Chinantecos. *In* Comas, 1943, La antropología física.

ALVA, B. DE
1634 Confesionario mayor y menor en lengua mexicana. Mexico.

ALVA IXTLILXOCHITL, F. DE
1838 Cruautés horribles des conquérants du Mexique. Paris.
1891–92 Obras históricas. A. Chavero, ed. Vol. 1: Relaciones. Vol. 2: Historia de la nación chichimeca. Mexico. (Reprinted 1952.)

ALVARADO, F. DE
1593 Vocabulario en lengua mixteca, hecha por los padres de la orden de predicadores, que residen en ella, y últimamente recopilado y acabado por el Padre . . . Vicario de Tamazulapa, de la misma orden. Facsimile ed., ed. by W. Jiménez Moreno. Inst. Nac. Indigenista and Inst. Nac. Antr. Hist. Mexico, 1962.

ALVARADO, J.
1959 Cardiopatías congénitas: estudio de 40 casos. Tesis de médico y cirujano, Facultad Cien. Méd., Univ. San Carlos de Guatemala.

ALVARADO, JOSÉ
1939 Hipótesis sobre la cerámica tarasca. *Rev. Artes Plásticas*, 2: 57–69. Mexico.

ALVARADO, P. DE
1838 Lettres à Fernand Cortés. *In* Ter-naux Compans, Recueil de pièces relatives à la conquête du Mexique, pp. 107–50. Paris.
1924 An account of the conquest of Guatemala in 1524. Ed. and tr. by S. J. Mackie. *Cortés Soc.*, no. 3. New York.

ALVARADO GARCÍA, E.
1958 Legislación indigenista de Honduras. *Inst. Indig. Interamer.*, Ed. Especiales, no. 35. Mexico.

ALVARADO TEZOZOMOC, H.
1878 Crónica mexicana escrita hacia el año de 1598. (Reprinted 1944.)
1949 Crónica mexicayotl. A. León, trans. *Univ. Nac. Autónoma Méx.*, Pub. Inst. Hist., 1st ser., no. 10.

ALVAREZ, C.
1953 Tifo exantemático — epidemiología. *Rev. Colegio Méd. Guatemala*, 4: 14–17.

ALVAREZ, I.
1955 A Yaqui Easter sermon. *Univ. Arizona, Social Sci. Bull.* 26.

ALVAREZ, M. F.
1900 Las ruinas de Mitla y la arquitectura. Mexico.

ALVAREZ MORALES, C. E.
1940 El problema del escleroma en Guatemala. Tesis de médico y cirujano, Facultad Cien. Méd., Univ. San Carlos de Guatemala.

ALVAREZ RUBIANO, P.
1944 Pedrarias Dávila. Inst. Gonzalo Fernández de Oviedo. Madrid.

AMAYA, J.
1951 Ameca, protofundación mexicana. Mexico.

AMEZQUITA BORJA, F.
1943 Música y danza de la sierra norte de Puebla. Puebla, Mexico.

AMIR, R. G.
1957 Magdalena Milpas Altas: 1880–1952. *In* R. N. Adams, 1957, Political changes, pp. 9–14.

AMRAM, D. W., JR.
1937 Eastern Chiapas, Mexico. *Amer. Geog. Rev.*, vol. 27, no. 1.
1948 Eastern Chiapas revisited. *Ibid.*, vol. 38, no. 1.

9

AMSDEN, C. A.
1935 The Pinto Basin artifacts. *In* Campbell and Campbell, 1935, pp. 33–51.
1936 A prehistoric rubber ball. *Masterkey*, 10 (1): 7–8.

AMSDEN, M.
1928 Archaeological reconnaissance in Sonora. *SW. Mus. Papers*, no. 1.

ANALES:
Cakchiquels
1953 The Annals of the Cakchiquels. A. Recinos and D. Goetz, trans. Univ. Oklahoma Press.

Cuauhtitlan
1938 Die Geschichte der Königreiche von Colhuacan und Mexiko. W. Lehmann, ed. and trans. Quellenwerke zur alten Geschichte Amerikas Aufgezeichnet in den Sprachen der Eingeborenen. *Ibero-Amerikanischen Inst.*, I. Berlin.
1945 Códice Chimalpopoca: Anales de Cuauhtitlan y Leyenda de los Soles. P. F. Velázquez, ed. and trans. *Univ. Nac. Autónoma Méx., Pub. Inst. Hist.*, 1st ser, no. 1.

Mexicanos
1903 Anales del Museo Nacional, ep. 1, 7: 49–74. Mexico.

Tecamachalco
1903 A. Peñafiel, ed. *In* Col. doc. para la historia mexicana. Mexico.

Tlatelolco
1939–40 Unos annales históricos de la nación mexicana: Die Manuscrits mexicains nr. 22 und 22bis der Bibliothèque Nationale de Paris. E. Mengin, ed. *Baessler-Archiv*, 22 (2–3): 73–168; 23 (4): 115–39. Berlin.
1945 Unos annales históricos de la nación mexicana: manuscrit mexicain nr. 22, nr. 22bis. E. Mengin, ed. *Corpus Codicum Americanorum Medii Aevi*, 2. Copenhagen.
1948 Anales de Tlatelolco: Unos annales históricos de la nación mexicana y códice de Tlatelolco. H. Berlin and R. H. Barlow, eds. *Fuentes para la historia de México*, 2. Mexico.

ANCIENT OAXACA
1966 Ancient Oaxaca: Discoveries in Mexican archeology and history. J. Paddock, ed. Stanford Univ. Press.

ANCONA, E.
1878 Historia de Yucatan desde la época más remota hasta nuestros días. Merida. 2d ed. 1889, Barcelona.

ANDERSON, A.
1957 Two Chol texts. *Tlalocan*, 3 (4): 313–16.

ANDERSON, A. E.
1932 Artifacts of the Rio Grande delta region. *Bull. Texas Archaeol. Paleontol. Soc.*, 4.

ANDERSON, A. H., AND H. J. COOK
1944 Archaeological finds near Douglas, British Honduras. *Carnegie Inst. Wash., Notes Middle Amer. Archaeol. Ethnol.*, no. 40.

ANDERSON, A. J. O.
1963 Materiales colorantes prehispánicos. *Inst. Hist., Estud. Cultura Náhuatl*, no. 4. Mexico.

—— AND C. E. DIBBLE
1950–69 *See* Sahagún, 1950–69.

ANDERSON, E.
1946 Report on maize from Cheran. *In* Beals, 1946, pp. 219–23.
1960 The evolution of domestication. *In* Tax, 1960, Evolution after Darwin, 2: 67–84.

—— AND R. H. BARLOW
1943 The maize tribute of Moctezuma's empire. *Ann. Missouri Botanical Garden*, 30: 413–20.

ANDERSON, J. E.
1965 Human skeletons of Tehuacan. *Science*, 148 (3669): 496–97.

ANDERSON, R. K., J. CALVO, G. SERRANO, AND G. C. PAYNE
1946 A study of the nutritional status and food habits of Otomi Indians in the Mezquital Valley of Mexico. *Amer. Jour. Public Health*, 36: 883–903.

—— AND OTHERS (J. CALVO, W. D. ROBINSON, G. SERRANO, AND G. C. PAYNE)
1948 Nutrition appraisals in Mexico. *Ibid.*, 38: 1126–35.

ANDERSON, J. G.
1932 Hunting magic in the animal style. *Mus. Far Eastern Antiquities*, Bull. 4, pp. 221–317.

ANDRADE, M.
1945 Investigación de la coccidioidiomico-
sis en la capital de Guatemala, por
medio de la intradermoreacción a la
coccidioidina. Tesis de médico y
cirujano, Facultad Cien. Méd., Univ.
San Carlos de Guatemala.

ANDRADE, M. J.
1940 A grammar of modern Yucatec. *Micro. Coll. MS Middle Amer. Cult.
Anthr.*, no. 41 (1957), Univ. Chicago
Library. 476 pp.
1946 Materials on the Quiche, Cakchiquel,
and Tzutuhil languages. *Ibid.*, no
11. 942 pp.
1946 Materiales sobre las lenguas Mam,
Jacalteca, Aguateca, Chuj, Bachahon,
Palencano, y Lacandone. *Maca*, 10.
1946 Materiales sobre las lenguas Quiche,
Cakchiquel y Tzutuhil. *Ibid.*, 11.
1946 Materiales sobre las lenguas Kekchi
y Pokomam. *Ibid.*, 12.

ANDREE, R.
1902 Die Älteste Nachricht ueber die sogennanten Azteken-Mikrocephalen.
*Ver. Berliner Gesellschaft für Anthr.,
Ethnol., und Urgeschichte*, pp. 219–
21.

ANDRESEN, P. H.
1948 The blood group system L—a new
blood group L2: a case of epistasy
within the blood groups. *Acta
Pathol., Microbiol. Scand.*, 25: 728–
31.

ANDREWS, E. W., IV
1939 A group of related sculptures from
Yucatan. *Carnegie Inst. Wash.*,
Pub. 509, Contrib. 26.
1940 Chronology and astronomy in the
Maya area. *In* The Maya and their
neighbors, pp. 150–61.
1942 Yucatan: architecture. *Carnegie
Inst. Wash.*, Year Book 41, pp. 257–
63.
1943 The archaeology of southwestern
Campeche. *Carnegie Inst. Wash.*,
Pub. 546, Contrib. 40.
1951 The Maya supplementary series. *In*
Tax, 1951, pp. 123–41.
1959 Dzibilchaltun: lost city of the Maya.
Nat. Geog. Mag., 115: 90–109.
1960 Excavations at Dzibilchaltun, north-

western Yucatan, Mexico. *Proc.
Amer. Phil. Soc.*, 104: 254–65.
1961 Excavations at the Gruta de Balan-
kanche, 1959. *Tulane Univ., Middle Amer. Research Inst., Misc. Ser.*,
no. 11, pp. 28–40 [appendix to next
entry].
1961 Preliminary report on the 1959–60
field season, National Geographic
Society–Tulane University Dzibilchaltun program. *Ibid.*, no. 11.
1962 Excavaciones en Dzibilchaltun, Yucatan, 1956–1962. *Univ. Nac. Autónoma Mex., Estud. Cultura Maya*,
2: 149–83.
1965 Archaeology and prehistory in the
northern Maya lowlands: an introduction. *In* Handbook of Middle American Indians, R. Wauchope, ed., vol.
2, art. 12.
1965 Progress report on the 1960–1964
field seasons, National Geographic Society—Tulane University Dzibilchaltun Project. *Tulane Univ., Middle
Amer. Research Inst.*, Pub. 31, pp.
23–67.

ANGEL, FR.
18thC [a] Arte de lengua cakchiquel. . . .
MS in Bibliothèque Nationale.
18thC [b] Vocabulario de la lengua cakchiquel. *Ibid.* 452 pp.
18thC [c] Vocabulario de la lengua cakchiquel. Photograph in Newberry Library. 718 pp.

ANGHIERA, P. M. D'
1612 De nouo orbe *or* The historie of the
West Indies. R. Eden and M. Lok,
trans. London.
1912 De orbe novo, the eight decades of
Peter Martyr d'Anghiera. Tr. from
Latin with notes and introduction by
F. A. McNutt. 2 vols. New York
and London.
1944 Décadas del nuevo mundo (1530).
Buenos Aires.

ANGULO, J. DE
1925 The linguistic tangle of Oaxaca.
Language, 1: 96–102.
1925 Kinship terms in some languages of
southern Mexico. *Amer. Anthr.*, 27:
103–07.

1926 Tone patterns and verb forms in a dialect of Zapotek. *Language*, 2: 238–50.

1926 The development of affixes in a group of monosyllabic languages of Oaxaca. *Ibid.*, 2: 46–61.

1932 The Chichimeco language (central Mexico). *Int. Jour. Amer. Ling.*, 7: 152–94.

—— AND L. S. FREELAND

1925 The Chontal language (dialect of Tequisistlan). *Anthropos*, 20: 1032–52.

1933–35 The Zapotekan linguistic group. *Int. Jour. Amer. Ling.*, 8: 1–38, 111–30.

ANLEO, B.

1744 Arte de lengua quiché.

1865 Arte de lengua Giche. *In* Squier, 1865.

ANONYMOUS

n.d. Chronicle of Oxkutzcab. MS. Peabody Mus., Harvard Univ.

n.d. Huichol and Aztec texts and dictionaries. *Univ. Chicago, Summer Inst. Ling.*, Microfilm 27.

n.d. Relation of the capital city of Atitlan. MS. Univ. Texas Library.

ca. 1580 Vocabulario en lengua Cakchiquel y Quiche. Photographic copy by W. E. Gates in Bowditch Coll., Peabody Mus., Harvard Univ.

1590 Dictionarium ex bismensi. . . . MS in Newberry Library. 314 pp.

1598 Vocabulario mexicano. Photograph in Newberry Library. 236 pp.

17thC? Bocabulario en lengua cakchiquel y quiche. Photograph in Newberry Library. 706 pp.

17thC? Bocabulario de lengua quiché. Photograph in Newberry Library. 78 pp.

17thC? Bocabulario de lengua quiché y castellana. Photograph in Newberry Library. 372 pp.

17thC? Calepino grande, castellano y quiché. Photograph in Newberry Library. 480 pp.

17thC Diccionario de San Francisco: maya-español, español-maya. Photograph in Newberry Library. 402 pp.

17thC Noticia breve de los vocablos más usuales de la lengua cakchiquel. MS in Bibliothèque Nationale. 182 pp.

17thC Vocabulario en lengua castellana y . . . cakchiquelchi. Photograph in Newberry Library. 500 pp.

18thC? Vocabulario de la lengua castellana y quiché. MS in Bibliothèque Nationale. 200 pp.

18thC Vocabulario hispano-hyaqui. MS in Newberry Library. 999 pp.

1733 Vocabulario de la lengua çoque. MS in John Carter Brown Library. 354 pp.

1750 Vocabulario otomí [Spanish-Otomi]. MS in Newberry Library. 571 pp.

1800 Arte zaapoteco. . . . MS in Newberry Library. 309 pp.

1838 Requête de plusieurs chefs indiens d'Atitlan à Philippe II. *In* H. Ternaux-Compans, Voyages, relations et mémoires originaux . . . : Receuil de pièces relatives à la conquête du Mexique. Paris.

1855 Les Aztèques: leur véritable caractère, leur origine, leurs aventures, leurs droits sociaux. *Le Moniteur des Hôpitaux*, ser. 1, 3: 753–54. Paris.

1862 Grammar of the Pima or Névome. . . . Buckingham Smith, ed. *J. G. Shea's Library of American Linguistics*, no. 5.

1863 Historia de Welinna, leyenda yucateca. Merida.

1875 Zaccicoxol ó baile de Cortés: Coban. *Univ. Pennsylvania, Univ. Mus., Berendt Coll.*, no. 56.

1884 A grammar of the Cakchiquel language. . . . *Proc. Amer. Phil. Soc.*, 21: 345–412.

1887 Gramática de la lengua zapoteca. . . . Antonio Peñafiel, ed. Mexico.

1890 Arte de la lengua cahita.

1893 Vocabulario castellano - zapoteco. . . . Mexico.

1893 Luces del otimí. Mexico.

1900 Zapoteken, grosser Eingeborenenstamm in Mexiko. *Handworterbuch der Zoologie, Anthropologie, und Ethnologie*, 8: 657–58. Breslau.

1902 Are va vuhil tioxilah evangelio rech ka nima ahaval Jesucristo kereka San Marcos. Belize. (San Jose, 1899.)

1912 Cuadros de Mestizos del Museo Nacional de México. *An. Mus. Nac. Arqueol., Hist., Etnog.,* ep. 3, 4: 237–48. Mexico.

1928 Anthropometric measurements of Mayas. *El Palacio,* 24: 85. Santa Fe.

1932 Natabal nu-tinamit—The memory of my village. *Maya Soc. Quar.,* 1 (2): 71.

1933 Aztec sculpture. *Amer. Mag. Art,* 26: 485–94. New York.

1939–48 Collected materials on Chol, Tojolabal, and Tzotzil. *Univ. Chicago, Summer Inst. Ling.,* Microfilm 26.

1944 Pastorela de viejos *Tlalocan,* 1 (3): 169–93.

1945 México: leyendas y costumbres, trajes y danzas. Mexico.

1946 Cuendú hanga: Mixteco. Summer Inst. Ling. Mexico.

1948 Primer congreso de la juventud zapoteca. *Bol. Indig.,* 8: 274–76.

1950 Alfabeto para los cuatro idiomas mayoritarios de Guatemala. *Pub. Especiales Inst. Ind. Nac.,* no. 10. Guatemala.

1952 El caballo endemoniado (tradición maya). *Yikal Maya Than,* 13 (145–50): 17–19.

1957 Data report: surface water temperatures at shore stations, United States west coast and Baja California, 1955. SIO Reference 57-28, 5 July 1957. (Baja California data taken under direction of Carl L. Hubbs, pp. 50–56.)

1958 Präkolumbische Kunst aus Mexiko und Mittelamerika. Haus der Kunst, München.

1960 Investigaciones arqueológicas. *Bol. Inst. Nac. Antr. Hist.,* 2: 5–9. Mexico.

ANONYMOUS CONQUEROR
   See Conquistador Anónimo, El.

ANTÓN, F.

1961 Mexiko, Indianerkunst aus präkolumbischer Zeit. Munich.

1965 Alt-Mexiko und seine Kunst. Leipzig.

—— AND F. DOCKSTADER

1968 Pre-Columbian art and later Indian tribal arts. New York.

ANTÓN, M.

1892 Antropología de los pueblos de América anteriores al descubrimiento. Madrid.

ARA, D. DE

16thC [Copanaguastla Tzeltal grammar.] MS in Newberry Library, subtitled Egregium opus. . . . 40 pp.

1571 Bocabulario en lengua tzeldal. Photograph in Newberry Library. 328 pp.

ARAGÓN, E. O.

1904 El ángulo útil (pelvimetría). Mexico.

1906 Algunas consideraciones sobre la mensuración torácica. *Rev. Med.,* 17: 249–56. Mexico.

ARAGÓN, J. O.

1931 Expansión territorial del imperio mexicano. *An. Mus. Nac. Arqueol. Hist. Etnog.,* ep. 4, 7 (1): 5–64.

ARAI, A. T.

1960 La arquitectura de Bonampak: ensayo de interpretación del arte maya; viaje a las ruinas de Bonampak. Mexico.

ARANA OSNAYA, F.

1953 Reconstrucción del Prototototonaco. *In* Huastecos, Totonacos y sus vecinos, pp. 123–30.

1957 Relaciones internas del tronco Mixteco. Master's thesis. [Published in 1960 in *An. Inst. Nac. Antr. Hist.,* pp. 22–73.]

1959 Relaciones internas del Mixteco-Trique. *An. Inst. Nac. Antr. Hist.,* 12: 219–73.

1959 Afinidades lingüísticas del Cuitlateco. *33d Int. Cong. Amer.* (San Jose, 1958), Acta, 2: 560–72.

1964 La posición lingüística del huave. *35th Int. Cong. Amer.* (Mexico, 1962), Acta, 2: 471–75.

1966 Posibles relaciones externas del grupo lingüístico maya. MS.

ARCHAEOLOGICAL SALVAGE PROGRAM FIELD OFFICE

1958 Appraisal of the archaeological resources of Diablo Reservoir, Val Verde County, Texas. Austin.

ARCHIVO DE LA NACIÓN, MEXICO
  Documents: Civil, 516; Inquisición, 37; Indios, 3, exp. 540; Tierras: 24, exp. 6; 34, exp. 1: 400, exp. 1: 3343.
  1935 Licencia para buscar antiguos tesoros. (General de parte 1587, vol. 3, p. 181.) *Bol. Archivo General de la Nación,* vol. 6.
  1935 Las pirámides de San Juan Teotihuacán en 1760. (General de parte 1760, vol. 41, fs. 225.) *Ibid.,* vol. 6.
ARCHIVO GENERAL DE INDIAS, SEVILLE
  1548–51 Un libro de tasaciones de los naturales de las provincias de Guatemala, Nicaragua, Yucatan, y pueblos de Comayagua. Guatemala, leg. 128.
  1604–07 Salinas. . . . Mexico, leg. 72. Extracted by E. B. Adams.
AREIZAGA MILLAN, M.
  1945 Estudio sanitario del municipio de Teziutlan, Puebla. Mexico.
ARELLANO, A. R. V.
  1946 Datos geológicos sobre la antigüedad del hombre en la cuenca de Mexico. *Mem. 2d Cong. Mex. Cienc. Sociales,* 5: 213–19.
  1946 El elefante fósil de Tepexpan y el hombre primitivo. *Rev. Mex. Estud. Antr.,* 8: 89–94.
  1951 The Becerra formation (latest Pleistocene) of central Mexico. *18th Int. Cong. Geol.,* pt. 11 (Proc. sec. K: Correlation of Continental Vertebrate-bearing Rocks), pp. 55–62. London.
  1951 Some new aspects of the Tepexpan Man case. *Bull. Texas Archaeol. and Paleontol. Soc.,* 22: 217–24.
  1953 Barrilaco Pedocal, a stratigraphic marker ca. 5000 B.C. and its climatic significance. *19th Int. Cong. Geol.,* Compte Rendu, sec. 7 (Déserts actuels et anciens, fascicule 1), pp. 53–76. Algiers.
  1953 Estratigrafía de la cuenca de Mexico. *Mem. Cong. Cien. de Mex.,* 3: 172–85.
  —— AND F. MÜLLER
  1948 La cueva encantada de Chimalacatlan, Morelos. *Bol. Soc. Mex. Georg. y Estad.,* 66: 483–91.

ARENAS, P. DE
  n.d. Vocabulario manual de las lenguas castellana y mexicana. . . . Calderón ed. 151 pp. (Other eds.: n.d., 1611, 1728; Puebla, 1793, 1887.)
ARÉVALO, R. A.
  1953 Labor desarrollada en el departamento de encuestas radiológico-pulmonares de la liga nacional contra la tuberculosis, de Mayo de 1949 a Junio de 1952. *Rev. Colegio Méd. Guatemala,* 4: 218–22.
ARGUEDAS R. DE LA BORBOLLA, S., AND L. AVELEYRA ARROYO DE ANDA
  1953 A Plainview point from northern Tamaulipas. *Amer. Antiquity,* 18: 392–93.
ARIAS, J.
  1959 Aspectos demográficos de la población indígena de Guatemala. *Bol. Estadístico,* nos. 1–2, pp. 18–38. Guatemala.
ARIAS LARRETA, A.
  1951 Literaturas aborígenes. Los Angeles.
ARIAS TEJADA, J. M.
  1957 Alcoholismo: urgente problema médico social. Tesis de médico y cirujano, Facultad Cien. Méd., Univ. San Carlos de Guatemala.
ARLEGUI, J.
  1737 Crónica de la Provincia de N.S.R.S. Francisco de Zacatecas. Mexico.
ARMENTA, J.
  1957 Hallazgos prehistóricos en el valle de Puebla. *Centro de Estud. Hist. de Puebla,* no. 2.
  1959 Hallazgo de un artefacto asociado con mamut, en el valle de Puebla. *Inst. Nac. Antr. e Hist.,* Pub. 7. Mexico.
ARMILLAS, P.
  1942–44 Oztuma, Guerrero, fortaleza de los mexicanos en la frontera de Michoacán. *Rev. Mex. Estud. Antr.,* 6: 165–75.
  1944 Exploraciones recientes en Teotihuacán, México. *Cuad. Amer.,* 16 (4): 121–36. Mexico.
  1945 Expediciones en el occidente de Guerrero. II: El grupo de Armillas, febrero-marzo, 1944. *Tlalocan,* 2: 73–85.
  1948 Arqueología del occidente de Guerre-

ro. *In* El Occidente de México, pp. 74–76.

1948 Fortalezas mexicanas. *Cuad. Amer.*, 41: 143–63.

1949 Notas sobre sistemas de cultivo en Mesoamérica. *An. Inst. Nac. Antr. Hist.*, 3: 85–113.

1949 Un pueblo de artesanos en la Sierra Madre del Sur, estado de Guerrero, México. *Amer. Indig.*, 9: 237–44.

1950 Teotihuacán, Tula y los Toltecas: las culturas post-arcaicas y pre-aztecas del centro de México: excavaciones y estudios, 1922–1950. *Runa*, 3: 37–70. Buenos Aires.

1951 Mesoamerican fortifications. *Antiquity*, 25: 77–86.

1951 Technology, socio-economic organization, and religion in Mesoamerica. *In* Tax, 1951, pp. 19–30. Tr. by A. J. Rubel.

1957 Programa de historia de la América indígena. Part 1: América precolombina. *Pan Amer. Union, Social Sci. Monogr.*, no. 2. (Also published in English, 1958.)

1962 Volumen y forma en la plástica aborigen. *In* Cuarenta siglos de plástica mexicana. Mexico.

1963 Investigaciones arqueológicas en el estado de Zacatecas. *Bol. Inst. Nac. Antr. Hist.*, 14: 16–17.

1964 Northern Mesoamerica. *In* Jennings and Norbeck, 1964, pp. 291–329.

1964 Condiciones ambientales y movimientos de pueblos en la frontera septentrional de Mesoamérica. *In* Homenaje Márquez-Miranda, pp. 62–82.

——, A. PALERM, AND E. R. WOLF

1956 A small irrigation system in the valley of Teotihuacan. *Amer. Antiquity*, 21: 396–99.

ARNDT, W. W.

1959 The performance of glottochronology in Germanic. *Language*, 35: 180–92.

ARNOLD, B. A.

1957 Late Pleistocene and Early Recent changes in land forms, climate, and archaeology in central Baja California. *Univ. California Pub. Geog.*, 10: 201–318.

ARNOLD, J. R., AND W. F. LIBBY

1950 Radiocarbon dates (September 1, 1950). Univ. Chicago, Inst. Nuclear Studies.

1951 Radiocarbon dates. *Science*, 113: 111–20.

ARPEE, L. H.

1935 Los indios tarahumaras de Chihuahua, México. *An. Mus. Nac. Arqueol. Hist. Etnog.*, ep. 5, 2: 461–77. Mexico.

ARREAGA, A.

1946 Los Pocomames orientales: su frontera lingüística. *Bol. Inst. Indig. Nac. Guatemala*, 1 (2–3): 47–52.

ARREGUI, D. L. DE

1946 Descripción de la Nueva Galicia. F. Chevalier, ed. Seville.

ARREOLA, J. M.

1921 *See* M. Gamio, 1921.

1922 Sellos, indumentaria, utensilios domésticos, utensilios industriales, objetos rituales, caracteres alfabéticos o numéricos. *In* M. Gamio, 1922, 1: 212–20.

ARRIAGA CERVANTES, E.

1944 Exploración sanitaria de Tlatlauqui, Puebla. Mexico.

ARRIOLA, J. L., ed.

1956 Integración social en Guatemala. *Seminario de Integración Social Guatemalteca*, Pub. 3. Guatemala.

1957 Integración económica de Centroamérica. Organización de Estados Centroamericanos. Guatemala.

ARROT, C. R.

1953 La cerámica moderna, hecha a mano en Santa Apolonia. *Antr. Hist. Guatemala*, 5:3–10.

ARROYAVE, G., H. SANDSTEAD, AND R. SCHUMACHER

1958 Relation of urinary creatinine and vitamins to nutritional status in preschool children. *Federation Proc.* 17: 469.

——, N. S. SCRIMSHAW, O. PINEDA, AND M. A. GUZMÁN

1960 Electrophoretic pattern of hyperproteinemic sera in a population group of rural Panama. *Amer. Jour. Tropical Med. and Hygiene*, 9: 81–84.

———, F. VITERI, M. BÉHAR, AND N. S. SCRIMSHAW
1959 Impairment of intestinal absorption of vitamin A palmitate in severe protein malnutrition (kwashiorkor). *Amer. Jour. Clinical Nutrition,* 7: 185–90.

ARSANDAUX, H., AND P. RIVET
1921 Contribution à l'étude de la métallurgie mexicaine. *Jour. Soc. Amer. Paris,* vol. 13.

ARTE PRECOLOMBINO DEL OCCIDENTE DE MÉXICO
1946 Monografía que la Dirección General de Educación Estética publica con motivo de su exposición. Estudios de S. Toscano, P. Kirchhoff, y D. Rubín de la Borbolla. Mexico.

ARTEAGA, C., M. SALAZAR-MALLÉN, E. L. UGALDE, AND A. VELÉZ-OROZCO
1952 Blood agglutinogens of the Mexicans. *Ann. Eugenics,* 16: 351–58.

ARZOBISPADO DE MÉXICO
1897 *See* García Pimentel, 1897; Paso y Troncoso, 1905–06, vol. 3.

ASCENSIÓN, A. DE LA
1916 Relation of the journey . . . Viscaino (1602). *In* Bolton, 1916.

ASCHER, R.
1962 Ethnography for archeology: a case from the Seri Indians. *Ethnology,* 1: 360–69.

——— AND F. J. CLUNE, JR.
1960 Waterfall Cave, southern Chihuahua, Mexico. *Amer. Antiquity,* 26: 270–74.

ASCHMANN, HERMAN P.
1946 Totonaco phonemes. *Int. Jour. Amer. Ling.,* 12: 34–43.

ASCHMANN, HOMER
1952 A fluted point from central Baja California. *Amer. Antiquity,* 17: 262–63.
1952 A primitive food preparation technique in Baja California. *SW. Jour. Anthr.,* 8: 36–39.
1959 The central desert of Baja California: demography and ecology. *Ibero-Amer.,* no. 42.
1960 The subsistence problem in Mesoamerican history. *Pan Amer. Union, Social Sci. Monogr.,* 10: 1–11.

ASCHMANN, P.
1956 Vocabulario totonaco: coordinación alfabética del totonaco de la Sierra de Veracruz y de Puebla. *Inst. Ling. Verano.* Mexico.

ASCOLI, W., N. S. SCRIMSHAW, AND A. BRUCH
1961 La vitamina A y su relación a la hiperqueratosis folicular y el bocio endémico en niños escolares de Ciudad Vieja, Guatemala. *Rev. Colegio Méd. Guatemala,* 12: 30–33.

ASKINASY, S.
1938 Notes anthropologiques: voyage au Yucatán, 1935. *Rev. Anthr.,* 48: 80–82. Paris.
1939 México indígena. Mexico.

ASTROV, M.
1946 The winged serpent: an anthology of American Indian prose and poetry. New York.

ASTURIAS, F.
1902 Historia de la medicina en Guatemala. Tesis de médico y cirujano, Facultad Cien. Méd., Univ. Nac. Guatemala.

ASTURIAS, M. A.
1948 Leyendas de Guatemala. Buenos Aires.

ATWOOD, E. B.
1953 A survey of verb forms in the eastern United States. *Studies Amer. English,* no. 2. Ann Arbor.

ATWOOD, W. W.
1933 Home of the ancient Maya civilization in Central America. *Proc. 5th Pac. Sci. Cong.,* 2: 1379–89. Toronto.

AUBERT DE LA RÜE, E.
1958 L'homme et les volcans. Paris.

AUBIN, J. M. A.
1885 Mémoires sur la peinture didactique et l'écriture figurative des anciens Mexicains. Paris.
1893 Histoire de la nation mexicaine depuis le départ d'Aztlan jusqu'à l'arrivée des conquérants espagnols (et au delà 1607). Paris.

AUBURTIN, E., LE BRET, AND L. A. GOSSE
1862 Instructions ethnologiques pour le Mexique. *Bull. Soc. Anthr. Paris,* 3: 212–37.

AUGUR, H.
1929 Blindness among Mexican Indians. *Science*, 70: xiv.
1954 Zapotec. New York.

AULIE, E., AND W. AULIE
1953 Terminos de parentesco en Chol. *Mem. Cong. Cien. Mex., Cien. Sociales*, 12: 151–58.

AUTRET, M., AND M. BÉHAR
1954 Síndrome policarencial infantil (kwashiorkor) and its prevention in Central America. *FAO Nutritional Studies*, no. 13. Rome, Italy, Food and Agriculture Organization of the United Nations.

AVELEYRA ARROYO DE ANDA, L.
1948 El hombre de Tamazulapan. *Mem. Acad. Mex. de Hist.*, 7: 3–15.
1950 Prehistoria de Mexico. Ediciones mexicanas, S.A.
1951 Reconocimiento arqueológico en la zona de la Presa Internacional Falcón, Tamaulipas y Texas. *Rev. Mex. Estud. Antr.*, 12: 31–59.
1954 Productos geológicos del valle de Mexico: marco cultural. *Ibid.*, 14: 41–52.
1955 El segundo mamut fósil de Santa Isabel Iztapan, Mexico, y artefactos asociados. *Inst. Nac. Antr. e Hist.*, Pub. 1.
1956 La Cueva de la Paila, cercana a Parras, Coahuila. *In* Cueva de la Candelaria, Aveleyra Arroyo de Anda and Maldonado-Koerdell, eds., vol. 1. *Mem. Inst. Nac. Antr. Hist.*, 5. Mexico.
1956 The second mammoth and associated artifacts at Santa Isabel Iztapan, Mexico. *Amer. Antiquity*, 22: 12–28.
1959 Los cazadores del mamut, primeros habitantes de México. *In* Esplendor del México antiguo, 1: 53–72. Centro Invest. Antr. de Mex.
1961 El primer hallazgo Folsom en territorio mexicano y su relación con el complejo de puntas acanaladas en Norteamérica. *In* Homenaje a Pablo Martínez del Río, pp. 31–48.
1962 Antigüedad del hombre en Mexico y Centroamérica: catálogo razonado de localidades y bibliografía selecta (1867–1961). *Cuad. Inst. Hist., Ser. Antr.*, no. 14.
1963 Le estela teotihuacana de La Ventilla. *Inst. Nac. Antr. Hist., Cuad. Mus. Nac. Antr.*, 1. Mexico.
1964 Obras selectas del arte prehispánico (adquisiciones recientes). Fotografías de I. Groth-Kimball. Consejo para la planeación e instalación del Museo Nacional de Antropología. Mexico.
1964 El sacro de Tequixquiac. *Cuad. Mus. Nac. Antr.*, no. 2.

—— AND M. MALDONADO-KOERDELL
1952 Asociación de artefactos con mamut en el Pleistoceno Superior de la cuenca de Mexico. *Rev. Mex. Estud. Antr.*, 13: 3–29.
1953 Association of artifacts with mammoth in the valley of Mexico. *Amer. Antiquity*, 18: 332–40.
1956 Cueva de la Candelaria. *Mem. Inst. Nac. Antr. Hist.*, no. 5.

AVENDAÑO ESTRADA, R.
1958 Drepanocitemia y anemia células falciformes en Guatemala. Tesis de médico y cirujano, Facultad Cien. Méd., Univ. San Carlos de Guatemala.

AVENDAÑO Y LOYOLA, A. DE
1696 Relación de las dos entradas que hize a la conversión de los gentiles itzaex y cehaches. MS in Ayer Coll., Newberry Library, Chicago.

AYMÉ, L. H.
1882 Notes on Mitla. *Proc. Amer. Antiquarian Soc.*, n.s., 2: 82–100.

BACA, F. M.
1897 Estudio craneométrico zapoteca. *11th Int. Cong. Amer.* (Mexico, 1895), Acta, pp. 237–64.

BACABS, RITUAL OF THE
n.d. Medical incantations and prescriptions. MS. Gates reproduction.

BAEGERT, J. J.
1773 Nachrichten von der Amerikanischen Halbinsel Californien, mit einen zweifachen Anhang falscher Nachrichten. Mannheim. Tr. by C. Rau, An account of the aboriginal inhabitants of the California peninsula. *Smithsoni-*

an Inst., ann. rept., 1863, pp. 352–69; 1864, pp. 378–99.

1942 Noticias de la peninsula americana de California. Tr. by Pedro Hendrichs. Mexico.

1952 Observations in Lower California. Tr. from German with introduction and notes by M. M. Brandenburg and C. L. Baumann. Univ. California Press.

BAER, P., AND M. BAER
1949 Notes on Lacandon marriage. *SW. Jour. Anthr.*, 5: 101–06.

BAEZ, V. D.
1909 Compendio de historia de Oaxaca. Oaxaca.

BAILEY, H. M.
1958 Santa Cruz of the Etla hills. Univ. Florida Press.

BAILLARGER, J. F. G.
1855 Discussion sur les Aztèques presentés à l'Academie Imperial de Médecine. *Bull. Acad. Nat. Méd.*, 2: 1158–59. Paris.

BAKER, A.
1887 Aboriginal Indian races of the state of Veracruz. *Proc. Royal Geog. Soc.*, n.s., 9: 568–74. London.

BAKER, C. L.
1930 Natural regions of Mexico. *Pan-Amer. Geol.*, 53: 311–12.

BAKER, P. T., et al.
1962 Ecology and anthropology: a symposium. *Amer. Anthr.*, 64: 15–59.

BAKER, R. H.
1963 The geographical distribution of terrestrial mammals in Middle America. *Amer. Midland Nat.*, 70: 208–49.

—— AND J. K. GREER
1962 The mammals of the Mexican state of Durango. *Pub. Mus., Michigan State Univ. Biol. Ser.*, 25: 25–154.

BALCASTRO, P.
1931 Vocabulario de la lengua Opata. MS in Bancroft Library. Reproduced in Radin, 1931.

BALES, R. F.
1958 Task roles and social roles in problem-solving groups. *In* Readings in social psychology, E. E. Maccoby, T. M. Newcomb, and E. L. Hartley, eds.

BALFOUR GOURLAY, W.
1940 Man and elephant in Central America. *Man*, 40: 86–88.

BALL, S. H.
1941 The mining of gems and ornamental stones by American Indians. *Smithsonian Inst., Bur. Amer. Ethnol.*, Bull. 128, Anthr. Papers, no. 13.

BALSALOBRE, G. DE
1892 Relación auténtica de las idolatrías, supersticiones, vanas observaciones de los indios del obispado de Oaxaca. *An. Mus. Nac. Mex.*, 6: 225–60. (Original ed. 1656.)

BALSER, C.
1953 El jade precolombino de Costa Rica. Mus. Nac. Costa Rica.

1955 A fertility vase from the old line, Costa Rica. *Amer. Antiquity*, 20: 384–87.

BANCROFT, H. H.
1874–76 The native races of the Pacific states of North America. 5 vols. San Francisco and New York. Reissued as his *Works*, vols. 1–5, 1882.

1882–90 Works. 39 vols. San Francisco.

BANDELIER, A. F.
1877 On the art of war and mode of warfare of the ancient Mexicans. *Peabody Mus., Harvard Univ.*, 10th ann. rept., 2: 95–161.

1878 On the distribution and tenure of land, and the customs with respect to inheritance among the ancient Mexicans. *Ibid.*, 11th ann. rept., 2: 385–448.

1880 On the social organization and mode of government of the ancient Mexicans. *Ibid.*, 12th and 13th ann. repts., 2: 557–699.

1880–85 Portfolio. Drawings without copy. Vatican Library, Vat. Lat. 14112–16. Microfilm.

1884 An excursion to Mitla. *Papers Archaeol. Inst. Amer., Amer. Ser.*, vol. 2. Boston.

1884 Report of an archaeological tour in Mexico. *Papers Archaeol. Inst. Amer., Amer. Ser.*, no. 2.

1890 The ruins of Casas Grandes. *The Nation*, Aug. 28 and Sept. 4.

1890 Final report of investigations among

the Indians of southwestern United States, Part 1. *Papers Archaeol. Inst. Amer., Amer. Ser.*, vol. 3.

1892 Final report of investigations among the Indians of southwestern United States, Part 2. *Ibid.*, vol. 4.

BANNON, J. F.
1955 The mission frontier in Sonora, 1620–1687. *U.S. Catholic Hist. Soc.*, Monogr. 26.

BARBA DE PIÑA CHAN, B.
1956 Tlapacoya: un sitio preclásico de transición. *Acta Anthr.*, ep. 2, vol. 1, no. 1. Mexico.

BARBERENA, S. J.
n.d. Quicheísmos. San Salvador.

BARBOUR, G. B.
1957 A note on jadeite from Manzanal, Guatemala. *Amer. Antiquity*, 22: 411–12.

BÁRCENA, J. M. R.
1862 Leyendas mexicanas. Mexico.

BÁRCENA, M.
1882 Descripción de un hueso labrado, de llama fósil, encontrado en los terrenos posterciarios de Tequixquiac. *An. Mus. Nac. Mex.*, ep. 1, 2: 439–44.

1886 The fossil man of Peñón, Mexico. *Amer. Naturalist*, 20: 633–35. Boston.

1886 Antropología mexicana: nuevos datos acerca de la antigüedad del hombre del Valle de México. *Naturaleza*, ser. 1, 7: 265–70.

1887 Contestación a las observaciones de la carta anterior. *Ibid.*, 7: 286–88.

1897 El hombre prehistórico en México. *11th Int. Cong. Amer.* (Mexico, 1895), Acta, pp. 73–78.

—— AND A. DEL CASTILLO
1885 Antropología mexicana: el hombre del Peñón. Mexico.

1885 Notice of some human remains found near the City of Mexico. *Amer. Naturalist*, 19: 739–44. Boston.

1886 Noticia acerca del hallazgo de restos humanos prehistóricos en el Valle de México. *Naturaleza*, ser. 1, 7: 257–64.

BARGHOORN, E. S., M. K. WOLFE, AND K. H. CLISBY
1954 Fossil maize from the valley of Mexico. *Bot. Mus. Leafl., Harvard Univ.*, 16: 229–40.

BARKER, G. C.
1957 Some aspects of penitential processions in Spain and the American Southwest. *Jour. Amer. Folklore*, 70: 137–42.

1957 The Yaqui Easter ceremony at Hermosillo. *Western Folklore*, 16: 256–62.

BARKER, H., AND C. J. MACKEY
1959 British Museum natural radiocarbon measurements I. *Amer. Jour. Sci., Radiocarbon Suppl.*, 1: 81–86.

1960 British Museum natural radiocarbon measurements II. *Ibid.*, 2: 26–30.

BARLOW, R. H.
1943 The periods of tribute collection in Moctezuma's empire. *Carnegie Inst. Wash., Notes Middle Amer. Archaeol. Ethnol.*, no. 23.

1944 Relación de Xiquilpan y su partido. *Tlalocan*, 1: 278–306.

1944 A western extension of Zapotec. *Ibid.*, 1: 267–68, 359–61.

1944 Los dioses del templo mayor de Tlatelolco. *Mem. Acad. Mex. Hist.*, 3: 530–40.

1945 Some remarks on the term "Aztec Empire." *The Americas*, 1: 344–49. Washington, D.C.

1945 Tlatelolco como tributario de la triple alianza. *Mem. Acad. Mex. Hist.*, 4: 200–15.

1945 Dos relaciones antiguas del pueblo de Cuilapa, estado de Oaxaca. *Tlalocan*, 2: 18–28.

1945 The Tlacotepec migration legend. *Ibid.*, 2: 70–73.

1946 Cerro de San Lorenzo, Coahuila: dos sitios arqueológicos. *Rev. Mex. Estud. Antr.*, 8: 266–67.

1946 Materiales para una cronología del imperio de los mexica. *Ibid.*, 8: 207–15.

1946 Some examples of Yeztla-Naranjo geometric ware. *Carnegie Inst. Wash., Notes Middle Amer. Archaeol. Ethnol.*, no. 73.

1946 The Tamiahua codices. *Ibid.*, no. 64.

1947 Relación de Tlalcozauhtitlan. *El México Antiguo*, 6: 383–91.

1947 Relación de Zacatula, 1580. *Tlalocan*, 2: 258–68.

1947 Conquistas de los antiguos mexicanos. *Jour. Soc. Amer. Paris*, 36: 215–22.

1947 Exploración en el occidente de Guerrero. III: Enero de 1948. *Tlalocan*, 2: 280–84.

1947–48 La fundación de la triple alianza (1427–1433). *An. Inst. Nac. Antr. Hist.*, 3: 147–55.

1948 La prensa tarasca de Paracho, Michoacan, 1939–40. *Int. Jour. Amer. Ling.*, 14: 49–52.

1948 Apuntes para la historia antigua de Guerrero. *In* El Occidente de México, pp. 181–90.

1948 Tres complejos de cerámica del norte del Rio Balsas. *Ibid.*, pp. 91–94.

1948 El derrumbe de Huexotzinco. *Cuad. Amer.*, 7: 147–60.

1949 The extent of the empire of the Culhua Mexica. *Ibero-Amer.*, no. 28.

1949 El Códice Azcatitlan. *Jour. Soc. Amer. Paris*, 38: 101–35.

1949 Las conquistas de Moctezuma Xocoyotzin. *Mem. Acad. Mex. Hist.*, 8: 159–72.

1949 Anales de Tula, Hidalgo. *Tlalocan*, 3: 2–13.

1950 Una nueva lámina del Mapa Quinatzin. *Jour. Soc. Amer. Paris*, 39: 111–24.

—— AND B. McAFEE, eds.

1949 Diccionario de elementos fonéticos en escritura jeroglífica (Códice Mendocino). *Univ. Nac. Autónoma Mex., Pub. Inst. Hist.*, 1st ser., no. 9.

BARNARD, J. G.

1852 The Isthmus of Tehuantepec, being the results of a survey for a railroad to connect the Atlantic and Pacific oceans. New York.

BARNES, A.

1947 The technique of blade production in Mesolithic and Neolithic times. *Proc. Prehist. Soc.*, 13: 101–113. Gloucester.

BARNETT, H. G.

1953 Innovation: the basis of cultural change. New York.

BARNETT, MADAME

1913 Quelques observations sur les petites têtes de Teotihuacan. *18th Int. Cong. Amer.* (London, 1912), Acta, p. 203.

BARNICOT, N. A., AND S. D. LAWLER

1953 A study of the Lewis, Kell, Lutheran and P blood group systems and the ABH secretion in West African Negroes. *Amer. Jour. Physical Anthr.*, n.s., 11: 83–90.

BAROCO, J. V.

1959 Map of the Tzeltal-Tzotzil area of Chiapas. *In* McQuown, 1959.

BARÓN CASTRO, R.

1942 La población de El Salvador. Madrid.

BARRAGÁN, E., C. CÁRDENAS, AND C. VALDÉS

1960 Conociendo a Coahuila, los laguneros o irritilas su cultura y sus restos. Univ. Coahuila. Saltillo.

BARRAGÁN, M.

1883 Datos antropométricos del recién nacido en México. Mexico.

BARRAGÁN, R., AND L. A. GONZÁLEZ BONILLA

1940 Vida actual de los tarascos. Mexico.

BARREDA, N. DE LA

1730 Doctrina cristiana en lengua chinanteca . . . México. Facsimile ed. *Mus. Nac. Antr., Ser. Cien.*, 6. *Papeles de la Chinantla*, 2. Introductory material by H. F. Cline (see Cline, 1961, Re-edición). Mexico.

BARRERA, F.

1745 Vocabulario castellano-quiché. Photograph in Newberry Library. 201 pp.

BARRERA GONZÁLEZ, M.

1949 Informe sanitario y problemas médicosociales del pueblo de Tepoztlan, Morelos. Mexico.

BARRERA VÁSQUEZ, A.

1935 Baltasar Mutul, autor de un libro de la pasión de Jesucristo y de un discurso sobre la Misa, en la langua maya. *Maya Research*, 2: 299–301.

1939 El Códice Pérez. *Rev. Mex. Estud. Antr.*, 3: 69–83.

1940 Idioma Quiché. *An. Inst. Nac. Antr. Hist.*, 1: 179–80.

1944 Canción de la danza del arquero flechador. *Tlalocan*, 1: 273–77.

1957 Códice de Calkini. *Bib. Campechana*, no. 4. Campeche.

—— AND S. G. MORLEY

1949 The Maya chronicles. *Carnegie Inst. Wash.*, Pub. 585, Contrib. 48.

—— AND S. RENDÓN

1948 El libro de los libros de Chilam Balam. Fondo de Cultura Económica. Mexico.

BARRETT, E. C.

1957 Baja California. [Bibliography.] Los Angeles.

BARRETT, W.

1956 The phonemic interpretation of "accent" in Father Rincón's "Arte mexicana." *General Ling.*, 2: 22–28. Lexington.

BARRIOS E., M.

1949 Textos de Hueyapan, Morelos. *Tlalocan*, 3 (1): 53–64.

BARTH, P. J.

1950 Franciscan education and the social order in Spanish North America, 1502–1821. Chicago.

BARTHEL, T. S.

1951 Maya-astronomie: lunare Inschriften aus dem Südreich. *Zeit. für Ethnol.*, 76: 216–38.

1952 Der Morgensternkult in den Darstellungen der Dresdener Mayahandschrift. *Ethnos*, 17: 73–112.

1953 Religion des Regengottes: zur Deutung der unteren Teile der Seiten 65–69 in der Dresdener Mayahandschrift. *Ibid.*, 18: 86–105.

1954 Maya epigraphy: some remarks on the affix 'al.' *30th Int. Cong. Amer.* (Cambridge, 1952), Acta, pp. 45–49.

1955 Maya-Palaeographik: die Hieroglyphe Strafe. *Ethnos*, 20: 146–51.

1955 Versuch über die Inschriften von Chichen Itza viejo. *Baessler Archiv*, n.s., 3: 5–33.

BARTHOLOMEW, D.

1959 Proto-Otomi-Pame. Master's thesis. [Expanded in his 1965.]

1960 Some revisions of Proto-Otomi consonants. *Int. Jour. Amer. Ling.*, 26: 317–29.

1965 The reconstruction of Otopamean (Mexico). Doctoral dissertation, Univ. Chicago.

BARTLETT, H. H.

1935 A method of procedure for field work in tropical American phytogeography based upon a botanical reconnaissance in parts of British Honduras and the Peten forest of Guatemala. *Carnegie Inst. Wash.*, Pub. 461, pp. 1–25.

BARTLETT, J. R.

1854 Personal narrative of explorations and incidents in Texas, New Mexico, California, Sonora and Chihuahua, connected with the United States and Mexican Boundary Commission, during the years 1850, '51, '52, and '53. New York.

BASALENQUE, D.

1640 Arte de la lengua matlaltzinga. Photograph in Newberry Library.

1642 Vocabulario . . . castellano . . . matlaltzinga. Photograph in Newberry Library. 411 pp.

1642 Vocabulario . . . matlaltzinga . . . castellano. Photograph in Newberry Library. 286 pp.

1886 Arte de la lengua tarasca. . . . Mexico.

BASAURI, C.

1926 The resistance of the Tarahumaras. *Mex. Folkways*, 2 (4): 40–47. Mexico.

1927 Creencias y prácticas de los Tarahumaras. *Ibid.*, 3: 218–34.

1928 La situación social actual de la población indígena de México. *Pub. Sec. Educación Pública*, vol. 16, no. 8. Mexico.

1928 Los tarascos de la Cañada de Chilchota. *In* his preceding entry.

1929 Monografía de los Tarahumaras. Talleres Gráficos de la Nación. Mexico.

1930 Apuntes etnográficos sobre los Indios Otomies del Valle del Mezquital.

1931 Tojolabales, Tzeltales y Mayas. Talleres Gráficos de la Nación. Mexico.

1940 La población indígena de México. 3 vols. Mexico.

1940 Tribu: chinantecas, h-me, wan-mi. *Ibid.*, 2: 545–68.

1940 Los indios triques de Oaxaca. *Ibid.*, 2: 427–63.

1940 Familia "zoque-mixeana": mixes. *Ibid.*, 3: 403–32.

1940 Familia "zoque-mixeana": zoques. *Ibid.*, 3: 387–402.

—— AND L. ARGOYTIA

1937 Antropometría. *In* Gómez Robleda and others, 1937, pp. 85–113.

BASAURI, M.

1938 Importancia de los grupos sanguíneos en los estudios etno-antropológicos. *Rev. Educación*, 2 (10): 18–20. Mexico.

BASLER, A., AND E. BRUMMER

1928 L'art précolombien. Paris.

BASSETA, D. DE

1698? Vocabulario de la lengua quiché. MS in Bibliothèque Nationale. 172 pp.

BASTIAN, A.

1881 Mexikanischer Graberschädel. *Ver. Berliner Gesellschaft für Anthr., Ethnol., und Urgeschichte*, p. 33.

BASURTO, I. R.

1900 Algunas consideraciones sobre la filiación antropométrica. Jalapa, Mexico.

BATALLA, M. A.

1945 Textile plants suitable for basketry. *Esta Semana*, March 3, 10, 17. Mexico.

BATRES, L.

1887 Informe que rinde el inspector y conservador de los monumentos arqueológicos de la República, de los trabajos llevados a cabo de octubre 1885 a abril 1886. *In* J. Baranda, Memoria que rinde al Congreso de la Unión, pp. lv, 377–93. Mexico.

1887 Estudio sobre los Toltecas. *Ibid.*, pp. 382–93. Mexico.

1889 Antropología mexicana: clasificación del tipo étnico de las tribus zapotecas del estado de Oaxaca y Acolhua del Valle de México. *Ibid.*, pp. 257–62. Mexico.

1889 Antropología mexicana: clasificación del tipo antropológico de las principales tribus aborígenes. *Rev. Nac.*

Letras y Ciencias, 1: 191–96. Mexico.

1889 Momia tolteca. Mexico.

1889 Teotihuacán o la ciudad sagrada de los Toltecas. Mexico.

1900 Anthropologie mexicaine, ostéologie. Paris.

1902 Exploraciones de Monte Albán. Mexico.

1902 Exploraciones arqueológicas en la Calle de las Escalerillas. Mexico.

1903 Visita a los monumentos arqueológicos de la Quemada, Zacatecas, México. Mexico.

1903 ¿Tlaloc? Exploración arqueológica en el oriente del Valle de México. Sec. Justicia e Instrucción Pública. Mexico.

1905 La lápida arqueológica de Tepatlaxco-Orizaba. Mexico.

1907 Teotihuacán. *15th Int. Cong. Amer.* (Quebec, 1906), Acta, 2: 277–82.

1908 Civilización prehistórica de las riberas del Papaloapan y costa de Sotavento, estado de Veracruz. Mexico.

BAUDEZ, C. F.

1959 Nuevos aspectos de la escultura lítica en el territorio Chorotega. *33rd Int. Cong. Amer.* (San Jose, 1958), Acta, 2: 286–95.

1962 Recherches archéologiques dans la vallée du Tempisque, Guanacaste, Costa Rica. *34th Int. Cong. Amer.* (Vienna, 1960), Acta.

1963 Cultural development in lower Central America. *In* Meggers and Evans, 1963, pp. 45–54.

—— AND M. D. COE

1962 Archaeological sequences in northwestern Costa Rica. *34th Int. Cong. Amer.* (Vienna, 1960), Acta, pp. 366–73.

BAUER-THOMA, W.

1916 Unter den Zapoteken und Mixes des Staates Oaxaca der Republik Mexiko: ethnographischen Studien. *Baessler Archiv*, 5: 75–97.

BAUTISTA, J. DE

1600 Advertencias para los confesores. Mexico.

BEAL, C. H.

1948 Reconnaissance of the geology and

oil possibilities of Baja California, Mexico. *Geol. Soc. Amer.*, Mem. 31.

BEALS, R. L.

n.d. The history of acculturation in Mexico. MS.

1932 The comparative ethnology of northern Mexico before 1750. *Ibero-Amer.*, no. 2.

1932 Unilateral organizations in Mexico. *Amer. Anthr.*, 34: 467–75.

1933 The Acaxee, a mountain tribe of Durango and Sinaloa. *Ibero-Amer.*, no. 6.

1934 A possible culture sequence at Mitla, Oaxaca. *Amer. Anthr.*, 36: 89–93.

1935 Two mountain Zapotec tales from Oaxaca, Mexico. *Jour. Amer. Folklore*, 48: 189–90.

1936 Problems in the study of Mixe marriage customs. *In* Essays in anthropology, presented to A. L. Kroeber, pp. 7–13.

1941 The western Mixe of Oaxaca. *Amer. Indig.*, 2: 45–50.

1942 Shell mounds and other sites in Sonora and northern Sinaloa. *Notebook Soc. Amer. Archaeol.*, 2: 38–40.

1943 The aboriginal culture of the Cáhita Indians. *Ibero-Amer.*, no. 19.

1944 Northern Mexico and the Southwest. *In* El Norte de México, pp. 191–99.

1944 Relations between Meso America and the Southwest. *Ibid.*, pp. 245–52.

1945 The contemporary culture of the Cáhita Indians. *Smithsonian Inst., Bur. Amer. Ethnol.*, Bull. 142.

1945 The ethnology of the western Mixe. *Univ. California Pub. Amer. Archaeol. Ethnol.*, 42: 1–176.

1946 Cheran: a sierra Tarascan village. *Smithsonian Inst., Inst. Social Anthr.*, Pub. 2.

1949 Conferencia sobre los indígenas contemporaneas de México. *Univ. Central de Ecuador, Filosofía y Letras*, pp. 38–52.

1951 History of acculturation in Mexico. *In* Homenaje Caso, pp. 73–82.

1951 Urbanism, urbanization and acculturation. *Amer. Anthr.*, 53: 1–10.

1952 Notes on acculturation. *In* Tax, 1952, Heritage, pp. 225–32.

1969 The Tarascans. *In* Handbook of Middle American Indians, R. Wauchope, ed., vol. 8, art. 35.

—— AND P. CARRASCO

1944 Games of the mountain Tarascans. *Amer. Anthr.*, 46: 516–22.

——, ——, AND T. McCORKLE

1944 Houses and house use of the sierra Tarascans. *Smithsonian Inst., Inst. Social Anthr.*, Pub. 1.

—— AND E. P. HATCHER

1943 The diet of a sierra Tarascan community. *Amer. Indig.*, 3: 295–304.

——, R. REDFIELD, AND S. TAX

1943 Anthropological research problems with reference to the contemporary peoples of Mexico and Guatemala. *Amer. Anthr.*, 45: 1–22.

BEARD, J. S.

1944 Climax vegetation in tropical America. *Ecology*, 25: 125–58.

1955 The classification of tropical American vegetation types. *Ibid.*, 36: 89–100.

BEAUMONT, P.

1855–56 Crónica de Michoacán, año de 1825. 2 vols. Morelia.

1932 Crónica de la Provincia de los Santos Apóstoles S. Pedro y S. Pablo de Michoacán (1565). Archivo General de la Nación, Pubs. 17, 18, 19. Mexico.

BECERRA, M. E.

1924 Breve noticia sobre la lengua e indios tsoques. *Mem. Soc. Cien. Antonio Alzate*, 43: 147–52.

1933 El antiguo calendario chiapaneco: estudio comparativo entre este y los calendarios precoloniales maya, quiche, y nahua. Mexico.

1937 Vocabulario de la lengua chol. *An. Mus. Nac. Arqueol., Hist., Etnol.*, s. 5, 2: 249–78.

BECERRA COBOS, J. DE LA L.

1944 Informe general sobre la exploración sanitaria del municipio de Amozoc de Mota, Puebla. Mexico.

BEEKMAN, J.

1956 The effect of education in an Indian village. *In* Estudios antropológicos, pp. 261–64.

BEESLEY, C.
1943 The religion of the Maya. *El Palacio*, 50 (1): 8–21.

BÉHAR ALCAHÉ, M.
1949 Elementos leptospiroides observados en la sangre (su posible confusión con leptospiras). Tesis de médico y cirujano, Facultad Cien. Méd., Univ. San Carlos de Guatemala.

1968 Prevalence of malnutrition among preschool children of developing countries. *In* Malnutrition, learning, and behavior, N. S. Scrimshaw and J. E. Gordon, eds. Massachusetts Inst. Technology Press.

——, W. ASCOLI, AND N. S. SCRIMSHAW
1958 An investigation into the causes of death in children in four rural communities in Guatemala. *Bull. World Health Org.*, 19: 1093–1102.

—— AND N. S. SCRIMSHAW
1959 Epidemiology of protein malnutrition. Presented at the Conference on Nutrition sponsored by the New York Academy of Medicine and the Institute of Social and Historical Medicine, Dec. 13–18, 1958. Harriman, N.Y.

—— AND OTHERS (G. ARROYAVE, C. TEJADA, F. VITERI, AND N. S. SCRIMSHAW)
1956 Desnutrición severa en la infancia. *Rev. Colegio Méd. Guatemala*, 7: 221–78.

BELDING, L.
1885 The Pericue Indians. *West Amer. Sci.*, vol. 1, no. 4.

BELL, B.
1960 Analysis of ceramic style: a west Mexican collection. Doctoral dissertation, Univ. California, Los Angeles.

BELL, R. E.
1958 Guide to the identification of certain American Indian projectile points. *Oklahoma Anthr. Soc.*, Special Bull. 1.

1960 Evidence of a fluted point tradition in Ecuador. *Amer. Antiquity*, 26: 102–06.

BELMAR, F.
1890 Cartilla del idioma zapoteco-serrano. Oaxaca.

1892 Códice Dehesa. Homenaje a Cristóbal Colón. Antigüedades mexicanas, publicadas por la junta colombina de México en el cuarto centenario del descubrimiento de América. Secretaria de Fomento. Mexico.

1892 Ligero estudio sobre la lengua mazateca. Oaxaca.

1897 Ensayo sobre la lengua trique. Lenguas indígenas del estado de Oaxaca. Oaxaca.

1898 Disertación sobre las lenguas zapoteca, chinanteca, mixe y trike, y comparación con zoke y el mixteco. MS in Newberry Library, Chicago.

1899 Idiomas indígenas del estado de Oaxaca: el Chocho. Oaxaca.

1900 Estudio de el chontal. Oaxaca.

1901 Los chochos: estudio lingüístico. Oaxaca.

1901 Investigación sobre el idioma amuzgo. . . . Oaxaca.

1901 Lenguas del estado de Oaxaca: estudio del huave. Oaxaca.

1902 Idiomas del estado de Oaxaca: el cuicateco. Oaxaca.

1902 Lenguas indígenas del estado de Oaxaca: estudio del idioma Ayook. Oaxaca.

1905 Lenguas indígenas de México. Familia mixteco-zapoteca y sus relaciones con el otomí. Familia zoque-mixe, chontal, huave y mexicano. Mexico.

1905 La familia mixteco-zapoteca en relación con la otomí. Mexico.

1905 Indian tribes of the state of Oaxaca and their languages. *13th Int. Cong. Amer.* (New York, 1902), Acta, pp. 193–202.

1921 Glotología indígena mexicana. Mexico.

BELTRÁN, E., ed.
1959 Los recursos naturales del sureste y su aprovachamiento. 3 vols. Inst. Mex. Recursos Naturales Renovables.

BELTRÁN DE SANTA ROSA, P.
1859 Arte del idioma maya reducido a succintas reglas y semilexicón yucateco. Merida. (Originally published 1746, Mexico.)

BELTRANENA, M.
1930 Informe semestral del jefe de sección

de enfermedades infecto-contagiosas. *Bol. Sanitario, Guatemala*, 1: 311–16.

BEMIS, S. F.
1943 The Latin American policy of the United States. New York.

BENASSINI, A., AND A. GARCÍA QUINTERO
1955–57 Recursos hidráulicos de la República Mexicana. *Ingeniería Hidráulica en Mexico*, vols. 9–11. Mexico.

BENAVENTE, T. DE
1903 *See* Motolinia, 1903.

BENAVIDES
1954 *See* Forrestal, 1954.

BENEDICT, F. G.
1928 Basal metabolism data on normal men and women. *Amer. Jour. Physiol.*, 85: 607–20.

—— AND M. STEGGERDA
1936 The food of the present-day Maya Indians of Yucatan. *Carnegie Inst. Wash.*, Pub. 456, Contr. 18.

BENÍTEZ P., A.
1943 Informe general sobre la exploración sanitaria de Tlaquiltenango, Morelos. Mexico.

BENNETT, E. B.
1963 An oceanographic atlas of the eastern tropical Pacific based on data from "Eastropic" Expedition, Oct.–Dec. 1955. *Bull. Inter-Amer. Tropical Tuna Comm.*, 8: 31–196.

—— AND M. B. SCHAEFER
1960 Studies of physical, chemical, and biological oceanography in the vicinity of the Revilla Gigedo Islands during the "Island Current Survey" of 1957. *Ibid.*, 4: 217–317.

BENNETT, H. H.
1925 The soils of Central America and northern South America. Rep. 5th Ann. Meeting, *Amer. Soil Survey Assoc.*, Bull. 6, vol. 1.

1926 Agriculture in Central America. *Ann. Assoc. Amer. Geog.*, 16: 63–84.

1929 Soil reconnaissance of the Panama Canal Zone and contiguous territory. U.S. Dept. Agriculture, Tech. Bull. 94.

1945 Soil conservation in Latin America. *In* Verdoorn, 1945, pp. 165–69.

BENNETT, J. W.
1944 Southeastern culture types and Middle American influence. *In* El Norte de México, pp. 223–41.

BENNETT, W. C.
1946 The archeology of Colombia. *In* Handbook of South American Indians, 2: 823–50.

1948 A reappraisal of Peruvian archaeology. *Soc. Amer. Archaeol.*, Mem. 4.

1950 The Gallinazo group, Viru valley, Peru. *Yale Univ. Pub. Anthr.*, no. 43.

—— AND J. B. BIRD
1949 Andean culture history. *Amer. Mus. Nat. Hist., Handbook Ser.*, no. 15.

—— AND R. M. ZINGG
1935 The Tarahumara, an Indian tribe of northern Mexico. Univ. Chicago Press.

BENNYHOFF, J.
1966 Chronology and periodization: continuity and change in the Teotihuacan ceramic tradition. *In* Teotihuacán, 1966.

BENSON, E., ed.
1968 Dumbarton Oaks conference on the Olmec. Washington, D.C.

BENZONI, G.
1857 History of the New World. Ed. and tr. by W. H. Smyth. Hakluyt Soc. London.

BERCKENHAGEN, H.
1894 Grammar of the Miskito language. Bluefields, Nicaragua.

BERENDT, C. H.
1869 An analytic alphabet for the Mexican and Central American languages. New York.

1870 Apuntes sobre la lengua chaneabal, con un vocabulario. Reproduction in Peabody Mus., Harvard Univ.

1873 Die Indianer des Isthmus von Tehuantepec. *Verhandlungen der Berliner Gesellschaft für Anthropologie, Ethnologie und Urgeschicht*, 5: 146–53.

1876 Remarks on the centers of ancient civilization in Central America and their geographical distribution. *Bull. Amer. Geog. Soc.*, 8 (2): 5–15.

BERGER, R., G. J. FERGUSSON, AND W. F. LIBBY
1965   UCLA radiocarbon dates, IV. *Radiocarbon*, 7: 336–71.
——, J. A. GRAHAM, AND R. F. HEIZER
1967   A reconsideration of the age of the La Venta site. *Contrib. Univ. California Archaeol. Research Facility*, 3: 1–24. Berkeley.
—— AND W. F. LIBBY
1966   UCLA radiocarbon dates, V. *Radiocarbon*, 8: 467–97.
1967   UCLA radiocarbon dates, VI. *Ibid.*, 9: 477–504.
——, R. E. TAYLOR, AND W. F. LIBBY
1966   Radiocarbon content of marine shells from the California and Mexican west coast. *Science*, 153 (3738): 864–66.
BERGSØE, P.
1937   The metallurgy and technology of gold and platinum among the pre-Columbian Indians. *Ingeniørvidenskabelige skrifter*, nr. A. 44. Copenhagen.
1938   The gilding process and the metallurgy of copper and lead among the pre-Columbian Indians. *Ibid.*, nr. A. 46.
BERLIN, H.
1940   Relaciones precolombinas entre Cuba y Yucatan. *Rev. Mex. Estud. Antr.*, 4: 141–60.
1943   Notes on Glyph C of the lunar series at Palenque. *Carnegie Inst. Wash., Notes Middle Amer. Archaeol. Ethnol.*, no. 24.
1946   Archaeological excavations in Chiapas. *Amer. Antiquity*, 12: 19–28.
1946   Three Zapotec stones. *Carnegie Inst. Wash., Notes Middle Amer. Archaeol. Ethnol.*, no. 66.
1947   Fragmentos desconocidos del códice de Yanhuitlan y otras investigaciones mixtecas. Mexico.
1947   Historia Tolteca-Chichimeca. Anales de Quauhtinchan. Mexico.
1947   Nota bibliográfica. *Bol. Bib. Antr. Amer.*, 9: 200–01.
1950   La historia de los Xpantzay. *Antr. Hist. Guatemala*, 2 (2): 40–53.
1951   The calendar of the Tzotzil Indians. *In* Tax, 1951, pp. 155–61.
1952   Excavaciones en Kaminal Juyu: Mon-
tículo D-III-13. *Antr. Hist. Guatemala*, 4 (1): 3–18.
1953   Archaeological reconnaissance in Tabasco. *Carnegie Inst. Wash., Current Reports*, no. 7.
1955   Selected pottery from Tabasco. *Carnegie Inst. Wash., Notes Middle Amer. Archaeol. Ethnol.*, no. 126.
1955   Apuntes sobre vasijas de Flores (El Peten). *Antr. Hist. Guatemala*, 7 (1): 15–17.
1956   Late pottery horizons of Tabasco, Mexico. *Carnegie Inst. Wash.*, Pub. 606, Contrib. 59.
1957   Las antiguas creencias en San Miguel Sola, Oaxaca, Mexico. *Beiträge zur mittelamerikanischen Völkerkunde, Herausgegeben von Hamburgischen Museum für Völkerkunde und Vorgeschichte*, no. 4.
1957   A survey of the Sola region in Oaxaca. *Ethnos*, 16: 1–17.
1958   El glifo "emblema" en las inscripciones mayas. *Jour. Soc. Amer. Paris*, 47: 111–19.
1963   The Palenque triad: a study in method. *Ibid.*, 52: 91–99.
—— AND R. H. BARLOW
1948   Anales de Tlatelolco: Unos annales históricos de la nación mexicana y códice de Tlatelolco. *Fuentes para la Historia de Mexico*, no. 2. Mexico.
BERLIN, O. B.
1962   The Tenejapa dialect of Tzeltal: an outline of morphology. *In* McQuown, 1962.
1962   Some further notes on Tenejapa syntax. *Ibid.*
BERNAL, I.
1946   La cerámica preclásica de Monte Alban. Thesis, Escuela Nac. Anthr. Hist. MS. Mexico.
1949   Exploraciones en Coixtlahuaca. *Rev. Mex. Estud. Antr.*, 10: 5–76.
1949   La cerámica grabada de Monte Alban. *An. Inst. Nac. Antr. Hist.*, 3: 59–78.
1949   La cerámica de Monte Alban III-A. Thesis, Univ. Nac. Autónoma de Mex.
1949   Distribución geográfica de las cul-

turas de Monte Alban. *El Mexico Antiguo*, 7: 209–16.

1950 Compendio de arte mesoamericano. *Enciclopedia Mex. Arte*, vol. 7. Mexico.

1951 Nuevos descubrimientos en Acapulco, México. *In* Tax, 1951, pp. 52–56.

1953 Excavations in the Mixteca Alta. *Mesoamer. Notes*, no. 3. Mexico.

1955 Excavations at Yagul, I. *Ibid.*, no. 4.

1958 México: pinturas prehispánicas. New York Graphic Soc. Col. UNESCO de Arte Mundial.

1958 Monte Alban and the Zapotecs. *Bol. Estud. Oaxaqueños*, no. 1. Mexico.

1958 Archaeology of the Mixteca. *Ibid.*, no. 7. Mexico.

1958 Exploraciones en Cuilapan de Guerrero, 1902–1954. *Inst. Nac. Antr. Hist.*, Informe 7. Mexico.

1958 Mexico: pinturas prehispánicas. New York Geog. Soc. Col. UNESCO de Arte Mundial.

1959 Tenochtitlan en una isla. *Inst. Nac. Antr. Hist., Hist. Ser.*, 2. Mexico.

1960 Exploraciones arqueológicas en Noriega, Oaxaca. *In* Homenaje a Rafael García Granados, pp. 83–88. Mexico.

1960 El palacio de los seis patios en Yagul. Mexico.

1962 Bibliografía de arqueología y etnografía: Mesoamérica y norte de México, 1514–1960. *Mem. Inst. Nac. Antr. Hist.*, no. 7. Mexico.

1963 [ed.] Teotihuacán: descubrimientos, reconstrucciones. Inst. Nac. Antr. Hist. Mexico.

1965 Teotihuacán: nuevas fechas de radiocarbono y su posible significado. *An. Antr.*, 2: 27–35. Mexico.

1965 Archaeological synthesis of Oaxaca. *In* Handbook of Middle American Indians, R. Wauchope, ed., vol. 3, art. 31.

1966 The Mixtecs in the archeology of the Valley of Oaxaca. *In* Paddock, 1966, Ancient Oaxaca, pp. 345–66.

1967 Teotihuacán: su prehistórica historia.

Conference, Mus. Nac. Antr. Mexico.

1968 Ancient Mexico in colour. Photographs by I. Groth-Kimball. London and New York.

1968 El mundo olmeca. Mexico.

1969 The Olmec world. D. Heyden and F. Horcasitas, trans. Berkeley and Los Angeles.

—— AND E. DÁVALOS HURTADO, eds.

1953 Huastecos, Totonacos y sus vecinos. *Rev. Mex. Estud. Antr.*, vol. 13, nos. 2 and 3.

——, R. PIÑA CHAN, AND F. CÁMARA BARBACHANO

1968 3000 years of art and life in Mexico as seen in the National Museum of Anthropology, Mexico City. New York.

—— AND B. VILLARET

1962 Arts anciens du Mexique: architecture et sculpture. Paris.

BERNSTEIN, F.

1931 Die geographische Verteilung der Blutgruppen und ihre anthropologische Bedeutung, pp. 227–43. Comitato Italiano per lo Studio dei Problemi della Populazione. Inst. Poligrafico dello Stato, Rome.

BERTHOLD, A. A.

1842 Ueber einen Schädel aus den Graebern des Alten Paläste von Mitla in Staat von Oaxaca. *Mem. des Curieux de la Nature*, 19: 441. Breslau-Bonn.

1886 Descripción y estudio de un cráneo extraido de uno de los palacios de Mitla. *An. Mus. Nac.*, 3: 115–21. Mexico.

BERTILLON, J.

1875 Les Aztèques. *La Nature*, pp. 65–67. Paris.

BETJEMAN, J., ed.

1959 Collins guide to English parish churches. London.

BEVAN, B.

1938 The Chinantec and their habitat. (The Chinantec: report on the central and southeastern Chinantec region, vol. 1.) *Inst. Panamer. Geog. Hist.*, Pub. 24. Mexico.

BEYER, H.

1918 La piedra de sacrificios (techcatl) del Museo Nacional de Arqueología, Historia y Etnología de México. *Disertaciones Científicas de Autores Alemanes en México*, 3: 35–46. Mexico.

1920 Algo sobre los "signos chinos" de Teotihuacán. *El México Antiguo*, 1: 211–17.

1921 El llamado "calendario azteca." Mexico.

1921 Nota bibliográfica y crítica sobre el quinto tomo de las memorias científicas de Seler. *Mem. y Rev. Soc. Cien. Antonio Alzate*, 40: 57–64.

1921 La gigantesca cabeza de la diosa Coyolxauhqui-Chantico. *Rev. de Rev.*, 569: 27–28.

1922 Sobre una plaqueta con una deidad teotihuacana. *Mem. y Rev. Soc. Cien. Antonio Alzate*, 40: 549–58.

1922 Relaciones entre la civilización teotihuacana y la azteca. *In* Gamio, 1922, 1: 273–93.

1924 Sobre algunas representaciones de los antiguos Totonacos. *Antropos*, 18: 253–57. Vienna.

1926 Die Verdopplung in der Hieroglyphenschrift der Maya. *Anthropos*, 21: 580–82. St. Gabriel Mödling bei Wien.

1927 Algunos datos sobre los "yugos" de piedra prehispánicos. *El México Antiguo*, 2: 269–78.

1930 A deity common to Teotihuacan and Totonac cultures. *23d Int. Cong. Amer.* (New York, 1928), Acta, pp. 82–84.

1932 Mayan hieroglyphs: some tun signs. *Tulane Univ., Middle Amer. Research Inst.*, Pub. 4, pp. 103–30.

1932 The stylistic history of the Maya hieroglyphs. *Ibid.*, Pub. 4, pp. 71–102.

1933 Shell ornament sets from the Huasteca, Mexico. *Ibid.*, Pub. 5, pp. 155–216.

1934–36 The position of the affixes in Maya writing. *Maya Research*, 1: 20–29, 101–08; 3: 102–04.

1937 Lunar glyphs of the supplementary series. *El Mexico Antiguo*, 4: 75–82.

1937 Studies on the inscriptions of Chichen Itza. *Carnegie Inst. Wash.*, Pub. 483, Contrib. 21.

1945 An incised Maya inscription in the Metropolitan Museum of Art, New York. *Tulane Univ., Middle Amer. Research Rec.*, 1: 85–88.

1955 La "Procesión de los Señores," decoración del primer teocalli de piedra en Mexico-Tenochtitlan. *El México Antiguo*, 8: 8–42.

1965 Mito y simbología del México antiguo. Segundo tomo especial de homenaje consagrado a honrar la memoria del ilustre antropólogo Doctor Hermann Beyer. . . . Primer tomo de sus obras completas recopiladas, traducidas y arregladas por C. Cook de Leonard. *El México Antiguo*, vol. 10.

1969 Cien años de arqueología mexicana: Humboldt-Beyer. Tercer tomo especial de homenaje a Hermann Beyer y segundo tomo de sus obras completas recopiladas, traducidas y arregladas por C. Cook de Leonard. Con un suplemento en honor a Alejandro de Humboldt. *El México Antiguo*, vol. 11.

BEZINA, A.

1959 Der mexikanische Federschild aus Ambras. Archiv für Völkerkunde. Vienna.

BIART, L.

1885 Les Aztèques: histoire, moeurs, coutumes. Paris.

1900 The Aztecs. Chicago.

BIASUTTI, R.

1941 L'umanità attuale: I caratteri somatici. *In* Le razze e i popoli della terra, R. Biasutti, ed., 1: 183–237. (2d ed. 1953.)

BIERHENKE, W., W. HABERLAND, U. JOHANSEN, AND G. ZIMMERMANN, eds.

1959 Amerikanistische Miszellen. Festband Franz Termer. *Mitteilungen aus dem Museum für Völkerkunde in Hamburg*, no. 25.

BILLIG, O., J. GILLIN, AND W. DAVIDSON

1947–48 Aspects of personality and culture

in a Guatemalan community. *Jour. Personality*, 16: 153–87, 326–68.

BIOCCA, E., AND E. WILLEMS
1947 Contribução para o estudo antropométrico dos índios Tukano, Tariana e Makú da região do alto Rio Negro (Amazonas). *Bol. Facultad Filos., Cién. e Letras*, 77: 33–38. Univ. São Paulo.

BIRD, J. B.
1948 Preceramic cultures in Chicama and Viru. *In* W. C. Bennett, 1948, pp. 21–29.
1951 South American radiocarbon dates. *In* F. Johnson, 1951, pp. 37–49.
1953 Two Guatemala wedding huipils. *Needle and Bobbin Club Bull.*, 37: 26–36.

BIRKNER, F.
1897 Das schädelwachstum der beiden amerikanischen Mikrocephalen Maximo und Bartola. *Correspondenzblatt der deutschen Gesellschaft für Anthr., Ethnol., und Urgeschichte*, 28: 153–54. Brunswick.
1898 Ueber die sogennanten Aztekon. *Archiv für Anthr.*, 25: 45–59. Brunswick.

BLACK, G. A.
1949 Tepexpan Man, a critique of method. *Amer. Antiquity*, 14: 344–46.

BLACKBURN, M.
1962 An oceanographic study of the Gulf of Tehuantepec. *U.S. Fish and Wildlife Service, Spec. Sci. Rept.—Fisheries*, no. 404.
1963 Distribution and abundance of tuna related to wind and ocean conditions in the Gulf of Tehuantepec, Mexico. *FAO Fisheries Rept. No. 6*, 3: 1557–82.

—— AND ASSOCIATES
1962 Tuna oceanography in the eastern tropical Pacific. *U.S. Fish and Wildlife Service, Spec. Sci. Rept.—Fisheries*, no. 400.

BLACKISTON, A. H.
1905 Cliff dwellers of northern Mexico. *Records of the Past*, 4: 355–61.
1906 Casas Grandian outposts. *Ibid.*, vol. 5.

1906 Ruins on the Cerro de Montezuma. *Amer. Anthr.*, 8: 256–61.
1909 Recently discovered cliff dwellers of the Sierra Madres. *Records of the Past*, 8: 20–32.
1910 Recent discoveries in Honduras. *Amer. Anthr.*, 12: 536–41.

BLAKE, W. W.
1891 The antiquities of Mexico as illustrated by the archaeological collections in its National Museum. New York.

BLAKNEY, R. B.
1955 The way of life, Lao Tzu. New York.

BLANCHARD, R.
1908 Les tableaux de métissage au Mexique. *Jour. Soc. Amer. Paris*, n.s., 5: 59–66.
1909 Sur quelques géants américaines. *Ibid.*, 6: 63–74.
1910 Encore sur les tableaux de métissage du Musée de Mexico. *Ibid.*, 7: 37–60.

BLANCO ESQUIVEL, M.
1957 Contribución al estudio de la familia: ancylostomatidae en Guatemala. Tesis de médico y cirujano, Facultad Cien. Méd., Univ. San Carlos de Guatemala.

BLANCO SALGADO, E.
1943 Contribución al estudio de los redúvidos hematófagos de Guatemala. *Ibid.*

BLÁSQUEZ LÓPEZ, L.
1943 La edad glacial en Mexico. *Bol. Soc. Mex. Geog. y Estad.*, 58: 263–305.
1956 Bosquejo fisiográfico y vulcanológico del occidente de Mexico. *In* Volcanismo terciario y reciente del eje volcánico de Mexico. Excursión A-15, pp. 9–17. *20th Cong. Geol. Int.* Mexico.

BLICK, J. C.
1937 Chinobampo skull. MS, Frick Laboratory, New York.

BLISS COLLECTION
See Handbook of the Robert Woods Bliss Collection.

BLOCH, I.
1906 Der Ursprung der Syphilis (Morbus americanus). *14th Int. Cong. Amer.* (Stuttgart, 1904), Acta, 1: 57–79.

BLOM, F.

1923 Las Chanecas of Tecuanapa. *Jour. Amer. Folklore*, 36: 200–02.

1927 Masterpieces of Maya art: the tomb at Comalcalco in the state of Chiapas, Mexico. *Art Soc. Washington*, vol. 24, no. 6.

1929 Preliminary report of the John Geddings Gray memorial expedition. Tulane Univ.

1930 Preliminary notes on two important Maya finds. *23d Int. Cong. Amer.* (New York, 1928), Acta, pp. 165–71.

1932 Commerce, trade, and monetary units of the Maya. *Tulane Univ., Middle Amer. Research Inst.*, Pub. 4, no. 14.

1932 The Maya ball-game *pok-ta-pok*. *Ibid.*, Pub. 4, no. 13.

1934 Short summary of recent explorations in the ruins of Uxmal, Yucatan. *24th Int. Cong. Amer.* (Hamburg, 1930), Acta, pp. 55–59.

1954 Ossuaries, cremation and secondary burials among the Maya of Chiapas, Mexico. *Jour. Soc. Amer. Paris*, 43: 123–35.

1959 Historical notes relating to the pre-Columbian amber trade from Chiapas. *In* Bierhenke, 1959, pp. 24–27.

—— AND G. DUBY

1949 Entre los indios Lacandones de México. *Amer. Indig.*, 9: 155–64.

1955–57 La selva lacandona: andanzas arqueológicas. 2 vols. Editorial Cultura. Mexico.

——, S. S. GROSJEAN, AND H. CUMMINS

1933 A Maya skull from the Uloa valley, Republic of Honduras. *Tulane Univ., Middle Amer. Research Inst.*, Pub. 5, no. 1. (Tr. into Spanish in *An. Soc. Geog. e Hist.*, 10: 32–40. Guatemala.)

—— AND O. LAFARGE

1926–27 Tribes and temples. 2 vols. *Tulane Univ., Middle Amer. Research Inst.*, Pub. 1.

BLOOMFIELD, L.

1933 Language. New York.

BLUMENBACH, J. F.

1790–1828 Collectio craniorum divers gen-

tium: 6 decades et novas pentas. Gotingue.

BLUMER, H.

1960 Early industrialization and the laboring class. *Sociol. Quar.*, 1: 5–14.

BOAS, F.

1890 Cranium from Progreso, Yucatan. *Proc. Amer. Antiquarian Soc.*, n.s., 6: 350–57.

1892 *See* F. Starr, 1902, Physical characters, p. 56.

1895 Anthropometrical observations on the Mission Indians of southern California. *Proc. Amer. Assoc. Advancement of Sci.*, 44: 261–69.

1895 Zur Anthropologie der nord-amerikanischen Indianer. *Ver. Berliner Anthr. Gesellschaft*, 27: 367–411.

1911 [ed.] Introduction. *In* Handbook of American Indian Languages, pt. 1. Washington.

1911–12 Álbum de colecciones arqueológicas. Pub. Escuela Internac. Arqueol. Etnol. Amer. Mexico. (See Gamio, 1921, for text.)

1912 Notes on Mexican folklore. *Jour. Amer. Folklore*, 25: 204–60.

1913 Archaeological investigations in the Valley of Mexico by the International School, 1911–12. *18th Int. Cong. Amer.* (London, 1912), Acta, pp. 176–79.

1913 Notes on the Chatino language of Mexico. *Amer. Anthr.*, 15: 78–86.

1962 Anthropology and modern life.

—— AND J. M. ARREOLA

1920 Cuentos en mexicano de Milpa Alta. *Jour. Amer. Folklore*, 33: 1–24.

—— AND H. K. HAEBERLIN

1924 Ten folktales in modern Nahuatl. *Ibid.*, 37: 345–70.

BOAS ANNIVERSARY VOLUME

1906 Anthropological papers written in honor of Franz Boas, presented to him on the twenty-fifth anniversary of his doctorate, ninth of August, nineteen hundred and six. New York.

BOBAN, E.

1891 Documents pour servir à l'histoire du Mexique. Catalogue raisonné de la collection de M. E. Eugène Goupil. 2 vols. Paris.

BOBAN CALENDAR WHEEL
1867 M. Doutrelaine, Rapport à son exc.
M. le Ministre de l'Instruction publique sur un manuscrit mexicain de
la collection Boban. *Archives Comm.
Scientifique du Mexique*, 3: 120–33.
Paris.

BODE, B. O.
1961 The dance of the conquest of Guatemala. *Tulane Univ., Middle Amer.
Research Inst.*, Pub. 27, pp. 205–92.

BOEKELMAN, H. J.
1935 Ethno- and archeo-conchological
notes on four Middle American
shells. *Maya Research*, 2: 255–77.
1935 Shell beads in the Caracol, Chichen
Itza. *Ibid.*, 2: 401–04.

BOGERT, C. M., AND J. A. OLIVER
1945 A preliminary analysis of the herpetofauna of Sonora. *Bull. Amer. Mus.
Nat. Hist.*, 83: 301–425.

BOGGS, R. S.
1939 Bibliografía del folklore mexicano.
Mexico.
1943 Notas sobre las excavaciones en la
hacienda "San Andres," Departamento de La Libertad. *Tzunpame*, 3:
104–26.
1943 Observaciones respecto a la importancia de "Tazumal" en la prehistoria
salvadoreña. *Ibid.*, 3: 127–33.
1944 A human-effigy pottery figure from
Chalchuapa, El Salvador. *Carnegie
Inst. Wash., Notes Middle Amer.
Archaeol. Ethnol.*, no. 31.
1944 A preconquest tomb on the Cerro del
Zapote, El Salvador. *Ibid.*, no. 32.
1944 Excavations in central and western El
Salvador. *In* Longyear, 1944, pp.
53–72.
1945 Informe sobre la tercera temporada
de excavaciones en las ruinas de
"Tazumal." *Tzunpame*, 5: 33–45.
1945 Archaeological material from the
Club Internacional, El Salvador.
*Carnegie Inst. Wash., Notes Middle
Amer. Archaeol. Ethnol.*, no. 60.
1945 Bibliografía completa, clasificada y
comentada, de los artículos de "Mexican Folkways," con índice. *Bol.
Bibliografía Antr. Amer.*, 3: 221–68.
1949 Mapa preliminar de las regiones folk-
lóricas de México. *Folklore Amer.*,
9: 1–4.
1949 Tlaloc incensarios in the Baratta collection, El Salvador. *Carnegie Inst.
Wash., Notes Middle Amer. Archaeol.
Ethnol.*, no. 94.
1950 "Olmec" pictographs in the Las Vic-
torias group, Chalchuapa archaeological zone, El Salvador. *Ibid.*, no. 99.

BOILEAU GRANT, J. C.
1936 Anthropometry of the Beaver, Sekani,
and Carrier Indians. *Canada Dept.
Mines, Nat. Mus. Canada*, Bull. 81.
Anthr. Ser., no. 18. Ottawa.

BOLETÍN ESTADÍSTICO
1959 Nos. 7–10. Guatemala.

BOLETÍN INDIGENISTA
1941– Published as a supplement to *America Indígena*, by Inst. Indig. Inter-
amer. Mexico.

BOLTON, H. E.
1916 Spanish explorations in the Southwest, 1542–1706. New York.
1919 Kino's historical memoir of Pimeria
Alta. 2 vols. Cleveland.
1927 Fray Juan Crespi: missionary explorer on the Pacific coast, 1769–
1774. Univ. California Press.
1936 Rim of Christendom. New York.

BONET, F.
1953 Datos sobre las cavernas y otros
fenómenos erosivos de las calizas de
la Sierra de El Abra. *Mem. Cong.
Cien. Mex.*, 3: 238–66.

BONILLA DOMÍNGUEZ, C.
1953 El proceso de cambio cultural en
medicina. *Inst. Nac. Indig.* Mexico.

BONILLA R., L.
1948 Exploración sanitaria y práctica de la
reacción de Mantoux en Tianguis-
tengo, Hidalgo. Mexico.

BONILLA Y SAN MARTÍN, A.
1923 Los mitos de la América precolombiana. Barcelona.

BONNARDEL, R., and R. SOLÍS QUIROGA
1948 Étude biométrique d'un groupe d'indiens du Mexique (Otomis). I:
Recherches psychométriques. *Le
Travail Humain*, 11: 1–68.

BONTÉ, A.
1864 Recherches faites et à faire sur l'orig-

ine de la race mexicaine indigène. *Rev. Orientaliste et Amer.*, 8: 263–80. Paris.

BOOK OF THE PEOPLE

1954 The book of the people: Popol Vuh, the national book of the ancient Quiche Maya. English version by D. Goetz and S. G. Morley from tr. into Spanish by A. Recinos, with pronouncing dictionary comp. by L. K. Weil and with illus. by E. G. Jackson. Los Angeles. *See* Popol Vuh, 1950; Edmonson, 1971.

BOPP, M.

1961 El análisis de polen, con referencia especial a dos perfiles polínicos de la cuenca de Mexico. *In* Homenaje a Pablo Martínez del Río, pp. 49–56.

BORAH, W. W.

1943 Silk raising in colonial Mexico. *Ibero-Amer.*, no. 20.

1951 New Spain's century of depression. *Ibid.*, no. 35.

1954 Early colonial trade and navigation between Mexico and Peru. *Ibid.*, no. 38.

1960 Sources and possibilities for the reconstruction of the demographic process of the Mixteca Alta, 1519–1895. *Rev. Mex. Estud. Antr.*, 16: 159–71.

—— AND S. F. COOK

1958 Price trends of some basic commodities in central Mexico, 1531–1570. *Ibero-Amer.*, no. 40.

1960 The population of central Mexico in 1548: an analysis of the Suma de Visitas de Pueblos. *Ibid.*, no. 43.

BORBOLLA, D. F.

See Rubín de la Borbolla, D. F.

BORBOLLA, S. A. R. DE LA, AND L. AVELEYRA ARROYO DE ANDA

1953 A Plainview point from northern Tamaulipas. *Amer. Antiquity*, 18: 392–93.

BORDAZ, J.

1964 Pre-Columbian ceramic kilns at Peñitas, a post-classic site in coastal Nayarit, Mexico. Doctoral dissertation, Columbia Univ.

BORHEGYI, S. F.

1950 Estudio arqueológico en la falda norte del Volcán de Agua. *Antr. Hist. Guatemala*, 2 (1): 3–22.

1950 Rim-head vessels and cone-shaped effigy prongs of the preclassic period at Kaminaljuyu, Guatemala. *Carnegie Inst. Wash., Notes Middle Amer. Archaeol. Ethnol.*, no. 97.

1950 Tlaloc effigy jar from the Guatemala National Museum. *Ibid.*, no. 96.

1950 A group of jointed figurines in the Guatemala National Museum. *Ibid.*, no. 100.

1950 Notas sobre sellos de barro existentes en el Museo Nacional de Arquelogía y Etnología de Guatemala. *Antr. Hist. Guatemala*, 2 (1): 16–26.

1951 A study of three-pronged incense burners from Guatemala and adjacent areas. *Carnegie Inst. Wash., Notes Middle Amer. Archaeol. Ethnol.*, no. 101.

1951 Further notes on three-pronged incense burners and rimhead vessels in Guatemala. *Ibid.*, no. 105.

1951 "Loop-nose" incense burners in the Guatemala National Museum. *Ibid.*, no. 103.

1952 Notes and comments on "duck-pots" from Guatemala. *Tulane Univ. Middle Amer. Research Rec.*, 2: 1–16.

1952 Travertine vase in the Guatemala National Museum. *Amer. Antiquity*, 17: 254–56.

1953 The miraculous shrines of Our Lord of Esquipulas in Guatemala and Chimayo, New Mexico. *El Palacio*, 60: 83–111.

1954 Jointed figurines in Mesoamerica and their cultural implications. *SW. Jour. Anthr.*, 10: 268–77.

1954 The cult of Our Lord of Esquipulas in Middle America and New Mexico. *El Palacio*, 61: 387–401.

1954 Figurinas articuladas de Mesoamerica. *Antr. Hist. Guatemala*, 6 (2): 3–9.

1955 Pottery mask tradition in Mesoamerica. *SW. Jour. Anthr.*, 11: 205–13.

1955 Chinese figurines in Mesoamerica. *Amer. Antiquity*, 20: 286–88.

1956 Settlement patterns in the Guatemala

highlands: past and present. *In* Willey, 1956, Prehistoric settlement patterns, pp. 101–06.

1956 The development of folk and complex cultures in the southern Maya area. *Amer. Antiquity,* 21: 343–56.

1956 Summer excavations in Guatemala. *Archaeology,* 9: 286–87.

1956 El incensario de "tres asas" de Kaminaljuyu, Guatemala. *Antr. Hist. Guatemala,* 8 (2): 3–7.

1957 Un raro cascabel de barro del período primitivo pre-clásico en Guatemala. *Ibid.,* 9 (1): 9–11.

1957 "Mushroom stones" of Middle America, arranged . . . geographically and chronologically by type. *In* Wasson and Wasson, 1957, vol. 2, folded leaf in pocket.

1957 Incensario de Purulha, Guatemala. *Antr. Hist. Guatemala,* 9 (1): 3–7.

1958 Figuras de incensarios de tres picos de la colección "Raul Moreno," Guatemala. *Ibid.,* 10 (2): 13–15.

1958 Aqualung archaeology. *Natural Hist.,* 67: 120–25.

1959 The composite or "assemble-it-yourself" censer: a new lowland Maya variety of the three-pronged incense burner. *Amer. Antiquity,* 25: 51–58.

1959 Underwater archaeology in the Maya highlands. *Sci. Amer.,* 200: 100–13.

1959 Pre-Columbian cultural connections between Mesoamerica and Ecuador. *Tulane Univ., Middle Amer. Research Records,* vol. 2, no. 6.

1960 Pre-Columbian cultural connections between Mesoamerica and Ecuador: addenda. *Ibid.,* vol. 2, no. 7.

1960 Underwater archaeology in Guatemala. *33d Int. Cong. Amer.* (San Jose, 1958), Acta, 2: 229–40.

1960 America's ball game. *Natural Hist.,* 69: 48–59.

1961 Miniature mushroom stones from Guatemala. *Amer. Antiquity,* 26: 498–504.

1961 Ball-game handstones and ball-game gloves. *In* Lothrop and others, 1961, pp. 126–51.

1961 Shark teeth, stingray spines, and shark fishing in ancient Mexico and Central America. *SW. Jour. Anthr.,* 17: 273–98.

1961 Underwater archaeological studies in Lake Amatitlan, highland Guatemala. *Amer. Phil. Soc.,* Year Book 1960, pp. 547–51.

1963 Pre-Columbian pottery mushrooms from Mesoamerica. *Amer. Antiquity,* 28: 328–38.

—— AND N. S. SCRIMSHAW

1957 Evidence for pre-Columbian goiter in Guatemala. *Amer. Antiquity,* 23: 174–76.

BORN, W.

1937 The use of purple among the Indians of Central America. *Ciba Rev.,* 4: 124–27.

BOSCH GARCÍA, C.

1944 La esclavitud prehispánica entre los aztecas. Fondo de Cultura Económica. Mexico.

BOSCH GIMPERA, P.

1958 *See* Miscelánea Paul Rivet.

BOSQUE, F. DEL

1675 Diary. *In* Bolton, 1916.

BOTERO ARANGO, G.

1942 Contribución al conocimiento de la petrografía del batolito antioqueño. *Mineria,* 20: 9318–30.

BOTURINI BENADUCI, L.

1746 Idea de una nueva historia general de la América septentrional. Madrid. (Other eds. 1871, 1887, 1933.)

BOURKE, J. G.

1886 An Apache campaign in the Sierra Madre. New York.

1893 Primitive distillation among the Tarascos. *Amer. Anthr.,* 6: 65–69.

BOVALLIUS, C.

1886 Nicaraguan antiquities. Stockholm.

BOWDITCH, C. P.

1904 [ed.] Mexican and Central American antiquities, calendar systems, and history. *Smithsonian Inst., Bur. Amer. Ethnol.,* Bull. 28.

1910 The numeration, calendar systems, and astronomical knowledge of the Mayas. Cambridge, Mass.

BOWER, B.

1946 Notes on shamanism among the

Tepehua Indians. *Amer. Anthr.*, 48: 680–83.

BOYD, W. C.

1939 *Tabulae Biologica Hague,* 17 (2): 113–240.

1950 Genetics and the races of man. Boston.

1959 A possible example of the action of selection in human blood groups. *Jour. Medical Education,* 34: 398–99.

—— AND L. G. BOYD

1937 Blood grouping tests on 300 mummies. *Jour. Immunology,* 32: 307–19.

1949 The blood groups and types of the Ramah Navaho. *Amer. Jour. Physical Anthr.,* n.s., 7: 569–74.

BRADEN, C.

1930 Religious aspects of the conquest of Mexico. Durham.

BRADFIELD, W.

1923 Preliminary report on excavating at Cameron Creek site. *El Palacio,* vol. 15, no. 5.

1931 Cameron Creek Village: a site in the Mimbres area in Grant County, New Mexico. *School Amer. Research,* Monogr. 1.

BRAIDWOOD, R. J.

1958 Near Eastern prehistory. *Science,* 127: 1419–30.

1960 The agricultural revolution. *Sci. Monthly,* 203: 131–48.

—— AND G. R. WILLEY

1962 Courses toward urban life. *Viking Fund Pub. Anthr.,* no. 32.

BRAINERD, G. W.

1941 Fine Orange pottery in Yucatan. *Rev. Mex. Estud. Antr.,* 5: 163–83.

1946 Wheel-made pottery in America? *Masterkey,* 20: 191–92.

1949 Forming of the jarro yucateco. *Ibid.,* 23: 56–58.

1951 Early ceramic horizons in Yucatan. *In* Tax, 1951, pp. 72–78.

1953 A cylindical stamp from Ecuador. *Masterkey,* 27: 14–27.

1954 The Maya civilization. Southwest Mus. Los Angeles.

1956 Changing living patterns of the Yucatan Maya. *Amer. Antiquity,* 22: 162–64.

1958 The archaeological ceramics of Yucatan. *Univ. California, Anthr. Records,* no. 19.

BRAMBILA, D.

1959 Psicología y educación del Tarahumar. *Amer. Indig.,* 19: 199–208. Mexico.

BRAMBILA, M.

1942 Mapa de suelos de Mexico. Sec. Agricultura y Fomento, Com. Nac. Irrigación. (Rev. eds. 1946, 1957.)

BRAND, D. D.

1932 Historical geography of northwest Chihuahua. Doctoral dissertation Univ. California.

1935 The distribution of pottery types in northwestern Mexico. *Amer. Anthr.,* 37: 287–305.

1936 Notes to accompany a vegetation map of northwest Mexico. *Univ. New Mexico Bull., Biol. Ser.,* vol. 4 no. 4.

1937 The natural landscape of northwestern Chihuahua. *Univ. New Mexico Bull., Geol. Ser.,* vol. 5, no. 2.

1938 Aboriginal trade routes for sea shells in the Southwest. *Yearbook Assoc. Pacific Coast Geog.,* 4: 3–10.

1939 Notes on the geography and archaeology of Zape, Durango. *In* Brand and Harvey, 1939, pp. 75–105.

1942 Recent archaeologic and geographic investigations in the basin of the Rio Balsas, Guerrero and Michoacan. *27th Int. Cong. Amer.* (Mexico, 1939), Acta, 1: 140–47.

1943 An historical sketch of anthropology and geography in the Tarascan region. Part I. *New Mexico Anthr.,* 6–7 (2): 37–108.

1943 Primitive and modern economy of the middle Rio Balsas, Guerrero and Michoacan. *Proc. 8th Amer. Sci. Cong.* (Washington, 1940), 9: 225–31.

1943 The Chihuahua culture area. *Univ. New Mexico Quar.,* 6: 115–58.

1944 Archaeological relations between northern Mexico and the Southwest. *In* El Norte de México, pp. 199–202.

1944 A note on the preceramic man in northern Mexico. *Ibid.,* p. 164.

1951 Quiroga: a Mexican municipio.

Smithsonian Inst., Inst. Social Anthr., Pub. 11.

1952 Bosquejo histórico de la geografía y la antropología en la región tarasca. Part I. *An. Mus. Michoacano*, ep. 2, 5: 41–163.

1957–58 Coastal study of southwest Mexico. Part I, 1957; Part II, 1958. Univ. Texas, Dept. Geography.

1960 Coalcoman and Motines del Oro: an ex-distrito of Michoacan, Mexico. Univ. Texas, Inst. Latin Amer. Studies. The Hague.

—— AND F. E. HARVEY, eds.

1939 So live the works of men. Seventieth anniversary volume honoring Edgar Lee Hewett. Univ. New Mexico and School Amer. Research.

BRANDHORST, W.

1958 Thermocline topography, zooplankton standing crop, and mechanisms for fertilization in the eastern tropical Pacific. *Jour. Conseil. Int. Expl. Mer*, 24: 16–31.

BRANSFORD, J. F.

1881 Archaeological researches in Nicaragua. *Smithsonian Contrib. Knowledge*, no. 25.

1882 Report on explorations in Central America in 1881. *Smithsonian Ann. Rept. 1882*.

BRASSEUR DE BOURBOURG, C. E.

1857–59 Histoire des nations civilisées du Mexique et de l'Amérique-Centrale durant les siècles antérieurs à Cristophe Colomb. 4 vols. Paris.

1861 Popul Vuh: le livre sacré et les mythes de l'antiquité américaine, avec les livres héroïques et historiques des Quichés. Paris.

1862 Grammaire de la langue Quiché servant d'introduction au Rabinal-Achi. Paris.

1864 Relation des choses de Yucatan de Diego de Landa . . . accompagné de documents divers historiques et chronologiques. . . . Paris.

1865 Mixtèques, Zapotèques, Mijes, Wabi, Chontales, et Chinantecas, etc., dans l'état d'Oaxaca. *Archives Comm. Sci. Mexique*, 1: 123–25.

1868 Quatre lettres sur Mexique. Paris.

1869–70 Manuscrit troano. Paris.

1871 Bibliothèque Mexicaine-Guatémalienne. Paris.

1872 Dictionnaire, grammaire et chrestomathie de la langue maya. . . . Paris.

BREITINGER, E.

1938 Zur Berechnung der Körperhöhe aus den langen Gliedmassenknochen. *Anthr. Anz.*, 14: 249–74.

1953 La misurazionne della capacita cranica. S.A.S., nos. 27–28, pp. 69–116.

BRETERNITZ, D. A.

1959 Excavations at Nantack Village, Point of Pines, Arizona. *Univ. Arizona, Anthr. Papers*, no. 1.

BRETON, A. C.

1908 Archaeology in Mexico. *Man*, 8 (17): 34–37. London.

1917 Relationships in ancient Guatemala. *Ibid.*, art. 119.

1919 Some Mexican clay heads. *Ibid.*, vol. 19, no. 3.

BRETZ, J. H.

1955 Cavern-making in a part of the Mexican plateau. *Jour. Geol.*, 63: 364–75.

BREW, J. O.

1940 Mexican influence upon the Indian cultures of the Southwestern United States in the sixteenth and seventeenth centuries. *In* The Maya and their neighbors, pp. 341–48.

1944 On the Pueblo IV and on the Katchina-Tlaloc relations. *In* El Norte de México, pp. 241–44.

1946 Archaeology of Alkali Ridge, southeastern Utah. *Papers Peabody Mus., Harvard Univ.*, vol. 21.

BRIGGS, E.

1961 Mitla Zapotec grammar. Inst. Ling. Verano and Centro Invest. Antr. Mexico. Mexico.

BRIGGS, J. C.

1951 A review of the clingfishes (Gobiesocidae) of the eastern Pacific with descriptions of new species. *Proc. Calif. Zool. Club*, 1: 57–108.

1955 A monograph of the clingfishes (order Xenopterygii). *Stanford Ichth. Bull.*, 6: 1–224.

BRIGGS, L. P.
1951 The ancient Khmer empire. *Trans. Amer. Phil. Soc.*, vol. 41, pt. 1.

BRIGHT, W.
1955 A bibliography of the Hokan-Coahuiltecan languages. *Int. Jour. Amer. Ling.*, 21: 276–85.

1956 Glottochronologic counts of Hokaltecan material. *Language*, 32: 42–48.

1960 Accent in classical Aztec. *Int. Jour. Amer. Ling.*, 26: 66–68.

BRINTON, D. G.
1882 The Maya chronicles. *Library Aboriginal Amer. Lit.*, no. 1. Philadelphia.

1882 American hero-myths. Philadelphia.

1883 Aboriginal American authors and their productions. Philadelphia.

1883 The folk-lore of Yucatan. *Folk-lore Jour.*, 1: 244–56.

1883 The Güegüence: a comedy ballet in the Nahuatl-Spanish dialect of Nicaragua. Philadelphia.

1885 The annals of the Cakchiquels. *Library Aboriginal Amer. Lit.*, no. 6. Philadelphia.

1885 On the Xinca Indians of Guatemala. *Proc. Amer. Phil. Soc.*, 22: 89–97.

1886 Notes on the Mangue dialect. *Ibid.*, 23: 238–57.

1887 On an ancient human footprint from Nicaragua. *Ibid.*, 24: 437–44.

1890 Essays of an Americanist. Philadelphia.

1890 Ancient Nahuatl poetry. *Library Aboriginal Amer. Lit.*, no. 7. Philadelphia.

1890 Rig-Veda Americanus. Philadelphia.

1891 The American race. New York.

1892 Chontales and Populucas: a contribution to Mexican ethnography. *8th Int. Cong. Amer.* (Paris, 1890), Acta, pp. 556–64.

1894 Nagualism: a study in native American folklore and history. *Proc. Amer. Phil. Soc.*, 33: 1–65.

1896 The myths of the New World. Philadelphia.

1897 The pillars of Ben. *Bull. Free Mus. Sci. and Art*, 1: 3–10.

BRITISH ASSOCIATION FOR THE ADVANCEMENT OF SCIENCE
1874 Notes and queries on anthropology. London.

BRITISH HONDURAS LAND USE SURVEY TEAM
1959 Land in British Honduras. *Colonial Research*, Pub. 24. London.

BROCA, P.
1865 Instructions générales pour les recherches et observations anthropologiques (anatomie et physiologie). *Mem. Soc. Anthr. Paris*, 2: 69–204.

BROCK, J. F.
1954 Survey of the world situation on kwashiorkor. *Ann. New York Acad. Sci.*, 57: 696–713.

BROCKINGTON, D.
1955 Brief report on the tombs at Yagul. *Mesoamer. Notes*, no. 4, pp. 70–71.

BRODKORB, P.
1943 Birds from the gulf lowlands of southern Mexico. *Univ. Mich., Mus. Zool.*, Misc. Pub. 55.

BROECKER, W. S., E. A. OLSON, AND J. B. BIRD
1959 Radiocarbon measurements on samples of known age. *Nature*, 183: 1582–84.

BROESIKE, G.
1877 Das anthropologische Material des Anatomischen Museums der Koeniglichen Universitat. *Anthr. Samml. Deutsch.*, pp. 52–57. Brunswick.

BROMAN, V. L.
1958 Jarmo figurines. M.A. thesis, Radcliffe College.

BROOKS, C. E. P.
1925 The distribution of thunderstorms over the earth. *Geophys. Mem.*, no. 24. British Meteorological Office. London.

BROOKS, C. W.
1875 Reports of Japanese vessels wrecked in the north Pacific, from the earliest records to the present time. *Proc. California Acad. Sci.*, 6: 50–66.

BROOKS, R. H., L. KAPLAN, H. C. CUTLER, AND T. W. WHITAKER
1962 Plant materials from a cave on the Río Zape, Durango, Mexico. *Amer. Antiquity*, 27: 356–69.

BROWN, K. S., B. L. HANNA, A. A. DAHLBERG, AND H. H. STRANDSKOV

1958 The distribution of blood group alleles among Indians of southwest North America. *Amer. Jour. Human Genetics*, 10: 175–95.

BROWN, W. L.

1960 Races of maize in the West Indies. *Nat. Acad. Sci., Nat. Research Council*, Pub. 792.

BRUCE S., R.

1965 Jerarquía maya entre los dioses lacandones. *An. Inst. Nac. Antr. Hist.*, 18: 99–108.

BRUGGE, D. M.

1956 Pima bajo basketry. *Kiva*, vol. 22, no. 1.

BRUNER, E. M.

1956 Cultural transmission and cultural change. *SW. Jour. Anthr.*, 12: 191–99.

BRUSH, C., AND E. BRUSH

n.d. Field notes on archaeological investigations on the Costa Grande and Costa Chica of Guerrero.

BRYAN, K.

1946 Comentario e intento de correlación con la cronología glacial. *Mem. 2d Cong. Mex. Cien. Sociales*, 5: 220–25.

1948 Los suelos complejos y fósiles de la altiplanicie de Mexico, en relación a los cambios climáticos. *Bol. Soc. Geol. Mex.*, 13: 1–20.

BUCK, J. L.

1930 Chinese farm economy. Univ. Chicago Press.

BUDOWSKI, G.

1956 Tropical savannas, a sequence of forest felling and repeated burnings. *Turrialba*, 6: 23–33. Inst. Interamer. Cien. Agrícolas. Turrialba, Costa Rica.

1959 Algunas relaciones entre la presente vegetación y antiguas actividades del hombre en el trópico americano. *33d Int. Cong. Amer.* (San Jose, 1958), Acta, 1: 257–63.

1959 The ecological status of fire in tropical American lowlands. *Ibid.*, 1: 264–78.

BUELNA, E.

1890 Arte de la lengua cáhita por un padre de la compañía de Jesús. Mexico.

1892 Peregrinación de los Aztecas y nombres geográficos indígenas de Sinaloa. 2d ed. Mexico.

BUITRÓN, A.

1961 El desarrollo de la comunidad en la teoría y en la práctica. *Amer. Indig.*, 21: 141–50.

BUKASOV, S. M.

1930 The cultivated plants of Mexico, Guatemala, and Colombia. *Bull. Appl. Bot. Gen. and Plant Breeding*, Suppl. 47. (English summary, pp. 470–553.)

BULL, T. H.

1959 Preliminary report on an archaeological site, district of Chame, province of Panama. *Panama Archaeol.*, vol. 2, no. 1.

BULLARD, F. M.

1956 Volcanic activity in Costa Rica and Nicaragua in 1954. *Trans. Amer. Geophys. Union*, 37: 75–82.

1957 Active volcanoes of Central America. *20th Int. Cong. Geol.*, sec. 1: Vulcanología del Cenozoico, 2: 351–71.

BULLARD, W. R., JR.

1960 Archaeological investigation of the Maya ruin of Topoxte, Peten, Guatemala. *Amer. Phil. Soc.*, Year Book, pp. 551–54.

1960 Maya settlement pattern in northeastern Peten, Guatemala. *Amer. Antiquity*, 25: 355–72.

BULOW, T. VON

1922 Contribución al estudio de la craneología costarricense. *Escuela Costarricense*, 8: 1–16. San Jose.

BUNZEL, R.

1940 The role of alcoholism in two Central American cultures. *Psychiatry*, 3: 361–87.

1952 Chichicastenango: a Guatemalan village. *Amer. Ethnol. Soc.*, Pub. 22.

1959 Chichicastenango and Chamula. *In* R. G. McCarthy, ed., Drinking and intoxication: selected readings in social attitudes and controls, pp. 73–86. Pub. Division Yale Center of Alcohol Studies. New Haven.

1960 El papel del alcoholismo en dos cul-
    turas centroamericanas. *Bol. Inst.
    Indig. Nac.*, 3: 27–81. Mexico.

BURG, A.
    n.d. La dentición en la población de La
        Candelaria, Coahuila. Inst. Nac.
        Antr. Hist. MS. Mexico.

BURGESS, D. M.
    1946 Quiche translation of the New Testa-
        ment. *Amer. Bible Soc.*

—— AND P. XEC
    1955 Popol Wuj. Quezaltenango.

BURGESS, P. (pseud. Bopal Resgubs)
    n.d. Quech'aw ri Awaj. Quezaltenango.
    n.d. Quincojon Che ri Dios Tataxel.
        Quezaltenango.
    n.d. Ri u Pix K'ak'. [Weekly.] Quezal-
        tenango.
    n.d. Himnario en Quiché. Quezaltenango.
    1924 Ch'abal Bixobal che ri kajawal Dios.
        Tip. "El Noticiero." Quezaltenango.
    1925 Ri utzilaj tzijobal jas ri xubij ri Xuan.
        Quezaltenango.

BURGOA, F. DE
    1670 Palestra historial de virtudes, y ex-
        emplares apostólicos. . . . Pub. Archi-
        vo General de la Nación (Mexico,
        1934).
    1674 Geográfica descripción de la parte
        septentrional del polo ártico de la
        América y nueva iglesia de las Indias
        Occidentales, y sitio astronómico de
        esta provincia de predicadores de
        Antequera, Valle de Oaxaca . . .
        México. *Pub. Archivo General de
        la Nación*, vols. 25, 26. (2d ed.
        1934, Mexico.)

BURKART, J.
    1836 Aufenthalt und Reisen in Mexiko in
        den Jahren 1825 bis 1824. Stutt-
        gart.

BURKITT, R.
    1920 The hills and the corn: a legend of
        the Kekchi Indians of Guatemala.
        *Univ. Pennsylvania, Univ. Mus.
        Anthr. Pub.*, 8: 183–227.
    1924 A journey in northern Guatemala.
        Mus. Jour., Univ. Pennsylvania, 15:
        115–44.
    1930 Excavations at Chocola. *Ibid.*, 21:
        5–40.
    1930 Explorations in the highlands of

western Guatemala. *Ibid.*, 21: 41–
    72.
    1933 Two stones in Guatemala. *An-
        thropos*, 28: 9–26.

BURLAND, C. A.
    1948 Art and life in ancient Mexico. Ox-
        ford.
    1949 Mexican deluge legends. *Atlantean
        Research*, 2 (4): 62–64.
    1958 The inscription on Stela 1, El Casti-
        llo, region of Santa Lucia Cotzumal-
        huapa, Guatemala. *32d Int. Cong.
        Amer.* (Copenhagen, 1956), Acta,
        pp. 326–30.
    1964 The bases of religion in Aztec Mexico.
        Guild of Pastoral Psychology, Guild
        Lecture 127. London.
    1967 The gods of Mexico. London.

BURT, W. H.
    1938 Faunal relationships and geographic
        distribution of mammals in Sonora,
        Mexico. *Univ. Mich., Mus. Zool.,*
        Misc. Pub. 39.

BURTON, R. V., AND J. W. M. WHITING
    1961 The absent father and cross-sex iden-
        tity. *Merrill-Palmer Quar. Behavior
        and Development*, vol. 7, no. 2.

BUSHNELL, G. H. S.
    1965 Ancient art of the Americas. Lon-
        don.

BUSHNELL, J.
    1958 La Virgen de Guadalupe as surrogate
        mother in San Juan Atzingo. *Amer.
        Anthr.*, 60: 261–65.

BUSIERRE, M. T.
    1863 L'empire mexicain: histoire des Tol-
        tèques, des Chichamèques, des Az-
        tèques et de la conquête espagnole.
        Paris.

BUSTAMANTE, M. E., AND G. VARELA
    1943 Una nueva rickettsiasis en México:
        existencia de la fiebre manchada en
        los estados de Sinaloa y Sonora.
        *Rev. Inst. Salubridad y Enfermedad
        Tropical Méx.*, 4: 189.

BUTLER, M.
    1935 A study of Maya mouldmade figu-
        rines. *Amer. Anthr.*, 37: 636–72.
    1935 Piedras Negras pottery. *Univ. Penn-
        sylvania Mus., Piedras Negras Pre-
        lim. Papers*, no. 4.
    1940 A pottery sequence from the Alta

38

Verapaz, Guatemala. *In* The Maya and their neighbors, pp. 250–67.

1959 Spanish contact at Chipal. *In* Bierhenke, pp. 28–35.

BUTTERWORTH, D. S.

1962 A study of the urbanization process among Mixtec migrants from Tilaltongo in Mexico City. *Amer. Indig.*, 22: 257–74.

—— AND J. PADDOCK, eds.

1962 The Mixtec and Zapotec cultures: the Zapotecs. *Bol. Estud. Oaxaqueños*, no. 21. The Mixtec and Zapotec cultures: the Mixtecs. *Ibid.*, no. 22. Relaciones of Oaxaca of the 16th and 18th centuries: relaciones of Cuilapan, 14th chapter of the relación of Chichicapa, and description of the city of Antequera. *Ibid.*, no. 23. Mexico.

BUXTON, L. H. D.

1925 Skulls from the valley of Mexico. *Rept. 92d meeting, British Assoc. Advancement of Science*, p. 421. London.

—— AND G. M. MORANT

1933 The essential craniological technique. I: Definitions of points and planes. *Jour. Royal Anthr. Inst.*, 63: 19–48. London.

BYERS, D. S.

1931 Physical measurements. *In* O. La Farge and D. Byers, The year bearer's people. *Tulane Univ., Middle Amer. Research Inst.*, Pub. 3.

1967 [ed.] The prehistory of the Tehuacan Valley. Vol. 1: Environment and subsistence. Published for the Robert S. Peabody Foundation, Phillips Academy, Andover, Mass. Univ. Texas Press.

1967 Climate and hydrology. *In* his preceding entry, 1: 48–65.

CABALLERO, D. J.

1880 Gramática del idioma mexicano. . . . Mexico.

CABEZA DE VACA, A. N.

1871 The narrative of Alvar Núñez Cabeza de Vaca. Tr. by T. Buckingham Smith. Washington.

CABRERA, A. J.

1876 La huaxteca potosina: ligeros apuntes sobre este país. San Luis Potosi.

CABRERA, L. G.

1920 Condiciones biológicas especiales a que están sometidos los habitantes de las diversas municipalidades del Distrito Federal. *Bol. Dirección Estud. Biol.*, 2: 387–91. Mexico.

1945 Descripción del esqueleto núm. 3 encontrado en la barranca del Aguila, Tepeaca. *An. Inst. Nac. Antr. Hist.*, 1: 75–79. Mexico.

CABRERA, M. A.

1950 Breve estudio sobre la repartición de los grupos sanguíneos entre nuestra población y la evolución de las investigación de la paternidad por medio de ellos en nuestro país. *Salubridad y Asistencia*, 3: 16–17.

—— AND J. R. DE LEÓN

1949 Historia del primer caso clínico de leishmaniosis visceral (kala azar) descubierto en Guatemala. *Univ. Guatemala, Inst. Invest. Cien.*, Pub. 2.

CABROL, A., AND L. COUTIER

1932 Contribution à l'étude de la taille de l'obsidienne au Mexique. *Bull. Soc. Préhist. Française*, 29: 579–82. Paris.

CACALCHEN, LIBRO DE

n.d. [Collection of wills, statutes, and other legal documents in Maya.] MS. Gates reproduction.

1647–1826 Manuscript. Photograph in Newberry Library. 167 pp.

CACHO A., R.

1961 La Cuidad de México. *Rev. Económica*, 24 (4): 23–33.

CADENA, C.

1892 Vocabulario Quiché. *In* León Fernández, ed., Lenguas indígenas de Centro-America en el siglo XVII. San Jose.

CAHILL, H.

1933 American sources of modern art. Mus. Modern Art. New York.

CAIN, S. A., AND G. M. DE OLIVEIRA CASTRO

1959 Manual of vegetation analysis. New York.

CALDERÓN, E.

1908 Estudios lingüísticos. I: Las lenguas

(sinca) de Yupiltepeque y del barrio norte de Chiquimulilla en Guatemala. II: Las lenguas de Oluta, Sayula, Texistepec en el Istmo de Tehuantepec en México. Guatemala.

CALDERÓN DE LA BARCA, F.
1843 Life in Mexico. Boston.

CALENDARIO DE LAS FIESTAS
1959 Calendario de las fiestas titulares de la Republica de Guatemala. Inst. Indig. Nac. Guatemala.

CALENDARIO MEXICANO
1919 Calendario mexicano, latino y castellano. *Bol. Biblioteca Nacional*, vol. 12, no. 5 Mexico.

CALKINI, CHILAM BALAM DE
n.d. Manuscript. Photograph in Newberry Library. 30 pp.

CALKINI, CRÓNICA DE
n.d. [Chronicle and geographical description of the Province of Ah Canul in Maya.] MS. Gates reproduction.

CALLEGARI, G. V.
1922–23 Scultura, lapidaria, oreficeria nel Messico precolombino. *Dedalo: Rassegna d'arte diretta de vgo ojetti*, 3: 541–66. Rome and Milan.

CALLEN, E., AND R. S. MACNEISH
n.d. Prehistoric Tamaulipas food remains as determined by a study of fecal remains. MS.

CALLENDER, S. R., AND R. R. RACE
1946 A serological and genetical study of multiple antibodies by a patient with lupus erythematosus diffusus. *Ann. Eugenics*, 13: 102–17.

CALNEK, E. E.
1959 Distribution and location of the Tzeltal and Tzotzil pueblos of the highlands of Chiapas from earliest time to the present. *In* McQuown, 1959.
1961 Report on Chiapas ethnohistory. Nat. Sci. Found., Seminar on Chiapas.
1962 Highland Chiapas before the Spanish conquest. Doctoral dissertation, Univ. Chicago.

CALVERT, P. P.
1908 The composition and ecological relations of the odonate fauna of Mexico and Central America. *Proc.*

Acad. Nat. Sci. Philadelphia, pp. 460–91.

CALVO, T.
1726 Bocabulario español-quiché. Photograph in Newberry Library. 144 pp.

CÁMARA BARBACHANO, F.
1946 Monografía sobre los Tzeltales de Tenejapa. *Univ. Chicago, Micro. Coll. MSS Middle Amer. Cult. Anthr.*, no. 5.
1946 Monografía de los Tzotziles de San Miguel Mitontik. *Ibid.*, no. 6.
1947 Culturas contemporáneas de México. *Amer. Indig.*, 7: 165–71.
1952 Instituciones religiosas y políticas indígenas. *In* Hechos y problemas del México rural. Seminario Mex. Sociol. Mexico.
1952 Organización religiosa y política de Tenejapa. *An. Inst. Nac. Antr. Hist.*, 4: 32.
1952 Religious and political organization. *In* Tax, 1952, Heritage of conquest, pp. 142–73.
1956 Factores causales respecto al bracero mexicano. *In* Estudios antropológicos, pp. 305–10.

CAMAVITTO, D.
1937 Premiers résultats d'une recherche anthropologique sur les Zambos de la Costa Chica, Guerrero (Mexico). *I Congrès d'Eugenique*. Dieppe.

CAMMAN, S. V. R.
1952 A Chinese soapstone carving from Yucatan. *Amer. Antiquity*, 18: 68–69.

CAMPBELL, E. W. C., AND W. H. CAMPBELL
1935 The Pinto Basin site. *Southwest Mus. Papers*, no. 9.

CAMPBELL, T. N.
1947 The Johnson site: type site of the Aransas focus of the Texas coast. *Bull. Texas Archaeol. Paleontol. Soc.*, 18: 40–76.
1958 Origin of the mescal bean cult. *Amer. Anthr.*, 60: 156–60.
1960 Archaeology of the central and southern sections of the Texas coast: a review of Texas archaeology, Part 1. *Bull. Texas Archaeol. Soc.*, 29: 145–75.

CAMPOBELLO, N., AND G. CAMPOBELLO
1940 Ritmos indígenas de México. Mexico.

CAMPOS, J. M.
1873 Paralelo entre las razas indígenas y criolla. Toluca.

CAMPOS, R. M.
1929 El folklore literario de México. Mexico.
1936 La producción literaria de los Aztecas. Mus. Nac. Arqueol. Hist. Etnog. Mexico.
1937 Tradiciones y leyendas mexicanas. An. Mus. Nac. Arqueol. Hist. Etnog., 2: 71–191.

CANBY, J. S.
1949 Excavations at Yarumela, Spanish Honduras. Doctoral dissertation, Harvard Univ.
1951 Possible chronological implications of the long ceramic sequence recovered at Yarumela, Spanish Honduras. In Tax, 1951, pp. 79–85.

CANCIAN, FRANCESCA M.
1963 Family interaction in Zinacantan. Doctoral dissertation, Harvard Univ.
1964 Interaction patterns in Zinacanteco families. Amer. Sociol. Rev., 29: 540–50.
1965 The effect of patrilocal households on nuclear family interaction in Zinacantan. Estud. Cultura Maya, 5: 299–315.

CANCIAN, FRANK
1963 Informant error and native prestige ranking in Zinacantan. Amer. Anthr., 65: 1068–75.
1964 Some aspects of the social and religious organization of a Maya society. 35th Int. Cong. Amer. (Mexico, 1962), Acta, 1: 335–43.
1965 Economics and prestige in a Maya community: the religious cargo system in Zinacantan. Stanford Univ. Press.
1965 Efectos de los programas económicos del gobierno mexicano en las tierras altas mayas de Zinacantan. Estud. Cultura Maya, 5: 281–97.

CANDOLLE, A. DE
1959 Origin of cultivated plants. New York. (1st ed. 1871, Paris.)

CANGAS Y QUIÑONES, S. DE
1928 Descripción de la Villa del Espíritu Santo. Relación de la vicaria y partido de Santa Cruz que en mexicano se dice Iztepec y en zapoteco Quialoo. Relación de los Pueblos Peñoles. Rev. Mex. Estud. Hist., 2 (app.): 176–91. [MS, dated 1580, in Univ. Texas Library.]

CANO, F.
1873 Testimonio del descubrimiento y posesión de la laguna del Nuevo Mexico, hecho por Francisco Cano, teniente de alcalde mayor de las minas de Mascipil en la Nueva Galicia, 1568. In Col. Doc. Inéditos del Archivo de las Indias, by Pacheco y Cárdenas. Mexico.

CANSECO, A. DE
1905 Relación de Tlacolula y Mitla. In Paso y Troncoso, 1905, 4: 144–54.

CANTARES MEXICANOS
1887 D. G. Brinton, Ancient Nahuatl poetry. Library Aboriginal Amer. Lit., no. 7. Philadelphia.
1899 A. Peñafiel, Cantares mexicanos: cantares en idioma mexicano, impresos según el manuscrito original que existe en la Biblioteca Nacional. In Col. doc. para la historia mexicana, vol. 2. Mexico.
1904 A. Peñafiel, Cantares en idioma mexicano: reproducción facsimilar del manuscrito original existente en la Biblioteca Nacional. Mexico.
1957 L. S. Schultze-Jena, Alt-Aztekische Gesänge. Quellenwerke zur alten Geschichte Amerikas Auggezeichnet in den Sprachen der Eingeborenen. Ibero-Amerikanischen Bibliothek, 6. Berlin.
1965 A. M. Garibay K., Poesía Náhuatl, II: Cantares mexicanos, manuscrito de la Biblioteca Nacional de México. Part I. Univ. Nac. Autónoma Méx., Inst. Invest. Hist., Fuentes Indígenas de la Cultura Náhuatl, no. 5.
1968 A. M. Garibay K., Poesía Náhuatl, III: Cantares mexicanos, manuscrito de la Biblioteca Nacional de México. Part II. Ibid., no. 6.

41

CANTELLANO ALVARADO, L.
1949 Exploración sanitaria del municipio de Hueytamalco, Puebla, y sus principales problemas médicos. Mexico.

CAPLOW, T.
1949 The social ecology of Guatemala City. *Social Forces*, 28: 113–33.
1952 The modern Latin American city. *In* Tax, 1952, Acculturation in the Americas, pp. 255–60.

CAPMANY, A.
1931 El baile y la danza. *In* F. Carreras y Candi, Folklore y costumbres de España, 2: 168–418. Barcelona.

CÁRDENAS, E.
1892 Algunas consideraciones sobre la medición torácica. Mexico.

CÁRDENAS, H.
1955 Informe agroeconómico de Jamiltepec, Oax. *Inst. Nac. Indigenista*, Ser. Mimeo., no. 8. Mexico.

CÁRDENAS, T. DE
17thC? Arte de la lengua cacchi de Coban. MS in Bibliothèque Nationale.

CARDOS DE M., A.
1959 El comercio de los Mayas antiguos. *Acta Anthr.*, ep. 2, vol. 2, no. 1. Mexico.

CARDOSO, J.
1948 Sangre de los tepehuanes. Mexico.

CAREY, H. A.
1931 An analysis of the northwestern Chihuahua culture. *Amer. Anthr.*, 33: 325–74.
1951 *Review of* The Pendleton ruin, Hidalgo County, New Mexico, by A. V. Kidder, H. S. and C. B. Cosgrove. *Amer. Antiquity*, 17: 156–57.
1954 Grant No. 1597 (1953), $750,000. The ancient Indian culture centering in the Casas Grandes Valley, northwestern Chihuahua, Mexico. *Year Book Amer. Phil. Soc.*, pp. 313–16.
1955 Grant No. 1779, $750,000. The Casas Grandes culture, Chihuahua, Mexico. *Ibid.*, pp. 314–16.

CARLO, A. M., ed.
1951 Historia de las Indias. Vols. 1–3. Mexico.

CARMACK, R. M.
1968 Toltec influence on the postclassic culture history of highland Guatemala. *Tulane Univ., Middle Amer. Research Inst.*, Pub. 26, pp. 49–92.

CARMICHAEL, J. H.
1959 Balsalobre on idolatry in Oaxaca. *Bol. Estud. Oaxaqueños*, Sept. 1, pp. 1–13.

CARNAP, R.
1942 Introduction to semantics. New York.

CARNEGIE INSTITUTION OF WASHINGTON
1935–54 Annual reports of the chairman of the Division of Historical Research or the Department of Archaeology. Year Books 34–53.
1952–57 Current reports. Dept. Archaeol.

CARO BAROJA, J.
1957 Vasconiana. Madrid.

CAROCHI, H.
1645 Arte de la lengua mexicana. *In* Col. de gramáticas, pp. 395–538. (Mexico, 1759, 1892.)

CARPENTER, R. H.
1954 Geology and ore deposits of the Rosario mining district and the San Juancito mountains, Honduras, Central America. *Bull. Geol. Soc. Amer.*, 65: 23–38.

CARR, A. F.
1949 La Montaña Llorana. *Sci. Monthly*, 68: 225–35.
1950 Outline for a classification of animal habitats in Honduras. *Bull. Amer. Mus. Nat. Hist.*, 94: 563–94.
1952 Handbook of turtles: the turtles of the United States, Canada, and Baja California. Ithaca, N.Y.

—— AND L. GIOVANNOLI
1957 The ecology and migrations of sea turtles: two results of field work in Costa Rica. *Amer. Mus. Novitates*, no. 1835.

CARR, M.
1952 The historical origin of the Middle American 'disease' concept [1937]. *Univ. Chicago, Micro. Coll. MSS Middle Amer. Cult. Anthr.*, no. 31.

CARR, R. F., AND J. E. HAZARD
1961 Map of the ruins of Tikal, El Peten, Guatemala. *Mus. Monogr., Univ. Pennsylvania, Tikal Reports*, no. 11.

CARRASCO PIZANA, P.
1945 Quetzalcoatl, dios de Coatepec de los

costales, Guerrero. *Tlalocan*, 2: 89–90.

1946 Paricutín volcano in Tarascan folklore. *El Palacio*, 53: 299–306.

1950 Los Otomíes: cultura e historia prehispánicas de los pueblos mesoamericanos de habla otomiana. *Univ. Nac. Autónoma Méx., Pub. Inst. Hist.*, 1st ser., no. 15.

1950 Middle American ethnography. *Pan Amer. Union, Social Sci. Monogr.*, no. 10.

1951 Las culturas indígenas de Oaxaca, México. *Amer. Indig.*, 2: 99–114.

1951 Una cuenta ritual entre los zapotecas del sur. *In* Homenaje Caso, pp. 91–100.

1952 El sol y la luna: versión mixe. *Tlalocan*, 3 (2): 168–69.

1952 Tarascan folk religion: an analysis of economic, social and religious interactions. *Tulane Univ., Middle Amer. Research Inst.*, Pub. 17, pp. 1–64.

1959 Kinship and territorial groups in pre-Spanish Guatemala. MS of paper delivered at meeting of Amer. Anthr. Assoc., 1959.

1960 Pagan rituals and beliefs among the Chontal Indians of Oaxaca, Mexico. *Univ. California Pub., Anthr. Records*, vol. 20, no. 3.

1961 The civil-religious hierarchy in Mesoamerican communities: pre-Spanish background and colonial development. *Amer. Anthr.*, 63: 483–97.

1961 Un mito y una ceremonia entre los chatinos de Oaxaca. *In* Homenaje Townsend, pp. 43–48.

1961 El barrio y la regulación del matrimonio en un pueblo del Valle de México en el siglo XVI. *Rev. Mex. Estud. Antr.*, 17: 7–26.

1963 Las tierras de dos indios nobles de Tepeaca en el siglo XVI. *Tlalocan*, 4: 97–119.

1964 Tres libros de tributos del Museo Nacional de México y su importancia para los estudios demográficos. *35th Int. Cong. Amer.* (Mexico, 1962), Acta, 3: 373–78.

1964 Family structure of sixteenth century

Tepoztlan. *In* Process and pattern in culture, R. A. Manners, ed., pp. 185–210.

1966 Documentos sobre el rango de Tecuhtli entre los nahuas tramontanos. *Tlalocan*, 5: 133–60.

1966 Sobre algunos términos de parentesco en el náhuatl clásico. *Inst. Hist., Estud. Cultura Náhuatl*, 6: 149–66. Mexico.

1971 Social organization of ancient Mexico. *In* Handbook of Middle American Indians, R. Wauchope, ed., vol. 10, art. 14.

in press Sucesión y alianzas matrimoniales en la dinastía teotihuacana. *Rev. Mex. Estud. Antr.*

——, W. MILLER, AND R. J. WEITLANER

1959 El calendario mixe. *El Mex. Antiguo*, 9: 153–72.

CARRASCO PUENTE, R.

1948 Bibliografía del Isthmus de Tehuantepec. Sec. Relaciones Exteriores. Mexico.

CARREÑO, A. DE LA O.

1951 Las provincias geohidrológicas de Mexico. *Inst. Geol., Univ. Nac. Autónoma de Mex.*, Bol. 56.

CARREÑO, A. M.

1912 La trepanación entre nuestros aborígenes. *17th Int. Cong. Amer.* (Mexico session, 1910), Acta, pp. 113–19.

CARRERA STAMPA, M.

1954 Los gremios mexicanos: la organización gremial en la Nueva España, 1521–1861. Mexico.

1955 [ed.] Memoria de los servicios que habia hecho Nuño de Guzmán, desde que fue nombrado gobernador de Pánuco en 1525. Mexico. (See also Fourth Anonymous.)

CARRERI, G.

1927 Viaje a la Nueva España. 2 vols. (Other eds. 1697, 1700, 1955.)

CARRIEDO, J. B.

1846 Estudios históricos y estadísticos del estado libre de Oaxaca. (2d ed. 1949.)

1851 Los palacios antiguos de Mitla. *Ilustración Mex.*, 2: 493–500.

1852 Leyenda zapoteca. *Ibid.*, 3: 336–45.

CARRIKER, M. A., JR.
1910 An annotated list of the birds of Costa Rica including Cocos Island. *Ann. Carnegie Mus.*, 6: 314–915.

CARRILLO, R.
1902 Datos sobre el desarrollo físico normal del niño mexicano. *Rev. Méd.*, 14: 269. Mexico.

CARRILLO GONZÁLEZ, M.
1950 Exposición de las condiciones sanitarias prevalentes en el municipio de San Sebastian Zinacatepec, Puebla. Mexico.

CARRILLO Y ANCONA, D. C.
1881 Historia antigua de Yucatan. Merida.

CARROLL, J. B., ed.
1956 Language, thought and reality. Selected writings of Benjamin Whorf.

CARTA DE UN RELIGIOSA
1951 Carta de un religiosa sobre la rebelión de indios mexicanos en 1692. *In* Biblioteca de historiadores mexicanas. Mexico.

CARTAS DE INDIAS
1877 Publícalas por primera vez el ministro de fomento. Madrid.

CARTER, G. F.
1945 Plant geography and culture history in the American southwest. *Viking Fund Pub. Anthr.*, no. 5.
1950 Plant evidence for early contacts with America. *SW. Jour. Anthr.*, 6: 161–82.
1957 Culture trails in the Pacific. *Johns Hopkins Mag.*, February.
1957 Pleistocene man at San Diego. Baltimore.

CARUS, C. G.
1856 Ueber die sogennanten Aztekenkinder. Berlin.

CASAGRANDE, J. B.
1948 Comanche baby language. *Int. Jour. Amer. Ling.*, 14: 11–14.
1954–55 Comanche linguistic acculturation. *Ibid.*, 20: 140–51, 217–37; 21: 8–25.
1959 Some observations on the study of intermediate societies. *In* Ray, 1959, pp. 1–10.

CASARES, D.
1905 A notice of Yucatan with some remarks on its water supply. *Amer.*

Antiquarian Soc. Papers, n.s., 17: 207–30.

CASARRUBIAS, V.
1945 Rebeliones indígenas de la Nueva España. Sec. Educación Pública. Mexico. (Extracts appear in supplement to González Obregón, 1952, 2d ed.)

CASE, H. A.
1911 Views on and of Yucatan. Merida.

CASO, A.
1924–27 Un antiguo juego mexicano, el patolli. *El Mex. Antiguo*, 2: 203–11.
1927 Una pintura desconocida en Mitla. *Rev. Mex. Estud. Hist.*, 1: 243–47.
1927 Las ruinas de Tizatlán, Tlax. *Ibid.*, 1: 139–72.
1927 El teocalli de la guerra sagrada. *Monogr. Mus. Nac. Arqueol. Hist. Etnog.*, no. 3. Mexico.
1928 Las estelas zapotecas. *Ibid.*, no. 3.
1930 Un códice en Otomí. *23d Int. Cong. Amer.* (New York, 1928), Acta, pp. 130–35.
1930 Informe preliminar de las exploraciones efectuadas en Michoacán. *An. Mus. Nac. Arqueol. Hist. Etnol.*, 6: 446–52. Mexico.
1932 Las exploraciones de Monte Alban, temporada 1931–32. *Inst. Panamer. Geog. Hist.*, Pub. 7.
1932 Las últimas exploraciones en Monte Alban. *Univ. Mexico*, 26: 100–07.
1932 La tumba de Monte Alban en Mixteca. *Ibid.*, 26: 117–50.
1932 Monte Alban, richest archaeological find in America. *Nat. Geog. Mag.*, 62: 487–512.
1932 El culto del dios de la lluvia en Tizapán. *Bol. Mus. Nac. Antr. Hist. Etnog.*, 1: 235–37. Mexico.
1932 Reading the riddle of ancient jewels. *Natural Hist.*, 32: 464–80.
1932 Notas sobre juegos antiguos. *Mex. Folkways*, 7: 56–60.
1933 Las tumbas de Monte Alban. *An. Mus. Nac. Mex.*, 8: 578–82.
1934 Sobre una figurilla de hueso del antiguo imperio Maya. *An. Mus. Nac. Arqueol. Hist. Etnog.*, ep. 5, 1: 11–16. Mexico.

1935 Las exploraciones en Monte Alban, temporada 1934–35. *Inst. Panamer. Geog. Hist.*, Pub. 18.

1935 Tenayuca. *In* Tenayuca, pp. 293–308.

1936 La religión de los aztecas. *Enciclopedia Ilustrada Mex.*, 1.

1936 Culturas mixteca y zapoteca. *Libro Cultura*, 6: 227–62. Barcelona.

1937 ¿Tenían los teotihuacanos conocimiento del Tonalpohualli? *El Mex. Antiguo*, 4: 131–43.

1938 Exploraciones en Oaxaca, quinta y sexta temporadas, 1936–37. *Inst. Panamer. Geog. Hist.*, Pub. 34.

1939 La correlación de los años azteca y cristiano. *Rev. Mex. Estud. Antr.*, 3: 11–45.

1940 El entierro del siglo. *Ibid.*, 4: 65–76.

1940 Pre-Spanish art. *In* Twenty centuries of Mexican art, pp. 26–66. Mus. Modern Art. New York.

1941 Culturas mixtecas y zapotecas. Bib. del Maestro, "El Nacional." Mexico.

1941 El complejo arqueológico de Tula y las grandes culturas indígenas de México. *Rev. Mex. Estud. Antr.*, 5: 85–95.

1942 El paraíso terrenal en Teotihuacán. *Cuad. Amer.*, 6: 127–36.

1942 Aztecas de México. *Ibid.*, 6. 155–60.

1942 Definición y extensión del complejo "Olmeca." *In* Mayas y Olmecas, pp. 43–46.

1944 El calendario de los Tarascos. *An. Mus. Michoacano*, pp. 11–36.

1946 El calendario Matlatzinca. *Rev. Mex. Estud. Antr.*, 8: 95–109.

1946 Contribución de las culturas indígenas de México a la cultura mundial. *In* México y la Cultura, pp. 51–80.

1947 Calendario y escritura de las antiguas culturas de Monte Albán. *In* M. O. de Mendizábal, Obras Completas, 1: 5–102.

1947 Resumen del informe de las exploraciones en Oaxaca durante la 7a y 8a temporadas, 1937–38 y 1938–39. *27th Int. Cong. Amer.* (Mexico, 1939), Acta, 2: 159–87.

1948 Definición del Indio y lo Indio. *Amer. Indig.*, 8: 239–47.

1949 El mapa de Teozacoalco. *Cuad. Amer.*, 8: 145–81.

1949 Una urna con el dios mariposa. *El Mexico Antiguo*, 7: 18–95.

1950 Una máscara azteca femenina. *México en el Arte*, 9: 2–9. Mexico.

1950 Explicación del reverso del códice Vindobonensis. *Mem. Colegio Nac.*, 5: 1–46. Mexico.

1951 Bases para la sincronología mixteca y cristiana. *Ibid.*, 6: 49–66.

1953 El pueblo del sol. Fondo de Cultura Económica. Mexico. (English ed., The Aztecs: people of the sun. Univ. Oklahoma Press, 1958. 2d ed. enlarged and corrected, Mexico, 1962.)

1953 New World culture history: Middle America. *In* Kroeber, Anthropology today, pp. 226–64.

1954 [ed.] Métodos y resultados de la política indigenista en México. *Inst. Nac. Indig.*, Mem. 6. Mexico.

1954 Instituciones indígenas precortesianas. *In* preceding entry, pp 13–27.

1954 Interpretación del códice Gómez de Orozco. Mexico.

1955 Vida y aventuras de 4 Viento "Serpiente de Fuego." *In* Misc. Estud. Fernando Ortíz, 1: 291–98. Havana.

1955 Der Jahresanfang bei den Mixteken. *Baessler Archiv*, n.s., 28 (3): 47–53.

1955 La orfebrería prehispánica. *Artes de Mexico*, año 3, no. 10.

1956 El calendario mixteco. *Hist. Mex.*, 5: 481–97.

1956 Los barrios antiguos de Tenochtitlán y Tlatelolco. *Mem. Acad. Mex. Hist.*, 15: 7–63. Mexico.

1958 Ideals of an action program. *Human Organization*, 17: 27–29.

1958 Indigenismo. Inst. Nac. Indig. Mexico.

1958 The Aztecs: people of the sun. Norman.

1958 El mapa de Xochitepec. *32d Int. Cong. Amer.* (Copenhagen, 1956), Acta, pp. 458–66.

1958 Lienzo de Yolotepec. *Mem. Colegio Nac.*, 3: 41–55. Mexico.

1958 El primer embajador conocido en América. *Cuad. Amer.*, 17: 285–93.

1958 Comentarios al códice Baranda. *In* Misc. Paul Rivet, 1: 373–93. Mexico.

1958 El calendario mexicano. *Mem. Acad. Mex. Hist.*, 17: 41–96.

1959 Nombres calendáricos de los dioses. *El México Antiguo*, 9: 77–100.

1959 Nuevos datos para la correlación de los años aztecas y cristianos. *Inst. Hist., Estud. Cultura Náhuatl*, 1: 9–25.

1959 Glifos teotihuacanos. *Rev. Mex. Estud. Antr.*, 15: 51–70. (Reprinted in his 1967, pp. 154–63.)

1959 La tenencia de la tierra entre los antiguos mexicanos. *Mem. Colegio Nac.*, 4: 29–54. Mexico.

1959 El dios 1 Muerte. *Mitteilungen Mus. für Völkerkunde*, 25: 40–43. Festband Franz Termer.

1960 La pintura mural en Mesoamérica. Conference, El Colegio Nacional. Mexico.

1960 Interpretación del códice Bodley 2858. Soc. Mex. Antr. Mexico.

1960 Valor histórico de los códices mixtecos. *Cuad. Amer.*, 19: 130–47.

1961 Los lienzos mixtecos de Ihuitlán y Antonio de León. *In* Homenaje Martínez del Río, pp. 237–74.

1962 The Mixtec and Zapotec cultures. *Bol. Estud. Oaxaqueños.*

1962 La pintura mural en Mesoamérica. *In* Cuarenta siglos de plástica mexicana. Mexico.

1962 Calendario y escritura en Xochicalco. *Rev. Mex. Estud. Antr.*, 18: 49–79.

1962 Vocabulario sacado del "Arte en lengua mixteca" de Fr. Antonio de los Reyes. *In* Vocabulario en lengua mixteca, W. Jiménez Moreno, ed., pp. 109–53.

1963 Representaciones de hongos en los códices. *Inst. Hist., Estud. Cultura Náhuatl*, 4: 27–38.

1964 Interpretación del códice Selden 3135 (A.2). Soc. Mex. Antr. Mexico.

1964 El lienzo de Filadelfia. *In* Homenaje Márquez Miranda, pp. 138–44. Madrid.

1964 Los señores de Yanhuitlán. *35th Int. Cong. Amer.* (Mexico, 1962), Acta, 1: 437–48.

1965 Sculpture and mural painting of Oaxaca. *In* Handbook of Middle American Indians, R. Wauchope, ed., vol. 3, art. 34.

1965 Lapidary work, goldwork, and copperwork from Oaxaca. *Ibid.*, vol. 3, art. 36.

1966 Interpretación del códice Colombino. Soc. Mex. Antr. Mexico.

1966 The lords of Yanhuitlan. *In* Paddock, 1966, Ancient Oaxaca, pp. 313–35.

1966 El culto al sol: notas a la interpretación de W. Lehmann. *Soc. Mex. Antr., Traducciones mesoamericanistas*, 1: 177–90.

1966 Dioses y signos teotihuacanos. *In* Teotihuacán, pp. 249–79.

1967 Los calendarios prehispánicos. *Univ. Nac. Autónoma Mex., Inst. Invest. Hist., Ser. Cultura Náhuatl*, Monogr. 6.

1967 Nombres calendáricos de los dioses. *See* 1959.

1967 Un antiguo imperio mesoamericano. Conference, Mus. Nac. Antr. Mexico.

1969 El tesoro de Monte Alban. *Mem. Inst. Nac. Antr. Hist.*, no. 3. Mexico.

—— AND G. AGUIRRE BELTRÁN

1960 Applied anthropology in Mexico. *In* Willey, Vogt, and Palerm, 1960, pp. 54–61.

—— AND I. BERNAL

1952 Urnas de Oaxaca. *Mem. Inst. Nac. Antr. Hist.*, no. 2. Mexico.

1965 Ceramics of Oaxaca. *In* Handbook of Middle American Indians, R. Wauchope, ed., vol. 3, art. 35.

——, ——, AND J. R. ACOSTA

1967 La cerámica de Monte Albán. *Mem. Inst. Nac. Antr. Hist.*, no. 13. Mexico.

—— AND L. GAMIO

1961 Informe de exploraciones en Huamelulpan. MS. in Archivo Inst. Nac. Antr. Hist.

—— AND M. G. PARRA
1950 Densidad de la población de habla indígena en la República Mexicana. *Inst. Nac. Indig.*, Mem. 1. Mexico.

—— AND D. F. RUBÍN DE LA BORBOLLA
1936 Exploraciones en Mitla, 1934–35. *Inst. Panamer. Geog. Hist.*, Pub. 21.

—— AND OTHERS
1946 ¿Conocieron la rueda los indígenas mesoamericanos? *Cuad. Amer.*, 25: 1–15.

CASON, J. F.
1952 Report on archaeological salvage in Falcon Reservoir, season of 1952. *Bull. Texas Archaeol. Paleontol. Soc.*, 23: 218–59.

CASSARETTO, M. A.
1956 El movimiento protestante en México, 1940–1955. Tesis profesional, Univ. Nac. Autónoma Mex.

CASSIRER, E.
1933 La langue et la construction du monde des objets. *Jour. Psychologie Normale et Pathologie*, 30: 18–44.
1944 An essay on man: an introduction to a philosophy of human culture. New Haven.

CASTAÑEDA, C. E.
1932 The first American play. *Catholic World*, January.

CASTAÑEDA, F. DE
1905 Relación de Tecciztlan y su partido. *In* Paso y Troncoso, 1905–06, 6: 209–30.
1905 Relación de Teutitlan del Camino. *Ibid.*, 4: 213–31. Originally published 1581.

CASTAÑEDA, P. DE
1896 Relación de la jornada de Cibola. *In* Winship, 1896, pp. 414–546.

CASTELLANOS, H., AND G. ARROYAVE
1961 Role of the adrenal cortical system in the response of children to severe protein malnutrition. *Amer. Jour. Clinical Nutrition*, 9: 186–95.

CASTELLANOS FERNÁNDEZ, H.
1950 Informe médico sanitario del municipio de Xochitlan Romero Rubio, Puebla, y el problema del bocio coloide. Mexico.

CASTELLS, F. DE P.
1904 The ruins of Indian Church in British

Honduras. *Amer. Antiquarian and Oriental Jour.*, 26: 32–37.

CASTETTER, E. F., AND W. H. BELL
1942 Pima and Papago Indian agriculture. *Univ. New Mexico, School Interamer. Affairs, Interamer. Ser.*, Studies 1.
1951 Yuman Indian agriculture. Univ. New Mexico Press.

CASTILLO, C. DEL
n.d. Migración de los mexicanos al país de Anahuac. Fin de su dominación y noticias de su calendario. Fragmentos históricos sacados de la obra escrita en lengua Nahuatl por Cristóbal del Castillo a fines del siglo 16. Bibliothèque Nationale. Paris.
1908 Fragmentos de la obra general sobre historia de los mexicanos, escrita in lengua náhuatl . . . a fines del siglo XVI. *Biblioteca Náhuatl*, 5: Tradiciones migraciones, Cuad. 2, pp. 43–107. Florence.

CASTILLO, I. M. DEL
1945 La alfabetización en lenguas indígenas: el proyecto tarasco. *Amer. Indig.*, 5: 139–51.

CASTILLO LEDÓN, L.
1917 Antigua literatura indígena mexicana. Mexico.

CASTILLO SÁNCHEZ, N.
1944 Informe general sobre la exploración sanitaria del municipio de San Jose Mihuatlan, distrito de Tehuacan, estado de Puebla. Mexico.

CASTILLO TEJERA, N.
1961 Conquista y colonización de Chiapas. *In* Los Mayas del sur, pp. 207–20.

CASTRO, C. A.
1955 La pluralización en pame meridional. *Rev. Mex. Estud. Antr.*, 14: 213–18.

CASTRO LEAL, A., ed.
1934 Escultura mexicana antigua. Exposición, Palacio de Bellas Artes. Mexico.

CATHERWOOD, F.
1844 Views of ancient monuments in Central America, Chiapas, and Yucatan. . . . London and New York. London and New York.

CAVE, A. J. E.
1939 Report on two skulls from British

47

Honduras. *Smithsonian Inst., Bur. Amer. Ethnol.*, Bull. 123, pp. 59–63.

CAZORLA VERA, E.
1935 Las problemas de la región zapoteca. *Neza*, 1 (4): 1, 5.
1937 La numeración zapoteca. *Ibid.*, 3 (2): 53–56.

CEBALLOS NOVELO, R.
1926 Informe al director de arqueología. *Bol. Sec. Educación Pública*, 5: 154–69. Mexico.

CEPEDA DE LA GARZA, R.
1944 Informe general sobre la exploración sanitaria de Villa de Xochitepec, cabecera del municipio de Xochitepec, estado de Morelos. Mexico.

CERDA SILVA, R. DE LA
1940 Los mixes. *Rev. Mex. Sociol.*, 2: 63–113.
1940 Los zoque. *Ibid.*, 2: 61–69.
1941 Los huave. *Ibid.*, 3: 81–111.
1942 Los cuicatecos. *Ibid.*, 4: 99–127.
1943 Los tepehuanes. *Ibid.*, 5: 541–67.
1943 Los coras. *Ibid.*, 5: 89–117.
1957 [ed.] Etnografía de México: síntesis monográfica. Inst. Invest. Soc., Univ. Nac. Autónoma Mex.
1957 Los mexicanos. *In* preceding entry.
1957 Los tzotziles. *Ibid.*
1957 Los choles. *Ibid.*
1957 Los triquis. *Ibid.*

CERECEDA, A. DE
1926 Relación. *In* Lothrop, 1926, 1: 28–29.

CERVANTES, N. C. DE
1732 Vocabulario en lengua castellana y cora. Reproduced in Radin, 1931.

CERVANTES, V.
1889 Ensayo de materia médica vegetal de México. Sec. de Fomento. Mexico.

CERVANTES DE SALAZAR, F.
1914 Crónica de la Nueva España. Madrid.
1936 Crónica de la Nueva España. *In* Paso y Troncoso, Papeles de Nueva España, 3d ser.

CERVANTES Y C., R.
1945 Un casamiento en Zoogocho. *Anuario Soc. Mex. Folklore*, vol. 3.

CHACÓN PINEDA, N.
1936 Xtagabene. *Neza*, 2: 2–6. Mexico.

CHADWICK, R.
1963 The god Malteutl in the "Histoire du Mechique." *Tlalocan*, vol. 4, no. 3.
1966 The "Olmeca-Xicallanca" of Teotihuacan: a preliminary study. *Mesoamerican Notes*, nos. 7–8. Mexico.
1967 Un posible glifo de Teotihuacán en el códice Nuttall. *Rev. Mex. Estud. Antr.*, 21: 17–41.
1968 The diffusion of a ceramic complex in the New World. MS.
1970 Un posible glifo de Xochicalco en los códices mixtecos. *Tlalocan*, 6: 216–28.
in press La correlación de las historias de Quetzalcoatl en los códices mixtecos con la versión del Códice Chimalpopoca. *An. Inst. Nac. Antr. Hist.* Mexico.
in press Estudio de los toponímicos mixtecos. *Ibid.*
—— AND R. S. MACNEISH
1967 Codex Borgia and the Venta Salada phase. *In* Byers, 1967, 1: 114–31.

CHALMERS, J. N. M., E. A. IKIN, AND A. E. MOURANT
1953 A study of two unusual blood group antigens in West Africans. *British Med. Jour.*, 2: 175–77.

CHAMBERLAIN, R. S.
1948 The conquest and colonization of Yucatan, 1517–1550. *Carnegie Inst. Wash.*, Pub. 582.
1953 The conquest and colonization of Honduras, 1502–1550. *Ibid.*, Pub. 598.

CHAMPE, J. L.
1946 Ash Hollow cave, a study of stratigraphic sequence in the central Great Plains. *Univ. Nebraska Studies*, n.s., no. 1.

CHAMPION, R.
1955 Acculturation among the Tarahumara of northwestern Mexico since 1890. *Trans. New York Acad. Sci.*, 17: 560–66.

CHAPEL, L. T.
1927 Winds and storms on the Isthmus of Panama. *Monthly Weather Rev.*, 55: 519–30.

CHAPMAN, A.
1947 Tzeltal stories. *In* A treasury of Mexican folkways, pp. 479–90.

CHAPMAN, A. M.
1957 Port of trade enclaves in Aztec and Maya civilizations. *In* Trade and market in the early empires, K. Polanyi, C. M. Arensberg, and H. W. Pearson, eds., pp. 114–53.
1960 Los Nicarao y los Chorotega según las fuentes históricas. Univ. Costa Rica.

CHAPMAN, F. M.
1917 The distribution of bird-life in Colombia. *Bull. Amer. Mus. Nat. Hist.*, no. 36.
1926 The distribution of bird-life in Ecuador. *Ibid.*, no. 55.

CHAPMAN, K. M.
1923 Casas Grandes pottery. *Art and Archaeol.*, 16: 25–34.

CHAPPLE, E. D., AND C. S. COON
1942 Principles of anthropology. New York.

CHARD, C. S.
1958 Organic tempering in northeast Asia and Alaska. *Amer. Antiquity*, 24: 193–94.
1958 An outline of the prehistory of Siberia. Part 1: The premetal period. *SW. Jour. Anthr.*, 14: 1–33.
1958 Nouveaux apports à la classification de l'homme américain. *In* Misc. Paul Rivet, 1: 107–36.

CHARDIN, P. TEILHARD DE
See Teilhard de Chardin, P.

CHARENCY, H. DE
1879 Vocabulaire Française-Nagranda. *Rev. Ling. et Philol. Comparée*, 12: 334–37.
1883 Des suffixes en lengua Quiché. Louvain.

CHARLOT, J.
1940 Twenty centuries of Mexican art. *Magazine of Art*, 33: 398–443. New York.

CHARNAY, D.
1863 Le Mexique: souvenirs et impressions de voyage, 1851–1861. Paris.
1880 The ruins of Central America. Part 4. *North Amer. Rev.*, 131: 519–27.
1884 Measurements of 5 Mixtecs, 16 Yuca-tecs and 1 Chocho. *In* Hamy, 1884, 1: 39–40.
1884 Mis descubrimientos en México y en la América Central. *In* América pintoresca: descripción de viajes al nuevo continente. Barcelona.
1885 Les anciennes villes du Nouveau Monde: voyages d'explorations au Mexique et dans l'Amérique Centrale. Paris.
1887 The ancient cities of the New World, being travels and explorations in Mexico and Central America from 1857 to 1882. London.
1887 Ma dernière expédition au Yucatan, 1886. *Tour du Monde*, 53: 273–320.

CHAVERO, A.
1877 La piedra del sol. Part 1. *An. Mus. Nac. Méx.*, 1: 353–86.
1882 *Idem*, part 2. *Ibid.*, 2: 3–46, 107–26, 233–36, 291–310, 403–30.
1886 *Idem*, part 3. *Ibid.*, 3: 3–26, 37–56, 100–14, 124–26.
1887 Historia antigua y de la conquista. *In* México a través de los siglos, Riva Palacio, ed., vol. 1. Mexico.
1901 Pinturas jeroglíficas de la Colección Chavero. 2 vols. Mexico.

CHÁVEZ, A. N.
1922 Bibliografía antropológica Otomi. *Ethnos*, 1: 68–73, 240–44. Mexico.

CHÁVEZ, G. DE
1865 Relación de la provincia de Meztitlan. *Col. Doc. Ineditos*, 4: 530–55.
1924 Relación de la provincia de Metztitlan. *Bol. Mus. Nac. Arqueol. Hist. Etnog.*, 4: 109–20. Mexico.

CHÁVEZ OROZCO, L.
1943 Las instituciones democráticas de los indígenas mexicanos en la época colonial. *Amer. Indig.*, 3: 73–82, 161–71, 265–76, 365–82.

CHÁVEZ TORRES, R.
1947 Exploración sanitaria de Zochitepec, estado de Morelos. Mexico.

CHEVALIER, F.
1952 La formation des grands domaines au Mexique: terre et société aux 16th–17th siècles. *Inst. Ethnol., Travaux et Mem.*, no. 16. Paris.

CHI, G. A.
1941 Relación. *In* Landa, 1941, pp. 230–32.

CHICAGO, UNIVERSITY OF
1959 *See* McQuown, 1959.

CHICXULUB, CRÓNICA DE
1542–62 Manuscript. Photograph in Newberry Library. 26 pp.

CHILDE, V. G.
1941 The dawn of European civilization. (6th ed. rev., 1957.)
1942 What happened in history. Penguin Books.
1950 The urban revolution. *Town Planning Rev.*, 21: 3–17. Univ. Liverpool.
1952 The birth of civilization. *Past and Present*, no. 2, pp. 1–10. London.

CHILTON, J.
1927 A notable discourse of M. John Chilton touching the people, manners, mines, cities, forces and other memorable things of New Spain. . . . *In* Hakluyt, 1927, 8: 264–79.

CHIMALPAHIN QUAUHTLEHUANITZIN, D. F.
1889 Annales de Domingo Francisco de San Antón Muñon Chimalpahin Quauhtlehuanitzin. Sixième et septième relations (1258–1612). Rémi Siméon, ed. and trans. *Bibliothèque Linguistique Américaine*, 12. Paris.
1949–52 Diferentes historias originales de los reynos de Culhuacan, y México, y de otras provincias. . . . Manuscrit mexicain, nr. 74. E. Mengin, ed. *Corpus Codicum Americanorum Medii Aevi*, 3. Copenhagen.
1958 Das Memorial Breve acerca de la fundación de la ciudad de Culhuacan und weitere ausgewahlte teile aus den "Diferentes historias originales" (Manuscrit mexicain nr. 74, Paris). Aztec text, with German translation by W. Lehmann and G. Kutscher. *Quellenwerke zur alten Geschichte Amerikas*, 7. Stuttgart.
1963 Die Relationen Chimalpahin's zur Geschichte Mexiko's. Part 1: Die Zeit bis zur Conquista 1521. Text herausgegeben von G. Zimmermann. Univ. Hamburg, Abhandlungen aus dem Gebeit de Auslandskunde, Band 68,

Reihe 8 (Völkerkunde, Kultur-geschichte und Sprachen), 38. Hamburg.
1965 *Idem.* Part 2: Das Jahrhundert nach der Conquista (1522–1615). Aztekischer Text herausgegeben von G. Zimmermann. *Ibid.*, Band 69, Reihe B (Völkerkunde, Kultur-geschichte und Sprachen), 39.
1965 Relaciones originales de Chalco Amaquemecan. Paleografiadas y traducidas del Náhuatl, con una introducción por S. Rendón. *Biblioteca Americana, Ser. Literatura Indigena.* Fondo de Cultura Económica. Mexico.

CHIMALPOPOCA GALICIA, F.
1869 Epítome ó modo fácile de aprender el idioma nahuatl. . . . Mexico.

CHINCHILLA AGUILAR, E.
1951 La danza del Tum-teleche o Loj-tum. *An. Soc. Antr. Hist. Guatemala*, 3 (2): 17–20.

CHONAY, D. J., AND D. GOETZ
1953 Titles of the lords of Totonicapan. Norman, Okla.

CHOWN, B., AND M. LEWIS
1953 The ABO, MNSs, P, Rh, Lutheran, Kell, Lewis, Duffy and Kidd blood groups and the secretor status of the Blackfeet Indians of Alberta, Canada. *Amer. Jour. Physical Anthr.*, n.s., 11: 369–83.
1955 The blood groups and secretor genes of the Stoney and Sarcee Indians of Alberta, Canada. *Ibid.*, 13: 181–89.
1957 The Kell antigen in American Indians with a note about anti-Kell sera. *Ibid.*, 15: 149–56.

CHOWNING, A.
1956 A round temple and its shrine at Mayapan. *Carnegie Inst. Wash., Current Reports*, no. 34.

—— AND D. E. THOMPSON
1956 A dwelling and shrine at Mayapan. *Ibid.*, no. 33.

CHRÉTIEN, C. D.
1956 Word distributions in southeastern Papua. *Language*, 32: 88–108.

CHRISTENSEN, B.
1937 The Acatlaxqui dance of Mexico. *Ethnos*, 4: 133–36.
1942 Notas sobre la fabricación del papel

indígena y su empleo para "brujerías" en la Sierra Norte de Puebla, México. *Rev. Mex. Estud. Antr.*, 6: 109–24.

1947 Otomi looms and quechquemitls from San Pablito, state of Puebla, and from Santa Ana Hueytlalpan, state of Hidalgo. *Carnegie Inst. Wash., Notes Middle Amer. Archaeol. Ethnol.*, no. 78.

1953 Los Otomies del estado de Puebla. *In* Huastecos, Totonacos, pp. 259–68.

1953 La pesca entre los otomíes de San Pablito, Puebla. *Yan*, no. 2.

CHRISTENSEN, L.

n.d. The Dominican missions in Oaxaca, Mexico. MS. Univ. California, Dept. Anthropology and Sociology.

CHU'Ü-HSUN, KAO

1959 The royal cemetery of the Yin dynasty at Anyang. *Nat. Taiwan Univ., Dept. Archaeol. and Anthr.*, Bull. 13, 14. Taipei.

CIUDAD REAL, A. DE

1600? Vocabulario en la lengua maya. MS in John Carter Brown Library. Maya Español, 465 f.; Español-Maya, 236 f. Photograph in Newberry Library. Constitutes Diccionario de Motul. First printed 1929, Merida.

1873 *See* A. Ponce, 1873.

1930 Diccionario de Motul maya-español atribuído a Fray Antonio de Ciudad Real y arte de la lengua maya por Fray Juan Coronel. J. Martínez Hernández, ed.

CLARK, J. C.

1912 The story of 8 Deer in Codex Colombino. London.

1938 *See* Codex Mendoza, 1938.

CLAVIGERO, F. J.

1780–81 Historia antigua de México. [For detailed listing of editions and translations see this *Handbook*, vol. 13, pp. 292–94.]

1937 The history of (Lower) California. Tr. by S. E. Lake and A. A. Gray. Stanford.

CLAYTON, H. H.

1927 World weather records. Washington.

1944 World weather records, 1921–1930. Washington.

—— AND F. L. CLAYTON

1947 World weather records, 1931–1940. Washington.

CLIMENT, J. A.

1869 Carta dirigida a Juan María Rodríguez sobre un caso distócico, ocasionada por el estrechamiento extraordinario de la pelvis. *Gaceta Méd. Méx.*, vol. 4.

CLINE, H. F.

1944 Lore and deities of the Lacandon Indians, Chiapas, Mexico. *Jour. Amer. Folklore*, 57: 107–15.

1945 Remarks on a selected bibliography of the Caste War and allied topics. *In* Villa Rojas, 1945, pp. 165–78.

1946 The terragueros of Guelatao, Oaxaca, Mexico: notes on the Sierra de Juarez and its XVIIth century Indian problems. *Acta Amer.*, 4: 161–84.

1947 Civil congregations of the Indians of New Spain, 1598–1606. *Hispanic Amer. Hist. Rev.*, 29: 349–69.

1952 Mexican community studies. *Ibid.*, 32: 212–42.

1953 Una subdivisión tentativa de los chinantecos históricos. *Rev. Mex. Estud. Antr.*, 12: 281–86.

1953 The United States and Mexico. Cambridge, Mass. (3d printing, 1966.)

1955 Civil congregation of the western Chinantla, New Spain, 1599–1604. *The Americas*, 12: 115–37.

1956 The Chinantla of northeastern Oaxaca, Mexico: bio-bibliographical notes on modern investigations. *In* Estudios antropológicos, pp. 635–56.

1957 Problems of Mexican ethno-history: the ancient Chinantla, a case study. *Hispanic Amer. Hist. Rev.*, 37: 273–95.

1959 The Patiño maps of 1580 and related documents: analysis of 16th century cartographic sources for the gulf coast of Mexico. *El Mexico Antiguo*, 9: 633–84.

1959 A preliminary report on Chinantec archaeology: excavations in Oaxaca,

Mexico, 1951. *33d Int. Cong. Amer.* (San Jose, 1958), Acta, 2: 158–70.

1960 *See* Barreda, 1730.

1961 Mapas and lienzos of the colonial Chinantec Indians, Oaxaca, Mexico. *In* Homenaje Townsend, pp. 49–77.

1961 Re-edición con notas y apéndices . . . Espinosa, 1910 [q.v.]. *Mus. Nac. Antr., Ser. Cien.,* 7. *Papeles de la Chinantla,* 3. Mexico.

1962 Mexico: revolution to evolution, 1940–1960. London.

1964 The Relaciones Geográficas of the Spanish Indies, 1577–1586. *Hispanic Amer. Hist. Rev.,* 46: 341–47.

CLISBY, K. H., AND P. B. SEARS

1955 Palynology in southern North America. Part 3: Microfossil profiles under Mexico City correlated with sedimentary profiles. *Bull. Geol. Soc. Amer.,* vol. 66.

CLUNE, D.

1960 Textiles and matting from Waterfall Cave, Chihuahua. *Amer. Antiquity,* 26: 274–77.

CLUNE, F. J., JR.

1963 A functional and historical analysis of the ball game in Mesoamerica. Doctoral dissertation, Univ. of California, Los Angeles.

COCKBURN, J.

1779 The unfortunate Englishmen. London.

CODICES:

Aubin

1893 Histoire de la nation mexicaine. Reproduction du Codex de 1576. Paris.

Azcatitlan

1949 Códice Azcatitlan. *Jour. Soc. Amer. Paris,* n.s., vol. 38, appendix.

Azoyu 2 (reverse)

1893 *In* E. Seler, Die mexikanischen Bilderhandschriften Alexander von Humboldt's in der Königlichen Bibliothek zu Berlin (atlas). Berlin.

1943 S. Toscano, Los códices Tlapanecas de Azoyú, p. 136. *Cuad. Amer.,* 10: 127–36.

1964 J. B. Glass, Catálogo de la colección de códices, fig. 119. Inst. Nac. Antr. Hist. Mexico.

CODICES—*continued*

Becker I, II

1961 Facsimile edition. Mus. für Völkerkunde. Vienna.

Bodley

1960 Facsimile edition of a Mexican painting preserved in the collection of Sir Thomas Bodley, Bodleian Library, Oxford. Interpreted by A. Caso, translated by R. Morales, revised by J. Paddock. Soc. Mex. Antr. Mexico.

Borbonicus

1899 Codex Borbonicus. Manuscrit mexicain de la Bibliothèque du Palais Bourbon. E. T. Hamy, ed. Facsimile. Paris.

Borgia

1898 Il manoscritto Messicano Borgiano del Museo Etnografico. . . . Loubat ed. Rome.

Carolino

1967 Códice Carolino. Manuscrito anónimo del siglo XVI en forma de adiciones a la primera edición del vocabulario de Molina. *Inst. Hist., Estud. Cultura Náhuatl,* 7: 13–58.

Chimalpopoca

1945 Códice Chimalpopoca: Anales de Cuauhtitlán y Leyenda de los Soles. P. F. Velázquez, trans. *Univ. Nac. Autónoma Méx., Pub. Inst. Hist.,* 1st ser., no. 1. Mexico.

Colombino

1892 Códice Colombino. Pintura precolombina de la raza mixteca. *In* Antigüedades mexicanas publicadas por la Junta Colombina. Mus. Nac. Mex.

Cospi (Bologna)

1898 Descripción del códice Cospiano. Manuscrito pictórico de los antiguos náhuas que se conserva en la biblioteca de la Universidad de Bolonia. Loubat reproduction. Rome.

Dehesa

See Belmar, 1892.

Dresden

See editions listed in Part II, p. 260, of this volume of the *Handbook.*

Féjérváry-Mayer

1901 Codex Féjérváry-Mayer. Manuscrit mexicain précolombien du Free Public Museum de Liverpool (12014/M).

CODICES—*continued*

Loubat reproduction. Paris. (See also Seler, 1901.)

Florentine

1905–07 *See* Sahagún, 1905–07.

1926 Edición completa en facsímile colorido del códice Florentino que se conserva en la Biblioteca Laurenzio Medicea de Florencia, Italia. F. del Paso y Troncoso, ed. Mexico.

1950–69 *See* Sahagún, 1950–69.

Franciscano

1941 Códice Franciscano, siglo XVI. J. García Icazbalceta, ed. Mexico.

Ixtlilxochitl

1891 *In* Boban, 1891, 2: 116–31; atlas, pls. 65–71. Paris.

1951 *In* D. Durán, Historia de la Indias de Nueva España y islas de tierra firme (atlas). Mexico.

Kingsborough

1912 Memorial de los Indios de Tepetlaoztoc al monarca español contra los encomenderos del pueblo. F. del Paso y Troncoso, ed. Madrid.

Laud

1831 *In* Kingsborough, 1831–48, vol. 2, pt. 2.

1961 Códice Laud. C. Martínez Marín, ed. *Inst. Nac. Antr. Hist., Ser. Invest.*, 5. Mexico.

1966 Codex Laud (MS Laud Misc. 678), Bodleian Library). True-colour facsimile of the old Mexican manuscript. Intro. by C. A. Burland. Graz, Austria.

Madrid (Cortesiano section)

1892 Códice maya denominado Cortesiano que se conserva en el Museo Arqueológico Nacional (Madrid). . . . Hecha y publicada bajo la dirección de D. Juan de Dios de la Rada y Delgado y D. Jerónimo López de Ayala y del Hierro. Madrid.

Madrid (Troano section)

1869–70 Manuscrit Troano. Études sur le système graphique et la langue des Mayas. By C. E. Brasseur de Bourbourg. 2 vols. Paris.

Magliabecchiano

1903 Z. Nuttall, ed., The book of life of the ancient Mexicans. . . . Part 1: Intro-

CODICES—*continued*

duction and facsimile. Univ. California, Berkeley.

1904 Codex Magliabecchiano XIII, 3. Manuscrit mexicain postcolombien de la Bibliothèque Nationale de Florence. Loubat reproduction. Rome.

Mariano Jiménez

1903 Códice Mariano Jiménez. Númina de tributos de los pueblos Otlazpan y Tepexic. En jeroglífico azteca y lengua castellana y nahuatl, 1549. N. León, ed. Mexico.

Matritense

1907 Códice Matritense de la Real Academia de la Historia. Textos en náhuatl de los indígenas informantes de Sahagún. F. del Paso y Troncoso, ed., vol. 8. Facsimile. Madrid.

Mendoza

1925 Colección de Mendoza o códice Mendocino, documento mexicano del siglo XVI que se conserva en la Biblioteca Bodleiana de Oxford, Inglaterra. F. del Paso y Troncoso [and J. Galindo y Villa], eds. Mexico.

1938 Codex Mendoza. The Mexican manuscript known as the Collection of Mendoza and preserved in the Bodleian Library, Oxford. James Cooper-Clark, ed. and trans. 3 vols. London.

Mexicanus

1952 Codex Mexicanus, n. 23–24 de la Bibliothèque Nationale de Paris. E. Mengin, ed. *Jour. Soc. Amer. Paris*, n.s. 41: 387–498 (facsimile reproduction in album).

Monteleone

1925 Códice del archivo de los duques de Monteleone. Declaración del indio Delmas en el juicio seguido por Hernan Cortés contra Nuño de Guzmán y otros sobre títulos de Huexotzingo. *An. Mus. Nac. Mex.*, ep. 2–3, pp. 58–64.

Nuttall

1902 Codex Nuttall. Facsimile of an ancient Mexican codex belonging to Lord Zouche of Harynworth, England. Intro. by Z. Nuttall. Pea-

Codices—*continued*

body Mus., Harvard Univ. Cambridge.

Osuna
1947 Códice Osuna. Reproducción facsimilar de la obra del mismo título, editada en Madrid, 1878. Mexico.

Paris
1887 Codex Peresianus. Manuscrit hiératique des anciens Indiens de l'Amérique Centrale conservé à la Bibliothèque Nationale de Paris, avec une introduction par Léon de Rosny. Publié en couleurs. Paris.

Pérez
ca. 1837 MS owned in Yucatan. Photograph made for Carnegie Inst. Wash.
1949 Códice Pérez. Tr. libre del Maya al Castellano. E. Solís Alcalá. Merida.

Porfirio Díaz (reverse)
1892 *In* Antigüedades mexicanas publicadas por la Junta Colombina. Homenaje a Cristóbal Colón. Atlas. Mexico.

Ramírez
1944 Códice Ramírez. Manuscrito del siglo XVI intitulado: Relación del origen de los indios que habitan esta Nueva España, según sus historias. M. Orozco y Berra, ed. Mexico.

Ríos
1900 *See* Codex Vaticanus A.

Selden 3135 (A.2)
1964 Interpretation of the codex by A. Caso, translated by J. Quirate, revised by J. Paddock, with a facsimile of the codex. Soc. Mex. Antr. Mexico.

Telleriano-Remensis
1830 *See* Kingsborough, 1831–48, vol. 1.
1899 Codex Telleriano-Remensis. Manuscrit mexicain. Loubat reproduction. Intro. by E. T. Hamy. Paris.

Tlaquiltenango (Mauricio de la Arena)
1926 M. Mazari, Códice Mauricio de la Arena. *An. Mus. Nac. Antr. Hist. Ethnog.*, ep. 4, 4: 273–78. Mexico.
1943 R. H. Barlow, The periods of tribute collection in Moctezuma's empire. *Carnegie Inst. Wash., Notes Middle Amer. Archaeol. Ethnol.*, no. 23.

Vaticanus A (3738)

Codices—*continued*
1900 Il manoscritto Messicano Vaticano 3738, detto il codice Ríos. Loubat reproduction. Rome.

Vaticanus B (3773)
1896 Il manoscritto Messicano Vaticano 3773. Loubat reproduction. Rome.
1902 Codex Vaticanus nr. 3773 (Codex Vaticanus B). Eine altmexikanische Bilderschrift der Vatikanischen Bibliothek. Loubat ed. Berlin. (See Seler, 1902.)

Veytia
1944 *In* Veytia, 1944. Text, 2: 339–46; illustrations, *passim*.

Vindobonensis Mexicanus I
1963 Facsimile ed. O. Adelhofer, ed. Graz, Austria. (See Seler, 1902–23.)

Yanhuitlan
1940 Ed. by W. Jiménez Moreno and S. Mateos Higuera. Mexico.

Xólotl
1951 *See* Dibble, 1951.

Coe, M. D.
1956 The funerary temple among the classic Maya. *SW. Jour. Anthr.*, 12: 387–94.
1957 Preclassic cultures in Mesoamerica: a comparative survey. *Papers Kroeber Anthr. Soc.*, 17: 7–37.
1957 Cycle 7 monuments in Middle America: a reconsideration. *Amer. Anthr.*, 59: 597–611.
1957 The Khmer settlement pattern: a possible analogy with that of the Maya. *Amer. Antiquity*, 22: 409–10.
1959 La Victoria, an early site on the Pacific coast of Guatemala. Ph.D. thesis, Harvard Univ.
1959 Una investigación arqueológica en la costa del Pacífico de Guatemala. *Antr. Hist. Guatemala*, 11 (1): 5–15.
1960 Archaeological linkages with North and South America at La Victoria, Guatemala. *Amer. Anthr.*, 62: 363–93.
1960 A fluted point from highland Guatemala. *Amer. Antiquity*, 25: 412–13.
1961 La Victoria, an early site on the Pacific coast of Guatemala. *Papers Peabody Mus., Harvard Univ.*, vol. 53.

1962 Preliminary report on archaeological investigations in coastal Guanacaste, Costa Rica. *34th Int. Cong. Amer.* (Vienna, 1960), Acta, pp. 358–65.

1962 An Olmec design on an early Peruvian vessel. *Amer. Antiquity*, 27: 579–80.

1963 Olmec and Chavin: rejoinder to Lanning. *Ibid.*, 29: 101–104.

1963 Cultural development in southeastern Mesoamerica. *In* Meggers and Evans, 1963, pp. 27–44.

1965 The jaguar's children: pre-classic central Mexico. Mus. Primitive Art. New York.

1965 The Olmec style and its distribution. *In* Handbook of Middle American Indians, R. Wauchope, ed., vol. 3, art. 29.

1965 Archaeological synthesis of southern Veracruz and Tabasco. *Ibid.*, vol. 3, art. 27.

1965 A model of ancient community structure in the Maya lowlands. *SW. Jour. Anthr.*, 21: 97–114.

1967 America's first civilization. New York. (Another ed. 1968, Princeton.)

1968 San Lorenzo and the Olmec civilization. *In* Benson, 1968, pp. 41–78.

1969 The archaeological sequence at San Lorenzo Tenochtitlan, Veracruz, Mexico. Paper presented to 34th annual meeting of Soc. Amer. Archaeol.

—— AND C. F. BAUDEZ

1961 The zoned bichrome period in northwestern Costa Rica. *Amer. Antiquity*, 26: 505–15.

——, R. A. DIEHL, AND M. STUIVER

1967 Olmec civilization, Veracruz, Mexico: dating of the San Lorenzo phase. *Science*, 155: 1399–1401.

COE, W. R.

n.d. Tikal caches 1–56. *Mus. Monogr., Univ. Pennsylvania, Tikal Reports*, no. 13.

1955 Early man in the Maya area. *Amer. Antiquity*, 20: 271–73.

1955 Excavations in El Salvador. *Bull. Univ. Pennsylvania Mus.*, 19: 15–21.

1957 A distinctive artifact common to Haiti and Central America. *Amer. Antiquity*, 22: 280–82.

1959 Piedras Negras archaeology: artifacts, caches, and burials. *Mus. Monogr., Univ. Pennsylvania*, no. 4.

1959 Tikal, 1959. *Expedition, Bull. Univ. Pennsylvania Mus.*, 1: 7–11.

1961 A summary of excavation and research at Tikal, Guatemala: 1956–1961. Univ. Pennsylvania Mus. Mimeographed.

1962 A summary of excavation and research at Tikal, Guatemala: 1956–1961. *Amer. Antiquity*, 27: 479–507.

1962 Maya mystery in Tikal. *Natural Hist.*, 71: 10–21, 44–53.

1965 Tikal, Guatemala, and emergent Maya civilization. *Science*, 147 (3664): 1401–19.

—— AND V. L. BROMAN

1958 Excavations in the Stela 23 group. *Mus. Monogr., Univ. Pennsylvania, Tikal Reports*, no. 2.

—— AND J. J. McGINN

1963 Tikal: the north acropolis and an early tomb. *Expedition, Bull. Univ. Pennsylvania Mus.*, 5 (2): 24–32.

——, E. M. SHOOK, AND L. SATTERTHWAITE

1961 The carved wooden lintels of Tikal. *Mus. Monogr., Univ. Pennsylvania, Tikal Reports*, no. 6.

COEDÉS, G.

1947 Pour mieux comprendre Angkor. Librairie d'Amérique et d'Orient. Paris.

1948 Les états hindouisés d'Indochine et d'Indonésie. *In* Histoire du Monde, vol. 8, ed. by M. E. Cavaignac. Paris.

COESTER, A.

1941 The danza de los conquistadores at Chichicastenango. *Hispania*, 24: 95–100.

COFIÑO, E., AND G. ARGUEDAS KLEE

1938 Contribución al estudio de ciertos edemas de la infancia (síndrome debido a carencia alimenticia múltiple). Trabajo presentado al V Cong. Méd. Centroamer. y Panamá. San Salvador.

COGHLAN, H. H.

1951 Notes on the prehistoric metallurgy of copper and bronze in the Old

World. Pitt Rivers Mus., Oxford Univ.

COGOLLUDO, D. L. DE
    See López de Cogolludo, D.

COINDET, L.
    1868 Le Mexique consideré au point de vue medico-chirurgical. 3 vols. Paris.

COLBY, B. N.
    1959 A field sketch of some recurring themes and tendencies in Zinacantan culture. Harvard Chiapas Project. Dittoed.
    1960 Ethnic relations in the highlands of Chiapas, Mexico. Doctoral dissertation, Harvard Univ.
    1960 Social relations and directed culture change among the Zinacantan. *Practical Anthr.*, 7: 241–50.
    1961 Outline for staff meeting discussion on values in Zinacantan. Harvard Chiapas Project. Dittoed.
    1961 Indian attitudes towards education and inter-ethnic contact in Mexico. *Practical Anthr.*, 8: 77–85.
    1963 Ethnographic notes and materials on the Ixil Indians of Nebaj, Guatemala. Unpublished material on file at Laboratory of Anthropology, Santa Fe.
    1964 Elements of a Mesoamerican personality pattern. *35th Int. Cong. Amer.* (Mexico, 1962), Acta, pp. 125–29.
    1966 Ethnic relations in the Chiapas highlands. Santa Fe.

—— AND P. L. VAN DEN BERGHE
    1960 Ethnic relations in southeastern Mexico. Harvard Univ. Mimeographed. Published in part in their 1961.
    1961 Ethnic relations in southeastern Mexico. *Amer. Anthr.*, 63: 772–92.

COLE, L. J.
    1910 The caverns and people of northern Yucatan. *Bull. Amer. Geog. Soc.*, 42: 321–36.

COLECCIÓN DE DOCUMENTOS
    1842–95 Colección de documentos inéditos para la historia de España. 112 vols. Madrid.
    1864–84 Colección de documentos inéditos relativos al descubrimiento, conquista y organización de las antiguas pose-

siones españolas de América y Oceanía, sacados de los archivos del reino, y muy especialmente del de Indias. J. Pacheco, F. de Cardenas, and L. Torres de Mendoza, eds. 42 vols. Madrid.
    1885–1932 Colección de documentos inéditos relativos al descubrimiento, conquista y organización de las antiguas posesiones españolas de ultramar. 25 vols. Madrid.

COLECCIÓN DE GRAMÁTICAS
    1904 Colección de gramáticas de la lengua mexicana. Vol. 1, 1457–1673. Mexico.

COLEMAN, S. N.
    1946 Volcanoes, new and old. New York.

COLLIER, A.
    1958 Gulf of Mexico physical and chemical data from *Alaska* cruises. U.S. Dept. Interior, *Fish and Wildlife Service*, Special Sci. Rept.: Fisheries, no. 249.

—— AND J. W. HEDGPETH
    1950 An introduction to the hydrography of tidal waters of Texas. *Inst. Marine Sci.*, 1: 123–94.

COLLIER, D.
    1959 Agriculture and civilization on the coast of Peru. Paper presented to annual meeting, Amer. Anthr. Assoc., Mexico City. Mimeographed. Chicago.
    1960 Aztec sculpture. *Bull. Chicago Natural Hist. Mus.*, 34 (6): 4–5.

——, A. E. HUDSON, AND A. FORD
    1942 Archaeology of the upper Columbia region. *Univ. Washington Pub. Anthr.*, 9: 1–178.

COLLIER, MRS. DONALD
    See Carr, M.

COLLIER, J. F.
    1968 Courtship and marriage in Zinacantan, Chiapas, Mexico. *Tulane Univ., Middle Amer. Research Inst.*, Pub. 25.

COLLINS, H. B.
    1927 Frequency and distribution of fossa pharingea in human crania. *Amer. Jour. Physical Anthr.*, 11: 101–06.

COLLINSON, J.
    1870 The Indians of the Mosquito Terri-

tory. *Mem. Anthr. Soc. London*, 3: 148–56.

COLÓN, H.

1947 Vida del Almirante Don Cristóbal Colón. Fondo de Cultura Económica. Mexico.

COLTON, H.

1943 Life history and economic possibilities of the American lac insect, *Tachardiella larrea. Plateau*, 16 (2): 21–32.

COLUMBUS, CHRISTOPHER

1930 The voyages of Christopher Columbus, being the journals of his first and last voyages, to which is now added the account of his second voyage written by Andrés Bernáldez, now newly translated and edited, with introduction and notes, by Cecil Jane. London.

COLUMBUS, FERDINAND

1867 Vita di Cristoforo Colombo, descritta da Ferdinando, e tradotta da Alfonso Ulloa. London.

COMAS, J.

1942 Contribution à l'étude du metopisme. *Archives Suisses Anthr. Générale*, 10: 273–412.

1942 El problema de la existencia de un tipo racial olmeca: conclusiones. *In* Mayas y Olmecas, pp. 69–70.

1942 El hueso interparietal epactal o inca en los cráneos mexicanos. *An. Escuela Nac. Ciencias Biol.*, 2: 469–90.

1942 El problema social de los indios triques en Oaxaca. *Amer. Indig.*, 2 (1): 51–57.

1943 El metopismo: sus causas y frecuencia en los cráneos mexicanos. *An. Inst. Etnog. Amer.*, 4: 121–59. Mendoza, Argentina.

1943 La antropología física en México y Centroamérica: estadísticas, bibliografía y mapas de distribución de caracteres somáticos. *Inst. Panamer. Geog. Hist.*, Pub. 68. Mexico.

1944 [with J. Faulhaber] Contribución al estudio antropométrico de los indios triques de Oaxaca, México. *An. Inst. Etnog. Amer.*, 5: 159–244. Mendoza, Argentina.

1945 Osteometría olmeca: informe prelimi-

nar sobre los restos hallados en Cerro de las Mesas, estado de Veracruz, México. *Ibid.*, 6: 169–206.

1950 Bosquejo histórico de la antropología en México. *Rev. Mex. Estud. Antr.*, 11: 97–192.

1951 *See* Homenaje al Doctor Alfonso Caso.

1952 Cálculo de la talla de Mexicanos del Valle de México a base de la longitud del fémur. *In* Tax, 1952, Acculturation, pp. 247–50.

1952 [with A. Marino Flores] Algunas caracteristicas del fémur entre mexicanos pre- y post-colombianos del Valle de México. *An. Soc. Geog. Hist.*, 26: 14–17. Guatemala.

1953 El problema social de los indios triques de Oaxaca. *In* Ensayos sobre indigenismo, pp. 1–9. Inst. Indig. Interamer. Mexico.

1953 Algunos datos para la historia del indigenismo en México. *Ibid.*, pp. 63–108.

1954 Los Congresos Internacionales de Americanistas: síntesis histórica e índice bibliográfico, 1875–1952. Inst. Indig. Interamer. Mexico.

1955 Un ensayo sobre raza y economía. *Amer. Indig.*, 15: 139–58.

1958 La deformación cefálica intencional en la región del Ucayali, Perú. *In* Misc. Paul Rivet, 2: 109–19. Mexico.

1959 El índice cnémico en tibias prehispánicas y modernas del Valle de México. *Cuad. Inst. Hist.*, ser. antr., no. 5. Mexico.

1960 Manual of physical anthropology. Springfield, Ill.

1960 Datos para la historia de la deformación craneal en México. *Hist. Mex.*, no. 36, pp. 509–20. Mexico.

1961 ¿Otra vez el racismo científico? *Amer. Indig.*, 21: 99–140.

1962 Las primeras instrucciones para la investigación antropológica en México: 1862. *Cuad. Inst. Hist.*, ser. antr., no. 16. Mexico.

1965 Crânes mexicains scaphocéphales. *L'Anthropologie*, 69: 273–301. Paris.

1966 Anthropologie der Sprachfamilie der Maya. *Homo*, 17: 1–36.

1966 Características físicas de la familia lingüística maya. *Inst. Invest. Hist.*, ser. antr., no. 20.

1966 Manual de antropología física. Revised and enlarged ed. Mexico.

1968 Dos microcéfalos 'aztecas': leyenda, historia, antropología. Inst. Invest. Hist., Sec. Antr., Univ. Nac. Autónoma Méx.

1969 Algunos cráneos de la región maya. *An. Antr.*, vol. 6. Mexico.

1969 Cráneos deformados de la Isla de Sacrificios, México. Inst. Invest. Hist., Sec. Antr., Univ. Nac. Autónoma Méx.

1969 Un precursor de la antropología física mexicana: E. Domenech, 1825–1904. *Ibid.*

—— AND J. FAULHABER

1944 *See* Comas, 1944.

1965 Somatometría de los indios triques de Oaxaca, México. Inst. Invest. Hist., Sec. Antr., Univ. Nac. Autónoma Méx.

—— AND S. GENOVÉS

1960 La antropología física en México, 1943–1959: inventario y programa de investigaciones. *Cuad. Inst. Hist., Ser. Antr.*, no. 10. Mexico.

COMMAILLE, J.

1913 Notes sur la décoration cambodgienne. *Bull. l'Ecole Française d'Extrême-Orient*, 13 (3): 1–38. Hanoi.

CONFIRMACIÓN DE CALPAN

1578 Confirmación de las elecciones de Calpan. Manuscrit mexicain nr. 73, Bibliothèque Nationale. Paris.

CONGRESO GEOLÓGICO INTERNACIONAL

1956 Carta geológica de la República Mexicana.

CONGRESO INDIGENISTA INTERAMERICANO

1949 Segundo congreso. Acta final. Inst. Indig. Interamer. Mexico.

1954 Tercero congreso. Acta final. *Ibid.*

1954 Tercero congreso. Número especial del *Bol. Indig.*, 14: 169–228.

1959 Cuarto congreso. *Ibid.*, 19: 125–80.

CONKLIN, H. C.

1956 Tagalog speech disguise. *Language*, 32: 136–39.

1959 Linguistic play in its cultural context. *Ibid.*, 35: 631–36.

CONNELL, C. H., AND J. B. CROSS

1950 Mass mortality of fish associated with the protozoan *Gonyaulax* in the Gulf of Mexico. *Science*, 112 (2909): 359–63.

CONQUISTADOR ANÓNIMO, EL

1858 Relación de algunas cosas de la Nueva España y de la gran ciudad de Temestitlán, México. *In* García Icazbalceta, 1858–66, 1: 368–98. (Other eds. 1556, 1563, 1606, 1838, 1938, and the following entries.)

1917 *Idem.* M. H. Saville, trans. *Cortés Soc.*, Pub. 1.

1941 *Idem.* L. Díaz Cárdenas, ed. Mexico.

CONSERVATION FOUNDATION

1954 Soil erosion survey of Latin America. In collaboration with Food and Agriculture Organization of the United Nations. Reprinted from *Jour. Soil and Water Conservation*, vol. 9, July, Sept., Nov.

CONTRERAS, D., AND H. CEREZO

1958 Geografía de Guatemala. Guatemala.

CONTRERAS ARIAS, A.

1959 Bosquejo climatológico. *In* Los recursos naturales del sureste y su aprovechamiento, ch. 3. 3 vols. Inst. Mex. Recursos Naturales Renovables. Mexico.

CONTRERAS R., J. D.

1951 Una rebelión indígena en el partido de Totonicapan en 1820: el Indio y la independencia. Guatemala.

CONTRERAS S., E.

1966 Trabajos de exploración en la zona arqueológica de Ixtlán del Río Nayarit. Inst. Nac. Antr. Hist. Mexico.

CONZATTI, C., AND OTHERS

1922 Flora y fauna de la región. *In* Gamio, 1922, 1: 19.

CONZEMIUS, E.

1923 The Jicaques of Honduras. *Int. Jour. Amer. Ling.*, 2: 163–70.

1928 Los Indios Payas de Honduras. *Estud. Geog., Hist., Etnog., y Ling.*

1930 Une tribu inconnue du Costa-Rica: les Indiens rama du Rio Zapote. *L'Anthropologie*, 40: 93–108. Paris.

1932 Ethnographical survey of the Miskito and Sumu Indians of Honduras and Nicaragua. *Smithsonian Inst., Bur. Amer. Ethnol.*, Bull. 106.

Cook, C.
    See Cook de Leonard, C.

Cook, O. F.
1909 Vegetation affected by agriculture in Central America. U.S. Dept. Agriculture, Bur. Plant Industry, Bull. 145.

1921 Milpa agriculture, a primitive tropical system. *Smithsonian Inst.*, ann. rept. 1919, pp. 307–26.

Cook, S. F.
1937 The extent and significance of disease among the Indians of Baja California, 1697–1773. *Ibero-Amer.*, no. 12.

1946 The incidence and significance of disease among the Aztecs and related tribes. *Hispanic Amer. Hist. Rev.*, 26: 320–25.

1949 The historical demography and ecology of the Teotlalpan. *Ibero-Amer.*, no. 33.

1949 Soil erosion and population in central Mexico. *Ibid.*, no. 34.

1958 Santa Maria Ixcatlan: habitat, population, subsistence. *Ibid.*, no. 41.

—— AND W. BORAH
1960 The Indian population of central Mexico, 1531–1610. *Ibid.*, no. 44.

1963 The aboriginal population of central Mexico on the eve of the Spanish conquest. *Ibid.*, no. 45.

—— AND L. B. SIMPSON
1948 The population of central Mexico in the sixteenth century. *Ibid.*, no. 31.

Cook de Leonard, C.
1952 Cronología de la cultura teotihuacana: comparación de los sistemas Pedro Armillas y George Vaillant. *Tlatoani*, 1 (2): 11–16.

1952 Teotihuacán: notas del interior. *Ibid.*, 3 (4): 49.

1953 Los Popolocas de Puebla: ensayo de una identificación etno-demográfica e histórico-arqueológica. *In* Huastecos, Totonacos, pp. 423–45.

1954 Dos extraordinarias vasijas del museo de Villa Hermosa (Tabasco). *Yan*, 3: 83–104.

1956 Algunos antecedentes de la cerámica tolteca. *Rev. Mex. Estud. Antr.*, 14: 37–43.

1956 Dos atlatl de la época teotihuacana. *In* Estudios antropológicos, pp. 183–200.

1957 El origen de la cerámica anaranjada delgada. MS. Tesis, Escuela Nac. Antr. Mexico.

1957 Excavaciones en la plaza no. 1, "Tres Palos," Teotihuacan. *Bol. Centro Invest. Antr. Mex.*, 4: 3–5. Mexico.

1959 Archäologisch-geographische Probleme der Insel Jaina, Campeche, Mexiko. *In* Bierhenke, 1959, pp. 44–47.

1959 [ed.] Esplendor del México antiguo. 2 vols. Mexico.

1959 El arte y sus técnicas: la escultura. *In* preceding entry, 2: 519–606.

1959 Ciencia y misticismo. *Ibid.*, 1: 127–40.

1959 La escultura. *Ibid.*, 2: 519–606.

1967 Sculptures and rock carvings at Chalcatzingo, Morelos. *Contrib. Univ. California Archaeol. Research Facility*, 3: 57–84. Berkeley.

—— AND D. LEONARD
1949 Costumbres mortuarias de los indios huaves: un viaje. *El Mex. Antiguo*, 7: 439–513.

Cooke, C. W.
1931 Why the Mayan cities of the Peten district, Guatemala, were abandoned. *Jour. Wash. Acad. Sci.*, 21: 283–87.

Coolidge, D., AND M. R. Coolidge
1939 The last of the Seris. New York.

Coomaraswamy, A.
1928–31 Yakshas. *Smithsonian Misc. Coll.*, no. 80.

Coon, C. S.
1931 Tribes of the Rif. *Peabody Mus. Harvard Univ., Harvard African Studies*, vol. 9.

1966 The living races of man. New York.

Cooper, J. M.
1949 Games and gambling. *In* Hand-

book of South American Indians, 5: 503–24.

COOPER-CLARK, J.
See Clark, J. C.

CORBETT, J. H.
1939 Ball courts and ball game of the ancient American Indians. Master's thesis, Univ. Southern California.

CÓRDOVA, J. DE
1578 Vocabulario castellano-zapoteco. Ed. with introduction and notes by W. Jiménez Moreno. (Mexico, 1942.)
1578 Arte del idioma zapoteca. Ed. Nicolás León. (Morelia, 1886.)

CORDRY, D. B.
1941 Zoque maize legend. *Masterkey*, 15: 58–59.
1947 Two Huichol tales from the sierra of Nayarit. *In* A treasury of Mexican folkways, pp. 499–501.
1947 Two Zoque serpent tales. *Ibid.*, pp. 501–02.

—— AND D. M. CORDRY
1940 Costumes and textiles of the Aztec Indians of the Cuetzalan region, Puebla, Mexico. *SW. Mus. Papers*, no. 14.
1941 Costumes and weaving of the Zoque Indians of Chiapas, Mexico. *Ibid.*, no. 15.

CORNEJO CABRERA, E.
1953 Estudio de psicología experimental en algunos grupos indígenas de México. Col. Cultura Mex. Mexico.
1961 Los Otomies: historia del grupo y de la cultura y su situación actual. *Rev. Mex. Sociol.*, 23: 53–90.

CORNWALL, I. W.
1962 Volcanoes, lakes, soils, and early man in and near the Mexico basin. *Man*, 86: 55–58.

CORNYN, J. H.
1925 Fábulas mexicanas. *Mex. Folkways*, 1: 13–16.
1932 Ixcit Cheel. *Maya Soc. Quar.*, 1: 47–55.
1932 X'tabay. *Ibid.*, 1: 107–11.
1935 Evil for good. *Real Mexico*, 2: 18–19.

—— AND B. McAFEE
1944 Tlacahuapehualiztli: educación de los hijos. *Tlalocan*, 1: 314–61.

CORONA NÚÑEZ, J.
n.d. Nayarit informes. MS filed at Inst. Nac. Antr. Hist. Mexico.
1946 La religión de los Tarascos. *An. Mus. Michoacano.*
1946 Cuiteo: estudio antropogeográfico. *Acta Anthr.*, vol. 2, no. 1, pt. 2.
1952 El templo de Quetzalcoatl en Ixtlán, Nayarit. *An. Inst. Nac. Antr. Hist.*, ep. 6, vol. 4, no. 32. Mexico.
1954 Diferentes tipos de tumbas prehispánicas en Nayarit. Centro Invest. Antr. Méx. *Yan*, 3: 46–50.
1955 Tumba de El Arenal, Etzatlán, Jalisco. *Inst. Nac. Antr. Hist., Dir. Monumentos Prehispánicos*, Informe 3. Mexico.
1957 Mitología tarasca. Mexico.
1960 Exploraciones en El Ixtepete. *Eco*, 2. Inst. Jalisciense de Antr. Hist. Guadalajara.
1960 Investigación arqueológica superficial hecha en el sur de Michoacán. *In* Brand, 1960, pp. 366–403.

CORONEL, J. DE
1620 Arte en lengua maya.... Mexico.

CORRAL, R.
1887 José María Leyva Cajeme: apuntes biográficos. *La Constitución* (official organ of state government of Sonora), vol. 9, nos. 16–28.

CORREA, G.
1955 El espíritu del mal en Guatemala. *Tulane Univ., Middle Amer. Research Inst.*, Pub. 19, pp. 37–104.
1958 Texto de un baile de diablos. *Ibid.*, Pub. 27, pp. 97–104.
1958 La loa en Guatemala. *Ibid.*, Pub. 27, pp. 1–96.

CORRIEDO, J. B.
1852 Leyenda zapoteca. *Ilustración Mex.*, 3: 336–45.

CORTÉS, H.
n.d. Cartas de Cortés. *In* Cartas de relación de la conquista de América. J. de Riverend, ed. Col. Atenea. Mexico.
1844 Carta del Marqués del Valle.... *In* Col. doc. España, 4: 193–201. Madrid.
1866 Cartas y relaciones de Hernán Cortés al emperador Carlos V. Paris.

1870 Cartas de relación dirigidas al emperador Carlos V. Five letters. *Bib. Hist. Iberia*, I. Mexico.

1877 Cartas de relación. *Historiadores Primitivos de Indias*, 1: 1–153. Madrid.

1908 Letters of Cortés. F. A. MacNutt, ed. and trans. 2 vols. New York.

1922 Cartas de relación de la conquista de Mexico. (Calpe ed.) Madrid.

1942 Cartas de relación de la conquista de Méjico. 2 vols. Madrid.

1960 Cartas de relación. *Col. "Sepan Cuantos . . .," no. 7. Mexico.

CORTÉS, M.

1865 Carta de D. Martín Cortés, segundo Marqués del Valle, al rey D. Felipe II. *In* Col. doc. Indias, 4: 440–62.

CORTÉS Y ZEDEÑO, J. T.

1765 Arte, vocabulario, y confessionario en el idioma mexicano. . . . Guadalajara, Puebla de los Angeles.

COSGROVE, C. B.

1947 Caves of the Upper Gila and Hueco areas, in New Mexico and Texas. *Papers Peabody Mus., Harvard Univ.*, vol. 24, no. 2.

COSGROVE, H. S., AND C. B. COSGROVE

1932 The Swartz ruin: a typical Mimbres site in southwestern New Mexico. *Ibid.*, vol. 15, no. 1.

COSIO VILLEGAS, D., ed.

1956 Historia moderna de México. 4 vols. Mexico.

COSTA RICA–PANAMA ARBITRATION

1913 Documents annexed to the argument of Costa Rica. Vol. 1.

COSTALES SAMANIEGO, A.

1956 Trabajas del Instituto Ecuatoriano de Antropología y Geografía. *Bol. Informaciones Cien. Nac.*, 8: 582–608. Quito.

COTNER, T. E., AND C. CASTAÑEDA

1958 Essays in Mexican history. Austin.

COTO, T.

17thC Vocabulario de la lengua cakchiquel. MS in American Philosophical Society. 955 pp.

COUNCIL ON FOREIGN RELATIONS

1961 Social change in Latin America today. New York.

COVARRUBIAS, M.

1942 Origen y desarrollo del estilo artístico olmeca. *In* Mayas y Olmecas, pp. 46–49.

1943 Tlatilco, archaic Mexican art and culture. *DYN*, 4–5: 40–46.

1946 El arte "Olmeca" o de La Venta. *Cuad. Amer.*, 28: 153–79.

1947 Mexico south: the isthmus of Tehuantepec. New York.

1948 Tipología de la industria de piedra tallada y pulida de la cuenca del Río Mezcala. *In* El Occidente de México, pp. 86–90.

1949 Las raices políticas del arte de Tenochtitlán. *México en el Arte*, vol. 8. Mexico.

1950 Tlatilco: el arte y la cultura preclásica del Valle de México. *Cuad. Amer.*, 51: 149–62.

1954 The eagle, the jaguar and the serpent: Indian art of the Americas. New York.

1957 Indian art of Mexico and Central America. New York.

COWAN, F. H.

1946 Notas etnográficas sobre los mazatecos de Oaxaca, México. *Amer. Indig.*, 6: 27–39.

1947 Linguistic and ethnological aspects of Mazateco kinship. *SW. Jour. Anthr.*, 3: 247–56.

1952 A Mazateco president speaks. *Amer. Indig.*, 12: 323–41.

—— AND G. M. COWAN

1947 Mazateco: locational and directional morphemes. *Aboriginal Ling.*, 1: 1–9.

COWAN, G. M.

1946 Mazateco house building. *SW. Jour. Anthr.*, 2: 375–90.

1947 Una visita a los indígenas amuzgos de México. *An. Inst. Nac. Antr. Hist.*, 2: 293–302.

1948 Mazateco whistle speech. *Language*, 24: 280–86.

1952 El idioma silbado entre los Mazatecos de Oaxaca y los Tepehuas de Hidalgo. *Sobretiro de Tlatoani*, 1: 31–33.

1954 La importancia social y política de la

faena mazateca. *Amer. Indig.*, 14: 67–92.

COWAN, M. M.
1962 A Christian movement in Mexico. *Practical Anthr.*, 9: 193–204.

COWGILL, G. L.
1959 Postclassic cultures in the southern Maya lowlands. MS of paper read at meeting of Amer. Anthr. Assoc.

COWGILL, U. M.
1959 Agriculture and population density in the southern Maya lowlands. MS of paper read at meeting of Amer. Anthr. Assoc.

1960 Soil fertility, population, and the ancient Maya. *Proc. Nat. Acad. Sci.*, 46: 1009–11.

CRABTREE, R. H., AND R. J. FITZWATER
n.d. Test excavations at Playa del Tesoro, Colima, Mexico. Mimeographed. Dept. Anthr., Univ. California, Los Angeles.

CRANE, H. R.
1956 University of Michigan radiocarbon dates, I. *Science*, 124: 664–72.

—— AND J. B. GRIFFIN
1958 University of Michigan radiocarbon dates, II. *Ibid.*, 127: 1098–1105.

1958 University of Michigan radiocarbon dates, III. *Ibid.*, 128: 1117–23.

1959 University of Michigan radiocarbon dates, IV. *Amer. Jour. Science, Radiocarbon Suppl.*, 1: 173–98.

1960 University of Michigan radiocarbon dates, V. *Ibid.*, 2: 31–48.

1961 University of Michigan radiocarbon dates, VI. *Ibid.*, 3: 105–25.

CRAWLEY, A. E.
1914 Pallone, pelota, and paume. *The Field*, vol. 123, suppl., p. xviii (April 25). London.

CREFAL
1959 CREFAL, its nature and purpose. [Centro Regional de Educación para la América Latina.] Patzcuaro, Michoacan, Mexico.

CRILE, G. W., AND D. P. QUIRING
1939 A study of the metabolism of the Maya Quiche Indian. *Jour. Nutrition*, 18: 369–74.

CROFT, K.
1951 Practical orthography for Matlapa Nahuatl. *Int. Jour. Amer. Ling.*, 17: 32–36.

1953 Matlapa Nahuatl II: affix list and morphophonemics. *Ibid.*, 19: 274–80.

1953 Six decades of Nahuatl: a bibliographical contribution. *Ibid.*, 19: 57–73.

1954 Matlapa Nahuatl III: morpheme arrangements. *Ibid.*, 20: 37–43.

1957 Nahuatl texts from Matlapa, San Luis Potosi. *Tlalocan*, 3: 317–33.

CROMWELL, T.
1958 Thermocline topography, horizontal currents and "ridging" in the eastern tropical Pacific. *Bull. Inter-Amer. Tropical Tuna Comm.*, 3: 133–64.

—— AND E. B. BENNETT
1959 Surface drift charts for the eastern tropical Pacific Ocean. *Ibid.*, 3: 215–37.

CROOK, W. W., JR., AND R. K. HARRIS
1957 Hearths and artifacts of early man near Lewisville, Texas, and associated faunal materials. *Bull. Texas Archaeol. Soc.*, 38: 7–97.

CRUXENT, J. M., AND I. ROUSE
1956 A lithic industry of Paleo-Indian type in Venezuela. *Amer. Antiquity*, 22: 172–79.

1958–59 An archeological chronology of Venezuela. 2 vols. *Pan Amer. Union, Social Sci. Monogr.*, no. 6.

CRUZ, E. T.
1939 Aun se practica la idolatría en Oaxaca. *Oaxaca en México*, vol. 2, no. 14.

CRUZ, H.
1960 Rinoescleroma en Guatemala: estudio etiopatogénico. Unpublished data.

CRUZ, J. DE LA
1571 Doctrina christiana en la lengua guasteca . . . compuesta por industria de un frayle de la orden del glorioso S. Agustín. Mexico.

CRUZ, W. C.
1935 El tonalamatl zapoteco: el mito y la leyenda zapoteca. Oaxaca.

1936 La hechicería entre los antiguos zapotecas. *Neza*, 2 (14): 3, 5.

1946 Oaxaca recóndita: razas, idiomas,

costumbres, leyendas y tradiciones del estado de Oaxaca. Mexico.

1947 Conceptos fundamentales de la civilización zapoteca. *27th Int. Cong. Amer.* (Mexico, 1939), Acta, 2: 390–98.

CUBILLOS, J. C.
1955 Tumaco (notas arqueológicas). Ministerio Educ., Dept. Extensión Cultural. Bogota.

CUEVA, P.
1607 Arte de la gramática de la lengua zapoteca conforme a la que de la gramática latina escribió Antonio de Lebrija. Mexico.

CUEVAS, M.
1914 [ed.] Documentos inéditos del siglo XVI para la historia de México. Mexico.

1940 Historia de la nación mexicana. Mexico.

1964 Prólogo. *In* Clavigero, Historia antigua de México, 1964 ed. (Porrúa, *Col. "Sepan cuantos,"* 29).

CULEBRO, C. A.
1937 Reseña histórico de Soconusco. Huixtla, Chiapas.

1939 Chiapas prehistórico: su arqueología. Folleto no. 1. Huixtla, Chiapas.

CULIN, S.
1907 Games. *In* Handbook of American Indians north of Mexico, 1: 483–86.

CULL, R.
1856 A brief notice of the Aztec race. *Jour. Ethnol. Soc. London,* 4: 120–28.

CUMMINGS, B. C.
1933 Cuicuilco and the archaic culture of Mexico. *Bull. Univ. Arizona,* vol. 4, no. 8.

CUMMINS, H.
1930 Dermatoglyphics in Indians of southern Mexico and Central America. *Amer. Jour. Physical Anthr.,* 15: 123–36.

1932 Dermatoglyphics in Indians of southern Mexico and Central America (Santa Eulalia, Tzeltal, Lacandon and Maya tribes). *Tulane Univ., Middle Amer. Research Inst.,* Pub. 4, pp. 181–208.

1936 A retabulation of the palmar dermato-

glyphics in Wilder's collection of Mayas, with a note on the Wilder collection of dermatoglyphics. *In* Cummins and others, 1936, pp. 197–203.

1941 Dermatoglyphics in North American Indians and Spanish-Americans. *Human Biol.,* 13: 177–88.

—— AND M. S. GOLDSTEIN
1932 Dermatoglyphics in Comanche Indians. *Amer. Jour. Physical Anthr.,* 17: 229–35.

—— AND C. MIDLO
1943 Fingerprints, palms and soles: an introduction to dermatoglyphics. Philadelphia.

—— AND M. STEGGERDA
1936 Plantar dermatoglyphics in Mayas. *Maya Research,* 3: 277–86.

1936 Fingerprints in Maya Indians. *In* Cummins and others, 1936, pp. 103–26.

—— AND OTHERS (M. S. LANE, S. M. LECHE, R. MILLAR, I. D. STEGGERDA, AND M. STEGGERDA)
1936 Measures of men. *Tulane Univ., Middle Amer. Research Inst.,* Pub. 7.

CURTH, W.
1938 Extracts from "Syphilis in the highlands of Guatemala." *In* Shattuck, 1938, pp. 144–47.

CURTIN, J.
1899 Creation myths in primitive America. London.

CURTIS, E. S.
1908 The North American Indian. Vol. 2.

CUSTER, J. L.
1951 Excavations at Culhuacan. Master's thesis, Univ. of the Americas. Mexico.

CUTBUSH, M., AND P. L. MOLLISON
1950 The Duffy blood group system. *Heredity,* 4: 383–89.

CUTLER, H. C.
1960 Cultivated plant remains from Waterfall Cave, Chihuahua. *Amer. Antiquity,* 26: 277–79.

—— AND T. W. WHITAKER
1961 History and distribution of the cultivated cucurbits in the Americas. *Ibid.,* 26: 469–85.

DABBS, J. A.
1958 The Indian policy of the second empire. *In* Cotner and Castañeda, 1958, pp. 113–26.

DADE, P. L.
1959 Tomb burials in southeastern Veraguas. *Panama Archaeol.*, vol. 2, no. 1.

DAHL, O. C.
1953 Malgache et maanjan: une comparaison linguistique. *Word*, 29: 577–97.

DAHLGREN DE JORDÁN, B.
1954 La mixteca: su cultura e historia prehispánicas. *Col. Cultura Mex.*, no. 11. Mexico.
1961 El nocheztli o la grana de cochinilla mexicana. *In* Homenaje Martínez del Río, pp. 387–99.
1963 Nocheztli: economía de una región. Nueva Biblioteca Mexicana de Obras Históricas. Porrúa. Mexico.

—— AND J. ROMERO
1951 La prehistórica Bajacaliforniana, redescubrimiento de pinturas rupestres. *Cuad. Amer.*, 4: 3–28.

DAMPIER, W.
1699 A new voyage around the world. 2 vols. 4th ed. London.

D'ANDRADE, R. G.
1962 Father absence and cross-sex identification. Doctoral dissertation, Harvard Univ.

DANSEREAU, P.
1951 Description and recording of vegetation upon a structural basis. *Ecology*, 32: 172–229.

DANSON, E. B.
1941 An archaeological survey of the Santa Cruz River valley from the headwaters to the town of Tubac in Arizona. MS report on file at Arizona State Mus.

DANZEL, T. W., AND E. FUHRMANN
1922 Mexiko. Schriften-Reihe: Kulturen der Erde. Material zur Kultur- und Kunstgeschichte aller Völker, Band 12, Mexiko. 3 vols. Hagen-Darmstadt.

DARÍO, R.
1954 Folklore de la América Central: representaciones y bailes populares en Nicaragua. *Nicaragua Indig.*, 2: 5–9. Managua.

DARK, P.
1958 Mixtec ethnohistory, a method of analysis of the codical art. Oxford Univ. Press.

DARLING, S. T.
1925 Comparative helminthology as an aid in the solution of ethnological problems. *Amer. Jour. Tropical Med.*, 5: 323–37.

DARLINGTON, P. J., JR.
1957 Zoogeography: the geographical distribution of animals. New York.

DAUBENMIRE, R. F.
1938 Merriam's life zones of North America. *Quar. Rev. Biol.*, 13: 327–32.

DÁVALOS HURTADO, E.
1945 La deformación craneana entre los tlatelolca. *Mem. Acad. Mex. Hist.*, 3: 31–50.
1951 La deformación craneana entre los tlatelolca. *Esc. Nac. Antr. Hist.*, tesis profesional. Mexico.
1953 Investigaciones osteopatológicas prehispánicas en México. *Mem. Cong. Cien. Mex.*, 12: 78–81.
1955 Un ejemplo de patología ósea prehispánica de México. *An. Inst. Nac. Antr. Hist.*, 7: 147–55.

—— AND A. MARINO FLORES
1956 Reflexiones acerca de la antropología mexicana. *Ibid.*, 8: 163–209.

—— AND L. VARGAS Y VARGAS
1956 La radiología en paleopatología. *An. Méd.*, 1: 159–62. Mexico.

—— AND OTHERS
1965 Museo Nacional de Antropología. *Artes de México*, año 12, ep. 2, no. 66/67.

DAVIDSOHN, I., K. STERN, E. R. STRAUSER, AND W. SPURRIER
1953 Be, a new "private" blood factor. *Blood*, 8: 747–54.

DÁVILA GARIBI, J. I.
1938 Epítome de raíces nahuas. Mexico.
1948 La escritura del idioma náhuatl a través de los siglos. 2d ed. Mexico.

DAVIS, A. L., AND R. I. McDAVID, JR.
1950 Northwestern Ohio: a transition area. *Language*, 26: 264–73.

DAVIS, A. P.
1900 Hydrography of Nicaragua. *U.S. Geol. Survey*, 20th ann. rept., pt. 4, pp. 563–637.

DAVIS, B.
1867 Thesaurus craniorum: catalogue of the skulls of various races of men. London.

DAVIS, C. C.
1948 *Gymnodinium breve* sp. nov., a cause of discolored water and animal mortality in the Gulf of Mexico. *Bot. Gaz.*, 109: 358–60.

DAVIS, E. H.
1920 Papago ceremony of Vikita. *Mus. Amer. Indian, Heye Found.*, 3 (4): 153–77.

DAVIS, E. M.
1953 Recent data from two Paleo-Indian sites on Medicine Creek, Nebraska. *Amer. Antiquity*, 18: 380–86.

DAWSON, E. Y.
1944 Some ethnobotanical notes on the Seri Indians. *Desert Plant Life*, 16: 132–38.

1945 Marine algae associated with upwelling along the northwestern coast of Baja California, Mexico. *Bull. Southern Calif. Acad. Sci.*, 44: 57–71.

1951 A further study of upwelling and associated vegetation along Pacific Baja California, Mexico. *Jour. Marine Research*, 10: 39–58.

1952 Circulation within Bahia Viscaino, and its effects on marine vegetation. *Amer. Jour. Botany*, 39: 425–32.

1960 The biogeography of California and adjacent seas. Part 2: A review of the ecology, distribution, and affinities of the benthic flora. *Syst. Zool.*, 9: 93–100.

DAVIS, J. T.
1959 Further notes on clay human figurines in the western United States, no. 71. *Univ. California Archaeol. Survey*, Rept. 48, pp. 16–31.

DE BUEN, F.
1943 Los lagos michoacanos. I: El lago de Zirahuen. *Rev. Soc. Mex. Hist. Natural*, 4: 211–32.

1944 Los lagos michoacanos II: Patzcuaro. *Ibid.*, 5: 99–125.

1945 Resultados de una campaña limnológica en Chapala y observaciones sobre otras aguas exploradas. *Ibid.*, 6: 129–44.

DECICCO, G.
1959 Ceremonias fúnebres de los chatinos. *Tlatoani*, 12: 22–24.

1969 The Chatino. *In* Handbook of Middle American Indians, R. Wauchope, ed., vol. 7, art. 17.

—— AND D. BROCKINGTON
1956 Reconocimiento arqueológico en el sudoeste de Oaxaca. *Inst. Nac. Antr. Hist.*, Informe 6.

—— AND F. HORCASITAS
1962 Los cuates. *Tlalocan*, 4: 74–79.

DECORME, G.
1941 La obra de los jesuítas mexicanos durante la época colonial, 1572–1767. 2 vols. Mexico.

DE CSERNA, Z.
1956 Tectónica de la Sierra Madre Oriental de Mexico, entre Torreon y Monterrey. Mexico.

1958 Notes on the tectonics of southern Mexico. *In* Habitat of Oil (Amer. Assoc. Petroleum Geol.).

DEDRICK, J. M.
1946 How Jobe?eso Ro?i got his name. *Tlalocan*, 2: 163–66.

DEEVEY, E. S.
1943 Intento para datar las culturas medias del valle de Mexico mediante análisis de polen. *Ciencia*, 4: 97–105.

1944 Pollen analysis and Mexican archaeology: an attempt to apply the method. *Amer. Antiquity*, 10: 135–49.

1955 Limnological studies in Guatemala and El Salvador. *Internationale Vereinigung für theoretische und angewandte Limnologie*, Verhandlungen, 12: 278–83.

1957 Limnologic studies in Middle America with a chapter on Aztec limnology. *Trans. Connecticut Acad. Arts and Sci.*, 39: 213–28.

——, R. F. FLINT, AND I. ROUSE, eds.
1963 Radiocarbon. *Amer. Jour. Science*, 261: 1–349.

——, L. J. GRALENSKI, AND V. HOFFREN
1959 Yale natural radiocarbon measure-

ments, IV. *Amer. Jour. Science, Radiocarbon Suppl.*, 1: 144–72.

DEGER, E. C.

1932 Las cenizas y arenas volcánicas de Guatemala y El Salvador en relación con su rol en la formación del suelo agrícola. Guatemala.

1932 Zur kenntnis der mittelamerikanischen Aschen. *Chemie der Erde*, 11: 249–55.

1939 Album petrográfico de la América Central. I: La zona de Amatitlan. Guatemala.

1942 Diferenciaciones magmáticas en la edificación de la Cordillera Andina de Centro-América. *Proc. 8th Amer. Sci. Cong.*, 4: 459–60.

DE LA FUENTE, JOSÉ M.

1905 Elementos de higiene pedagógica. *Mem. Soc. Cien. Antonio Alzate*, 23: 119–81.

DE LA FUENTE, JULIO

1938 Yalalag. *Indoamérica*, vol. 1, no. 6.

1941 Creencias indígenas sobre la onchocercosis, el paludismo y otras enfermedades. *Amer. Indig.*, 1 (1): 43–47.

1942 Un reporte sobre los sitios arqueológicos existentes en los distritos de Villa Alta, Choapam, Ixtlan y Tlacolula. MS in Archivo Inst. Nac. Antr. Hist.

1947 Las ceremonias de la lluvia entre los zapotecos de hoy. *27th Int. Cong. Amer.* (Mexico, 1939), Acta, 2: 479–84.

1947 Definición, pase y desaparición del indio en México. *Amer. Indig.*, 7: 63–69.

1947 Discriminación y negación del indio. *Ibid.*, 7: 211–15.

1947 Los Zapotecos de Choapan, Oaxaca. *An. Inst. Nac. Antr. Hist.*, 2: 143–206.

1947 Notas sobre lugares de Oaxaca, con especial referencia a la toponimia zapoteca. *Ibid.*, 2: 279–92.

1948 Cambios socio-culturales en México. *Acta Anthr.*, vol. 3, no. 4.

1949 Documentos para la etnografía e historia zapoteca. *An. Inst. Nac. Antr. Hist.* 3: 175–97.

1949 Yalalag: una villa zapoteca serrana. *Mus. Nac. Antr., Ser. Cien.*, no. 1. Mexico.

1952 Ethnic and communal relations. *In* Tax, 1952, Heritage, pp. 76–96.

1952 Algunos problemas etnológicas de Oaxaca. *An. Inst. Nac. Antr. Hist.*, 4: 241–52.

1958 Relaciones étnicas en Chiapas. Mimeographed.

1958 Results of an action program. *Human Organization*, 17: 30–33.

1959 Los programas de cambio dirigido, sus características y sus resultados. *In* Stone, 1959, 1: 380–85.

1960 La cultura zapoteca. *Rev. Mex. Estud. Antr.*, 16: 233–46.

DELGADO, A.

1957 Exploración de tumbas en la Chinantla. MS in Archivo Inst. Nac. Antr. Hist.

1960 Investigaciones en la parte alta de la Chinantla. *Bol. Inst. Nac. Antr. Hist.*, 2: 7.

1960 Exploraciones en la Chinantla. *Rev. Mex. Estud. Antr.*, 16: 105–23.

1961 Exploraciones en Tehuantepec. *In* Los Mayas del sur y sus relaciones con los Nahuas meridionales, pp. 93–104. Soc. Mex. Antr.

DELGADO, A. I.

1950 La danza "cadenitas," una expresión folklórica. *Cuauhtémoc: Rev. Cultura y Actualidad*, 2: 48–49.

DELGADO, H. S.

n.d. Archaeological textiles from Durango, Zacatecas, and Sinaloa. MS.

DE LIMA, P. E.

1947 Impressões digitais dos Indios tenetehára. *Bol. Mus. Nac.*, n.s., 7: 1–11. Rio de Janeiro.

DELLA SANTA, E.

1959 Les Cupisniques et l'origine des Olmèques. *Rev. Univ. Bruxelles*, 5: 1–24.

DEMAREST, D., AND C. TAYLOR

1956 The dark virgin: the book of our lady of Guadalupe. New York.

DEMBOA, A., AND J. IMBELLONI

1938 Deformaciones intencionales del cuerpo humano de carácter étnico. *Hu-*

manior. Bibl. Amer. Moderno, sec. A, vol. 3. Buenos Aires.

DeNatale, A., and others (A. Cahan, J. A. Jack, R. R. Race, and R. Sanger)
1955 Blood groups—Rh (V). *Jour. Amer. Med. Assoc.*, 159: 247–50.

Denevan, W. M.
1958 The upland pine forests of Nicaragua. M.A. thesis, Univ. California.
1961 The upland pine forests of Nicaragua: a study in cultural plant geography. *Univ. Calif. Pub. Geog.*, 12: 251–320.

Deniker, J.
1895 Sur les ossements humaines recueillés par M. Diguet dans la Basse Californie. *Bull. Mus. Hist. Naturelle*, 1: 33–35. Paris.
1926 Les races et les peuples de la terre. Paris.

Densidad
1950 *See* Instituto Nacional Indigenista (Mexico), 1950.

Desarrollo Cultural de los Mayas
1964 Desarrollo cultural de los Mayas. E. Z. Vogt and A. Ruz Lhuillier, eds. Wenner-Gren symposium at Burg Wartestein on the cultural development of the Maya. Univ. Nac. Autónoma Mex.

Descripción . . . Antequera
1946 Descripción de la ciudad de Antequera. *Tlalocan*, 2: 134–37.

Descripción de Indios
1912 *In* Codex Kingsborough, pp. 199–202.

Descripción del Arzobispado de México
1905 *In* Paso y Troncoso, 1905–06, vol. 3.

Descripción . . . Pueblo de Guauchinango
1948 Descripción del pueblo de Guauchinango y de otros pueblos de su jurisdicción, sacada de la relación hecha por el alcalde mayor de aquel pueblo en 13 de Mayo de 1609. *In* Toussaint, 1948, pp. 293–303. (Also in Col. doc. Indias, 9: 120–32.)

Descripción . . . Provincia de Pánuco
1948 Descripción de los pueblos de la provincia de Pánuco, sacada de las relaciones hechas por Pedro Martínez, capitán y alcalde mayor de la provincia. *Ibid.*, pp. 271–81. (Also in Col. doc. Indias, 9: 150–66.)

Descripción . . . Villa de Pánuco
1948 Descripción de la villa de Pánuco, sacada de las relaciones hechas por Pedro Martínez, capitán y alcalde mayor de aquella provincia. *Ibid.*, pp. 261–70. (Also in Col. doc. Indias, 9: 133–49.)

Descripción . . . Villa de Tampico
1948 Descripción de la villa de Tampico, sacada de las relaciones hechas por Pedro Martínez, capitán y alcalde mayor de aquella provincia. *Ibid.*, pp. 283–91. (Also in Col. doc. Indias, 9: 167–79.)

Deshon, S. K.
1959 Women's position on a Yucatecan henequen hacienda. Doctoral dissertation, Yale Univ.

Dessaint, A. Y.
1962 Effects of the hacienda and plantation systems on Guatemala's Indians. *Amer. Indig.*, 22: 323–54.

De Terra, H.
1946 New evidence for the antiquity of early man in Mexico. *Rev. Mex. Estud. Antr.*, 8: 69–88.
1946 Discovery of an upper Pleistocene human fossil at Tepexpan, Valley of Mexico. *Ibid.*, 8: 287–88.
1947 Preliminary note on the discovery of fossil man at Tepexpan in the Valley of Mexico. *Amer. Antiquity*, 13: 40–44.
1947 Teoría de una cronología geológica para el valle de Mexico. *Rev. Mex. Estud. Antr.*, 9: 11–26.
1949 Early man in Mexico. *In* Tepexpan man, pp. 13–86. *Viking Fund Pub. Anthr.*, no. 11.
1950 Los cambios climatológicos y la conservación del suelo en Mexico. *Turrialba*, 1: 28–31.
1951 Comments on radiocarbon dates from Mexico. *Mem. Soc. Amer. Archaeol.*, 8: 33–36.
1951 Radiocarbon age measurements and fossil man in Mexico. *Science*, 113: 124–25.
1951 Comments on radiocarbon dates from Mexico. *In* Homenaje Caso, pp. 377–88.

1957 Man and mammoth in Mexico. London.

1959 A successor of Tepexpan man in the valley of Mexico. *Science*, 129 (3348): 563–64.

——, J. Romero, and T. D. Stewart
1949 Tepexpan man. *Viking Fund Pub. Anthr.*, no. 11.

Deuel, T., ed.
1952 Hopewellian communities in Illinois. *Illinois State Mus. Sci. Papers*, vol. 5, no. 3.

Deurden, J. E.
1897 Aboriginal Indian remains in Jamaica. *Jour. Inst. Jamaica*, 2 (4): 1–52. Kingston.

DeVries, H.
1958 Groningen radiocarbon dates. *Science*, 127:123–37.

—— and H. T. Waterbolk
1958 Groningen radiocarbon dates II. *Science*, 127 (3290).

Dewar, J.
1957 Blanket for tortillas, an Otomi textile. *Masterkey*, 31: 105–06.

d'Harcourt, R.
1942 Archéologie de la province d'Esmeraldas, Equateur. *Jour. Soc. Amer. Paris*, 34: 61–200.

1948 Arts de l'Amérique. Paris.

1950 Primitive art of the Americas. Paris. (English trans. of his 1948.)

1958 Representation de textiles dans la statuaire Maya. *32d Int. Cong. Amer.* (Copenhagen, 1956), Acta, pp. 415–21.

Diamond, S., ed.
1960 Culture in history: essays in honor of Paul Radin. New York.

Díaz, A. F.
1952 El tokelau en Guatemala. *Rev. Colegio Méd. Guatemala*, 3: 253–55.

Díaz del Castillo, B.
1632 Historia verdadera de la conquista de la Nueva España. Madrid. (Various eds. 1904, 1908–16, 1912, 1927, 1928, 1933–34, 1938, 1939, 1942, 1944, 1950.)

Díaz de Salas, M.
1960–61 Field notes of San Bartolome de las Casas. MS, Chiapas Project files, Univ. Chicago, Dept. Anthropology.

Díaz Lozano, E.
1917 Diatomeas fósiles mexicanas. *An. Inst. Geol. de Mex.*, 1 (1): 1–27.

1920 Depósitos diatomíferos en el valle de Toxi, Ixtlahuaca, Mexico. *Ibid.*, 1 (9): 1–19.

1922 Rocas y minerales del Valle. *In* Gamio, 1922, 2: 31–66.

1927 Los restos fósiles de elephas encontrados en terrenos de la hacienda de Tepexpan, Mexico. *An. Inst. Geol. de Mex.*, 2 (6–10): 201–202.

Dibble, C. E.
1942 Códice en Cruz. Mexico.

1951 Códice Xolotl. *Univ. Nac. Autónoma Méx., Pub. Inst. Hist.*, 1st ser., no. 22. Mexico.

—— and A. J. O. Anderson
1950–69 *See* Sahagún, 1950–69.

Diccionario de Motul
1929 Maya-Español. Juan Martínez Hernández, ed. Merida.

Dice, L. R.
1943 The biotic provinces of North America. Univ. Michigan Press.

1952 Natural communities. Univ. Michigan Press.

Dick, H. W.
1952 Evidences of early man in Bat Cave and on the plains of San Augustin, New Mexico. *In* Tax, 1952, Indian tribes, pp. 158–63.

—— and B. Mountain
1960 The Claypool site: a Cody complex site in northeastern Colorado. *Amer. Antiquity*, 26: 223–35.

Dickey, D. R., and A. J. van Rossem
1938 The birds of El Salvador. *Field Mus. Nat. Hist., Zool. Ser.*, no. 23.

Diebold, A. R., Jr.
1960 Determining the centers of dispersal of language groups. *Int. Jour. Amer. Ling.*, 26: 1–10.

1961 Incipient bilingualism. *Language*, 37: 97–112.

1966 The reflection of coresidence in Mareño kinship terminology. *Ethnology*, 5: 37–39.

DIESELDORFF, E. P.

1903　Old titles of the Queccki Indians. MS in Peabody Mus., Harvard Univ.

1904　A pottery vase with figure painting from a grave in Chama. *Smithsonian Inst., Bur. Amer. Ethnol.*, Bull. 28, pp. 639–50.

1926–33　Kunst und Religion der Mayavölker im alten und heutigen Mittelamerika. 3 vols. Berlin.

1928–29.　Religión y arte de las mayas. *An. Soc. Geog. Hist.*, vol. 4, nos. 1–4. Guatemala.

1930　The Aztec calendar stone and its significance. *23d Int. Cong. Amer.* (New York, 1928), Acta, pp. 211–22.

1940　Las plantas medicinales del departamento de Alta Verapaz. *An. Soc. Geog. Hist.*, vol. 16, no. 3.

DIETSCHY, H.

1945　Alt-Mexiko. Führer durch das Museum für Völkerkunde. Basel.

1948　La coiffure de plumes mexicaines du Musée de Vienne: critique iconographique et notes ethno-psychologiques. *28th Int. Cong. Amer.* (Paris, 1947), Acta, pp. 381–92.

DIGUET, L.

1899　Rapport sur une mission scientifique dans la Basse Californie. *Nouvelles Archives des Missions Scientifiques,* 9: 1–53. Paris.

1899　La sierra de Nayarit et ses indigènes. Paris.

1903　Le Chimalhuacan et ses populations avant la conquête espagnole. *Jour. Soc. Amer. Paris*, 1: 1–57.

1905　Anciennes sépultures indigènes de la Basse Californie méridionale. *Ibid.*, 2: 329–33.

1911　Idiome huichol. *Ibid.*, 8: 23–54.

DIMICK, J.

1941　El Salvador. *Carnegie Inst. Wash.*, Year Book 40.

DIPESO, C. C.

1950　Painted stone slabs of Point of Pines, Arizona. *Amer. Antiquity*, 16: 57–65.

1951　The Babocomari village site on the Babocomari River, southeastern Arizona. *Amerind Found.*, no. 5.

1955　Two Cerro Guamas Clovis fluted points from Sonora, Mexico. *Kiva,* 21 (1, 2): 13–15.

1956　The Upper Pima of San Cayetano del Tumacacori. *Amerind Found.*, no. 7.

—— AND H. C. CUTLER

1958　The Reeve ruin of southeastern Arizona: a study of a prehistoric western Pueblo migration into the middle San Pedro valley. *Ibid.*, no. 8.

DIRECCIÓN DE MONUMENTOS PREHISPÁNICOS

1933　Monumentos arqueológicos de México. Pub. Sec. Educación Pública, Depto. Monumentos Prehispánicos. Mexico.

DIRECCIÓN GENERAL DE ASUNTOS INDÍGENAS, MEXICO

[1958]　Seis años de labor.

DIRECCIÓN GENERAL DE ESTADÍSTICA, GUATEMALA

1953　Sexto censo de población. Guatemala.

1959　*Boletín estadístico*, nos. 1–2. Guatemala.

DIRECCIÓN GENERAL DE IRRIGACIÓN

1954–55　Estadística hidrológica. Servicio de Hidrometría Nacional. Tegucigalpa, Honduras.

DIRINGER, D.

[1948]　The alphabet, a key to the history of mankind. London.

DISSELHOFF, H. D.

1932　Note sur le résultat de quelques fouilles archéologiques faites à Colima (Mexique). *Rev. Inst. Etnol., Univ. Nac. Tucumán.* Tucumán, Argentina. (25th Int. Cong. Amer.)

DIXON, K. A.

1958　Two masterpieces of Middle American bone sculpture. *Amer. Antiquity*, 24: 53–62.

1959　Two carved human bones from Chiapas. *Archaeology*, 12: 106–10.

1959　Ceramics from two preclassic periods at Chiapa de Corzo, Chiapas, Mexico. *Papers New World Archaeol. Found.*, no. 5.

DIXON, R. B.

1923　The racial history of man. New York.

—— AND A. L. KROEBER

1919　Indian linguistic families of California.

Univ. California Pub. Archaeol. Ethnol., 16: 47–118.

DOCKSTADER, F. J.
1961 A figurine cache from Kino Bay, Sonora. *In* Lothrop and others, 1961, pp. 182–91.
1964 Indian art in Middle America. Greenwich, Conn.

DOCTRINA CRISTIANA
1944 Doctrina cristiana en lengua española y mexicana por los religiosos de la orden de Santo Domingo. Madrid. (Facsimile ed. of 1548 ed.)

DOCUMENTOS:
n.d. Documentos de tierras de la hacienda Sn. Juan Bautista Tavi en idioma maya o yucateca. MS in Tulane Univ.
16thC Documentos inéditos . . . México. *See* Cuevas, 1914.
16thC–17thC Documentos inéditos . . . Tampico. *See* Meade, 1939.
16thC–17thC Documentos . . . México colonial. *See* Scholes and Adams, 1955–61.
1642–1761 Documentos de Ticul. Manuscript. Photograph in Newberry Library. 62 pp.
1842–95 Colección de documentos inéditos . . . España. *See* Colección de Documentos, 1842–95.
1853–57 Documentos para la historia de México. *See* García Torres, 1853–57.
1858–66 Colección de documentos . . . México. *See* García Icazbalceta, 1858–66.
1864–84 Colección de documentos inéditos . . . . Indias. *See* Colección de Documentos, 1864–84.
1884 Documentos relativos al axe o ni-in. *Naturaleza*, 6: 372–84. Mexico.
1885–1932 Colección de documentos inéditos . . . ultramar. *See* Colección de Documentos, 1885–1932.
1886–92 Nueva colección de documentos . . . México. *See* García Icazbalceta, 1886–92.
1897–99 Colección de documentos . . . San Luis Potosí. *See* Velázquez, 1897–99.
1897–1903 Colección de documentos . . .

DOCUMENTOS—*continued*
historia mexicana. *See* Peñafiel, 1897–1903.
1903–07 Documentos históricos de México. *See* García Pimentel, 1903–07.
1956 Documentos históricos de Chiapas. *Archivo General del Estado*, Bol. 6. Tuxtla Gutierrez.

DOLL, E. E.
1952 The stewardship of the saint in Mexico and Guatemala [1943]. *Univ. Chicago, Micro. Coll. MSS Middle Amer. Cult. Anthr.*, no. 31, item B.

DOLLFUS, A., AND E. DE MONTSERRAT
1868 Voyage géologique dans les républiques de Guatemala et de Salvador. Paris.

DOLORES, J.
1911–14 Papago verb stems. *Univ. California Pub. Amer. Archaeol. Ethnol.*, 10: 241–63.
1923 Papago nominal stems. *Ibid.*, 20: 19–31.

DOMÍNGUEZ, F.
1939 Dos sones zapotecas. *Neza*, 4 (1): supplement.
1939 Telayuu (melodía de la madrugada). *Ibid.*
1939 Trío de músicos zapotecas. *Ibid.*, 4 (1): 9–15.

DONDÉ IBARRA, J.
1884 El ni-in. *Naturaleza*, 6: 200–04. Mexico.

DONDÉ Y LÓPEZ, T.
1941 Costumbres cuitlatecas. *El Mex. Antiguo*, 5 (7–10): 233–38.

DONDOLI, C.
1940 Rocas de Costa Rica, determinación y estudio petrográfico (cuarzo-diorita andesino). *Centro Nac. Agronómico*, pp. 73–78. San Jose, Costa Rica.
1940 Rocas de Costa Rica, determinación y estudio petrográfico (andesita labradorítica). *Bol. Técnico Dept. Nac. de Agricultura*, no. 32. San Jose, Costa Rica.
1943 La región de El General, condiciones geológicas y geoagronómicas de la zona. *Ibid.*, no. 44.
1943 Relación entre el terreno y la roca. *Ibid.*, nos. 45, 46.

DOS RELACIONES . . . CUILAPA
1945 Dos relaciones antiguos del pueblo de Cuilapa, estado de Oaxaca. *Tlalocan*, 2: 18–28.

DOTSON, F., AND L. O. DOTSON
1956 Urban centralization and decentralization in Mexico. *Rural Sociol.*, 21: 41–49.
1957 La estructura ecológica de las ciudades mexicanas. *Rev. Mex. Sociol.*, 19: 39–66.

DOUTRELAINE, COLONEL
1867 Rapport sur les ruines de Mitla. *In* Archives de la Commission Scientifique du Mexique, 3: 104–11. Paris.

DOWNEY, J. E.
1927 Types of dextrality among North American Indians. *Jour. Experimental Psychol.*, 10: 478–88.

DOWNING, T.
1940 The marigolds of Mitla. *Mex. Life*, 16 (7): 21–23, 53–59.

DOWNS, C. M., H. P. JONES, AND K. KOERBER
1929 Incidence and properties of isohemolysis. *Jour. Infectious Diseases*, 44: 412–19.

DOZIER, C. L.
1958 Indigenous tropical agriculture in Central America. *Nat. Acad. Sci., Nat. Research Council*, Pub. 594.

DOZIER, E. P.
1956 Two examples of linguistic acculturation: the Yaqui of Sonora and Arizona and the Tewa of New Mexico. *Language*, 32: 146–57.

DRESSLER, R. L.
1953 The pre-Columbian cultivated plants of Mexico. *Bot. Mus. Leafl. Harvard Univ.*, 16: 115–72.

DREWITT, B.
1966 Planeación en la antigua ciudad de Teotihuacán. *In* Teotihuacán, pp. 79–94.

DRIVER, H. E., AND W. DRIVER
1963 Ethnography and acculturation of the Chichimeca-Jonaz of northeast Mexico. *Indiana Univ. Research Center in Anthr., Folklore, Ling.*, Pub. 26.

—— AND W. C. MASSEY
1957 Comparative studies of North American Indians. *Trans. Amer. Phil. Soc.*, 47 (part 2): 165–456.

DRUCKER, P.
n.d. Field and laboratory notes, Soconusco survey of 1947. MS in Smithsonian Inst. Washington.
1941 Culture element distributions: XVII Yuman-Piman. *Univ. California, Anthr. Rec.*, vol. 6, no. 3.
1941 Yuman-Piman. Univ. California Press.
1943 Ceramic stratigraphy at Cerro de las Mesas, Veracruz, Mexico. *Smithsonian Inst., Bur. Amer. Ethnol.*, Bull. 141.
1943 Ceramic sequences at Tres Zapotes, Veracruz, Mexico. *Ibid.*, Bull. 140.
1948 Preliminary notes on an archaeological survey of the Chiapas coast. *Tulane Univ., Middle Amer. Research Rec.*, vol. 1, no. 11.
1952 La Venta, Tabasco: a study of Olmec ceramics and art. *Smithsonian Inst., Bur. Amer. Ethnol.*, Bull. 153.
1952 Two aboriginal works of art from the Veracruz coast. *Smithsonian Misc. Coll.*, 117: 1–7.
1955 The Cerro de las Mesas offering of jade and other materials. *Smithsonian Inst., Bur. Amer. Ethnol.*, Bull. 157, pp. 25–68.
1958 The native brotherhoods. *Ibid.*, Bull. 168.

—— AND R. F. HEIZER
1960 A study of the milpa system of the La Venta island and its archaeological implications. *SW. Jour. Anthr.*, 16: 36–45.

——, ——, AND R. J. SQUIER
1957 Radiocarbon dates from La Venta, Tabasco. *Science*, 126: 72–73.
1959 Excavations at La Venta, Tabasco, 1955. *Smithsonian Inst., Bur. Amer. Ethnol.*, Bull. 170.

DRUCKER, S.
1959 Field notes on Jamiltepec, a Mixtec and Mestizo village of Oaxaca, Mexico. MS.
1963 Cambio de indumentaria. *Col. Antr. Social*. Inst. Nac. Indig. Mexico.

——, R. ESCALANTE, AND R. J. WEITLANER
1969 The Cuitlatec. *In* Handbook of Middle American Indians, R. Wauchope, ed., vol. 7, art. 30.

DRUMMOND, K. H., AND G. B. AUSTIN
1958 Some aspects of the physical oceanography of the Gulf of Mexico. *In*
A. Collier, 1958.

DUBY, G.
1944 Los lacandones: su pasado y su presente. *Bib. Enciclopedica Popular,*
no. 30. Mexico.
1955 Los lacandones: el mundo y su influencia sobre ellos. *Novedades,*
Aug. 14.
1961 Chiapas indígena. Univ. Nac. Autónoma Mex.

DUCRUE, N.
1765 Description of California. *In* O'-
Crouley, n.d.

DUELLMAN, W. E.
1960 A distributional study of the amphibians of the Isthmus of Tehuantepec,
Mexico. *Univ. Kansas Pub., Mus.
Nat. Hist.,* 13: 19–72.

DUGÉS, A.
1891 La *Llaveia dorsalis, nobis. Naturaleza,* ser. 2, 1: 160–61.

DUGGINS, O. H., AND M. TROTTER
1956 Characteristics of hair of Yupa Indians. *Proc. Amer. Phil. Soc.,* 100:
220–22.

DUNLOP, R. G.
1847 Travels in Central America. London.

DUNN, E. R.
1931 The herpetological fauna of the
Americas. *Copeia,* 3: 106–19.
1940 Some aspects of herpetology in lower Central America. *Trans. New
York Acad. Sci.,* 2: 156–58.

DUNNE, P. M.
1940 Pioneer Black Robes on the west
coast. Univ. California Press.
1944 Pioneer Jesuits in northern Mexico.
Ibid.
1948 Early Jesuit missions in Tarahumara.
Ibid.

DUPAIX, G.
1834 Antiquités mexicaines: relation des
trois expéditions du Capitaine Dupaix,
ordonnées en 1805, 1806, et 1807,
pour la recherche des antiquités du
pays, notamment celles de Mitla et
de Palenque; accompagnée des dessins de Castañeda. . . . 2 vols. and
atlas. Paris.

DUPERTUIS, C. W., AND J. A. HADDEN, JR.
1951 On the reconstruction of stature from
long bones. *Amer. Jour. Physical
Anthr.,* 9: 15–53.

DUQUE DE ESTRADA, J.
1902 Contribution à l'étude des formations
pelviennes à Mexico. *Mem. Soc.
Cien. Antonio Alzate,* 17: 63–111;
18: 35–72. Mexico.
1910 Procedimiento fácil y rápido para la
mensuración del diámetro bi-isquiático. *Crónica Méd. Méx.,* vol. 8.
1911 Contribución al estudio de la deformaciones pélvicas en México. Mexico.
1916 Pelvis infundibuliformes mexicanas.
Bol. Dirección Estud. Biol., 3: 171–
210. Mexico.

DURÁN, D.
1868–80 Historia de las Indias de Nueva
España y islas de tierra firme. 2 vols.
and atlas. Mexico.
1951 *Idem,* reprinted.
1967 *Idem.* Ed. paleográfica del manuscrito
autógrafo de Madrid, con introduc-
ciones, notas y vocabularios de palabras indígenas y arcaicas. A. M.
Garibay K., ed. 2 vols. *Bibloteca
Porrúa,* 36. Mexico.

DURÁN OCHOA, J.
1955 Población, México. Fondo de Cultura Económica. Mexico.
1961 La explosión demográfica. *In* México: 50 años de revolución, 2: 3–28.

DURHAM, J. W., AND E. C. ALLISON
1960 The biogeography of Baja California
and adjacent seas. Part 1: The geologic history of Baja California and
its marine faunas. *Syst. Zool.,* 9:
47–91.

DU SOLIER, W.
1939 Informe sobre la zona de Tuzapan,
Veracruz, año de 1939. Inst. Nac.
Antr. Hist., Archivo Técnico de Monumentos Prehispánicos. Mexico.
1939 Una representación pictórica de Quetzalcoatl en una cueva. *Rev. Mex.
Estud. Antr.,* 3: 129–41.
1943 A reconnaissance on Isla de Sacrificios, Veracruz, Mexico. *Carnegie*

Inst. Wash., Notes Middle Amer. Archaeol. Ethnol., no. 14.

1945 La cerámica arqueológica de El Tajín. *An. Mus. Nac. Arqueol. Hist. Etnog.*, ep. 5, 3: 147–92.

1945 Estudio arquitectónico de los edificios huastecos. *Ibid.*, 1: 121–46.

1946 Primer fresco mural huasteco. *Cuad. Amer.*, año 5, no. 6, pp. 151–59.

1947 Cerámica arqueológica de San Cristóbal Ecatepec. *An. Inst. Nac. Antr. Hist.*, 3: 27–58.

1947 Sistema de entierros entre los huastecos prehispánicos. *Jour. Soc. Amer. Paris*, n.s., 36: 195–214.

1950 Ancient Mexican costume. Mexico.

——, A. D. KRIEGER, AND J. B. GRIFFIN

1947 The archaeological zone of Buena Vista, Huaxcama, San Luis Potosi, Mexico. *Amer. Antiquity*, 13: 15–32.

DUTTON, B. P.

1939 La fiesta de San Francisco de Assisi, Tecpan, Guatemala. *El Palacio*, 46: 73–78.

1939 All Saints' Day ceremonies in Todos Santos, Guatemala. *Ibid.*, 46: 169–82, 205–17.

1943 A history of plumbate ware. *Papers School Amer. Research*, no. 31. Santa Fe. (Reprinted from *El Palacio*, 49: 205–19, 229–47, 257–71.)

1955 Tula of the Toltecs. *El Palacio*, 62: 195–251.

1956 A brief discussion of Chichen Itza. *Ibid.*, 63: 202–32.

1958 Studies in ancient Soconusco. *Archaeology*, 11: 48–54.

—— AND H. R. HOBBS

1943 Excavations at Tajumulco, Guatemala. *Monogr. School Amer. Research*, no. 9.

DUVALIER, A.

1960 La laca de Chiapa de Corzo: síntesis. *Acta Politécnica Mex.*, vol. 1, no. 6.

DYEN, I.

1953 *Review of* O. C. Dahl, Malgache et Maanjan: une comparaison linguistique. *Language*, 29: 577–90.

1956 The Ngaju-Dayak 'old speech stratum.' *Ibid.*, 32: 83–87.

1956 Language distribution and migration theory. *Ibid.*, 32: 611–26.

DYK, A.

1959 Mixteco texts. *Summer Inst. Ling., Ling. Ser.*, no. 3. Norman.

EARDLEY, A. J.

1951 Structural geology of North America. New York.

1954 Tectonic relations of North and South America. *Bull. Amer. Assoc. Petroleum Geol.*, 38: 707–73.

EASBY, D. T.

1956 Orfebrería y orfebres precolombinos. *An. Inst. Arte Amer.*, no. 9. Buenos Aires.

1957 Sahagún y los orfebres precolombinos de Mexico. *An. Inst. Nac. Antr. Hist.*, 9: 85–117.

1962 A man of the people. *Metropolitan Mus. Art Bull.* (December), pp. 133–40.

EASBY, E. K.

1961 The Squier jades from Tonina, Chiapas. *In* Lothrop and others, 1961, pp. 60–80.

—— AND D. T. EASBY

1953 Apuntes sobre la técnica de tallar el jade en Mesoamerica. *An. Inst. Arte Amer.*, no. 6. Buenos Aires.

EBERHARD, W.

1942 Kultur und Siedlung der Randvölker Chinas. Leyden.

EBNETER, T.

1960 Report on classical Quiché. Mimeo. Austin.

ECHEVERRÍA, A. R.

1956 Los aglutinogenos de grupo sanguíneo, sistemas ABO y Rh en los indígenas tarahumaras. Doctoral dissertation, Inst. Politécnico. Mexico.

ECKER, A.

1877 Catalog der anthropologischen Sammlungen der Universität Freiburg. *Anthr. Samml. Deutsch.*, p. 44. Brunswick.

ECKER, L.

1930 Los términos de parentesco en Otomi, Nahua, Tarasco y Maya. MS in Mus. Nac. Antr. Hist. Mexico.

1937 Los dos "metoros": un cuento Otomi. *Invest. Ling.*, 4: 254–61. Mexico.

1939 Relationship of Mixtec to the Otomian languages. *El Mex. Antiguo*, 4: 209–40.

EDMONSON, C. N.

n.d. Field notes on Barrio Libre, Tucson, Arizona. MS in the possession of E. H. Spicer, Univ. Arizona.

EDMONSON, M. S.

1953 [ed.] Synoptic studies of Mexican culture. *Tulane Univ., Middle Amer. Research Inst.*, Pub. 17.

1959 The Mexican truck driver. *Ibid.*, Pub. 25, pp. 73–88.

1960 Nativism, syncretism and anthropological science. *Ibid.*, Pub. 19, pp. 181–203.

1961 Field notes on western Guatemala, 1960–61. MS.

1961 Neolithic diffusion rates. *Current Anthr.*, 2: 71–102.

1965 Quiche-English dictionary. *Tulane Univ., Middle Amer. Research Inst.*, Pub. 30.

1971 The Book of Counsel: The Popol Vuh of the Quiche Maya of Guatemala. *Ibid.*, Pub. 35.

EDWARDS, C.

1954 Geographical reconnaissance in the Yucatan Peninsula. Rept. field work carried out under ONR Contract 222(11) NR 388 067. Univ. California, Dept. Geography.

1957 Quintana Roo: Mexico's empty quarter. *Ibid.*

EDWARDS, J. D.

1956 Estudio sobre algunos de los conglomerados rojos del Terciario Inferior del centro de Mexico. *20th Cong. Geol. Int.*

EGGAN, F.

1934 The Maya kinship system and cross-cousin marriage. *Amer. Anthr.*, 36: 188–202.

EGLER, F. E.

1942 Vegetation as an object of study. *Philosophy of Sci.*, 9: 245–60.

EICKSTEDT, E. F. VON

1933–34 Rassenkunde und rassengeschichte der Menschheit. Stuttgart.

EISENMANN, E.

1955 The species of Middle American birds. *Trans. Linn. Soc. New York*, vol. 7.

EKHOLM, G. F.

1939 Results of an archaeological survey of Sonora and northern Sinaloa. *Rev. Mex. Estud. Antr.*, 3: 7–10.

1940 Prehistoric "lacquer" from Sinaloa. *Ibid.*, 4: 10–15.

1940 The archaeology of northern and western Mexico. *In* The Maya and their neighbors, pp. 320–30.

1942 Excavations at Guasave, Sinaloa, Mexico. *Amer. Mus. Natural Hist., Anthr. Papers*, vol. 38, pt. 2.

1944 Excavations at Tampico and Panuco in the Huasteca, Mexico. *Ibid.*, vol. 38, pt. 5.

1945 A pyrite mirror from Queretaro, Mexico. *Carnegie Inst. Wash., Notes Middle Amer. Archaeol. Ethnol.*, no. 53.

1946 The probable use of Mexican stone yokes. *Amer. Anthr.*, 48: 593–606.

1946 Wheeled toys in Mexico. *Amer. Antiquity*, 11: 223–28.

1948 Ceramic stratigraphy at Acapulco, Guerrero. *In* El Occidente de México, pp. 95–104.

1949 Palmate stones and thin stone heads: suggestions on their possible use. *Amer. Antiquity*, 15: 1–9.

1950 Is American Indian culture Asiatic? *Natural Hist.*, 59: 344–51, 382.

1953 A possible focus of Asiatic influence in the late classic cultures of Mesoamerica. *Mem. Soc. Amer. Archaeol.*, 9: 72–89.

1953 Notas arqueológicas sobre el valle de Tuxpan y areas circunvecinas. *In* Huastecos, Totonacos, pp. 413–21.

1955 The new orientation toward problems of Asiatic-American relationships. *In* Meggers and Evans, 1955, pp. 95–109.

1958 Regional sequences in Mesoamerica and their relationships. *In* Willey, Vogt, and Palerm, eds., Middle American Anthropology, pp. 15–24. *Pan Amer. Union, Social Sci. Monogr.*, no. 5.

1959 Stone sculpture from Mexico. Mus. Primitive Art. New York.

1961 Puerto Rican stone "collars" as ball-game belts. *In* Lothrop and others, 1961, pp. 356–71.

1964 Possible Chinese origin of Teotihuacan cylindrical tripod pottery and certain related traits. *35th Int. Cong. Amer.* (Mexico 1962), Acta, 1: 31–45.

1964 Transpacific contacts. *In* Jennings and Norbeck, eds., Prehistoric man in the New World, pp. 489–510.

EKMAN, V. W.

1905 On the influence of the earth's rotation on ocean currents. *Ark. Mat., Astr. och Fysik, K. Svenska Vetenskapsakad.*, 2 (11): 1–52.

ELLEGÅRD, A.

1959 Statistical measurement of linguistic relationship. *Language*, 35: 131–56.

ELSON, B. F.

1947 The Homshuk: a Sierra Popoluca text. *Tlalocan*, 2: 193–214.

1947 Sierra Popoluca syllable structure. *Int. Jour. Amer. Ling.*, 13: 13–17.

1948 Sierra Popoluca personal names. *Ibid.*, 14: 191–93.

1951 *Review of* Foster and Foster, Sierra Popoluca Speech. *Ibid.*, 17: 57–61.

1954 Sierra Popoluca intonation. Master's thesis, Cornell Univ.

1958 Beginning morphology-syntax. *Summer Inst. Ling.* Glendale.

1960 Sierra Popoluca morphology. *Int. Jour. Amer. Ling.*, 26: 206–23.

1960 Gramática del Popoluca de la Sierra. *Bib. Facultad Filosofia y Letras*, no. 6. Univ. Veracruzana. Jalapa.

1960 Person markers and related morphemes in Sierra Popoluca. In following entry.

1960 [ed.] A William Cameron Townsend en el vigésimoquinto aniversario del Instituto Lingüístico de Verano. Mexico.

EMBER, M.

1959 The nonunilinear descent groups of Samoa. *Amer. Anthr.*, 61: 573–77.

EMENEAU, M. B.

1956 India as a linguistic area. *Language*, 32: 3–16.

EMERY, K. O.

1960 The sea off southern California: a modern habitat of petroleum. New York and London.

EMMERICH, A.

1959 Savages never carved these stones. *Amer. Heritage*, 10: 46–57.

1963 Art before Columbus: the art of ancient Mexico, from the archaic villages of the second millennium B.C. to the splendor of the Aztecs. New York.

EMMONS, A. B.

1913 A study of the variations in the female pelvis, based on observations made on 217 specimens of the American Indian squaw. *Biometrika*, 9: 34–57. Cambridge.

EMMONS, G. T.

1923 Jade in British Columbia and Alaska, and its use by the natives. *Mus. Amer. Indian, Heye Found., Indian Notes and Monogr.*, no. 35.

EMORY, K. P.

1943 Polynesian stone remains. *In* Coon and Andrews, Studies in the anthropology of Oceania and Asia, pp. 9–21. *Papers Peabody Mus., Harvard Univ.*, vol. 20.

ENCICLOPEDIA YUCATANENSE

1944–47 Ed. by C. A. Echánove Trujillo. 8 vols. Mexico.

ENCISO, J.

1933 Pintura sobre madera en Michoacán y en Guerrero. *Mex. Folkways*, 8: 4–34.

1947 Sellos del antiguo México. Mexico.

ENGEL, F.

1956 Curayacu, a Chavinoid site. *Archaeology*, 9: 98–105.

1957 Early sites on the Peruvian coast. *SW. Jour. Anthr.*, 13: 54–68.

1957 Sites et établissements sans céramique de la côte Péruvienne. *Jour. Soc. Amer. Paris*, 46: 65–155.

ENGELHARDT, Z.

1929 The missions and missionaries of California. Vol. 1, Lower California. (2d ed.) Santa Barbara.

ENGELS, F.

1884 Der Ursprung der Familie, des Privateigenthums, und des Staats.

ENGERRAND, G.

1908–10 Les métissages au Mexique. *Bull. et Mem. Soc. Anthr.*, ser. 5, 9: 712–16; ser. 6, 1: 18. Paris.

1910 Etude preliminaire d'un cas de croise-

ment entre un chinois et une yuca-
tèque. *Ibid.*, ser. 6, 1: 264–66.

1912 Un caso de cruzamiento entre un
chino y una yucateca de origen indígena. *17th Int. Cong. Amer.* (Mexico, 1910), Acta, pp. 105–06.

1917 Les mutilations dentaires chez les anciens Mayas. *Rev. Anthr.*, 27: 488–
93. Paris.

—— AND F. URBINA

1908 Las ciencias antropológicas en Eu-
ropa, en los Estados Unidos y en la
América Latina. *Mem. Soc. Cien.
Antonio Alzate*, 27: 81–123. Mexico.

1908 Algo que se ha descuidado en el
problema de la educación. *Ibid.*, 27:
181–223.

ENGLEKIRK, J. E.

1957 El teatro folklórico hispanoamericano. *Folklore Amer.*, 17: 1–36.

EPISTOLARIO DE NUEVA ESPAÑA

1505–1818 *See* Paso y Troncoso, 1939–42.

EPSTEIN, J. F.

1957 Late ceramic horizons in northeastern
Honduras. Doctoral dissertation,
Univ. Pennsylvania.

1959 Dating the Ulua polychrome complex. *Amer. Antiquity*, 25: 125–29.

1960 Centipede and Damp caves: excavations in Val Verde County, Texas,
1958. Austin.

1960 Burins from Texas. *Amer. Antiquity*,
26: 93–97.

1961 The San Isidro and Puntita Negra
sites: evidence of early man horizons
in Nuevo Leon, Mexico. *In* Homenaje a Pablo Martínez del Río, pp.
71–74.

ERASMUS, C. J.

1948 The economic life of a Mayo village.
MS in Dept. Anthropology, Univ.
Arizona.

1950 Patolli, pachisi, and the limitation of
possibilities. *SW. Jour. Anthr.*, 6:
369–87.

1950 Current theories on incest prohibition
in the light of ceremonial kinship.
Papers Kroeber Anthr. Soc., 2: 42–
50.

1955 Work patterns in a Mayo village.
Amer. Anthr., 57: 322–33.

1961 Man takes control: cultural develop-

ment and American aid. Univ. Minnesota Press.

ERBEN, H. K., U. ERBEN, C. COOK DE LEONARD,
D. J. LEONARD, G. O'NEIL, N. O'NEIL

1956 Una contribución geológico-arqueoló-
gica al problema de niveles de lagos
de la cuenca de México. *Rev. Mex.
Estud. Antr.*, 14: 23–39.

ERBEN, K. G.

1957 Paleogeographic reconstructions for
the Lower and Middle Jurassic and
for the Callovian of Mexico. *20th
Cong. Geol. Int.*, sec. 2, El Mesozoico del hemisferio occidental y sus
correlaciones mundiales, pp. 35–41.

1957 New biostratigraphic correlations in
the Jurassic of eastern and south-
central Mexico. *Ibid.*, pp. 43–52.

ERIKSON, E.

1950 Childhood and society. New York.

ERNST, A.

1892 Notes on some stone yokes from Mexico. *Internat. Archiv für Ethnog.*, 5:
71–76. Leiden.

EROSA P., I. R.

1932 El Kan Cah. Merida.

EROSA P., J. A.

1948 Guide book to the ruins of Uxmal.
Merida.

ESCALANTE, R.

1958 Field notes. MS. Mexico.

—— AND L. FAIER

1959 Relaciones del Linca y Xinca. Paper
presented to annual meeting, Amer.
Anthr. Assoc.

ESCALONA RAMOS, A.

1946 Algunas ruinas prehistóricas en
Quintana Roo. *Bol. Soc. Mex.
Geog. Estad.*, 61: 513–628.

1953 Xochicalco en la cronología de la
América Media. *In* Huastecos, Totonacos y sus vecinos, pp. 351–70.

ESCOBAR P., J.

1945 Contribución al estudio del mal del
pinto en Guatemala. Tesis de médico y cirujano, Facultad Cien. Méd.,
Univ. San Carlos de Guatemala.

ESCOBAR VILLATORO, C.

1953 Cáncer: su frecuencia en Guatemala.
Ibid.

ESCUDERO, J.
1834 Noticias estadísticas del estado de Chihuahua. Mexico.

ESPEJO, A.
1945 Las ofrendas halladas en Tlatelolco. *Tlatelolco a través de los tiempos*, 4: 15–29.

1949 Fragmentos de vasijas de barro con decoración en relieve. Introduction to C. Seler-Sachs, 1913. *El México Antiguo*, 7: 96–104.

1953 Dos tipos de alfarería negro-sobre-anaranjado en la cuenca de México y en el Totonacapan. *Rev. Mex. Estud. Antr.*, 13: 403–12.

ESPINOSA, GASPAR DE
1519 Relación a proceso quel Licenciado Gaspar de Espinosa, . . . ciudad de Panama a las provincias de Paris e Nata. . . . *Col. Doc. Ined. Amer. y Oceania*, 1864–84, 20: 5–119.

1892 Relación hecha por Gaspar de Espinosa, alcalde mayor de Castilla de Oro, dada á Pedranas de Avila, lugar-teniente general de aquellas provincias, de todo lo que sucedió en la entrada. *In* Doc. Ined. Colombia, vol. 2.

ESPINOSA, I. F. DE
1742 El peregrino septentrional Atlante delineado en la exemplarissima vida del . . . Antonio Margil de Jesus. Valencia.

1746 Crónica apostólica y seráfica de todos los colegios de propaganda fide de esta Nueva España. Mexico.

ESPINOSA, M.
1910 Apuntes históricos de las tribus chinantecas, matzatecas, y popolucas. Recuerdo del centenario. Mexico. [For re-edition see Cline, 1961.]

ESPINOSA RAMOS, A.
1949 El folklore literario de México. *Orientación Musical*, no. 89, pp. 5–7. Mexico.

ESPINOZA, G.
1934–35 Ruinas de Guaytan. *Rev. Agrícola*, 7: 215–64; 8: 54–58. Guatemala.

ESPLENDOR DEL MÉXICO ANTIGUO
1959 Esplendor del México antiguo. R. Noriega and C. Cook de Leonard, eds. 2 vols. Centro Invest. Antr. Mex. Mexico.

ESQUIVEL, D. DE
1579 Relación de la chinantla. *In* Paso y Troncoso, 1905–06, 4: 58–68. [Tr in Bevan, 1938, pp. 135–44.]

ESSAYS IN ANTHROPOLOGY
1936 Essays in anthropology, presented to A. L. Kroeber. Univ. California Press.

ESTADO ACTUAL
1928 Estado actual de los principales edificios arqueológicos de Mexico. Sec. Educ. Pub. Mexico.

ESTADO . . . COATZACOALCOS
1945 Estado en que se hallaba la provincia de Coatzacoalcos en el año de 1599. *Bol. Archivo General Nación*, 16: 195–246, 429–79.

ESTÉVEZ MASELLA, F.
1946 Contribución al estudio de la enfermedad de chagas, por la intradermo-reacción de Montenegro. Tesis de médico y cirujano, Facultad Cien. Méd., Univ. San Carlos de Guatemala.

ESTRADA, E.
1956 Valdivia: un sitio arqueológico formativo en la costa de la provincia del Guayas, Ecuador. *Mus. Victor Emilio Estrada*, Pub. 1. Guayaquil.

1957 Ultimas civilizaciones pre-históricas de la cuenca del Rio Guayas. *Ibid.*, Pub. 2.

1957 Los Huancavilcas, ultimas civilizaciones pre-históricas de la costa del Guayas. *Ibid.*, Pub. 3.

1957 Prehistoria de Manabi. *Ibid.*, Pub. 4.

1958 Las cultural pre-clásicas, formativas o arcaicas del Ecuador. *Ibid.*, Pub. 5.

1960 Newspaper article. Guayaquil.

1962 Arqueología de Manabi central. *Mus. Victor Emilio Estrada*, Pub. 7.

——— AND C. EVANS
1963 Cultural development in Ecuador. *In* Meggers and Evans, 1963, pp. 77–88.

ESTRADA, G.
1937 El arte mexicano en España. *In* Enciclopedia ilustrada mexicana, no. 5. Mexico.

ESTRADA BALMORI, E., AND R. PIÑA CHAN
1948 Funeraria en Chupícuaro, Guanajuato. *An. Inst. Nac. Antr. Hist.*, 3: 79–84.
1948 Complejo funerario en Chupícuaro. *In* El Occidente de México, pp. 40–41.

ESTUDIOS ANTROPOLÓGICOS
1956 Estudios antropológicos publicados en homenaje al doctor Manuel Gamio. Univ. Nac. Autónoma Méx., Soc. Mex. Antr. Mexico.

ESTUDIOS DE CULTURA NÁHUATL
1959, 1960, 1962, 1964, 1965 Yearbook of the Seminario de Cultura Náhuatl I–V. Univ. Nacional. Mexico.

ESTUDIOS HISTÓRICOS AMERICANOS
1953 Estudios históricos americanos. Homenaje a Silvio Zavala. Mexico.

EVANS, C., AND B. J. MEGGERS
1957 Formative period cultures in the Guayas basin, coastal Ecuador. *Amer. Antiquity*, 22: 235–47.
1958 Valdivia, an early formative culture. *Archaeology*, 11: 3.
1960 A new dating method using obsidian. Part 2: an archaeological evaluation of the method. *Amer. Antiquity*, 25: 523–37.

——, ——, AND E. ESTRADA
1959 Cultura Valdivia. *Mus. Victor Emilio Estrada*, Pub. 6.

EWALD, R. H.
1954 San Antonio Sacatepéquez: culture change in a Guatemalan community. Doctoral dissertation, Univ. Michigan.
1957 San Antonio Sacatepéquez: 1932–53. *In* R. N. Adams, 1957, Political changes, pp. 18–22.
1957 San Antonio Sacatepéquez: culture change in a Guatemalan community. *Social Forces*, 36: 160–65.

EWING, J. F.
1950 Hyperbrachycephaly as influenced by cultural conditioning. *Papers Peabody Mus., Harvard Univ.*, vol. 23, no. 2.

EXQUEMELIN, A. O.
1686 Histoire des aventuriers qui se sont signalez dans les Indes. 2 vols. Paris.

1893 Bucaniers of America. London.

EZELL, P. H.
1954 An archaeological survey of northwestern Papagueria. *Kiva*, 19 (2–4): 1–26.
1955 Indians under the law: Mexico 1821–1847. *Amer. Indig.*, 15: 199–214.

FABILA, A.
1940 Las tribus yaquis de Sonora: su cultura y anhelada autodeterminación. Depto. Asuntos Indígenas. Mexico.
1949 Sierra norte de Puebla. Mexico.
1959 Los huicholes de Jalisco. Inst. Nac. Indig. Mexico.

—— AND G. FABILA
1951 México: ensayo socioeconómico del estado. 2 vols. Mexico.

——, ——, M. MESA ANDRACA, AND O. SOBERÓN M.
1955 Tlaxcala: tenencia y aprovechamiento de la tierra. Centro Invest. Agrarias. Mexico.

—— AND OTHERS
1962 Problemas de los indios nahuas, mixtecos y tlapanecos de la parte oriental de la Sierra Madre del Sur del estado de Guerrero. MS. Inst. Nac. Indig. Mexico.

FAHSEN, A.
1935 Contribución al estudio del pian en Guatemala. Tesis de médico y cirujano, Facultad Cien. Med., Univ. Nac. Guatemala.

FALCÓN, E.
1949 La venta del cochino, leyenda yucateca. *Yikal Maya Than*, 10 (116–17): 47–48.

FALERO, J.
1886 Influencia de la civilización en la atrofia y desaparición del tercer molar. *El Observador Méd.*, ep. 2, no. 4. Mexico.

FARRINGTON, O. C.
1897 Observations on Popocatepetl and Ixtaccihuatl, with a review of the geographic and geologic features of the mountains. *Field Columbian Mus., Biol. Ser.*, 1: 66–120.

FASTLICHT, S.
1947 Estudio dental y radiográfico de las mutilaciones dentarias. *An. Inst. Nac. Antr. Hist.*, 2: 7–13.

1950 La odontología en el México prehispánico. *Rev. Asoc. Dental Mex.*, 7
(2): 67–89.

1951 Contribución al estudio del pegamen-
to de las incrustaciones. *In* Homenaje Caso, pp. 153–65.

1960 Las mutilaciones dentarias entre los
Mayas: un nuevo dato sobre las in-
crustaciones dentarias. *An. Inst. Nac.
Antr. Hist.*, 12: 111–30. Mexico.

—— AND J. ROMERO
1951 El arte de las mutilaciones dentarias.
Encic. Mex. Arte, no. 14. Mexico.

FAULHABER, J.
n.d. Algunos aspectos antropológicos de la
población de Tepoztlán, Mor. MS.

1947 Análisis de algunos caracteres somáti-
cos de la población de San Miguel
Totolapan, estado de Guerrero. *An.
Inst. Nac. Antr. Hist.*, 2: 15–59.
Mexico.

1948–49 Restos óseos de la Huasteca.
Rev. Mex. Estud. Antr., 10: 77–98.

1950–56 Antropología física de Veracruz.
2 vols. Veracruz.

1952 El tipo somático de San Miguel Totolapan en relación con algunas otras
poblaciones del estado de Guerrero.
An. Inst. Nac. Antr. Hist., 4: 223–28.
Mexico.

1953 Los Huastecos y Mexicanos en relación con otras poblaciones de la faja
costera del Golfo de México. *In*
Huastecos, Totonacos, 1953, pp. 79–
93.

1953 Algunos rasgos morfológico-funcio-
nales de dos grupos de campesinos
del norte de Veracruz. *Mem. Cong.
Cien. Mex.*, 12: 87–92.

1953 [Informe sobre los restos óseos de la
cueva de La Candelaria.] *In* Martínez del Río, 1953, La cueva, pp.
187–89.

1953 [Descripción preliminar de los restos
óseos de la cueva de La Candelaria.]
In Martínez del Río, 1953, Preliminary report, pp. 215–21.

1960 Breve análisis osteológico de los restos
humanos de La Quemada, Zacatecas.
An. Inst. Nac. Antr. Hist., 12: 131–
49. Mexico.

1965 La población de Tlatilco, México,
caracterizada por sus entierros. *In*
Homenaje Comas, 2: 83–121.

FAURÉ, E.
1931 Some observations on Aztec art.
California Arts and Architecture, 40
(6): 21–22, 50. San Francisco.

FAVRE, H.
1964 Notas sobre el homicido entre los
chamulas. *Estud. Cultura Maya*, 4:
305–22.

FAY, G. E.
1953 The archaeological cultures of the
southern half of Sonora, Mexico.
Year Book Amer. Phil. Soc., pp. 266–
69.

1955 Pre-pottery lithic complex from Sonora, Mexico. *Science*, 121 (3152):
777–78.

1956 Peralta complex, a Sonoran variant of
the Cochise culture. *Science*, 124:
1029.

1956 A Seri fertility figurine from Bahia
Kino, Sonora. *Kiva*, 21 (3, 4): 11–
12.

1957 A prepottery lithic complex from
Sonora, Mexico. *Man*, 57: 98–99.

1957 Peralta complex, a Sonoran variant
of the Cochise culture. *New World
Antiquity*, 4 (3): 41–44.

1958 The Peralta complex, a Sonoran va-
riant of the Cochise culture. *32d Int.
Cong. Amer.* (Copenhagen, 1956),
Acta, pp. 491–93.

1959 Handbook of pottery types of Nayarit,
Mexico. *Inst. Interamer., Misc. Pa-
pers, Archaeol. Ser.*, no. 1. Magnolia,
Arkansas.

1959 Peralta complex, a Sonoran variant
of the Cochise culture: new data,
1958. *El Palacio*, 66: 21–24.

FEARING, F.
1954 An examination of the conceptions of
Benjamin Whorf in the light of the
theories of perception and cognition.
In Language in culture, *Amer. Anthr.
Assoc.*, Memoir 79.

FELDMAN, L. H.
1967 Archaeological mollusks of west Mexico. MS.

FELIPE SEGUNDO
1573 Ordenanzas para descubrimientos,

nuevas poblaciones y pacificaciones. MS.

FELIX, J., AND H. LENK
1892 Über die tecktonischen Verhältnisse der Republik Mexiko. *Zeit. der Deutschen Geol. Gesellschaft,* 44: 303–23.

FENNEMAN, N. M.
1928 Physiographic divisions of the United States. *Ann. Assoc. Amer. Geog.,* 18: 261–353.

FENOCHI, A.
1913 Villa Alta. *Bol. Soc. Mex. Geog. Estad.* 6: 212–20.

FERDON, E. N.
1953 Tonala, Mexico: an archaeological survey. *Monogr. School Amer. Research,* no. 16. Santa Fe.
1955 A trial survey of Mexican-Southwestern architectural parallels. *Ibid.,* no. 21.

FERGUSON, C. A.
1956 Arabic baby talk. *In* Halle, Lunt, McLean, and Van Schooneveld, 1956, pp. 121–28.
1959 Diglossia. *Word,* 15: 325–40.

—— AND J. J. GUMPERZ, eds.
1960 Linguistic diversity in South Asia: studies in regional, social and functional variation. *Indiana Univ. Research Center Anthr., Folklore, Ling.,* Pub. 13.

FERGUSSON, G. J., AND W. F. LIBBY
1963 UCLA radiocarbon dates, II. *Radiocarbon,* 5: 1–22.

FERIZ, H.
1959 Zwischen Peru und Mexiko. 2 vols. Kónongluk Inst. Tropen. Amsterdam.

FERNÁNDEZ, J.
n.d. Escultura prehispánica de México. Mexico.
1937 Diccionario poconchí. *An. Soc. Geog. Hist.,* 14: 47–70, 184–200.
1954 Coatlicue: estética del arte indígena antiguo. Centro Estud. Filosóficos, Univ. Nac. Autónoma Méx.
1958 Arte mexicano de sus origines a nuestros dias. Mexico.
1959 El arte. *In* Esplendor del México antiguo, 1: 305–22.
1959 Coatlicue: estética del arte indígena antiguo. 2d ed., augmented, of his 1954.

—— AND V. T. MENDOZA
1941 Danzas de los concheros de San Miguel de Allende, Mexico. Mexico.

FERNÁNDEZ, L.
1881–1907 Colección de documentos para la historia de Costa Rica. 10 vols. San Jose, Paris, Barcelona.

FERNÁNDEZ, M. A.
1925 El juego de pelota de Chichén-Itzá, Yucatan. *An. Mus. Nac. Arqueol. Hist. Etnog.,* ep. 4, 3: 363–72.
1941 El templo num. 5 de Tulum, Quintana Roo. *In* Los Mayas Antiguos, pp. 155–80.
1943 New discoveries in the Temple of the Sun in Palenque. *DYN,* 4–5: 55–58.
1945 Las ruinas de Tulum, I. *An. Mus. Nac. Arqueol. Hist.,* 3: 109–15.
1945 Las ruinas de Tulum, II. *Ibid.,* 1: 95–105.
1945 Exploraciones arqueológicas en la Isla Cozumel. *Ibid.,* 1: 107–20.

——, C. LIZARDI R., AND R. ROZO
1945 Las pinturas de la galería sur del Templo de los Frescos, Tulum. *Ibid.,* 3: 117–31.

FERNÁNDEZ DE CÓRDOBA, J.
1944 Tres impresos en lengua tarasco del siglo XIX. Mexico.

FERNÁNDEZ DE MIRANDA, M. T.
1951 Reconstrucción del Protopopoloca. *Rev. Mex. Estud. Antr.,* 12: 61–93.
1956 Glotocronología de la familia Popoloca. *Mus. Nac. Antr., Ser. Cien.,* no. 4. Mexico.
1959 Fonémica del ixcateco. Inst. Nac. Antr. Hist. Mexico.
1960 Reflejos consonánticos de Proto-Zapoteco. MS.
1961 Toponimia popoloca. *In* Homenaje Townsend, pp. 431–47.

——, M. SWADESH, AND R. J. WEITLANER
1959 Some findings on Oaxaca language classification and cultural terms. *Int. Jour. Amer. Ling.,* 25: 54–58.
1960 El panorama etno-lingüístico de Oaxaca y el istmo. *Rev. Mex. Estud. Antr.,* 16: 137–57.

—— AND R. J. WEITLANER
1961 Sobre algunas relaciones de la familia mangue. *Anthr. Ling.*, 3 (7): 1–99.

FERNÁNDEZ DE NAVARRETE, M.
1945 Colección de los viajes y descubrimientos que hicieron los Españoles desde fines del siglo XV. 5 vols. Buenos Aires.

FERNÁNDEZ DE OVIEDO Y VALDÉS, G.
1851–55 Historia natural y general de las Indias. Madrid.
1959 Historia general y natural de las Indias. *Bib. Autores Españoles*, vols. 67–71. Madrid.
1959 Natural history of the West Indies. Tr. and ed. by S. A. Stoudemire. *Univ. North Carolina Studies Romance Lang. and Lit.*, no. 32.

FERNÁNDEZ FERRAZ, J.
1902 Síntesis de constructiva gramatical de la lengua Quiché: ensayo lingüístico. San Jose.

FERNÁNDEZ GUARDIA, R.
1908 Cartas de Juan Vázquez de Coronado. Barcelona.

FERNÁNDEZ ORTIGOSA, I.
1909 El asunto Courmont. *Crónica Méd. Mex.*, 12: 226–44. Mexico.

FERRERA, J.
1920 Pequeña gramática y diccionario de la lengua tarahumara. Reproduced in Radin, 1931.

FESTINGER, L.
1957 A theory of cognitive dissonance. Evanston.

FEWKES, J. W.
1893 A Central American ceremony which suggests the snake dance of the Tusayan villages. *Amer. Anthr.*, o.s., 6: 284–306.
1898 Archaeological expedition to Arizona in 1895. *Smithsonian Inst., Bur. Amer. Ethnol.*, 17th ann. rept., pp. 519–752.
1907 Certain antiquities of eastern Mexico. *Ibid.*, 25th ann. rept., pp. 221–96.
1912 Casa Grande, Arizona. *Ibid.*, 28th ann. rept., pp. 25–180.
1919 Antiquities of the gulf coast of Mexico. *Smithsonian Inst., Smithsonian Misc. Coll.*, vol. 70, no. 2.
1922 A prehistoric island culture area of America. *Smithsonian Inst., Bur. Amer. Ethnol.*, 34th ann. rept., pp. 35–281.

FIELD, H.
1948 Early man in Mexico. *Man*, 48 (14–24): 17–19. London.
1954 Los indios de Tepoztlán (México). Univ. Miami Press.

FIGUEROA, H.
1924 Unpublished data.

FIGEROA A., J.
1960 Mexican national report on seismology. 12th General Assembly of the I.U.G.G., Helsinki, Finland. Inst. de Geofísica, U.N.A.M., Mexico (mimeographed).

FIGUEROA GARCÍA, L. N.
1958 Leishmaniosis visceral (kala azar): segundo caso clínico descubierto en Guatemala. Tesis de médico y cirujano, Facultad Cien. Med., Univ. San Carlos de Guatemala.

FISCHER, E., AND K. SALLER
1928 Eine neue Haarfarbentafel. *Anthr. Anz.*, 5: 238–44.

FISCHER, J. L.
1958 Social influences on the choice of a linguistic variant. *Word*, 14: 47–56.

FISHBURNE, J. H.
1962 Courtship and marriage of Zinacantan. Honors thesis, Radcliffe College.
See also Collier, J. F., 1968.

FISHER, G.
1953 Directed culture change in Nayarit, Mexico. *Tulane Univ., Middle Amer. Research Inst.*, Pub. 17, pp. 65–176.

FLEMING, R. H.
1935 Oceanographic studies in the Central American Pacific. Doctoral dissertation, Univ. California.
1938 Tides and tidal currents in the Gulf of Panama. *Jour. Marine Research*, 1: 193–206.
1941 A contribution to the oceanography of the Central American region. *Proc. 6th Pacific Sci. Cong.*, 3: 167–75.

FLINT, E.
n.d. Letters to Prof. F. W. Putnam, Pea-

body Museum, Harvard University. MS.

FLINT, F. R., AND E. S. DEEVEY
1959 Radiocarbon supplement. *Amer. Jour. Sci.*, vol. 1.

FLORES, E.
1950 Los braceros mexicanos en Wisconsin. *Trimestre Econ.*, 17: 23–80. Mexico.

FLORES, F.
1881 Ligeros apuntes de pelvimetría comparada. *Rev. Méd. Méx.*, 2: 294.
1886 Antropología: las razas nativas de América. *El Observador Méd.*, ep. 2, 1: 73–80, 101–07, 121–27. Mexico.

FLORES, I. J.
1753 Arte de la lengua metropolitana del reyno cakchiquel. . . . Antigua.

FLORES, M., Z. FLORES, AND B. MENESES
1957 Estudios de hábitos dietéticos en poblaciones de Guatemala. IX: Santa Catarina Barahona. *Archivo Venezolano Nutrición*, 8: 57–82.

—— AND B. GARCÍA
1960 The nutritional status of children of pre-school age in the Guatemalan community of Amatitlan. I: Comparison of family and child diets. *British Jour. Nutrition*, 14: 207–15.

——, B. GARCÍA, C. SÁENZ, AND A. DE SIERRA
1962 Estudios de hábitos dietéticos en poblaciones de Guatemala. X: La Fragua, Departamento de Zacapa. Pub. Cien. Inst. Nutrición de Centro América y Panamá, Recopilación no. 4. Organización Panamericana de la Salud, Pub. Cien. no. 59, pp. 106–16. Washington, D.C.

——, B. MENESES, Z. FLORES, AND M. DE LEÓN
1956 Estudios de hábitos dietéticos en poblaciones de Guatemala. VII: Hacienda "Chocolá." *Bol. Oficina Sanitaria Panamer.*, 40: 504–20.

—— AND E. REH
1955 Estudios de hábitos dietéticos en poblaciones de Guatemala. I: Magdalena Milpas Altas. *Ibid.*, suppl. 2, pp. 90–128.
1955 Estudios de hábitos dietéticos en poblaciones de Guatemala. II: Santo Domingo Xenacoj. *Ibid.*, suppl. 2, pp. 129–48.
1955 Estudios de hábitos dietéticos en poblaciones de Guatemala. III: San Antonio Aguas Calientes y su aldea San Andrés Ceballos. *Ibid.*, suppl. 2, pp. 149–62.
1955 Estudios de hábitos dietéticos en poblaciones de Guatemala. IV: Santa María Cauqué. *Ibid.*, suppl. 2, pp. 163–73.

FLORES GUERRERO, R.
1958 Castillo de Teayo. *An. Inst. Invest. Estéticas*, 7 (27): 5–15. Univ. Nac. Autónoma Méx.
1962 Historia general del arte mexicano: época prehispánica. Mexico.

FLORES R., N.
1944 Carencias nutritivas (síndrome de policarencia en la infancia). Tesis de médico y cirujano, Facultad Cien. Méd., Univ. Nac. Guatemala.

FLORES RUIZ, E.
1954 El sumidero, la leyenda de los Chiapas (el marco, la leyenda, la historia). *Abside*, 18: 415–35. Mexico.

FLOWER, W. R.
1879 Catalogue of the Royal College of Surgeons' Museum. London.

FOLLETT, P. H. F.
1932 War and weapons of the Maya. *Tulane Univ., Middle Amer. Research Inst.*, Pub. 4, pp. 375–410.

FONCERRADA DE MOLINA, M.
1962 La arquitectura Puuc dentro de los estilos de Yucatan. *Univ. Nac. Autónoma Mex., Estud. Cultura Maya*, 2: 225–38.

FONDO EDITORIAL DE LA PLÁSTICA MEXICANA
1964 Flor y canto del arte prehispánico de México. Mexico.

FONSECA, R.
1949 Investigaciones sobre la existencia de histoplasmosis pulmonar en Guatemala. Tesis de médico y cirujano, Facultad Cien. Méd., Univ. San Carlos de Guatemala.

FOR THE DEAN
1950 For the dean: essays in anthropology in honor of Byron Cummings. E. K.

Reed and D. S. King, eds. Tucson and Santa Fe.

FORBES, J. D.
1957 The Janos, Jacomes, Mansos and Su-mas Indians. *New Mexico Hist. Rev.*, 32: 319–34.
1960 Apache, Navaho and Spaniard. Univ. Oklahoma Press.

FORBES, R. J.
1950 Metallurgy in antiquity. Leiden.

FORD, J. A.
1944 Excavations in the vicinity of Cali, Colombia. *Yale Univ. Pub. Anthr.*, no. 31.
1951 Greenhouse: a Troyville–Coles Creek period site in Avoyelles Parish, Loui-siana. *Amer. Mus. Natural Hist., Anthr. Papers*, vol. 44, no. 1.
1954 The history of a Peruvian valley. *Sci. Amer.* (August), pp. 28–34.
1969 A comparison of Formative cultures in the Americas. *Smithsonian Inst., Smithsonian Contrib. Knowledge*, vol. 11.

—— AND G. I. QUIMBY
1945 The Tchefuncte culture, an early oc-cupation of the lower Mississippi Val-ley. *Mem. Soc. Amer. Archaeol.*, no. 2.

—— AND C. H. WEBB
1956 Poverty Point, a late archaic site in Louisiana. *Amer. Mus. Natural Hist., Anthr. Papers*, vol. 46, pt. 1.

—— AND G. R. WILLEY
1940 Crooks site, a Marksville period burial mound in La Salle Parish, Louisiana. *Dept. Conservation, Louisiana Geol. Survey, Anthr. Study*, no. 3. New Orleans.

FORD, S. L.
1948 Informe sobre la tribu chinanteca, re-gión de Yólox, Ixtlán de Juárez, Oaxaca. *Bol. Indig.*, 8: 290–98.

FORDE, C. D.
1934 Habitat, economy and society: a geo-graphical introduction to ethnology. London.

FORRESTAL, P. R., tr.
1954 Benavides' Memorial of 1630. *Pub. Acad. Amer. Franciscan Hist., Doc. Ser.*, vol. 2.

FÖRSTEMANN, E. W.
1880, 1882, 1892 *See* Part II, p. 260, of this volume of the *Handbook*.
1904 Various papers *in* Bowditch, 1904, pp. 393–590.
1906 Commentary on the Maya manu-script in the Royal Public Library of Dresden. *Papers Peabody Mus. Harvard Univ.*, vol. 4, no. 2.

FORSTER, J. R.
1955 Notas sobre la arqueología de Te-huantepec. *An. Inst. Nac. Antr. Hist.*, 7: 77–100.

FORTÚN DE PONCE, J. E.
1957 La navidad en Bolivia. Ministerio de Educación, Depto. Folklore. La Paz.

FOSHAG, W. F.
1954 Estudios mineralógicos sobre el jade de Guatemala. *Antr. Hist. Guate-mala*, 6 (1): 3–47.
1955 Chalchihuitl, a study in jade. *Amer. Mineral.*, 40: 1062–70.
1957 Mineralogical studies on Guatemalan jade. *Smithsonian Inst., Smithsonian Misc. Coll.*, vol. 135, no. 5.

—— AND J. GONZÁLES REYNA
1956 Birth and development of Paricutin volcano, Mexico. *U.S. Geol. Survey*, Bull. 965-D.

—— AND R. LESLIE
1955 Jadeite from Manzanal, Guatemala. *Amer. Antiquity*, 21: 81–83.

FOSTER, G. M.
1940 Notes on the Popoluca of Vera Cruz. *Inst. Panamer. Geog. Hist.*, Pub. 51. Mexico.
1942 A primitive Mexican economy. *Monogr. Amer. Ethnol. Soc.*, 5: 1–115.
1942 Indigenous apiculture among the Po-poluca of Veracruz. *Amer. Anthr.*, 44: 538–42.
1943 The geographical, linguistic, and cultural position of the Popoluca of Vera Cruz. *Ibid.*, 45: 531–46.
1944 Nagualism in Mexico and Guate-mala. *Acta Amer.*, 2: 85–103.
1945 Sierra Popoluca folklore and beliefs. *Univ. California Pub. Amer. Archae-ol. Ethnol.*, 42: 177–250.
1946 Expedición etnológica de la región

del lago de Pátzcuaro. *An. Mus. Michoacano*, ep. 2, no. 4, pp. 65–67.

1948 Empire's children: the people of Tzintzuntzan. *Smithsonian Inst., Inst. Social Anthr.*, Pub. 6.

1948 The folk economy of rural Mexico with special reference to marketing. *Jour. Marketing*, 13: 153–62.

1948 Some implications of modern Mexican mold-made pottery. *SW. Jour. Anthr.*, 4: 356–70.

1949 Sierra Popoluca kinship terminology and its wider relationships. *Ibid.*, 5: 330–34.

1950 Mexican and Central American Indian folklore. *In* Standard dictionary of folklore, mythology, and legend, M. Leach, ed., 2: 711–16.

1951 Some wider implications of soul-loss illness among the Sierra Popoluca. *In* Homenaje Caso, pp. 167–74.

1952 Relationships between theoretical and applied anthropology: a public health program analysis. *Human Organization*, 11: 5–15.

1953 Cofradía and compadrazgo in Spain and Spanish America. *SW. Jour. Anthr.*, 9: 1–28.

1953 Relationships between Spanish and Spanish-American folk medicine. *Jour. Amer. Folklore*, 66: 201–17.

1953 What is folk culture? *Amer. Anthr.*, 55: 159–73.

1955 Contemporary pottery techniques in southern and central Mexico. *Tulane Univ., Middle Amer. Research Inst.*, Pub. 22, pp. 1–48.

1959 The Coyotepec *molde* and some associated problems of the potter's wheel. *SW. Jour. Anthr.*, 15: 53–63.

1959 The potter's wheel: an analysis of idea and artifact in invention. *Ibid.*, 15: 99–119.

1960 Culture and conquest: America's Spanish heritage. *Viking Fund Pub. Anthr.*, no. 27.

1960 Life expectancy of utilitarian pottery in Tzintzuntzan. *Amer. Antiquity*, 25: 606–09.

1960 Archaeological implications of the modern pottery of Acatlan, Puebla, Mexico. *Ibid.*, 26: 205–14.

1961 The dyadic contract: a model for the social structure of a Mexican peasant village. *Amer. Anthr.*, 63: 1173–92.

1961 Traditional cultures and the impact of technological change. New York.

FOSTER, M. L., AND G. M. FOSTER

1948 Sierra Popoluca speech. *Smithsonian Inst., Inst. Social Anthr.*, Pub. 8.

FOUGHT, J. G.

1967 Chorti (Mayan) phonology, morphophonemics and morphology. Doctoral dissertation, Yale Univ.

FOURTH ANONYMOUS

1955 Memoria de los servicios que habia hecho Nuño de Guzmán, desde que fue nombrado gobernador de Pánuco en 1525. M. Carrera Stampa, ed. Mexico. Reproduces (pp. 93–128) Cuarta relación anónima de la jornada que hizo Nuño de Guzmán a la Nueva Galicia. (See also García Icazbalceta, 1858–66, 2: 461–83.)

FRAGOSO, D.

1934 Constantes biométricas del recién nacido mexicano. Mexico.

FRANCO, N.

1885 El tacto vaginal durante el trabajo del parto. Mexico.

FRANCO C., J. L.

1945 Comentarios sobre tipología y filogenia de la decoración negra sobre color natural del barro en la cerámica "Azteca II." *Rev. Mex. Estud. Antr.*, 7: 163–86.

1949 Algunos problemas relativos a la cerámica azteca. *El México Antiguo*, 7: 162–208.

1955 Sobre un molde para vasijas con decoración en relieve. *Ibid.*, 8: 76–84.

1956 Malacates del complejo Tula-Mazapan. *In* Estudios antropológicos, pp. 201–12.

1957 Motivos decorativos en la cerámica azteca. *Mus. Nac. Antr., Ser. Cien.*, 5: 7–36. Mexico.

1958 Un oyohualli mixteco. *Bol. Centro Invest. Antr. Méx.*, 5: 13–15.

1959 La escritura y los códices. *In* Esplendor del México antiguo, pp. 361–78.

1960 Mezcala, Guerrero (I, II, III). *Bol. Centro Invest. Antr. Méx.*, 7: 4–6, 8: 1–5, 9: 8–12.

FRANCO MARTÍNEZ, R.
1951 Informe sanitario del municipio de San Gabriel Chilac, estado de Puebla. Mexico.

FRENCH, D.
1958 Cultural matrices of Chinookan non-casual language. *Int. Jour. Amer. Ling.*, 24: 258–63.

FRIAS, D. V.
1907 Foc-lor de los pueblos de San Bartolome Aguascalientes. Nicolás León, ed.

FRIAS, H.
1898 Páginas nacionales. Cosijoopii: leyenda zapoteca. *El Imparcial*, 5: 562.

FRIED, J.
1952 Ideal norms and social control in Tarahumara society. Doctoral dissertation, Yale Univ.
1953 The relation of ideal norms to actual behavior in Tarahumara society. *SW. Jour. Anthr.*, 9: 286–95.
1961 An interpretation of Tarahumara interpersonal relations. *Anthr. Quar.*, 34: 110–20.

FRIEDLAENDER, I.
1930 Über die mexikanischen Vulkane Pico de Orizaba, Cerro de Tequila, und Colima. *Zeit. für Vulkanologie*, 13: 154–64.

—— AND R. A. SONDER
1923 Über das Vulkangebiet von San Martin Tuxtla in Mexiko. *Zeit. für Vulkanologie*, 7: 162–87.

FRIEDMAN, I., AND R. L. SMITH
1960 A new dating method using obsidian. *Amer. Antiquity*, 25: 476–537.

FRIEDRICH, J.
1955 Kurze Grammatik der alten Quiché-Sprache im Popol Vuh. *Akad. der Wissenschaften und der Literatur in Mainz, Abhand. der Geistes-u. Soz.-Wissenschaftlichen Klasse*, Jahr. 1955, no. 4. Wiesbaden.

FRIEDRICH, P.
1957 Community study of a Tarascan community. Doctoral dissertation, Yale Univ.

1958 A Tarascan cacicazgo: structure and function. *In* V. F. Ray, ed., Systems of political control and bureaucracy in human societies, pp. 23–39. *Proc. Amer. Ethnol. Soc.*

FRIES, C.
1960 Geología del estado de Morelos y partes adyacentes de Mexico y Guerrero, región central meridional de Mexico. *Inst. Geol., Univ. Nac. Autónoma de Mex.*, Bol. 60.

FRIES, C. C., AND K. L. PIKE
1949 Coexistent phonemic systems. *Language*, 25: 29–50.

FRY, E. I.
1956 Skeletal remains from Mayapan. *Carnegie Inst. Wash., Current Reports*, no. 38.

FUENTE, J. DE LA
See De la Fuente, J.

FUENTES L., L. G.
1961 Estado actual de los grupos sanguíneos en Amerindios y su investigación en Indios Guatusos de Costa Rica. Tesis de Grade, Dept. Microbiol., Univ. Costa Rica.

FUENTES Y GUZMÁN, F. A. DE
1882–83 Historia de Guatemala o recordación florida escrita el siglo XVII. 2 vols. Madrid.
1932–33 Recordación florida: discurso historial y demostración natural, material, militar y política del reyno de Guatemala. *Bib. Goathemala*, vols. 6–8. Guatemala.

FUGLISTER, F. C.
1947 Average monthly sea surface temperatures of the western North Atlantic. *Papers Physical Oceanogr. and Meteorol.*, 10: 3–25.

FUHRMANN, E.
1922 *See* Danzel and Fuhrmann, 1922.

FUNKHOUSER, W. D., AND W. S. WEBB
1929 The so-called "ash caves" in Lee County, Kentucky. *Univ. Dept. Anthr. and Archaeol.*, vol. 1, no. 2.

FURST, P. T.
1965 Radiocarbon dates from a tomb in Mexico. *Science*, 147 (3658): 612–13.
1965 West Mexico, the Caribbean, and northern South America: some prob-

lems in New World interrelationships. *Antropológica*, 14: 1–37. Inst. Caribe Antr. Sociol. de la Fundación La Salle. Caracas.

1965 West Mexican tomb sculpture as evidence for shamanism in prehispanic Mesoamerica. *Ibid.*, 15: 29–81.

1966 Shaft tombs, shell trumpets, and shamanism: a culture-historical approach to problems in west Mexican archaeology. Doctoral dissertation, Univ. California, Los Angeles.

1967 Tumbas de tiro y cámara: un posible eslabón entre México y los Andes. *Eco*, 26: 1–6. Inst. Jalisciense Antr. Hist. Guadalajara.

GABEL, N. E.
1949 A comparative racial study of the Papago. Univ. New Mexico Press.

1950 The skeletal remains of Ventana Cave. *In* Haury, 1950, pp. 473–520.

GADOW, H.
1908 Through southern Mexico, being an account of the travels of a naturalist. London.

1930 Jorullo: the history of the volcano Jorullo and the reclamation of the devastated district by animals and plants. Cambridge.

GAGE, T.
1648 The English American or a new survey of the West Indies. London.

1702 A survey of the Spanish West Indies, being a journal of 3000 and 300 miles on the continent of America. London.

1908 Viajes de Tomás Gage en la Nueva España, sus diversas aventuras. 2 vols. Paris.

GAILLARD, G.
1895 Les Pápagos de l'Arizona et de la Sonora. *L'Anthropologie*, 6: 212. Paris.

GAITÁN, L.
1936 De como luchó Guatemala contra el cólera morbus en el siglo pasado. Trabajo presentado al IV Cong. Méd. Centroamer. y Panamá. *Bol. Sanitario, Guatemala*, 7: 93.

GAJDUSEK, D. C., AND N. G. ROGERS
1955 Specific serum antibodies to infectious disease agents in Tarahumara adolescents of northwestern Mexico. *Pediatrics*, 16: 819–34.

GALDO GUZMÁN, D. DE
1642 Arte mexicano. *In* Col. de gramáticas, pp. 281–394.

GALICH, L. F.
1953 El tifo exantemático en Guatemala. *Rev. Colegio Méd. Guatemala*, 4: 9.

GALINDO, M.
1922 Bosquejo de la geografía arqueológica del estado de Colima. *An. Mus. Nac. Arqueol. Hist. Etnog.*, ep. 4, vol. 1. Mexico.

GALINDO Y VILLA, J.
1902 [ed.] Álbum de antigüedades indígenas que se conservan en el Museo Nacional de México.

1903 La escultura nahua. *An. Mus. Nac. Méx.*, ep. 2, 1: 195–234.

1904 Catálogo del departamento de arqueología del Museo Nacional. Part 1: Galería de monolitos. 4th ed. Mexico.

1921 Los yugos. *Mem. Soc. Cien. Antonio Alzate*, 39: 219–29.

GALLENKAMP, C.
1959 Maya: the riddle and rediscovery of a lost civilization. New York.

GALTSOFF, P., ed.
1954 Gulf of Mexico: its origin, waters, and marine life. U.S. Dept. Interior, Fish and Wildlife Service, Fishery Bull., vol. 55.

GAMBOA, F., ed.
1963 Masterworks of Mexican art from pre-Columbian times to the present. Los Angeles County Mus. Art. Los Angeles.

GAMBOA, R. P., ed.
1942 *See* Mayas y Olmecas.

GÁMEZ, E.
1955 El valle del Fuerte. Los Mochis.

GAMIO, L.
1950 Informe relacionado con la zona de Quiotepec. MS in Archivo Inst. Nac. Antr. Hist.

1954 Inspección de las zonas arqueológicas de la Costa Rica. MS *ibid*.

1957 Zona arqueológica de San Martin Huamelulpan. MS *ibid*.

GAMIO, M.
1910 Los monumentos arqueológicas de las

inmediaciones de Chalchihuites, Zacatecas. *An. Mus. Nac. Arqueol. Hist. Etnog.*, ep. 3, 2: 469–92.

1913 Arqueología de Azcapotzalco, D.F., Mexico. *18th Int. Cong. Amer.* (London, 1912), Acta, pp. 180–93.

1917 Investigaciones arqueológicas en México, 1914–1915. *19th Int. Cong. Amer.* (Washington, 1915), Acta, pp. 125–33.

1920 Las excavaciones del Pedregal de San Angel y la cultura arcaica del Valle de México. *Amer. Anthr.*, 22: 127–43.

1921 Álbum de colecciones arqueológicas: texto. Pub. Escuela Internac. Arqueol. Etnol. Amer. Mexico. (See Boas, 1911–12, for photographs.)

1921 Una mascara falsificada. *Ethnos*, 1: 260.

1922 La población del valle de Teotihuacan, Mexico. 3 vols. Sec. Agricultura y Fomento. Mexico.

1922 Las pequeñas esculturas. *In* preceding entry, 1: 179–86.

1924 Sequence of cultures in Mexico. *Amer. Anthr.*, 26: 307–22.

1926–27 Cultural evolution in Guatemala and its geographic and historic handicaps. *Art and Archaeol.*, 22: 203–22, 23: 17–32, 71–78, 129–33.

1930 The Mexican immigrant: his life story. Chicago.

1930 The Mexican immigrant in the United States: a study in human migration and adjustment. Chicago.

1930 Mexican immigration to the United States. Chicago.

1933 Sources and distribution of Mexican immigration into the United States. Mexico.

1937 Cultural patterns in modern Mexico. *Pan Amer. Inst. Geog. Hist., Proc. 2d General Assembly* (1935). Washington.

1937 La importancia del folklore yaqui. *Mex. Folkways*, July, pp. 45–51.

1939 El índice cultural y el biotipo. *Quar. Inter-Amer. Relations*, April.

1942 Consideraciones sobre el problema indígena de América. *Amer. Indig.*, 2 (2): 17–24.

1942 Las características culturales y los censos indígenas. *Ibid.*, 2 (3): 15–19.

1946 La identificación del indio. *Ibid.*, 6: 99–103.

1946 Exploración económico-cultural en la región oncocercosa de Chiapas, Mexico. *Ibid.*, vol. 6, no. 3.

——, F. GONZÁLEZ DE COSSÍO, AND OTHERS
1958 Legislación indígena de México. *Inst. Indig. Interamer.*, Ed. Especiales, no. 38.

GÁMIZ, E.
1948 Monografía de la nación tepehuana que habita en la región sur del estado de Durango. Mexico.

GANGOLY, O. C.
1920 A note on Kirtimukha: being the life-history of an Indian architectural ornament. *Rupam*, 1: 11–19. Calcutta.

GANN, T. W. F.
1900 Mounds in northern Honduras. *Smithsonian Inst., Bur. Amer. Ethnol.*, 19th ann. rept., pt. 2, pp. 655–92.

1914–16 Report on some excavations in British Honduras. *Univ. Liverpool, Ann. Archaeol. Anthr.*, 7: 28–42.

1917 The chachac or rain ceremony as practiced by the Maya of southern Yucatan and northern British Honduras. *19th Int. Cong. Amer.* (Washington, 1915), Acta, pp. 409–18.

1918 The Maya Indians of southern Yucatan and northern British Honduras. *Smithsonian Inst., Bur. Amer. Ethnol.*, Bull. 64.

1925 Mystery cities: exploration and adventure in Lubaantun. London.

1925 Maya jades. *21st Int. Cong. Amer.*, (Goteborg, 1924), Acta, pp. 274–82.

1926 Ancient cities and modern tribes: exploration and adventure in Maya lands. London.

1928 Discoveries and adventures in Central America. London.

1928 Maya cities. New York.

1932 Worshippers of the long-nosed god. *Illustr. London News*, 101: 1006-07.

1939 Glories of the Maya. London.

—— AND M. GANN
1939 Archaeological investigations in the Corozal district of British Honduras. *Smithsonian Inst., Bur. Amer. Ethnol.,* Bull. 123, pp. 1–66.

—— AND J. E. S. THOMPSON
1931 The history of the Maya from the earliest times to the present day. New York.

GANTE, C. DE
1921 Narraciones tlaxcaltecas. 2 vols. Puebla.

GANTE, P. DE
n.d. Cartas de Fr. Pedro de Gante, O.F.M., primer educador de América. Comp. by Fr. Fidel de Chauvet, O.F.M. Printed by Fr. Junipero Serra, Provincia del Santo Evangelio de México.

GÁRATE DE GARCÍA, C.
1960 Los trastornos emocionales como causa de la enfermedad en Tehuantepec. *Amér. Indig.,* 20: 201–06. Mexico.

GARBELL, M. A.
1947 Tropical and equatorial meteorology. New York and Chicago.

GARCÍA, D.
1899–1901 Diverso grosor de algunas regiones del cráneo en la raza mixta latinoamericana. *Crónica Méd. Mex.,* 4: 265–70 (Mexico); *El Progreso Méd.,* 1: 63–68 (San Luis Potosi).

GARCÍA, E.
1918 Crónica de la provincia agustiniana del santísimo nombre de Jesús de México. Madrid.

GARCÍA, J. M.
1859 Apéndice a José María Murguía y Galardi. *Bol. Soc. Mex. Geog. Estad.,* 7: 159–275.

GARCÍA A., J. L.
1942 Leyendas indígenas de Guatemala. Guatemala.

GARCÍA CONDE, P.
1842 Ensayo estadístico sobre el estado de Chihuahua. Chihuahua.
1849 El album mexicana. Mexico.

GARCÍA COOK, A.
1967 Análisis tipológico de artefactos. *Inst. Nac. Antr. Hist., Ser. Invest.,* no. 12. Mexico.

GARCÍA CUBAS, A.
1907 Mis últimas exploraciones arqueológicas: excursión a Teotihuacán. *Mem. Soc. Cien. Antonio Alzate,* 24: 261–77.

GARCÍA DE PALACIO, D.
1860 Carta dirijida al rey de España, año 1576. *In* Squier, 1860.

GARCÍA GRANADOS, R.
1935 Contribución para la geografía, etnográfica y lingüística de Oaxaca. *Bol. Soc. Mex. Geog. Estad.,* 44: 401–10.
1939 Mexican feather mosaics. *Mexican Art and Life,* no. 5, pp. 1–4. Mexico.
1942 Antigüedades mexicanas en Europa. *Mem. Acad. Mex. Hist.,* vol. 1, no. 2.
1946 El arte plumario. *In* México Prehispánico, pp. 576–81.
1952–53 Diccionario biográfico de historia antigua de México. 3 vols. Inst. Historia. Mexico.

GARCÍA ICAZBALCETA, J.
1858–66 Colección de documentos para la historia de México. 2 vols. Mexico.
1886 Bibliografía mexicana del siglo XVI: catálogo razonado de libros impresos en México de 1539 a 1600 con biografías de autores y otras ilustraciones. [Index by C. A. Janvier, 1890.] Mexico.
1889–92 Nueva colección de documentos para la historia de México. 5 vols. Mexico. (2d ed. 1941.)

GARCÍA PAYÓN, J.
n.d. Informes de los trabajos de exploración y conservación llevados a cabo en El Tajín, abarcan el período de 1938 a 1962. Inst. Nac. Antr. Hist., Archivo Técnico. Mexico.
n.d. Las artes menores de los Totonacos de Zempoala.
1938 La zona arqueológica de Tecaxic-Calixtlahuaca y los Matlatzincas. Part 2. 2 vols. Mexico.
1939 Exploraciones y comentarios sobre la zona arqueológica de El Tajín, temporada de 1938–1939. Inst. Nac. Antr. Hist., Archivo Técnico. Mexico.
1941 Estudio preliminar de la zona arqueológica de Texmelincan, estado de Gue-

rrero. *El México Antiguo*, 5: 341–64.

1941 La cerámica del valle de Toluca. *Rev. Mex. Estud. Antr.*, 5: 209–38.

1942 Interpretación de la vida de los pueblos matlatzincas. *El Mex. Antiguo*, 6: 73–90.

1943 Interpretación cultural de la zona arqueológica de El Tajín, seguida de un ensayo de una bibliografía antropológica del Totonacapan y región sur del estado de Veracruz. Univ. Nac. Autónoma Méx.

1944 Notas de campo.

1944 Un templo de Xolotl descubierto en Zempoala, Veracruz. *El Dictámen*, Feb. 6.

1945 Notas de campo.

1945 Mausolea in central Veracruz. *Carnegie Inst. Wash., Notes Middle Amer. Archaeol. Ethnol.*, no. 59.

1946 Los monumentos arqueológicos de Malinalco, estado de México. *Rev. Mex. Estud. Antr.*, 8: 5–63.

1947 Conclusiones de mis exploraciones en el Totonacapan meridional, temporada 1939. *27th Int. Cong. Amer.* (Mexico, 1939), Acta, 2: 88–96.

1947 Sinopsis de algunos problemas arqueológicos de Totonacapan. *El México Antiguo*, 6: 301–32.

1947 Exploraciones arqueológicas en el Totonacapan meridional (región de Misantla). *An. Inst. Nac. Antr. Hist.*, 2: 73–111. Mexico.

1949 Arqueología de El Tajín. I: ensayo de interpretación del monolito con relieve del monumento V de El Tajín. *Uni-Ver*, 1: 299–305. Jalapa.

1949 Notable relieve con sorprendentes revelaciones. *Ibid.*, 1: 351–59.

1949 La zona arqueológica de Zempoala, I. *Ibid.*, 1: 11–19.

1949 Arqueología de Zempoala, II. *Ibid.*, 1: 134–39.

1949 Zempoala: compendio de su estudio arqueológico. *Ibid.*, 1: 449–76.

1949 Arqueología de Zempoala, III. *Ibid.*, 1: 534–48.

1949 La zona arqueológica de Oceloapan, Ver. *Ibid.*, 1: 492–504.

1949 Arqueología de El Tajín. II: Un palacio totonaca. *Ibid.*, 1: 581–95.

1949 Arqueología de Zempoala, IV. *Ibid.*, 1: 636–56.

1950 Palmas y hachas votivas. *Ibid.*, 2: 63–66.

1950 Restos de una cultura prehispánica encontrados en la región de Zempoala, Veracruz. *Ibid.*, 2: 90–130.

1950 Castillo de Teayo: noticias sobre su arqueología. *Ibid.*, 2: 155–64.

1950 Exploraciones en Xiuhtetelco, Puebla. *Ibid.*, 2: 397–426, 447–76.

1950 Las tumbas con mausoleos de la región central de Veracruz. *Ibid.*, 2: 7–23.

1950 Restos de una cultura prehistórica encontrados en la región de Zempoala, Veracruz. *Ibid.*, 2: 90–130.

1950 Notas de campo.

1951 La pirámide de El Tajín: estudio analítico. *Cuad. Amer.*, 10 (6): 153–77.

1951 La ciudad arqueológica de El Tajín. Contrib. Univ. Veracruzana, Reunión de Mesa Redonda Antr. Jalapa.

1951 Breves apuntes sobre la arqueología de Chachalacas. *Ibid.*

1951 La cerámica de fondo "sellado" de Zempoala, Veracruz. *In* Homenaje Caso, pp. 181–98.

1952 Totonacos y Olmecas: un ensayo de correlación histórico-arqueológica. *Uni-Ver*, 3: 27–52.

1953 ¿Qué es lo Totonaco? *In* Huastecos, Totonacos y sus vecinos, pp. 379–87.

1954 El Tajín: descripción y comentarios. *Uni-Ver*, 4: 18–63.

1956–57 Síntesis de las investigaciones en Tecaxic-Calixtlahuaca. *Rev. Mex. Estud. Antr.*, 14: 157–59.

1959–61 Ensayo de interpretación de los tableros del juego de pelota sur de El Tajín. *El México Antiguo*, 9: 445–60.

1963 Quienes construyeron El Tajín y resultados de las últimas exploraciones de la temporada 1961–1962. *Palabra y Hombre* (Revista de la Univ. Veracruzana), pp. 243–52. Jalapa.

1965 [ed.] Descripción del pueblo de Gueytlalpan (Zacatlán, Jujupango,

Matlatlán y Chila, Papantla) por el alcalde mayor Juan de Carrion, 30 de Mayo de 1581. Jalapa.

1966 Prehistoria de Mesoamérica: excavaciones en Trapiche y Chalahuite, Veracruz, México, 1942, 1951 y 1959. *Cuad. Facultad Filosofía, Letras y Ciencias*, no. 31. Univ. Veracruzana. Jalapa.

GARCÍA PELÁEZ, F. DE P.
1851–52 Memorias para la historia del antiguo reino de Guatemala. 3 vols. Guatemala.

GARCÍA PÉREZ, A.
1863 Descripción de la ciudad de Uruapan .... *Bol. Soc. Mex. Geog. Estad.*, 10: 469–77.

GARCÍA PÉREZ, H.
1943 Exploración sanitaria de Altepexi, distrito de Tehuacan, Puebla. Mexico.

GARCÍA PIMENTEL, L., ed.
1897 Descripción del arzobispado de México hecha en 1570 y otros documentos. Mexico.
1903–07 Documentos históricos de México. 5 vols. Mexico, Paris, Madrid.
1904 Relación de los obispados de Tlaxcala, Michoacan, Oaxaca y otros lugares en el siglo XVI. *In* his 1903–07, vol. 2.

GARCÍA TORRES, V., ed.
1853–57 Documentos para la historia de México. 20 vols. Mexico.

GARCÍA VALLE, M.
1947 Breves apuntes sobre onchocercosis. Tesis de Graduación, Facultad Cien. Méd., Univ. San Carlos de Guatemala.

GARFÍAS, V. R., AND T. C. CHAPÍN
1949 Geología de Mexico. Mexico.

GARIBAY K., A. M.
1940 Llave del Náhuatl. (2d ed. 1961.) Otumba, Mexico.
1940 La poesía indígena de la altiplanicie. *Bib. Estudiante Universitario*, no. 11. Mexico. (3d ed. 1962.)
1943 Huehuetlatolli, documento A. *Tlalocan*, 1: 31–53, 81–107.
1943 Paralipómenos de Sahagún. *Ibid.*, 1: 307–13.
1945 Épica Náhuatl. *Bib Estudiante Uni-*

versitario, no. 57. Mexico. (Another ed. 1964.)
1946 Paralipómenos de Sahagún. *Tlalocan*, 2: 167–74, 249–320.
1948 Relación breve de las fiestas de los dioses, fray Bernardino de Sahagún. *Ibid.*, 2: 289–320.
1953–54 Historia de la literatura Náhuatl. 2 vols. Mexico.
1957 Supervivencias de cultura intelectual precolombina entre los Otomies de Huizquilucan, estado de México. *Amer. Indig.*, 17: 319–33.
1958 [ed.] Veinte himnos sacros de los Nahuas. *Informantes indígenas de Sahagún*, no. 2. Univ. Nac., Seminario de Cultura Náhuatl. Mexico.
1961 [ed.] Vida económica de Tenochtitlan y Pochtecáyotl. *Ibid.*, no. 3.
1964 [ed.] Poesía Náhuatl. I: Romances de los señores de la Nueva España. Manuscrito de Juan Bautista de Pomar, Tezcoco, 1582. Univ. Nac. Autónoma Méx., Inst. Hist., Seminario de Cultura Náhuatl, Fuentes Indígenas de la Cultura Náhuatl. Mexico.
1965 Teogonía e historia de los mexicanos: tres opúsculos del siglo XVI. *Col. "Sepan Cuantos,"* no. 37. Mexico.
1965 Poesía Náhuatl. II: Cantares mexicanos. Manuscrito de la Bib. Nac. Méx. Part 1. Mexico.

GARTH, J. S.
1960 The biogeography of Baja California and adjacent seas. Part 2: Distribution and affinities of the brachyuran Crustacea. *Syst. Zool.*, 9: 105–23.

GARVIN, P. L.
1947 Distinctive features in Zoque phonemic acculturation. *Studies in Ling.*, 5: 13–20.
1953 *Review of* Preliminaries to speech analysis: the distinctive features and their correlates, by R. Jakobson, C. G. M. Fant, and M. Halle. *Language*, 29: 472–81.

GATES, W. E.
1920 Distribution of the several branches of the Mayance linguistic stock. *Carnegie Inst. Wash.*, Pub. 219, pp. 605–15.

1924 The William Gates Collection. American Art Assoc. New York.

1931 An outline dictionary of Maya glyphs. *Maya Soc.*, Pub. 1.

1932 The Mayance nations. *Maya Soc. Quar.*, 1: 97–106.

1938 A grammar of Maya. Maya Soc. Baltimore.

GAVAN, J. A.

1949 The skeletal material from Tuxcacuesco. *In* Kelly, 1949, pp. 213–14.

GAY, C. T. E.

1966 Rock carvings of Chalcacingo: bas reliefs add to knowledge of ancient Olmec culture in Mexico. *Natural Hist.*, 75: 57–61.

GAY, J. A.

1881 Historia de Oaxaca. 2 vols. Mexico. (Another ed. 1933.)

GAYANGOS, P. DE, ed.

1866 Cartas y relaciones de Hernán Cortés al emperador Carlos V. Paris.

GEIPEL, G.

1955 Tastleistenbefund bei Yupa-Indianern West-Venezuelas. *Zeitschr. für Morph. und Anthr.*, 47: 127–46.

GENIN, A. M. A.

1928 Note sur les objets précortesiens nommés indûment yugos ou jougs. *22d Int. Cong. Amer.* (Rome, 1926), Acta, 1: 521–28.

GENNA, G. E.

1934 Missione per lo studio delle popolazioni indigeni del Messico. *Rev. Antr.*, 30: 489–92. Rome.

1943 I Serie: la loro costituzione scheletrica. Com. Italiano per lo studio dei problemi della popolazione. Florence.

1953 I caratteri serologici e i gruppi sanguigni. *In* Le razze e i popoli della terra, R. Biasutti, ed., pp. 257–80. (2d ed.). Torino.

GENOVÉS T., S.

1958 Estudio de los restos óseos de Coixtlahuaca, estado de Oaxaca. *In* Misc. Paul Rivet, 1: 455–84. Mexico.

1959 El surco pre-auricular y las cavidades dorso-sinfisiales del hueso coxal en algunos restos del Laboratorio de Antropología del Museo Nacional, México. *33d Int. Cong. Amer.* (San Jose, 1958), Acta, 2: 27–33.

1960 Revaluation of the age, stature, and sex of the Tepexpan remains, Mexico. *Amer. Jour. Physical Anthr.*, 18: 205–18.

1964 Introducción al estudio de la proporción entre huesos largos y la reconstrucción de la estatura en restos mesoamericanos. *An. Antr.*, 1: 47–62. Mexico.

1966 La proporcionalidad entre los huesos largos y su relación con la estatura en restos mesoamericanos. *Inst. Invest. Hist., Ser. Antr.*, Cuad. 19. Mexico.

1966 El supuesto aumento secular de la estatura a partir de circa 1800 d.c. *An. Antr.*, 3: 69–98. Mexico.

1966 Some comments on the secular trend of stature in the last generations. *Amer. Anthr.*, 68: 499–504.

1967 Long bone proportionality and its relation to stature in Mesoamerican populations. *Amer. Jour. Physical Anthr.*, 26: 67–78.

—— AND J. COMAS

1964 La antropología física en México, 1943–1964: inventario bibliográfico. *Cuad. Inst. Hist., Ser. Antr.*, no. 17. Mexico.

—— AND M. MESSMACHER

1959 Valor de los patrones tradicionales para la determinación de la edad por medio de las suturas en cráneos mexicanos, indígenas y mestizos. *Ibid.*, no. 7. Mexico.

GERALD, R.

1957 A historic house excavation near Janos, northwest Chihuahua, Mexico. M.A. thesis, Univ. Pennsylvania.

GERHARD, P.

n.d. Aboriginal population of Baja California. MS.

1964 Emperor's dye of the Mixtecs. *Natural Hist.*, 73: 26–31.

1964 Shellfish dye in America. *35th Int. Cong. Amer.* (Mexico, 1962), Acta, 3: 177–91.

—— AND H. E. GULICK

1958 Lower California guidebook: a descriptive traveler's guide. Glendale.

GERSTENHAUER, A.
1960 Der tropische Kegelkarst in Tabasco (Mexico). *Zeit. für Geomorphologie, Suppl.*, 2: 22–48. Berlin.

GERTH, T. H.
1955 Der geologische Bau der Südamerikanische Kordillere. Berlin.

GESSAIN, R.
1938 Contribution à l'étude des cultes et des cérémonies indigènes de la region de Huehuetla, Hidalgo: les "muñecos," figures rituelles. *Jour. Soc. Amer. Paris,* 30: 323–70.
1953 Les Indiens Tepehuas de Huehuetla. *In* Huastecos, Totonacos, pp. 187–211.

GIBLETT, E. R.
1958 Js, a "new" blood-group antigen found in Negroes. *Nature,* 181: 1221–22. London.

——, J. CHASE, AND A. G. MOTULSKY
1957 Studies on anti-V, a recently discovered Rh antibody. *Jour. Laboratory Clinical Med.,* 49: 433–39.

GIBSON, C.
n.d. The pre-conquest Tepanec zone and the labor drafts of the sixteenth century. MS.
1952 Tlaxcala in the sixteenth century. *Yale Hist. Pub.,* Miscellany, no. 56.
1955 The transformation of the Indian community in New Spain, 1500–1810. *Jour. World Hist.,* 2: 581–601.
1956 Llamamiento general, repartimiento, and the empire of Acolhuacan. *Hispanic Amer. Hist. Rev.,* 36: 1–27.
1960 The Aztec aristocracy in colonial Mexico. *Comparative Studies in Society and Hist.,* 2: 169–196.

GIBSON, G. D.
1960 Bibliography of anthropological bibliographies: the Americas. *Current Anthr.,* 1: 61–73.

GIBSON, L. F.
1956 Pame (Otomi) phonemics and morphophonemics. *Int. Jour. Amer. Ling.,* 22: 242–65.

GIDDINGS, R. W.
1959 Yaqui myths and legends. *Univ. Arizona, Anthr. Papers,* no. 2.

GIERLOFF-EMDEN, H. G.
1959 Die Küste von El Salvador. Eine morphologische-ozeanographische Monographie. *Acta Humboldtiana, Series Geog. et Ethnog.,* no. 2. Wiesbaden.

GIFFORD, E. W.
1933 The Cocopa. *Univ. California Pub. Amer. Archaeol. Ethnol.,* vol. 31, no. 5.
1946 Archaeology in the Punta Peñasco region, Sonora. *Amer. Antiquity,* 11: 215–21.
1950 Surface archaeology of Ixtlan del Rio, Nayarit. *Univ. California Pub. Amer. Archaeol. Ethnol.,* vol. 43, no. 2.

—— AND R. H. LOWIE
1928 Notes on the Akwa'ala Indians of Lower California. *Ibid.,* vol. 23, no. 7.

GIFFORD, J. C.
1960 The type-variety method of ceramic classification as an indicator of cultural phenomena. *Amer. Antiquity,* 25: 341–47.

GILBERTI, M.
1558 Arte de la lengua tarasca ó de Michoacán. (Mexico, 1898.)
1559 Diccionario de la lengua tarasca ó de Michoacán. (Mexico, 1901.)

GILES, H. A.
1923 The travels of Fa-hsien (399–414 A.D.) or record of the Buddhistic kingdoms. Cambridge.

GILL, M.
1957 La conquista del valle del Fuerte. Mexico.

GILLIN, J.
1943 Houses, food, and the contact of cultures in a Guatemalan town. *Acta Amer.,* 1: 344–59.
1945 Parallel cultures and the inhibitions to acculturation in a Guatemalan community. *Social Forces,* 24: 1–14.
1948 "Race" relations without conflict: a Guatemalan town. *Amer. Jour. Sociol.,* 53: 337–43.
1948 Magical fright. *Psychiatry,* 11: 387–400.
1951 The culture of security in San Carlos: a study of a Guatemalan community

of Indians and Ladinos. *Tulane Univ., Middle Amer. Research Inst.,* Pub. 16.

1952 Ethos and cultural aspects of personality. *In* Tax, 1952, Heritage, pp. 193–224.

1957 San Luis Jilotepeque: 1942–55. *In* R. N. Adams, 1957, Political changes, pp. 23–27.

1958 San Luis Jilotepeque. Tr. by J. Noval. *Seminario de Integración Social Guatemalteca,* no. 7. Guatemala.

—— AND G. NICHOLSON

1951 The security function of cultural systems. *Social Forces,* 30: 179–84.

GILLMOR, F.

1949 Flute of the smoking mirror: a portrait of Nezahualcoyotl, poet-king of the Aztecs. Univ. New Mexico Press.

GILLOW, E. G.

1889 Apuntes históricos. Mexico.

GILMORE, R. M.

1947 Report on a collection of mammal bones from archaeologic cave-sites in Coahuila, Mexico. *Jour. Mammalogy,* 28: 147–65.

1950 Fauna and ethnozoology of South America. *In* Handbook of South American Indians, 6: 345–463.

1957 Whales aground in Cortes' sea. *Pacific Discovery,* 10: 22–27.

1959 On the mass strandings of sperm whales. *Pacific Naturalist,* 1: 9–16.

GINI, C.

1934–35 Premiers resultats d'une expedition italo-mexicaine parmi les populations indigènes et métisses du Mexique. *Genus,* pp. 147–77 (Rome). *Bol. Soc. Mex. Geog. Estad.,* 45: 97–134 (Mexico).

GINSBURG, I.

1930 Commercial snappers (*Lutianidae*) of Gulf of Mexico. U.S. Bur. Fisheries, Bull. 46, pp. 265–76.

GIRARD, R.

1944 El baile de los gigantes. *An. Soc. Geog. Hist. Guatemala,* 19: 427–45.

1949 Los chortis ante el problema maya: historia de los culturas indígenas de América, desde su origin hasta hoy.

5 vols. Col. Cultura Precolombiana. Mexico.

1962 Los Mayas eternos. Mexico.

GLADWIN, H. S.

1937 Excavations at Snaketown, II: Comparisons and theories. *Medallion Papers,* no. 26.

1957 A history of the ancient Southwest. Portland, Me.

——, E. W. HAURY, E. B. SAYLES, AND N. GLADWIN

1937 Excavations at Snaketown: material culture. *Medallion Papers,* no. 25.

GLADWIN, W., AND H. S. GLADWIN

1929 The red-on-buff culture of the Papagueria. *Ibid.,* no. 4.

GLASS, B., AND C. C. LI

1953 The dynamics of racial intermixture: an analysis based on the American Negro. *Amer. Jour. Human Genetics,* 5: 1–20.

GLASSOW, M. A.

1967 The ceramics of Huistla, a west Mexican site in the municipality of Etzatlan, Jalisco. *Amer. Antiquity,* 32: 64–83.

GLEASON, H. A., JR.

1959 Counting and calculating for historical reconstruction. *Anthr. Ling.,* 2: 22–32.

GODDARD, P. E.

1920 The cultural and somatic correlations of Uto-Aztecan. *Amer. Anthr.,* 22: 244–47.

GODIN, P.

1903 Recherches anthropométriques sur la croissance des diverses parties du corps. Paris.

GODSKE, C. L., T. BERGERON, J. BJERKNES, AND R. C. BUNDGAARD

1957 Dynamic meteorology and weather forecasting. Amer. Meteorol. Soc. and Carnegie Inst. Wash.

GOETZ, D., AND S. G. MORLEY

1950 Popol Vuh: the sacred book of the ancient Quiche Maya. Norman, Okla.

GOFF, C. W.

1948 Anthropometry of a Mam-speaking group of Indians from Guatemala. *Amer. Jour. Physical Anthr.,* 6: 429–

48. (Reprinted in Woodbury and Trik, 1953, pp. 288–311.)

1953 New evidence of pre-Columbian bone syphilis in Guatemala. *In* Woodbury and Trik, 1953, pp. 312–19.

GOGGIN, J. M.
1943 An archaeological survey of the Rio Tepalcatepec basin, Michoacan, Mexico. *Amer. Antiquity*, 9: 44–58.
1960 The Spanish olive jar, an introductory study. *Yale Univ. Pub. Anthr.*, no. 62.

GOLDMAN, E. A.
1920 Mammals of Panama. *Smithsonian Inst., Misc. Coll.*, vol. 69, no. 5.
1951 Biological investigations in Mexico. *Ibid.*, vol. 115.

—— AND R. T. MOORE
1946 The biotic provinces of Mexico. *Jour. Mammalogy*, 26: 347–60.

GOLDSCHMIDT, W. R.
1952 The interrelations between cultural factors and the acquisition of new technical skills. *In* Hoselitz, 1952, pp. 135–51.

GOLDSTEIN, M. S.
1943 Demographic and bodily changes in descendants of Mexican immigrants. Univ. Texas, Inst. Latin-Amer. Studies.
1943 Observations on Mexican crania. *Amer. Jour. Physical Anthr.*, 1: 83–93.
1957 Skeletal pathology of early Indians in Texas. *Ibid.*, 15: 299–311.

CÓMEZ, A. M.
1935 Estudios gramaticales de la lengua cora. *Invest. Ling.*, 3: 79–142.

GÓMEZ, E. A.
1944 El Popol Vuh. Mexico.

GÓMEZ, F., R. RAMOS GALVÁN, J. CRAVIOTO, AND S. FRENK
1952 Desnutrición de tercer grado en México (kwashiorkor en Africa). *Bol. Méd. Hospital Infantil Méx.*, 9: 281–84.
1954 Malnutrition and kwashiorkor. *Acta Paediatrics*, 43: 336–57.
1958 Prevention and treatment of chronic severe infantile malnutrition (kwashiorkor). *Ann. New York Acad. Sci.*, 69: 969–81.

—— AND OTHERS (R. RAMOS GALVÁN, J. CRAVIOTO, S. FRENK, C. DE LA PEÑA, M. E. MORENO, AND M. E. VILLA)
1957 Protein metabolism in chronic severe malnutrition (kwashiorkor): absorption and retention of nitrogen from a typical poor Mexican diet. *British Jour. Nutrition*, 11: 229–33.

GÓMEZ, H.
1934 Grupos sanguíneos de los niños mexicanos del Distrito Federal. Mexico.

GÓMEZ, W. G.
1913 Promedios de peso y estatura de los alumnos de las escuelas primarias del Distrito Federal según los datos recogidos en los años 1910 a 1912. *An. Higiene Escolar*, vol. 2, no. 4. Mexico.

GÓMEZ CAÑEDO, L.
1959 Nuevos datos acerca del cronista Fray Antonio Tello. *Estud. Hist.*, 1: 117–21. Guadalajara.

GÓMEZ DE OROZCO, F.
1928 Relaciones histórico-geográficas del obispado de Oaxaca. *Rev. Mex. Estud. Hist.*, 2: 113–91.
1945 Costumbres, fiestas, enterramientos y diversas formas de proceder de los Indios de Nueva España. Copy of part of text of Madrid Museo de América codex cognate with Codex Magliabecchiano. *Tlalocan*, 2: 37–63.

GÓMEZ-MAILLEFERT, E. M.
1923 Folk-lore de Oaxaca. *Jour. Amer. Folklore*, 36: 199–200.

GÓMEZ ROBLEDA, J.
1930 Algunas consideraciones sobre antropología criminal. *Quetzalcoatl*, 1 (3): 8–10. Mexico.
1940 Ensayo biotipológico sobre los indios tarascos. *In* Mendieta y Núñez, 1940, pp. 119–26.

—— AND L. ARGOYTIA
1940 Deportistas: características y correlaciones somáticas y funcionales. Mexico.

——, A. QUIROZ QUARÓN, L. ARGOYTIA, AND A. MERCADO
1949 Estudio biotipológico de los Zapotecos. *In* Mendieta y Núñez, 1949, pp. 263–414.

—— AND OTHERS
1937 Características biológicas de los niños proletarios. Inst. Nac. Psicopedagogía. Mexico.
1943 Pescadores y campesinos tarascos. Sec. Educación Pública. Mexico.
1961 Estudio biotipológico de los Otomies. Inst. Invest. Sociales, UNAM. Mexico.

GÓMEZ TAGLE, C.
1904 Cefalometría. Mexico.

GONZÁLEZ, J. E.
1885 Obras completas. Monterrey.

GONZÁLEZ, L.
1672 Arte breve y vocabulario de la lengua tzoque . . . de Tecpatlan. MS in Bibliothèque Nationale.

GONZÁLEZ, M. N.
1954 Instituciones indígenas en México independiente. In Caso, 1954, Métodos, pp. 113–69.

GONZÁLEZ, M. T., AND A. R. OLIVARES
1887 Estudios obstetriciales. Guanajuato.

GONZÁLEZ, P. D.
1897 Algunos puntos y objetos monumentales antiguos del estado de Guanajuato. 11th Int. Cong. Amer. (Mexico, 1895), Acta, pp. 149–59.

GONZÁLEZ BONILLA, L. A.
1939 Los huastecos. Rev. Mex. Sociol., 1: 29–56.

GONZÁLEZ CASANOVA, P.
1920 Cuento en mexicano de Milpa Alta, D. F. Jour. Amer. Folklore, 33: 25–27.
1925 Los idiomas popolocas y su clasificación. An. Mus. Nac. Arqueol. Hist. Etnog., 3: 497–538.
1927 El Tapachulteca no. 2, sin relación conocido. Rev. Mex. Estud. Hist., 1: 18–26.
1928 El ciclo legendario del Tepoztecatl. Mex. Folkways, 4: 206–29.
1946 Cuentos indígenas. Univ. Nac. Autónoma Mex.

GONZÁLEZ DE COSSÍO, F.
1952 El libro de las tasaciones de pueblos de la Nueva España, siglo XVI. Mexico.

GONZÁLEZ OBREGÓN, L.
1952 Rebeliones indígenas y precursores de la independencia mexicana en los siglos 16, 17 y 18. 2d ed. Mexico.

GONZÁLEZ PEÑA, C.
1940 Historia de la literatura mexicana desde los orígenes hasta nuestros días. Mexico.

GONZÁLEZ ROSA, J. M.
1949 Morras o yucas. A la uñita. La mojiganga. Convite al aire. (Folklore.) Rev. Archivo y Biblioteca Nac., 27: 357–64. Tegucigalpa.

GONZÁLEZ RUL, F.
1959 Una punta acanalada del rancho La Chuparrosa. Inst. Nac. Antr. Hist., Pub. 8.

—— AND F. MOOSER
1961 Erupciones volcánicas y el hombre primitivo en la cuenca de Mexico. In Homenaje a Pablo Martínez del Río, pp. 137–41.

GONZÁLEZ TENORIO, G.
1941 Informe general sobre la exploración sanitaria del municipio de Acaxochitlan, distrito de Tulancingo, estado de Hidalgo. Mexico.

GOODENOUGH, W. H.
1959 A problem in Malayo-Polynesian social organization. Amer. Anthr., 55: 557–72.

GOODMAN, J. T.
1897 The archaic Maya inscriptions. In appendix to Maudslay, 1889–1902.

GOODNER, K.
1930 Incidence of blood groups among the Maya Indians of Yucatan. Jour. Immunology, 18: 432–35.

GOODSPEED, T. H.
1954 The genus Nicotiana. Chronica Botanica.

GORDON, B. L.
1957 A domesticated, wax-producing scale insect kept by the Guaymí Indians of Panama. Ethnos, 22: 36–49.

GORDON, G. B.
1896 Prehistoric ruins of Copan, Honduras. Mem. Peabody Mus., Harvard Univ., vol. 1, no. 1.
1898 Caverns of Copan, Honduras. Ibid., vol. 1, no. 5.
1898 Researches in the Uloa valley. Ibid., vol. 1, no. 4.

1913   *Introduction to* The Book of Chilam Balam of Chumayel.   *Univ. Mus. Anthr. Pub.*, vol. 5.   Philadelphia.

1915   Guatemala myths.   *Mus. Jour., Univ. Pennsylvania*, 6: 103–44.

—— AND J. A. MASON

1925–43   Examples of Maya pottery in the museum and other collections.   3 parts.   *Univ. Pennsylvania Mus.*

GORDON, J. E., A. A. J. JANSEN, AND W. ASCOLI

1965   Measles in rural Guatemala.   *Jour. Pediatrics*, 66: 779–86.

—— AND OTHERS (W. ASCOLI, L. J. MATA, M. A. GUZMÁN, AND N. S. SCRIMSHAW)

1968   Nutrition and infection field study in Guatemalan villages, 1959–1964.   VI. Acute diarrheal disease and nutritional disorders in general disease incidence.   *Arch. Environ. Health*, 16: 424–37.

GOSSE, L. A.

1855   Essais sur les déformations artificielles du crâne.   *Ann. Hygiène Publique et Méd. Légale*, ser. 2, 3: 317–93; 4: 1–83.   Paris.

1861   Presentation d'un crâne deformé de Nahoa, trouvé dans la vallée de Ghovel, Mexique.   *Bull. Soc. Anthr. Paris*, 2: 567–77.

GOUBAUD CARRERA, A.

1935   El "Guajxaquip báts"—ceremonia calendárica indígena.   *An. Soc. Geog. Hist. Guatemala*, 12: 39–50.

1945   Discurso pronunciado en la inauguración del Instituto Indigenista Nacional de Guatemala.   *Bol. Indig.*, 5: 372–86.

1946   Distribución de las lenguas indígenas actuales de Guatemala.   *Bol. Inst. Indig. Nac.*, 1 (2, 3): 63–76.   Guatemala.

1946   La población de habla indígena en Guatemala.   *Ibid.*, 1 (4): 17–21.

1948   Some aspects of the character structure of the Guatemala Indians.   *Amer. Indig.*, 8: 95–105.

1949   Notes on the Indians of the finca Nueva Granada.   *Univ. Chicago, Micro. Coll. MSS Middle Amer. Cult. Anthr.*, no. 21.

1949   Notes on the Indians of eastern Guatemala.   *Ibid.*, no. 22.

1949   Notes on San Juan Chamelco, Alta Verapaz.   *Ibid.*, no. 23.

1949   Problemas etnológicos del Popol Vuh. I: Procedencia y lenguaje de los Quiches.   *Antr. Hist. Guatemala*, 1 (1): 35–42.

1952   Indian adjustments to modern national culture.   *In* Tax, 1952, Heritage, pp. 244–48.

——, J. DE DÍOS ROSALES, AND S. TAX

1947   Reconnaissance of northern Guatemala, 1944.   *Univ. Chicago, Micro. Coll. MSS Middle Amer. Cult. Anthr.*, no. 17.

GOULD, H. N.

1946   Anthropometry of the Chol Indians of Chiapas, Mexico.   *Tulane Univ., Middle Amer. Research Inst.*, Pub. 15, no. 9.

GOWER, C. D.

1927   The northern and southern affiliations of Antillean culture.   *Mem. Amer. Anthr. Assoc.*, no. 35.

GRACE, G. W.

1959   The position of the Polynesian languages within the Austronesian (Malayo-Polynesian) language family.   *Indiana Univ. Pub. Anthr. Ling.*, Memoir 16.

GRACIEUX, P.

1918   A propos de la tâche mongolique au Mexique: notes preliminaires.   *Bull. et Mem. Soc. Anthr. Paris*, ser. 6, 9: 6–9.

GRAEBNER, F.

1920–21   Alt- und neuweltliche Kalender.   *Zeit. für Ethnol.*, 52/53: 6–37.

GRAHAM, J., ed.

1966   Ancient Mesoamerica: selected readings.   Palo Alto.

GRAJEDA, J. A.

1925   Algunas consideraciones sobre el rinoescleroma: su tratamiento por el radium.   Tesis de médico y cirujano, Facultad Cien. Méd., Univ. Nac. Guatemala.

GRANLUND, J.

1953   Birdskin caps: a cultural element of the Arctic and northern countries.   *Ethnos*, 18: 125–42.

GRASSERIE, R. DE LA

See La Grasserie, R. de.

GRATIOLET, P.

1860　Sur un crâne de Totonaque. *Bull. Soc. Anthr. Paris,* 1: 562–65.

1860　Description d'un crâne de mexicain Totonaque des environs d'Orizaba. *Mem. Soc. Anthr. Paris,* 1: 391–98.

1861　Sur la forme et la cavité cranienne d'un Totonaque, avec reflexions sur la signification du volume de l'encéphale. *Bull. Soc. Anthr. Paris,* 2: 66–71.

GREENBERG, J. H.

1948　Linguistics and ethnology. *SW. Jour. Anthr.,* 4: 140–47.

1954　A quantitative approach to the morphological typology of language. *In* R. F. Spencer, ed., Method and perspective in anthropology: papers in honor of Wilson D. Wallis. Reprinted in *Int. Jour. Amer. Ling.,* 26: 178–94.

1957　Essays in linguistics. *Viking Fund Pub. Anthr.,* no. 24.

1957　The nature and uses of linguistic typologies. *Int. Jour. Amer. Ling.,* 23: 68–77.

1960　A quantitative approach to the morphological typology of language. *Ibid.,* 26: 178–94.

—— AND M. SWADESH

1953　Jicaque as a Hokan language. *Ibid.,* 19: 216–22.

GREENGO, R. E.

1952　The Olmec phase in eastern Mexico. *Bull. Texas Archaeol. Paleontol. Soc.,* 23: 260–92.

1960　Rocker-stamped pottery in the Old and New World. *In* Wallace, 1960, pp. 553–65.

GREULICH, W. W., AND S. I. PYLE

1959　Radiographic atlas of skeletal development of the hand and wrist. 2d ed. Stanford Univ. Press.

GRIFFEN, W. B.

1959　Notes on Seri Indian culture, Sonora, Mexico. *Univ. Florida School Inter-Amer. Studies, Latin Amer. Monogr.,* no. 10.

GRIFFIN, JAMES B.

1944　Archaeological horizons in the southeast and their connections with the Mexican area. *In* El Norte de México, pp. 283–86.

1945　The ceramic affiliations of the Ohio Valley Adena culture. *In* Webb and Snow, 1945, pp. 220–46.

1946　Culture change and continuity in eastern United States archaeology. *Papers Peabody Found. Archaeol.,* 3: 37–96. Andover, Mass.

1949　Meso-America and the southeast: a commentary. *In* John W. Griffin, 1949, pp. 77–99.

1952　[ed.] Archaeology of eastern United States. Univ. Chicago Press.

1952　Some early and middle Woodland pottery types in Illinois. *In* Deuel, 1952, pp. 93–129.

1952　An interpretation of the place of Spiro in southeastern archaeology. *Missouri Archaeol.,* 14: 89–106.

1953　Prehistoric chronology estimates in the eastern United States and central Mexico, 1940–50. *In* Huastecos, Totonacos, pp. 485–96.

1955　Notes on the grooved axe in North America. *Pennsylvania Archaeol.,* 25: 32–44.

1956　Prehistoric settlement patterns in the northern Mississippi Valley and the upper Great Lakes. *In* Willey, 1956, Prehistoric settlement patterns, pp. 63–71.

1958　The chronological position of the Hopewellian culture in the eastern United States. *Univ. Michigan, Mus. Anthr., Anthr. Papers,* no. 12.

1960　Some prehistoric connections between Siberia and America. *Science,* 131: 801–12.

1960　Climatic change: a contributory cause of growth and decline of northern Hopewellian culture. *Wisconsin Archaeol.,* 41: 21–33.

1960　A hypothesis for the prehistory of Winnebago. *In* Diamond, 1960, pp. 809–65.

1961　Commentary on "Neolithic diffusion rates," by Munro S. Edmonson. *Current Anthr.,* 2: 92–93.

1961　Some correlations of climatic and cultural change in eastern North American prehistory. *Ann. New York Acad. Sci.*, 95: 710–17.

1962 A discussion of prehistoric similarities and connections between the Arctic and Temperate zones of North America. *In* J. M. Campbell, ed., Prehistoric cultural relations between the Arctic and Temperate zones of North America. *Arctic Inst. North Amer., Tech. Papers*, no. 11, pp. 154–63.

—— AND A. ESPEJO

1947 La alfarería correspondiente al último período de ocupación nahua del Valle de México, I. *Tlatelolco a Través de los Tiempos*, 9: 10–26.

1950 La alfarería correspondiente al último período de ocupación nahua del Valle de México, II: Culhuacan, Tenayuca, Tenochtitlan y Tlatelolco. *Ibid.*, 11: 15–16.

—— AND A. D. KRIEGER

1947 Notes on some ceramic techniques and intrusions in central Mexico. *Amer. Antiquity*, 12: 156–69.

——, W. C. McKERN, AND P. F. TITTERINGTON

1945 Painted pottery figurines from Illinois. *Ibid.*, 10: 295–302.

—— AND R. G. MORGAN, eds.

1941 Contributions to the archaeology of the Illinois River valley. *Trans. Amer. Phil. Soc.*, 32: 1–208.

GRIFFIN, JOHN W., ed.

1949 The Florida Indian and his neighbors. Inter American Center, Rollins College. Winter Park.

GRIJALVA, J. DE

1624 Crónica de la orden de nuestro padre San Agustin en las provincias de la Nueva España. Mexico. (2d ed. 1924.)

GRIMAUX, G.

1900 Une peuplade qui s'éteint: les coucapah du Rio Colorado, Mexique septentrional. *Rev. Scien.*, 14: 807–09. Paris.

GRIMES, J. E.

1955 Style in Huichol structure. *Language*, 31: 31–35.

1959 Huichol tone and intonation. *Int. Jour. Amer. Ling.*, 25: 221–32.

1960 Spanish-Nahuatl-Huichol monetary terms. *Ibid.*, 26: 162–65.

1961 Huichol economics. *Amer. Indig.*, 21: 280–306.

1964 Huichol syntax. The Hague.

—— AND B. F. GRIMES

1962 Semantic distinctions in Huichol (Uto-Aztecan) kinship. *Amer. Anthr.*, 64: 104–14.

GRISCOM, L.

1926 Nicaragua. *In* Shelford, 1926, pp. 604–07.

1932 The distribution of bird-life in Guatemala. *Bull. Amer. Mus. Nat. Hist.*, no. 44.

1934 The ornithology of Guerrero, Mexico. *Bull. Mus. Comp. Zool., Harvard Univ.*, 75: 365–422.

1935 The ornithology of the Republic of Panama. *Ibid.*, 78: 260–382.

1940 Origin and relationships of the faunal areas of Central America. *Proc. 8th Amer. Sci. Cong.*, 3: 425–30.

1950 Distribution and origin of the birds of Mexico. *Bull. Mus. Comp. Zool., Harvard Univ.*, 103: 341–82.

GROBMAN, A., W. SALHUANA, AND R. SEVILLA, IN COLLABORATION WITH P. C. MANGELSDORF

1961 Races of maize in Peru: their origins, evolution and classification. *Nat. Acad. Sci.*, Pub. 915.

GROLLIG, F. X.

1959 San Miguel Acatan, Huehuetenango, Guatemala: a modern Mayan village. Doctoral dissertation, Indiana Univ.

GROPP, A. E.

1934 Manuscripts in the Department of Middle American Research. *Tulane Univ., Middle Amer. Research Inst.*, Pub. 5.

GROSSCUP, G. L.

1961 A sequence of figurines from west Mexico. *Amer. Antiquity*, 26: 390–406.

1964 The ceramics of west Mexico. Doctoral dissertation, Univ. California, Los Angeles.

GROSSMAN, F. E.

1871 The Pima Indians of Arizona. *Smithsonian Inst.*, ann. rept. Bound in *Anthr. Pamphlets*, 19: 407–19.

GROTH-KIMBALL, I., AND F. FEUCHTWANGER

1953 Kunst im alten Mexiko. Zurich-Freiburg.

1954 The art of ancient Mexico. English trans. of their 1953. London and New York.

GROUSSET, R.
1959 Chinese art and culture. London.

GROVE, D.
1968 Chalcatzingo, Morelos, Mexico: a reappraisal of the Olmec rock carvings. *Amer. Antiquity*, 33: 486–91.

GROVES, G. W., AND J. L. REID, JR.
1958 Estudios oceanográficos sobre las aguas de Baja California. Mem. Primer Cong. de Hist. Regional. Dir. General de Acción Cívica y Cultural, Gobierno del Estado de Baja California, Mexicali, pp. 81–121.

GRUBB, R.
1951 Observations on the human group system Lewis. *Acta Pathol. Microbiol. Scand.*, 28: 61–82.

GRUENING, E.
1928 Mexico and its heritage. New York.

GRUNING, E. L.
1930 Report on the British Museum expedition to British Honduras, 1930. *Jour. Royal Anthr. Inst.*, 60: 477–83.

GUATEMALA, DIRECCIÓN GENERAL DE ESTADÍSTICA
1957 Sexto censo general de población, Abril 18 de 1950.

GUATEMALA, MINISTERIO DE EDUCACIÓN PÚBLICA
1960 Memoria de labores realizadas por la Dirección General de Desarrollo Socio-Educativo Rural durante en año de 1959.
1960 Prospecto de los cursos de profesionalización para maestros rurales empíricos en servicio.
1960 Extracto del proyecto piloto de nutrición y horticultura.
1960 Plan del trabajo de la Dirección General de Desarrollo Socio-Educativo Rural para el año de 1960.

GUDSCHINSKY, S. C.
1955 Lexico-statistical skewing from dialect borrowing. *Int. Jour. Amer. Ling.*, 21: 138–49.
1958 Mazatec dialect history: a study in miniature. *Language*, 34: 469–81.

1958 Native reactions to tones and words in Mazatec. *Word*, 14: 338–45.
1959 Proto-Popotecan. *Int. Jour. Amer. Ling.*, Mem. 15.
1959 Discourse analysis of a Mazatec text. *Ibid.*, 25: 139–46.
1959 Mazatec kernel constructions and transformations. *Ibid.*, 25: 81–89.
1959 Proto-Popotecan: a comparative study of Popolocan and Mixtecan. *Indiana Univ. Pub. Anthr. Ling.*, Memoir 15.

GUÉRIN, J.
1853 Les microcéphales Aztèques. *Gazette Méd. Paris*, 42: 647–49.

GUERRA, J.
1692 Arte de la lengua mexicana . . . de Guadalaxara. Mexico. (2d ed., Guadalajara, 1900.)

GUERRERO, RAÚL G.
1939 La fiesta tradicional de Juchitan. *Rev. Mex. Estud. Antr.*, 3: 242–56.
1939 La música zapoteca. *Neza*, 4 (1): 16–20.
1944 El hombre y la mujer. *Tlalocan*, 1: 253–58.
1950 Alfajayucan, etnografía y folklore de un grupo otomí del valle del Mezquital, estado de Hidalgo. MS. Bib. Inst. Indig. Interamer. Mexico.
1950 Etnografía y folklore de la zona otomí del estado de Hidalgo. MS. *Ibid.*

GUERRERO, ROSALÍA
1950 La mujer otomí. MS. *Ibid.*

GUERRERO C., J. N.
1955 Historia de los ejidos de Boaco. *Nicaragua Indig.*, ep. 2, no. 7, pp. 33–39.
1956 El pueblo extranjero. Monografía de Chontales. Managua.

GUEVARA CALENDAR (TLAXCALTECA)
1901 *In* Chavero, 1901, 1: 31–38.

GUIGNABAUDET, P.
1953 Nuevos descubrimientos arqueológicos en las tolas de Huaraqui. *Bol. Informaciones Cien. Nac.*, 6: 168–86. Quito.

GUILLEMÍN, J. F.
1958 La pirámide B-6 de Mixco Viejo y el sacrificatorio de Utatlan. *Antr. Hist. Guatemala*, 10 (1): 21–28.
1959 Iximche. *Ibid.*, 11 (2): 22–64.

GUILLEMIN-TARAYRE, E.

1867 Rapport sur l'exploration minéralogique des régions mexicaines. *Archives Com. Sci. du Mexique*, 3: 173–470. Paris.

1867 Notes archéologiques et ethnographiques: vestiges laissés par les migrations américaines dans le nord du Mexique. *Ibid.*, 3: 341–470.

1869 Exploration minéralogique des régions mexicaines. Paris.

1869 Informe sobre las ruinas de la Quemada.

GUITERAS HOLMES, C.

n.d. World view and belief system. *In* World view in San Pedro Chenalho.

1946 Informe de Cancuc. *Univ. Chicago, Micro. Coll. MSS Middle Amer. Cult. Anthr.*, no. 8.

1946 Informe de San Pedro Chenalhó. *Ibid.*, no. 14.

1947 Clanes y sistema de parentesco de Cancuc, México. *Acta Amer.*, 5: 1–17.

1948 Organización social de tzeltales y tzotziles, México. *Amer. Indig.*, 8: 45–62.

1948 Sistema de parentesco huasteco. *Acta Amer.*, 6: 152–72.

1951 El calpulli de San Pablo Chalchihuitan. *In* Homenaje Caso, pp. 199–206.

1952 Sayula. *Soc. Mex. Geog. Estad.* Mexico.

1952 Social organization. *In* Tax, 1952, Heritage, pp. 97–118.

1956 Background of a changing kinship system among the Tzotzil Indians of Chiapas. MS. [Also dated 1960.]

1960 La familia Tzotzil. *Tlatoani*, no. 13.

1961 La magia en la crisis del embarazo y parto en los actuales grupos mayances de Chiapas. *Estud. Cultura Maya*, 1: 159–66.

1961 Perils of the soul: the world view of a Tzotzil Indian. *Univ. Chicago Press.*

1961 Informe sobre Bachajon. MS.

GUNTER, G.

1941 Relative numbers of shallow water fishes of the northern Gulf of Mexico, with some records of rare fishes from the Texas coast. *Amer. Midl. Nat.*, vol. 26, no. 1.

GUTHE, C. E.

1921 A possible solution of the number series on pages 51 to 58 of the Dresden Codex. *Papers Peabody Mus., Harvard Univ.*, vol. 6, no. 2.

GUTIÉRREZ, J. F.

1899 Contribución al estudio del rinoescleroma. Tesis de médico y cirujano, Facultad Cien. Méd., Univ. Nac. Guatemala.

GUTIÉRREZ DE LIÉVANA, J.

1905 Relación de la villa de Tepuztlan. *In* Paso y Troncoso, 1905–06, 6: 237–50.

GUTIÉRREZ GARCÍA, D.

1946 Exploración sanitaria del municipio de Acaxochitlan, estado de Hidalgo. Mexico.

GUTIÉRREZ ZAVALA, M.

1895 Apuntamiento para el estudio comparativo de la pelvis mexicana y la europea, y consecuencias prácticas a que da lugar la especial conformación de la primera. *Trans. 1st Pan Amer. Med. Cong.* Washington.

GUZMÁN, A. DE

16thC Bocabulario de lengua tzeldal. . . . Photograph in Newberry Library. 294 pp.

GUZMÁN, E.

1933 Caracteres fundamentales del arte antiguo mexicano: su sentido fundamental. *Univ. México*, 5: 117–55, 408–29.

1934 Exploración arqueológica en la Mixteca alta. *An. Mus. Nac. Arqueol. Hist. Etnog.*, 1: 17–42.

1934 Los relieves de las rocas del Cerro de la Cantera, Jonacatepec, Morelos. *Ibid.*, 1: 237–51. Mexico.

1938 [ed.] Un manuscrito de la Colección Boturíni que trata de los antiguos señores de Teotihuacán. *Ethnos*, 3: 89–103.

1946 Caracteres fundamentales del arte. *In* Vivó, 1946, pp. 545–51.

1959 Huipil y máxtlatl. *In* Esplendor del México antiguo, 2: 959–82.

GUZMÁN, E. J., AND Z. DE CSERNA

1960 Outline of the tectonic history of Mexico. MS.

GUZMÁN, L. E.
1958 The agricultural terraces of the ancient highland Maya. *Ann. Assoc. Amer. Geog.*, 48: 266.

GUZMÁN, M. A.
1968 Impaired physical growth and maturation in malnourished populations. *In* Malnutrition, learning, and behavior, N. S. Scrimshaw and J. E. Gordon, eds. Massachusetts Inst. Technology Press.

——, G. ARROYAVE, AND N. S. SCRIMSHAW
1961 Serum ascorbic acid, riboflavin, carotene, vitamin A, vitamin E and alkaline phosphatase values in Central American school children. *Amer. Jour. Clinical Nutrition*, 9: 164–69.

HAAS, M. R.
1959 Tonkawa and Algonkian. *Anthr. Ling.*, 1: 1–6.

HABEL, S.
1878 The sculptures of Santa Lucia Cosumalwhuapa in Guatemala. *Smithsonian Contrib. Knowledge*, vol. 22.

HABERLAND, W.
1953 Die regionale Verteilung von Schmuckelementen im Bereiche der klassichen Maya-Kultur. *Beitrage zur mittelamerikanischen Völkerkunde*, no. 2.
1955 Preliminary report on the Aguas Buenas culture, Costa Rica. *Ethnos*, 20: 224–30.
1957 Excavations in Costa Rica and Panama. *Archaeology*, 10: 258–63.
1957 Black-on-red painted ware and associated features in intermediate area. *Ethnos*, 22: 148–61.
1958 A pre-classic complex of western El Salvador, C. A. *32d Int. Cong. Amer.* (Copenhagen, 1956), Acta, pp. 485–90.
1959 Archäologische Untersuchungen in Südost – Costa Rica. *Acta Humboldtiana, Ser. Geog. Ethnog.*, no. 1. Wiesbaden.
1959 Chiriquian pottery types. *Panama Archaeol.*, vol. 2, no. 1.
1959 A re-appraisal of Chiriquian pottery types. *33d Int. Cong. Amer.* (San Jose, 1958), Acta, 2: 339–46.
1960 Ceramic sequences in El Salvador. *Amer. Antiquity*, 26: 21–29.
1960 Cien años de arqueología en Panama. *Pub. Rev. "Loteria,"* no. 12.
1960 Die Steinfiguren von Barriles in Panama. Die Umschau in Wissenschaft und Technik. Heft 23, 1 Dizember. Frankfurt am Main.
1960 Villalba, pt. I. *Panama Archaeol.*, 3: 9–21.
1962 The scarified ware and the early cultures of Chiriqui (Panama). *34th Int. Cong. Amer.* (Vienna, 1960), Acta, pp. 381–89.
in press Observaciones en la península de Osa. *Informe Semestral*, Inst. Geog. Nac., Costa Rica.

—— AND W. H. GREBE
1957 Prehistoric footprints from El Salvador. *Amer. Antiquity*, 22: 282–85.

HACKETT, C. W., ed.
1923–37 Historical documents relating to New Mexico, Nueva Vizcaya and approaches thereto, to 1773, collected by Adolph F. A. Bandelier and Fanny R. Bandelier. 3 vols. *Carnegie Inst. Wash.*, Pub. 330.

HADEN-GUEST, S., J. K. WRIGHT, AND E. M. TECLAF, eds.
1956 A world geography of forest resources. New York.

HAGEN, V. W. VON
1945 La fabricación del papel entre los aztecas y los mayas. Nuevo Mundo. Mexico.

HAHN, P. G.
1961 A relative chronology of the Cuban nonceramic tradition. Doctoral dissertation, Yale Univ.

HAJDA, Y.
1959 Dialect areas as determined by isogloss bundles (transect map). *In* McQuown, 1959, Man-in-Nature, fig. 17.
1959 Linguistic cross-influences: phonemic isoglosses on lexicostatistical clustering diagram. *Ibid.*, fig. 18.
1959 Linguistic cross-influences: grammatical isogloss on lexicostatistical clustering diagram. *Ibid.*, fig. 19.
1959 Linguistic cross-influence: phonetic

isoglosses on lexicostatistical clustering diagram. *Ibid.*, fig. 20.

1959 Linguistic cross-influences: lexical isoglosses on lexicostatistical clustering diagram. *Ibid.*, fig. 21.

1959 Loan word charts. *Ibid.*, fig. 22.

—— AND M. E. VERBITSKY

1959 Percentages of retention of native Mayan lexicon on pre-Hispanic traits map. *Ibid.*, fig. 40.

1959 Percentages of early Spanish loans on colonial Spanish introductions map. *Ibid.*, fig. 41.

1959 Percentages of recent Spanish loans on recent Mexican introductions map. *Ibid.*, fig. 42.

HAKLUYT, R.

1927 The principal navigations, voyages, traffiques and discoveries of the English nation. 8 vols. London, Toronto, New York.

HALE, K.

1958 Internal diversity in Uto-Aztecan: I. *Int. Jour. Amer. Ling.*, 24: 101–07.

1959 Internal diversity in Uto-Aztecan: II. *Ibid.*, 25: 114–21.

HALL, E. R., AND K. R. KELSON

1959 The mammals of North America. 2 vols. New York.

HALL, R. A., JR.

1958 Creolized language and "genetic relationships." *Word*, 14: 367–73.

HALLE, M., H. G. LUNT, H. MCLEAN, AND C. H. VAN SCHOONEVELD, comps.

1956 For Roman Jakobson. The Hague.

HALPERN, A. M.

1942 A theory of Maya tš-sounds. *Carnegie Inst. Wash., Notes on Middle Amer. Archaeol. Ethnol.*, no. 13.

HAMBLY, W. D.

1937 Skeletal material from San Jose ruin, British Honduras. *Field Mus. Natural Hist., Anthr. Mem.*, 25: 1–19.

HAMILTON, A.

1901 Maori art. Wellington.

HAMILTON, H. W.

1952 The Spiro mound. *Missouri Archaeol.*, 14: 17–276.

HAMILTON, P.

n.d. Jade and two cultures. MS.

—— AND D. LEONARD

1966 There is native jade in Mexico. *Intercambio* (November). Mexico.

HAMMOND, E. H.

1954 A geomorphic study of the cape region of Baja California. *Univ. California Pub. Geog.*, 10: 45–112.

HAMMOND, G. P., AND A. REY, trans. and eds.

1928 Obregón's history of the 16th century explorations in western America. Los Angeles.

HAMP, E. P.

1954 Componential restatement of syllable structure in Trique. *Int. Jour. Amer. Ling.*, 20: 206–09.

1958 Protopopoloca internal relationships. *Ibid.*, 24: 150–53.

1960 Chocho-Popoloca innovations. *Ibid.*, 26: 62.

1963 *Discussion and criticism of* Aboriginal languages of Latin America, S. Tax, ed. *Current Anthr.*, 4: 317.

HAMY, E. T.

1875 Quelques observations ethnologiques au sujet de deux microcéphales américains, designés sous le nom d'Aztèques. *Bull. Soc. Anthr. Paris*, ser. 2, 10: 39–54.

1878 L'ancienneté del l'homme au Mexique. *La Nature*, 251: 262–64. Paris.

1882 Les mutilations dentaires au Mexique et dans le Yucatan. *Bull. Soc. Anthr. Paris*, ser. 3, 5: 879–87; *La Nature*, 11: 403–06.

1883 Mutilations dentaires des Huaxtèques modernes. *Bull. Soc. Anthr. Paris*, ser. 3, 6: 644–45.

1884 Anthropologie du Mexique. *Mission Scientifique au Mexique et dans l'Amérique Centrale*, Part 1. Paris.

1886 Coup d'oeil d'ensemble sur les resultats des fouilles de M. D. Charnay dans le massif du Popocatepetl. *Bull. Soc. Anthr. Paris*, ser. 3, 9: 187–201.

1891 Sur le pretendu crâne de Moctezuma II. *Compte-rendu Acad. Sci.*, 112: 745–47. Paris.

1897 Galerie américaine du Musée d'ethnographie au Trocadéro: choix de pièces archéologiques et ethnographiques, décrites et figurées. Paris.

1897 Momie de Comatlan, Oaxaca. *In* preceding entry.

1897 Contribution à l'anthropologie du Nayarit. *Bull. Mus. Hist. Naturelle*, 6: 190–93. Paris. In Spanish in *Mem. Soc. Cien. Antonio Alzate*, 12: 30–32, 41–42. Mexico.

1899 Note sur un crâne perforé de Tarahumar de la cueva de Picachic, Chihuahua. *Bull. Mus. Hist. Naturelle*, 7: 339–41. Paris. Also in *Rev. Cien. Bibliog.*, 15 (3–4): 36–37. Mexico.

1899 *See* Codex Borbonicus.

HANDBOOK . . . BLISS COLLECTION
1963 Handbook of the Robert Woods Bliss Collection of pre-Columbian art. Dumbarton Oaks. Washington. (See also Lothrop, 1956; Lothrop, Foshag, and Mahler, 1957.)

HANDBOOK OF AMERICAN INDIANS NORTH OF MEXICO
1907 Handbook of American Indians north of Mexico. F. W. Hodge, ed. 2 vols. *Smithsonian Inst., Bur. Amer. Ethnol.*, Bull. 30.

HANDBOOK OF SOUTH AMERICAN INDIANS
1946–59 Handbook of South American Indians. J. H. Steward, ed. 7 vols. *Ibid.*, Bull. 143.

HANKE, L.
1949 The Spanish struggle for justice in the conquest of America. Philadelphia.

1959 Aristotle and the American Indian. Chicago.

HANSEN, A. T.
1934 The ecology of a Latin American city. *In* Reuter, 1934, pp. 124–42.

HANSON, H. C.
1958 Principles concerned in the formation and classification of communities. *Botanical Rev.*, 24: 65–125.

HARCUM, C. G.
1923 Indian pottery from the Casas Grandes region, Chihuahua, Mexico. *Bull. Royal Ontario Mus. Archaeol.* (December), pp. 4–11.

HARDY, A.
1960 Was man more aquatic in the past? *New Scientist*, 7: 642–45.

HARDY, R. W. H.
1829 Travels in the interior of Mexico. London.

HARO, J.
1944 Un poco de folklore del istmo. *Anuario Soc. Folklórica Mex.*, 5: 255–73.

HARRINGTON, M. R.
1933 Gypsum Cave, Nevada. *SW. Mus. Papers*, no. 8.

—— AND R. D. SIMPSON
1961 Tule Springs, Nevada, with other evidences of Pleistocene man in North America. *Ibid.*, no. 18.

HARRIS, M.
1946 An introduction to the Chontal of Tabasco, Mexico. *Amer. Indig.*, 6: 247–55.

1959 Caste, class, and minority. *Social Forces*, 37: 248–54.

HARRISON, W. R.
1952 The mason: a Zoque text. *Tlalocan*, 3: 193–204.

HARSHBERGER, J. W.
1911 Phytogeographic survey of North America. A consideration of the phytogeography of the North American continent, including Mexico, Central America and the West Indies, together with the evolution of North American plant distribution. Leipzig.

HART, M. V. D., H. BOSMAN, AND J. J. VAN LOGHEM
1954 Two rare human blood group antigens. *Vox Sanguinis*, 4: 108–16.

HARTE, E. M.
1958 Guacamaya Indian culture. *Panama*, February.

HARTE, N. A.
1958 A Madden Lake cave. *Panama Archaeol.*, vol. 1, no. 1.

1960 Preliminary report on petroglyphs of the Republic of Panama.

HARTMAN, C. V.
1901 Archaeological researches in Costa Rica. Stockholm.

1907 Archaeological researches on the Pacific coast of Costa Rica. *Mem. Carnegie Mus.*, vol. 3, no. 1.

1907 Mythology of the Aztecs of Salvador. *Jour. Amer. Folklore*, 20: 143–50.

1910 Le calebassier de l'Amérique tropicale (*Crescentia*): étude d'ethnobotanique. *Jour. Soc. Amer. Paris*, n.s., 7: 131–43.

HASKINS, W. C.
1940 In the land of the Zapotecs. *Mex. Life*, 16: 14–15.

HASLER, J. A.
n.d. Las formas de salutación en el Pipil del golfo. MS.
1954–55 Los cuatro dialectos de la lengua Nahua. *Rev. Mex. Estud. Antr.*, 14: 145–46.
1954–55 Cinco elementos clasificatorios del Nahua del oeste. *Ibid.*, 14: 147.
1954–55 Método de clasificación dialectal por correspondencia. *Ibid.*, 14: 148.
1960 El mundo físico-espiritual de los mazatecos de Ichcatlan. *Ibid.*, 16: 257–69.

HASTINGS, W., ed.
1916 Encyclopedia of religion and ethics. 8 vols. New York.

HATCH, N. S.
1954 Colonia Juarez, an intimate account of a Mormon village. Salt Lake City.

HATT, R. T.
1953 Faunal and archeological researches in Yucatan caves. *Cranbrook Inst. Sci.*, Bull. 33.

HATTORI, S.
1960 *Discussion of* D. H. Hymes, Lexicostatistics so far. *Current Anthr.*, 1: 40–42.

HAUGEN, E.
1949 Problems of bilingualism. *Lingua*, 2: 271–90.
1950 The analysis of linguistic borrowing. *Language*, 26: 210–31.
1953 The Norwegian language in America: a study in bilingual behavior. 2 vols. Univ. Pennsylvania Press.
1954 Some pleasures and problems of bilingual research. *Int. Jour. Amer. Ling.*, 20: 116–22.
1956 Bilingualism in the Americas: a bibliography and research guide. *Amer. Dialect Soc.*, Pub. 26.

HAURY, E. W.
1933 Maya textile weaves. MS.

1936 Some southwestern pottery types, series IV. *Medallion Papers*, no. 19.
1936 The Mogollon culture of southwestern New Mexico. *Ibid.*, no. 20.
1944 Mexico and the southwestern United States. *In* El Norte de México, pp. 203–05.
1945 The excavation of Los Muertos and neighboring ruins in the Salt River valley, southern Arizona. *Papers Peabody Mus., Harvard Univ.*, vol. 24, no. 1.
1945 The problem of contacts between the southwestern United States and Mexico. *SW. Jour. Anthr.*, 1: 55–74.
1950 [ed.] The stratigraphy and archaeology of Ventana Cave, Arizona. Univ. New Mexico Press and Univ. Arizona Press.
1950 Summary of the archaeology of Papagueria. *In* preceding entry.
1960 Association of fossil fauna and artifacts of the Sulphur Spring stage, Cochise culture. *Amer. Antiquity*, 25: 609–10.
1962 The greater American Southwest. *In* Braidwood and Willey, 1962, pp. 106–31.

——, E. B. SAYLES, AND W. W. WASLEY
1959 The Lehner mammoth site, southeastern Arizona. *Amer. Antiquity*, 25: 2–30.

—— AND OTHERS
1959 *American Antiquity*, vol. 24, no. 3. (Complete issue devoted to study of North American archaic cultures.)

HAUSWALDT, J. G.
1940 Kurze Notiz über eine, im Tal von Mexiko gefundene "palma." *El México Antiguo*, 5: 202–03.

HAWLEY, F. M.
1936 Field manual of prehistoric Southwestern pottery types. *Univ. New Mexico Bull., Anthr. Ser.*, vol. 1, no. 4. (Rev. ed. 1950.)

HAY, C. L., AND OTHERS, eds.
1940 The Maya and their neighbors. New York.

HAYDEN, J. D.
1956 Notes on the archaeology of the central coast of Sonora, Mexico. *Kiva*, 21 (3, 4): 19–23.

HAYNER, N.
1944 Oaxaca, city of old Mexico. *Sociol. and Social Research*, 29: 87–95.

HEACOCK, J. G., AND J. L. WORZEL
1955 Submarine topography west of Mexico and Central America. *Bull. Geol. Soc. Amer.*, 66: 773–76.

HEALEY, G. G.
1950 The Lacanja valley. *Archaeology*, 3: 12–15.

HEATH-JONES [*no given name*]
1959 Definition of an ancestral Maya civilization in Miraflores phase: Kaminaljuyu. *In* Suhm, 1959, p. 37.

HEFLIN, A. A.
1961 Bone spindle whorls in the Valley of Mexico. *Bol. Centro Invest. Antr. Méx.*, 12: 9–12.

HEGER, F.
1913 Eine weitere neue Serie von Gebilden welche die Mischungsverhaeltnisse der verschiedenen Rassen in Mexiko zur Darstellung bringt. *18th Int. Cong. Amer.* (London, 1912), Acta, pp. 461–63.

HEILPRIN, A.
1891 Geological researches in Yucatan. *Proc. Philadelphia Acad. Natural Sci.*, pp. 136–58.

HEIM, A.
1934 El Bernal de Horcasitas, a volcanic plug in the Tampico plain. *Zeit. für Vulkanologie*, 15: 254–60.

1940 The front ranges of Sierra Madre Oriental, from C. Victoria to Tamazunchale. *Ecologae Geol. Helvetiae*, 33: 313–62. Basel.

HEIM, R., AND R. G. WASSON
1958 Les champignons hallucinogènes du Mexique: études ethnologiques, taxonomiques, biologiques, physiologiques et chimiques. *Archives du Mus. Nat. d'Histoire Naturelle*, vol. 6.

HEINE-GELDERN, R.
1937 L'art prébouddique de la Chine et de l'Asie du Sud-Est et son influence en Océanie. *Rev. Arts Asiatiques*, 11: 177–206.

1952 Some problems of migration in the Pacific. *In* Koppers, Heine-Geldern, and Haekel, eds., Kultur und Sprache. *Wiener Beiträge zur Kulturgeschichte und Linguistik*, 9: 313–62.

1952 Die asiatische Herkunft der südamerikanischen Metalltechnik. *Paideuma*, 5: 347–423.

1956 Conceptions of state and kingship in southeast Asia. *Southeast Asia Program, Dept. Far Eastern Studies, Cornell Univ.*, Data Paper 18.

1956 Herkunft und Ausbreitung der Hochkulturen. *Osterreichische Akad. Wissenschaften*, Almanach (1955), Jahrgang 105, pp. 252–67.

1956–57 La escritura de la Isla de Pascua y sus relaciones con otras escrituras (observaciones al articulo del Dr. Thomas Barthel). *Runa*, 8: 5–27.

1958 Kulturpflanzengeographie und das Problem vorkolumbischer Kulturbeziehungen zwischen Alter und Neuer Welt. *Anthropos*, 53: 361–402.

1959 Chinese influences in Mexico and Central America: the Tajin style of Mexico and the marble vases from Honduras. *33d Int. Cong. Amer.* (San Jose, 1958), Acta, 1: 195–206.

1959 Chinese influence in the pottery of Mexico, Central America, and Colombia. *Ibid.*, 1: 207–10.

1959 Representations of the Asiatic tiger in the art of the Chavin culture: a proof of early contacts between China and Peru. *Ibid.*, 1: 321–26.

1964 Indonesian cultures. *Encyclopedia World Art*, vol. 8, columns 41–59.

1964 Traces of Indian and southeast Asiatic Hindu-Buddhist influences in Mesoamerica. *35th Int. Cong. Amer.* (Mexico, 1962), Acta, 1: 47–54.

—— AND G. F. EKHOLM
1951 Significant parallels in the symbolic arts of southern Asia and Middle America. *In* Tax, 1951, pp. 299–309.

HEISER, C. B., JR.
1955 The origin and development of the cultivated sunflower. *Amer. Biol. Teacher*, 17: 161–67.

1965 Cultivated plants and cultural diffusion in nuclear America. *Amer. Anthr.*, 67: 930–49.

HEIZER, R. F.

1942 Ancient grooved clubs and modern rabbit sticks. *Amer. Antiquity,* 8: 41–56.

1943 Aboriginal use of bitumen by the California Indians. *California Div. Mines,* 118: 73–75.

1953 Additional notes on Chinese soapstone carvings from Mesoamerica. *Amer. Antiquity,* 19: 81.

—— AND S. F. COOK

1959 New evidence of antiquity of Tepexpan man and other human remains from the valley of Mexico. *SW. Jour. Anthr.,* 15: 36–42.

—— AND E. M. LEMERT

1947 Observations on archaeological sites in Topanga Canyon, California. *Univ. California Pub. Amer. Archaeol. Ethnol.,* 44: 237–58.

—— AND W. C. MASSEY

1953 Aboriginal navigation off the coasts of Upper and Baja California. *Smithsonian Inst., Bur. Amer. Ethnol.,* Bull. 151, pp. 285–311.

—— AND T. SMITH

1964 Olmec structure and stone working: a bibliography. *Contrib. Univ. California Archaeol. Research Facility,* 1: 71–87. Berkeley.

—— AND H. WILLIAMS

1965 Stones used for colossal sculpture at or near Teotihuacan. *Ibid.,* 1: 55–70.

——, ——, AND J. A. GRAHAM

1965 Notes on Mesoamerican obsidians and their significance in archaeological studies. *Ibid.,* 1: 94–103.

HELBIG, K. M.

1959 Die Landschaft von Nordost-Honduras. *Petermanns Mitt.,* Ergänzungsheft 286. Gotha.

1964 La cuenca superior del Río Grijalva: un estudio regional de Chiapas, sureste de México. Inst. Cien. y Artes de Chiapas. Tuxtla Gutierrez.

HELBRÜGER, E.

1874 Album de vistas fotográficas de las antiguas ruinas de los palacios de Mitla. Oaxaca.

HENCKEL, K. O.

1933 Sobre la disposición de las crestas palares de las falangitas en los indígenas de la provincia de Cautín. *Bol. Soc. Biol.,* 7: 53–60. Concepción, Chile.

HENDERSON, R.

1952 Lost silver ledge of Santa Catarina. *Desert Mag.,* vol. 15, no. 11.

1952 Tribesmen of Santa Catarina. *Ibid.,* vol. 15, no. 7.

HENDRICHS PÉREZ, P. R.

1939 Un estudio preliminar sobre la lengua cuitlateca de San Miguel Totolapan, Guerrero. *El Mex. Antiguo,* 4: 329–62.

1940 ¿Es el arco de Oztuma de construcción azteca? *Ibid.,* 5: 142–47.

1943 Tlachtemalacates y otros monumentos de la zona arqueológica de La Soledad, Gro. *Ibid.,* 6: 120–30.

1945–46 Por tierras ignotas: viajes y observaciones en la región del Río de las Balsas. 2 vols. Mexico.

HENESTROSA, A.

1933 Estudios sobre la lengua zapoteca. *Invest. Ling.,* 1: 27–30.

1936 Vini-gunday-zaa. *Neza,* 2 (10): 1–6. Mexico.

1936 Niza-Rindani. *Ibid.,* 2 (14): 1–4.

1936 Estudios sobre la lengua zapoteca. *Ibid.,* 2: 19.

1936 Los sones zapotecas. *Ibid.,* vol. 2.

1947 La viva raíz de Juchitan. *Univ. Mexico,* 1 (9): 16–17.

HENNING, P.

1911 Los Otomies del distrito de Lerma. *An. Mus. Nac.,* 3 (3a): 58–85. Mexico.

1912 Informe del colector de documentos etnológicos sobre su excursión a Tuxtepec. *Bol. Mus. Nac. Arqueol. Hist. Etnol.,* 1: 229–35.

1918 El Xipe del Tazumal de Chalchuapa, Departamento de Santa Ana, República de El Salvador. *Disertaciones Cien. Autores Alemanes en Mex.,* no. 4.

1919 Palangónen en zapoteco, que se usa en Zaachila, distrito de Zimatlan, estado de Oaxaca, para pedir la novia. *El Mex. Antiguo,* 1: 91–96.

HENSCHEN, F.

1956 Sonderdruck aus den Verhandlungen

der Deutschen Gesellschaft für Pathologie. Stuttgart.

HEPNER, H. E.
1904 The Aztecs of today. *Southern Workman*, 33: 528–35. Hampton, Va.
1906 Tepehuanes of Chihuahua and Durango. *Ibid.*, 35: 157–63.

HERAS, N.
1940 Yugo de uso entre los zapotecos. *El Nacional*, May 10.

HERBERTSON, A. J.
1905 The major natural regions of the world. *Geog. Jour.*, 25: 300–10. London.

HEREDIA, M. A.
1959 Tuberculosis meníngea, nuestra experiencia en los servicios de medicina de niños. Tesis de médico y cirujano, Facultad Cien. Méd., Univ. San Carlos de Guatemala.

HERMITTE, E.
1958–60 Field notes of Pinola. MS, Chiapas Project files, Univ. Chicago, Dept. Anthropology.

HERNÁNDEZ, FORTUNATO
1902 Las razas indígenas de Sonora y la guerra del Yaqui. Mexico.
1902 Particularidadea anatómicas de los cráneos otomíes. *Gaceta Méd. Méx.*, 2: 19–23.

HERNÁNDEZ, FRANCISCO
1926 De antiquitatibus Novae Hispaniae. (Códice de la Real Academia de la Historia en Madrid.) Ed. facsimilar. Mus. Nac. México.
1959–60 Obras completas. 3 vols. Mexico.

HERNÁNDEZ, FRANCISCO JAVIER
1946 Holidays and festivals in Mexico. Pan Amer. Union, Travel Division. Washington.
1959 El Museo Nacional de Antropología. Bib. Popular de Arte Mexicano.

HERNÁNDEZ, J.
1923 The temperature of Mexico. *Monthly Weather Rev.*, Suppl. 23.

HERNÁNDEZ, P. M.
1905 De los primeros habitantes de la venturosa yucateca. Merida.

HERNÁNDEZ BOLAÑOS, J.
1958 Escleroma, revisión de 170 casos.

Tesis de médico y cirujano, Facultad Cien. Méd., Univ. San Carlos de Guatemala.

HERNÁNDEZ MORENO, J., AND S. NAHMAD
1961 La política económica del estado como factor del desarrollo social regional. *Rev. Mex. Sociol.*, 23: 147–68.

HERNÁNDEZ RODRÍGUEZ, R.
1952 El valle de Toluca: su historia, época prehispánica y siglo XVI. *Bol. Soc. Mex. Geog. Estad.*, 74: 7–124.

HERNÁNDEZ SOTO, E.
1959 La fiebre amarilla en Guatemala. Tesis de médico y cirujano, Facultad Cien. Méd., Univ. San Carlos de Guatemala.

HERNÁNDEZ SPINA, V.
1932 Calendario Quiché. *Maya Soc. Quar.*, March.

[HERNÁNDEZ Y DÁVALOS, J., comp.]
1878 Noticias varias de Nueva Galicia, intendencia de Guadalajara. Guadalajara.

HERRARTE, A.
1955 La unión de Centroamérica: tragedias y esperanza. Guatemala.

HERRERA, A. L.
1884 El aje. *Naturaleza*, 6: 198–200.
1893 El hombre prehistórico de México. *Mem. Soc. Cien. Antonio Alzate*, 7: 17–56.
1896 Estudios de antropología mexicana. *Naturaleza*, ser. 2, 2: 462–69. Mexico.
1897 Nota relativa a las causas que producen atrofia de los pelos: refutación a un argumento de M. de Quatrefages. *An. Mus. Nac. Méx.*, ep. 1, 4: 216–24.

—— AND R. E. CICERO
1895 Catálogo de las colecciones antropológicas del Museo Nacional. Mexico.

—— AND D. VERGARA LOPE
1899 La vie sur les hauts plateaux. Mexico.

HERRERA, M.
1922 Esculturas zoomorfas. *In* Gamio, 1922, 1: 187–96.
1925 Las representaciones zoomorfas en el arte antiguo mexicano. *Pub. Sec. Educación Púb.*, 2: 8. Mexico.

1935 Estudio comparativo de las serpientes de la pirámide con los crótalos vivos. *In* Tenayuca, pp. 203–32.

HERRERA Y GUTIÉRREZ, M.

1890 La dolomía del distrito de Uruapan. *Mem. Soc. Cien. Antonio Alzate*, vol. 3.

1891 *Idem. Naturaleza*, 2d ser., 1: 397–99.

HERRERA Y TORDESILLAS, A. DE

1601–15 Historia general de los hechos de los castellanos en las islas y tierra firme del mar océano. . . . 4 vols. Madrid. (Other eds. 1725, 1726, 1726–30, 1934, 1945.)

HERSHKOVITZ, P.

1958 A geographical classification of Neotropical mammals. *Fieldiana* (Zoology), 36: 581–620.

HERSKOVITS, M. J.

1938 Acculturation: the study of cultural contact. New York.

1948 Man and his works. New York.

HERVÁS Y PANDURO, L.

1800 Catálogo de las lenguas de las naciones conocidas. 6 vols. Madrid. (Lenguas y naciones americanas in vol. 1.)

HERZOG, G.

1941 Culture change and language: shifts in the Pima vocabulary. *In* Spier, Hallowell, and Newman, 1941.

HESS, H. H.

1938 Gravity anomalies and island arc structure with particular reference to the West Indies. *Proc. Amer. Phil. Soc.*, 79: 71–96.

HESTER, J. A.

1952 Agriculture, economy and population densities of the Maya. *Carnegie Inst. Wash.*, Year Book 51, pp. 266–71.

1953 Agriculture, economy and population densities of the Maya. *Ibid.*, Year Book 52, pp. 289–92.

1954 Natural and cultural bases of ancient Maya subsistence economy. Doctoral dissertation, Univ. California.

HEWES, L.

1935 Huapec: an agricultural village of Sonora, Mexico. *Econ. Geog.*, 11: 284–92.

HEWETT, E. L.

1908 Les communautés anciennes dans le désert américain. Librairie Kündig. Geneva.

1913 The excavation of Quirigua, Guatemala, by the School of American Archaeology. *18th Int. Cong. Amer.* (London, 1912), Acta, pp. 241–48.

1923 Anahuac and Aztlan: retracing the legendary footsteps of the Aztecs. *Art and Archaeol.*, 16: 35–50.

1930 Ancient life in the American Southwest. Indianapolis.

1936 Ancient life in Mexico and Central America. Indianapolis.

HEYERDAHL, T., AND A. SKJÖLSVOLD

1956 Archeological evidence of pre-Spanish visits to the Galapagos Islands. *Soc. Amer. Archaeol.*, Mem. 12.

HIBBARD, C. W.

1955 Pleistocene vertebrates from the Upper Becerra (Becerra Superior) formation, valley of Tequixquiac, Mexico, with notes on other Pleistocene forms. *Univ. Michigan, Contrib. Mus. Paleontol.*, 12 (5): 47–96.

HIBBEN, F. C.

1941 Evidences of early occupation of Sandia Cave, New Mexico, and other sites in the Sandia-Manzano region. *Smithsonian Inst., Misc. Coll.*, vol. 99, no. 23.

HICKS, F., AND H. B. NICHOLSON

1964 The transition from classic to postclassic at Cerro Portezuelo, Valley of Mexico. *35th Int. Cong. Amer.* (Mexico, 1962), Acta, 1: 493–506.

—— AND C. E. ROZAIRE

1960 Mound 13, Chiapa de Corzo, Chiapas, Mexico. *Papers New World Archaeol. Found.*, no. 10.

HIGBEE, E.

1947 The agricultural regions of Guatemala. *Geog. Rev.*, 37: 177–201.

HILDEBRAND, S. F.

1925 Fishes of the Republic of El Salvador. U.S. Bur. Fisheries, Bull. 41, pp. 237–87.

1938 A new catalogue of the fresh-water fishes of Panama. *Field Mus. Nat. Hist., Zool. Ser.*, 22: 219–359.

HILL, A. F.
1952 Economic botany. 2d ed. New York.

HILL, R. T.
1898 The geological history of the Isthmus of Panama and portions of Costa Rica. *Bull. Mus. Comp. Zool., Harvard Univ.*, 28: 151–285.

HILTON, K.
1948 Raramuri oseríame: cuentos de los Tarahumaras. Summer Inst. Ling. Mexico.

HINSHAW, R.
1966 Structure and stability of belief in Panajachel. Doctoral dissertation, Univ. Chicago.

HINTON, T. B.
1955 A survey of archaeological sites in the Altar valley, Sonora. *Kiva*, 21 (1, 2): 1–12.
1955 The Seri girls' puberty rite at Desemboque, Sonora. *Kiva*, vol. 20, no. 4.
1959 A survey of Indian assimilation in eastern Sonora. *Univ. Arizona, Anthr. Papers*, no. 4.
1961 The village hierarchy as a factor in Cora Indian acculturation. Doctoral dissertation, Univ. California, Los Angeles.
1964 The Cora village: a civil-religious hierarchy in northern Mexico. *In* Culture change and stability: essays in memory of Olive Ruth Barker and George C. Barker, Jr., pp. 44–62. Univ. California, Los Angeles.

—— AND R. C. OWEN
1957 Some surviving Yuman groups in northern Baja California. *Amer. Indig.*, 17: 87–102.

HIRTZEL, J. S. H.
1930 Le manteau de plumes dit de "Montezuma" des Musées Royaux du Cinquantenaire de Bruxelles. *23d Int. Cong. Amer.* (New York, 1928), Acta, pp. 649–51.

HISSINK, K.
1934 Masken als fassadenschmuk. *Akad. Abh. Kulturgeschichte*, vol. 3, no. 2.

HISTORIA DE LOS MEXICANOS POR SUS PINTURAS
1941 Historia de los Mexicanos por sus pinturas. *In* García Icazbalceta, 1941, 3: 207–40.

1965 *Idem. In* Garibay K., 1965, Teogonía, pp. 23–90.

HISTORIA TOLTECA-CHICHIMECA
1937–38 Die mexikanische Bilderhandschrift Historia Tolteca-Chichimeca. Die Manuskripte 46–58bis der Nationalbibliothek in Paris. K. T. Preuss and E. Mengin, eds. and trans. *Baessler-Archiv*, 20, Beiheft 9, 21: 1–66. Berlin.
1942 Historia Tolteca-Chichimeca. E. Mengin, ed. *Corpus Codicum Americanorum Medii Aevi*, 1. Copenhagen.
1947 Historia Tolteca-Chichimeca: anales de Quauhtinchan. H. Berlin in collaboration with S. Rendón, eds. Prologue by P. Kirchhoff. *Fuentes para la Historia de México*, 1. Mexico.

HISTOYRE DU MECHIQUE
1905 Histoyre du Mechique: manuscrit français inédit du XVIe siècle. E. de Jonghe, ed. *Jour. Soc. Amer. Paris*, n.s., 2: 1–41.
1961 Histoyre du Mechique. Retraducción del francés al castellano por Joaquín Meade, con notas de W. Jiménez Moreno. *Mem. Acad. Mex. Hist.*, 20: 183–210.
1965 *Idem. In* Garibay K., 1965, Teogonía, pp. 91–120. (Spanish trans.)

HO, PING-TI
1955 The introduction of American food plants into China. *Amer. Anthr.*, 57: 191–201.

HOCKETT, C. F.
1947 Componential analysis of Sierra Popoluca. *Int. Jour. Amer. Ling.*, 13: 258–67.
1955 A manual of phonology. *Indiana Univ. Pub. Anthr. Ling.*, Memoir 11.

HODGMAN, C. D.
1948 Handbook of chemistry and physics. 13th ed. Cleveland.

HOENIGSWALD, H. M.
1960 Language change and linguistic reconstruction. Chicago.

HOFFSTETTER, R., AND OTHERS
1960 Lexique stratigraphique international. Vol. 5: Amérique Latine. Paris.

HOHENTHAL, W. D.

1951 The mountain tribes of northern Baja California, Mexico. MS.

1960 The Tipai and their neighbors of northern Baja California, Mexico. MS.

HOIJER, H.

1948 Linguistic and cultural change. *Language*, 24: 335–45.

1954 The Sapir-Whorf hypothesis. *In* Language in culture, *Amer. Anthr. Assoc.*, Memoir 79.

1956 Language and writing. *In* Man, culture, and society, H. L. Shapiro, ed., pp. 196–223.

—— AND OTHERS

1946 Linguistic structures of native America. *Viking Fund Pub. Anthr.*, no. 6.

HOLDEN, J.

1957 The postclassic stage in Mesoamerica. *Papers Kroeber Anthr. Soc.*, no. 17, pp. 75–108.

HOLDEN, W. C., AND OTHERS

1936 Studies of the Yaqui Indians of Sonora, Mexico. *Texas Tech. College Bull.*, vol. 12, no. 1.

HOLDRIDGE, L. R.

1947 Determination of world formations from simple climatic data. *Science*, 105 (2727): 367–68.

1956 Middle America. *In* Haden-Guest, Wright, and Teclaf, 1956, pp. 183–200.

HOLLAND, W. R.

1959 Dialect variations of the Mixtec and Cuicatec areas of Oaxaca, Mexico. *Anthr. Ling.*, 1 (8): 25–31.

1961 Relaciones entre la religión tzotzil contemporánea y la maya antigua. *An. Inst. Nac. Antr. Hist.*, 13: 113–31.

1961 El tonalismo y el nagualismo entre los tzotziles. *Estud. Cultura Maya*, 1: 167–81.

1963 Medicina maya en los altos de Chiapas: un estudio del cambio sociocultural. *Inst. Nac. Indig., Col. Antr. Social*, no. 2.

1963 Psicoterapia maya en los altos de Chiapas. *Estud. Cultura Maya*, 3: 261–77.

1965 Contemporary Tzotzil cosmological concepts as a basis for interpreting prehistoric Maya civilization. *Amer. Antiquity*, 29: 301–06.

—— AND R. G. THARP

1964 Highland Maya psychotherapy. *Amer. Anthr.*, 66: 41–52.

HOLLERAN, M. P.

1949 Church and state in Guatemala. New York.

HOLMAN, C. A.

1953 A new rare human blood group antigen (Wrᵃ). *Lancet*, 2: 119–20.

HOLMES, R. W., AND M. BLACKBURN

1960 Physical, chemical, and biological observations in the eastern tropical Pacific Ocean Scot Expedition, April–June 1958. *U.S. Fish and Wildlife Service, Spec. Sci. Rept.—Fisheries*, no. 345.

HOLMES, W. H.

1887 The use of gold and other metals among the ancient inhabitants of Chiriqui, Isthmus of Darien. *Smithsonian Inst., Bur. Amer. Ethnol.*, Bull. 3.

1888 Ancient art of the province of Chiriqui. *Ibid.*, 6th ann. rept., pp. 13–187.

1895–97 Archaeological studies among the ancient cities of Mexico. *Field Columbian Mus., Anthr. Ser.*, vol. 1, no. 1.

1903 Aboriginal pottery of the eastern United States. *Smithsonian Inst., Bur. Amer. Ethnol.*, 20th ann. rept.

1907 On a nephrite statuette from San Andres Tuxtla, Vera Cruz, Mexico. *Amer. Anthr.*, 9: 691–701.

1916 Masterpieces of aboriginal American art. IV: Sculpture in the round. *Art and Archaeol.*, 3: 71–85. Washington.

1919 Handbook of aboriginal American antiquities. Part 1: The lithic industries. *Smithsonian Inst., Bur. Amer. Ethnol.*, Bull. 60.

HOLMES ANNIVERSARY VOLUME

1916 Anthropological essays presented to William Henry Holmes in honor of his seventieth birthday. Washington.

HOLZKAMPER, F. M.
1956 Artifacts from Estero de Tastiota, Sonora. *Kiva*, 21 (3, 4): 12–19.

HOMENAJES:
Beyer *See* Beyer, 1965 and 1969.
Boas *See* Boas Anniversary Volume, 1906.
Caso
1951 Homenaje al doctor Alfonso Caso. Juan Comas and others, eds. Nuevo Mundo. Mexico.
Colón
1892 Códice Dehesa. Homenaje a Cristóbal Colón. Antigüedades mexicanas, publicadas por la Junta Colombina de México en el cuarto centenario del descubrimiento de América. Secretaria de Fomento. Mexico.
Comas
1965 Homenaje a Juan Comas en su 65 aniversario. 2 vols. Mexico.
Cummings *See* For the Dean, 1950.
Gamio *See* Estudios antropológicos, 1956.
García Granados
1960 Homenaje a Rafael García Granados. Inst. Nac. Antr. Hist. Mexico.
Hewett *See* So Live the Works of Men, 1939.
Holmes *See* Holmes Anniversary Volume, 1916.
Kroeber *See* Essays in Anthropology, 1936.
Márquez Miranda
1964 Homenaje a Fernando Márquez Miranda. Madrid and Seville.
Martínez del Río
1961 Homenaje a Pablo Martínez del Río en el XXV aniversario de la primera edición de Los Orígenes Americanos. Inst. Nac. Antr. Hist. Mexico.
Putnam *See* Putnam Anniversary Volume, 1909.
Radin
1960 Culture in history: essays in honor of Paul Radin. S. Diamond, ed. New York.
Rivet *See* Miscelánea Paul Rivet, 1958.
Stephens *See* Los Mayas antiguos, 1941.
Termer
1959 Amerikanistische Miszellen. Festband Franz Termer. W. Bierhenke, W. Haberland, U. Johansen, and G. Zimmermann, eds. *Mitteilungen aus*

HOMENAJES—*continued*
dem Museum für Völkerkunde in Hamburg, no. 25.
Townsend
1961 A William Cameron Townsend en el vigésimoquinto aniversario del Instituto Lingüístico del Verano. B. F. Elson, ed. Mexico.
Tozzer *See* The Maya and their Neighbors, 1940.
Wallis
1954 Method and perspective in anthropology: papers in honor of Wilson D. Wallis. R. F. Spencer, ed.
Weitlaner *See* Summa anthropologica, 1966.
Zavala *See* Estudios históricos americanos, 1953.

HOOGSHAGEN, S. A.
1959 Notes on the sacred (narcotic) mushroom from Coatlan, Oaxaca, Mexico. *Bull. Oklahoma Anthr. Soc.*, 7: 71–74.
1960 Elección, instalación y aseguramiento de los funcionarios en Coatlan. *Rev. Mex. Estud. Anthr.*, 16: 247–55.
—— AND W. R. MERRIFIELD
1961 Coatlan Mixe kinship. *SW. Jour. Anthr.*, 17: 219–25.

HOOPER, E. T.
1952 A systematic review of the harvest mice (genus *Reithrodontomys*) of Latin America. *Univ. Michigan, Mus. Zool.*, Misc. Pub. 77.

HOOTON, E. A.
1930 The Indians of Pecos pueblo: a study of their skeletal remains. Yale Univ. Press.
1940 Skeletons from the Cenote of Sacrifice at Chichen Itza. *In* The Maya and their neighbors, pp. 272–80.
1946 Up from the ape. New York.

HOOVER, J. W.
1935 Generic descent of the Papago villages. *Amer. Anthr.*, 37: 445–64.

HOPKINS, D. M.
1959 Cenozoic history of the Bering land bridge. *Science*, 129: 1519–28.

HOPKINS, N. A.
1962 A phonology of Zinacantan Tzotzil. Master's thesis, Univ. Texas. *Also in* McQuown, 1962.

1962 A short sketch of Chalchihuitan Tzotzil. *In* McQuown, 1962.

HOPPE, W. A.
1960 Field notes. MS. Mexico.
1961 Field notes. MS. Mexico.

HORCASITAS PIMENTEL, F.
1949 Piezas teatrales en lengua Náhuatl: bibliografía descriptiva. *Bol. Bibliográfico Antr. Amer.*, 11: 154–64.

HOSELITZ, B., ed.
1952 The progress of underdeveloped areas. Chicago.

HOSTOS, A. DE
1948 The ethnography of Puerto Rico. *In* Handbook of South American Indians, 4: 540–42.

HOTCHKISS, J.
1959 A summary of Chanal, Teopisca and San Bartolome. Working paper. Chicago.
1960–61 Field notes of Teopisca. MS, Chiapas Project files. Univ. Chicago, Dept. Anthropology.

HOUGH, W.
1923 Casas Grandes pottery in the National Museum. *Art and Archaeol.*, 16: 34.

HOUSEHOLDER, F. W., JR.
1960 First thoughts on syntactic indices. *Int. Jour. Amer. Ling.*, 26: 195–97.

HOVANITZ, W.
1958 Distribution of butterflies in the New World. *Zoogeography, Amer. Assoc. Advancement Sci.*, Pub. 51, pp. 321–68.

HOVEY, E. O.
1905 The western Sierra Madre of the state of Chihuahua. *Bull. Amer. Geog. Soc.*, 37: 531.
1907 A geological reconnaissance in the western Sierra Madre of the state of Chihuahua. *Amer. Mus. Nat. Hist.*, Bull. 23, pp. 401–42.

HOWARD, A. M.
1957 Navacoyan: a preliminary survey. *Bull. Texas Archaeol. Soc.*, 28: 181–89.

HOWELLS, W. W.
1936 Some uses of the standard deviation in anthropometry. *Human Biol.*, 8: 592.
1937 The designation of the principal anthropometric landmarks on the head and skull. *Amer. Jour. Physical Anthr.*, 22: 477–94.

HOWENSTINE, W.
1963 Lecture. Chicago Teachers' College North. MS.

HOYT, E. E.
1951 Want development in undeveloped areas (Guatemala). *Jour. Polit. Econ.*, 59: 194–202.
1955 El trabajador indígena en las fincas cafeteleras de Guatemala. *Cien. Sociales*, 6 (35): 258–68.

HRDLIČKA, A.
1898 Report on skeletal remains. *In* McGee, 1898, pp. 140–47.
1899 Description of an ancient anomalous skeleton from the Valley of Mexico, with special reference to supernumerary and bicipital ribs in man. *Amer. Mus. Nat. Hist.*, Bull. 12, pp. 81–107.
1899 An anomalous ulna, supra-capital foramen. *Amer. Anthr.*, 1: 246–50.
1901 A painted skeleton from northern Mexico, with notes on bone painting among the American aborigines. *Ibid.*, 3: 701–25.
1902 The Aztecs of yesterday and today. *Harpers Monthly Mag.* (December), pp. 35–42.
1902 Anthropological work in the southwestern United States and northern Mexico. *Jour. Amer. Mus. Natural Hist.*, 2 (7): 68–72.
1902 Particularidades anatómicas de los cráneos otomíes: rectificación al trabajo del señor doctor F. Hernández. *Crónica Méd. Mex.*, 5: 72–75.
1903 Descripción de un antiguo esqueleto humano anormal del Valle de México. *An. Mus. Nac. Méx.*, ep. 1, 7: 75–92.
1903 The Chichimec and their ancient culture, with notes on the Tepecanos and the ruin of La Quemada, Mexico. *Amer. Anthr.*, 5: 385–440.
1904 Notes on the Indians of Sonora, Mexico. *Ibid.*, 6: 51–89.
1904 Cora dances. *Ibid.*, 6: 744–45.
1905 A Cora cradle. *Ibid.*, 7: 361–62.
1905 Diseases of the Indians, more especially of the southwestern United

States and northern Mexico. *Washington Med. Ann.*, 4: 372–94.

1906 Contribution to the physical anthropology of California. *Univ. California Pub. Amer. Archaeol. Ethnol.*, 4: 49–64.

1907 Skeletal remains suggesting or attributed to early man in North America. *Smithsonian Inst., Bur. Amer. Ethnol.*, Bull. 33.

1908 Physiological and medical observations among the Indians of southwestern United States and northern Mexico. *Ibid.*, Bull. 34.

1909 On the stature of the Indians of the Southwest and northern Mexico. *In* Putnam Anniversary Vol., pp. 405–26.

1912 The natives of Kharga Oasis, Egypt. *Smithsonian Misc. Coll.*, 59: 1–118.

1912 An ancient sepulchre at San Juan Teotihuacan, with anthropological notes on the Teotihuacan people. *17th Int. Cong. Amer.* (Mexico, 1910), Acta, pp. 3–7.

1916 Physical anthropology of the Lenape or Delawares and of the eastern Indians in general. *Smithsonian Inst., Bur. Amer. Ethnol.*, Bull. 62.

1918 Physical anthropology: its scope and aims, its history and present status in America. *Amer. Jour. Physical Anthr.*, 1: 133–82, 267–303, 377–414.

1920 Anthropometry. Wistar Inst. Anatomy and Biology. Philadelphia.

1924 Catalogue of human crania in the United States National Museum collections. *Smithsonian Inst., U.S. Nat. Mus., Proc. U.S.*, vol. 63, art. 12.

1926 The Indians of Panama: their physical relations to the Maya. *Amer. Jour. Physical Anthr.*, 9: 1–15.

1927 Catalogue of human crania in the United States National Museum collections: the Algonkin and related Iroquois, Siouan, Caddoan, Salish and Sahaptin, Shoshonean, and California Indians. *Smithsonian Inst., U.S. Nat. Mus., Proc. U.S.*, vol. 69, art. 5.

1932 The humerus: septal apertures. *Anthropologie*, 1: 31–96. Prague.

1935 The Pueblos, with comparative data on the bulk of the tribes of the Southwest and northern Mexico. *Amer. Jour. Physical Anthr.*, 20: 235–460.

1935 Ear exostoses. *Smithsonian Misc. Coll.*, vol. 93, no. 6.

—— AND C. LUMHOLTZ

1898 Marked human bones from a prehistoric Tarasco Indian burial place in the state of Michoacan. *Bull. Amer. Mus. Natural Hist.*, 10: 61–79.

HUASTECOS, TOTONACOS

1953 Huastecos, Totonacos y sus vecinos. I. Bernal and E. Dávalos Hurtado, eds. *Rev. Mex. Estud. Antr.*, vol. 13, nos. 2 and 3.

HUBBS, CARL L.

1948 Changes in the fish fauna of western North America correlated with changes in ocean temperatures. *Jour. Marine Research*, 7: 459–82.

1952 Antitropical distribution of fishes and other organisms. *In* Symposium on problems of bipolarity and of pan-temperate faunas. *Proc. 7th Pacific Sci. Cong.*, 3: 324–29.

1958 Recent climatic history in California and adjacent areas. Proc. Conference on Recent Research in Climatology, Scripps Inst. Oceanogr. Comm. on Research in Water Resources, Univ. California, pp. 10–22.

1960 Quaternary paleoclimatology of the Pacific coast of North America. *Repts. California Coop. Oceanic Fish. Invest.*, 7: 105–12.

1960 The biogeography of Baja California and adjacent seas. Part 2: The marine vertebrates of the outer coast. *Syst. Zool.*, 9: 134–47.

——, G. S. BIEN, AND H. E. SUESS

1960 La Jolla natural radiocarbon measurements I. *Amer. Jour. Sci., Radiocarbon Suppl.*, 2: 197–223.

1962 La Jolla natural radiocarbon measurements II. *Radiocarbon*, 4: 204–38.

1963 La Jolla natural radiocarbon measurements III. *Radiocarbon*, 5: 254–72.

—— AND L. C. HUBBS

1960 Shoreline surface-temperature data between La Jolla, California, and Punta Baja, Baja California. *In* Surface water temperatures at shore stations. U.S. west coast and Baja California, 1956–59. SIO Reference 60–27, 15 Sept. 1960, pp. 78–95.

1961 *Idem,* 1960. SIO Reference 61–14, 28 Apr. 1961, pp. 38–43.

1962 *Idem,* 1961. SIO Reference 62–11, 2 Apr. 1962, pp. 36–41.

1963 *Idem,* 1962. SIO Reference 63–17, 17 June 1963, pp. 34–39.

HUBBS, CLARK
1952 A contribution to the classification of the blennioid fishes of the family Clinidae, with a partial revision of the eastern Pacific forms. *Stanford Ichth. Bull.,* 4: 41–165.

1953 Revision of the eastern Pacific fishes of the clinid genus *Labrisomus. Zoologica,* 38: 113–36.

HUGHES, A. E.
1935 The beginnings of Spanish settlement in the El Paso district. *Univ. California Pub. Hist.,* vol. 1, no. 3.

HUGHES, J. T.
1947 An archaeological reconnaissance in Tamaulipas, Mexico. *Amer. Antiquity,* 13: 33–39.

HUGHES, L. H.
1950 The Mexican cultural mission programme. *Monogr. Fundamental Education,* no. 3. UNESCO, Paris.

HULSE, F. S.
1945 Skeletal material from the excavations at Culiacan, Sinaloa. *In* Kelly, 1945, pp. 187–98.

1955 Blood types and mating patterns among northwest coast Indians. *SW. Jour. Anthr.,* 11: 93–104.

1957 Linguistic barriers to gene flow: the blood groups of the Yakima, Okanagon and Swinomish Indians. *Amer. Jour. Physical Anthr.,* 15: 235–46.

1960 Adaptation, selection and plasticity in ongoing human evolution. *Human Biol.,* 32: 63–79.

HUMBOLDT, A. VON
1810 Vues de cordillères et monuments des peuples indigènes de l'Amérique. Paris. (Other eds. 1814, 1816.)

1811 Essai politique sur le royaume de la Nouvelle-Espagne. 5 vols. Paris.

1814 Researches concerning the institutions and monuments of the ancient inhabitants of America. Tr. by H. M. Williams of his 1810. London.

1856 Lettre à Mr. Morris. *Froriep's Notizen aus dem Gebiete der Natur- und Heilkunde,* 2: 102–03.

HUMPHREY, W. E.
1956 Tectonic framework of northeast Mexico. *Trans. Gulf Coast Assoc. Geol. Soc.,* 6: 26–35.

HUMPHREYS, E. W.
1916 *Sphenozamites rogersianus* Fontaine, an addition to the Rhaetic flora of San Juancito, Honduras. *Jour. New York Bot. Garden,* 17: 52–58.

HUNT, A.
1960 Archeology of the Death Valley salt pan, California. *Univ. Utah, Anthr. Papers,* no. 47.

HUNT, M. E.
1962 The dynamics of the domestic group in two Tzeltal villages: a contrastive comparison. Doctoral dissertation, Univ. Chicago.

1963 The family and domestic group in the highlands of Chiapas. MS, Chiapas Project files. Univ. Chicago, Dept. Anthropology.

HUNTER, W. A.
1960 The Calderonian auto sacramental *El gran teatro del mundo:* an edition and translation of a Nahuatl version. *Tulane Univ., Middle Amer. Research Inst.,* Pub. 27, pp. 105–202.

HURD, W. E.
1929 Tropical cyclones in the eastern north Pacific. *Monthly Weather Rev.,* 57: 43–49.

1929 Northers in the Gulf of Tehuantepec. *Ibid.,* 57: 192–94.

HURTARTE, A. E., AND N. S. SCRIMSHAW
1955 Dental findings in a nutritional study of school children in five Guatemalan highland villages. *Jour. Dental Research,* 34: 390–96.

HUTCHINS, L. W.
1947 The bases for temperature zonation in geographical distribution. *Ecol. Monogr.,* 17: 325–35.

HUTCHINSON, J. B., R. A. SILOW, AND S. G. STEPHENS
1947 The evolution of Gossypium and the differentiation of the cultivated cottons. London.

HVIDTFELDT, A.
1958 Teotl and Ixiptlatli: some central conceptions in ancient Mexican religion. Copenhagen.

HYMAN, L. H., ed.
1960 Symposium: the biogeography of Baja California and adjacent areas. Part 3: Terrestrial and fresh-water biotas. *Syst. Zool.*, 9: 47–232.

HYMES, D. H.
1958 Linguistic features peculiar to Chinookan myths. *Int. Jour. Amer. Ling.*, 24: 253–57.
1959 Genetic classification: retrospect and prospect. *Anthr. Ling.*, 1 (2): 50–66.
1960 Lexicostatistics so far. *Current Anthr.*, 1: 3–44.

IBARRA, A.
1941 Cuentos y leyendas. Mexico.
1942 Juegos y deportes en México. *Anuario Soc. Folklórica Mex.* (1938–40), 1: 41–49.

IBARRA GRASSO, D. E.
1958 Lenguas indígenas americanas. Buenos Aires.

ICAZA, F. A. DE
1928 Miscelánea histórica. *Bib. Rev. Mex. Estud. Hist.*, 2: 15.

ICAZA, I. L. DE, AND I. R. GONDRA
1827 Colección de antigüedades mexicanas que existen en el Museo Nacional. Litografiadas por Federico Waldeck e impresas por Pedro Robert. Mexico. (Facsimile ed. 1927.)

IGLESIAS, A.
1856 Soteapan. *In* M. Orozco y Berra, ed., Apéndice al diccionario universal de historia y de geografía, 3: 433–38.

IGLESIAS, J. M.
1831 Los departamentos de Acayucan y Jalapa. Cuaderno segundo, Estadística del estado libre y soberano de Veracruz.

IKIN, E. A., AND E. A. MOURANT
1951 A rare blood group antigen occurring in Negroes. *British Med. Jour.*, 1: 456–57.

IMBELLONI, J.
1938 Tabla classificatoria de los Indios. *Physis* (*Rev. Soc. Argentina Cien. Naturales*), 12: 229–49.
1950 Cephalic deformations of the Indians of Argentina. *In* Handbook of South American Indians, 6: 53–55.
1953 Le genti indigene dell'America. *In* Le razze e i popoli della terra, R. Biasutti, ed., 4: 307–30. 2d ed.

IMENDIA, C. A.
1951 Del folklore salvadoreño: la canoa blanca. *An. Mus. Nac. David J. Guzmán*, 2 (8): 89–91. San Salvador.

IMLAY, R. W.
1939 Possible interoceanic connection across Mexico during the Jurassic and Cretaceous periods. *Proc. 6th Pacific Sci. Cong., Geophys. and Geol.*, pp. 423–27.
1943 Jurassic formations of the gulf region. *Bull. Amer. Assoc. Petroleum Geol.*, 27: 1407–1533.
1944 Correlation of Cretaceous formations of the Greater Antilles, Central America and Mexico. *Bull. Geol. Soc. Amer.*, 55: 1005–45.
1944 Cretaceous formations of Central America and Mexico. *Bull. Amer. Assoc. Petroleum Geol.*, 28: 1077–98.
1952 Correlation of the Jurassic formations of North America, exclusive of Canada. *Bull. Geol. Soc. Amer.*, 63: 953–62.

INDIANIST YEARBOOK
1962 Indians in the hemisphere today: Guatemala. Guide to the Indian population. *Inter-Amer. Indian Inst.*, vol. 22. Mexico.

INFORMANTES DE SAHAGÚN
See Codex Matritense, 1907.

INFORME DE LOS PADRES
1697 Informe de los padres misioneros Fray Francisco de San Joseph y Fray Pablo de Rebullida. Talamanca. *Archivos Nacionales*, doc. 5226. San Jose, Costa Rica.

INSTITUTO DE INVESTIGACIONES SOCIALES
1957 Etnografía de México. Mexico.

INSTITUTO DE NUTRICIÓN DE CENTRO AMÉRICA
Y PANAMÁ
1955 Recomendaciones nutricionales diarias
para las poblaciones de Centro América y Panamá. *Bol. Oficina Sanitaria
Panamer.*, suppl. 2, pp. 225–26.
1960 [Unpublished data.]

INSTITUTO INDIGENISTA INTERAMERICANO
1958 Recientes datos estadísticos sobre la
población de América. *Bol. Indig.*,
18: 6–7. Mexico.
1960 Guatemala: informe del Instituto Indigenista Nacional, 1959. *Ibid.*, 20:
119–32.

INSTITUTO INDIGENISTA NACIONAL (GUATE-
MALA)
1948 Chuarrancho. *Special publications,
Inst. Indig. Nac.*, no. 2.
1948 San Juan Sacatepequez. *Ibid.*, no.
3.
1948 Chinautla. *Ibid.*, no. 4.
1948 Parramos. *Ibid.*, no. 5.
1948 San Antonio Aguas Calientes. *Ibid.*,
no. 6.
1948 Santa Catarina Barahona. *Ibid.*, no.
7.
1949 Santo Domingo Xenacoj. *Ibid.*, no.
8.
1949 San Bartolomé Milpas Altas. *Ibid.*,
no. 9.

INSTITUTO INTERAMERICANO DE ESTADÍSTICA,
UNIÓN PANAMERICANA
1960 La estructura demográfica de las
naciones americanas. *País de naci-
miento, nacionalidad y lengua, características generales de la población*,
1: 3. Washington.

INSTITUTO NACIONAL DE ANTROPOLOGÍA E
HISTORIA
1946 Pre-Hispanic art of Mexico. Mexico.
1956 Guía oficial: Museo Nacional de Antropología. Mexico. (Another ed.
1967.)

INSTITUTO NACIONAL INDIGENISTA (MEXICO)
n.d. Memoirs, no. 1.
n.d. La deuda del sol, y otros cuentos.
Nuestros Cuentos, no. 1.
n.d. El muchacho en la cueva, y otros
cuentos. *Ibid.*, no. 2.

n.d. La casa de los tigres, y otros cuentos.
Ibid., no. 3.
1950 Densidad de la población de habla
indígena en la República Mexicana
(por entidades federativas y municipio, conforme al censo de 1940).
Prologo de A. Caso. Introducción de
M. G. Parra. *Mem. Inst. Nac.
Indig.*, vol. 1, no. 1.
1955 ¿Que es el I.N.I.?

INSTITUTO NACIONAL INDIGENISTA
(NICARAGUA)
1947 *Nicaragua Indígena*, vol. 1, nos. 4–6.
Managua.

INTEGRACIÓN SOCIAL
1956 Integración social en Guatemala.
Seminario de Integración Social.
Guatemala.

INTERNATIONAL LABOR OFFICE
1953 Indigenous peoples. Geneva.

INVENTARIO DE ASUNTOS PENALES
1953–63 Inventario de asuntos penales.
Archivos del distrito de Villa Alta.

IRRIGATION CIVILIZATIONS
1955 *See* Steward, 1955.

IRWIN, H. J., AND C. C. IRWIN
1959 Excavations at the Lodaiska site in
the Denver, Colorado, area. *Proc.
Denver Mus. Nat. Hist.*, no. 8.

ISLAS, L.
1912 El hogar del indio zapoteca. *Bol.
Mus. Nac.*, 2: 4–10. Mexico.

ITURBIDE, J., AND C. E. GUZMÁN
1953 Consideraciones sobre el tétanos ne-
onatorum. *Rev. Colegio Méd. Guatemala*, 4: 237–39.

ITURRIBARRÍA, J. F.
1941 Historia de Oaxaca. Mexico.
1955 Oaxaca en la historia: de la época
precolombina a los tiempos actuales.
Mexico.
1960 Yagul: mestizo product of Mixtecs
and Zapotecs. *Bol. Estud. Oaxaqueños*, no. 17.

IVES, R. L.
1935 Recent volcanism in northwestern
Mexico. *Pan-Amer. Geol.*, 63: 335–
38.
1963 The problem of the Sonoral littoral
cultures. *Kiva*, 28 (3): 28–32.
1963 The bell of San Marcelo. *Ibid.*, 29
(1): 14–22.

IXTLILXOCHITL, F. DE A.
See Alva Ixtlilxochitl, F. de.

IZIL, CHILAM BALAM DE
n.d. Manuscript. Photograph in Newberry Library. 85 pp.

IZQUIERDO, J. J.
1922 Estudio fisiológico del indígena adul-
to del valle de Teotihuacán. *In*
Gamio, 1922, 2: 167–86.
1922–28 Contribución a la fisiología de la
respiración en las altitudes; el gasto
respiratorio máximo. *Mem. Soc.
Cien. Antonio Alzate,* 41: 109–49;
49: 37–60.

IZUMI, S., AND T. SONO
1963 Andes 2: excavations at Kotosh, Peru.
Univ. Tokyo Exped. to the Andes,
1960. Tokyo.

JACKS, G. V.
1954 Multilingual vocabulary of soil
science. Food and Agriculture Organization of the United Nations.

JACKSON, R. L., AND H. G. KELLY
1945 Growth charts for use in pediatric
practice. *Jour. Pediatrics,* 27: 215–
29.

JACOBS-MÜLLER, E. F.
See Müller, E. F. J.

JAEGER, E. C.
1957 The North American deserts. Stanford.

JAEGER, F.
1926 Forschungen über das Diluviale
Klima in Mexiko. *Petermanns Mitt.,*
Ergänzungsheft 190. Gotha.

JAKEMAN, M. W.
1947 The ancient Middle American calendar system: its origin and development. *Brigham Young Univ., Pub.
Archaeol. and Hist.,* no. 1.

JAMES, P. E., AND C. F. JONES, eds.
1954 American geography: inventory and
prospect. Syracuse Univ. Press.

JANSE, O. R. T.
1947 Archaeological research in Indo-
China. Vol. 1.

JANTZ, R. L.
1968 Fingerprint dermatoglyphics of the
Cashinahua Indians. *Amer. Jour.
Physical Anthr.,* 29: 122, abstract 7.

JAUREGUI, S.
1948 Estudio del izote (*Yucca elephan-*

tipes) como planta auxiliar. *Café
de El Salvador* (April), pp. 277–91.

JAYASWAL, K. P.
1933 Metal images of Kurkihar monastery.
Jour. Indian Soc. Oriental Art, vol. 1.
Calcutta.

JELKS, E. B., E. M. DAVIS, AND H. B. STURGIS
1960 A review of Texas archaeology.
Bull. Texas Archaeol. Soc., vol. 29
(for 1958).

JENKINS, J.
1946 San Gregorio, an Otomi village of the
highlands of Hidalgo, Mexico. *Amer.
Indig.,* 6: 345–49.

JENKINS, K. D.
1964 Aje or ni-in (the fat of a scale insect): painting medium and unguent.
35th Int. Cong. Amer. (Mexico,
1962), Acta, 1: 625–36.
1967 Lacquer. *In* Handbook of Middle
American Indians, R. Wauchope, ed.,
vol. 6, art. 7.

JENNINGS, J. D.
1956 [ed.] The American Southwest: a
problem in cultural isolation. *In*
Wauchope, 1956, pp. 59–127.
1957 Danger Cave. *Mem. Soc. Amer.
Archaeol.,* no. 14.

—— AND G. NEUMANN
1940 A variation of Southwestern Pueblo
culture: analysis of the skeletal
material. *Lab. Anthr., Tech. Ser.,*
Bull. 10. Santa Fe.

—— AND E. NORBECK, eds.
1964 Prehistoric man in the New World.
Univ. Chicago Press.

—— AND E. K. REED
See Wauchope, 1956.

JIJÓN Y CAAMAÑO, J.
1914 Contribución al conocimiento de los
aborígenes de la provincia de Imba-
bura. *Estud. Prehist. Amer.,* II.
Madrid.
1930 Una gran marea cultural en el N. O.
de Sud America. *Jour. Soc. Amer.
Paris,* 22: 107–97.
1938 Sebastian de Benalcazar. Vol. 2.
Editorial Ecuatoriana. Quito.
1951 Antropología prehispánica del Ecuador, 1945. Quito.

JIMÉNEZ, T. F.
1957 El monolito de Cayagunca. *An.*

Mus. Nac. David J. Guzmán, 7: 11–17. El Salvador.

JIMÉNEZ MORENO, W.

1937 Materiales para una bibliografía etnográfica de la América Latina. *Bol. Bibliog. Antr. Amer.,* vol. 1, nos. 1 and 2. Mexico.

1939 Origen y significación del nombre "Otomí." *Rev. Mex. Estud. Antr.,* 3: 62–68.

1941 Tula y los Toltecas según las fuentes históricas. *Ibid.,* 5: 79–83.

1942 El enigma de los olmecas. *Cuad. Amer.,* 5: 113–45.

1942 Fr. Juan de Córdova y la lengua zapoteca. Mexico.

1944 Tribus e idiomas del norte de México. *In* El Norte de México, pp. 121–23.

1945 Introducción. *In* Ruz Lhuillier, 1945, pp. 7–18.

1948 Historia antigua de la zona tarasca. *In* El Occidente de México, pp. 146–57.

1953 Historia antigua de México. Mimeographed. Soc. Alumnos de la Escuela Nac. Antr. Hist. Mexico. (2d ed. 1956.)

1953 Cronología de la historia de Veracruz. *In* Huastecos, Totonacos, pp. 311–13.

1954–55 Síntesis de la historia precolonial del Valle de México. *Rev. Mex. Estud. Antr.,* 14: 219–36.

1956 La conquista: choque y fusión de dos mundos. *Hist. Mex.,* 6: 1–8. Mexico.

1958 The Indians of America and Christianity. *In* History of religion in the New World, *Americas,* 14 (4): 75–95.

1959 Síntesis de la historia pretolteca de Mesoamérica. *In* Esplendor del México antiguo, 2: 1019–1108.

1962 Etimología de toponímicos mixtecos. *In* F. de Alvarado, Vocabulario en lengua mixteca, 1593. Facsimile ed. Mexico.

1962 La historiografía Tetzcocana y sus problemas. *Rev. Mex. Estud. Antr.,* 19: 81–86.

1966 Mesoamerica before the Toltecs. *In* Paddock, 1966, Ancient Oaxaca, pp. 1–82.

—— AND S. MATEOS HIGUERA

1940 Códice de Yanhuitlán. *Inst. Nac. Antr. Hist.* Mexico.

JIMÉNEZ RUEDA, J.

1950 Historia de la cultura en México: el virrienato. Ediciones cultura. Mexico. (2d ed. 1951.)

JOHANNESSEN, C. L.

1957 Man's role in the distribution of the corozo palm (*Orbignya* spp.). *Yearbook Assoc. Pacific Coast Geog.,* 19: 29–33.

1959 The geography of the savannas of interior Honduras. Univ. California, Dept. Geography.

1963 Savannas of interior Honduras. *Ibero-Amer.,* no. 46.

JOHNSON, A. E.

1960 The place of the Trincheras culture of northern Sonora in Southwestern archaeology. M. A. thesis, Univ. Arizona.

1963 The Trincheras culture of northern Sonora. *Amer. Antiquity,* 29: 174–86.

JOHNSON, A. S.

1958 Similarities in Hohokam and Chalchihuites artifacts. *Amer. Antiquity,* 24: 126–30.

JOHNSON, F.

1940 The linguistic map of Mexico and Central America. *In* The Maya and their neighbors, pp. 88–114.

1951 [ed.] Radiocarbon dating. *Mem. Soc. Amer. Archaeol.,* no. 8.

JOHNSON, I. W.

n.d. Tejidos de la Cueva de La Candelaria, Coahuila. MS.

1936 A Chinantec calendar. *Amer. Anthr.,* 38: 197–201.

1953 El quechquemitl y el huipil. *In* Huastecos, Totonacos, pp. 241–57.

1954 Chiptic cave textiles from Chiapas, Mexico. *Jour. Soc. Amer. Paris,* 43: 137–47.

1956 Análisis de un tejido de Tlatelolco. Tlatelolco a través de los tiempos, no. 12. *Mem. Acad. Mex. Hist.,* 15: 127–28.

1957 Survival of feather ornamented huipiles in Chiapas, Mexico. *Jour. Soc. Amer. Paris,* n.s., 46: 189–96.

1957 An analysis of some textile fragments from Yagul. *Mesoamer. Notes*, 5: 77–81. Mexico City College, Dept. Anthropology.

1958 Twine-plaiting in the New World. *32d Int. Cong. Amer.* (Copenhagen, 1956), Acta, pp. 198–213.

1958–59 Un antiguo huipil de ofrenda decorado con pintura. *Rev. Mex. Estud. Antr.*, 15: 115–22.

1959 Hilado y tejido. *In* Esplendor del México antiguo, 1: 439–78.

1960 Un tzotzopaztli antiguo de la región de Tehuacán. *An. Inst. Nac. Antr. Hist.*, 11: 75–85.

1964 Copper preserved textiles from Michoacan and Guerrero. *35th Int. Cong. Amer.* (Mexico, 1962), Acta, 1: 525–36.

1966 Análisis textil del Lienzo de Ocotepec. *In* Pompa y Pompa, pp. 139–44.

1966–67 Miniature garments found in Mixteca Alta caves, Mexico. *Folk*, 8–9: 179–90. Copenhagen.

1967 Textiles. *In* The prehistory of the Tehuacan Valley, 2: 189–226.

1970 A painted cloth from Tenancingo, Mexico. Paper presented to 35th annual meeting, Society for American Archaeology, Mexico, 1970.

1970 Textiles. *In* Minería prehispánica en la sierra de Querétaro, pp. 37–44. Sec. Patrimonio Nacional. Mexico.

—— AND J. L. FRANCO C.
1967 Un *huipilli* precolombino de Chilapa, Guerrero. *Rev. Mex. Estud. Antr.*, 21: 149–89.

—— AND J. B. JOHNSON
1939 Un cuento mazateco popoloca. *Ibid.*, 3: 217–26.

JOHNSON, J. B.
1939 The elements of Mazatec witchcraft. *Ethnol. Studies*, 9: 128–50. Göteborg.

1939 Oaxaca market. [San Lucas, Zoquiapan.] *SW. Rev.*, 24: 333.

1939 Some notes on the Mazatec. *Rev. Mex. Estud. Antr.*, 3: 142–56.

1940 Three Mexican tar baby stories. *Jour. Amer. Folklore*, 53: 215–17.

1943 A clear case of linguistic acculturation. *Amer. Anthr.*, 45: 427–34.

1950 The Opata: an inland tribe of Sonora. *Univ. New Mexico Pub. Anthr.*, no. 6.

JOHNSON, L.
1960 Preliminary pollen analysis of Damp and Centipede rockshelters. *In* Epstein, 1960, Centipede and Damp caves, pp. 167–73.

JONES, C. L.
1940 Guatemala, past and present. Univ. Minnesota Press.

JONES, J.
1963 Bibliography for Olmec sculpture. Mus. Primitive Art. *Primitive Art Bibliographies*, no. 2. New York.

1964 Sculpture from Mexico in the collection of the Museum of Primitive Art. Mus. Primitive Art. New York.

JONES, M. R.
1952 Map of the ruins of Mayapan, Yucatan, Mexico. *Carnegie Inst. Wash., Current Reports*, no. 1.

JONES, V. H., AND R. L. FONNER
1954 Plant materials from the Durango area. *In* E. H. Morris and R. F. Burgh, Basket Maker II sites near Durango, Colorado, pp. 93–115. *Carnegie Inst. Wash.*, Pub. 604.

JORDAN, D. S., AND B. W. EVERMANN
1896–1900 The fishes of North and Middle America. 4 vols. *Smithsonian Inst., U.S. Nat. Mus.*, Bull. 47.

JOSEPH, A., R. B. SPICER, AND J. CHESKY
1949 The desert people: a study of the Papago Indians. Univ. Chicago Press.

JOURDANET, D.
1861 Les altitudes de l'Amérique tropical comparées au niveau des mers au point de vue de la constitution médicale. Paris.

JOYCE, T. A.
1912 A short guide to the American antiquities in the British Museum. London.

1916 Central American and West Indian archaeology. London.

1920 Mexican archaeology. London and New York.

1926 Report on the investigations at Lubaantun, British Honduras, in 1926. *Jour. Royal Anthr. Inst.*, 56: 207–30.

1927 Maya and Mexican art. London.

1929 Report on the British Museum expedition to British Honduras. *Jour. Royal Anthr. Inst.*, 59: 439–59.

1933 The pottery whistle-figurines of Lubaantun. *Ibid.*, 63: xv–xxv.

——, J. Cooper-Clark, and J. E. S. Thompson

1927 Report on the British Museum expedition to British Honduras, 1927. *Ibid.*, 57: 295–323.

Juárez, T., and P. Valentín

1554 Tiburcio Juárez y Pedro Valentín, sobre tierras, 1554. MS. Archivo General de la Nación, ramo de Tierras, 13, exped. 4. Mexico.

Juarros, D.

1823 A statistical and commercial history of the kingdom of Guatemala in Spanish America. Tr. by J. Baily. London.

Judd, N. M.

1954 The material culture of Pueblo Bonito. *Smithsonian Misc. Coll.*, vol. 123.

Junqueira, P. C., and P. J. Wishart

1956 Blood groups of Brazilian Indians (Carajas). *Nature*, 177: 40. London.

—— and others (P. J. Wishart, F. Ottensooser, R. Pasqualin, P. L. Fernandes, and H. Kalmus)

1956 The Diego blood factor in Brazilian Indians. *Ibid.*, 177:41.

Kamar Al-Shimas

1922 The Mexican southland. Fowler, Indiana.

Kamer, Aga-Oglu

1955 Late Ming and early Ch'ing porcelain fragments from archaeological sites in Florida. *Florida Anthr.*, 8: 91–110.

Kaplan, B. A.

1951 Changing functions of the Hunancha dance at the Corpus Christi festival in Paracho, Michoacan, Mexico. *Jour. Amer. Folklore*, 64: 383–92.

1953 Technological and social change: Paracho, a case in point. Doctoral dissertation, Univ. Chicago.

1954 Environment and human plasticity. *Amer. Anthr.*, 56: 780–800.

1960 Mechanization in Paracho, a craft community. *In* Leslie, 1960, Social anthropology, pp. 59–65.

Kaplan, L., and R. S. MacNeish

1960 Prehistoric bean remains from caves in the Ocampo region of Tamaulipas, Mexico. *Bot. Mus. Leafl., Harvard Univ.*, 19: 33–56.

Kate, H. F. C. ten

See ten Kate, H. F. C.

Katz, F.

1956 Die sozialökonomischen Verhältnisse bei den Azteken im 15. und 16. Jahrhundert. *Ethnographische-archäologische Forschungen*, vol. 3, part 2. Berlin.

1958 The evolution of Aztec society. *Past and Present*, 13: 14–25. London.

1966 Situación social e económica de los aztecas durante los siglos XV y XVI. Univ. Nac. Mexico.

Kaufman, T. S.

1961 Tzeltal grammar code. Mimeographed. Stanford Univ., Anthr. Research Center. *Also in* McQuown, 1962.

1962 A sketch of Tenejapa Tzeltal syntax. *In* McQuown, 1962.

Kean, B. H.

1944 The blood pressure of the Cuna Indians. *Amer. Jour. Tropical Med.*, 24: 341–43.

Keane, H. A.

1908 Veytia's "Calendarios mexicanos." *Atheneum*, 1: 193–94. London.

Keen, E. N.

1953 Estimation of stature from the long bones: a discussion of its reliability. *Jour. Forensic Med.*, 1: 46–51.

Keith, H. H.

1924 Racial differences in the papillary lines of the palm. *Amer. Jour. Physical Anthr.*, 7: 165–206.

Kelemen, P.

1939 Pre-Columbian jades. *Parnassus*, 11 (4): 4–10.

1943 Medieval American art. 2 vols. New York. (2d ed. 1956, 3d ed. 1969.)

Keller, J. H.

1955 The atlatl in North America. *Indiana Hist. Soc., Prehist. Research Ser.*, vol. 3, no. 3.

KELLER, K., AND M. HARRIS
1946 Masculine crab and mosquitoes. *Tlalocan*, 2: 138–40.

KELLEY, D. H.
1955 Quetzalcoatl and his coyote origins. *El Mexico Antiguo*, 8: 397–413.
1960 Calendar animals and deities. *SW. Jour. Anthr.*, 16: 317–37.

KELLEY, J. C.
1947 The cultural affiliations and chronological position of the Clear Fork focus. *Amer. Antiquity*, 13: 97–109.
1952 Some geographic and cultural factors involved in Mexican-southeastern contacts. *In* Tax, 1952, Indian tribes, pp. 139–44.
1953 Reconnaissance and excavation in Durango and southern Chihuahua, Mexico. *Amer. Phil. Soc.*, Year Book (1953), pp. 172–76. Philadelphia.
1955 Juan Sabeata and diffusion in aboriginal Texas. *Amer. Anthr.*, 57: 981–95.
1956 Settlement patterns in north central Mexico. *In* Willey, 1956, Prehistoric settlement patterns, pp. 128–39.
1957 North Mexico and the correlation of Mesoamerican and Southwestern cultural sequences. MS.
1959 The desert cultures and the Balcones phase: archaic manifestations in the Southwest and Texas. *Amer. Antiquity*, 24: 276–88.
1960 North Mexico and the correlation of Mesoamerican and Southwestern cultural sequences. *In* Wallace, 1960, pp. 566–73.
1963 Northern frontier of Mesoamerica. First ann. rept., Aug. 15, 1961–Aug. 15, 1962. A report of research under the auspices of the National Science Foundation (Grant 18586) and the University Museum and Mesoamerican Cooperative Research Program of the Southern Illinois University. Carbondale.
1966 Mesoamerica and the southwestern United States. *In* Handbook of Middle American Indians, R. Wauchope, ed., vol. 4, art. 5.

—— AND E. ABBOTT
1966 The cultural sequence on the north central frontier of Mesoamerica. *36th Int. Cong. Amer.* (Seville, 1964), Acta, 1: 326–37.

——, T. N. CAMPBELL, AND D. J. LEHMER
1940 The association of archaeological materials with geological deposits in the Big Bend region of Texas. *West Texas Hist. and Sci. Soc.*, no. 10.

—— AND W. J. SHACKELFORD
1954 Preliminary notes on the Weicker site, Durango, Mexico. *El Palacio*, 61: 145–50. Santa Fe.

—— AND H. D. WINTERS
1958 Graphic survey of work at the Schroeder site (LCAJI-I), Durango, Mexico. MS.
1960 A revision of the archaeological sequence in Sinaloa, Mexico. *Amer. Antiquity*, 25: 547–61.

KELLOGG, C. E.
1949 The soils that support us. New York.
1949 Special issue of *Soil Science* (vol. 67, no. 2) devoted to soil classification.

KELLY, I. T.
1938 Excavations at Chametla, Sinaloa. *Ibero-Amer.*, no. 14.
1941 The relationship between Tula and Sinaloa. *Rev. Mex. Estud. Antr.*, 5: 199–207.
1943 Notes on a west coast survival of the ancient Mexican ball game. *Carnegie Inst. Wash., Notes Middle Amer. Archaeol. Ethnol.*, no. 26.
1944 Worked gourds from Jalisco. *Ibid.*, no. 43.
1944 West Mexico and the Hohokam. *In* El Norte de México, pp. 206–22.
1945 Excavations at Culiacan, Sinaloa. *Ibero-Amer.*, no. 25.
1945 The archaeology of the Autlan-Tuxcacuesco area of Jalisco. I: The Autlan zone. *Ibid.*, no. 26.
1945 Report on grant for study and analysis of a large collection of potsherds gathered during extensive surveys in the Sayula basin of west central Mexico. *Amer. Phil. Soc.*, Year Book (1944), pp. 209–12.
1947 An archaeological reconnaissance of the west coast: Nayarit to Michoacan.

27th Int. Cong. Amer. (Mexico, 1939), Acta, 2: 74–77.

1947 Excavations at Apatzingan, Michoacan. *Viking Fund. Pub. Anthr.*, no. 7.

1948 Ceramic provinces of northwestern Mexico. *In* El Occidente de México, pp. 55–71.

1949 The archaeology of the Autlan-Tuxcacuesco area of Jalisco. II: The Tuxcacuesco-Zapotitlan zone. *Ibero-Amer.*, no. 27.

1953 The modern Totonac. *In* Huastecos, Totonacos, pp. 175–86.

1965 Folk practices in north Mexico. *Inst. Latin Amer. Studies, Latin Amer. Monogr.*, no. 2.

1966 World view of a highland Totonac pueblo. *In* Pompa y Pompa, 1966, pp. 395–411.

—— AND B. BRANIFF DE TORRES
1966 Una relación cerámica entre occidente y la mesa central. *Bol. Inst. Nac. Antr. Hist.*, 23: 26–27.

—— AND A. PALERM
1952 The Tajin Totonac. Part 1: History, subsistence, shelter and technology. *Smithsonian Inst., Inst. Social Anthr.*, Pub. 13.

KELLY, W. H.
1942 Cocopa gentes. *Amer. Anthr.*, 44: 675–91.

1944 A preliminary study of the Cocopa Indians, with an analysis of the influence of geographical position and physical environment on certain aspects of the culture. Doctoral dissertation, Harvard Univ.

1949 Cocopa attitudes and practices with respect to death and mourning. *SW. Jour. Anthr.*, 5: 151–64.

KELMAN, H.
1958 Compliance, identification and internalization: three processes of attitude change. *Jour. Conflict Resolution*, 2: 51–60.

KEMPTON, J. H.
1935 Preliminary report of the agricultural survey of Yucatan of 1935. Mimeographed. Carnegie Inst. Wash.

KENT, K. P.
1957 The cultivation and weaving of cotton in the prehistoric southwestern United States. *Trans. Amer. Phil. Soc.*, n.s., 47: 457–732.

KERR, R.
1814 A general history and collection of voyages and travels. Edinburgh.

KEY, H.
1952–53 Algunas observaciones preliminares de la distribución dialectal de náhuatl en el área Hidalgo-Veracruz-Puebla. *Rev. Mex. Estud. Antr.*, 13: 131–43.

1960 Stem construction and affixation of Sierra Nahuat verbs. *Int. Jour. Amer. Ling.*, 26: 130–45.

—— AND M. KEY
1953 The phonemes of Sierra Nahuat. *Ibid.*, 19: 53–56.

KIDDER, II, A.
1949 Mexican stone yokes. *Bull. Fogg Mus. Art.*, 11: 3–10. Cambridge, Mass.

—— AND C. SAMAYOA CHINCHILLA
1959 The art of the ancient Maya. New York.

KIDDER, A. V.
1916 The pottery of the Casas Grandes district, Chihuahua. *In* Holmes Anniversary Volume, pp. 253–68.

1924 An introduction to the study of Southwestern archaeology. *Phillips Acad., Dept. Archaeol., Papers SW. Expedition*, no. 1.

1935 Notes on the ruins of San Agustin Acasaguastlan, Guatemala. *Carnegie Inst. Wash.*, Pub. 456, Contrib. 15.

1939 Notes on the archaeology of the Babicora district, Chihuahua. *In* Brand and Harvey, 1939, pp. 221–32.

1940 Clay heads from Chiapas, Mexico. *Carnegie Inst. Wash., Notes on Middle Amer. Archaeol. Ethnol.*, no. 1.

1942 Archaeological specimens from Yucatan and Guatemala. *Ibid.*, no. 9.

1943 Grooved stone axes from Central America. *Ibid.*, no. 29.

1945 Excavations at Kaminaljuyu, Guatemala. *Amer. Antiquity*, 11: 65–75.

1947 The artifacts of Uaxactun, Guatemala. *Carnegie Inst. Wash.*, Pub. 576.

1948 Kaminaljuyu, Guatemala: addenda and corrigenda. *Carnegie Inst.*

122

Wash., Notes on Middle Amer. Archaeol. Ethnol., no. 89.

1949 Jades from Guatemala. *Ibid.*, no. 91.

1949 Certain archaeological specimens from Guatemala, I. *Ibid.*, no. 92.

1950 Certain archaeological specimens from Guatemala, II. *Ibid.*, no. 95.

1954 Miscellaneous archaeological specimens from Mesoamerica. *Ibid.*, no. 117.

1961 Archaeological investigations at Kaminaljuyu, Guatemala. *Proc. Amer. Phil. Soc.*, 105: 559–70.

——, AND H. S. AND C. B. COSGROVE

1949 The Pendleton ruin, Hidalgo County, New Mexico. *Carnegie Inst. Wash.*, Pub. 585, Contrib. 50.

—— AND G. F. EKHOLM

1951 Some archaeological specimens from Pomona, British Honduras. *Carnegie Inst. Wash., Notes on Middle Amer. Archaeol. Ethnol.*, no. 102.

——, J. D. JENNINGS, AND E. M. SHOOK

1946 Excavations at Kaminaljuyu, Guatemala. With technological notes by A. O. Shepard. *Carnegie Inst. Wash.*, Pub. 561.

—— AND A. O. SHEPARD

1944 Stucco decoration of early Guatemala pottery. *Carnegie Inst. Wash., Notes on Middle Amer. Archaeol. Ethnol.*, no. 35.

—— AND E. M. SHOOK

1946 "Rim-head" vessels from Kaminaljuyu, Guatemala. *Ibid.*, no. 69.

1959 A unique ancient Maya sweathouse, Guatemala. *In* Bierhenke, 1959, pp. 70–74.

1961 A possibly unique type of formative figurine from Guatemala. *In* Lothrop and others, 1961, pp. 176–81.

KIDDLE, L. B.

1944 The Spanish word *jícara*: a word history with an appendix on the manufacture of *jícaras* in Olinala, Guerrero. *Tulane Univ., Middle Amer. Research Inst., Philol. and Doc. Studies*, vol. 1, no. 4.

KING, A. R.

1952 Changing cultural goals and patterns in Guatemala. *Amer. Anthr.*, 54: 139–42.

1955 Archaeological remains from the Cintalapa region, Chiapas, Mexico. *Tulane Univ., Middle Amer. Research Rec.*, vol. 2, no. 4.

KING, E.

See Kingsborough, Lord.

KINGSBOROUGH, LORD [EDWARD KING]

1831–48 Antiquities of Mexico, comprising facsimiles of ancient Mexican paintings and hieroglyphics. 9 vols. London.

1964 Antigüedades de México, basadas en la recopilación de Lord Kingsborough. Palabras preliminares, Antonio Ortiz Mena. Prólogo, Agustín Yáñez. Estudio e interpretación, José Corona Núñez. 2 vols. Sec. Hacienda y Crédito Público. Mexico.

KINNAIRD, L., ed.

1958 The frontiers of New Spain: Nicolas de LaFora's description 1766–1768. *Quivira Soc. Pub.*, 13: 98–99.

KINO, E. F.

1913–22 Las misiones de Sonora y Arizona, comprendiendo la crónica titulada "Favores celestiales" y la "Relación diaria de la entrada al noroeste." *Archivo General de la Nación*, Pub. 8.

KIRCHHOFF, P.

1940 Los pueblos de la Historia Tolteca-Chichimeca: sus migraciones y parentesco. *Rev. Mex. Antr. Hist.*, 4: 77–104.

1942 Las tribas de la Baja California y el libro de Padre Baegert. *In* Baegert, 1942.

1943 Mesoamérica: sus límites geográficas, composición étnica y caracteres culturales. *Acta Amer.*, 1: 92–107.

1944 Los recolectores-cazadores del norte de México. *In* El Norte de México, pp. 133–44.

1946 Cronología de la historia precolombina de México. *In* Vivó, 1946, pp. 99–108.

1946 El papel de México en la América precolombina. *Ibid.*, pp. 82–90.

1946 La cultura del occidente de México a través de su arte. *In* Arte Precolombino del Occidente de México, pp. 49–69.

1948 Etnografía antigua. *In* El Occidente de México, pp. 134–36.

1954 Gatherers and farmers in the greater Southwest: a problem in classification. *Amer. Anthr.*, 56:529–61.

1954–55 Calendarios Tenochca, Tlatelolca y otros. *Rev. Mex. Estud. Antr.*, 14: 257–67.

1955 Quetzalcoatl, Huemac y el fin de Tula. *Cuad. Amer.*, 14: 163–96.

1955 The principles of clanship in human society. *Davidson Jour. Anthr.*, 1: 1–10.

1956 Land tenure in ancient Mexico: a preliminary sketch. *Rev. Mex. Estud. Antr.*, 14: 351–61.

1956 La relación de Michoacán como fuente para la historia de la sociedad y cultura Tarascas. *In* Relación de las ceremonias y ritos y población y gobierno de los Indios de la provincia de Michoacan (1541). Madrid.

1956 Composición étnica y organización política de Chalco según las relaciones de Chimalpahin. *Rev. Mex. Estud. Antr.*, 14: 297–302.

1961 Das Toltekenreich und sein Untergang. *Saeculum*, 12: 248–65.

1961 ¿Se puede localizer Aztlán? *Univ. Nac. Autónoma Méx., Anuario Hist.*, año 1, pp. 59–73.

1964 La aportación de Chimalpahin a la historia tolteca. *An. Antr.*, 1: 77–90.

1964 The diffusion of a great religious system from India to Mexico. *35th Int. Cong. Amer.* (Mexico, 1962), Acta, 1: 73–100.

KIRSTEIN, L.
1935 Dance: a short history of classical theatrical dancing. New York.

KLAUSNER, S. Z.
1955 Phonetics, personality and status in Israel. *Word*, 11: 209–15.

KLINEBERG, O.
1934 Notes on the Huichol. *Amer. Anthr.*, 36: 446–60.
1952 Raza y psicología: la cuestión racial ante la ciencia. UNESCO, Paris.

KLUCKHOHN, F. R., AND F. L. STRODTBECK
1961 Variations in value orientations. New York.

KNAUTH, L.
1961 El juego de pelota y el rito de la decapitación. *Univ. Nac. Autónoma Mex., Estud. Cultura Maya*, 1: 183–98.

KNOROZOV, Y. V.
1952 Drevnyaya Pis'menost Tsentralnoy Ameriki [The ancient script of Central America]. *Sovietskaya Etnografiya*, no. 3, pp. 100–18. Moscow.
1955 La escritura de los antiguos Mayas (ensayo de descrifado). In Russian and Spanish. Inst. Etnografi Akad. Nauk. Moscow.
1958 The problem of the study of the Maya hieroglyphic writing. *Amer. Antiquity*, 23: 284–91.
1958 New data on the Maya written language. *32d Int. Cong. Amer.* (Copenhagen, 1956), Acta, pp. 467–75.

KOEPPEN, W.
1900 Versuch einer Klassifikation der Klimat, vorzugsweise nach ihren Beziehungen zur Pflanzenwelt. *Geog. Zeit.*, 6: 593–611, 657–79. Leipzig.
1948 Climatología. Mexico.
—— AND R. GEIGER, eds.
1930–39 Handbuch der Klimatologie. 4 vols. Berlin.

KOHL, J. G.
1863 Aelteste Geschichte der Entdeckung und Erforschung des Golf von Mexiko und der ihn umgebenden Küsten durch die Spanier von 1492 bis 1543. *Zeit. für Allegemeine Erdkunde*, 15: 1–40, 169–94. Berlin.

KOPPERS, W.
1957 Das Problem der Universalgeschichte im Lichte von Ethnologie und Prähistorie. *Anthropos*, 52: 369–89.

KOVAR, P. A.
1945 Idea general de la vegetación de El Salvador. *In* Verdoorn, 1945, pp. 56–57.

KRAMER, F. L.
1957 The pepper tree, *Schinus molle*. *Economic Botany*, 11: 322–26.

KRAUSE, R.
1855 Bericht ueber zwei Schaedel aus Totonicapan. *Alt-Mexiko archaeolo-*

gische Beitrage zur Kulturgeschichte seiner Bewohner, pp. 101–06. Hamburg and Leipzig.

KRETZENBACHER, L.

1952 Folk songs in the folk plays of the Austrian alpine regions. *Jour. Int. Folk Music Council*, 4: 45–49. London.

KRICKEBERG, W.

1918–25 Die Totonaken: ein Beitrag zur historischen Ethnographie Mittelamerikas. *Baesseler Archiv*, 7: 1–55; 9: 1–75.

1933 Los Totonaca. Tr. from the German by Porfirio Aguirre. *Pub. Mus. Nac.* Mexico.

1948 Das mittelamerikanische Ballspiel und seine religiöse Symbolik. *Paideuma, Mitteilungen zur Kultur-Kunde*, 3 (3–5): 118–90.

1949 Felsplastik und Felsbilder bei den Kulturvölkern Altamerikas mit besonderer Beruck sichtigung Mexikos. I: Die Andenlander. II: Die Felsentempel in Mexiko. Berlin.

1950 Ostasien-Amerika: Bemerkungen eines Amerikanisten zu zwei Büchern Carl Hentzes. *Sinologica*, 2: 195–233. Basel.

1956 Altmexikanische Kulturen. Berlin. (2d ed. 1966.)

1958 Bermerkungen zu den Skulpturen und Felsbildern von Cozumalhuapa. *In* Misc. Paul Rivet, 1: 495–513.

1960 Altmexikanischer Felsbilder. *Tribus*, 9: 172–84.

1961 Die Religionen der Kulturvölker Mesoamerikas. Die Religionen des Alten Amerika (Religionen der Menschheit, 7), pp. 1–89. Stuttgart.

1961 Las antiguas culturas mexicanas. Mexico. (Spanish trans. of his 1956; 2d ed. 1964.)

1966 Altmexikanische Kulturen (mit einem Anhang über die Kunst Altmexikos von G. Kutscher). Berlin. (2d ed. of his 1956.)

1968 Felsplastik und Felsbilder bei den kulturvölken Altamerikas Band II: Felsbilder Mexikos als historische, religiöse und Kunstdenkmäler. Aus dem Nachlass herausgegeben von K.

Hahn-Hissink, M.-B. Franke und D. Eisleb. Berlin.

1968 Mesoamerica. *In* Pre-Columbian American religions, pp. 5–82. London. (English trans. of his 1961, Die Religionen.)

KRIEGER, A. D.

1945 An inquiry into supposed Mexican influence on a prehistoric "cult" in the southern United States. *Amer. Anthr.*, 47: 483–515.

1950 *Review of* De Terra, Romero, and Stewart, Tepexpan Man. *Amer. Antiquity*, 15: 343–49.

1951 Notes and news: early man. *Ibid.*, 17: 77–78.

1951 Stephenson's "Culture chronology in Texas." *Ibid.*, 16: 265–67.

1953 New World culture history: Anglo-America. *In* Kroeber, 1953, pp. 238–64.

1953 Recent developments in the problem of relationships between Mexican gulf coast and eastern United States. *In* Huastecos, Totonacos, pp. 497–518.

1956 Some Mexican figurine heads in Texas. *Bull. Texas Archaeol. Soc.*, 27: 258–65.

—— AND J. T. HUGHES

1950 Archaeological salvage in the Falcon reservoir area: progress report no. 1. Mimeographed. Austin.

KRMPOTIC, M. D.

1923 The life and works of the Reverend Ferdinand Konscak, S. J. Boston.

KROEBER, A. L.

1915 Serian, Tequistlatecan and Hokan. *Univ. California Pub. Amer. Archaeol. Ethnol.*, 11: 279–90.

1925 Archaic culture horizons in the Valley of Mexico. *Ibid.*, 17: 373–408.

1925 Handbook of the Indians of California. *Smithsonian Inst., Bur. Amer. Ethnol.*, Bull. 78.

1931 The Seri. *SW. Mus. Papers*, no. 6.

1932 The Patwin and their neighbors. *Univ. California Pub. Amer. Archaeol. Ethnol.*, 29: 253–423.

1934 Uto-Aztecan languages of Mexico. *Ibero-Amer.*, no. 8.

1939 The cultural and natural areas of native North America. *Univ. Cali-*

fornia Pub. Amer. Archaeol. Ethnol., vol. 38. (2d ed. 1958.)

1939–44 The historical position of Chicomuceltec in Maya. *Int. Jour. Amer. Ling.*, 10: 159–60.

1940 Language history and culture history. *In* The Maya and their neighbors, pp. 463–70.

1940 Conclusions: The present status of Americanistic problems. *Ibid.*, pp. 460–87.

1948 Anthropology. New York.

1952 The nature of culture. Univ. Chicago Press.

1953 [ed.] Anthropology today. Chicago.

1960 Statistics, Indo-European, and taxonomy. *Language*, 36: 1–21.

1960 On typological indices I: ranking of languages. *Int. Jour. Amer. Ling.*, 26: 171–77.

—— AND C. D. CHRÉTIEN

1937 Quantitative classification of Indo-European languages. *Language*, 13: 83–103.

KRYNINE, P. D.

1935 Arkose deposits in the humid tropics: a study of sedimentation in southern Mexico. *Amer. Jour. Sci.*, 229: 353–63.

KUBLER, G.

1942 Population movements in Mexico, 1520–1600. *Hispanic Amer. Hist. Rev.*, 22: 606–43.

1943 The cycle of life and death in metropolitan Aztec culture. *Gazette des Beaux Arts*, 23: 257–68. New York.

1948 *Review of* The population of central Mexico in the sixteenth century, by S. F. Cook and L. B. Simpson. *Hispanic Amer. Hist. Rev.*, 28: 556–59.

1948 Mexican architecture of the sixteenth century. 2 vols. Yale Univ. Press.

1954 The Louise and Walter Arensberg collection: pre-Columbian sculpture. Mus. Art. Philadelphia.

1958 The design of space in Maya architecture. *In* Misc. Paul Rivet, 1: 515–31.

1961 Chichen-Itza y Tula. *Estud. Cultura Maya*, 1: 47–80.

1962 The art and architecture of ancient America: the Mexican, Maya, and Andean peoples. Penguin Books.

1967 The iconography of the art of Teotihuacan: the pre-Columbian collection, Dumbarton Oaks. *Studies in Pre-Columbian Art and Archaeol.*, no. 4. Washington.

—— AND C. GIBSON

1951 The Tovar calendar. *Mem. Connecticut Acad. Arts and Sci.*, vol. 11. New Haven.

KULP, J. L., H. W. FEELY, AND L. E. TRYON

1951 Lamont natural radiocarbon measurements, I. *Science*, 114: 565–68.

KUNST, J.

1915 Some animal fables of the Chuh Indians. *Jour. Amer. Folklore*, 28: 353–57.

KUNZ, G. F.

1907 Gems and precious stones of Mexico. *In* Compt rendu, 10th sess., Cong. Geol. Int. Mexico.

KURATH, G. P.

1946 Los Concheros. *Jour. Amer. Folklore*, 59: 387–99.

1947 Los arrieros of Acopilco, Mexico. *Western Folklore*, 6: 232–36.

1949 Mexican moriscas. *Jour. Amer. Folklore*, 62: 87–106.

1950 Penitentes. *In* Standard dictionary of folklore, mythology, and legend, M. Leach, ed., 2: 851–52.

1952 Dance acculturation. *In* Tax, 1952, Heritage, pp. 233–42.

1956 Dance relatives of mid-Europe and Middle America. *Jour. Amer. Folklore*, 69: 286–98.

1958 La transculturación en la danza hispano-americana. *Folklore Amer.*, 18 (2): 17–25. Coral Gables.

1960 The sena'asom rattle of the Yaqui Indian pascolas. *Ethnomusicology*, 4: 60–62.

1963 Stylistic blends in Afro-American dance cults of Catholic origin. *Papers Michigan Acad. Sci. Arts Letters*, 18: 577–84.

—— AND S. MARTÍ

1964 Dances of Anahuac. *Viking Fund. Pub. Anthr.*, no. 38.

KURATH, W., AND E. H. SPICER

1947 A brief introduction to Yaqui, a native language of Sonora. *Univ. Arizona Social Sci. Bull.*, no. 15.

KURTZ, E. B., H. TUCKER, AND J. L. LIVERMAN
1960 Reliability of identification of fossil pollen as corn. *Amer. Antiquity*, 25: 605–06.

KUTSCHER, G.
1958 *Introduction to* Präkolumbische Kunst aus Mexiko und Mittelamerika. Munich.

LADD, J.
1957 A stratigraphic trench at Sitio Conte, Panama. *Amer. Antiquity*, 22: 265–71.

LaFARGE, O.
1927 Adaptations of Christianity among the Jacalteca Indians of Guatemala. *Thought*, December. New York.
1927 Comparative wordlists: Yocotan, Chontal, Tzeltal, Chaneabal, Jacalteca. *In* Blom and LaFarge, Tribes and temples, 2: 487–98. *Tulane Univ., Middle Amer. Research Inst.*, Pub. 1.
1930 The ceremonial year at Jacaltenango. *23d Int. Cong. Amer.* (New York, 1928), Acta, pp. 656–60.
1931 Post-Columbian dates and the Maya correlation problem. *Maya Research*, 1: 109–24.
1940 Maya ethnology: the sequence of cultures. *In* The Maya and their neighbors, pp. 281–91.
1947 Santa Eulalia: the religion of a Cuchumatan Indian town. Univ. Chicago Press.

—— AND D. BYERS
1931 The year bearer's people. *Tulane Univ., Middle Amer. Research Inst.*, Pub. 3.
1931 The Jacalteca language. *In* preceding entry, pp. 244–366.

LA GRASSERIE, R. DE
1896 Langue tarasque. *Bibliothèque Linguistique Amer.*, vol. 19. Paris.
1898 Langue zoque et langue mixe. Paris.

LAGUNAS, J. P. DE
1574 Arte y diccionario tarascos. Mexico. (Morelia, 1890.)

LAHEY, M. E., M. BÉHAR, F. VITERI, AND N. S. SCRIMSHAW
1958 Values for copper, iron and iron-binding capacity in the serum in kwashiorkor. *Pediatrics*, 22: 72–79.

LAMB, S. M.
1958 Linguistic prehistory in the Great Basin. *Int. Jour. Amer. Ling.*, 24: 95–100.
1959 Some proposals for linguistic taxonomy. *Anthr. Ling.*, 1: 33–49.

LAMBERT, J. C., ed.
1961 Mexique précolombien. *Art et Style*, Pub. 2. Paris.

LAMBRECHTS, A., AND K. HOLEMANS
1958 Le problème du phosphore et du calcium en zone rural. *Ann. Soc. Belge Med. Tropical*, 38: 459.

LANDA, DIEGO DE
1864 Relación de las cosas de Yucatan. C. E. Brasseur de Bourbourg, ed. Paris.
1938 *Idem.* Pérez Martinez, ed. Merida.
1941 *Idem.* Tr. and ed. with notes by A. M. Tozzer. *Papers Peabody Mus., Harvard Univ.*, vol. 18.
1959 *Idem.* Intro. por A. M. Garibay K., con un apéndice en el que se publican varios documentos importantes y cartas del autor. 8th ed., Porrúa. Mexico.

LANDA, E.
1910 El índice cefálico de los niños recién nacidos. *Mem. IV Cong. Méd. Nac.*, pp. 505–08. Mexico.
1912 Contribución al estudio de la forma de la cabeza en los niños recién nacidos. *Gaceta Méd. Méx.*, 7: 41–47.

LANDERO, P. A. DE
1922 Rocas y minerales del valle: canteras. *In* Gamio, 1922, 2: 67–79.

LANDSTEINER, K., AND P. LEVINE
1929 On the racial distribution of some agglutinable structures of human blood. *Jour. Immunology*, 16: 123–31.

——, A. S. WIENER, AND G. A. MATSON
1942 Distribution of the Rh factor in American Indians. *Jour. Experimental Med.*, 76: 73–78.

LANKS, H. C.
1938 Otomi Indians, Mezquital Valley, Hidalgo. *Econ. Geog.*, 14: 184–94.

LANNING, E. P.

1960 Cerámica antigua de la costa peruana: nuevos descubrimientos. (2d
ed., rev.) Inst. Andean Studies.
Berkeley.

1960 Chronological and cultural relation-
ships of early pottery styles in ancient
Peru. Doctoral dissertation, Univ.
California.

1961 Cerámica pintada pre-Chavin de la
costa central del Peru. *Rev. Mus.
Nac.*, 30: 78–83. Lima.

1963 Olmec and Chavin: reply to Michael
D. Coe. *Amer. Antiquity*, 29: 99–
101.

LARDÉ Y LARÍN, J.

1952 Guía histórica de El Salvador. *Biblioteca de Pueblo*, no. 13. San Salvador.

1953 La población de El Salvador: su
origen y su distribución geográfica.
An. Mus. Nac. David J. Guzmán,
vol. 4, no. 12. San Salvador.

LARSEN, A. E.

1936 Variation of cosmopolitan diseases in
tropical and temperate zones. *Amer.
Jour. Tropical Med.*, 16: 91–100.

LARSEN, H.

1937 The Mexican Indian flying pole
dance. *Nat. Geog.*, 71: 387–400.

LARSON, K.

1949 Huasteco baby talk. *El Mex. Antiguo*, 7: 295–98.

LARSON, R.

1953 Procliticos pronominales del dialecto
huasteco que se habla en el estado de
San Luis Potosí. *In* Huastecos,
Totonacos, pp. 117–18.

LAS CASAS, B. DE

n.d. Historia de las Indias. Apéndice
apologética historia. Aguilar, ed.
Madrid.

1875–76 Historia de las Indias. Col. doc.
inéditos para la historia de España.
5 vols. Madrid.

1909 Apologética historia de las Indias.
Nueva Biblioteca Autores Españoles,
no. 13. M. Serrano y Sanz, ed. Madrid.

1951 Historia de las Indias. Millares
Carlo, ed. Mexico.

1967 Apologética historia sumaria. 2 vols.

Inst. Invest. Hist., Univ. Nac. Autónoma Méx.

LASKER, G. W.

1952 An anthropometric study of returned
Mexican emigrants. *29th Int. Cong.
Amer.* (New York, 1949), Acta, 3:
242–46.

1952 Environmental growth factors and se-
lective migration. *Human Biol.*, 24:
262–89.

1953 The age factor in bodily measurements of adult male and female Mexicans. *Ibid.*, 25: 50–63.

1954 Human evolution in contemporary
communities. *SW. Jour. Anthr.*, 10:
353–65.

1954 Photoelectric measurement of skin
color in a Mexican Mestizo population. *Amer. Jour. Physical Anthr.*,
n.s., 12: 115–21.

1954 The question of physical selection of
Mexican migrants to the U.S.A. *Human Biol.*, 26: 52–58.

LATHRAP, D. W.

1957 The classic stage in Mesoamerica.
Papers Kroeber Anthr. Soc., 17: 38–
74.

1958 The cultural sequence at Yarinacocha,
eastern Peru. *Amer. Antiquity*, 23:
379–88.

1960 *Review of* Cultura Valdivia, by
Evans, Meggers, and Estrada. *Ibid.*,
26: 125–27.

1962 Yarinacocha, stratigraphic excavations in the Peruvian montaña.
Doctoral dissertation, Harvard Univ.

1963 Los Andes centrales y la montaña.
Rev. Mus. Nac., 32: 197–202.
Lima.

1965 Origins of central Andean civilization: new evidence. *Review of*
Izumi and Sono, 1963. *Science*,
148: 796–98.

LAUER, W.

1956 Vegetation, Landnutzung und Agrar-
potential in El Salvador (Zentralamerika). *Schriften Geog. Inst. Univ.
Kiel*, no. 16.

1959 Klimatische und pflanzengeograph-
ische Grundzüge Zentralamerikas.
Erdkunde, 13: 344–54.

LAUFER, B.
1909 Chinese pottery of the Han dynasty. Leiden.

LAUGHLIN, R. M.
1962 Through the looking glass: reflections on Zinacantan courtship and marriage. Doctoral dissertation, Harvard Univ.
1962 El símbolo de la flor en la religión de Zinacantan. *Estud. Cultura Maya*, 2: 123–39.

LAW, H. W.
1948 Greeting forms of the gulf Aztecs. *SW. Jour. Anthr.*, 4: 43–48.
1957 Tamakasti: a gulf Nahuatl text. *Tlalocan*, 3: 344–60.
1958 Morphological structure of Isthmus Nahuat. *Int. Jour. Amer. Ling.*, 24: 108–29.
1960 Linguistic acculturation in Mexico. *Univ. Texas, Dept. Anthropology, Student Papers Anthr.*, 3: 1–31.

LAYRISSE, M., AND T. ARENDS
1956 High incidence blood group found in Venezuelan Indians. *Science*, 123: 633.
1956 The Diego blood factor in Chinese and Japanese. *Nature*, 177: 1083. London.

—— AND J. WILBERT
1960 El antígeno del sistema sanguíneo Diego. La Fundación Creole y la Fundación Eugenio Mendoza. Caracas, Venezuela.

LAZO DE LA VEGA, L.
1956 The miraculous apparition of the beloved Virgin Mary, our lady of Guadalupe, at Tepeyacac, near Mexico City. *In* Demarest and Taylor, 1956, pp. 39–53.

LAZO DE LA VEGA, M.
1908 Investigaciones sobre la topografía fisiológica de la sensibilidad cutánea. Tesis del año 1907, pp. 170–89, Facultad Méd. Mexico.

LEACH, E.
1954 Political systems of highland Burma. London.

LEACH, E. R.
1966 Lévi-Strauss in the Garden of Eden: an examination of some recent developments in the analysis of myth.

In Reader in comparative religion, W. Lessa and E. Z. Vogt, eds., pp. 574–92. 2d ed.

LEAL, M.
1950 Patterns of tone substitution in Zapotec morphology. *Int. Jour. Amer. Ling.*, 16: 132–36.
1954 Noun possession in Villa Alta Zapotec. *Ibid.*, 20: 215–16.

LEBRÓN DE QUIÑONES, L.
1945 Memoria de los pueblos de la provincia de Colima. Mexico.

LECHE, S. M.
1933 Dermatoglyphics and functional lateral dominance in Mexican Indians (Mayas and Tarahumaras). *Tulane Univ., Middle Amer. Research Inst.*, Pub. 5, pp. 29–42.
1936 Dermatoglyphics and functional lateral dominance in Mexican Indians: II Aztecas. *In* Cummins and others, 1936, pp. 207–23.
1936 Dermatoglyphics and functional lateral dominance in Mexican Indians: III Zapotecas and Mixtecas. *Ibid.*, pp. 225–84.
1936 Dermatoglyphics and functional lateral dominance in Mexican Indians: IV Chamulas. *Ibid.*, pp. 287–312.
1936 The dermatoglyphics of the Tarascan Indians of Mexico, from the collection of Dr. D. F. Rubín de la Borbolla. *Ibid.*, pp. 315–29.

——, H. N. GOULD, AND D. THARP
1944 Dermatoglyphics and functional lateral dominance in Mexican Indians: V Zinancantecs, Huixtecs, Amatenangos, and Finca Tzeltals. *Tulane Univ., Middle Amer. Research Inst.*, Pub. 15, pp. 21–84.

LECONTE, J.
1852 The "Aztec" dwarfs.

LE DOUBLE, F.
1903 Traité des variations des os du crâne de l'homme, et de leur signification au point de vue de l'anthropologie zoologique. Paris.

LEES, R. B.
1953 The basis of glottochronology. *Language*, 29: 113–27.

LEGTERS, D. B.
1937   The story of a hunter.   *Invest. Ling.*,
       4: 302–05.

LEHMANN, H.
1948   Résultat d'un voyage de prospection
       archéologique sur les côtes du Pacific
       (nord de l'état de Guerrero et sud de
       l'état de Michoacán).   *28th Int.
       Cong. Amer.* (Paris, 1947), Acta, pp.
       425–39.

1951   Le personnage couché sur le dos:
       sujet commun dans l'archéologie du
       Mexique et de l'Equateur.   *In* Tax,
       1951, pp. 291–98.

1953   On Noel Morss' "Cradled infant figu-
       rines."   *Amer. Antiquity,* 19: 78–80.

1959   Les céramiques précolombiennes.
       Paris.

1960   L'art précolombien.   Paris.

—— AND M. CUTBUSH
1952   Sub-division of some southern Indian
       communities according to the inci-
       dence of sickle-cell trait and blood
       groups.   *Trans. Royal Soc. Tropical
       Med.,* 46: 380–83.

LEHMANN, W.
1905   Die fünf im Kindbett gestorbenen
       Frauen und die fünf Götter des Sü-
       dens in der mexikanischen Mythol-
       ogie.   *Zeit. für Ethnol.,* 37: 848–71.
       Berlin.

1905   Les peintures Mixteco-Zapotèques et
       quelques documents apparentés.
       Jour. Soc. Amer. Paris, 2: 241–80.

1906   Traditions des anciens Mexicains:
       texte inédit et original en langue
       Nahuatl avec traduction en Latin.
       Ibid., 3: 239–97.

1908   Reisebericht aus San Jose de Costa
       Rica.   *Zeit. für Ethnol.,* 40: 439–46.
       Berlin.

1910   Ergebnisse einer Forschungsreise in
       Mittelamerika und Mexiko, 1907–09.
       Ibid., 42: 687–749.

1913   Die Archäologie Costa Rica.   *Ab-
       handlungen der Naturhistorischen
       Gesellschaft Nürnberg,* vol. 20.

1915   Ueber die Stellung und Verwandt-
       schaft der Subtiaba-Sprache der Pazi-
       fischen Kuste Nicaraguas.   *Zeit. für
       Ethnol.,* 47: 1–34.

1920   Zentral-Amerika: die Sprachen Zen-
       tral-Amerikas in ihren Beziehungen
       Zueinander sowie zu Süd-Amerika
       und Mexiko.   2 vols.   Berlin.

1921   Altmexikanische Kunstgeschichte:
       eine Entwurf in Unrissen.   "Orbis
       Pictus": Weltkunst-Bucherei-Band, 8.
       Berlin.

1922   The history of ancient Mexican art:
       an essay in outline.   "Orbis Pictus":
       the Universal Library of Art, vol. 8.
       New York.   (English trans. of his
       1921.)

1922   [ed.]   Festschrift Eduard Seler.
       Stuttgart.

1928   Ergebnisse einer mit Unterstützung
       der Notgemeinschaft der Deutschen
       Wissenschaft in den Jahren 1925/
       1926 ausgeführten Forschungsreise
       nach Mexiko und Guatemala.   *An-
       thropos,* 23: 747–91.

1938   Die Geschichte der Königreiche von
       Colhuacan und Mexiko.   *Quellen-
       werke zur alten Geschichte Amerikas,*
       vol. 1.   Berlin.

1938   *See* Anales de Cuauhtitlan, 1938.

1949   Sterbende Götter und christliche
       Heilsbotschaft: wechselreden indian-
       ischer Vornehmer und spanischer
       Glaubensapostel in Mexiko 1524.
       ("Coloquios y doctrina christiana"
       des Fray Bernardino de Sahagún aus
       dem Jahre 1564.)   *Quellenwerke zur
       alten Geschichte Amerikas,* vol. 3.
       Stuttgart.

1958   *See* Chimalpahin, 1958.

1966   Las cinco mujeres del oeste muertas
       en el parto y los cinco dioses del sur
       en la mitología mexicana.   *Soc. Mex.
       Antr., Traducciones Mesoamericanis-
       tas,* 1: 147–75.   (Spanish trans. of
       his 1905.)

—— AND G. KUTSCHER, eds.
1958   Das 'Memorial breve acerca de la
       fundación de la ciudad de Culhuacán'
       von Domingo de S. Anton Muñon
       Chimalpahin.   *Quellenwerke zur al-
       ten Geschichte Amerikas,* vol. 7.
       Stuttgart.

LEHMANN-NITSCHE, R.
1926   Mitología centroamericana.   *An.
       Soc. Geog. Hist. Guatemala,* 2: 408–
       14.

Lehmer, D. J.
1948 The Jornada branch of the Mogollon. *Bull. Univ. Arizona*, vol. 19, no. 2.
1949 Archaeological survey of Sonora, Mexico. *Chicago Natural Hist. Mus.*, Bull. 20, no. 12, pp. 4–5.
1960 A review of trans-Pecos Texas archaeology. *In* Jelks, Davis, and Sturgis, 1960.

Leigh, H.
1960 Notes on Mitla lore and language. *Bol. Estud. Oaxaqueños*, no. 18, pp. 1–3.
1960 The Zapotec name for the Zapotecs. *Ibid.*, no. 18, pp. 4–7.
1961 Head shrinking in ancient Mexico. *Sci. Man*, 2: 4–7.

Lejeal, L.
1903 Campagnes archéologiques récentes dans l'Oaxaca (Mitla et les "mogotes" de Xoxo). *Jour. Soc. Amer. Paris*, 4: 174–89.

Lekis, L.
1958 Folk dances of Latin America. New York.

Lemley, H. V.
n.d. Unpublished material.
1949 Three Tlapaneco stories from Tlacoapa, Guerrero. *Tlalocan*, 3: 76–82.

Lemoine V., E.
1954 Ensayo de división municipal del estado de Oaxaca. *Yan*, no. 3, pp. 69–74.

Lenz, H.
1948 El papel indígena mexicano: historia y supervivencia. Mexico.

León, Adrián, ed.
1949 Crónica mexicáyotl, by F. Alvarado Tezozómoc. Mexico.

León, Alonso de
1909 Relación y discursos del descubrimiento, población y pacificación de este nuevo reino de Leon [1649]. *In* Doc. inéditos o muy raros para la historia de Mexico, by Genaro García, vol. 25. Mexico.

León, F. de P.
1939 Los esmaltes de Uruapan. Departamento Autónoma de Prensa y Publicidad. Mexico.

León, J. R. de
1942 Nota preliminar acerca de la enfermedad de chagas en Guatemala: casos encontrados en el oriente de la república y probable existencia de un nuevo trypanosoma humano. *Rev. Cruz Roja*, 9: 131–32.
1943 La trypanosomiasis americana o enfermedad de chagas en Guatemala. *Gaceta Méd. Centroamer.*, 1: 57–60.
1947 Contribución al estudio de la enfermedad de chagas en Guatemala. *Univ. San Carlos de Guatemala, Pub. Trimestral*, 9: 127–44.
1949 Sobre la prioridad en el descubrimiento de los primeros casos de trypanosomiasis humana causados por Trypanosoma Rangeli en Guatemala. *Univ. San Carlos de Guatemala, Inst. Invest. Cien.*, Pub. 4.

—— and L. N. Figueroa
1959 Descubrimiento de la primera zona endémica de kala azar Guatemalense y sus condiciones epidemiológicas. *Rev. Colegio Méd. Guatemala*, 10: 240–45.

León, M. de
1611 Camino del cielo en lengua mexicana. Mexico.

León, N.
1887 Nombres de algunos vegetales, en tarasco, con su correspondiente clasificación científica. *El Monitor Médico-Farmacéutico e Industrial*, December. Morelia.
1887 Nombres de animales, en tarasco y castellano, con su correspondiente clasificación científica. *Ibid.*
1889 El matrimonio entre los tarascos precolombianos y sus actuales usos. *An. Mus. Michoacano*, 2: 155–65.
1889 Adición al estudio "Matrimonio entre los tarascos." *Ibid.*, 2: 135–86.
1890 Anomalías y mutilaciones étnicas del sistema dentario entre los Tarascos precolombinos. *Ibid.*, 3: 168–73.
1892 Anomalies et mutilations dentaires des Tarasques. *8th Int. Cong. Amer.* (Paris, 1890), Acta, pp. 339–40.
1901 Los dientes caninos en los indios de México: quien primero los estudió y publicó sus observaciones. *Crónica Méd. Mex.*, 4: 270.
1901 Apuntes para una bibliografía antro-

pológica de México (somatología). *Rev. Cien. Bibliog.*, 15: 63–78. Mexico.

1901 Lyobaa o Mictlan. Guía histórico-descriptiva. Mexico.

1901 Familias lingüísticas de México. *Mem. Soc. Cien. Antonio Alzate*, 15: 275–87. Mexico.

1901 Los huavi: estudio etno-antropológico. *Rev. Cien. Bibliog. Soc. Antonio Alzate*, 16: 103–29.

1902 Carta lingüística de México. *An. Mus. Nac.* Mexico.

1902 La caza de aves con el tzipaqui en el lago de Patzcuaro. *In* Lumholtz, 1902.

1902 Familias lingüísticas de México. *Mus. Nac.* Mexico.

1902 Occipital cuadrado en un cráneo de mestizo Otomí moderno. *Crónica Méd. Mex.*, 5: 170. (English version in *Science*, Aug. 8, 1902.)

1902 Carta lingüística de México. *Mus. Nac.* Mexico.

1903 Los Tarascos, notas históricas, étnicas y antropológicas. *An. Mus. Nac.*, 11: 392–502.

1903 Familias lingüísticas de México. *Ibid.*, 7: 279–335.

1903 Vocabulario en lengua cuitlateca de San Miguel Totolapan, Guerrero. Mexico.

1904 Catálogo de la colección de antigüedades huavis del estado de Oaxaca, existente en el Museo Nacional de México. Mexico.

1904 Los Tarascos: notas históricas, étnicas y antropológicas. *An. Mus. Nac.*, ep. 2, 1: 392–502. Mexico.

1905 Los Popolocas. *Ibid.*, 12: 103–20.

1906 Los tarascos: etnografía postcortesiana y actual. Part 3. *Ibid.*, ep. 2, vol. 3.

1907 Bibliografía mexicana del siglo XVIII. *Bol. Inst. Bib.*, vol. 8.

1911 Programa del curso de antropología física [del Museo Nacional de México]. (Reprinted in *Bol. Mus. Nac. Arqueol. Hist. Etnol.*, 1: 44–46. Mexico.)

1912 Vocabulario de la lengua popoloca

chocha ó chuchona. . . . *An. Mus. Nac.*, 3d ser., 3: 1–48.

1912 Nuevo modelo de cédula antropométrica para el Departamento de Antropometría Escolar. *Bol. Instrucción Pública*, 18: 357–58.

1912 Cefalometría fetal: notas de antropometría obstétrica. Mexico.

1913 Guía para la nomenclatura en las observaciones de la cédula antropométrica del Dr. Aleš Hrdlička. Mexico.

1914 Técnica osteométrica: notas para los alumnos de la clase de antropología física del Museo Nacional. Mexico.

1915 Programa de la cátedra de antropología física del Museo Nacional de México: curso del año 1915. *Documentos relativos a la translación de las clases que actualmente se cursan en el Museo de la Escuela Nacional de Altos Estudios*, pp. 28–41. Mexico.

1919 Historia de la antropología física en México. *Amer. Jour. Physical Anthr.*, 2: 229–64.

1921 Supervivencias precolombinas: la pintura al aje de Uruapan. *Amer. Española*, 1: 332–39, 412–18.

1922 Familias lingüísticas de México. 5th rev. ed., abridged.

1922 Huellas humanas impresas sobre roca en territorio mexicano. *El Mex. Antiguo*, 1: 204–10.

1922 La antropología física y la antropología en México: notas históricas. *An. Mus. Nac. Arqueol. Hist. Etnog.*, ep. 4, 1: 99–136. Mexico.

1922 Tablas cromáticas, según Broca, Martin y Fischer de los colores de la piel, ojos y pelo, mas comunes en los indios de México. Mexico.

1924 ¿Que es la antropología física y con qué objeto hay un departamento de ese nombre en el Museo Nacional de Arqueología, Etnografía e Historia? Cartilla de vulgarización del Museo Nacional de México.

1924 Las castas del México colonial: noticias etno-antropológicas. Mexico.

1928 La capacidad craneana en algunas tribus indígenas de la República Mexicana. *20th Int. Cong. Amer.*

(Rio de Janeiro, 1922), Acta, 2: 37–53.

1934 Los indios Tarascos del lago de Pátzcuaro. *An. Mus. Nac. Arqueol. Hist. Etnog.*, ep. 5, 1: 149–68.

1967 La pintura al aje de Uruapan (Michoacan). *Bol. Centro Invest. Antr. Méx.*, no. 14, pp. 1–15. (MS 1910?)

LEÓN BLANCO, F.

1940 Nota sobre la evolución histórica de nuestros conocimientos acerca del mal de pinto o carate. *Rev. Méd. Tropical y Parasitol., Bacteriol. Clin. y Lab.*, 6: 289.

LEÓN M., A. F., AND H. CONTRERAS A.

1944 Pastorela de viejos, para el año 1912. *Tlalocan*, 1: 169–93.

LEÓN-PORTILLA, M.

1956 La filosofía Náhuatl, estudiada en sus fuentes. *Special ed., Inst. Indigenista Interamer.*, Pub. 26. Mexico. (2d ed. 1959). English trans., Aztec thought and culture: a study of the ancient Nahuatl mind, 1963, Norman, Okla. (3d ed. 1966, Mexico.)

1958 Ritos, sacerdotes y atavíos de los dioses. Univ. Nac. Autónoma Méx., Inst. Hist., Seminario de Cultura Náhuatl, *Textos de los Informantes de Sahagún*, no. 1.

1959 Panorama de la población indígena de México. *Amer. Indig.*, 19: 43–73 (2d ed.). Mexico.

1961 Mythology of ancient Mexico. *In* Mythologies of the ancient world, S. N. Kramer, ed., pp. 443–72. New York.

1961 Los antiguos mexicanos a través de sus crónicas y cantares. Fondo de Cultura Económica. Mexico.

1962 La institución cultural del comercio prehispánico. *Estud. Cultura Nahuatl*, 3: 23–54.

1967 El proceso de aculturación de los Chichimecas de Xolótl. *Ibid.*, 7: 59–86.

—— AND A. M. GARIBAY K.

1959 Visión de los vencidos: relaciones indígenas de la conquista. *Bib. Estudiante Universitario*, no. 81. Mexico.

LEÓN Y GAMA, A.

1832 Descripción histórica y cronológica de las Dos Piedras que con ocasión del nuevo empedrado que se está formando en la plaza principal de México, se hallaron en ella el año de 1790. 2d ed., C. M. Bustamante, ed. Mexico.

LEOPOLD, A. S.

1950 Vegetation zones of Mexico. *Ecology*, 31: 507–18.

1959 Wildlife of Mexico: the game birds and mammals. Univ. California Press.

LE PLONGEON, A. D.

1886 Here and there in Yucatan. New York.

LES AZTÈQUES

See Anonymous, 1855.

LESLIE, C. M.

1960 Now we are civilized: a study of the world view of the Zapotec Indians of Mitla, Oaxaca. Wayne State Univ. Press.

1960 [ed.] The social anthropology of Middle America. *Alpha Kappa Deltan*, vol. 30, no. 1 (special issue).

LESSER, A.

1928 Bibliography of American folklore, 1915–1928. *Jour. Amer. Folklore*, 41: 1–60.

LESTRANGE, M. DE

1953 Recherches critiques sur les méthodes de notation des dessins papillaires digitaux. *L'Anthropologie*, 57: 240–71.

1954 Dermatoglyphes digitaux et palmaires de 33 Indiens Caincangues, Paraná, Brésil. *Bull. et Mem. Soc. Anthr. Paris*, 10: 310–11.

1954 Dermatoglyphes digitaux et palmaires de 47 Indiens du Brésil. *Ibid.*, 10: 85–86.

LEUBUSCHER, R.

1856 Ueber die sogenannten Azteken (amerikanische Mikrocephalen). *Froriep's Notizen aus dem Gebiete der Natur- und Heilkunde*, 2: 81–89, 97–105.

LEVINE, M. H.

1958 An area co-tradition for Mesoamerica. *Papers Kroeber Anthr. Soc.*, no. 18.

LEVINE, P., AND OTHERS (E. A. ROBINSON, M. LAYRISSE, T. ARENDS, AND R. DOMINGUEZ SISCO)

1956   The Diego blood factor. *Nature*, 177: 40–41. London.

LEWIS, M., B. CHOWN, AND H. KAITA

1956   Further observations on the blood factor Di^a. *Ibid.*, 178: 1125.

LEWIS, O.

1947   Wealth differences in a Mexican village. *Sci. Monthly*, 65: 127–32.

1949   Husbands and wives in a Mexican village: a study of role conflict. *Amer. Anthr.*, 51: 602–10.

1951   Life in a Mexican village: Tepoztlan restudied. Univ. Illinois Press.

1952   Urbanization without breakdown: a case study. *Sci. Monthly*, 75: 31–41.

1955   Medicine and politics in a Mexican village. *In* B. D. Paul, 1955, pp. 403–34.

1957   Urbanización sin desorganización: las familias tepoztecas en la ciudad de México. *Amer. Indig.*, 17: 231–46.

1958   México desde 1940. *Invest. Econ.*, vol. 18, no. 70. Mexico.

1959   The culture of the vecindad in Mexico City: two case studies. *In* Stone, 1959, pp. 387–402.

1959   Five families: Mexican case studies in the culture of poverty. New York.

1960   Tepoztlan, village in Mexico. New York.

1961   The children of Sanchez: autobiography of a Mexican family. New York.

1961   Mexico since Cárdenas. *In* Council on Foreign Relations, 1961, pp. 283–345.

——— AND E. E. MAES

1945   Base para una nueva definición práctica del Indio. *Amer. Indig.*, 5: 107–18.

LEWY, E.

1937   Die Sprache der Quiche (Kiče) von Guatemala. *Anthropos*, 32: 929–58. Mödling.

LEYENDA DE LOS SOLES

1903   Leyenda de los Soles, continuada con otras leyendas y noticias: relación anónima escrita en lengua mexicana el año 1558. F. del Paso y Troncoso,

ed. and trans. *Bib. Náhuatl, 5: Tradiciones, Migraciones*, Cuad. 1, pp. 1–40. Florence.

1938   *See* Anales de Cuauhtitlan, 1938, pp. 322–88.

1945   *See* Anales de Cuauhtitlan, 1945, pp. 119–42.

LIBBY, W. F.

1951   Radiocarbon dates, II. *Science*, 114: 291–96.

1952   Radiocarbon dates, III. *Ibid.*, 116: 673–81.

1952   Radiocarbon dating. Univ. Chicago Press.

1954   Chicago radiocarbon dates, V. *Science*, 120: 733–42.

1955   Radiocarbon dating. 2d ed. Univ. Chicago Press.

LI CH'IAO-P'ING

1948   The chemical arts of old China. Easton.

LIEBAN, R. W.

1960   Sorcery, illness, and social control in a Philippine municipality. *SW. Jour. Anthr.*, 16: 127–43.

LIEKENS, E.

1952   Los zapotecas no son zapotecas sin itzaes Villahermosa, Tabasco.

LIENZO DE TLAXCALA

1892   Lienzo de Tlaxcala. *In* Antigüedades mexicanas publicadas por la Junta Colombina de Mexico. 2 vols.

LIFE EN ESPAÑOL

1959   Issue of November 16, pp. 84–87.

LIFE MAGAZINE

1959   Issue of October 26, pp. 93–96.

LINCK, W.

n.d.   Carte. *In* Doc. para la Historia de Mexico, 1853–57.

LINCOLN, J. S.

1939   The southeastern Chinantla of Mexico. *Sci. Monthly*, 69: 57–65.

1942   The Maya calendar of the Ixil of Guatemala. *Carnegie Inst. Wash.*, Pub. 528, Contrib. 38.

1946   An ethnological study of the Ixil Indians of the Guatemala highlands. *Univ. Chicago, Micro. Coll. MSS Middle Amer. Cult. Anthr.*, no. 1.

LINDIG, W.

1959   Die Seri: ein Hoka-wildbeuterstamm in Sonora, Mexiko. Leiden.

134

LINDSAY, A. J., JR.
1968   Northern Mexico. *Amer. Antiquity*, 33: 122.

LINDZEY, G.
1961   Projective techniques and cross-cultural research. New York.

LING, SHUN-SHENG
1956   Patu found in Taiwan and other east Asiatic regions and its parallels in Oceania and America. *Nat. Taiwan Univ., Bull. Dept. Archaeol. and Anthr.*, 7: 1–22, 82–104. Taipei.

LINNÉ, S.
1929   Darién in the past. *Götesborg Kungl. Veterskaps – och Vitterhets – Samhälles Handlinar*, Femte Följden, Ser. A, 1, 3.
1934   Archaeological researches at Teotihuacan, Mexico. *Ethnog. Mus. Sweden*, n.s., Pub. 1. Stockholm.
1936   The expeditions to Mexico sent out in 1934–35 by the Ethnographical Museum of Sweden. *Ethnos*, 1: 39–48.
1938   Zapotecan antiquities and the Paulson collection in the Ethnographical Museum of Sweden. *Ethnog. Mus. Sweden*, Pub. 4. Stockholm.
1941   Teotihuacan symbols. *Ethnos*, 6: 174–86.
1942   Mexican highland cultures: archaeological researches at Teotihuacan, Calpulalpan and Chalchicomula in 1934–35. *Ethnog. Mus. Sweden*, n.s., Pub. 7.
1947   The thin orange pottery of Mexico and Guatemala. *Ethnos*, 12: 127–36.
1951   A wheeled toy from Guerrero, Mexico. *Ibid.*, 16: 141–52.
1956   Radiocarbon dates in Teotihuacan. *Ibid.*, 21: 180–93.
1956   Treasures of Mexican art: two thousand years of art and art handicraft. A. Read, trans. Swedish-Mexican Exhibition Comm. Stockholm.
1960   The art of Mexico and Central America. *In* The art of ancient America: civilizations of Central and South America, pp. 13–134. New York.

LINTON, R.
1922   The sacrifice to the morning star by the Skidi Pawnee. *Field Mus. Natural Hist.*, Leaflet 6.
1936   The study of man. New York.
1940   Acculturation in seven American Indian tribes. New York.

LIPSCHÜTZ, A.
1944   El indio-americanismo y el problema racial en las Américas. 2d ed. Santiago, Chile.

LISTER, R. H.
1939   A report on the excavations made at Agua Zarca and La Morita in Chihuahua. *Univ. New Mexico, Research Graduate School*, vol. 3, no. 1.
1941   Cerro Oztuma, Guerrero. *El Mex. Antiguo*, 5: 209–20.
1946   Survey of archaeological remains in northwestern Chihuahua. *SW. Jour. Anthr.*, 2: 433–54.
1947   Archaeology of the middle Rio Balsas basin, Mexico. *Amer. Antiquity*, 13: 67–78.
1948   An archaeological survey of the region about Teloloapan, Guerrero. *In* El Occidente de México, pp. 107–22.
1949   Excavations at Cojumatlan, Michoacan, Mexico. *Univ. New Mexico Pub. Anthr.*, no. 5.
1953   The stemmed, indented base point, a possible horizon marker. *Amer. Antiquity*, 18: 265.
1953   Excavations in Cave valley, Chihuahua, Mexico: a preliminary note. *Ibid.*, 19: 166–69.
1955   The present status of the archaeology of western Mexico: a distributional study. *Univ. Colorado Studies, Anthr. Ser.*, no. 5.
1958   Archaeological excavations in the northern Sierra Madre Occidental, Chihuahua and Sonora, Mexico. *Ibid.*, no. 7.

—— AND A. M. HOWARD
1955   The Chalchihuites culture of northwestern Mexico. *Amer. Antiquity*, 21: 122–29.

LITTMANN, E. R.
1958   Ancient Mesoamerican mortars, plasters, and stuccos: the composition and origin of *sascab*. *Amer. Antiquity*, 24: 172–76.

LITVAK KING, J.

1968 Excavaciones de rescate en la presa de La Villita. *Bol. Inst. Nac. Antr. Hist.*, 31: 28–30.

LIZANA, B. DE

1893 Historia de Yucatan. Devocionario de Ntra. Sra. de Izamal y conquista espiritual. Mexico. (1st ed. 1633.)

LIZARDI RAMOS, C.

1939 Exploraciones arqueológicas en Quintana Roo. *Rev. Mex. Estud. Antr.*, 3: 46–53.

1940 Exploraciones en Quintana Roo. Mexico.

1941 [ed.] Los Mayas antiguos: monografías de arqueología, etnografía y lingüística mayas. . . . Colegio de Mexico.

1944 El chacmool mexicano. *Cuad. Amer.*, 14: 137–48.

1949 Mas fechas mayas. *El Mex. Antiguo*, 7: 238–60.

1955 ¿Conocían el xihuitl los teotihuacanos? *Ibid.*, 8: 219–23.

1956–57 Arquitectura de Huapalcalco, Tulancingo. *Rev. Mex. Estud. Antr.*, 14 (part 2): 111–16.

1959 El calendario maya-mexicano. *In* Esplendor del México Antiguo, 1: 221–42.

LLAVE, P. DE LA

1832 Sobre el Axin, especie nueva de Coccus, y sobre la grasa que de él se extrae. *Registro Trimestre*, 1: 147–52. Mexico.

LLERGO, C. L. DE

1927 Hipótesis sobre la morfogenia del tipo yucateco. *Mem. Soc. Cien. Antonio Alzate*, 47: 59–71.

LOCKE, L. L.

1923 The ancient Quipu or Peruvian knot record. Amer. Mus. Nat. Hist.

LOGHEM, J. J. VAN, M. V. D. HART, J. BOK, AND P. C. BRINKERINK

1955 Two further examples of the antibody anti-Wr[a]. *Vox Sanguinis*, 5: 130–34.

LOMBARDO, N.

1702 Arte de la lengua teguima llamada vulgarmente ópata. Mexico.

LOMBARDO TOLEDANO, V.

1931 Geografía de las lenguas de la sierra de Puebla, con algunas observaciones sobre sus primeros y sus actuales pobladores. *Univ. México*, 2 (13): 14–96.

LONG, R. C. E.

1926 The Zouche codex. *Jour. Royal Anthr. Inst.*, 56: 239–58.

1942 The payment of tribute in the codex Mendoza. *Carnegie Inst. Wash., Notes Middle Amer. Archaeol. Ethnol.*, no. 10.

1948 Some remarks on Maya arithmetic. *Ibid.*, no. 88.

LONG, S. V.

1965 Shaft-tombs and hollow figurines from the Magdalena lake basin of Jalisco, Mexico. Doctoral dissertation, Univ. California, Los Angeles.

1967 Form and distribution of shaft-and-chamber tombs. *Rev. Univ. de los Andes*, no. 1. Bogota.

—— AND R. E. TAYLOR

1966 Chronology of a west Mexican shaft tomb. *Nature*, 212 (5062): 651–52.

1966 Suggested revision for west Mexican archaeological sequences. *Science*, 154 (3755): 1456–59.

—— AND M. V. V. WIRE

1966 Excavations at Barra de Navidad, Jalisco. Inst. Caribe Antr. Sociol. de la Fundación La Salle. *Antropológica*, no. 18. Caracas.

LONGACRE, R. E.

1952 Five phonemic pitch levels in Trique. *Acta Ling.*, 7: 62–82.

1955 Rejoinder to Hamp's componential restatement to syllable structure in Trique. *Int. Jour. Amer. Ling.*, 21: 189–94.

1957 Proto-Mixtecan. *Indiana Univ. Research Center Anthr., Folklore, Ling.*, Pub. 5.

1959 Trique tone morphemics. *Anthr. Ling.*, 1: 5–42.

1960 String constituent analysis. *Language*, 36: 63–88.

1961 Swadesh's Macro-Mixtecan hypothesis. *Int. Jour. Amer. Ling.*, 27: 9–29.

1961 *Review of* M. Swadesh, Mapas de clasificación lingüística de México y las Américas. *Language*, 36: 397–410.

1964 Grammar discovery procedures. The Hague.

1966 On linguistic affinities of Amuzgo. *Int. Jour. Amer. Ling.*, 32: 46–49.

—— AND R. MILLON

1961 Proto-Mixtecan and Proto-Amuzgo-Mixtecan vocabularies: a preliminary cultural analysis. *Anthr. Ling.*, 3 (4): 1–44.

LONGYEAR, J. M.

1940 A Maya old empire skeleton from Copan, Honduras. *Amer. Jour. Physical Anthr.*, 27: 151–54.

1944 Archaeological investigations in El Salvador. *Mem. Peabody Mus., Harvard Univ.*, vol. 9, no. 2.

1947 Cultures and peoples of the south-eastern Maya frontier. *Carnegie Inst. Wash., Theoretical Approaches to Problems*, no. 3.

1948 A sub-pottery deposit at Copan, Honduras. *Amer. Antiquity*, 13: 248–49.

1952 Copan ceramics: a study of southeastern Maya pottery. *Carnegie Inst. Wash.*, Pub. 597.

LÓPEZ, J. J.

1892 Cachiquel, Quiché y Sutugil. *In* León Fernández, ed., Lenguas indígenas de Centroamérica en el siglo XVIII. San Jose.

LÓPEZ AUSTIN, A.

1961 El abogado náhuatl. *Debate*, 2: 22–24. Ciudad Juarez.

1961 La constitución real de México-Tenochtitlan. Univ. Nac. México.

1967 Cuarenta clases de magos del mundo Náhuatl. *Inst. Hist., Estud. Cultura Náhuatl*, 7: 87–117.

LÓPEZ CHIÑAS, GABRIEL

1936 El paisaje en la vida de Juchitan. *Neza*, 2 (12): 1, 5.

1937 Los parientes: antecesores zapotecas. *Ibid.*, 3 (1): 33–37.

1939 La música aborigen de Juchitan. *Ibid.*, 4 (1): 21–24.

1945 El concepto de la muerte entre los zapotecas. *Anuario Soc. Folklórica Mex.*, 4: 485–91.

1949 Breve estudio sobre la evolución social y jurídica de la familia zapoteca. Tesis, Escuela Nac. Jurisprudencia. Mexico.

1958 Vinni Gulasa: cuentos de Juchitan. (2d ed.) Mexico.

LÓPEZ CHIÑAS, JEREMÍAS

1936 La vida militar zapoteca. *Neza*, 1 (9): 2.

1937 Algunos animales y plantas que conocierón los antiguos zapotecas. *Ibid.*, 3 (1): 12–24.

1939 La música zapoteca en la capital. *Ibid.*, 4 (1): 25–27.

LÓPEZ DE COGOLLUDO, D.

1867–68 Historia de Yucatan. 2 vols. 3d ed. Merida. (1st ed. 1688, Madrid; 4th ed. 1955, Campeche.)

LÓPEZ DE GÓMARA, F. DE

1852 Primera y segunda partes de la historia general de las Indias. *Bib. Autores Españoles, desde la formación del lenguaje hasta nuestros días*, vol. 1. Madrid.

1931 Hispania victrix. Primera y segunda parte de la historia general de las Indias. *In* Historiadores primitivos de Indias, pp. 155–455. Madrid.

1941 Historia general de Las Indias. 2 vols. Madrid.

1943 Historia de la conquista de México. 2 vols. P. Robredo, ed. Mexico.

LÓPEZ DE LLERGO, R.

1953 Las provincias fisiográficas de la República Mexicana. *Mem. Cong. Cien. Mex.*, 4: 274–77.

1960 Principales rasgos fisiográficos de la región comprendida entre el paralelo 19° y el istmo de Tehuantepec. *Rev. Mex. Estud. Antr.*, 16: 21–29.

LÓPEZ DE MENESES, A.

1948 Tecuichpochtzin, hija de Moteczuma (¿1510?-1550). *In* Estudios cortesianos recopilados con motivo de la IV centenario de la muerte de Hernán Cortés (1547–1947), pp. 471–95. Madrid.

LÓPEZ MEDEL, T.

1941 Relación. *In* Landa, 1941, pp. 221–29.

LÓPEZ OTERO, D.

1914 Gramática maya. Merida.

LÓPEZ RAMOS, E.

1956 Visita a las localidades tipo de las

formaciones del Eoceno, Oligoceno y Mioceno de la cuenca sedimentaria de Tampico-Misantla, en la llanura costera del Golfo de Mexico, entre Poza Rica, Ver. – Tampico, Tamps. y Ciudad Valles, San Luis Potosi. *20th Cong. Geol. Int.*, Field Guide, no. 1.

López Ruiz, M., and M. Martínez Gracida
1906 Ita Andehui: leyenda mixteca. Oaxaca.

López Vera, T.
1935 Juchitan y Tehuantepec. *Neza*, 1 (1): 2.

López y López, G.
1947 En pos de la filosofía zapoteca. *Filosofía y Letras*, 27: 9–20, 57–59, 85–98 (1955).

Lorenzo, J. L.
1953 A fluted point from Durango, Mexico. *Amer. Antiquity*, 18: 394–95.
1955 Los concheros de la costa de Chiapas. *An. Inst. Antr. Hist.*, 7: 41–50.
1958 Un sitio precerámico en Yanhuitlan, Oaxaca. *Inst. Nac. Antr. Hist.*, *Dir. Prehistoria*, Pub. 6.
1958 Préhistoire et Quaternaire récent au Mexique: état actuel des connaissances. *L'Anthropologie*, 62: 62–83. Paris.
1958 Una hipótesis paleoclimática para la cuenca de Mexico. *In* Misc. Paul Rivet, 1: 579–84.
1959 La colección Leon Diguet de la Baja California en el Museo del Hombre, Paris: el material lítico. Paper presented to annual meeting, Amer. Anthr. Assoc., Mexico City.
1959 Glaciología mexicana. *Bol. Bibl. Geofísica y Oceanogr. Amer.*, 1: 131–36.
1959 Los glaciares de Mexico. *Monogr. Inst. Geofísica*, no. 1. Univ. Nac. Autónoma de Mex.
1960 Sobre un hallazgo de carácter prehistórico en el estado de Puebla. *Tlatoani*, ep. 2, no. 13, pp. 37–40.
1961 La revolución neolítica en Mesoamerica. *Inst. Nac. Antr. Hist.*, *Dir. Prehistoria*, Pub. 11.
1964 Primer informe sobre los trabajos arqueológicos de rescate efectuados en el vaso de la presa de El Infiernillo, Guerrero y Michoacán. *Bol. Inst. Nac. Antr. Hist.*, 17: 24–31. Mexico.
1965 Tlatilco: artefactos. *Inst. Nac. Antr. Hist., Ser. Invest.*, 7. Mexico.

Lothrop, R. W., and S. K. Lothrop
1927 The use of plaster on Porto Rican stone carvings. *Amer. Anthr.*, 29: 728–30.

Lothrop, S. K.
1919 The discovery of gold in the graves of Chiriqui. *Mus. Amer. Indian, Heye Found., Indian Notes and Monogr.*, vol. 6, no. 2.
1923 Stone yokes from Mexico and Central America. *Man*, 23: 97–98. London.
1924 Tulum: an archaeological study of the east coast of Yucatan. *Carnegie Inst. Wash.*, Pub. 335.
1926 Stone sculptures from the Finca Arevalo ruins, Guatemala. *Mus. Amer. Indian, Heye Found., Indian Notes*, 3: 147–71.
1926 Pottery of Costa Rica and Nicaragua. *Mus. Amer. Indian, Heye Found.*, Contrib. 8. 2 vols. New York.
1927 The museum Central American expedition, 1925–1926. *Mus. Amer. Indian, Heye Found., Indian Notes*, 4: 12–33.
1927 Pottery types and their sequence in El Salvador. *Ibid.*, vol. 1, no. 4.
1927 A note on Indian ceremonies in Guatemala. *Ibid.*, vol. 4, no. 1.
1927 The potters of Guatajiagua, El Salvador. *Ibid.*, 4: 109–18.
1928 Santiago Atitlan, Guatemala. *Ibid.*, vol. 5, no. 4.
1929 Christian and pagan in Guatemala. *Nation*, vol. 128, no. 3315 (Jan. 16).
1929 Further notes on Indian ceremonies in Guatemala. *Mus. Amer. Indian, Heye Found., Indian Notes*, vol. 6, no. 1.
1930 A modern survival of the ancient Maya calendar. *23d Int. Cong. Amer.* (New York, 1928), Acta, pp. 652–55.
1933 Atitlan: an archaeological study of ancient remains on the borders of

Lake Atitlan, Guatemala. *Carnegie Inst. Wash.*, Pub. 444.

1936 Zacualpa: a study of ancient Quiche artifacts. *Ibid.*, Pub. 472.

1937–42 Cocle: an archaeological study of central Panama. *Mem. Peabody Mus., Harvard Univ.*, vols. 7, 8.

1939 The southeastern frontier of the Maya. *Amer. Anthr.*, 41: 42–54.

1941 Gold ornaments of Chavin style from Chongoyape, Peru. *Amer. Antiquity*, 6: 250–62.

1942 The Sigua: southernmost Aztec outpost. *Proc. 8th Amer. Sci. Cong., Anthr. Sci., Native Amer. Cultures*, 2: 109–16.

1950 An exhibition of ancient American gold and jade. Taft Mus. Cincinnati.

1950 Archaeology of southern Veraguas, Panama. *Mem. Peabody Mus., Harvard Univ.*, vol. 9, no. 3.

1951 Gold artifacts of Chavin style. *Amer. Antiquity*, 16: 226–40.

1952 Metals from the cenote of sacrifice, Chichen Itza, Yucatan. *Mem. Peabody Mus., Harvard Univ.*, vol. 10, no. 2.

1955 Jade and string sawing in northeastern Costa Rica. *Amer. Antiquity*, 21: 43–51.

1956 Indigenous art of the Americas: catalogue of the collection of Robert Woods Bliss. London. (See also Lothrop, Foshag, and Mahler, 1957; Handbook . . . Bliss Collection, 1963.)

1963 Archaeology of the Diquis delta, Costa Rica. *Papers Peabody Mus., Harvard Univ.*, vol. 51.

1964 Treasures of ancient America: the arts of the pre-Columbian civilizations from Mexico to Peru. Geneva.

——, W. F. FOSHAG, AND J. MAHLER
1957 Pre-Columbian art: Robert Woods Bliss Collection. Phaidon Press. London.

—— AND OTHERS
1961 Essays in pre-Columbian art and archaeology. Harvard Univ. Press.

LOU, D. WING-SOU
1957 Rain-worship among the ancient Chinese and the Nahua-Maya Indians. *Acad. Sinica, Bull. Inst. Ethnol.*, 4: 31–102. Taipei.

LOVÉN, S.
1924 Über die Wurzeln der Tainischen Kultur. Göteborg.

1935 Origins of the Tainan culture, West Indies. Göteborg.

LOWE, G. W.
1956 Summary of New World Archaeological Foundation investigations at Chiapa de Corzo, Chiapas, 1955. *New World Archaeol. Found.*, Pub. 1, pp. 38–42.

1959 The long sequence of preclassic architectural development at Chiapa de Corzo, Chiapas. 24th ann. meeting, Soc. Amer. Archaeol., abstracts of papers, p. 38.

1959 The Chiapas project, 1955–1958: report of the field director. *Papers New World Archaeol. Found.*, no. 1.

1959 Archaeological exploration of the upper Grijalva River, Chiapas, Mexico. *Ibid.*, no. 2.

1962 Mound 5 and minor excavations, Chiapa de Corzo, Chiapas, Mexico. *Ibid.*, no. 12.

—— AND C. NAVARRETE
1959 Research in Chiapas, Mexico. *New World Archaeol. Found.*, Pub. 3.

LOWIE, R. H.
1958 The culture area concept as applied to North and South America. *32d Int. Cong. Amer.* (Copenhagen, 1956), Acta, pp. 73–78.

LOZANO GARCÍA, R.
1945 El gas natural y la turba en la cuenca de Mexico. *Inst. Geol., Univ. Nac. Autónoma de Mex., Estud. Geol.-Econ.*, no. 1.

LUCK, J. V.
1950 Bone and joint diseases. Springfield, Ill.

LUDEWIG, H. E.
1858 The literature of American aboriginal languages. London.

LUMHOLTZ, C.
1891 Explorations in the Sierra Madre. *Scribner's Mag.*, vol. 10, no. 5.

1897 A case of trephining in northeastern

Mexico. *Proc. Amer. Acad. Arts and Sci.* Boston.

1898 Explorations au Mexique, de 1894 à 1897. *Jour. Soc. Amer. Paris*, 2: 179–84.

1898 The Huichol Indians of Mexico. *Bull. Amer. Mus. Natural Hist.*, 10: 1–14.

1900 Symbolism of the Huichol Indians. *Amer. Mus. Natural Hist., Mem. Anthr.*, vol. 2, no. 1.

1902 Unknown Mexico. 2 vols. New York.

1904 El México desconocido. Balbino Dávalos, tr. Spanish edition of his 1902.

1904 Decorative art of the Huichol Indians. *Amer. Mus. Natural Hist., Mem. Anthr.*, 2: 279–326.

1907 Among the Tarahumaras: the American cave dwellers. *Scribner's Mag.*, July.

1912 New trails in Mexico. New York.

—— AND A. HRDLIČKA

1897 Trephining in Mexico. *Amer. Anthr.*, 10: 389–96.

LUNDELL, C. L.

1934 Preliminary sketch of the phytogeography of the Yucatan peninsula. *Carnegie Inst. Wash.*, Pub. 436, Contrib. 12.

1937 The vegetation of the Peten. *Ibid.*, Pub. 478.

1945 The vegetation and natural resources of British Honduras. *In* Verdoorn, 1945, pp. 270–73.

LUSCHAN, F. VON

1916 Ueber Hautfarbentafeln. *Zeitschr. für Ethnol.*, 48: 402–06.

MCAFEE, B.

1952 Danza de la gran conquista. *Tlalocan*, 3: 246–73.

MCARTHUR, H. S.

1961 La estructura político-religiosa de Aguacatán. *Guatemala Indíg.*, 1: 41–56.

MCBIRNEY, A. R.

1958 Active volcanoes of Nicaragua and Costa Rica. Catalogue of Active Volcanoes of the World, pt. 4, pp. 107–46. Naples.

MCBRIDE, G. M.

1923 The land systems of Mexico. *Amer. Geog. Soc., Research Ser.*, no. 12.

MCBRYDE, F. W.

1934 Solola, a Guatemalan town and Cakchiquel market-center. *Tulane Univ., Middle Amer. Research Inst.*, Pub. 5, pp. 45–152.

1943 The black lacquer mystery of the Guatemala Maya. *Sci. Monthly*, 57: 113–18.

1947 Cultural and historical geography of southwest Guatemala. *Smithsonian Inst., Inst. Social Anthr.*, Pub. 4.

MCCLENDON, J. J. C.

1961 An ethnographic sketch of Topiltepec and Pochahuixco. MS.

MACCURDY, G. G.

1910 An Aztec "calendar stone" in Yale University Museum. *Amer. Anthr.*, 12: 481–96.

1911 A study of Chiriquian antiquities. *Mem. Connecticut Acad. Arts and Sci.*, vol. 3.

MCDAVID, R. I., JR.

1946 Dialect geography and social science problems. *Social Forces*, 25: 168–72.

1951 Dialect differences and inter-group tensions. *Studies in Ling.*, 9: 27–33.

—— AND V. G. MCDAVID

1952 *h* before semivowels in the eastern United States. *Language*, 28: 41–62.

MACDONELL, W. R.

1904 A study of the variation and correlation of the human skull, with special reference to the English crania. *Biometrika*, 3: 191–244.

MCDOUGALL, E.

1946 Observations on altar sites in the Quiche region, Guatemala. *Carnegie Inst. Wash., Notes Middle Amer. Archaeol. Ethnol.*, no. 62.

1947 Easter ceremonies at San Antonio Palopo, Guatemala. *Ibid.*, no. 81.

1955 Easter ceremonies at Santiago Atitlan in 1930. *Ibid.*, no. 123.

MACDOUGALL, T., AND I. W. JOHNSON

1966 *Chichicaztli* fiber: the spinning and weaving of it in southern Mexico.

Archiv für Völkerkunde, 20: 65–73. Vienna.

MACE, C.
1957 Collection of dances from Rabinal (Baja Verapaz), Guatemala. MS. Tulane Univ., Middle Amer. Research Inst.

McEWEN, G. F.
1916 Summary and interpretation of the hydrographic observations made by the Scripps Institution for Biological Research of the University of California, 1908 to 1915. *Univ. California Pub. Zool.*, 15: 255–356.

McGEE, W. J.
1898 The Seri Indians. *Smithsonian Inst., Bur. Amer. Ethnol.*, 17th ann. rept. (1895–96).

McGILL, H. C., JR., ed.
1968 The geographic pathology of atherosclerosis. *Laboratory Investigation*, 18 (5): 463–653.

MacGILLAVRY, H. J.
1934 Some rudistids from the Alta Verapaz. *Proc. Koninklijke Nederlandsche Akad. van Wetenschappen Amsterdam*, 37: 232–38.

1937 Geology of the province of Camaguey, Cuba, with revisional studies in rudistid paleontology. Dissertation, Univ. Utrecht.

McGIMSEY, C. R.
1956 Cerro Mangote: a preceramic site in Panama. *Amer. Antiquity*, 22: 151–61.

1957 Further data and a date from Cerro Mangote, Panama. *Ibid.*, 23: 434–35.

MacGOWAN, K., AND J. A. HESTER
1962 Early man in the New World. *Natural Hist. Library*, no. 22, pp. 136–39. Garden City, N.Y.

McGREGOR, J. C.
1943 Burial of an early American magician. *Proc. Amer. Phil. Soc.*, 86: 270–98.

MACÍAS, C.
1912 Los tehuantepecanos actuales. *Bol. Mus. Nac.*, 2: 18–29. Mexico.

1912 Caracteres étnicos en general. *An. Mus. Nac. Arqueol. Hist. Etnog.*, ep. 3, 4: 169–83.

—— AND A. RODRÍGUEZ GIL
1910 Estudio etnográfico de los actuales indios Tuxpaneca del estado de Jalisco. *Ibid.*, ep. 3, 2: 195–219.

MACÍAS VILLADA, M.
1954 Estudio agrológico de gran visión de la península de Yucatan. Sec. Rec. Hidráulicos.

1960 Suelos de la República Mexicana. *Ingeniería Hidráulica en México*, 14: (2) 51–71; (3) 63–73.

McINTOSH, J. B.
1945 Huichol phonemes. *Int. Jour. Amer. Ling.*, 11: 31–35.

1949 Cosmogonía huichol. *Tlalocan*, 3: 14–21.

—— AND J. GRIMES
1954 Niuqui 'iquisicayari: vocabulario huichol-castellano, castellano-huichol. Inst. Ling. Verano. Mexico.

MacIVER, R. M., AND C. H. PAGE
1949 Society: an introductory analysis. New York.

McKAUGHAN, H. P.
1954 Chatino formulas and phonemes. *Int. Jour. Amer. Ling.*, 20: 23–27.

—— AND B. McKAUGHAN
1951 Diccionario de la lengua chatino. Inst. Ling. Verano. Mexico.

MacKIE, E. W.
1961 New light on the end of the classic Maya culture at Benque Viejo, British Honduras. *Amer. Antiquity*, 27: 216–24.

MACKIE, W. W.
1943 Origin, dispersal and variability of the lima bean, *Phaseolus lunatus*. *Hilgardia*, 15: 1–29.

McKINLAY, A.
1945 Visits with Mexico's Indians. Mexico.

McKUSICK, M. B.
1960 Aboriginal canoes in the West Indies. *Yale Univ. Pub. Anthr.*, no. 63.

—— AND A. T. GILMAN
1959 An acorn grinding site in Baja California. *Univ. California Archaeol. Survey*, ann. rept., pp. 47–58.

McMAHON, A.
1967 Phonemes and phonemic units of Cora (Mexico). *Int. Jour. Amer. Ling.*, 33: 128–34.

—— AND M. J. McMahon

1959 Vocabulario Cora. Ser. Vocabularios Indígenas Mariano Silva y Aceves, no. 2. Inst. Ling. Verano. Mexico.

MacNeish, R. S.

n.d. Midseason report of the second Tamaulipas archaeological expedition. MS, File 565, Technical Archives, Inst. Nac. Antr.

n.d. Culture and agriculture in prehistoric southwest Tamaulipas, Mexico. MS.

1947 A preliminary report on coastal Tamaulipas, Mexico. *Amer. Antiquity*, 13: 1–13.

1948 Prehistoric relationships between the cultures of the southeastern United States and Mexico in light of an archaeological survey of the state of Tamaulipas, Mexico. Doctoral dissertation, Univ. Chicago.

1950 A synopsis of the archaeological sequence in the Sierra de Tamaulipas. *Rev. Mex. Estud. Antr.*, 11: 79–96.

1954 An early archaeological site near Panuco, Vera Cruz. *Trans. Amer. Phil. Soc.*, 44: 539–641.

1954 The Pointed Mountain site near Fort Liard, Northwest Territories, Canada. *Amer. Antiquity*, 19: 234–53.

1956 Prehistoric settlement patterns on the northeastern periphery of Mesoamerica. *In* Willey, 1956, Prehistoric settlement patterns, pp. 140–47.

1958 Preliminary archaeological investigations in the Sierra de Tamaulipas, Mexico. *Trans. Amer. Phil. Soc.*, 48: 1–209.

1959 A speculative framework of northern North American prehistory as of April, 1959. *Anthropologica*, n.s., 1 (1, 2): 7–23. Ottawa.

1959 Origin and spread of some domesticated plants as seen from Tamaulipas, Mexico. MS presented to annual meeting, Amer. Anthr. Assoc.

1960 Rejoinder to Taylor. *Amer. Antiquity*, 25: 591–93.

1961 Recent finds concerned with the incipient agriculture stage in prehistoric Meso-America. *In* Homenaje Martínez del Río, pp. 91–101.

1961 Restos precerámicos de la cueva de Coxcatlan en el sur de Puebla. *Inst. Nac. Antr. Hist., Dir. Prehistoria*, Pub. 10.

1961 First annual report of the Tehuacan archaeological-botanical project. Robert S. Peabody Found. Archaeol., Phillips Acad. Andover, Mass.

1962 Second annual report of the Tehuacan archaeological-botanical project. *Ibid.*

1964 Ancient Mesoamerican civilization. *Science*, 143: 531–37.

1964 The origins of New World civilization. *Sci. Amer.*, 211: 29–37.

——, A. Nelken-Terner, and I. W. Johnson

1967 Nonceramic artifacts. Vol. 2 of The prehistory of the Tehuacan Valley.

—— AND F. A. Peterson

1962 The Santa Marta rock shelter, Ocozocoautla, Chiapas, Mexico. *Papers New World Archaeol. Found.*, no. 14.

——, ——, AND K. V. Flannery

1970 Ceramics. Vol. 3 of The prehistory of the Tehuacan Valley.

MacNutt, F. A.

1908 Letters of Cortés: the five letters of relation from Hernando Cortés to the Emperor Charles V. 2 vols. New York.

McQuown, N. A.

n.d. Quiché phonemes and vocabulary. Univ. Chicago, Dept. Anthropology.

1941 La fonémica del cuitlateco, Mexico. *El Mex. Antiguo*, 5: 239–54.

1942 Una posible síntesis lingüística Macro-Mayance. *In* Mayas y Olmecas, 2: 37–38.

1942 La fonémica de un dialecto olmeco-mexicano de la sierra norte de Puebla. *El Mex. Antiguo*, 6: 61–72.

1954 Content analysis of language in culture. *In* Language in culture, *Amer. Anthr. Assoc.*, Memoir 79.

1955 *Review of* Chrétien, Beeler, Emeneau, and Haas, eds., Papers from the symposium on American Indian linguistics. *Int. Jour. Amer. Ling.*, 21: 73–77.

1955 The indigenous languages of Latin America. *Amer. Anthr.*, 57: 501–70.

1956   The classification of the Mayan languages. *Int. Jour. Amer. Ling.*, 22: 191–95.

1957   Linguistic transcription and specification of psychiatric interview materials. *Psychiatry*, 20: 79–86.

1959   [ed.] Report on the "Man-in-Nature" project of the department of anthropology of the University of Chicago in the Tzeltal-Tzotzil-speaking region of the state of Chiapas, Mexico. 3 vols. Hectographed.

1959   Overview and preview. *Ibid.*, ch. 4.

1959   Measures of dialect distance in Tzeltal-Tzotzil. *Ibid.*, ch. 21.

1960   Discussion of the symposium on translation between language and culture. *Anthr. Ling.*, 2 (2): 79–80.

1960   Middle American linguistics: 1955. *Pan Amer. Union, Middle Amer. Anthr.*, 2: 12–36.

1962   [ed.] Report on the 'Natural History' of the Tzeltal-Tzotzil speaking region of the state of Chiapas, Mexico. MS.

1964   Los orígines y la diferenciación de los mayas según se infiere del estudio comparativo de las lenguas mayanas. *In* Desarrollo cultural de los Mayas, pp. 49–80.

—— AND OTHERS
1959   Internal linguistic groupings in the transect communities. *In* his 1959, fig. 23.

McVAUGH, R.
1956   Edward Palmer: plant explorer of the American west. Univ. Oklahoma Press.

MADSEN, C.
1966   A study of change in Mexican folk medicine. *Tulane Univ., Middle Amer. Research Inst.*, Pub. 25, pp. 89–138.

MADSEN, W.
1955   Shamanism in Mexico. *SW. Jour. Anthr.*, 11: 48–57.

1955   Hot and cold in the universe of San Francisco Tecospa, valley of Mexico. *Jour. Amer. Folklore*, 68: 123–39.

1956   Aztec morals. *In* Encyclopedia of Morals, pp. 41–45. Philosophical Library of New York.

1957   Christo-paganism: a study of Mexican

religious syncretism. *Tulane Univ., Middle Amer. Research Inst.*, Pub. 19, pp. 105–80.

1960   The Virgin's children: life in an Aztec village today. Univ. Texas Press.

—— AND C. MADSEN
1948   The human birds of Papantla. *Travel Mag.*, 91: 24–28.

MAHONEY, R.
1961   Caballito Blanco (Oaxaca) again. *Katunob*, 2: 12.

MAK, C.
1959   Mixtec medical beliefs and practices. *Amer. Indig.*, 19: 125–51.

—— AND R. E. LONGACRE
1960   Proto-Mixtec phonology. *Int. Jour. Amer. Ling.*, 26: 23–40.

MAKEMSON, M. W.
1943   The astronomical tables of the Maya. *Carnegie Inst. Wash.*, Pub. 546, Contrib. 42.

1946   The Maya correlation problem. *Vassar College Observatory*, Pub. 5.

1951   The book of the jaguar priest: a translation of the book of Chilam Balam of Tizimin. New York.

MALDONADO, F.
16thC   Arte, pronunciación y ortografía de . . . cakchiquel. Photograph in Newberry Library.

MALDONADO, P. R.
1895   Estudio antropológico del niño. Puebla, Mex.

1899   La antropología criminal y pedagógica. *Mem. Soc. Cien. Antonio Alzate*, 14: 23–30.

MALDONADO-KOERDELL, M.
1947   Antecedentes del descubrimiento del hombre de Tepexpan. *Anthropos*, 1: 33–36.

1947–49   Bibliografía mexicana de prehistoria. *Bol. Bibliog. Antr. Amer.*, 9: 66–71; 10: 98–102; 11: 148–53.

1948   Los vertebrados fósiles del Cuaternario en Mexico. *Rev. Soc. Mex. Hist. Natural*, 9: 1–35.

1952   Formaciones con fusulínidos del Permo-Carbonífero Superior de Mexico. *Ciencia*, 12: 235–47.

1953   Plantas del rético-liásico y otros fósiles Tríasicos de Honduras (Centroamerica). *Ibid.*, 12: 294–96.

1953 Mamíferos recientes y fósiles de Mexico. *Ibid.*, 13: 79–84.

1954 La formación y caracteres del pedregal de San Angel. *Tlatoani*, nos. 8, 9, pp. 2–6.

1954 Nomenclatura, bibliografía y correlación de las formaciones arqueozoicas y paleozoicas de Mexico. *Bol. Asoc. Mex. Geol. Petroleros*, 6: 113–38.

1954–55 La historia geohidrológica de la cuenca de Mexico. *Rev. Mex. Estud. Antr.*, 14: 15–21.

1958 Recientes adelantos en geofísica y geología submarinas en las areas del océano Pacífico próximas a Mexico. *Ciencia*, 18: 105–13.

1958 Nomenclatura, bibliografía y correlación de las formaciones continentales (y algunas marinas) del Mesozoico de Mexico. *Bol. Asoc. Mex. Geol. Petroleros*, 10: 287–308.

1958 Bibliografía geológica y paleontológica de America Central. *Inst. Panamer. Geog. e Hist.*, Pub. 204.

—— AND L. AVELEYRA ARROYO DE ANDA

1949 Nota preliminar sobre dos artefactos del Pleistoceno Superior hallados en la región de Tequixquiac, Mexico. *El Mex. Antiguo*, 7: 154–61.

MALER, T.

1895 Yukatekische forschungen. *Globus*, 68: 247–60, 277–92.

1901–03 Researches in the central portion of the Usumatsintla valley. *Mem. Peabody Mus., Harvard Univ.*, vol. 2, nos. 1, 2.

1902 Yukatekische forschungen. *Globus*, 82: 197–230.

1908 Explorations of the upper Usumatsintla and adjacent region: Altar de Sacrificios; Seibal; Itsimte-Sacluk; Cancuen. *Mem. Peabody Mus., Harvard Univ.*, vol. 4, no. 1.

1908 Explorations in the Department of Peten, Guatemala, and adjacent region: Topoxte; Yaxha; Benque Viejo; Naranjo. *Ibid.*, vol. 4, no. 2.

1911 Explorations in the Department of Peten, Guatemala: Tikal. *Ibid.*, vol. 5, no. 1.

1912 Lista de las ilustraciones para una proyectada publicación, de Teobert Maler, en el libro de recuerdos del Congreso Americanistas, 1910. *17th Int. Cong. Amer.*, Reseña 2d sess.

1942 Descubrimiento de una tumba real zapoteca en Tehuantepec, en el año de 1875. *El Mexico Antiguo*, 6: 1–5.

MALINOWSKI, B., AND J. DE LA FUENTE

1957 La económica de un sistema de mercados en México. *Acta Anthr.*, ser. 2, vol. 1, no. 2. Mexico.

MANDELBAUM, D. G., ed.

1949 Selected writings of Edward Sapir, in language, culture, and personality. Berkeley.

MANGELSDORF, P. C.

1954 New evidence on the origin and ancestry of maize. *Amer. Antiquity*, 19: 409–10.

—— AND R. H. LISTER

1956 Archaeological evidence on the evolution of maize in northwestern Mexico. *Bot. Mus. Leafl., Harvard Univ.*, 17: 151–78.

—— R. S. MACNEISH, AND W. C. GALINAT

1956 Archaeological evidence on the diffusion and evolution of maize in northeastern Mexico. *Ibid.*, 17: 125–50.

1964 Domestication of corn. *Science*, 143 (3606): 538–45.

—— AND D. L. OLIVER

1951 Whence came maize to Asia? *Bot. Mus. Leafl., Harvard Univ.*, 14: 263–91.

—— AND R. G. REEVES

1939 The origin of Indian corn and its relatives. *Texas Agric. Expt. Sta.*, Bull. 574.

1959 The origin of corn. III: Modern races, the product of teosinte introgression. *Bot. Mus. Leafl., Harvard Univ.*, 18: 389–411.

1959 The origin of corn. IV: Place and time of origin. *Ibid.*, 18: 413–27.

—— AND C. E. SMITH

1949 New archaeological evidence on evolution in maize. *Ibid.*, 13: 213–47.

MANJE, J. M.

1954 Luz de tierra incognita. Part 2. H. J. Karns, trans. Tucson.

MANN, C. E.
1958 Ethnography of the lowland Mixe. Master's thesis, Mexico City College.
—— AND R. CHADWICK
1960 Present-day use of ancient calendars among the lowland Mixe. *Bol. Estud. Oaxaqueños*, no. 19.

MANN, G. V., J. A. MUÑOZ, AND N. S. SCRIMSHAW
1954 Serum lipid levels of Central Americans. *Federation Proc.*, 13: 467.

MANNERS, R. A.
1956 Functionalism, realpolitik and anthropology in underdeveloped areas. *Amer. Indig.*, 16: 7–33.

MANÓ, J. C.
1883 Primer informe presentado a la secretaría de fomento, por . . . comisionado por el supremo gobierno para estudiar la República de Guatemala bajo el punto de vista mineralógico. *An. Soc. Geog. e Hist. de Guatemala*, 16: 304–07 (1939–40).
1883 Segundo informe. . . . *Ibid.*, 16: 384–400 (1939–40).

MANOUVRIER, L.
1888 Mémoire sur la platycnémie chez l'homme et chez les anthropoïdes. *Mem. Soc. Anthr. Paris*, ser. 2, 3: 469–548.
1893 La détermination de la taille d'après les grands os des membres. *Ibid.*, vol. 4.

MANRIQUE CASTAÑEDA, L.
1957 Notas de campo sobre el área pame. Inst. Nac. Antr. Hist., Depto. Invest. Antr. Mexico.
1959 Sobre la clasificación del otomí-pame. *33d Int. Cong. Amer.* (San Jose, 1958), Acta, 2: 551–59.
1959 Field notes. MS.
1960 Dos gramáticas pames del siglo XVIII. *An. Inst. Nac. Antr. Hist.*, vol. 11, no. 40.
1961 La organización social de Jiliapan, Hidalgo. *Ibid.*, 13: 95–111.
1967 Jiliapan Pame. *In* Handbook of Middle American Indians, vol. 5, art. 7G.

MANUEL, H. T.
1934 Physical measurements of Mexican

children in American schools. *Child Development*, 5: 237–52.

MANZO DE CONTRERAS, C.
1661 Relación cierta y verdadera de lo que sucedió y ha sucedido en esta villa de Guadalcazar, provincia de Tehuantepec. . . . Mexico.

MAPS
1904 Nuevo mapa oficial de estado de Sonora. Sonora News Co., Nogales, by C. E. Herbert.
1948 U.S.A.F. preliminary base. Sec. 4718 (Douglas) Aeronautical Chart Service. Washington.
1958 World aeronautical chart. Secs. 405 (Gila River), 406 (Estacado Plains), 471 (Sonora), 470 (Santiago Mts.). U.S. Coast and Geodetic Survey.
1958 Estados Unidos Mexicanos. Com. Intersecretarial Coordinadora del Levantamiento de la Carta Geográfica de la República Mexicana. Hermosillo, 12R-IV; Chihuahua, 13R-III; Nogales, 12R-II; Ciudad Juarez, 13R-I. Mexico.

MAQUEO CASTELLANOS, E.
1936 El espectro de Guiengola: leyenda zapoteca. *Neza*, 2 (13): 4–7.

MARCHAL, H.
1951 Le décor et la sculpture Khmers. *Etudes d'Art et d'Ethnol. Asiatiques*, vol. 3. Paris.

MARDEN, L.
1959 Dzibilchaltun: up from the well of time. *Nat. Geog. Mag.*, 115: 110–29.

MARGÁIN, C. R.
1939 Escultura náhoa. *Artes Plásticas*, 1: 57–69.
1944 Zonas arqueológicas de Querétaro, Guanajuato, Aguascalientes, y Zacatecas. *In* El Norte de México, pp. 145–48.
1956 La habitación popular en el México prehispánico. Soc. Arquitectos Mexicanos, Colegio Nac. de Arquitectos de México, *Ciclo de Conferencias sobre Vivienda Popular*, no. 5.
1966 Sobre sistemas y materiales de construcción en Teotihuacán. *In* Teotihuacán, pp. 157–211.

1968 Sobre la policromía del llamado "Calendario Azteca." MS.

MARÍN TAMAYO, F.
1960 La división racial en Puebla de los Angeles bajo el régimen colonial. Puebla.

MARINA ARREOLA, A.
1961 Población de los altos de Chiapas durante el siglo XVII e inicios del XVIII. *In* Los Mayas del sur, pp. 247–64.

MARINGER, J.
1950 Contributions to the prehistory of Mongolia. *Sino-Swedish Exped.*, Pub. 34, no. 7. Stockholm.

MARINO FLORES, A.
1945 La criminología y una nueva técnica de craneología constitucionalista. *Rev. Mex. Estud. Antr.*, 7: 113–49.
1952 *See* Comas, 1952.
1956 Indígenas de México: algunas consideraciones demográficas. *Amer. Indig.*, 16: 41–48.
1957 Bibliografía lingüística de la República Mexicana. *Inst. Ind. Interamer.* Mexico.
1958–59 Grupos lingüísticos del estado de Guerrero. *Rev. Mex. Estud. Antr.*, 15: 95–114.
1963 Distribución municipal de los hablantes de lenguas indígenas en la República Mexicana. Inst. Nac. Antr. Hist. Mexico.
—— AND A. CASTRO DE LA FUENTE
1960 La población agrícola y la educación en la República Mexicana. *Inst. Nac. Antr. Hist.*, Pub. 4. Mexico.

MARISCAL, F.
1928 Estudio arquitectónico de las ruinas mayas: Yucatan y Campeche. Sec. Educ. Púb. Mexico.

MARMER, H. A.
1926 The tide. New York and London.

MARQUINA, I.
1928 Estudio arquitectónico comparativo de los monumentos arqueológicos de Mexico. *Contrib. of Mexico to 23d Int. Cong. Amer.*, pp. 1–86.
1939 Atlas arqueológico de la República Mexicana. *Inst. Panamer. Geog. Hist.*, Pub. 41.
1944 Los monumentos de Mexico y los del suroeste y sureste de Estados Unidos. *In* El Norte de México, pp. 252–54.
1951 Arquitectura prehispánica. *Inst. Nac. Antr. Hist.*, Mem. 1. Mexico. (2d ed., enlarged, 1964.)
1960 El Templo Mayor de México. Inst. Nac. Antr. Hist. Mexico.
1964 Arquitectura prehispánica. (2d ed. of his 1951.)
1968 Exploraciones en la pirámide de Cholula. *Bol. Inst. Nac. Antr. Hist.*, 32: 12–19.

MARROQUÍN, A. D.
1954 Tlaxiaco: una ciudad mercado. *Inst. Nac. Indig.*, Ed. Mimeográficas, no. 4. Mexico.
1955 Factor económico y cambio social. *Amer. Indig.*, 15: 215–26.
1956 Consideraciones sobre el problema económico de la región Tzeltal-Tzotzil. *Ibid.*, 16: 191–203.
1957 La ciudad mercado (Tlaxiaco). Mexico.

MARTÍ, S.
1955 Instrumentos musicales precortesianos. Inst. Nac. Antr. Hist. Mexico.

MARTIN, N. F.
1957 Los vagabundos en la Nueva España en el siglo 16. Mexico.

MARTIN, PAUL SCHULTZ
1958 A biogeography of reptiles and amphibians in the Gomez Farias region, Tamaulipas, Mexico. *Univ. Michigan, Mus. Zool.*, Misc. Pub. 101.

MARTIN, PAUL SIDNEY, J. B. RINALDO, AND OTHERS
1952 Mogollon cultural continuity and change: the stratigraphic analysis of Tularosa and Cordova caves. *Fieldiana: Anthr.*, vol. 40.
1954 Caves of the Reserve area. *Ibid.*, vol. 42.
1961 Mineral Creek site and Hooper Ranch pueblo, eastern Arizona. *Ibid.*, vol. 52.
1962 Chapters in the prehistory of eastern Arizona, I. *Ibid.*, vol. 53.

MARTIN, R.
1928 Lehrbuch der Anthropologie, in systematischer Darstellung. 3 vols. 2d ed. Jena.

—— AND K. SALLER

1957 Lehrbuch der Anthropologie in systematischer Darstellung. Vol. 1. 3d ed. Stuttgart.

MARTINET, A.

1954 Dialect. *Romance Philology*, 8: 1–11.

MARTÍNEZ, L.

1937 Caracteristicas hematológicas de los indios otomies. *An. Inst. Biol.*, 8: 273–306. Mexico.

MARTÍNEZ, M.

1936 Plantas utiles de México. Mexico.

1959 Plantas medicinales de México. Mexico.

1959 Plantas utiles de la flora mexicana. Ed. Botas. Mexico.

MARTÍNEZ, P. L.

1956 Historia de Baja California. Mexico.

1958 El magonismo en Baja California: documentos. Mexico.

MARTÍNEZ BACA, F.

1897 Estudio craneométrico zapoteca. *11th Int. Cong. Amer.* (Mexico, 1895), Acta, pp. 237–64.

—— AND M. VERGARA

1892 Estudios de antropología criminal. Puebla, Mex.

MARTÍNEZ DEL RÍO, P.

1947 El hombre fósil de Tepexpan. *Cuad. Amer.*, no. 4, pp. 139–50.

1952 Los orígenes americanos. 3d ed. Mexico.

1952 El mamut de Santa Isabel Iztapan. *Cuad. Amer.*, no. 4, pp. 149–70.

1953 La cueva mortuoria de La Candelaria, Coahuila. *Ibid.*, no. 4, pp. 177–204.

1953 A preliminary report on the mortuary cave of Candelaria, Coahuila, Mexico. *Bull. Texas Archaeol. Paleontol. Soc.*, 24: 208–56.

1954 La comarca lagunera a fines del siglo XVI y principios del XVII según las fuentes escritas. *Univ. Nac. Autónoma Méx., Pub. Inst. Hist.*, 1st ser., no. 30.

MARTÍNEZ DURÁN, C.

1964 Las ciencias médicas en Guatemala. 3d ed. Guatemala.

MARTÍNEZ ESPINOSA, E.

1959 Una nueva escultura olmeca de Ton-

ala, Chiapas. *Inst. Cien. Artes Chiapas*, 1: 79–81. Tuxtla Gutierrez.

MARTÍNEZ GRACIDA, M.

1883 Catálogo etimológico de los nombres de los pueblos, haciendas y ranchos del estado de Oaxaca. Oaxaca.

1883 Colección de cuadros sinópticos. Anexo no. 50 a la memoria administrativa. Oaxaca.

1897 Minería y su industria. *11th Int. Cong. Amer.* (Mexico, 1895), Acta, pp. 426–42.

1898 Mitología mixteca. *Mem. y Rev. Soc. Cien. Antonio Alzate*, 11: 421–34.

1910 Civilización chontal: historia antigua de la Chontalpa oaxaqueña. *Ibid.*, 30: 29–104, 223–325.

MARTÍNEZ HERNÁNDEZ, J.

1909 Las crónicas mayas. Revisión y traducción del texto de las crónicas de Chicxulub, de Maní, de Tizimín, de Chumayel. MS. Biblioteca Cepeda. Merida.

1909 El Chilam Balam de Maní. Códice Pérez. Merida.

1926 Crónicas mayas: crónica de Yaxkukul. Merida.

1929 Diccionario de Motul: Prólogo; Arte de lengua maya [por Fray Juan Coronel, 1620]; Carta de los diez caciques [1567]; Diccionario Maya-Español [Fray Antonio de Ciudad Real, 1600?]. Merida.

MÁRTIR DE ANGLERÍA

See Anghiera, P. M. d'

MARTYR, P.

See Anghiera, P. M. d'

MASON, G.

1927 Silver cities of Yucatan. New York.

MASON, J. A.

n.d. Notes and observations on the northern Tepehuan Indians. MS. [See his 1952, same title.]

1912 The fiesta of the pinole at Azqueltan (Tepehuan). *Mus. Jour., Univ. Pennsylvania*, 3 (3): 44–50.

1913 The Tepehuan Indians of Azqueltan. *18th Int. Cong. Amer.* (London, 1912), Acta, pp. 344–51.

1917 Tepecano, a Piman language of western Mexico. *Ann. New York Acad. Sci.*, 25: 309–416.

1918 Tepecano prayers. *Int. Jour. Amer. Ling.*, 1: 91–153.

1920 The Papago harvest festival. *Amer. Anthr.*, 22: 13–25.

1921 The Papago migration legend. *Jour. Amer. Folklore*, 34: 254–68.

1923 A preliminary sketch of the Yaqui language. *Univ. California Pub. Amer. Archaeol. Ethnol.*, 20: 193–212.

1927 Native American jades. *Mus. Jour., Univ. Pennsylvania*, 18: 47–73.

1935 Preserving ancient America's finest sculptures. *Nat. Geog. Mag.*, 68: 537–70.

1935 The place of Texas in pre-Columbian relationships between the United States and Mexico. *Bull. Texas Archaeol. Paleontol. Soc.*, 7: 29–46.

1936 Classification of the Sonoran languages. *In* Essays in anthropology, presented to A. L. Kroeber, pp. 183–98.

1936 Archaeological work in Durango during March, 1936. *Bull. Univ. Pennsylvania Mus.*, 6: 136–37.

1937 Late archaeological sites in Durango, Mexico, from Chalchihuites to Zape. *Pub. Philadelphia Anthr. Soc., Twenty-fifth Anniversary Studies*, 1: 127–46.

1939 Los quatro grandes filones lingüísticos de México y Centro América. *27th Int. Cong. Amer.* (Mexico, 1939), Acta, 2: 282–88.

1940 The native languages of Middle America. *In* The Maya and their neighbors, pp. 52–87.

1942 New excavations at the Sitio Conte, Cocle, Panama. *Proc. 8th Amer. Sci. Cong.*, vol. 2. Washington.

1943 The American collections of the University Museum: the ancient civilizations of Middle America. *Bull. Univ. Pennsylvania Mus.*, 10: 1–2.

1945 Costa Rican stonework: the Minor C. Keith Collection. *Amer. Mus. Natural Hist., Anthr. Papers*, vol. 39, no. 3.

1948 The Tepehuan and other aborigines of the Mexican Sierra Madre Occidental. *Amer. Indig.*, 8: 289–300.

1950 The language of the Papago of Arizona. *Univ. Pennsylvania, Mus. Monogr.*

1951 On two Chinese figurines found in Mesoamerica. *In* Homenaje Caso, pp. 271–76.

1952 Some initial phones and combinations in Utaztecan stems. *Int. Jour. Amer. Ling.*, 18: 9–11.

1952 Notes and observations on the Tepehuan. *Amer. Indig.*, 12: 33–50.

1959 The Tepehuan of northern Mexico. *Mitteilungen aus dem Museum für Völkerkunde in Hamburg*, 25: 91–96.

1960 Mound 12, Chiapa de Corzo, Chiapas, Mexico. *Papers New World Archaeol. Found.*, no. 9.

1960 The terrace to north of Mound 13, Chiapa de Corzo, Chiapas, Mexico. *Ibid.*, no. 11.

—— AND D. M. BRUGGE

1958 Notes on the lower Pima. *In* Misc. Paul Rivet, 1: 277–97.

—— AND A. M. ESPINOSA

1914 Folktales of the Tepecanos. *Jour. Amer. Folklore*, 27: 148–210.

MASON, O. T.

1881 Noticia de una momia encontrada en una cueva llamada del Coyote, en Coahuila. *Smithsonian Inst.*, ann. rept. 1880, p. 445.

1904 Aboriginal American basketry: studies in a textile art without machinery. *Ibid.*, ann. rept. for year ending 1902, pp. 171–548.

MASSEY, W. C.

n.d. Archaeology in central and southern Baja California: the Castaldí Collection. MS.

n.d. The historical ethnography of Baja California. MS.

1947 Brief report on archaeological investigations in Baja California. *SW. Jour. Anthr.*, 3: 344–59.

1949 Tribes and languages of Baja California. *Ibid.*, 5: 272–307.

1955 Culture history in the cape region of Baja California. Doctoral dissertation, Univ. California.

1961   The survival of the dart-throwers on the peninsula of Baja California. *SW. Jour. Anthr.*, 17: 81–93.

1961   The cultural distinction of aboriginal Baja California. Soc. Mex. Antr. Mexico.

—— AND C. M. OSBORNE
1961   A burial cave in Lower California: the Palmer Collection, 1887. *Univ. California Anthr. Records*, vol. 16, no. 8.

—— AND D. R. TUOHY
n.d.   Caves of the Sierra de la Giganta.
n.d.   Petroglyphs of Baja California.
n.d.   Pottery from the northwest coast of Baja California Norte, Mexico.

MASTACHE, A. G.
1966   Técnicas prehispánicas de tejido. Master's thesis, Esc. Nac. Antr. Hist., Inst. Nac. Antr. Hist. Mexico.

1970   Tejidos arqueológicos de una cueva seca de la región de Caltepec, Puebla. Paper presented to 35th annual meeting, Society for American Archaeology, Mexico, 1970.

MATEOS HIGUERA, S.
1930   Breve monografía y reglas del "patolli." Mexico.

1948   La pictografía tarasca. *In* El Occidente de México, pp. 160–74.

MATIENZO, J. DE
1910   Obra escrita en el siglo XVI por el Lic. don Juan Matienzo, oidor de la Real Audiencia de Charcos. Facultad Filosofía y Letras, Sec. Hist. Lima.

MATOS MOCTEZUMA, E.
1968   Piezas de saqueo procedentes de Jerécuaro, Gto. *Bol. Inst. Nac. Antr. Hist.*, 33: 30–35.

MATRÍCULA DE HUEXOTZINCO
1560   Matrícula de Huexotzinco, manuscrit mexicain 387. Bibliothèque Nationale. Paris.

MATRÍCULA DE TRIBUTOS
1890   *See* Peñafiel, 1890, vol. 2, pls. 228–59.

MATSON, D. S., AND A. H. SCHROEDER
1957   Cordero's description of the Apache, 1796. *New Mexico Hist. Rev.*, 32: 335–56.

MATSON, G. A.
1938   Blood groups and ageusia in Indians of Montana and Alberta. *Amer. Jour. Physical Anthr.*, 24: 81–89.

1941   Distribution of the blood groups among the Sioux, Omaha, and Winnebago Indians. *Ibid.*, 28: 313–18.

——, E. A. KOCH, AND P. LEVINE
1954   A study of the hereditary blood factors among the Chippewa Indians of Minnesota. *Ibid.*, n.s., 12: 413–26.

—— AND G. L. PIPER
1947   Distribution of the blood groups, M-N, Rh types and secretors among the Ute Indians of Utah. *Ibid.*, n.s., 5: 357–68.

—— AND H. F. SCHRADER
1933   Blood grouping among "Blackfeet" and "Blood" tribes of American Indians. *Jour. Immunology*, 25: 155–63.

—— AND J. SWANSON
1959   Distribution of hereditary blood antigens among the Maya and non-Maya Indians in Mexico and Guatemala. *Amer. Jour. Physical Anthr.*, n.s., 17: 49–74.

1960   [Unpublished data.]

1961   Distribution of hereditary blood antigens among Indians in Middle America: Lacandon and other Maya. *Amer. Anthr.*, 63: 1292–1322.

1963   Distribution of hereditary blood antigens among Indians in Middle America: II, Tzotzil and other Maya. *Amer. Jour. Physical Anthr.*, n.s., 21: 1–14.

1963   Distribution of hereditary blood antigens among Indians in Middle America: III, In Guatemala. *Ibid.*, 21: 301–17.

1963   Distribution of blood groups among Indians in Middle America: IV, In Honduras. *Ibid.*, 21: 319–33.

1963   Distribution of hereditary blood antigens among Indians in Middle America: V, In Nicaragua. *Ibid.*, 21: 545–59.

1964   Distribution of hereditary blood antigens among Indians in Middle America: VI, In British Honduras. *Ibid.*, 22: 271–84.

1965 Distribution of hereditary blood antigens among Indians in Middle America: VII, In Costa Rica. *Ibid.*, 23: 107–22.

1965 Distribution of hereditary blood antigens among Indians in Middle America: VIII, In Panama. *Ibid.*, 23: 413–26.

—— AND OTHERS

1958 (J. Swanson, J. Noades, R. Sanger, and R. R. Race). A "new" antigen and antibody in the P system. *Proc. 7th Int. Cong. Blood Transfusion*, pp. 581–86. Rome.

1959 (J. Swanson, J. Noades, R. Sanger, and R. R. Race). A "new" antigen and antibody belonging to the P blood group system. *Amer. Jour. Human Genetics*, 11: 26–34.

1966 (H. E. Sutton, J. Swanson, A. Robinson, and A. Santiana). Distribution of hereditary blood antigens among Indians in South America: I, In Ecuador. *Amer. Jour. Physical Anthr.*, 24: 51–70.

MATTHEWS, W.

1891 The human bones of the Hemenway collection in the U.S. Army Medical Museum at Washington. *Mem. Nat. Acad. Sci.*, 6: 141–286.

MATUS, V. E.

1935 Nuestro istmo zapoteca. *Neza*, 1 (4): 1, 5.

1935 Tópicos de mi tierra. *Ibid.*, 1 (5): 1, 5.

1939 Comentarios sobre zapoteco y nahuatl. *El Universo Gráfico*, 18 (7677): 8, 15.

1939 Lecciones de escritura comparada zapoteca. *Ibid.*, 18 (7659): 8, 19.

1939 ¿Zapoteco moderno? *Ibid.*, 18 (7749): 9, 13.

1940 Sandunga tehuantepecana. *Oaxaca en México*, special issue, October, pp. 32–34.

1940 El verbo zapoteco. *El Universo Gráfico*, 19 (8024): 11.

1941 El zapoteco. *Istmo*, 2 (2, 12): 4–5.

1942 Poesía zapoteca. *Ibid.*, 2 (2, 13): 4.

1945 Zapotecos del istmo de Oaxaca. *In* L. Alvárez y Alvárez de la Cadena,

ed., Leyendas y costumbres, trajes y danzas, pp. 359–65. Mexico.

MAUDSLAY, A. C., AND A. P. MAUDSLAY

1899 A glimpse at Guatemala and some notes on the ancient monuments of Central America. London.

MAUDSLAY, A. P.

1889–1902 Archaeology. *In* Biologia Centrali-Americana. 5 vols. London.

MAYA AND THEIR NEIGHBORS, THE

1940 The Maya and their neighbors. C. L. Hay and others, eds. New York.

MAYA SOCIETY

1937 The Maya society and its work. Baltimore.

MAYAS ANTIGUOS, LOS

1941 Los Mayas antiguos: monografías de arqueología, etnografía y lingüística mayas, publicadas con motivo del centenario de la exploración de Yucatán por John L. Stephens y Frederick Catherwood en los años 1841–42. C. Lizardi Ramos, ed. Colegio de Mex. Mexico.

MAYAS DEL SUR, LOS

1961 Los mayas del sur y sus relaciones con los nahuas meridionales. VIII mesa redonda, San Cristobal de las Casas, Chiapas. Soc. Mex. Antr. Mexico.

MAYAS Y OLMECAS

1942 Mayas y Olmecas. Rafael Pascacio Gamboa, ed. Segunda reunión de mesa redonda sobre problemas antropológicos de México y Centro América, Tuxtla Gutiérrez. Soc. Mex. Antr.

MAYER, B.

1844 Mexico: Aztec, Spanish and Republican. New York. (2d ed. 1953, Mexico.)

1857 Observations on Mexican history and archaeology, with a special notice of Zapotec remains. *Smithsonian Contrib. Knowledge*, 9: 1–33.

MAYER, M.

1958 Poconchi texts. Summer Inst. Ling. Norman.

MAYER-OAKES, W. J.

1959 A stratigraphic excavation at El Risco, Mexico. *Proc. Amer. Phil. Soc.*, 103: 332–73.

1963 Early man in the Andes. *Sci. Amer.*, 208: 116–28.

—— AND R. E. BELL

1960 Early man site found in highland Ecuador. *Science*, 131: 1805–06.

MAYERS, M. K.

1959 Maya area linguistics. *In* McQuown, 1959, fig. 14.

1960 The linguistic unity of Pocomam-Pocomchi. *Int. Jour. Amer. Ling.*, 26: 317–29.

1960 The phonemes of Pocomchi. *Anthr. Ling.*, 2: 1–39.

1966 Languages of Guatemala.

——, Y. HAJDA, AND N. A. McQUOWN

1959 Tzeltal-Tzotzil linguistics description, distributions, relations. *In* McQuown, 1959, ch. 8.

—— AND N. A. McQUOWN

1959 Lexicostatistics of transect informant short list. *Ibid.*, fig. 15.

1959 Dialect areas as determined by lexicostatistical distance counts (transect map). *Ibid.*, fig. 16.

MAYR, E.

1946 History of the North American bird fauna. *Wilson Bull.*, 58: 1–41.

MAZA, A. DE LA

1947 La nación pame. *Bol. Soc. Mex. Geog. Estad.*, vol. 63, no. 2.

1953 La Pamería a través de los tiempos. *In* Huastecos, Totonacos, pp. 269–80.

MAZA, F. DE LA

1959 La ciudad de Cholula y sus iglesias. Inst. Invest. Estéticas. Mexico.

MAZZOTTI, L.

1934 Grupos sanguíneos de los indios Seri. *Salubridad*, 5 January-March. Mexico.

1942 Existence of Microfilaria Ozzardi in Mexico. *Rev. Inst. Salubridad y Enfermedad Tropical Méx.*, 3: 223.

MEADE, J.

1939 Documentos inéditos para la historia de Tampico, siglos XVI y XVII. Mexico.

1940 ¿Fué la nación Maguage la misma que la Olive? *Divulgación histórica*, 2: 28–31. Mexico.

1942 La Huasteca: época antigua. Mexico.

1948 Arqueología de San Luis Potosi. Mexico.

1950 Fray Andrés de Olmos. *Mem. Acad. Mex. Hist.*, 9: 374–452. Mexico.

1953 Historia prehispánica de la Huasteca. *In* Huastecos, Totonacos, pp. 291–302.

MEANS, P. A.

1917 History of the Spanish conquest of Yucatan and of the Itzas. *Papers Peabody Mus., Harvard Univ.*, vol. 7.

MEAVE, J. A. DE

1791 Memoria sobre la pintura del pueblo de Olinalan de la jurisdicción de Tlalpam dispuesta por su cura propietario y juez eclesiástico D. Joaquín Alejo de Meave. *Gaceta de Literatura*, 2: 173–78. Mexico.

1831 *Idem. Gaceta de Literatura de México*, 2: 213–20. Puebla.

MECHAM, J. L.

1938 The origin of federalism in Mexico. *Hispanic Amer. Hist. Rev.*, 18: 164–82.

MECHLING, W. II.

1912 Indian linguistic stocks of Oaxaca, Mexico. *Amer. Anthr.*, 14: 643–82.

1912 Stories from Tuxtepec, Oaxaca. *Jour. Amer. Folklore*, 25: 199–203.

1916 Stories and songs from the southern Atlantic coastal region of Mexico. *Ibid.*, 29: 547–58.

MEDELLÍN ZENIL, A.

1950 Arqueología de Remojadas. MS in Archivo Inst. Antr. Veracruz. Jalapa.

1952 Distribución geográfica de la "Cultura de Remojadas": exploraciones arqueológicas de 1952. MS, *ibid.*

1952 Exploraciones en Quauhtochco. Gobierno del estado de Veracruz, Depto. Antr. Jalapa.

1953 Exploraciones en Los Cerros y Dicha Tuerta. MS in Archivo Técnico, Inst. Antr., Univ. Veracruzana. Jalapa.

1953 Secuencia cronológico-cultural en el centro de Veracruz. *In* Huastecos, Totonacos, pp. 371–78.

1955 Desarrollo de la cultura prehispánica central veracruzana. *An. Inst. Nac. Antr. Hist.*, 7: 101 110.

151

1955 Exploraciónes en la Isla de Sacrificios. Gobierno del estado de Veracruz. Jalapa.

1960 Cerámicas del Totonacapan: exploraciones arqueológicas en el centro de Veracruz. Jalapa.

1960 Nopiloa: un sitio clásico del Veracruz central. *Palabra y Hombre*, 13: 37–48.

1960 Monolitos inéditos olmecas. *Ibid.*, 16: pp. 75–98.

1962 El monolito de Maltrata, Veracruz. *Ibid.*, 24: 555–62.

——, O. Paz, and F. Beveride

1962 Magia de la risa. Mexico.

—— and F. A. Peterson

1954 A smiling head complex from central Veracruz, Mexico. *Amer. Antiquity*, 20: 162–69.

Medina, A.

1960 Field notes. MS.

1961 Informe preliminar sobre un paraje de Tenejapa. MS, Chiapas Project files, Univ. Chicago, Dept. Anthropology.

1961–62 Notas de campo y reportes sobre Tenejapa. *Ibid.*

Medina, J. T.

1912 Monedas usadas por los Indios de América al tiempo del descubrimiento según los antiguos documentos y cronistas españoles. *17th Int. Cong. Amer.* (Mexico, 1910), Acta, pp. 556–57.

Medina de la Torre, F.

1934 Monumentos arqueológicos en el oriente del estado de Jalisco. *Bol. Junta Auxiliar Jalisciense de la Soc. Mex. Geog. y Estad.* Guadalajara.

Medinilla, M.

1883 Una idea de los idiomas . . . caminos, ríos, hamacas . . . [district of Tuxtepec]. *In* Martínez Gracida, 1883, Colección.

Médioni, G.

1950 Art maya du Mexique et du Guatemala. Ancien Empire. Paris.

1952 L'art tarasque du Mexique: Mexique occidental. Paris.

—— and M. T. Pinto

1941 Art in ancient Mexico. Collection of Diego Rivera. New York.

Médiz Bolio, A.

1941 Literatura indígena moderna. Mexico.

1943 Introducción al estudio de la lengua maya. Mexico.

Meek, S. E.

1904 The freshwater fishes of Mexico north of the Isthmus of Tehuantepec. *Field Columbia Mus., Zool. Ser.,* Pub. 93, vol. 5.

1907 Synopsis of the fishes of the Great Lakes of Nicaragua. *Ibid.*, Pub. 121, 7: 97–157.

1908 Zoology of lakes Amatitlan and Atitlan, Guatemala, with special reference to ichthyology. *Ibid.*, Pub. 127, 7: 159–206.

Meggers, B. J.

1954 Environmental limitation on the development of culture. *Amer. Anthr.*, 56: 801–24.

1963 Cultural development in Latin America: an interpretative overview. *In* Meggers and Evans, 1963, pp. 131–45.

—— and C. Evans

1955 [eds.] New interpretations of aboriginal American culture history. *Anthr. Soc. Washington*, 75th anniv. vol.

1957 Archeological investigations at the mouth of the Amazon. *Smithsonian Inst., Bur. Amer. Ethnol.*, Bull. 167.

1962 The Machalilla culture: an early formative complex on the Ecuadorian coast. *Amer. Antiquity*, 28: 186–92.

1963 [eds.] Aboriginal cultural development in Latin America: an interpretative review. *Smithsonian Misc. Coll.*, vol. 146, no. 1.

1964 Especulaciones sobre rutas tempranas de difusión de la cerámica entre Sur y Mesoamérica. *Hombre y Cultura*, 1 (3): 1–5. Panama.

Meighan, C. W.

1950 Excavations in sixteenth century shell-mounds at Drake's Bay, Marin County. *Univ. California Archaeol. Survey*, Rept. 9, pp. 27–32.

1959 New findings in west Mexican archaeology. *Kiva*, 25: 1–7.

1960 Prehistoric copper objects from western Mexico. *Science*, 131 (3412): 1534.

1961   Interrelationships of New World cultures: field activities of Project A (west Mexico), 1960–1961. Mimeographed. Dept. Anthropology, Univ. California, Los Angeles.

—— AND R. F. HEIZER

1952   Archaeological exploration of sixteenth-century Indian mounds at Drake's Bay. *California Hist. Soc. Quar.*, 31: 98–108.

MEIGS, J. A.

1866   Observations upon the cranial forms of the American aborigines. *Proc. Acad. Natural Sci.*, 18: 197–235.

MEIGS, P.

1935   The Dominican mission frontier of Lower California. *Univ. California, Pub. Geog.*, no. 7.

1939   The Kiliwa Indians of Lower California. *Ibero-Amer.*, no. 15.

MEILLET, A., AND M. COHEN

1924   Les langues du monde. Paris. (Rev. ed., 1952.)

MEJÍA, D.

1876   Nuevo aparato para medir con precisión todos los diámetros del cráneo. *Gaceta Méd. Méx.*, 11: 261–68.

MEJÍA, J. V.

1927   Geografía de la República de Guatemala. 2d ed. Guatemala.

MELGAREJO VIVANCO, J. L.

1947   La provincia de Tzicoac. Jalapa.

1943   Totonacapan. Jalapa.

1950   Historia de Veracruz (época prehispánica). Jalapa.

MELHUS, I. E., ed.

1949   Plant research in the tropics. Agricultural Exp. Station, Iowa State College.

MEMORIA . . . SANTA ANA

1565   Memoria título de Santa Ana. MSS in Pokom, no. 6 in volume of photographs of Kekchi documents prepared by W. Gates.

MEMORIAL DE SOLOLA

1950   Memorial de Solola. Anales de los Cakchiqueles. Bib. Amer., Ser. Lit. Indígena.

MEMORIAL . . . TLACUPAN

1939–42 Memorial de los pueblos sujetos al señorio de Tlacupan, y de los que tributaban a México, Tezcuco y Tlacupan. *In* Paso y Troncoso, 1939–42, 14: 118–22.

MEN AND CULTURES

1960   *See* Wallace, 1960.

MENA, C.

n.d.   [Medicina maya.] MS. Photograph in Newberry Library. 159 pp.

MENA, R.

1911   Los dientes de los indios. *Mem. Soc. Cien. Antonio Alzate*, 30: 211–13.

1913   El trabajo de la obsidiana en México: ejemplares de la colección arqueológica de la Sociedad Mexicana de Geografía y Estadística. *Bol. Soc. Mex. Geog. Estad.*, 6: 203–11.

1924   Arqueología: monolitos. Cartillas de vulgarización del Museo Nacional de México.

1930   Educación intelectual y física entre los náhuas y mayas precolombinos. Mexico.

MENARD, H. W.

1955   Deformation of the northeastern Pacific basin and the west coast of North America. *Bull. Geol. Soc. Amer.*, 66: 1149–98.

1959   Geology of the Pacific sea floor. *Experientia*, 15: 205, 244.

1960   The east Pacific rise. *Science*, 132: 1737–46.

MENDELSON, E. M.

1956   Les Maya des hautes terres. *Critique*, 115: 1076–87. Paris. [Also in Seminario de Integración Social Guatemalteca, Cuad. 6.]

1958   The king, the traitor and the cross: an interpretation of a highland Maya religious conflict. *Diogenes*, 21: 1–10. Chicago.

1958   A Guatemalan sacred bundle. *Man*, 58 (art. 170): 121–26.

1959   Maximón: an iconographical introduction. *Ibid.*, 59 (art. 87): 57–60.

1962   Religion and world-view in Santiago Atitlan. *Univ. Chicago, Micro. Coll. MSS Middle Amer. Cult. Anthr.*, no. 52.

1965   Los escándalos de Maximón. *Seminario de Integración Social Guatemalteca.*

153

MÉNDEZ, A. C. DE
1959 El comercio de los Mayas antiguos. *Acta Anthr.*, vol. 2, no. 1.

MÉNDEZ, J., AND C. BEHRHORST
1963 The anthropometric characteristics of Indians and urban Guatemalans. *Human Biol.*, 35: 457–83.

MÉNDEZ DE LA VEGA, J., M. A. GUZMÁN, AND F. AGUIRE
1952 Niveles de vitaminas y proteinas, valores hematológicos y hallazgos parasitológicos en diversos grupos de población. *Rev. Colegio Med. Guatemala*, 3: 17–23.

MENDIETA, G. DE
1870 Historia eclesiástica indiana. J. García Icazbalceta, ed. Mexico.
1945 *Idem*. S. Chávez Hayhoe, ed. 4 vols. Mexico.

MENDIETA HUERTA, E.
1939 La economía de los pueblos indígenas huastecos de San Luis Potosi. *Rev. Mex. Sociol.*, 1: 57–68. Mexico.

MENDIETA Y NÚÑEZ, L., ed.
1940 Los tarascos: monografía histórica, etnográfica y económica. Inst. Invest. Sociales. Mexico.
1949 Los zapotecos: monografía histórica, etnográfica y económica. Mexico.

MENDIZABAL, M. O. DE
1928 Influencia de la sal en la distribución geográfica de los grupos indígenas de México. Mus. Nac. Arqueol. Hist. Etnog. Mexico. *Also in* his 1946–47, 2: 181–340.
1939 La demografía mexicana: época colonial 1519–1810. *Bol. Soc. Mex. Geog. Estad.*, 48: 301–41.
1946 La evolución del noroeste de México. *In* his 1946–47, 3: 7–86.
1946 Charts at end of vol. 5 in his 1946–47.
1946–47 Obras completas. 6 vols. Mexico.
1947 Evolución económica y social del valle de Mezquital. *In* his 1946–47, vol. 6.
1947 Industrias de los otomíes contemporáneos. *In* his 1946–47, vol. 6.
—— AND W. JIMÉNEZ MORENO
1936 Mapa lingüístico de Norte- y Centro-

América. *Inst. Panamer. Geog. Hist.* Mexico.
1937 Distribución prehispánica de las lenguas indígenas de México. Mapa. *Ibid.*
1939 Lenguas indígenas de México. Mapa de su distribución prehispánica. *Ibid.*
——, ——, AND E. ARANA OSNAYA
1959 Linguistic map. *In* Esplendor del México antiguo, p. 97.

MENDNER, S.
1956 Das Ballspiel im Leben der Völker. Münster.

MENDOZA, V. T.
1955 La danza durante la colonia de México. *Tradición, Rev. peruana cultura*, 19–20: 13–18. Cuzco.
1956 Panorama de la música tradicional de México. Mexico.

MENGET, P.
1968 Death in Chamula. *Natural Hist.*, 67: 48–57.

MENGIN, E., ed.
1942–50 Corpus codicum Americanorum medii aevi. 6 vols. Copenhagen.
1945 *See* Anales de Tlatelolco, 1945.
1950 Diferentes historias originales de los reynos de Culhuacan y de México y de otras provincias. 5a Relación de Chimalpahin. *Mitteilungen aus dem Mus. für Völkerkunde in Hamburg*, 22.
1952 Commentaire du Codex Mexicanus nrs. 23–24 de la Bibliothèque Nationale de Paris. *Jour. Soc. Amer. Paris*, 41: 387–498.

MENZEL, D., J. H. ROWE, AND L. DAWSON
1964 The Paracas pottery of Ica, a study in style and time. *Univ. California Pub. Amer. Archaeol. Ethnol.*, vol. 50.

MERCADO SÁNCHEZ, P.
1959 Breve reseña sobre las principales artes de pesca usadas en Mexico. Sec. Industria y Comercio, Dir. General de Pesca e Industrias Conexas, pp. 1–79.
1961 Corrección y modernización del sistema de captura del camarón en aguas interiores del noroeste de Mexico. *Acta Zool. Mex.*, 4: 1–11.

MERCER, H. C.

1896　The hill caves of Yucatan. Philadelphia.

MERCK GARCÍA, C.

1958　Consideraciones sobre difteria en Guatemala (revisión de 87 casos). Tesis de médico y cirujano, Facultad Cien. Méd., Univ. San Carlos de Guatemala.

MEREJKOWSKY, C.

1882　Sur quelques crânes americaines. *Bull. Soc. Anthr. Paris*, 5: 170–80.

MÉRIDA, C.

1938　Pre-hispanic dance theater. *Theater Arts Monthly*, 22: 561–68.

1940　Carnavales de México. Mexico.

MERRIAM, C.

1932　Zapotecan funeral. *Mex. Life*, 8 (9): 11–13.

MERRIAM, C. H.

1891　The geographic distribution of life in North America. *Smithsonian Inst.*, ann. rept., pp. 365–415.

1898　Life zones and crop zones of the United States. U.S. Dept. Agriculture. *Biol. Survey*, Bull. 10.

MERRIFIELD, W. R.

1959　Chinantec kinship in Palantla, Oaxaca, Mexico. *Amer. Anthr.*, 61: 875–81.

1966　Linguistic clues for the reconstruction of Chinantec prehistory. *In* Pompa y Pompa, 1966, pp. 579–96.

MERRILL, R. H.

1945　Maya sun calendar dictum disproved. *Amer. Antiquity*, 10: 307–11.

MERTON, R.

1957　Social theory and social structure. Glencoe.

MERWIN, R. E.

1909–10　Note book no. 4. Peabody Mus., Harvard Univ.

1913　The ruins of the southern part of the peninsula of Yucatan with special reference to their place in the Maya area. Doctoral dissertation, Harvard Univ. MS in Peabody Mus.

—— AND G. C. VAILLANT

1932　The ruins of Holmul, Guatemala. *Mem. Peabody Mus., Harvard Univ.*, vol. 3, no. 2.

MERZ, A.

1906　Beiträge zur Klimatologie und Hydrographie Mittelamerikas. *Mitt. des Vereins für Erdkunde zu Leipzig*, 1906: 1–96.

METEOROLOGICAL OFFICE

1956　Monthly meteorological charts of the eastern Pacific Ocean. *British Meteorological Office*, 518: 1–122. London.

METZGER, B.

1959　The social structure of three Tzeltal communities: Omaha systems in change. *In* McQuown, 1959, sec. 25.

1960　Notes on the history of Indian-Ladino relations in Chiapas. MS. Laboratory Social Relations, Harvard Univ.

METZGER, D.

n.d.　An interpretation of drinking performances in Aguacatenango. MS.

1959　The social organization of Aguacatenango, Chiapas: a preliminary statement. MS.

1959　A preliminary evaluation of institutionalized social control and its contribution to cultural pluralism in the highlands of Chiapas. *In* McQuown, 1959, sec. 23.

1960　Report on Aguacatenango. MS.

—— AND R. RAVICZ

1966　Field notes on Tenejapa Tzeltal. MS.

—— AND G. WILLIAMS

1963　A formal ethnographic analysis of Tenejapa Ladino weddings. *Amer. Anthr.*, 65: 1076–1101.

1963　Tenejapa medicine. I: the curer. *SW. Jour. Anthr.*, 19: 216–34.

MÉXICO, DEPARTAMENTO DE MONUMENTOS

1935　*See* Tenayuca, 1935.

MÉXICO, DIRECCIÓN GENERAL DE ESTADÍSTICA

1943　Sexto censo de población (1940).

1944　Mapas lingüísticos de la República Mexicana. Depto. Asuntos Indígenas. Mexico.

1953　Séptimo censo . . . (1950).

1963　Octavo censo . . . (1960).

MÉXICO, MINISTERIO DE FOMENTO, COLONIZACIÓN E INDUSTRIA

1884　Trabajos de la Secretaría de Fomento

de la República Mexicana sobre el Axe.

MÉXICO PREHISPÁNICO
1946 México prehispánico: culturas, deidades, monumentos. J. A. Vivó, ed. Mexico.

MÉXICO Y LA CULTURA
1946 México y la cultura. Sec. Educación Pública. Mexico. (2d ed. 1961.)

MEXICO CITY COLLEGIAN
1960 Issue of August 4.

MEYER-ABICH, H.
1952 Das Erdbeben von Jucuapa en El Salvador vom 6 und 7 Mai 1951. *Neues Jahrbuch für Mineralogie und Geologie*, Abhandlungen, 95: 311–36.
1952–53 Consideraciones generales acerca de la planta eléctrica proyectada en el lugar "Chorrera del Guayabo" en el Rio Lempa. *Comunicaciones Inst. Tropical Invest. Cien. Univ. El Salvador*, 1: 1–6.
1953 Los ausoles de El Salvador, con un sumario geológico-tectónico de la zona volcánica occidental. *Ibid.*, 2: 55–94.
1956 Los volcanes activos de Guatemala y El Salvador. *An. Servicio Geol., El Salvador*, Bol. 3.
1958 Active volcanoes of Guatemala and El Salvador. *In* Mooser, Meyer-Abich, and McBirney, 1958, pp. 37–105.

MEZA, C.
1954 Hacia el panorama psiquiátrico en Guatemala. *Rev. Colegio Méd. Guatemala*, 5: 63–76.

MEZA, O.
1934 Leyendas aztecas. Mexico.

MEZA CALIX, U.
1916 Geografía de Honduras. Tegucigalpa.

MICHEL, C.
1951 Cantos indígenas de México. Inst. Nac. Indig. Mexico.

MICHELSEN, R.
1967 Pecked metates of Baja California. *Masterkey*, 41 (2): 73–77.
—— AND R. C. OWEN
1967 A keruk ceremony at Santa Catarina, Baja California, Mexico. *Pacific Coast Archaeol. Soc. Quar.*, vol. 3, no. 1.

MILES, S. W.
1948 A comparative analysis of the survivals of the ancient Maya calendar. Master's thesis, Univ. Chicago.
1952 An analysis of modern Middle American calendars: a study in conservatism. *In* Tax, 1952, Acculturation, pp. 273–84.
1957 The sixteenth-century Pokom-Maya: a documentary analysis of social structure and archaeological setting. *Trans. Amer. Phil. Soc.*, 47: 731–81.
1957 Maya settlement patterns: a problem for ethnology and archaeology. *SW. Jour. Anthr.*, 13: 239–48.
1958 An urban type: extended boundary towns. *Ibid.*, 14: 339–51.

MILLA, J. D.
1879 Historia de la América Central desde los primeros españoles (1502) hasta su independencia de la España (1821). Guatemala.

MILLÁN MALDONADO, A.
1942 Folklore. Univ. Nac. Autónoma. Mexico.

MILLER, A. G.
1967 The birds of Quetzalpapalotl. *Ethnos*, 32: 5–17.

MILLER, E. B., R. E. ROSENFIELD, AND P. VOGEL
1951 On the incidence of some of the new blood agglutinogens in Chinese and Negroes. *Amer. Jour. Physical Anthr.*, n.s., 9: 115–26.

MILLER, F. C.
1959 Social structure and changing medical practices in a Mexican Indian community. *In* McQuown, 1959, sec. 3.
1959 Social structure and medical change in a Mexican Indian community. Doctoral dissertation, Harvard Univ.
1960 The influence of decision-making on the process of change: the case of Yalcuc. *In* Leslie, 1960, Social Anthropology, pp. 29–35.
1964 Tzotzil domestic groups. *Jour. Royal Anthr. Inst.*, 94: 172–82. London.
1965 Cultural change as decision-making: a Tzotzil example. *Ethnology*, 4: 53–65.

MILLER, G. S., AND R. KELLOGG
1955 List of North American recent mammals. *Smithsonian Inst., U.S. Nat. Mus.*, Bull. 205.

MILLER, R. R.
1958 Origin and affinities of the freshwater fish fauna of western North America. *In* Zoogeography, Amer. Assoc. Advancement Sci., Pub. 51, pp. 187–222.

MILLER, W. S.
1956 Cuentos mixes. *Inst. Nac. Indig., Biblioteca Folklore Indig.*, no. 2. Mexico.
1961 Notes on the Mixe. MS.

MILLON, R. F.
1954 Irrigation at Teotihuacan. *Amer. Antiquity*, 20: 176–80.
1957 Irrigation systems in the valley of Teotihuacan. *Ibid.*, 23: 160–66.
1957 New data on Teotihuacan I in Teotihuacan. *Bol. Centro Invest. Antr. Mex.*, no. 4, pp. 12–17.
1959 La agricultura como inicio de la civilización. *In* Esplendor del México antiguo, 2: 997–1018.
1960 Chronological and developmental classifications in Mesoamerican prehistory. MS presented to annual meeting (1959), Amer. Anthr. Assoc.
1960 The beginnings of Teotihuacan. *Amer. Antiquity*, 26: 1–10.
1964 Valley of Teotihuacan chronology. Mimeographed chart, dated 1964, distributed during 11th Round Table meeting, Soc. Mex. Antr., 1966. Mexico.
1966 Cronología y periodificación: datos estratigráficos sobre períodos cerámicos y sus relaciones con la pintura mural. *In* Teotihuacán, pp. 1–18.
1966 Décimaprimera mesa redonda de antropología. *Bol. Inst. Nac. Antr. Hist.*, no. 25.
1966 Extensión y población de la ciudad de Teotihuacán en sus diferentes períodos: un cálculo provisional. *In* Teotihuacán, pp. 57–78.
1967 Teotihuacan. *Sci. Amer.*, 216: 38–48.

—— AND J. A. BENNYHOFF
1961 A long architectural sequence at Teotihuacan. *Amer. Antiquity*, 26: 516–23.

——, B. DREWITT, AND J. A. BENNYHOFF
1965 The Pyramid of the Sun at Teotihuacan: 1959 investigations. *Trans. Amer. Phil. Soc.*, vol. 55, part 6.

—— AND R. E. LONGACRE
1961 Proto-Mixtecan and Proto-Amuzgo-Mixtecan vocabularies: a preliminary cultural analysis. *Anthr. Ling.*, 3 (4): 1–44.

MILLS, C. A.
1942 Climatic effects on growth and development with particular reference to the effects of tropical residence. *Amer. Anthr.*, 44: 1–13.

MINTZ, S. W.
1953 The folk urban continuum and the rural proletarian community. *Amer. Jour. Sociol.*, 59: 136–45.

—— AND E. R. WOLF
1950 An analysis of ritual co-parenthood (compadrazgo). *SW. Jour. Anthr.*, 6: 341–68.

MIRAMBELL, L.
1961 Evangelización y organización eclesiástica en la época colonial. *In* Los Mayas del Sur, pp. 221–32.

MIRAMONTES, F.
1936 Geografía económica agrícola del estado de Michoacán. *In* Cámara de Diputados, vol. 4. Mexico.

MIRANDA, F.
1947 Rasgos de la vegetación de la cuenca del Rio de las Balsas. *Rev. Soc. Mex. Hist. Natural*, 8: 95–114.
1948 Datos sobre la vegetación en la cuenca alta del Papaloapan. *An. Inst. Biol. Univ. Nac. Autónoma de Mex.*, 19: 333–64.
1952–53 La vegetación de Chiapas. 2 vols. Tuxtla Gutierrez, Depto. Prensa y Turismo.
1959 Estudios acera de la vegetación. *In* Beltrán, 1959, pp. 215–71.

—— AND A. J. SHARP
1950 Characteristics of vegetation in certain temperate regions of eastern Mexico. *Ecology*, 31: 313–33.

MIRANDA, J.
1952 El tributo indígena en la Nueva Es-

paña durante el siglo XVI.   Colegio de México.   Mexico.

—— AND S. ZAVALA
1954   Instituciones indígenas en la colonia. *In* Caso, 1954, Métodos, pp. 29–167.

MISCELÁNEA PAUL RIVET
1958   Miscelánea Paul Rivet, octogenario dicata. 2 vols. Presentation by P. Bosch Gimpera. Univ. Nac. Autónoma Mex.

MITCHELL, R. H.
1959   Projectile points from Panama. *Panama Archaeol.*, vol. 2, no. 1.
1959   An unreported pottery vessel from Panama. *Ibid.*, vol. 2, no. 1.
in press   Wooden artifacts from cave urnburials in Madden Lake. *Ethnos.*

MODIANO, N.
1964   Mental testing among Tzeltal and Tzotzil children. *35th Int. Cong. Amer.* (Mexico, 1962), Acta, 3: 65–78.
1968   A Chamula life. *Natural Hist.*, 67: 58–63.

MOEDANO KOER, H.
1941   Estudio preliminar de la cerámica de Tzintzuntzan: temporada III. *Rev. Mex. Estud. Antr.*, 5: 21–42.
1942   Estudio general sobre la situación de la fortaleza de Oztuma. *27th Int. Cong. Amer.* (Mexico, 1939), Acta, 1: 557–63.
1944   La diosa raptada. *Nosotros*, 1 (19): 24–26.   Mexico.
1944   El octavo xiuhmolpilli. *El Nacional*, March 22, section 1, pp. 3–4.
1946   La cerámica de Zinapécuaro, Michoacán. *An. Mus. Michoacano*, ep. 2, no. 4, pp. 39–49.
1946   Jaina: un cementerio maya. *Rev. Mex. Estud. Antr.*, 8: 217–42.
1947   El friso de los caciques. *An. Inst. Nac. Antr. Hist.*, 2: 113–36.   Mexico.
1948   Breve noticia sobre la zona de Oztotitlan, Guerrero. *In* El Occidente de México, pp. 105–06.

MOEN, M. L., AND INCAP STUDENTS
1953   Consumo de alimentos de trece familias de los empleados de una fábrica de textiles en Quezaltenango, Guatemala, C. A. *Bol. Oficina Sanitaria Panamer.*, suppl. 1, pp. 37–49.

MOLINA, A. DE
1555   Aquí comiença un vocabulario en lengua castellana y mexicana. . . .   Mexico.
1571   Arte de la lengua mexicana y castellana.   *In* Col. de gramáticas, pp. 127–224.   (2d ed., 1576.)
1571   Vocabulario de la lengua mexicana. Mexico.   (Leipzig, 1880.)
1944   Vocabulario en lengua castellana y mexicana. *In* Colección de incunables americanos, siglo XVI, vol. 4. Ediciones Cultura Hispánica (facsimile ed. of 1571 ed.).   Madrid.

MOLINA, A. G.
1892   El jazmín del istmo: principios generales para aprender a leer, escribir y hablar la lengua zapoteca.   Oaxaca.
1894   La rosa de amor: frases en español y zapoteca.   San Blas Tehuantepec.

MOLINA ENRÍQUEZ, R.
1925   Las lacas de México. *Ethnos*, ep. 3, 1: 115–24.   Mexico.
1928   Lacas de México: los baules de Olinalá. *Forma*, 1 (6): 15–22. Mexico.

MOLINA SOLÍS, J. F.
1896   Historia del descubrimiento y conquista de Yucatan con una reseña de la historia antigua de esta península. Merida.

MOLINS FABREGA, N.
1956   El Códice Mendocino y la economía de Tenochtitlan.   Mexico.

MONGES CALDERA, J.
1960   Trabajos gravimétricos en las Americas. *Bol. Biblio. Geofísica y Oceanogr. Amer.*, 2: 341–51.

MONTAGU, R.
1958   Preliminary summary of a survey in the Tojolabal region, Chiapas, Mexico.   MS.
1959   Preliminary report on the city of San Cristobal.   MS, Chiapas Project files, Univ. Chicago, Dept. Anthropology.
1960–61   Field notes of the fincas of the region of Ocosingo. *Ibid.*

—— AND E. HUNT
1962   Nombre, autoridad y el sistema de creencias en los altos de Chiapas. *Estud. Cultura Maya*, 2: 141–47.

MONTELL, G.
1937 Statens etnografiska museums expedition till Mexico 1934–35: de etnografiska undersökningarna. *Ethnos*, 2: 301–18. Stockholm.

MONTEMAYOR, F.
1950–56 La población de Veracruz; historia de las lenguas; culturas actuales; rasgos físicos de la población. Mexico.

MONTENEGRO, M. L.
1943 Consideraciones sobre la tripanosomiasis americana o enfermedad de chagas en Guatemala. Tesis de médico y cirujano, Facultad Cien. Méd., Univ. Nac. Guatemala.

MONTERDE, F.
1955 Teatro indígena prehispánico: Rabinal Achí. *Bib. Estudiante Universitario*, no. 71. Mexico.

MONTERDE, J. M.
1842–45 Información sobre las ruinas de Casas Grandes, Chihuahua.

MONTOYA, J. J., J. M. VÁZQUEZ, AND M. E. MORALES
1961 Informe sobre el trabajo de campo en San Pablito, Puebla. MS en Depto. Invest. Antr., Inst. Nac. Antr. Hist. Mexico.

MONTÚFAR, L.
1879 Reseña histórica de Centro-América. 7 vols. (1878–87). Guatemala.

MONZÓN, A.
1945 Restos de clanes exogámicos entre los cora de Nayarit. *Escuela Nac. Antr.*, Pub. 4, pp. 12–16. Mexico.
1945 Teogonía trique. *Tlalocan*, 2: 3–9.
1947 Planteamiento de algunos problemas indígenas. *Amer. Indig.*, 7: 323–31.
1949 El calpulli en la organización social de los tenochca. *Univ. Nac. Autónoma Méx.*, Pub. Inst. Hist., 1st ser., no. 14.

—— AND A. ESPEJO
1945 Algunas notas sobre organización social de los tlatelolca. *Mem. Acad. Mex. Hist.*, 4: 484–89.

MONZÓN MALICE, C. M.
1951 Consideraciones sobre el tema de poliomielitis, e informe sobre los casos observados durante el año de 1949. *Rev. Colegio Méd. Guatemala*, 2 (2): 5–11.

MOONEY, G. X.
1957 Mexican folk dances for American schools. Univ. Miami Press.

MOORE, C. B.
1905 Certain aboriginal remains of the Black Warrior River. *Jour. Acad. Natural Sci. Philadelphia*, 13: 337–405.

MOORE, R., ed.
1962 Evolution. Life Nature Library. New York.

MOORE, R. T.
1945 The transverse volcanic biotic province of central Mexico and its relationship to adjacent provinces. *Trans. San Diego Soc. Nat. Hist.*, 10: 217–36.

MOORE, S. F.
1958 Power and property in Inca Peru. New York.

MOORE, W. E.
1950 Utilization of human resources through industrialization. *Milbank Mem. Fund Quar.*, 28: 52–67. New York.
1951 Industrialization and labor: social aspects of economic development. New York.

MOOSER, F.
1957 Los ciclos de vulcanismo que formaron la cuenca de Mexico. *20th Cong. Geol. Int.*, pp. 337–48.
1958 Active volcanoes of Mexico. *In* Catalogue of the Active Volcanoes of the World, pt. 4, pp. 1–36. Naples.

—— AND F. GONZÁLEZ R.
1961 Erupciones volcánicas y el hombre primitivo en la Cuenca de México. *In* Homenaje Martínez del Río, pp. 137–41.

—— AND M. MALDONADO-KOERDELL
1961 Tectónica penecontemporanea a lo largo de la costa mexicana del Oceano Pacifico. *Geofísica Int.*, 1: 3–20.

——, H. MEYER-ABICH, AND A. R. MCBIRNEY
1958 Catalogue of the active volcanoes of the world. Pt. 4. Int. Volcanological Assoc. Naples.

——, S. E. WHITE, AND J. L. LORENZO
1956 La cuenca de Mexico: considera-

ciones geológicas y arqueológicas. *Inst. Nac. Antr. Hist.*, Pub. 2.

MORALES, S. A.
1950 Modos de vida otomí. MS en Bib. Inst. Indig. Interamer. Mexico.
1952 Relaciones étnicas en Chiapas. Notas de campo. MS.

MORALES GÓMEZ, A.
1944 El tlilamatl o libro de los dioses. Mexico.

MORALES HENESTROSA, B.
1936 Semblanzas zapotecas: fiestas y ropaje. *Neza*, 2 (15): 2, 5.
1937 Semblanzas zapotecas: perfiles de la sandunga. *Ibid.*, 3 (2): 57–59.

MORALES PATIÑO, O.
1949 Los Mayas de Honduras y los indígenas antillanos precolombinos. *Tzunpame*, año 7, no. 6–7, pp. 9–40.
1950 Los Mayas de Honduras y los indígenas antillanos precolombinos. *Rev. Arqueol. Ethnol.*, 2d ep., no. 10–11, pp. 69–100. Havana.

MORÁN, FRANCISCO
1685–95 Arte en lengua cholti. MS.

MORÁN, FRANCISCO
1914 Las arcadas dentarias en relación con las tendencias criminales del individuo. Mexico.

MORÁN, PEDRO
n.d. Bocabulario de solo los nombres de la lengua pokoman. . . . Photograph in Newberry Library. 242 pp.
1720 Arte breve y compendiosa de la lengua pocomchi. . . . MS in Bibliothèque Nationale.

MORANT, G. M.
1949 Changes in the size of British people in the past hundred years. *In* Homenaje a don Luis de Hoyos Sainz, pp. 235–42. Madrid.

MORENO, D. A.
1958 Los factores demográficos en la planeación económica. Ed. de la camara nacional de la industria de la transformación. Mexico.

MORENO, M. M.
1931 La organización política y social de los aztecas. Univ. Nac. Autónoma Méx.

MORENO DE LOS ARCOS, R.
1967 Los cinco soles cosmogónicos. *Univ.*

Nac. Autónoma Méx., Estud. Cultura Náhuatl, 7: 183–210.

MORGADANES, D.
1940 Similarity between the Mixco (Guatemala) and the Yalalag (Oaxaca, Mexico) costumes. *Amer. Anthr.*, 42: 359–64.

MORGAN, L. H.
1878 Ancient society or researches in the lines of human progress from savagery through barbarism to civilization. New York.

MORIARTY, J. M.
1964 The influence of strand plain morphology on the development of primitive industries along the Costa de Nayarit, Mexico. Part 1. *Amér. Indígena*, 24: 365–97.
1965 *Idem*, part 2. *Ibid.*, 25: 65–78.

MORISON, S. E.
1942 Admiral of the ocean sea: a life of Christopher Columbus. 2 vols. Boston.

MORLEY, S. G.
1915 An introduction to the study of the Maya hieroglyphs. *Smithsonian Inst., Bur. Amer. Ethnol.*, Bull. 57.
1916 The supplementary series in the Maya inscriptions. *In* Holmes Anniversary Volume, pp. 366–96.
1920 The inscriptions at Copan. *Carnegie Inst. Wash.*, Pub. 219.
1935 Guide book to the ruins of Quirigua. *Ibid.*, Supp. Pub. 16.
1937–38 The inscriptions of Peten. 5 vols. *Ibid.*, Pub. 437.
1946 The ancient Maya. Stanford Univ. Press. (2d ed. 1947; 3d ed. 1956, revised by G. W. Brainerd; reprinted 1963.)

—— AND F. R. MORLEY
1938 The age and provenance of the Leyden Plate. *Carnegie Inst. Wash.*, Pub. 509, Contrib. 24.

MORRIS, E. H.
1919 Preliminary account of the antiquities of the region between the Mancos and La Plata rivers in southwestern Colorado. *Smithsonian Inst., Bur. Amer. Ethnol.*, 33d ann. rept., pp. 155–206.
1927 The beginnings of pottery making in

the San Juan area: unfired prototypes and the wares of the earliest ceramic period. *Amer. Mus. Natural Hist., Anthr. Papers,* vol. 28, pt. 2.

1931 The Temple of the Warriors: the adventure of exploring and restoring a masterpiece of native American architecture in the ruined Maya city of Chichen Itza, Yucatan. New York.

——, J. CHARLOT, AND A. A. MORRIS

1931 The Temple of the Warriors at Chichen Itza, Yucatan. 2 vols. *Carnegie Inst. Wash.,* Pub. 406.

MORRISON, H.

1928 A classification of the higher groups and genera of the Coccid family Margarodidae. U.S. Dept. Agriculture, Technical Bull. 52.

MORTON, N. E., H. KRIEGER, A. G. STEINBERG, AND R. E. ROSENFIELD

1965 Genetic evidence confirming the localization of Sutter in the Kell blood group systems. *Vox Sanguinis,* 10: 608–13.

MORTON, S. G.

1839 Crania americana: or a comparative view of the skulls of various aboriginal nations of North and South America. Philadelphia and London.

1841 Mexican crania: Otomi, Chichimec, Tlascalan, Aztec. *Proc. Acad. Natural Sci.,* 1: 50–51.

1842 Yucatan (Ticul) skeleton. *Ibid.,* 1: 203–04.

1842 An inquiry into the distinctive characteristics of the aboriginal race of America. Boston.

MOSCOSO PASTRANA, P.

1961 El complejo ladino en los altos de Chiapas. *In* Los Mayas del Sur, pp. 265–78.

MOSS, M. L.

1960 A reevaluation of the dental status and chronological age of the Tepexpan remains. *Amer. Jour. Physical Anthr.,* 18: 71–72.

MOSS, W. L., AND J. A. KENNEDY

1929 Blood groups in Peru, Santo Domingo, Yucatan and among the Mexicans at the Blue Ridge prison farm in Texas. *Jour. Immunology,* 16: 159–74.

MOTA PADILLA, M. DE LA

1870 Historia de la conquista de la provincia de la Nueva Galicia. Mexico.

MOTA Y ESCOBAR, A. DE LA

1939–40 Memoriales del obispo de Tlaxcala Fray Alonso de la Mota y Escobar. *An. Inst. Nac. Antr. Hist.,* 1: 191–306.

1940 Descripción geográfica de los reinos de Nueva Galicia, Nueva Viscaya y Nuevo León. Intro. by J. Ramírez Cabanas. Mexico.

MOTOLINÍA, TORIBIO (FRAY TORIBIO DE BENAVENTE)

1541 Historia de los indios de la Nueva España. Barcelona. (Other eds. 1914, 1950.)

1858 *Idem. In* J. García Icazbalceta, Col. Doc. para la Historia de Mexico, 1: 1–249.

1903 Memoriales. *In* García Pimentel, 1903–07, vol. 1.

1914 Historia de los indios de la Nueva España. Barcelona.

1941 *Idem.* S. Chávez Hayhoe, ed. Mexico.

1950 History of the Indians of New Spain. *In* Documents and narratives concerning the discovery and conquest of Latin America, n.s., no. 4. E. A. Foster, ed. and trans. Cortés Soc. Berkeley.

MOTUL DICTIONARY

See Martínez Hernández, 1929.

MOURANT, A. E.

1954 The distribution of the human blood groups. Blackwell Sci. Pub. Oxford.

——, A. C. KOPÉC, AND K. DOMANIEWSKA-SOBCZAK

1958 The ABO blood groups: comprehensive tables and maps of world distribution. *Ibid.*

MUIR, J. M.

1926 Data on the structure of pre-Columbian Huastec mounds in the Tampico region, Mexico. *Jour. Royal Anthr. Inst.,* 56: 231–38. London.

MULLER, C. H.

1939 Relations of the vegetation and climatic types in Nuevo Leon, Mexico. *Amer. Midl. Naturalist,* 21: 687–729.

1947 Vegetation and climate of Coahuila. *Madroño*, 9: 33–57.

MÜLLER, E. F. J.
1956–57 El valle de Tulancingo. *Rev. Mex. Estud. Antr.*, 14: 129–38.

1961 Tres objetos de piedra de Huapalcaldo, estado de Hidalgo. *In* Homenaje a Pablo Martínez del Río, pp. 319–22.

1966 Instrumental y armas. *In* Teotihuacán, pp. 225–38.

MULLER, H. P. N.
1903 The Mitla ruins and the Mexican natives. *Hand. Nederl. Anthr. Ver.*, 1: 14–25. The Hague.

MÜLLER, M.
1888 Grundriss der Sprachwissenschaft. Vienna.

MÜLLERRIED, F. K. G.
1934 Sobre artefactos de piedra en la porción oriental del estado de Coahuila. *An. Mus. Nac. Arqueol. Hist. Ethnol.*, pp. 205–19.

1942 The Mesozoic of Mexico and northwestern Central America. *Proc. 8th Amer. Sci. Cong.*, 4: 124–47.

1942 Contribution to the geology of northwestern Central America. *Ibid.*, 4: 469–82.

1942 Valle de Tixtla, cuenca de desagüe subterráneo temporal en el estado de Guerrero. *Rev. Geog.*, 2: 17–48.

1944 El mapa geológico de la América Central. *Rev. Geog. Inst. Panamer. Geog. e Hist.*, 4: 35–64.

1945 Contribución a la geología de Mexico y noroeste de América Central. Mexico.

1947 Acerca del descubrimiento del hombre de Tepexpan (valle de Mexico). *Bol. Biblio. Antr. Amer.*, 9: 60–64.

1947 El mapa geológico de Centro-América. *An. Soc. Geog. e Hist. de Guatemala*, 22: 143–65.

1948 Las facies de fauna y flora del Mesozoico en el noroeste de la América Central (del Istmo de Tehuantepec a Nicaragua). *18th Int. Geol. Cong.*, Volume of Titles and Abstracts, sec. J, Faunal and Floral Correlations, p. 71.

1949 Rectificación de la estratigrafía del Mesozoico en el noroeste de América Central (del Istmo de Tehuantepec a Nicaragua). *Ciencia*, 9: 219–23.

1949 La orogénesis del sur y del sureste de México. *Bol. Soc. Geol. Mex.*, 14: 73–101.

1957 La geología de Chiapas. Gobierno constitucional del estado de Chiapas. Tuxtla Gutierrez.

——— AND H. VON WINNING
1943 El "Cerrito" al este de Tepotzotlán, México, en el Valle de México. *El Méx. Antiguo*, 6: 131–39.

MUMFORD, L.
1952 Art and technics. 2d ed. Columbia Univ. Press.

MUÑIZ, M., AND W. J. McGEE
1897 Primitive trephining in Peru. *Smithsonian Inst., Bur. Amer. Ethnol.*, 16th ann. rept. 1894–95, pp. 7–72.

MÜNNICH, K. O., H. G. OSTLUND, H. DE VRIES, AND H. BARKER
1958 Carbon 14 activity during the past 5000 years. *Nature*, 182: 1432–33.

MUÑOZ, J. A., C. PÉREZ, AND N. S. SCRIMSHAW
1955 Endemic goiter in Guatemala. *Amer. Jour. Tropical Med.*, 4: 963–69.

MUÑOZ, M.
1950 Notas preliminares sobre el municipio Tasquillo, estado de Hidalgo, México. MS en Bib. Inst. Indig. Interamer. Mexico.

1963 Mixteca Nahua-Tlapaneca. *Inst. Nac. Indig.*, Mem. 9. Mexico.

MUÑOZ CAMARGO, D.
1892 Historia de Tlaxcala. Annotated by A. Chavero. Mexico. (3d ed. 1947, Mexico; ed. with notes by L. E. Rossell and A. Escalona Ramos.)

MUÑOZ Y MANZANO, C.
1892 Bibliografía española de lenguas indígenas de América. Madrid.

MUNSCH, A.
1943 Some magico-religious observances of the present-day Maya Indians of British Honduras and Yucatan. *Primitive Man*, 16: 31–43. Catholic Anthr. Conference. Washington.

MURDOCK, G. P.
1949 Social structure. New York.

1957 World ethnographic sample. *Amer. Anthr.*, 59: 664–87.

MURGUÍA Y GALARDI, J. M. DE

1859 Apuntamientos estadísticos de la provincia de Oaxaca en esta Nueva España, que comprenden dos partes: la primera sobre sus antigüedades y la segunda sobre su actual estado. Año de 1818. Oaxaca.

MURIEL, J.

1948 Reflexiones sobre Hernán Cortés. *Rev. Indias*, año 9, pp. 229–45.

MURRAY, G. E.

1961 Atlantic and gulf coast geology of North America. New York.

MUSÉE DE L'HOMME

1965 Chefs-d'oeuvre du Musée de l'Homme. Musée de l'Homme, Caisse Nationale des Monuments Historiques. Paris.

MUSEO NACIONAL DE ARTES E INDUSTRIAS POPULARES

1951 Native dress of the Sierra de Puebla. No. 2. Mexico.

1953 Obras selectas del arte popular. No. 5. Mexico.

1954 Los Huicholes. No. 7. Mexico.

NADAILLAC, J. F. DE

1899 Les Zapotèques. *La Nature*, 27: 177–79. Paris.

1901 Les Seris. *Correspondant*. Paris.

NADER, L.

1960 Social grouping and conflict in a Mexican village. MS.

1964 Talea and Juquila: a comparison in Zapotec social organization. *Univ. California Pub. Amer. Archaeol. Ethnol.*, 48: 195–296.

1966 Variations in Zapotec legal procedure. *In* Pompa y Pompa, 1966.

1969 The Trique of Oaxaca. *In* Handbook of Middle American Indians, R. Wauchope, ed., vol. 7, art. 19.

—— AND D. METZGER

1963 Conflict resolution in two Mexican villages. *Amer. Anthr.*, 65: 584–92.

NAH, CHILAM BALAM DE

n.d. Manuscript. Photograph in Newberry Library. 56 pp.

NAHMAD, S., AND L. BEVILLE

1959 Field notes. MS.

NÁJERA, M. DE SAN JUAN CRISÓSTOMO

1870 Gramática del tarasco. Morelia.

NASH, J. C.

1959 Amatenango del Valle. *In* McQuown, 1959, sec. 10.

1959 Social structure and social organization in Oxchuc, Chiapas. *Ibid.*, sec. 24.

1960 Protestantism in an Indian village in the western highlands of Guatemala. *In* Leslie, 1960, Social anthropology, pp. 49–58.

1960 Social relations in Amatenango del Valle: an activity analysis. Doctoral dissertation, Univ. Chicago.

NASH, M.

1953–54 Field notes, Cantel. MS.

1955 The reaction of a civil-religious hierarchy to a factory in Guatemala. *Human Organization*, 13: 26–28.

1956 Recruitment of wage labor and development of new skills. *Ann. Amer. Acad. Political and Social Sci.*, 305: 23–31.

1957 The multiple society in economic development: Mexico and Guatemala. *Amer. Anthr.*, 59: 825–33.

1957 Cultural persistences and social structure: the Mesoamerican calendar survivals. *SW. Jour. Anthr.*, 13: 149–55.

1958 Machine age Maya: the industrialization of a Guatemalan community. *Amer. Anthr. Assoc.*, Mem. 87.

1958 Political relations in Guatemala. *Social and Econ. Studies*, 7: 65–75.

1960 Witchcraft as social process in a Tzeltal community. *Amer. Indig.*, 20: 121–26.

1961 The social context of economic choice in a small community. *Man*, 61: 186–91.

——, M. E. VERBITSKY, J. C. HOTCHKISS, AND N. A. McQUOWN

1959 Present-day socio-cultural-linguistic-ethnohistorical correlations. *In* McQuown, 1959, ch. 3.

NATIONAL ARCHIVES OF SEVILLE

1600 Guatemala II. May 15, Doc. 38 (2).

NATIONAL RESEARCH COUNCIL
1948 Recommended dietary allowances. *Circular Ser.*, no. 129. Washington.

NATIONAL SCIENCE FOUNDATION
1959 Vegetation project, Univ. Chicago.

NATURALEZA, LA
La Naturaleza: periódico científico de la Sociedad Mexicana de Historia Natural. Mexico.

NAUDOU, J.
1962 À propos d'un eventuel emprunt de l'art maya aux arts de l'Inde extérieure. *34th Int. Cong. Amer.* (Vienna, 1960), Acta, pp. 340–47.

NAVARRETE, C.
n.d. Investigaciones arqueológicas acerca del problema chiapaneco. MS of paper presented to VII Mesa Redonda, Soc. Mex. Antr. (1959).
1959 Explorations at San Agustin, Chiapas, Mexico. *Papers New World Archaeol. Found.*, no. 3.
1959 A brief reconnaissance in the region of Tonala, Chiapas. *Ibid.*, no. 4.
1960 Archaeological explorations in the region of the Frailesca, Chiapas, Mexico. *Ibid.*, no. 7.

NAVARRETE, M. F. DE
1825–37 Colección de los viajes y descubrimientos, que hicieron por mar los españoles desde fines del siglo XV. 5 vols. Madrid.

NAVARRO Y NORIEGA, F.
1943 Catálogo de los curatos y misiones de la Nueva España. (1st ed. 1813.) Mexico.

NAZAREO, P., AND OTHERS
1940 Carta al rey don Felipe II . . . 17 de Marzo de 1566. *In* Paso y Troncoso, 1939–42, 10: 89–129.

NEBEL, C.
1839 Viaje pintoresco y arqueológico sobre la República Mexicana, 1829–1834. Paris.

NEBRIJA, E. A. DE
1492 Gramática castellana. 2 vols. (Madrid, 1946.)

NEEL, J. V., AND OTHERS (F. M. SALZANO, P. C. JUNQUEIRA, F. KEITER, AND D. MAYBURY-LEWIS)
1964 Studies on the Xavante Indians of the Brazilian Mato Grosso. *Amer. Jour. Human Genetics*, 16: 52–140.

NELLIS, J. G.
1947 Sierra Zapotec forms of address. *Int. Jour. Amer. Ling.*, 13: 231–32.

NELSON, E. W.
1921 Lower California and its natural resources. *Mem. Nat. Acad. Sci.*, 16: 1–194.

NEPEAN, E.
1844 Letter to Samuel Birch upon the antiquities discovered in the Island of Sacrificios. *Soc. Antiquaries London, Archaeologia*, 30: 339–41. London.
1857 Excavations in the Island of Sacrificios. *Ibid.*, 30: 138–339.

NESBITT, P. H.
1931 The ancient Mimbreños based on investigations at the Mattocks ruin, Mimbres Valley, New Mexico. *Logan Mus.*, Bull. 4.

NEWBERRY, J. S.
1887 Discusiones acerca del hombre del Peñón. *Naturaleza*, 1st ser., 7: 284–85.
1888 Rhaetic plants from Honduras. *Amer. Jour. Sci. and Arts*, 3d ser., 36: 342–51.
1888 Triassic plants from Honduras. *Trans. New York Acad. Sci.*, 7: 113–15.

NEWBOLD, S.
1957 Receptivity to communist fomented agitation in rural Guatemala. *Econ. Development and Cult. Change*, 5: 338–61.

NEWELL, H. P., AND A. D. KRIEGER
1949 The George C. Davis site, Cherokee County, Texas. *Soc. Amer. Archaeol.*, Mem. 5.

NEWELL, N. D.
1959 Corals. Part 1: Questions of the coral reefs. *Natural Hist.*, 68: 118–31.
1959 The coral reefs. Part 2: Biology of the corals. *Ibid.*, 68: 226–35.

NEWMAN, M. T.
n.d. Palm and fingerprints of Quechua Indians from the north central Peruvian sierra. MS.
n.d. Blood groups in Quechua Indians from Hacienda Vicos in the north cen-

tral Peruvian sierra. Part 2: History and comparative analysis. MS.

1949 Nuevos rasgos característicos encontrados en Xochicalco. *Rev. Mex. Estud. Antr.*, 10: 115–19.

1953 The application of ecological rules to the racial anthropology of the aboriginal New World. *Amer. Anthr.*, 55: 311–27.

1958 A trial formulation presenting evidence from physical anthropology for migrations from Mexico to South America. *In* R. H. Thompson, 1958, Migrations, pp. 33–40.

1960 Adaptations in the physique of American aborigines to nutritional factors. *Human Biol.*, 32: 288–313.

1960 Population analysis of finger and palm prints in highland and lowland Maya Indians. *Amer. Jour. Physical Anthr.*, n.s., 18: 45–58.

1962 Evolutionary changes in body size and head form in American Indians. *Amer. Anthr.*, 64: 237–57.

NEWMAN, S.

1955 Vocabulary levels: Zuñi sacred and slang usage. *SW Jour. Anthr.*, 11: 345–54.

1964 Comparison of Zuñi and Californian Penutian. *Int. Jour. Amer. Ling.*, 30: 1–13.

—— AND R. J. WEITLANER

1950 Central Otomian I: Proto-Otomi reconstructions. *Ibid.*, 16: 1–19.

1950 Central Otomian II: primitive central Otomian reconstructions. *Ibid.*, 16: 73–81.

NEVE Y MOLINA, L. DE

1767 Reglas de ortografía, diccionario, y arte del idioma othomi. . . . Mexico. (Mexico, 1863.)

NEZA

1935–39 Organo mensual de la sociedad nueva de estudiantes juchitecos.

NICARAGUA, DIRECCIÓN GENERAL DE ESTADÍSTICA Y CENSOS

1954 Censo general de población. Managua.

NICHOLSON, H. B.

1953 On a supposed Mesoamerican "Thin Orange" vessel from Ecuador. *Amer. Antiquity*, 19: 164–66.

1955 Aztec style calendric inscriptions of possible historical significance: a survey. Mimeographed. Mexico.

1955 The temalacatl of Tehuacan. *El Mex. Antiguo*, 8: 95–134.

1957 Topiltzin Quetzalcoatl of Tollan: a problem in Mesoamerican ethnohistory. Doctoral dissertation, Harvard Univ.

1958 An Aztec monument dedicated to Tezcatlipoca. *In* Misc. Paul Rivet, 1: 593–607.

1959 The Chapultepec cliff sculpture of Motescuhzoma Xocoyotzin. *El Mex. Antiguo*, 9: 379–444.

1959 Los principales dioses mesoamericanos. *In* Esplendor del México antiguo, 1: 161–78.

1960 The Mixteca-Puebla concept in Mesoamerican archeology: a re-examination. *In* Wallace, 1960, pp. 612–17. (Reprinted in Graham, 1966, pp. 258–63.)

1961 Interrelationships of New World cultures: Project A, central Pacific coast of Mexico. Mimeographed. Dept. Anthropology, Univ. California, Los Angeles.

1961 Notes and news: Middle America. *Amer. Antiquity*, 26: 594–600.

1961 The use of the term 'Mixtec' in Mesoamerican archaeology. *Ibid.*, 26: 431–33.

1962 Notes and news: Middle America. *Ibid.*, 27: 617–24.

1963 Interrelationships of New World cultures: Project A, central Pacific coast of Mexico. 1961–62 season. *Katunob*, 4: 39–51.

1966 The problem of the provenience of the members of the "Codex Borgia group": a summary. *In* Pompa y Pompa, 1966, pp. 145–58.

1967 A "royal headband" of the Tlaxcalteca. *Rev. Mex. Estud. Antr.*, 21: 71–106.

1968 *Review of* Alfonso Caso, Interpretación del Códice Colombino. *An. Antr.*, 5: 280–87. Mexico.

—— AND J. SMITH

1960 Interrelationships of New World cultures: Project A, central and south

Pacific coast, Mexico. 1960 season. Mimeographed. Dept. Anthropology, Univ. California, Los Angeles.

NICHOLSON, I.
1967 Mexican and Central American mythology. London.

NICKERSON, N. H.
1953 Variation in cob morphology among certain archaeological and ethnological races of maize. *Ann. Missouri Bot. Garden*, 40: 79–111.

NICOLAU D'OLWER, L.
1952 Fray Bernardino de Sahagún (1499–1590). *Inst. Panamer. Geog. Hist., Comisión de Historia, Historiadores de América*, no. 9. Mexico.

NICOLI, J. P.
1885 El estado de Sonora: Yaquis y Mayos; estudio histórico de León. Mexico.

NIDA, E. A., AND M. ROMERO C.
1950 The pronominal series in Maya (Yucatec). *Int. Jour. Amer. Ling.*, 16: 193–97.

NIGG, C.
1926 A study of the blood groups among the American Indians. *Jour. Immunology*, 11: 319–22.

NIJENHUIS, L. E.
1953 The Henshaw blood group (He) in Papuans and Congo Negroes. *Vox Sanguinis*, 3: 112–14.

NISWANDER, J. D., F. KEITER, AND J. V. NEEL
1967 Further studies on the Xavante Indians. II: Some anthropometric, dermatoglyphic and nonquantitative morphological traits of the Xavantes of Simões Lopes. *Amer. Jour. Human Genetics*, 19: 490–501.

NOGUERA, E.
1925 Las representaciones del buho en la cultura teotihuacana. *An. Mus. Nac. Mex.*, ep. 4, 3: 444–48.
1926 Ruinas arqueológicas de Casas Grandes, Chihuahua. Mexico.
1930 Ruinas arqueológicas del norte de México, Casas Grandes (Chihuahua), La Quemada, Chalchihuites (Zacatecas). *Pub. Sec. Educ. Pública, Talleres Gráficos de la Nación*, pp. 5–27. Mexico.
1931 Excavaciones arqueológicas en las regiones de Zamora y Pátzcuaro, estado de Michoacán. *An. Mus. Nac. Arqueol. Hist. Etnog.*, ep. 4, 7: 89–103.
1932 Extensiones cronológico-culturales y geográficas de las cerámicas de México. Mexico.
1935 Antecedentes y relaciones de la cultura teotihuacana. *El Mex. Antiguo*, 3 (5–8): 3–90, 93–95.
1935 La cerámica de Tenayuca y las excavaciones estratigráficas. *In* Tenayuca, pp. 141–201.
1936 Los petroglifos de Maltrata. *Mapa*, 3 (26): 39–41.
1937 El altar de los cráneos esculpidos de Cholula. Mexico.
1938 Guide book to the National Museum of Archaeology, History, and Ethnology. Popular Library of Mexican Culture. Mexico.
1940 Excavations at Tehuacan. *In* The Maya and their neighbors, pp. 306–19.
1940 Tribu: yalaltecos. *In* Basauri, 1940, 2: 467–96.
1942 Cultura tarasca. Biblioteca del Maestro. Mexico.
1942 Exploraciones en "El Opeño," Michoacán. *27th Int. Cong. Amer.* (Mexico, 1939), Acta, 1: 574–86.
1943 Excavaciones en El Tepalcate, Chimalhuacán, México. *Amer. Antiquity*, 9: 33–43.
1944 Exploraciones en Jiquilpan. *An. Mus. Michoacano*, ep. 2, 3: 37–54.
1945 Exploraciones en Xochicalco. *Cuad. Amer.*, año 4, no. 1.
1946 Cultura de El Opeño. *In* Mexico prehispánico, pp. 150–54.
1946 La escultura. *Ibid.*, pp. 583–90.
1947 Cerámica de Xochicalco. *El Mex. Antiguo*, 6: 273–98.
1948 Estado actual de los conocimientos acerca de la arqueología del noroeste de Michoacán. *In* El Occidente de México, pp. 38–39.
1951 Exploraciones en Xochicalco. *In* Tax, 1951.
1954 La cerámica arqueológica de Cholula. Ed. Guaranía. Mexico.

166

1955 Extraordinario hallazgo en Teotihuacán. *El Mex. Antiguo*, 8: 43–56.

1958 Reconocimiento arqueológico en Sonora. *Inst. Nac. Antr. Hist.*, Informe 10. Mexico.

1958 Tallas prehispánicas en madera. Ed. Guaranía. Mexico.

1960 La Quemada, Chalchihuites. Guía oficial del Inst. Nac. Antr. Hist. Mexico.

1960 Zonas arqueológicas del estado de Morelos. Guía oficial del Inst. Nac. Antr. Hist. Mexico.

1961 Últimos descubrimientos en Xochicalco. *Rev. Mex. Estud Antr.*, 17: 33–37.

1962 Nueva clasificación de figurillas del horizonte clásico. *Cuad. Amer.*, no. 5. Mexico.

1965 La cerámica arqueológica de Mesoamérica. *Univ. Nac. Autónoma Méx., Inst. Invest. Hist.*, 1st ser., no. 86.

—— AND D. J. LEONARD
1957 Descubrimiento de la Casa de las Águilas, en Teotihuacán. *Bol. Centro Invest. Antr. Méx.*, 4: 6–9.

—— AND R. PIÑA CHAN
1956–57 Estratigrafía de Teopanzolco. *Rev. Mex. Estud. Antr.*, 14: 139–56.

NOLASCO A., M.
1965 Los Papagos, habitantes del desierto. *An. Inst. Nac. Antr. Hist.*, 45 de la colección. Mexico.

NOMLAND, G. A.
1932 Proboscis statue from the isthmus of Tehuantepec. *Amer. Anthr.*, 34: 591–93.

NORDENSKIÖLD, E.
1927 The Choco Indians. *Discovery*, 8: 95.

NORIEGA, R., AND C. COOK DE LEONARD, eds.
1959 *See* Esplendor del México antiguo.

NORIEGA HOPE, C.
1922 Apuntes etnográficos. *In* Gamio, 1922, 2: 207–81.

NORMAN, J.
1959 In Mexico: where to look, how to buy Mexican popular arts and crafts. New York.

NORTE DE MÉXICO, EL
1944 El norte de México y el sur de Estados Unidos. Tercera reunión de mesa redonda sobre problemas antropológicos de México y Centro América. Soc. Mex. Antr. Mexico.

NORTH, A. W.
1908 The native tribes of Lower California. *Amer. Anthr.*, 10: 236–50.

1910 Camp and camino in Lower California. New York.

NOTES AND NEWS
1946 Notes and news: Middle American area. *Amer. Antiquity*, 11: 207–08.

NOTT, J. C., AND G. R. GLIDDON
1857 Indigenous races of the earth or new chapters of ethnological inquiry. Philadelphia.

NOTTEBOHM, K. H.
1945 A second Tlaloc gold plaque from Guatemala. *Carnegie Inst. Wash., Notes Middle Amer. Archaeol. Ethnol.*, no. 51.

NOWOTNY, K. A.
n.d. Farben und Weltrichtungen. MS.

1959 Die Hieroglyphen des Codex Mendoza. *Mitteilungen aus dem Museum für Völkerkunde in Hamburg*, vol. 25. Hamburg.

1960 Mexikanische Kostbarkeiten aus Kunstkammern der Renaissance, im Museum für Völkerkunde Wien und in der Nationalbibliothek Wien. Mus. für Völkerkunde. Vienna.

1961 Tlacuilolli: die mexikanischen Bilderhandschriften, Stil und Inhalt: mit einem Katalog der Codex-Borgia-Gruppe. *Ibero-Amerikanischen Bibliothek, Monumenta Americana*, 3. Berlin.

NOYES, E.
1932 *See* A. Ponce, 1932.

NUEVOS DOCUMENTOS . . . CORTÉS
1946 Nuevos documentos relativos a los bienes de Hernán Cortés. Archivo General de la Nación. Mexico.

NÚÑEZ, A. A.
1777 Carta edificante histórico-curiosa escrita desde la misión de Sta. María de Baserac en los finos de Sonora. *In* Noticias de varias misiones, vol. 76. Bib. Nac. de Mexico.

NÚÑEZ CABEZA DE VACA, A.
1906 Relación de los naufragios y comen-

tarios, ilustrados con varios documentos inéditos. *In* Doc. referentes a la historia de América. 2 vols. Madrid.

NÚÑEZ CHINCHILLA, J.
1959 Panorama indigenista actual de la República de Honduras. *Bol. Indig.,* 19: 230–32. Mexico.

NÚÑEZ DE LA VEGA, F.
1702 Constituciones diocesanas del obispado de Chiapa. Rome.

NUTINI, H. G.
1961 Clan organization in a Nahuatl-speaking village of the state of Tlaxcala, Mexico. *Amer. Anthr.,* 63: 62–78.

NUTTALL, Z.
1886 Terra cotta heads of San Juan Teotihuacan. *Amer. Jour. Archaeol.,* 2: 151–318.
1892 On ancient Mexican shields. *Internat. Archiv für Ethnog.,* 5: 34–53, 89. Leiden.
1901 Chalchihuitl in ancient Mexico. *Amer. Anthr.,* 3: 227–38.
1902 *See* Codex Nuttall.
1903 *See* Codex Magliabecchiano, 1903.
1904 A penitential rite of the ancient Mexicans. *Papers Peabody Mus., Harvard Univ.,* vol. 1, no. 7.
1909 A curious survival in Mexico of the use of the *Purpura* shellfish for dyeing. *In* Putnam Anniversary Volume, pp. 368–84.
1910 The Island of Sacrifice. *Amer. Anthr.,* n.s., 12: 257–95.
1927 [ed.] El libro perdido de los pláticas o coloquios de los doce primeros misioneros de México, por Fr. Bernardino de Sahagún. *Rev. Mex. Estud. Hist.,* 1: 101–39.

NYGREN, W. E.
1950 Bolivar geosyncline of northwestern South America. *Bull. Amer. Assoc. Petroleum Geol.,* 34: 1998–2006.

OAKES, H., AND J. THORP
1950 Dark-clay soils of warm regions variously called Rendzina, black cotton soils, regur, and tirs. *Proc. Soils Sci. Soc. Amer.,* 15: 347–54.

OAKES, M.
1951 The two crosses of Todos Santos: survivals of Mayan religious ritual. *Bollingen Ser.,* no. 27.
1951 Beyond the windy place: life in the Guatemalan highlands. New York.

OAXACA
1956 División territorial del estado de Oaxaca. Oaxaca.

OBER, F. A.
1884 Travels in Mexico and life among the Mexicans. Boston.

OCAMPO, M.
1950 Historia de la misión de la tarahumara. Mexico.

OCARANZA, F.
1923 Hematologie de l'indien du plateau central du Mexique. *Compte-rendu Soc. Biol.,* 88: 554–55. Paris.
1933 Los Franciscanos en las provincias internas de Sonora y Ostimuri. Mexico.

OCCIDENTE DE MÉXICO, EL
1948 El occidente de México. Cuarta reunión de mesa redonda sobre problemas antropológicos de México y Centro América. Soc. Mex. Antr. Mexico.

OCHOA, J. C.
1945 The phantom lover. *Tlalocan,* 2: 34.

O'CROULEY, P. A.
n.d. Ydea compendiosa del reyno de Nueva España. Photostat. MS in Sauer Coll., Bib. Nacional, Madrid.

OETTEKING, B.
1923 On the morphological significance of certain cranio-vertebral variations. *Anatomical Record,* 25: 339–53.

OETTING, M. I.
1949 Hand- und fingerleisten einiger Guayaki-Indianer. *Zeitschr. für Morph. und Anthr.,* 41: 275–83.

OGLESBY, C.
1938 The potters of Mexico. *Mex. Life,* 15 (8): 20–22.
1940 Weavings for use and sale. *Ibid.,* 16 (2): 17–20, 54–56.

O'GORMAN, E.
1941 Noticia sobre los Indios guastecos de la provincia de Pánuco y su religión. Primer tercio del siglo XVII. *Bol. Archivo General de la Nación,* 12: 215–21. Mexico.

OKADA, F. E.
1951   Some characteristics of Mongolian-type lames. *Amer. Antiquity,* 16: 254.

OKLADNIKOV, A. P.
1959   Dalekoye proshloye primorya. [The remote past of the maritime province.] Vladivostok.

OLIVER, J. P.
1955   Architectural similarities of Mitla and Yagul. *Mesoamer. Notes,* 4: 49–67.

OLIVERA SEDANO, A.
1956   Cuitlahuac. *Rev. Mex. Estud. Antr.,* 14: 299–302.

OLIVIER, G.
1960   Pratique anthropologique. Paris.

OLMOS, A. DE
1547   Arte para aprender la lengua mexicana. *In* Col. de gramáticas, pp. 1–126.

OLMSTED, D. L.
1950   Ethnolinguistics so far. *Studies in Ling.,* 2.
1958   Tequistlatec kinship terminology. *SW. Jour. Anthr.,* 14: 449–53.
1961   Lexicostatistics as 'proof' of genetic relationship: the case of "Macro Manguean." *Anthr. Ling.,* 3 (6): 9–14.
1967   Tequistlatec ceremonies and the analysis of stereotypy. *In* Studies in Southwestern ethnolinguistics, D. H. Hymes and W. E. Bittle, eds., pp. 68–88. The Hague.

OLSON, E. A., AND W. S. BROECKER
1959   Lamont natural radiocarbon measurements V. *Amer. Jour. Sci., Radiocarbon Suppl.,* 1: 1–28.

OLSON, E. C., AND P. O. MCGREW
1941   Mammalian fauna from the Pliocene to Honduras. *Bull. Geol. Soc. Amer.,* 52: 1219–44.

OLSON, R. D.
1964   Mayan affinities with Chipaya of Bolivia I: correspondences. *Int. Jour. Amer. Ling.,* 30: 313–24.
1965   Mayan affinities with Chipaya of Bolivia II: cognates. *Ibid.,* 31: 29–38.

OLSON, R. L.
1933   Clan and moiety in native America.

Univ. California Pub. Amer. Archaeol. Ethnol., 33: 351–432.

OLSSON, A. A.
1932   Contributions to the Tertiary paleontology of northern Peru. Part 5: The Peruvian Miocene. *Bull. Amer. Paleontol.,* 19: 1–272.

OLVERA, J.
1956   El arte de las lacas en Chiapas. *El Maestro Mex.,* ser. 3, 6: 38–40.
1959   *Idem. El Sol de Chiapas,* January 21, 22. Tuxtla Gutierrez.

O'NEALE, L. M.
1942   Early textiles from Chiapas, Mexico. *Tulane Univ., Middle Amer. Research Rec.,* vol. 1, no. 1.
1945   Textiles of highland Guatemala. *Carnegie Inst. Wash.,* Pub. 567.
1948   Textiles of pre-Columbian Chihuahua. *Carnegie Inst. Wash.,* Pub. 574, Contrib. 45.

O'NEILL, G. C.
1954   Notes and news: early man. *Amer. Antiquity,* 19: 304.
1956–57   Preliminary report on stratigraphic excavations in the southern Valley of Mexico: Chalco-Xico. *Rev. Mex. Estud. Antr.,* 14: 45–52.

OPLER, M. E., AND H. HOIJER
1940   The raid and war-path language of the Chiricahua Apache. *Amer. Anthr.,* 42: 617–34.

ORCHARD, W. C.
1925   Minute gold bead from La Tolita, Ecuador. *Mus. Amer. Indian, Heye Found., Indian Notes,* vol. 2, no. 1.

ORDEN . . . TECUTLES
n.d.   La orden que los yndios tenian en su tiempo para hacerse tecutles. MS. in Rich Collection, New York Public Library.

ORDÓÑEZ, E.
1903–06   Los xalapazcos del estado de Puebla. *Inst. Geol. de Mex., Parergones,* 1: 295–393.
1906   Guide géologique au Mexique. Part 8: De Mexico à Patzcuaro et Uruapan. *10th Cong. Geol. Int.* Mexico.
1922   Escultura: la labra de piedra. *In* Gamio, 1922, 1: 164–68.
1936   Principal physiographic provinces of

Mexico. *Bull. Amer. Assoc. Petroleum Geol.*, 20: 1277–1307.

1941 Las provincias fisiográficas de Mexico. *Rev. Geog.*, 1: 133–81.

1945 Las huellas de pisadas humanas en Rincon de Guadalupe, Amanalco de Becerra, estado de México. MS, Inst. Geol. library. Mexico.

ORDÓÑEZ Y AGUIAR, R. DE

1907 Historia de la creación del cielo, y de la tierra, conforme al systema de la gentilidad americana. *In* N. León, 1907, 5: 1–272.

ORELLANA G., R. A.

1950 Estudios sobre aspectos técnicos del censo de población. Univ. Autónoma de San Carlos de Guatemala.

ORELLANA TAPIA, R.

1952 Zona arqueológica de Izapa. *Tlatoani*, 1: 17–25.

1954 El vaso de Ixtapa, Chiapas. *Yan*, no. 3, pp. 114–18.

1954 Ixtapa, Chinkultic, Tenam-Puente, Mox. y Tonina. *Ibid.*, no. 3, pp. 125–26.

1955 Nueva lápida olmecoide de Izapa, Chiapas, Estela 21. *El Mex. Antiguo*, 8: 157–68.

ORIGEN DE LOS MEXICANOS

1941 Origen de los mexicanos. *In* García Icazbalceta, 1941, 3: 256–80.

OROPEZA CASTRO, M.

1947 El diluvio totonaco. *Tlalocan*, 2: 269–75.

1968 Teotihuacán: escultura. *Inst. Nac. Antr. Hist., Mus. Nac. Antr., Col. Breve*, no. 3. Mexico.

OROZCO, G.

1946 Tradiciones y leyendas del istmo de Tehuantepec. Mexico.

OROZCO Y BERRA, M.

1858 San Juan Yalalag. *In* Diccionario Universal, app. 2. Mexico.

1864 Geografía de las lenguas y carta etnográfica de México. Mexico.

1864 Memoria para la carta hidrográfica del valle de México. Mexico.

1877 El cuauhxicalli de Tizoc. *An. Mus. Nac. Mex.*, 1: 3–36.

1880 Historia antigua y de la conquista de México. 4 vols. and atlas. Mexico.

1960 *Idem*, 2d ed. Con un estudio previo

de A. M. Garibay K. y biografía del autor más tres bibliografías referentes al mismo de M. León-Portilla. Mexico.

ORTEGA, A.

1873 Un caso de craneotomía y cefalotripsia: enanismo. *Gaceta Méd. Méx.*, 8: 123–27.

ORTEGA, J. DE

1732 Vocabulario en lengua castellana y cora. . . . Mexico. (Tepic, 1888.)

1754 Conquista de Nayarit. Barcelona. (Mexico, 1944.)

1887 Historia de Nayarit, Sonora, Sinaloa y ambas Californias. Mexico.

ORTEGA, M. F.

1940 Extensión y límites de la provincia de los Yopes a mediados del siglo XVI. *El Mex. Antiguo*, 5: 48–53.

ORTELIUS, A.

1584 Theatrum orbis terrarum. Antwerp.

ORTIZ, F.

1947 El huracán, su mitología y sus símbolos. Mexico.

ORTIZ, S.

1940 Lingüística familia Choko. *Univ. Católica Bolivariana*, 6.

ORTIZ MONASTERIO, R.

1950 Reconocimiento agrológico regional del estado de Yucatan. *Bol. Soc. Mex. Geog. y Estad.*, 69: 245–324.

1955–57 Los recursos agrológicos de la República Mexicana. *Ingeniería Hidráulica en Mexico*, vols. 9–11. Sec. Recursos Hidráulicos.

OSBORN, H. F.

1905 Recent vertebrate paleontology: fossil mammals of Mexico. *Science*, 21 (546): 931–32.

OSBORNE, D.

1943 An archaeological reconnaissance in southeastern Michoacan. *Amer. Antiquity*, 9: 59–73.

—— AND A. HAYES

1938 Some archaeological notes from southern Hidalgo County, New Mexico. *New Mexico Anthr.*, 3 (3): 21–23.

OSBORNE, L. DE J.

1935 Guatemala textiles. *Tulane Univ., Middle Amer. Research Inst.*, Pub. 6.

1945 Costumes and wedding customs at

Mixco, Guatemala. *Carnegie Inst. Wash., Notes Middle Amer. Archaeol. Ethnol.*, no. 48.

1956 Four keys to El Salvador. New York.

OSGOOD, C.
1935 The archaeological problem in Chiriqui. *Amer. Anthr.*, 37: 234–43.

OSGOOD, C. E., AND P. TANNENBAUM
1955 The principle of congruity and the prediction of attitude change. *Psychol. Rev.*, 62: 42–55.

OSORIO-TAFALL, B. F.
1943 El Mar de Cortes y la productividad fitoplanctónica de sus aguas. *An. Escuela Nac. Cien. Biol.*, 3: 73–118.

1946 Algunos problemas de la hidrología mexicana. *In* Tamayo, 1946, pp. 385–417.

OTIS, G. A.
1880 List of the specimens in the anatomical section of the U.S. Army Medical Museum. Washington.

OTTENSOOSER, F.
1944 Calculo do grau de mistiera racial atraves dos grupos sanguineos. *Rev. Brasil. Biol.*, 4: 531–37.

OUTWATER, J. O., JR.
1957 The pre-Columbian stonecutting techniques of the Mexican plateau. *Amer. Antiquity*, 22: 258–64.

OVIEDO Y VALDÉS, G. F. DE
1851–55 Historia general y natural de las Indias, islas y tierra-firme del mar océano. J. Amador de los Ríos, ed. 4 vols. Madrid.

1943–45 *Idem*, another ed. Paragua.

OWEN, R.
1856 Description of the so-called Aztec children. *Jour. Ethnol. Soc. London*, 4: 128–37.

OWEN, R. C.
1956 Some clay figurines and Seri dolls from coastal Sonora, Mexico. *Kiva*, 21 (3, 4): 1–11.

1957 Paddle and anvil appearance of some Sonoran pottery. *Amer. Antiquity*, 22: 291.

1958 Easter ceremonies among Opata descendents of northern Sonora, Mexico. *Kiva*, vol. 23, no. 4.

1959 Marobavi: a study of an assimilated group in northern Sonora. *Univ. Arizona, Anthr. Papers*, no. 3.

1960 Paipai ethnography. MS.

1960 Concepts of disease and the curing practices of the Indians of ex-Mission Santa Catarina, Baja California Norte, Mexico. MS.

1962 The Indians of Santa Catarina, Baja California, Mexico: concepts of disease and curing. Doctoral dissertation, Univ. California at Los Angeles.

1963 Indians and revolution: the 1911 invasion of Baja California, Mexico. *Ethnohistory*, 10: 373–95.

1963 The use of plants and non-magical techniques in curing illness among the Paipai, Santa Catarina, Baja California, Mexico. *Amer. Indig.*, 23: 319–44.

1965 The patrilocal band: a linguistically and culturally hybrid social unit. *Amer. Anthr.*, 67: 675–90.

OWER, L. H.
1928 Geology of British Honduras. *Jour. Geol.*, 36: 494–509.

PACHECO DA SILVA, F.
1686 Doctrina cristiana en lengua zapoteca nexitza. Mexico.

1687 Doctrina cristiana traducida de la lengua castellana en lengua zapoteca nexitza. Mexico.

PACHECO CRUZ, S.
1920 Compendio del idioma maya. Merida. (Merida, 1938; Mexico, 1948.)

1939 Léxico de la fauna yucateca. Merida. (Merida, 1919.)

1947 Usos, costumbres, religión, y supersticiones de los Mayas. Merida.

PACHECO LUNA, R.
1946 Notes on oncocercosis in Guatemala. *British Jour. Ophthalmology*, 30: 234–37.

PADDOCK, J.
1957 The 1956 season at Yagul. *Mesoamer. Notes*, 5: 13–36.

1958 Comments on some problems of Oaxaca archeology. *Bol. Estud. Oaxaqueños*, no. 4.

1960 Exploración en Yagul, Oaxaca. *Rev. Mex. Estud. Antr.*, 16: 91–96.

1966 Distribución de rasgos teotihuacanos en Mesoamérica. Mimeographed and distributed during 11th Round Table meeting, Soc. Mex. Antr. Mexico.

1966 [ed.] *Mesoamerican Notes*, 6–7. Dept. Anthropology, Univ. of the Americas. Mexico.

1966 [ed.] Ancient Oaxaca: discoveries in Mexican archeology and history. Stanford Univ. Press.

1966 Mixtec ethnohistory and Monte Alban V. *Ibid.*, pp. 367–86.

1966 Oaxaca in ancient Mesoamerica. *Ibid.*, pp. 83–242.

1967 Western Mesoamerica. *Amer. Antiquity*, 32: 422–27.

1968 Western Mesoamerica. *Ibid.*, 33: 122–28.

——, J. R. Mogor, and M. D. Lind
1968 Lambityeco, Tomb 2: a preliminary report. *Bol. Estud. Oaxaqueños*, no. 25. Mexico.

Padilla, M. R.
1956 Observaciones sobre Fasciola Hepática en Guatemala. *Rev. Colegio Méd. Guatemala*, 7: 145–51.

Padilla, V. M.
1953 La chorrera del Celaque (folklore). *Honduras Rotaria*, 9 (119–20): 11, 23. Tegucigalpa.

Padilla Borjes, E.
1959 Histoplasmina: reporte sobre mil docientas intradermoreacciones. Tesis de médico y cirujano, Facultad Cien. Méd., Univ. San Carlos de Guatemala.

Padrones de Tlaxcala
n.d. Padrones de Tlaxcala del siglo XVI. *Mus. Nac. Méx., Archivo Histórico, Col. Antigua* 377.

Páez Brotchie, L.
1940 La Nueva Galicia a través de su viejo archivo judicial. *Bib. Hist. Mex. Obras Inéd.*, no. 18. Mexico.

Page, J. L.
1930 Climate of Mexico. *Monthly Weather Rev.*, Suppl. 33.

Painter, M. T.
1960 Easter at Pascua village. Univ. Arizona Press.

——, R. Savala, and I. Alvárez
1955 A Yaqui Easter sermon. *Univ. Arizona, Social Sci. Bull.*, no. 26.

Paiz, C. R.
1959 Estudio preliminar de las hemoglobinas en Guatemala. Tesis de médico y cirujano, Facultad Cien. Méd., Univ. San Carlos de Guatemala.

Palacio, Licenciado
1864–84 Relación hecha por el Licenciado Palacio al rey Felipe II, en la que describe la provincia de Guatemala, las costumbres de los indios y otras cosas notables. *In* Col. doc. Indias, 1864–84, 6: 5–40.

Palacios, E. J.
1917 Puebla: su territorio y sus habitantes. *Mem. Soc. Cien. Antonio Alzate*, 36: 1–750.

1923 Otra ciudad desconocida en Hueyaltepetl. *Bol. Mus. Nac. Arqueol. Hist. Etnog.*, 2: 21–32. Mexico.

1923 Documentos relativos a la exploración de Hueyaltepetl. *Ibid.*, 2: 33–35.

1928 En los confines de la selva lacandona. Sec. Educación Pública. Mexico.

1928 Monumentos de Etzna-Tixmucuy. *In* Estado actual, pp. 167–78.

1929 La piedra del escudo nacional de México. *Pub. Sec. Educación Pública*, vol. 22, no. 9. Mexico.

1937 Mas gemas del arte maya en Palenque. *An. Mus. Nac. Arqueol. Hist. Etnog.*, 2: 193–225.

1939 Enbozo de prehistoria de México. *Mem. Soc. Cien. Antonio Alzate*, 54: 401–49.

1940 El simbolismo del chacmool: su interpretación. *Rev. Mex. Estud. Antr.*, vol. 4, nos. 1, 2.

1941 Cien años después de Stephens. *In* Los Mayas antiguos, pp. 275–342.

1943 Los yugos y su simbolismo: contribución al VI Congreso Mexicano de Historia, con sede en Jalapa, Veracruz. Mexico.

1945 Exploración en Tuzapan y zonas comarcanas. *An. Mus. Nac. Arqueol. Hist. Etnog.*, 3: 133–37. Mexico.

1945 Guía arqueológica de Chacmultun, Labna, Sayil, Kabah, Uxmal, Chichen Itza y Tulum. *In* Enciclopedia Yucatanense, 2: 405–554.

1945 Arquitectura, escultura, pintura, orfebrería y lapidaria. *Ibid.*, 2: 343–404.

PALAZUELOS, R.

1937 Informe antropológico sobre las dos momias de Durango. *Bol. Mus. Nac.*, ep. 6, 1: 15–23. Mexico.

—— AND J. ROMERO

1933 Informe preliminar de los trabajos antropológicos efectuados en las pirámides de Cholula. *An. Mus. Nac. Arqueol. Hist. Etnog.*, ep. 4, 8: 211–20. Mexico.

PALERM, A.

1927 Notas preliminares sobre vestigios glaciales en el estado de Hidalgo y en el valle de Mexico. *Mem. y Rev. Soc. Cien. Antonio Alzate*, 48: 1–13.

1953 Etnografía antigua totonaca en el oriente de México. *In* Huastecos, Totonacos, pp. 163–73.

1954 La distribución del regadío en el área central de Mesoamérica. *Pan Amer. Union, Cien. Sociales*, 5: 2–15; 6: 64–74. Washington.

1955 The agricultural bases of urban civilizations in Mesoamerica. *In* Irrigation civilizations: a comparative study, J. H. Steward and others, eds., pp. 28–42.

1956 Notas sobre las construcciones militares y la guerra en Mesoamerica. *Cien. Sociales*, 7 (39): 189–202.

1956 Comentario. *In* Arriola, 1956.

1957 Ecological potential and cultural development in Mesoamerica. *In* Studies in Human Ecology, pp. 1–37. *Pan Amer. Union, Social Sci. Monogr.*, no. 3.

—— AND E. R. WOLF

1956 El desarrollo del área clave del imperio texcocano. *Rev. Mex. Estud. Antr.*, 14: 337–49.

PALES, L.

1930 Paléopathologie et pathologie comparative. Paris.

PALLEGOIX

1854 Description du royaume Thai ou Siam. Vol. 1. Paris.

PALMA, M. T.

1886 Gramática de la lengua azteca. . . . Puebla.

PALMER, E.

1882 Mexican caves with human remains. *Amer. Naturalist*, 16: 306–11.

1888 Dr. Palmer's unpublished notes on the Coahuila caves.

PALMER, R. H.

1926 Tectonic setting of Lago de Chapala. *Pan-Amer. Geol.*, 45: 125–234.

PAN AMERICAN INST. GEOGRAPHY AND HISTORY

1953–54 Los estudios sobre los recursos naturales en las Americas. 9 vols. Mexico.

PAN AMERICAN SANITARY BUREAU

1958 Summary of four-year reports on health conditions in the Americas. *Sci. Pub. 40.* Regional Office, World Health Organization.

PANAMA

1958 Carta hidrológica. Inst. Fomento Económico.

PANIAGUA, F. A.

1876 Catecismo elemental de historia y estadística de Chiapas. San Cristobal de las Casas.

1908 Documentos y datos para un diccionario etimológico, histórico, y geográfico de Chiapas. 3 vols. San Cristobal de las Casas.

PANTIN, A. M., AND J. C. JUNQUEIRA

1952 Blood groups in Brazilian Indians. *Amer. Jour. Physical Anthr.*, n.s., 10: 395–405.

—— AND R. KALLSEN

1953 The blood groups of the Diegueño Indians. *Ibid.*, 11: 91–96.

PAPALOAPAN, EL

1949 El Papaloapan: obra del presidente Alemán. Sec. Recursos Hidráulicos. Mexico.

PAPELES DE NUEVA ESPAÑA

See Paso y Troncoso, 1905–06.

PAREYÓN MORENO, E.

1960 Exploraciones arqueológicas en Ciudad Vieja de Quiotepec, Oaxaca. *Rev. Mex. Estud. Antr.*, 16: 97–104.

PARKER, R. R.

1938 Rocky Mountain spotted fever. *Jour. Amer. Med. Assoc.*, 110: 1185–88, 1273–78.

PARMENTIER, H.

1922 Les sculptures chames au Musée de Tourane. *Ars Asiatica*, vol. 4. Paris.

1954 L'Art du Laos. Vol. 1. Paris and Hanoi.

PARR, A. E.
1935 Report on hydrographic observations in the Gulf of Mexico and the adjacent straits made during the Yale oceanographic expedition on the *Mabel Taylor* in 1932. *Bull. Bingham Oceanogr. Coll., Peabody Mus. Natural Hist., Yale Univ.*, vol. 5, art. 1.
1937 A contribution to the hydrography of the Caribbean and Cayman seas. *Ibid.*, vol. 5, art. 4.
1938 Further observations on the hydrography of the eastern Caribbean and adjacent Atlantic waters. *Ibid.*, vol. 6, art. 4.

PARRA, M. G.
1950 Densidad de la población de habla indígena en la República Mexicana. *Inst. Nac. Indig.*, Mem. 1. Mexico.
1954 Las grandes tendencias de la evolución histórica de la política indigenista moderna en México. *In* Parra and Jiménez Moreno, 1954, pp. xvii-ci.

—— AND W. JIMÉNEZ MORENO
1954 Bibliografía indigenista de México y Centroamérica (1850–1950). *Inst. Nac. Indig.*, Mem. 4. Mexico.

PARRES ARIAS, J.
1962 Nuevas adquisiones del Museo de Arqueología. *Eco*, 12: 6–7, 12. Inst. Jalisciense Antr. Hist. Guadalajara.
1963 Cofradía: nueva zona arqueológica en Jalisco. *Ibid.*, 14: 5–6.

PARSONS, E. C.
1928 Notes on the Pima. *Amer. Anthr.*, 30: 445–64.
1930 Spanish elements in the kachina cult of the Pueblos. *23d Int. Cong. Amer.* (New York, 1928), Acta, pp. 582–603.
1930 La institución de la mayordomía. *Mex. Folkways*, 6: 72–78.
1930 Entierro de un angelito. *Ibid.*, 6: 141–45.
1930 Ritos zapotecos de año nuevo. *Ibid.*, 6: 38–46.

1931 Curanderos in Oaxaca, Mexico. *Sci. Monthly*, 32: 60–68.
1932 Zapotecan and Spanish tales of Mitla, Oaxaca. *Jour. Amer. Folklore*, 45: 277–317.
1932 Folklore from Santa Ana Xalmimilulco, Puebla. *Ibid.*, 45: 318–62.
1932 Las varas. *Mex. Folkways*, 7: 81–86.
1932 Casándose en Mitla, Oaxaca. *Ibid.*, 7: 129–37.
1936 Mitla: town of the souls. Univ. Chicago Press.
1939 Pueblo Indian religion. 2 vols. Univ. Chicago Press.

PARSONS, J. J.
1955 The Miskito pine savanna of Nicaragua and Honduras. *Ann. Assoc. Amer. Geog.*, 45: 36–63.

PARSONS, L. A.
1957 The nature of horizon markers in Middle American archaeology. *Anthr. Tomorrow*, 5: 98–121. Anthr. Club, Univ. Chicago.

——, S. F. BORHEGYI, P. JENSON, AND R. RITZENTHALER
1963 Excavaciones en Bilbao, Santa Lucia Cotzumalhuapa: informe preliminar. *Antr. Hist. Guatemala*, 15 (1): 3–14.

PASCHAL, F. C., AND L. R. SULLIVAN
1925 Racial influence in the mental and physical development of Mexican children. *Comparative Psychol. Monogr.*, 3: 1–75.

PASO Y TRONCOSO, F. DEL
1890 Invención de la Santa Cruz por Santa Elena. Coloquio escrito en mexicano por el Br. D. Manuel de los Santos y Salazar. Lo tradujo libremente al castellano F. P. T. Museo Nacional. Mexico.
1891 Informes a la Secretaría de Instrucción Pública acerca de sus exploraciones en la Villa Rica y Cempoala. *Diario Oficial* (April 18), vol. 24, no. 93. Mexico.
1893 Catálogo de los objetos que presenta la República de México en la Exposición Histórico-Americana de Madrid. 2 vols. Madrid.
1898 Códice del Palais Bourbon de París. Florence.

1902 Comédies en náhuatl. *12th Int. Cong. Amer.* (Paris, 1900), Acta, pp. 309–16.

1903 Leyenda de los Soles continuada con otras leyendas y noticias. Relación anónima escrita en lengua mexicana el año 1558. (Biblioteca Nahuatl, 5 (1): 1–40). Florence.

1905 Las guerras con las tribus yaqui y mayo del estado de Sonora. Mexico.

1905–06 Papeles de Nueva España. Segunda Serie, Geografía y Estadística. 6 vols. Vol. 1: Suma de visitas de los pueblos de la Nueva España. Vol. 2: Not published. Vol. 3: Descripción del Arzobispado de México, 1571. Vol. 4: Relaciones geográficas de la diócesis de Oaxaca, 1579–81. Vol. 5: Relaciones geográficas de la diócesis de Tlaxcala, 1580–82. Vol. 6: Relaciones geográficas de la diócesis de México, 1579–82. Vol. 7: Relaciones geográficas de la diócesis de México y de la de Michoacán, 1579–82. Madrid.

1906–07 Códices Matritenses del Palacio Nacional y de la Real Academia de la Historia. Vols. 6–8. Madrid.

1912 Codice Kingsborough. Memorial de los Indios de Tepetlaoztoc al monarca español contra los encomenderos del pueblo. . . . Primera parte. . . . Madrid. [Part 2 not published.]

1928–31 Indice de documentos de Nueva España existentes en el archivo de Indias de Sevilla. 4 vols. *Monogr. Bibliográficas Mexicanas*, nos. 12, 14, 22, 23.

1939–42 Epistolario de Nueva España, 1505–1818. 16 vols. Bib. Histórica Mexicana de Obras Inéditas, 2d ser. Mexico.

1954 Tratado de las idolatrías, supersticiones, dioses, ritos, hechicerías y otras costumbres gentílicas de las razas aborígenes de México. 2 vols. Mexico.

—— AND F. GALICIA CHIMALPOPOCA

1897 Lista de los pueblos principales que pertenecían antiguamente a Tetzcoco. *An. Mus. Nac. Mex.*, 4: 48–56.

PASSARGE, S.

1919 Grundlagen der Landschaftskunde. 2 vols. Hamburg.

PASSIN, H.

1942 Sorcery as a phase of Tarahumara economic relations. *Man*, 42: 11–15.

1942 Tarahumara prevarication: a problem in field method. *Amer. Anthr.*, 44: 235–47.

1943 The place of kinship in Tarahumara social organization. *Acta Amer.*, 1: 361–89, 469–95.

PATIÑO, C.

1907 Vocabulario totonaco. Jalapa.

PATIÑO, L., A. AFANADOR, AND J. H. PAUL

1937 Spotted fever in Tobia, Columbia: preliminary report. *Amer. Jour. Tropical Med.*, 17: 639–53.

PATIÑO, L. R.

1955 Posibilidades agrícolas y de colonización de la zona costanera de Oaxaca entre los ríos Salado y Mixtepec. Informes agroeconómicos de la Mixteca de la Costa. *Inst. Nac. Indigenista*, Ser. Mimeo., no. 8.

—— AND H. CÁRDENAS

1955 Informes agroeconómicos de la Mixteca de la costa. *Ibid.*

PATTIE, J. O.

1905 *See* Thwaites, 1905.

PATTULLO, J., W. H. MUNK, R. REVELLE, AND E. STRONG

1955 The seasonal oscillation in sea level. *Jour. Marine Research*, 14: 88–155.

PAUL, B. D.

1942 Ritual kinship: with special reference to godparenthood in Middle America. Doctoral dissertation, Univ. Chicago.

1950 Life in a Guatemalan Indian village. *In* Patterns for modern living, division 3: cultural patterns, pp. 468–515. Delphian Soc. Chicago.

1950 Symbolic sibling rivalry in a Guatemalan Indian village. *Amer. Anthr.*, 52: 205–18.

1953 Mental disorder and self-regulating processes in culture: a Guatemalan illustration. *In* Interrelations between the social environment and psychiatric disorders, pp. 51–67. Milbank Mem. Fund. New York.

1955 [ed.] Health, culture and community: case studies of public reaction to health programs. Russell Sage Found. New York.

—— AND L. PAUL

1952 The life cycle. *In* Tax, 1952, Heritage, pp. 174–92.

1962 Ethnographic materials on San Pedro la Laguna, Solola, Guatemala. *Univ. Chicago, Micro. Coll. MSS Middle Amer. Cult. Anthr.*, no. 54.

1963 Changing marriage patterns in a highland Guatemalan community. *SW. Jour. Anthr.*, 19: 131–48.

PAUL-BONCOUR, G.

1912 Anthropologie anatomique: crâne—face—tête sur le vivant. Paris.

PAULS, F. P., B. B. VICTORS, AND M. W. DODSON

1953 Distribution of blood groups among the Eskimos, Indians, and Whites of western Alaska. *Amer. Jour. Human Genetics*, 5: 252–56.

PAYNE, E. J.

1892 History of the new world called America. New York.

PAYNTER, R. A., JR.

1955 The ornithogeography of the Yucatan peninsula. *Peabody Mus. Natural Hist., Yale Univ.*, Bull. 9.

PEABODY MUSEUM

1896 Prehistoric ruins of Copan, Honduras. *Mem. Peabody Mus., Harvard Univ.*, vol. 1, no. 1.

PEARCE, J. E., AND A. T. JACKSON

1933 A prehistoric rock shelter in Val Verde county, Texas. *Univ. Texas Bull., Anthr. Papers*, vol. 1, no. 3.

PEARL, R. M.

1961 Rocks and minerals. New York.

PEARSE, A. S., AND OTHERS

1936 The cenotes of Yucatan. *Carnegie Inst. Wash.*, Pub. 457.

PEARSON, K.

1899 On the reconstruction of the stature of prehistoric races. *Mathematical Contrib. to the Theory of Evolution*, 5. *Philos. Trans. Royal Soc.*, ser. A, 192: 170–244. London.

PEISSE, L.

1855 Les Aztèques à l'Academie de Méde-cine: leur histoire. *Gazette Méd. Paris*, 26 July, p. 463.

PEITHMAN, R. I.

1961 Cultural history and significance of Nayar white-on-red. Master's thesis, Dept. Anthropology, Southern Illinois Univ.

PELLICER, C., AND OTHERS

1965 Anahuacalli: Museo Diego Rivera. *Artes de México*, año 12, ep. 2, no. 66/67.

PELLIOT, P.

1925 Quelques textes chinois concernant l'Indochine hindouisée. *In* Études asiatiques publiées à l'occasion du vingt-cinquième anniversaire de l'École Française d'Extrême-Orient, 2: 243–63.

PEÑA, M. T. DE LA

1950 Problemas sociales y económicos de las mixtecas. *Inst. Nac. Indig.*, Mem. 2. Mexico.

1951 Chiapas económico. 4 vols. Gobierno del estado de Chiapas, depto. prensa y turismo. Tuxtla Gutierrez.

PEÑAFIEL, A.

1884 Memoria sobre las aguas potables de la capital de Mexico. Sec. Fomento. Mexico.

1885 *See* his 1967.

1887 [ed.] Gramática de la lengua zapoteca por un autor anónimo (con bibliografía de la lengua zapoteca de tierra caliente o de Tehuantepec). Mexico.

1890 Monumentos de arte mexicano antiguo: ornamentación, mitología, tributos y monumentos. 3 vols. in 5 bindings. Berlin.

1897–1903 Colección de documentos para la historia mexicana. 6 vols. Sec. de Fomento. Mexico.

1900 Teotihuacán: estudio histórico y arqueológico. Mexico.

1900 Cráneo antiguo de Coatlinchán. *Ibid.*, pls. 89, 90.

1903 *See* Anales de Tecamachalco, 1903.

1903 Indumentaria antigua: armas y vestidos guerreros y civiles de los antiguos Mexicanos. Mexico.

1904 *See* Cantares mexicanos, 1904.

1909 Ciudades coloniales y capitales de la

República Mexicana. 2 vols. Mexico.

1910 Destrucción del Templo Mayor de México antiguo y los monumentos encontrados en la ciudad, en las excavaciones de 1897 y 1902. Mexico.

1967 Nombres geográficos de México: catálogo alfabético de los nombres de lugar pertenecientes al idioma 'Náhuatl': estudio jeroglífico de la Matrícula de los Tributos del Códice Mendocino. Guadalajara. (Original ed. 1885.)

PEÑALVER, L. M.
1953 Estado actual de la enfermedad de chagas en Guatemala. *Rev. Colegio Méd. Guatemala*, 4: 294–308.

——, F. J. AGUILAR, F. ARTHÉS S., AND G. ARAMBURÚ
1955 Notas previas sobre tramatoidiasis en Guatemala. *Ibid.*, 6: 101–06.

PENDERGAST, D. M.
1960 The distribution of metal artifacts in prehispanic America. Doctoral dissertation, Univ. California, Los Angeles.

PENDLETON, R. L.
1943 General soil conditions in Central America. *Proc. Soil Sci. Soc. Amer.*, 8: 403–07.

1945 Some important soils of Central America. *In* Verdoorn, 1945, pp. 163–65.

PENNINGTON, C. W.
1963 The Tarahumar of Mexico: their environment and material culture. Salt Lake City.

PEÓN CONTRERAS, J.
1872 Idiotía microcefálica. *Gaceta Méd. Méx.*, vol. 7.

PEPPER, G. H.
1906 Human effigy vases from Chaco Canyon, New Mexico. *In* Boas Anniversary Volume, pp. 320–34.

1916 Yácatas in the Tierra Caliente, Michoacan. *In* Holmes Anniversary Volume, pp. 415–20.

1920 Pueblo Bonito. *Amer. Mus. Natural Hist., Anthr. Papers*, vol. 27.

PERALTA, M. M. DE
1883 Costa-Rica Nicaragua y Panama en el siglo XVI. Madrid.

1890 Límites de Costa Rica y Colombia. Madrid.

1898 Costa Rica y Costa de Mosquitos. Madrid.

PERET, B., AND M. ALVAREZ BRAVO
1943 Los tesoros del Museo Nacional de México: escultura azteca. Mexico.

PÉREZ, J. P.
n.d. [Recetarios de indios; indices de plantas medicinales y de enfermedades coordinadas.] MS. Photograph in Newberry Library. 58 pp.

1843 Cronología antigua de Yucatan y examen del método con que los indios contaban el tiempo, sacados de varios documentos antiguos. Peto. (Copies published in Registro Yucateco and in Brasseur de Bourbourg, 1864.)

1866–67 Diccionario de la lengua maya. Merida.

1898 Coordinación alfabética de las voces del idioma maya. Merida.

PÉREZ ARCEO, L.
1923 Iktili . . . a fable from the Maya. *El Agricultor*, 10 (18), November 15. Mexico.

1954 U tzicablil Xtabay (la leyenda de la Xtabay). *Yikal Maya Than*, 15 (176): 56–59.

PÉREZ AVENDAÑO, C.
1955 Estudios sobre la edad ósea en niños guatemaltecos. *Rev. Colegio Méd. Guatemala*, 6: 44–47.

—— AND R. COMPARINI ANDERSON
1960 Niveles de hemoglobina y parasitismo intestinal en pacientes de las salas de medicina del hospital Roosevelt. *Ibid.*, 11: 127–29.

——, A. A. PAIZ, AND E. MAZA
1955 Estudios clínicos nutricionales en poblaciones de El Salvador. *Bull. Oficina Sanitaria Panamer.*, suppl. 2, p. 22.

——, AND N. S. SCRIMSHAW
1955 Endemic goiter in Guatemala. *Amer. Jour. Tropical Med. and Hygiene*, 4: 963–69.

PÉREZ DE RIBAS, A.
1645 Historia de los triunfos de nuestra santa fe entre gentes las más bárbaras y fieras del nuevo orbe. Madrid.

1944 *Idem*, another ed. Mexico.

PÉREZ ESTRADA, F.
1954 Teatro folklórico hispanoamericano. *Nicaragua Indig.*, 2a ep., 1: 34–39.
1955 Las comunidades indígenas en Nicaragua. *Ibid.*, 2a ep., 8: 5–19.

PÉREZ GARCÍA, R.
1956 La Sierra Juarez. 2 vols. Mexico.

PÉREZ SALAZAR, A.
1881 Breve estudio sobre los diámetros del feto maduro, considerado bajo el punto de vista de la obstetricia y de la medicina legal. Mexico.

PÉREZ SERRANO, M.
1942 Leyenda zapoteca: el "betooc" o señor de los bosques. *Anuario Soc. Folklórica Mex.*, 3: 173–175.

PERICOT, L.
1936 Historia de América. Vol. 1. *América Indígena*. Barcelona.

PÉRIER, J. A. N.
1860–68 Essais sur les croisements ethniques. *Mem. Soc. Anthr. Paris*, 1: 69–92, 187–236; 2: 261–374; 3: 211–96.

PÉRIGNY, M. DE
1908 Yucatan inconnu. *Jour. Soc. Amer. Paris*, 5: 67–84.

PERRY, E.
1922 Central American union. *Hispanic Amer. Hist. Rev.*, 5: 30–51.

PETERS, J. A.
1955 Use and misuse of the biotic province concept. *Amer. Naturalist*, 89: 21–28.

PETERSON, C. L.
1960 The physical oceanography of the Gulf of Nicoya, Costa Rica, a tropical estuary. *Bull. Inter-Amer. Tropical Tuna Comm.*, 4: 137–216.

PETERSON, F. A.
1952 Caritas sonrientes de la región maya. *Tlatoani*, 1: 63–64.
1959 Las fiestas. *In* Esplendor del México antiguo, 2: 819–36.
1959 Ancient Mexico: an introduction to the pre-Hispanic cultures. London.
1963 Some ceramics from Mirador, Chiapas, Mexico. *Papers New World Archaeol. Found.*, no. 15.

—— AND F. HORCASITAS
1957 Recent finds at Tlatilco. *Tlalocan*, 3: 363–65.

PETTERSSEN, S.
1941 Introduction to meteorology. New York and London.

PFEFFERKORN, I.
1949 Sonora, a description of the province. Tr. by T. E. Treutlein. Univ. New Mexico Press.

PHELAN, J. L.
1956 The millennial kingdom of the Franciscans in the New World: a study of the writing of Gerónimo de Mendieta (1525–1604). *Univ. California Pub. Hist.*, no. 52.

PHILLIPS, P.
1940 Middle American influences on the archaeology of the southeastern United States. *In* The Maya and their neighbors, pp. 349–67.

——, J. A. FORD, AND J. B. GRIFFIN
1951 Archaeological survey in the lower Mississippi alluvial valley, 1940–1947. *Papers Peabody Mus., Harvard Univ.*, vol. 25.

—— AND J. C. GIFFORD
1959 A review of the taxonomic nomenclature essential to ceramic analysis in archaeology. MS in Peabody Mus., Harvard Univ. (Mimeographed.)

PICKETT, V. B.
1946 Cartillas I and II. Inst. Ling. Verano. Mexico.
1948 Problems in Zapotec tone analysis. *Int. Jour. Amer. Ling.*, 14: 161–70.
1951 Nonphonemic stress: a problem in stress placement in Isthmus Zapotec. *Word*, 7: 60–65.
1953 Isthmus Zapotec verb analysis I. *Int. Jour. Amer. Ling.*, 19: 292–96.
1955 Isthmus Zapotec verb analysis II. *Ibid.*, 21: 217–32.
1959 Castellano-zapoteco, zapoteco-castellano. Inst. Ling. Verano. Mexico.
1960 The grammatical hierarchy of isthmus Zapotec. *Language*, suppl. 56.

PICOLO, F. M.
1919 Report on the state of the new Christianity of California (1701.) *In* Bolton, 1919, 1: 46–67.

PIJOAN, J.
1946 Arte precolombiano, mexicano y maya. *In* his Summa artis: historia general del arte, vol. 10. Madrid. (3d ed. 1958.)

PIJOAN, M.
1946 The health and customs of the Miskito Indians of northern Nicaragua: interrelations in a medical program. *Amer. Indig.*, 6: 157–83.

PIKE, E. V.
1948 Head-washing and other elements in the Mazateco marriage ceremony. *Amer. Indig.*, 8: 219–22.

1948 Problems in Zapotec tone analysis. *Int. Jour. Amer. Ling.*, 14: 161–70.

1954 Phonetic rank and subordination in consonant patterning and historical change. *Misc. Phonetica*, 2: 25–41.

1956 Tonally differentiated allomorphs in Soyaltepec Mazatec. *Int. Jour. Amer. Ling.*, 22: 57–71.

—— AND B. F. ELSON
1962 An introduction to morphology and syntax. *Summer Inst. Ling.* Santa Ana.

PIKE, F. B., ed.
1959 Freedom and reform in Latin America. Notre Dame, Indiana.

PIKE, K. L.
1937 Una leyenda mixteca: cuenta chihi. *Invest. Ling.*, 4: 262–70.

1944 Analysis of a Mixteco text. *Int. Jour. Amer. Ling.*, 10: 113–38.

1945 Tone puns in Mixteco. *Ibid.*, 11: 129–39.

1945 Mock Spanish of a Mixteco Indian. *Ibid.*, 11: 219–24.

1946 Another Mixtec tone pun. *Ibid.*, 12: 22–24.

1946 Phonemic pitch in Maya. *Ibid.*, 12: 82–88.

1947 A text involving inadequate Spanish of Mixteco Indians. *Ibid.*, 13: 251–57.

1947 Phonemics. *Univ. Michigan Pub. Ling.*, no. 3.

1948 Tone languages. Univ. Michigan Press.

1948–49 Cuento mixteco de un conejo, un coyote y la luna. *Rev. Mex. Estud. Antr.*, 10: 133–34.

1954 Language in relation to a unified theory of the structure of human behavior, part I. *Summer Inst. Ling.* Glendale.

1955 *Idem*, part II.

1956 Towards a theory of the structure of human behavior. *In* Estudios antropológicos publicados en homenaje al doctor Manuel Gamio. *Soc. Mex. Antr.* Mexico.

1958 On tagmemes, née gramemes. *Int. Jour. Amer. Ling.*, 24: 273–78.

1959 Language as particle, wave and field. *Texas Quar.*, 2 (2): 37–54.

1960 Language in relation to a unified theory of the structure of human behavior, part III. *See* his 1954, 1955.

—— AND E. V. PIKE
1947 Immediate constituents of Mazateco syllables. *Int. Jour. Amer. Ling.*, 13: 78–91.

PILSBRY, H. A.
1926 The land mollusks of the Republic of Panama and the Canal Zone. *Proc. Acad. Nat. Sci. Philadelphia*, pp. 57–133.

1930 Results of the Pinchot South Seas expedition. Part 2: Land mollusks of the Canal Zone, the Republic of Panama, and the Cayman Islands. *Ibid.*, pp. 339–65.

PIM, CAPTAIN, AND B. SEEMANN
1869 Dottings on the roadside in Panama, Nicaragua, and Mosquito. London.

PIMENTEL, F.
1874–75 Cuadro descriptivo y comparativo de las lenguas indígenas de México. 3 vols. 2d ed. Mexico. (Another ed. 1904.)

1903 Obras completas. Vol. 2. Mexico.

PIMENTEL NEZAHUALCOYOTL, H.
1880 Sacado de un memorial dirigido al rey. . . . *In* Orozco y Berra, 1880, 2: 201–03.

PIMENTEL S., J.
1954 Narración tradicional. *Anuario Soc. Folklórica Mex.*, 9: 9–24.

1957 Miscelánea de creencias en la congregación de los angeles, Simojovel, Chiapas. *Ibid.*, 11: 207–24.

PIÑA CHAN, R.
1948 Breve estudio sobre la funeraria de

Jaina, Campeche. *Mus. Arqueol. Etnog. Hist.*, Cuad. 7. Campeche.

1952 Tlatilco y la cultura preclásica del Valle de México. *An. Inst. Nac. Antr. Hist.* (1949–50), ep. 6, 4 (32): 33–43.

1955 Chalcatzingo, Morelos. *Inst. Nac. Antr. Hist., Dir. Monumentos Prehispánicos*, Informe 4. Mexico.

1955 Las culturas preclásicas de la cuenca de México. Fondo de Cultura Económica. Mexico.

1958 Tlatilco. *Inst. Nac. Antr. Hist., Ser. Invest.*, nos. 1, 2.

1959 Museo de la cultura huasteca. Guía oficial. Inst. Nac. Antr. Hist. Mexico.

1960 Mesoamérica: ensayo histórico cultural. *Mem. Inst. Nac. Antr. Hist.*, vol. 6.

1960 Algunos sitios arquelógicos de Oaxaca y Guerrero. *Rev. Mex. Estud. Antr.*, 16: 65–76.

1960 Reconocimientos arqueológicos en el estado de Chiapas. MS, VII Mesa Redonda, Soc. Mex. Antr. San Cristobal de las Casas.

1960 Descubrimiento arqueológico en Xochicalco, Morelos. *Bol. Inst. Nac. Antr. Hist.*, 2: 1–4.

1963 Las culturas prehispánicas en Jalisco. *Eco*, 14: 3–4. Inst. Jalisciense Antr. Hist. Guadalajara.

1963 Excavaciones en el rancho "La Ventanilla." *In* Bernal, 1963, pp. 50–52.

1963 Cultural development in central Mesoamerica. *In* Meggers and Evans, 1963, pp. 17–26.

PINART, A. L.

n.d. Vocabularies of the Hehúe dialect of Opata. MS. Pinart Coll., Bancroft Library, Univ. California.

PINEDA, E.

1845 Descripción geográfica de Chiapas y Soconusco. Mexico.

PINEDA, V.

1888 Gramática de la lengua tzeltal y diccionario. . . . Chiapas.

1888 Historia de las sublevaciones indígenas habidas en el estado de Chiapas. San Cristobal de las Casas.

PINTO, R. G.

1941 Los indígenas y la República Mexicana.

PINTURA DE MÉXICO

1891 Pintura de México. *In* Alva Ixtlilxochitl, 1891, pp. 258–61.

PITTIER, H. F.

1895 Exploración en Talamanca. San Jose.

1912 Kostarika. Beiträge zur Orographie und Hydrographie. *Petermanns Mitt.*, Ergänzungsheft 175. Gotha.

PITTMAN, R. S.

1945 La historia de Pedro Sa-kinemilea. *Tlalocan*, 2: 10–17.

1948 Nahuatl honorifics. *Int. Jour. Amer. Ling.*, 14: 236–39.

1954 A grammar of Tetelcingo (Morelos) Nahuatl. *Ling. Soc. Amer.*, Language Dissertation 50.

PITT-RIVERS, J. A.

1954 The people of the sierra. London.

1963 Political organization in Chiapas. MS, Chiapas Project files, Univ. Chicago, Dept. Anthropology.

PLANCARTE, F. M.

1954 El problema indígena tarahumara. *Inst. Nac. Indig.*, Mem. 5. Mexico.

PLANCARTE Y NAVARRETE, F.

1893 Archeologic explorations in Michoacan, Mexico. *Amer. Anthr.*, o.s., 6: 79–84.

1923 Prehistoria de Mexico. Tlalpan, D.F.

POCOCK, R. I.

1902 Arachnida, scorpiones, pedipalpi, and solifugae. *In* Biologia Centrali-Americana, Zoology, vol. 12.

POLANYI, K., C. M. ARENSBERG, AND H. W. PEARSON

1957 Trade and market in early empires. Glencoe, Ill.

POLLOCK, H. E. D.

1936 Round structures of aboriginal Middle America. *Carnegie Inst. Wash.*, Pub. 471.

1940 Sources and methods in the study of Maya architecture. *In* The Maya and their neighbors, pp. 179–201.

1940 Architectural survey of Yucatan. *Carnegie Inst. Wash.*, Year Book 39, pp. 265–67.

1952   Department of archaeology. *Ibid.*, Year Book 51, pp. 235–43.

——, R. L. Roys, T. Proskouriakoff, and A. L. Smith

1962   Mayapan, Yucatan, Mexico. *Carnegie Inst. Wash.*, Pub. 619.

—— and G. Stromsvik

1953   Chacchob, Yucatan. *Carnegie Inst. Wash., Current Reports*, no. 6.

Polunin, I., and P. H. A. Sneath

1953   Studies on blood groups in southeast Asia. *Jour. Royal Anthr. Inst.*, 83: 215–51.

Pomar, J. B.

1891   Relación de Tezcoco. *In* García Icazbalceta, 1889–1902, 3: 1–69.

1941   *Idem. In* García Icazbalceta, 1941, 3: 1–64.

1964   *Idem. In* Garibay K., 1964, 4: 149–228.

Pompa y Pompa, A., ed.

1966   Summa anthropologica: en homenaje a Roberto J. Weitlaner. Inst. Nac. Antr. Hist. Mexico.

Ponce, A.

1873   Relación breve y verdadera de algunas cosas de las muchas que sucedieron al Padre Fray Alonso Ponce en las provincias de la Nueva España. 2 vols. Madrid. (Originally issued in Col. doc. España, vols. 57 and 58, Madrid, 1872. Almost certainly the work of Antonio Ciudad Real.)

1892   Breve relación de los dioses y ritos de la gentilidad. *An. Mus. Nac. Mex.*, ep. 1–6, pp. 3–12.

1932   Fray Alonso Ponce in Yucatan, 1588. E. Noyes, ed. and trans. *Tulane Univ., Middle Amer. Research Inst.*, Pub. 4, pp. 297–372.

1953   Breve relación de los dioses y ritos de la gentilidad. *In* Tratado de las idolatrías, supersticiones, dioses, ritos, hechicerías y otras costumbres gentílicas de las razas aborígenes de México. *Ediciones Fuente Cultural*, 10: 371–80. Mexico. (1st ed. 1892.)

1965   Tratado de los dioses y ritos de la gentilidad. *In* Garibay K., 1965, Teogonía, pp. 121–32.

Ponce de León, L.

1882   Relación de la provincia de Soconus-
co, together with a covering letter dated 1574. *In* Fuentes y Guzmán, 1882, 1: 423–28.

Popenoe, D. H.

1934   Some excavations at Playa de los Muertos, Ulua River, Honduras. *Maya Research*, 1: 61–81.

1936   The ruins of Tenampua, Honduras. *Smithsonian Inst.*, ann. rept. 1935, pp. 559–72.

Popenoe, H.

1960   Effects of shifting cultivation on natural soil constituents in Central America. Doctoral dissertation, Univ. Florida.

Popenoe, W.

1926   Guatemala. *In* Shelford, 1926, pp. 596–601.

Popol Vuh

1950   Popol Vuh: the sacred book of the ancient Quiche Maya. Norman, Okla. *See* Book of the People, 1954; Edmonson, 1971.

Porter, K. W.

1951   The Seminole in Mexico, 1850–1861. *Hispanic Amer. Hist. Rev.*, 31: 1–36.

Porter, M. N.

1948   Pipas precortesianas. *Acta Anthr.*, 3: 130–251.

1948   Pottery found at Chupicuaro, Guanajuato. *In* El Occidente de México, pp. 42–47.

1953   Tlatilco and the pre-classic cultures of the New World. *Viking Fund Pub. Anthr.*, no. 19.

1955   Material preclásico de San Salvador. *Inst. Tropical Invest. Cien.*, 4: 105–12. San Salvador.

1956   Excavations at Chupicuaro, Guanajuato, Mexico. *Trans. Amer. Phil. Soc.*, vol. 46, pt. 5.

Porter, W. W.

1932   The Coahuila piedmont, a physiographic province in northeastern Mexico. *Jour. Geol.*, 40: 338–52.

Portillo, E. L.

1886   Apuntes para la historia antigua de Coahuila y Texas. Saltillo.

1897   Catecismo geográfico político e histórico del estado de Coahuila de Zaragoza. Saltillo.

POWERS, S.
1918 Notes on the geology of eastern Guatemala and northwestern Spanish Honduras. *Jour. Geol.*, 26: 507–23.

POZAS A., R.
1944 Monografía de Chamula, Chiapas. *Univ. Chicago, Micro. Coll. MSS Middle Amer. Cult. Anthr.*, no. 15.

1945 El fraccionamiento de la tierra por el mecanismo de herencia en Chamula. *Rev. Mex. Estud. Antr.*, 7: 187–97.

1949 La alfarería de Patambam. *An. Inst. Nac. Antr. Hist.*, 3: 115–45.

1952 Juan Pérez Jolote: biografía de un Tzotzil. Fondo de Cultura Económica. Mexico. (3d ed. 1959.) [See his 1962.]

1952 El trabajo en las plantaciones de café y el cambio socio-cultural del indio. *Rev. Mex. Estud. Antr.*, 13: 31–48.

1959 Chamula: un pueblo indio de los altos de Chiapas. *Mem. Inst. Nac. Indig.*, vol. 8.

1959 El mundo mágico de los chamulas. *Acad. Mex. Pediatría*, no. 16, pp. 3–10. Mexico.

1959 Los cambios sociales y la industrialización. *In* Stone, 1959, pp. 373–79.

1960 Etnografía de los mazatecos. *Rev. Mex. Estud. Antr.*, 16: 211–26.

1962 Juan the Chamula: an ethnological re-creation of the life of a Mexican Indian. Tr. from the Spanish by L. Kemp. Univ. California Press. [Tr. of Pozas, 1952.]

POZAS, I. H. DE
1949 Notas etnográficas de Eloxochitlan, Oaxaca. MS.

PREHISTORIC MAN IN THE NEW WORLD
1964 Prehistoric man in the New World. J. D. Jennings and E. Norbeck, eds. Univ. Chicago Press.

PREHISTORY OF THE TEHUACAN VALLEY
See Byers, 1967; MacNeish and others, 1967, 1970.

PRESCOTT, W. H.
1844 History of the conquest of Mexico, with a preliminary view of the ancient Mexican civilization and the life of the conqueror Hernando Cortés. 3 vols. London.

PREUSS, K. T.
1904 Der Ursprung der Religion und Kunst. *Globus*, 86: 321–27. Brunswick.

1912 Die Nayarit-Expedition, Textaufnahmen und Beobachtungen unter mexikanischen Indianern. Band I: Die Religion der Cora Indianer. Leipzig.

1930 Mexikanische Religion. *In* Bilderatlas zur Religiongeschichte, H. Haas, ed., vol. 16. Leipzig.

1932 Au sujet du caractère des mythes et chants Huichols que j'ai recueillis. *Univ. Tucuman, Inst. Etnol.*, 2: 445–57. Tucuman, Argentina.

1932 Grammatik der Cora-Sprache. *Int. Jour. Amer. Ling.*, 7: 1–84.

1935 Wörterbuch Deutsch-Cora. *Ibid.*, 8: 79–102.

1955 El concepto de la estrella matutina según textos recogidos entre los Mexicanos del estado de Durango, Mexico. *El Mex. Antiguo*, 8: 375–93.

—— AND E. MENGIN
1937–38 Die mexikanische Bilderhandschrift Historia Tolteca-Chichimeca. Parts I and II. *Baessler Archiv.* Berlin.

PRICE, H. W.
1899 Excavations on the Sittee River, British Honduras. Proc. Soc. Antiquaries.

PRICE, S. H.
1966 I was Pashku and my husband was Telesh. *Radcliffe Quar.*, May-June, pp. 4–8.

PRIDE, K.
1961 Numerals in Chatino. *Anthr. Ling.*, 3: 1–10.

PRIESTLEY, H. I.
1923 The Mexican nation, a history. New York.

PRIETO, A.
1873 Historia, geografía y estadística del estado de Tamaulipas, Mexico.

PRIMERA RELACIÓN DE . . . GUZMÁN
1858–66 Primera relación anónima de la jornada que hizo Nuño de Guzmán a la Nueva Galicia. *In* García Icazbalceta, 1858–66, 2: 288–95.

PROCESOS DE INDIOS
1912   Procesos de Indios idólatras y hechi-
        ceros. *Archivo General de la Na-*
        ción, Pub. 3. Mexico.

PROMPTUARIO MANUAL MEXICANO
1759   Promptuario manual mexicano. Bi-
        bliotheca Mexicana. Mexico.

PROSKOURIAKOFF, T.
1944   An inscription on a jade probably
        carved at Piedras Negras. *Carnegie*
        Inst. Wash., Notes Middle Amer. Ar-
        chaeol. Ethnol., no. 47.
1946   An album of Maya architecture.
        Carnegie Inst. Wash., Pub. 558.
1950   A study of classic Maya sculpture.
        Ibid., Pub. 593.
1951   Some non-classic traits in the sculp-
        ture of Yucatan. *In* Tax, 1951, pp.
        108–18.
1952   Sculpture and artifacts of Mayapan.
        Carnegie Inst. Wash., Year Book 51,
        pp. 256–59.
1952   The survival of the Maya tun count
        in colonial times. *Carnegie Inst.*
        Wash., Notes Middle Amer. Archaeol.
        Ethnol., no. 112.
1953   Scroll patterns (entrelaces en Vera-
        cruz). *In* Huastecos, Totonacos, pp.
        389–401.
1954   Varieties of classic central Veracruz
        sculpture. *Carnegie Inst. Wash.*,
        Pub. 606, Contrib. 58.
1957   Notes and news: Middle America.
        Amer. Antiquity, 22: 333–34.
1957   Notes and news: Middle America.
        Ibid., 23: 218–20.
1958   Studies on Middle American art.
        In Willey, Vogt, and Palerm, 1958,
        pp. 29–35.
1960   Historical implications of a pattern
        of dates at Piedras Negras, Guate-
        mala. *Amer. Antiquity*, 25: 454–75.
1961   Portraits of women in Maya art.
        In Lothrop and others, 1961, pp. 81–
        99.
1962   Civic and religious structures of
        Mayapan. *Carnegie Inst. Wash.*,
        Pub. 619, pp. 87–164.
1962   The artifacts of Mayapan. *Ibid.*, pp.
        321–442.
1962   *Review of* More human than divine,

by William Spratling. *Amer. Antiq-*
        uity, 27: 439.
1968   Olmec and Maya art: problems of
        their stylistic relation. *In* Benson,
        1968, pp. 119–34.
——— AND C. R. TEMPLE
1955   A residential quadrangle: Structures
        R-85 to R-90. *Carnegie Inst. Wash.,*
        Current Reports, no. 29.
——— AND J. E. S. THOMPSON
1947   Maya calendar round dates such as
        9 Ahau 3 Mol. *Carnegie Inst.*
        Wash., Notes Middle Amer. Ar-
        chaeol. Ethnol., no. 79.

PUENTE Y OLEA, M. DE LA
1889   Relación de la comarca y minas de
        Temascaltepec hecha en 1579 por D.
        Gaspar de Covarrubias. *Mem. Soc.*
        Cien. Antonio Alzate, 3: 203–14.

PULGRAM, E.
1956   On prehistoric linguistic expansion.
        In Halle, Lunt, McLean, and Van
        Schooneveld, 1956, pp. 411–17.

PUTNAM, F. W.
1872   Note on ancient races of America,
        their crania, migrations, and greatest
        development in Mexico and Peru.
        Bull. Essex Inst., 4: 228–29. Salem,
        Mass.
1872   An ancient human cranium from
        southern Mexico. *Proc. Boston Soc.*
        Natural Hist., 15: 228–29.
1884   Human footprints found in tufa near
        the shore of Lake Managua, Nicara-
        gua. *Abstr. Proc. Amer. Antiquarian*
        Soc., n.s., 3: 92–93.
1892   An ancient human cranium from Yu-
        catan. *Proc. Amer. Assoc. Advance-*
        ment Sci., 40: 376.
1899   A problem in American anthropology.
        Proc. Amer. Acad. Arts and Sci., 48:
        1–17.

PUTNAM ANNIVERSARY VOLUME
1909   Anthropological essays presented to
        Frederic Ward Putnam in honor of
        his seventieth birthday. New York.

QUATREFAGES, A. DE
1889   Introduction à l'étude des races hu-
        maines. A. Hennuyer, ed. Paris.
——— AND E. T. HAMY
1882   Crania ethnica. Paris.

QUEVEDO, J.
1949 El escleroma en Guatemala. *Rev. Federación Méd. Guatemala*, vol. 3, no. 14.

QUEVEDO Y ZUBIETA, S.
1894 Del hallux valgus. Tesis. Mexico.

QUIJADA, H.
1579 Relación de Usila. *In* Paso y Troncoso, 1905–06, 4: 45–52. [Tr. in Bevan, 1938, pp. 129–34.]

QUINTANA, A. DE
1729 Arte de la lengua mixe. Puebla. (Reprinted 1891.)

QUINTANA, J. N.
1906 Pelvis oblicua triangular. Puebla.

RABASA, R.
1895 El estado de Chiapas: geografía y estadística. Mexico.

RACE, R. R., AND R. SANGER
1858 Blood groups in man. Blackwell Sci. Pub. Oxford.

—— AND OTHERS (R. SANGER, F. H. ALLEN, L. K. DIAMOND, AND B. NIEDZIELA)
1951 Inheritance of the human blood-group antigen Jk^a. *Nature*, 168: 207. London.

RADA Y DELGADO, J. DE LA, AND J. LÓPEZ DE AYALA Y DEL HIERRO
1892 Códice maya denominado cortesiano. Madrid.

RADCLIFFE, L.
1922 Fisheries and market for fishery products in Mexico, Central America, South America, West Indies, and Bermudas. Rept. U.S. Comm. Fisheries, App. 8.

RADHAKRISHNAN, R.
1962 An outline of Pinolteca [Tzeltal] morphology. Master's thesis, Univ. Chicago. *Also in* McQuown, 1962.

RADIN, P.
1915 Folktales from Oaxaca. *Jour. Amer. Folklore*, 28: 390–408.
1916 On the relationship of Huave and Mixe. *Amer. Anthr.*, 18: 411–23.
1917 El folklore de Oaxaca. New York.
1919 The genetic relationship of the North American Indian languages. *Univ. California Pub. Amer. Archaeol. Ethnol.*, 14: 489–502.
1920 The sources and authenticity of the history of the ancient Mexicans. *Ibid.*, 17: 1–150.
1925 The distribution and phonetics of the Zapotec dialects: a preliminary sketch. *Jour. Soc. Amer. Paris*, 17: 27–76.
1925 Maya, Nahuatl, and Tarascan kinship terms. *Amer. Anthr.*, 27: 101–03.
1927 The story of the American Indian. New York.
1929 Huave texts. *Int. Jour. Amer. Ling.*, 5: 1–56.
1930 Preliminary sketch of the Zapotec language. *Language*, 6: 64–85.
1931 Mexican kinship systems. *Univ. California Pub. Amer. Archaeol. Ethnol.*, 31: 1–14.
1933 Mixe texts. *Jour. Soc. Amer. Paris*, 25: 41–64.
1935 An historical legend of the Zapotecs. *Ibero-Amer.*, no. 9.
1935 Notes on the Tlappanecan language of Guerrero. *Int. Jour. Amer. Ling.*, 8: 45–72.
1935 Tehuano vocabulary and Tehuano texts. MS, Library of Miguel Covarrubias, Tizapan.
1940 Notes on Schultze-Jena's Tlappanec. *Bol. Bibliográfico Antr. Amer.*, 4: 70–74.
1943–44 Cuentos y leyendas de los zapotecos. *Tlalocan*, 1: 3–30, 134–54, 194–226.
1944 The classification of the languages of Mexico. *Ibid.*, 2: 259–65.
1945 Cuentos de Mitla. *Ibid.*, vol. 2, nos. 1, 2, 3.
1946 Zapotec texts: dialect of Juchitan Tehuano. *Int. Jour. Amer. Ling.*, 12: 152–72.

RADLEY, J.
1960 The physical geography of the east coast of Nicaragua. Rept. field work carried out under ONR Contract 222(11) NR 388 067. Univ. California, Dept. Geography.

RAISZ, E.
1959 Landforms of Mexico. [Map with text.] Cambridge, Mass.

RALPH, E. K.
1965 Review of radiocarbon dates from

Tikal and the Maya correlation problem. *Amer. Antiquity*, 30: 421–27.

RAMÍREZ, J.
1897 Las leyes biológicas permiten asegurar que las razas primitivas de América son autóctonas. *11th Int. Cong. Amer.* (Mexico, 1895), Acta, pp. 360–63.

RAMÍREZ, J. F.
1949 Noticias sacadas de un manuscrito intitulado Relaciones de todas las cosas que en el Nuevo México . . . desde el año 1538 hasta el de 1626 por Fr. Gerónimo de Zárate S. . . . Mexico.

RAMÍREZ DE FUENLEAL, S.
1866 Parecer de Don Sebastián Ramírez de Fuenleal. . . . *In* García Icazbalceta, 1858–66, 2: 165–89.
1870 Carta a su magestad del obispo de Santo Domingo. . . . *In* Col. doc. Indias, 13: 233–37.
1870 Carta a su magestad del obispo de Santo Domingo. . . . *Ibid.*, 13: 250–61.

RAMÍREZ FLORES, J.
1935 La arqueología en el sur de Jalisco. Bol. Junta Auxiliar Jalisciense, Soc. Mex. Geografía y Estadística, 4 (2): 41–56. Guadalajara.

RAMÍREZ VÁSQUEZ, P., AND OTHERS
1968 The National Museum of Anthropology, Mexico: art, architecture, archaeology, ethnography. New York.

RAMMOW, H.
1964 Die Verwandschaftsbezeichnungen im klassischen Aztekischen. Mus. für Völkerkunde und Vorgeschichte. Hamburg.

RAMÓN Y LLIGE, A.
n.d. Estudio de las puntas arrojadizas de la altiplanicie de México. Tesis, Escuela Nacional de Antropología. Mexico.
1959 Útiles de piedra. *In* Esplendor de México antiguo, 2: 480–84.

RAMOS, G.
1918 As impressões digitaes dos selvagens. *Amazonas Med.*, 1: 3–14.

RAMOS B., J.
1945 The phantom lover. *Tlalocan*, 2: 30–33.

RAMOS GALVÁN, R., AND OTHERS
1964 Aplicación de la prueba de Goodenough a escolares mexicanos de distintos grupos socioculturales y diverso estado de nutrición. *Bol. Méd. Hospital Infantil Méx.*, 21: 157–64, 173–77.

RANDS, B. C.
1954 Ceramics associated with the Temple of the Inscriptions, Palenque, Chiapas, Mexico. Master's thesis, Univ. New Mexico.
—— AND R. L. RANDS
1959 Preliminary notes on Group 4, Pit 5, Palenque, Chiapas: burials 1959. MS.

RANDS, R. L.
1952 Some evidences of warfare in classic Maya art. Doctoral dissertation, Columbia Univ.
1953 The water lily in Maya art: a complex of alleged Asiatic origin. *Smithsonian Inst., Bur. Amer. Ethnol.*, Bull. 151, pp. 75–153.
1954 Artistic connections between the Chichen Itza Toltec and the classic Maya. *Amer. Antiquity*, 19: 281–82.
1955 Some manifestations of water in Mesoamerican art. *Smithsonian Inst., Bur. Amer. Ethnol.*, Bull. 157, pp. 265–393.
1957 Comparative notes on the hand-eye and related motifs. *Amer. Antiquity*, 22: 247–57.
1961 Elaboration and invention in ceramic traditions. *Ibid.*, 26: 331–40.
1961 The ceramic history of Palenque, Chiapas, Mexico. *Amer. Phil. Soc.*, Year Book 1960, pp. 566–68.
—— AND B. C. RANDS
1957 The ceramic position of Palenque, Chiapas. *Amer. Antiquity*, 23: 140–50.
1959 The incensario complex of Palenque, Chiapas. *Ibid.*, 25: 225–36.
1960 Ceramic investigations at Palenque, Mexico. *Bol. Bib. Antr. Amer.*, vol. 21-22, pt. 1, pp. 218–20.
—— AND R. E. SMITH
1965 Pottery of the Guatemalan highlands. *In* Handbook of Middle American In-

dians, R. Wauchope, ed., vol. 2, art. 4.

RATTRAY, E. C.
1966 Teotihuacan chronology. [Chart.] *Mesoamerican Notes*, 6–7. Mexico.
1966 An archaeological and stylistic study of Coyotlatelco pottery. *Ibid.*, 7–8, pp. 87–211.

RAVENEAU DE LUSSAN
1869 Journal du voyage fait à la Mer du Sur, par les flibustiers de l'Amérique en 1684 et années suivantes. Paris.

RAVICZ, R.
1958 A comparative study of selected aspects of Mixtec social organization. Doctoral dissertation, Harvard Univ.
1959 Field notes on Cuauhtenco, a Nahuatl-speaking village of Tlaxcala, Mexico. MS.
1960 Field notes on Xochistlahuaca, an Amuzgo-speaking village of Guerrero, Mexico. MS.
1961 Field notes on Trique and Mixtec speakers of Oaxaca and Nahuatl speakers of Guerrero, Mexico. MS.
1961 La mixteca en el estudio comparativo del hongo alucinante. *An. Inst. Nac. Antr. Hist.*, 13: 73–92.
1962–65 Field notes on Mixtec. MS.
1965 Organización social de los Mixtecos. *Inst. Nac. Indig., Col. Antr. Social*, no. 5. Mexico.
1966 The washing of the hands: a structural element in indigenous interpretation of Christian baptism. *In* Pompa y Pompa, 1966.
—— AND A. K. ROMNEY
1955 Sixteen centuries of Mixtec kinship. MS.

RAY, S. M., AND W. B. WILSON
1956 The occurrence of *Gymnodinium breve* in the western Gulf of Mexico. *Ecology*, 2: 388.

RAY, V. F., ed.
1959 Intermediate societies, social mobility, and communication. *Amer. Ethnol. Soc.*, Proc. annual spring meeting.

RECINOS, A.
1913 Monografía del departamento de Huehuetenango, República de Guatemala. Guatemala. (2d ed. 1954.)
1916 Estudios de antropología y etnografía: razas y lenguas indígenas de Guatemala. *Centroamérica*, 8: 607–18. Guatemala.
1917 Lenguas indígenas de Guatemala. *Proc. 2d Pan Amer. Sci. Cong. Anthr.*, 1: 209–19.
1947 Popol Vuh: las antiguas historias del Quiché. Mexico.
1950 The Popol Vuh. Univ. Oklahoma Press.
1950 [ed.] Memorial de Sololá: anales de los Cakchiqueles seguido del título de los señores de Totonicapán. Mexico.
1953 [ed.] The Annals of the Cakchiquels. Univ. Oklahoma Press.
1957 Crónicas indígenas de Guatemala. Guatemala.

RECORD, S. J., AND R. W. HESS
1943 Timbers of the New World. New Haven.

REDFIELD, M. P.
1935 Folk literature of a Yucatecan town. *Carnegie Inst. Wash.*, Pub. 456, Contrib. 14.

REDFIELD, R.
1928 The calpulli-barrio in a present day Mexican pueblo. *Amer. Anthr.*, 30: 282–94.
1930 Tepoztlan, a Mexican village. Univ. Chicago Press.
1934 Culture changes in Yucatan. *Amer. Anthr.*, 36: 57–69.
1938 Primitive merchants of Guatemala. *Quar. Jour. Inter-Amer. Relations*, 1 (4): 42–56.
1939 Culture contact without conflict. *Amer. Anthr.*, 41: 514–17.
1940 The Indian in Mexico. *In* Mexico today, T. Sallin, ed. *Ann. Amer. Acad. Polit. Social Sci.*, 208: 132–43.
1941 The folk culture of Yucatan. Univ. Chicago Press.
1946 Ethnographic materials on Agua Escondida. *Univ. Chicago, Micro. Coll. MSS Middle Amer. Cult. Anthr.*, no. 3.
1946 Notes on San Antonio Palopo. *Ibid.*, no. 4.
1950 A village that chose progress: Chan Kom revisited. Univ. Chicago Press.

1953 The primitive world and its transformations. Ithaca, N.Y.

1954 *Foreword to* Language in culture. *Amer. Anthr. Assoc.*, Memoir 79.

1956 Peasant society and culture: an anthropological approach to civilization. Univ. Chicago Press.

1960 The little community. Univ. Chicago Press.

—— AND M. P. REDFIELD

1940 Disease and its treatment in Dzitas, Yucatan. *Carnegie Inst. Wash.*, Pub. 523, Contrib. 32.

—— AND S. TAX

1952 General characteristics of present-day Mesoamerican Indian society. *In* Tax, 1952, Heritage, pp. 31–39.

—— AND A. VILLA ROJAS

1934 Chan Kom, a Maya village. *Carnegie Inst. Wash.*, Pub. 448.

1939 Notes on the ethnography of the Tzeltal communities of Chiapas. *Ibid.*, Pub. 509, Contrib. 28.

1962 Chan Kom, a Maya village. Rev. ed. Univ. Chicago Press.

REED, D. W., AND J. L. SPICER

1952 Correlation methods of comparing idiolects in a transition area. *Language*, 28: 348–59.

REED, E. K.

1951 Cultural areas of the pre-Spanish Southwest. *New Mexico Quar. Rev.*, 21: 428–39.

REED, N.

1964 The caste war of Yucatan. Stanford Univ. Press.

REED, W. W.

1923 Climatological data for Central America. *Monthly Weather Rev.*, 51: 133–41.

1926 Climatological data for the West Indian islands. *Ibid.*, 54: 133–60.

REESIDE, J. B., JR., AND OTHERS

1957 Correlation of the Triassic formations of North America, exclusive of Canada. *Bull. Geol. Soc. Amer.*, 68: 1151–1614.

REGAN, C. T.

1906–08 Pisces. *In* Biologia Centrali-Americana, Zoology, vol. 8.

REH, E., S. BENÍTEZ, AND M. FLORES

1951 Estudio de dieta en Centro América.

Rev. Colegio Méd. Guatemala, 2 (4): 2–22.

——, A. CASTELLANOS, AND Y. B. DE RUEDA

1954 Estudios de hábitos dietéticos en poblaciones de Guatemala: VI, Estudio de la dieta y de las condiciones de vida existentes entre los trabajadores de una plantación azucarera de Guatemala. *Bol. Oficina Sanitaria Panamer.*, 37: 32–52.

REHM, P.

1914 Anomalie encephalique chez un indien Yaqui. *Bull. et Mem. Soc. Anthr. Paris*, ser. 6, 5: 277–81.

REICHEL-DOLMATOFF, G.

1955 Excavaciones en los Conchales de la costa de Barlovento. *Rev. Colombiana Anthr.*, 4: 249–72. Bogota.

1961 Puerto Hormiga: un complejo prehistórico marginal de Colombia. *Ibid.*, 10: 349–54.

1961 Anthropomorphic figurines from Colombia, their magic and art. *In* Lothrop and others, 1961, pp. 229–41.

1965 Excavaciones arqueológicas en Puerto Hormiga (Departamento de Bolivar). *Antropología*, 2. Bogota.

—— AND A. REICHEL-DOLMATOFF

1956 Momil: excavaciones en el Sinu. *Rev. Colombiana Antr.*, 5: 111–333.

REID, J. L., JR.

1960 [ed.] The NORPAC atlas. Oceanic observations of the Pacific, 1955. Univ. California Press and Univ. Tokyo Press.

——, G. I. RODEN, AND J. G. WYLLIE

1958 Studies of the California Current system. *Calif. Coop. Fisheries Invest.*, Progress Rept., 1956–58, pp. 27–57.

REINA, R. E.

1957 Chinautla: 1944–53. *In* R. N. Adams, 1957, pp. 32–37.

1957 Chinautla, a Guatemalan Indian community: a field study in the relationship of community culture and national change. Doctoral dissertation, Univ. North Carolina.

1958 Continuidad de la cultura indígena en una comunidad guatemalteca.

Rev. Cien. Sociales, 2: 243–59. Puerto Rico.

1959 Continuidad de la cultura indígena en una comunidad guatemalteca. *Cuad. Seminario Integración Social Guatemalteca*, no. 4.

1959 Two patterns of friendship in a Guatemalan community. *Amer. Anthr.*, 61: 44–50.

1959 Political crisis and cultural revitalization: the Guatemalan case. *Human Organization*, 17: 14–18.

1960 Chinautla, a Guatemalan Indian community: a study in the relationship of community culture and national change. *Tulane Univ., Middle Amer. Research Inst.*, Pub. 24, pp. 55–130.

1961 Culture retention and culture change among Itzas of Peten and British Honduras. *Univ. Pennsylvania, Mus. Monogr.*

1963 Chinautla, comunidad indígena guatemalteca: estudio de las relaciones entre la cultura de comunidad y el cambio nacional. *Guatemala Indig.*, 3: 31–150.

1963 The potter and the farmer: the fate of two innovators in a Maya village. *Expedition*, 5 (4): 18–31.

1967 The law of the saints: a Pokomam pueblo and its community culture. New York.

REJÓN GARCÍA, M.

1905 Supersticiones y leyendas mayas. Merida.

1926 Tix'iz: a Isidra. *Bol. Univ. Nac. Sureste*, pp. 125–27. Merida.

REKO, B. P.

1945 Mitobotánica zapoteca. Tacubaya.

REKO, V. A., AND F. HESTERMANN

1931 Quellenschriften zur mexikanischen Linguistik. Das verschollene Manuskript des Gaspar de los Reyes, "Gramática zapoteca del valle" (1700). *Mitteilungen der Anthr. Gesellschaft in Wien*, 61: 331–50.

RELACIONES:

Ajuchitlan

1579 Relación de Ajuchitlan. *In* Paso y Troncoso, 1905–06, 5: 81–98.

Breve y verdadera

See Ponce, 1873.

RELACIONES—*continued*

Espinosa

See Espinosa, Gaspar de, 1892.

Genealogía

1941 Relación de la genealogía y linaje de los señores. . . . *In* García Icazbalceta, 1941, 3: 240–56.

Metztitlán

1865 Relación de la provincia de Metztitlán, hecha por Gabriel de Chávez, alcalde mayor de esta provincia, por S. M. de orden del Virrey de Nueva España. *In* Col. doc. Indias, 4: 530–555.

1924 *See* G. de Chávez, 1924.

Mexico

1905–06 Relaciones geográficas de la diócesis de México. *In* Paso y Troncoso, 1905–06, vol. 6.

Michoacan

1869 Relación de las ceremonias y ritos y población y gobierno de los indios de la provincia de Michoacán (1541). *Col. Doc. Ined. para la Historia de España*, vol. 53. Madrid.

1875 *Idem.* Reissued fraudulently with new covers.

1903 *Idem.* Morelia.

1956 *Idem.* Limited new edition with analysis by P. Kirchhoff. Madrid.

1956 *Idem.* Reproducción facsímil de MS c. IV 5 de El Escorial, con transcripción, prólogo, introducción y notas por José Tudela. . . . Madrid.

1958 Relaciones geográficas de la diócesis de Michoacán, 1579–80. 2 vols. Guadalajara.

Ocopetlayuca

1905–06 Relación de Ocopetlayuca. *In* Paso y Troncoso, 1905–06, 6: 257.

Tecciztlan

1905 Relación de Tecciztlan. *See* F. de Castañeda, 1905.

Tepuztlan

1905 Relación de la villa de Tepuztlan. *See* Gutiérrez de Liévana, 1905.

Tetela del Rio

1579 Relación de Tetela del Río. *In* Paso y Troncoso, 1905–06, 5: 124–73.

RELACIONES—*continued*

Teutitlan
1905 Relación de Teutitlan del Camino. *See* F. de Castañeda, 1905.

Tezcoco
See Pomar, 1891, 1941, 1964.

Tlacolula y Mitla
1955 Relación de Tlacolula y Mitla. Notes and trans. by F. Horcasitas and R. George. Mexico City College, *Mesoamer. Notes*, 4: 13–24.

Tlaxcala
1904 *See* García Pimentel, 1904.
1940 Relación del distrito y pueblos del obispado de Tlaxcala. *In* Paso y Troncoso, 1939–42, 14: 70–101.

Tuzantla
1965 The relación geográfica of Tuzantla, Michoacan, 1579. H. F. Cline, ed. *Tlalocan*, 5: 58–73.

Uexutla
1905–06 Relación de Uexutla. *In* Paso y Troncoso, 1905–06, 6: 183–92.

Yucatan
1898–1900 Relaciones de Yucatan. *In* Colección de documentos inéditos relativos al descubrimiento, conquista y organización de las antiguas posesiones españolas de ultramar. 2d ser., vols. 11, 13. Madrid.

Zempoala
1949 Relación de Zempoala y su partido, 1580. *Tlalocan*, 3: 29–41.

REMESAL, A. DE
1908 Historia de San Vicente de Chiapas y Guatemala. Madrid.
1932 Historia general de las Indias occidentales y particular de la gobernación de Chiapa y Guatemala. 2 vols. Guatemala.

RENDÓN, S.
1947 La alimentación tarasca. *An. Inst. Nac. Antr. Hist.*, 2: 202–27. Mexico.
1950 Aspectos de ceremonias civiles tarascas. *Amer. Indíg.*, 10: 91–98.
1965 [ed.] Relaciones originales de Chalco Amaquemecan por Francisco de San Anton Muñón Chimalpahin Cuauhtlehuanitzin. Mexico and Buenos Aires.

RENDÓN MONZÓN, J.
1960 Relaciones internas de la familia zapoteca-chatina. *In* Gloto-cronología y las lenguas oto-mangues. Cuad. Inst. Hist., Univ. Nac. Autónoma Mex.

RESTREPO, C., AND C. TEJADA
1963 Toxoplasmosis congenita: estudio clínico patológico de los siete primeros casos observados en Guatemala. *Rev. Colegio Méd. Guatemala*, 14: 73–88.

RETI, A.
1908 Frambuesia tropical. Presented at 5th Panamer. Med. Cong.

RETZIUS, G.
1901 Om trepanation of hufvud-skalen, sasom folksed i forna och nyara tider. *Ymer*, 21: 11–28. Stockholm.

REUTER, E. B., ed.
1934 Race and culture contacts. New York.

REVELLE, R.
1950 1940 *E. W. Scripps* cruise to the Gulf of California. Part 5: Sedimentation and oceanography: summary of field observations. *Geol. Soc. Amer. Mem.*, 43: 1–6.

REYES, A. DE LOS
1593 Arte en lengua mixteca.... Mexico. (Reprinted 1750, Puebla; 1889, Alençon; 1890, Paris.)

REYES, A. E.
1923 Los elefantes de la cuenca de Mexico. *Rev. Mex. Biol.*, 3: 227–44.
1927 Ejemplar no. 213 del Museo Paleontológico del Instituto Geológico de Mexico. *An. Inst. Geol. de Mex.*, 2: 203–04.

REYES, G. DE LOS
1891 Gramática de las lenguas zapoteca-serrana y zapoteca del valle. Oaxaca.

REYES, L. G.
1963 Nonohualco. *El Dia*, April 27. [Article in honor of Roberto J. Weitlaner.]

REYGADAS V., J.
1928 Chacmultun, Chacbolay y Kom, Kiuic, Labna, Zayi, Kabah, Uxmal. *In* Estado Actual, pp. 179–235.

REYNOLDS, D.
1956 Danzas guatemaltecas. *Americas*, 8 (2): 31–35.

REYNOSO, D. DE
1644 Arte y vocabulario en lengua mame. Mexico. (Charencey reprint, 1892.)

RIBAS, A. P. DE
1645 Historia de los triunfos de nuestra santa fe, en las misiones de la provincia de Nueva España. *In* Beals, 1943, pp. 66, 67.

RICARD, R.
1933 La "conquête spirituelle" du Mexique. *Univ. Paris, Inst. Ethnol., Travaux et Mem.*, no. 20.

RICHARDS, P. W.
1957 The tropical rain forest: an ecological study. Cambridge Univ. Press.

RICHARDSON, F. B.
1940 Non-Maya monumental sculpture of Central America. *In* The Maya and their neighbors, pp. 395–416.
1941 Nicaragua. *Carnegie Inst. Wash.*, Year Book 40, pp. 300–02.
1942 Some problems relating to the archaeology of southern Central America. *Proc. 8th Amer. Sci. Cong.*, 2: 93–99.

——— AND K. RUPPERT
1942 Nicaragua. *Carnegie Inst. Wash.*, Year Book 41, pp. 269–71.

RICKARDS, C. G.
1910 The ruins of Mexico. London.

RICKETSON, O. G., JR.
1925 Burials in the Maya area. *Amer. Anthr.*, 27: 381–401.
1929 Excavations at Baking Pot, British Honduras. *Carnegie Inst. Wash.*, Pub. 403, Contrib. 1.
1932 Las excavaciones en Uaxactun. *An. Soc. Geog. Hist. Guatemala*, 9: 34–57.
1935 Maya pottery well from Quirigua farm, Guatemala. *Maya Research*, 2: 103–05.
1936 Ruins of Tzalcani, Guatemala. *Ibid.*, 3: 18–23.
1939 Municipal organization of an Indian township in Guatemala. *Geog. Rev.*, 29: 643–47.
1940 An outline of basic physical factors affecting Middle America. *In* The Maya and their neighbors, pp. 10–31.

——— AND A. V. KIDDER
1930 An archaeological reconnaissance by air in Central America. *Geog. Rev.*, 20: 177–206.

——— AND E. B. RICKETSON
1937 Uaxactun, Guatemala: Group E—1926–1931. *Carnegie Inst. Wash.*, Pub. 477.

RIDE, L.
1935 Anthropological studies amongst North American Indians of British Columbia. *Caduceus* (Univ. Hong Kong), 14: 205–16.

RIDGWAY, R.
1912 Color standards and color nomenclature. Washington.

RIDLEY, F.
1960 Transatlantic contacts of primitive man: eastern Canada and northwestern Russia. *Pennsylvania Archaeol.*, 30: 46–57.

RIES, M.
1932 Stamping: a mass-production printing method 2000 years old. *Tulane Univ., Middle Amer. Research Inst.*, Pub. 4, pp. 411–83.

RIFE, D. C.
1953 Finger prints as criteria of ethnic relationship. *Amer. Jour. Human Genetics*, 5: 389–99.
1968 Finger and palmar dermatoglyphics in Seminole Indians of Florida. *Amer. Jour. Physical Anthr.*, 28: 119–26.

RIFE, D. W.
1932 Blood groups of Indians in certain Maya areas of Central America. *Jour. Immunology*, 22: 207–09.

RILEY, C. L., AND J. HOBGOOD
1959 A recent nativistic movement among the southern Tepehuan Indians. *SW. Jour. Anthr.*, 15: 355–60.

——— AND H. D. WINTERS
1963 The prehistoric Tepehuan of northern Mexico. *Ibid.*, 19: 177–85.

RILEY, C. V.
1881 [A mummy cave in Mexico.] *Abstr. Trans. Anthr. Soc. Washington*, pp. 29–30.

RINALDINI, B.
1743 Arte de la lengua tépeguana. . . . Mexico.

RINCÓN, A. DEL
1595 Arte mexicana. *In* Col. de gramáticas, pp. 225–80.

RÍO, A. DEL
1822 Description of the ruins of an ancient city, discovered near Palenque, in the kingdom of Guatemala, in Spanish America. London.

RÍOS, P. DE
1900 Il manoscritto Messicano. Vaticano 3738 detto il codice Rios. Rome.

RÍOS VARGAS, A.
1936 Indice cefalométrico. Mexico.

RIPPEN, B. VAN
1917 Pre-Columbian operative density of the Indians of Middle and South America. *Dental Cosmos*, 59: 861–73.
1917–18 Mutilations and decorations of teeth among the Indians of North, Central and South America. *Jour. Allied Dental Soc. New York*, 13: 219–42.

RIVERA, P. DE
1736 Diario y derrotero. Guatemala.

RIVERTE, J. M., AND C. PÉREZ
1955 Estudios clínicos nutricionales en poblaciones de Panamá. *Bol. Oficina Sanitaria Panamer.*, suppl. 2, p. 27.

RIVET, P.
1908 Note sur deux crânes du Yucatan. *Jour. Soc. Amer. Paris*, 5: 251–59.
1909 Recherches anthropologiques sur la Basse Californie. *Ibid.*, 6: 147–253.
1910 Recherches sur le prognathisme. *L'Anthropologie*, 21: 504–18, 637–59. Paris.
1911 Observations au sujet des recherches anthropologiques sur la Basse Californie. *Ibid.*, 22: 37–40.

—— AND H. ARSANDAUX
1946 La métallurgie en Amérique précolombienne. *Travaux et Mem. Inst. Ethnol.*, vol. 39. Paris.

—— AND G. FREUND
1954 Mexique précolombien. Coll. des Idées Photographiques, no. 8. Paris.

ROBB, J. D.
1961 The matachines dance: a ritual folk dance. *Western Folklore*, 20: 87–101.

ROBELO, C. A.
1951 Diccionario de mitología nahoa. *Ediciones Fuente Cultural*. Mexico. (Other eds., 1905–08, 1911.)

ROBERTS, D. F.
1952 Basal metabolism, race and climate. *Jour. Royal Anthr. Inst.*, 82: 169.
1952 An ecological approach to physical anthropology. *Proc. 4th Int. Cong. Anthr. Ethnol. Sci.*, 1: 145.

ROBERTS, F. H. H.
1945 The New World Paleo-Indian. *Smithsonian Inst.*, ann. rept. 1944, pp. 403–34.

ROBERTS, L. M., U. J. GRANT, R. RAMIREZ E., W. H. HATHEWAY, AND D. L. SMITH in collaboration with P. C. MANGELSDORF
1957 Races of maize in Colombia. *Nat. Acad. Sci., Nat. Research Council*, Pub. 510.

ROBERTS, O. W.
1827 Narrative of voyages and excursions on the east coast and in the interior of Central America. *Constable's Miscellany*, vol. 17. Edinburgh.

ROBERTS, R. E. T.
1948 A comparison of ethnic relations in two Guatemalan communities. *Acta Amer.*, 6: 135–51.

ROBERTS, R. J., AND E. M. IRVING
1957 Mineral deposits of Central America. *U. S. Geol. Survey*, Bull. 1034.

ROBERTSON, D.
1959 Mexican manuscript painting of the early colonial period: the metropolitan schools. Yale Univ. Press.
1963 The style of the Borgia group of Mexican pre-conquest manuscripts. *In* Studies in western art, M. Meiss and others, eds., vol. 3 (Latin American art and the Baroque period in Europe), pp. 148–64. *20th Int. Cong. History of Art* (New York, 1961).
1963 Pre-Columbian architecture. *In* The great ages of world architecture, G. Braziller, ed. New York.
1964 Los manuscritos religiosos mixtecos. *35th Int. Cong. Amer.* (Mexico, 1962), Acta, 1: 425–35. (English trans. in Paddock, 1966, Ancient Oaxaca, pp. 298–312.)

1968 The Tulum murals: the international style of the Late Postclassic. Paper presented to 38th Int. Cong. Amer. (Stuttgart, 1968).

ROBINA, R. DE
1956 Estudio preliminar de las ruinas de Hochob, municipio de Hopelchen, Campeche. Mexico.
1959 La arquitectura. *In* Esplendor del México antiguo, 2: 607–50.

ROBINSON, U., AND OTHERS (M. BÉHAR, F. VITERI, G. ARROYAVE, AND N. S. SCRIMSHAW)
1957 Protein and fat balance studies in children recovering from kwashiorkor. *Jour. Tropical Pediatrics*, 2: 217–23.

ROBLES, C.
1929 La región arqueológica de Casas Grandes. Mexico.

ROBLES, R.
1917 Oncochercose humaine au Guatemala produisant la cecité et l'eysipele du littoral. *Bull. Soc. Pathol. Exotique*, vol. 12, no. 7.

ROBLES RAMOS, R.
1942 Orogénisis de la República Mexicana en relación a su relieve actual. *Irrigación en Mex.*, 23: 6–61.
1944 Algunas ideas sobre la glaciología y morfología del Iztaccihuatl. *Rev. Geog. Inst. Panamer. Geog. Hist.*, 4: 65–98.
1950 Apuntes sobre la morfología de Yucatan. *Bol. Soc. Mex. Geog. Estad.*, 69: 27–106.
1959 Geología y geohidrología. *In* Beltrán, 1959, pp. 55–92.

ROBLES URIBE, C.
1962 Manual del Tzeltal (gramática Tzeltal de Bachajón). *Univ. Iberoamericana* (Antropología: Lingüística I).

—— AND OTHERS
1967 Los Lacandones: bibliografía y reseña crítica de materiales publicados. Inst. Nac. Antr. Hist. Mexico.

RÖCK, F.
1922 Kalender, Sternglaube und Weltbilder der Tolteken als Zeugen verschollener Kulturbeziehungen zur Alten Welt. *Mitteilungen Anthr. Gesellschaft in Wien*, 52: 43–136.

RODAS N., F.
n.d. Vocabulario en idioma kiché. Guatemala.

——, O. RODAS CORZO, AND L. F. HAWKINS
1940 Chichicastenango: the Kiche Indians. Guatemala.

RODEN, G. I.
1958 Oceanographic and meteorological aspects of the Gulf of California. *Pacific Sci.*, 12: 21–45.
1959 On the heat and salt balance of the California Current region. *Jour. Marine Research*, 18: 36–61.
1960 On the nonseasonal variations in sea level along the west coast of North America. *Jour. Geophys. Research*, 65: 2809–26.
1961 On seasonal temperature and salinity variations along the west coast of the United States and Canada. *California Coop. Oceanic Fisheries Invest.*, Rept. 8, pp. 95–119.
1961 On the wind driven circulation in the Gulf of Tehuantepec and its effect upon surface temperatures. *Geofis. Internac. Mex.*, 1: 55–76.
1962 Oceanographic aspects of the eastern equatorial Pacific. *Ibid.*, 2: 77–92.
1963 Sea level variations at Panama. *Jour. Geophys. Research*, 68: 5701–10.
1964 Oceanographic aspects of the Gulf of California. *In* Marine Geology of the Gulf of California, *Amer. Assoc. Petroleum Geol.*, Mem. 3, pp. 30–58.

—— AND G. W. GROVES
1959 Recent oceanographic investigations in the Gulf of California. *Jour. Marine Research*, 18: 10–35.

RODOZ, J. DE
1723 Arte de la lengua Tzotzlen o Tzinacantan. (Paris Dictionary.)

RODRÍGUEZ, H., F. B. ELISA, B. P. ALVAR LORIA, AND R. LISKER
1962 Estudios sobre algunas caracteristicas hematológicas hereditarias en la población mexicana: I, Grupos sanguíneos en tarascos, nahoas y mixtecos. *Rev. Invest. Clínicas*, 14: 319–28.

RODRÍGUEZ, J. M.
1869 Pelvis viciada por estrechez absoluta. *Gaceta Méd. Méx.*, vol. 4.

1875 Enanismo. *An. Soc. Humboldt*, 2: 8–24. Mexico.

1885 Guía clínica del arte de los partos: cuadro de la figura, dimensiones y ejes del canal pélvico y particularidades que representan las mexicanas. 3d ed. Mexico.

RODRÍGUEZ GIL, A.

1907 Los indios ocuiltecas actuales. MS en Depto. Invest. Antr., Inst. Nac. Antr. Hist. Mexico.

ROGERS, M. J.

1939 Early lithic industries of the lower basin of the Colorado River and adjacent desert areas. *San Diego Mus. Papers*, no. 3.

1945 An outline of Yuman prehistory. *SW. Jour. Anthr.*, 1: 167–98.

1958 San Dieguito implements from the terraces of the Rincon-Pantano and Rillito drainage system. *Kiva*, 24 (1): 1–23.

ROGERS, W.

1928 A cruising voyage around the world (1712). New York.

ROHRSHEIM, L.

1928 Una visita a los huavis. *Mex. Folkways*, 4: 49–65.

ROJAS, G. DE

1927 Descripción de Cholula. *Rev. Mex. Estud. Antr.*, 1: 158–70.

ROJAS, M. J.

1933 Ecaliztli ihuicpan tepoztecatl (batalla contra el tepozteco). *In* D. Castañeda and V. T. Mendoza, Instrumental precortesiano. Mexico.

ROJAS GARCIDUEÑAS, J.

1935 El teatro de Nueva España en el siglo XVI. Mexico.

1942 Fiestas en México en 1578. *An. Inst. Invest. Estéticas*, 9: 33–57.

ROJAS GONZÁLEZ, F.

1943 La institución del compadrazgo entre los indios de México. *Rev. Mex. Sociol.*, 5: 201–13. Mexico.

1949 Los zapotecos en la época prehispánica. *In* Mendieta y Núñez, 1949, pp. 35–102.

1949 Los zapotecos en la época colonial. *Ibid.*, pp. 105–56.

1949 Los zapotecos en la época independiente. *Ibid.*, pp. 157–95.

1957 Los huastecos. *In* Cerda Silva, 1957, pp. 581–91.

—— AND R. DE LA CERDA SILVA

1941 Los tzotziles. *Rev. Mex. Sociol.*, 3: 113–42.

1949 Etnografía general de los zapotecos. *In* Mendieta y Núñez, 1949, pp. 201–61.

ROMANCES DE LOS SEÑORES

1964 Romances de los señores de la Nueva España. *In* Garibay K., 1964.

ROMANO, A.

1952 Relaciones étnicas en Chiapas. Notas de campo. MS.

1953 La Cueva de La Candelaria en el Valle de las Delicias: informe preliminar. *Tlatoani*, ep. 2, 7: 5–12.

1955 Nota preliminar sobre los restos humanos subfósiles de Santa María Astahuacan, D.F. *An. Inst. Nac. Antr. Hist.*, 7: 65–74. Mexico.

1956 Los restos óseos humanos de la Cueva de La Candelaria, Coah. Tesis profesional, Escuela Nac. Antr. Hist. MS.

1963 Breve informe de los hallazgos en San Vicente Chicoloapan, México. *An. Inst. Nac. Antr. Hist.*, 15: 245–59. Mexico.

1965 Estudio morfológico de la deformación craneana en Tamuín, S. L. P., y en la Isla del Idolo, Ver. *Inst. Nac. Antr. Hist., Ser. Invest.*, no. 10. Mexico.

ROMERO, J.

n.d. La población indígena de Tilantongo, Oaxaca. MS.

n.d. Estudio somatológico de la población de Tianguisolco, Guerrero. MS.

n.d. Estudio somatológico de los habitantes valle de Mezquital.

1934 Estudio de la osamenta procedente de las excavaciones de la plaza del Seminario. *An. Mus. Nac. Arqueol. Hist. Etnog.*, ep. 5, 1: 287–90. Mexico.

1935 Estudio de los entierros de la pirámide de Cholula. *Ibid.*, ep. 5, 2: 5–36.

1935 Cráneos trepanados de Monte Albán. MS.

1937 Aportación osteométrica. *In* Noguera, 1937, pp. 23–37.

1939 Breves notas acerca de la colección de cráneos de delincuentes del Museo Nacional. *Rev. Mex. Estud. Antr.*, 3: 167–76.

1946 Aplicación del coeficiente de divergencia tipológica de Pearson. *Mem. Segundo Cong. Mex. Ciencias Sociales*, 5: 181–212. Mexico.

1949 The physical aspects of Tepexpan man. *In* De Terra, Romero, and Stewart, 1949, pp. 87–121.

1951 Monte Negro (Oaxaca), centro de interés antropológico. *In* Homenaje Caso, pp. 317–29.

1951 La prehistoria bajacaliforniana. *Cuad. Amer.*, 10: 158–62.

1952 Los patrones de la mutilación dentaria prehispánica. *An. Inst. Nac. Antr. Hist.*, 4: 177–221. Mexico.

1952 Sobre la estatura de la población campesina de México. *Ibid.*, 4: 229–37.

1955 Datos tensionales de nuestra juventud mexicana. *Ibid.*, 6: 59–80.

1956 Aspectos psicobiométricos y sociales de una muestra de la juventud mexicana. *Inst. Nac. Antr. Hist.*, *Dir. Invest. Antr.*, no. 1. Mexico.

1958 Mutilaciones dentarias prehispánicas de México y América en general. *Ibid.*, no. 3.

1960 Una experiencia con la prueba abreviada de matrices progresivas de Raven. *An. Inst. Nac. Antr. Hist.*, 11: 259–79. Mexico.

1960 Ultimos hallazgos de mutilaciones dentarias en México. *Ibid.*, 12: 151–215.

1961 Tiempos de reacción ante excitaciones auditivas y visuales. *In* Homenaje Martínez del Río, pp. 193–206.

1962 Doce años de investigación psicobiológica sobre la juventud. *Rev. Mex. Estud. Antr.*, 18: 21–44.

1965 Recientes adiciones a la colección de dientes mutilados. *An. Inst. Nac. Antr. Hist.*, 17: 199–256.

1965 Valor de los estudios psicobiológicos y sociales en el ejército. *Rev. Ejército*, 22: 3–14. Mexico.

—— AND J. VALENZUELA
1945 Expedición a la Sierra Azul, Ocampo, Tamaulipas. *An. Inst. Nac. Antr. Hist.*, 1: 7–15.

—— AND OTHERS
1955 Ensayo de geometría craneana. Inst. Nac. Antr. Hist. Mexico.

ROMERO ALVÁREZ, J.
1952 Estudio de las principales parásitos intestinales en el municipio de Jaltocan, Hidalgo. Mexico.

ROMERO DE TERREROS Y VINENT, M.
1918 Arte colonial. Mexico.

1923 Las artes industriales en la Nueva España. Mexico.

1951 El arte en México durante el virreinato: resumen histórico. Mexico.

ROMERO FLORES, J.
1946 Historia de Michoacán. 2 vols. Mexico.

ROMERO FUENTES, L. C.
1910 La lengua maya al alcance de todos. Merida.

ROMNEY, A. K.
1957 The genetic model and Uto-Aztecan time perspective. *Davidson Jour. Anthr.*, 3: 35–41.

1967 Kinship and family. *In* Handbook of Middle American Indians, R. Wauchope, ed., vol. 6, art. 11.

—— AND R. ROMNEY
1963 The Mixtecans of Juxtlahuaca, Mexico. *In* Six cultures: studies of child rearing, B. B. Whiting, ed., pp. 541–692.

RONEY, J. G., JR.
1959 Palaeopathology of a California archaeological site. *Bull. Hist. Med.*, vol. 33, no. 2.

ROOT, W. C.
1951 Gold-copper alloys in ancient America. *In* Symposium on Archaeological Chemistry. *Jour. Chem. Educ.*, vol. 28, no. 2.

RORTY, J.
1960 ¿Hay discriminación en México? La experiencia indigenista de Chiapas. *Amer. Indig.*, 20: 217–28.

ROSADO OJEDA, V.
1945 Estudio del códice mixteco post-cortesiano, no. 36. *An. Inst. Nac. Antr. Hist.*, 1: 147–55.

1948 Interpretación de la grada jeroglífica del Chanal, Colima. *In* El Occidente de México, pp. 72–73.

ROSAL H., V. H.
1944 Apuntes sobre tifus exantemático en la ciudad capital de Guatemala en el año de 1944. Tesis de médico y cirujano, Facultad Cien. Méd., Univ. San Carlos de Guatemala.

ROSALES, J. DE D.
1949 Notes on Aguacatan. *Univ. Chicago, Micro. Coll. MSS Middle Amer. Cult. Anthr.*, no. 24.
1949 Notes on San Pedro La Laguna. *Ibid.*, no. 25.
1950 Notes on Santiago Chimaltenango. *Ibid.*, no. 30.
1959 Indígenas de Guatemala. *Amer. Indig.*, 19: 115–24.

ROSE, R. H.
1904 Utilla: past and present. Danville, N.Y.

ROSEN, D. E., AND R. M. BAILEY
1963 The poeciliid fishes (Cyprinodontiformes), their structure, zoogeography, and systematics. *Bull. Amer. Mus. Nat. Hist.*, 126: 1–176.

ROSENBLAT, A.
1945 La población indígena de América desde 1492 hasta la actualidad. *Inst. Cultural Española*. Buenos Aires.
1954 La población indígena y el mestizaje en América. 2 vols. *Editorial Nova*. Buenos Aires.

ROSENBLATT, R. H.
1959 A revisionary study of the blennioid fish family Tripterygiidae. Doctoral dissertation, Univ. California.

ROSENFIELD, R. E., AND OTHERS (P. VOGEL, N. GIBBEL, G. OHNO, AND G. HABER)
1953 Anti-Jk^a: three new examples of the isoantibody: frequency of the factor in Caucasians, Negroes and Chinese of New York City. *Amer. Jour. Clinical Pathol.*, 23: 1222–25.

ROSENZWEIG, F.
1959 Demografía de la peninsula de Yucatan. MS en Depto. Invest. del Banco de México.

ROSNY, L. DE
1887 Codex Peresianus manuscrit hiéra-

tique des anciens Indiens de l'Amérique Centrale. Paris.

ROSS, V.
1939 Some pottery types of the highlands of western Mexico. Master's thesis, Yale Univ.

ROSSBY, C. G.
1954 Las bases científicas de la moderna meteorología. *Bol. Soc. Mex. Geog. y Estad.*, 78: 103–87.

ROUAIX, FR., G. DECORME, AND A. G. SARAVIA
1952 Manual de historia de Durango. Editorial Jus, S.A. Mexico.

ROUJOU, A.
1873 Photographies mexicaines établissant l'existence dans ce pays de Mongoloïdes et Caucasoïdes. *Bull. Soc. Anthr. Paris*, ser. 2, 8: 492–93.

ROUSE, I.
1948 The West Indies. *In* Handbook of South American Indians, 4: 495–565.
1951 Areas and periods of culture in the Greater Antilles. *SW. Jour. Anthr.*, 7: 248–65.
1953 The circum-Caribbean theory, an archaeological test. *Amer. Anthr.*, 55: 188–200.
1954 Reply to Stern. *Ibid.*, 56: 107–08.
1960 The entry of man into the West Indies. *Yale Univ. Pub. Anthr.*, no. 61.
1960 Recent developments in American archaeology. *In* Wallace, 1960, pp. 64–73.
1964 Prehistory of the West Indies. *Science*, 144: 499–513.

——— AND J. M. CRUXENT
1963 Venezuelan archaeology. *Yale Caribbean Ser.*, no. 6.

ROWE, J. H.
1946 Inca culture at the time of the Spanish conquest. *In* Handbook of South American Indians, 2: 183–330.
1960 Cultural unity and diversification in Peruvian archaeology. *In* Wallace, 1960, pp. 627–31.
1962 Chavin art, an inquiry into its form and meaning. New York Graphic Soc. Greenwich.

ROY, S. K.
1957 The present status of the volcanoes

of Central America. *Fieldiana* (Geology), 10: 335–39.

Roys, L.

1933 The Maya correlation problem today. *Amer. Anthr.*, 35: 403–17.

1934 The engineering knowledge of the Maya. *Carnegie Inst. Wash.*, Pub. 436, Contrib. 6.

1958 The use of the term "classic" in Maya archaeology. *Davenport Public Mus. Quar.*, 3: 1–5.

Roys, R. L.

1920 A Maya account of creation. *Amer. Anthr.*, 22: 360–66.

1929 Annotated transcription of the Chilam Balam of Kaua. MS. Tulane Univ., Middle Amer. Research Inst.

1931 The ethno-botany of the Maya. *Ibid.*, Pub. 2.

1932 Antonio de Ciudad Real, ethnographer. *Amer. Anthr.*, 34: 118–26.

1933 The book of Chilam Balam of Chumayel. *Carnegie Inst. Wash.*, Pub. 438.

1939 The titles of Ebtun. *Ibid.*, Pub. 505.

1940 Personal names of the Maya of Yucatan. *Ibid.*, Pub. 523, Contrib. 31.

1941 The Xiu chronicle, pt. 2. MS in Peabody Mus., Harvard Univ.

1943 The Indian background of colonial Yucatan. *Carnegie Inst. Wash.*, Pub. 548.

1944 The Vienna dictionary. *Ibid., Notes on Middle Amer. Archaeol. Ethnol.*, no. 41.

1949 Guide to the Codex Pérez. *Ibid.*, Pub. 585, Contrib. 49.

1949 The prophecies for the Maya tuns or years in the books of Chilam Balam of Tizimin and Mani. *Ibid.*, Pub. 585, Contrib. 51.

1954 The Maya katun prophecies of the books of Chilam Balam, Series I. *Ibid.*, Pub. 606, Contrib. 57.

1957 Political geography of the Yucatan Maya. *Ibid.*, Pub. 613.

——, F. V. Scholes, and E. B. Adams

1940 Report and census of the Indians of Cozumel, 1570. *Ibid.*, Pub. 523, Contrib. 30.

1959 Census and inspection of the town of Pencuyut, Yucatan, in 1583 by Diego García de Palacio, oidor of the audiencia of Guatemala. *Ethnohistory*, 6: 195–225.

Rubel, A. J.

1950 Field notes on the Chinantec of Ojitlan. MS.

1955 Ritual relationships in Ojitlan, Mexico. *Amer. Anthr.*, 57: 1038–40.

1957 Notes on the Tzotzil-speakers of San Bartolome de los Llanos, Chiapas. MS.

1960 Concepts of disease in Mexican-American culture. *Amer. Anthr.*, 62: 795–814.

1964 The epidemiology of a folk illness: susto in Hispanic America. *Ethnology*, 3: 268–83.

Rubin, M., and C. Alexander

1960 United States Geological Survey radiocarbon dates V. *Amer. Jour. Sci., Radiocarbon Suppl.*, 2: 129–85.

Rubín de la Borbolla, D. F.

1930 Estudio de las particularidades que presentan algunos cráneos de la colección del Departamento de Antropología Física del Museo Nacional. *An. Mus. Nac. Arqueol. Hist. Etnog.*, ep. 4, 6: 429–34. Mexico.

1933 Crania azteca. *Ibid.*, ep. 4, 8: 97–106.

1933 Informe de los trabajos de antropología realizados durante la segunda temporada de exploraciones en Monte Albán, Oaxaca. *Ibid.*, ep. 4, 8: 189–202.

1933 Contribución a la antropología física de México. *Ibid.*, ep. 4, 8: 333–45.

1939 Antropología: Tzintzuntzan-Ihuatzio, temporadas I y II: Entierros tarascos. *Rev. Mex. Estud. Antr.*, 3: 99–121.

1940 Types of tooth mutilation found in Mexico. *Amer. Jour. Physical Anthr.*, 26: 349–65.

1941 Exploraciones arqueológicas en Michoacán: Tzintzuntzan, temporada III. *Rev. Mex. Estud. Antr.*, 5: 5–20.

1944 Orfebrería tarasca. *Cuad. Amer.*, 3: 125–38.

1946 Arqueología del sur de Durango. *Rev. Mex. Estud. Antr.*, 8: 111–20.

1947 Teotihuacán: ofrendas de los templos de Quetzalcoatl. *An. Inst. Nac. Antr. Hist.*, 2: 61–72.

1948 Arqueología tarasca. *In* El Occidente de México, pp. 29–33.

1953 México: monumentos históricos y arqueológicos. Libro primero: México precolombino. *Inst. Panamer. Geog. Hist.*, Pub. 145. Mexico.

1963 Arte popular mexicano. *In* Arte popular de México (special issue of Artes de México).

—— AND R. L. BEALS
1940 The Tarascan project: a cooperative enterprise of the National Polytechnic Institute, Mexican Bureau of Indian Affairs, and the University of California. *Amer. Anthr.*, 42: 708–12.

RUDINGER, N.
1892 Die Rassen-Schaedel und Skelette in der Anatomischen Anstalt in München. *Anthr. Samml. Deutsch.*, pp. 192–93. Brunswick.

RUIZ, B.
1884 Relación de los primeros descubrimientos de Francisco Pizarro y Diego de Almagro. *In* Col. doc. inéd. para la hist. España, 5: 193–201.

RUIZ, D.
1785 La pirámide de Papantla. *Gaceta de México*, 1: 349–51.

RUIZ, E.
1940 Michoacán: paisajes, tradiciones y leyendas. Mexico. (Other eds. 1891, 1900.)

RUIZ, J. B.
1925 Distancia interpupilar y anchura del cráneo en la región bitemporal, en relación con las razas de la república. Mexico.

RUIZ COLMENERO, J.
1903 Abstract of linguistic data, from Visita General of 1648–1649, made by A. Santoscoy. Published 1902 in *Diario de Jalisco*; reprinted by N. Léon in *An. Mus. Nac. Méx.*, 7: 309–11 and passim to p. 335.

RUIZ DE ALARCÓN, H.
1892 Tratado de las supersticiones y costumbres gentílicas que hoy viven entre los indios naturales de esta Nueva España. *An. Mus. Nac. Mex.*, ep. 1, 6: 123–224. (2d ed. 1948; 3d ed. 1953 in Tratados de las idolatrías, supersticiones, dioses, ritos, hechicerías y otras costumbres gentílicas de las razas aborígenes de México. *Ediciones Fuente Cultural*, 20: 17–180. Mexico.)

RUIZ U., R. E.
1956 The struggle for a national culture in rural education. *In* Estudios antropológicos, pp. 473–90.

RUPPERT, K.
1931 The Temple of the Wall Panels, Chichen Itza. *Carnegie Inst. Wash.*, Pub. 403, Contrib. 3.

1935 The Caracol at Chichen Itza, Yucatan, Mexico. *Ibid.*, Pub. 454.

1940 A special assemblage of Maya structures. *In* The Maya and their neighbors, pp. 222–31.

1943 The Mercado, Chichen Itza, Yucatan. *Carnegie Inst. Wash.*, Pub. 546, Contrib. 43.

1950 Gallery-patio type structures at Chichen Itza. *In* For the Dean, pp. 249–58.

1952 Chichen Itza: architectural notes and plans. *Carnegie Inst. Wash.*, Pub. 595.

—— AND J. H. DENISON
1943 Archaeological reconnaissance in Campeche, Quintana Roo, and Peten. *Ibid.*, Pub. 543.

—— AND A. L. SMITH
1952 Excavations in house mounds at Mayapan: I. *Carnegie Inst. Wash., Current Reports*, no. 4.

1954 Excavations in house mounds at Mayapan: III. *Ibid.*, no. 17.

1957 House types in the environs of Mayapan and at Uxmal, Kabah, Sayil, Chichen Itza, and Chacchob. *Ibid.*, no. 39.

——, J. E. S. THOMPSON, AND T. PROSKOURIAKOFF
1955 Bonampak, Chiapas, Mexico. *Carnegie Inst. Wash.*, Pub. 602.

RUSSELL, F.
1900 Studies in cranial variation. *Amer. Naturalist*, 34: 737–43.

1905 The Pima Indians. *Smithsonian*

Inst., Bur. Amer. Ethnol., 26th ann. rept., pp. 5–391.

RUSSELL, S. R.

1954 A new type of archaic ruins in Chiapas, Mexico. *Amer. Antiquity*, 20: 62–64.

RUZ LHUILLIER, A.

1945 La costa de Campeche en los tiempos prehispánicos. M.S. thesis, Univ. Nac. Autónoma de Mexico.

1945 Campeche en la arqueología maya. *Acta Anthr.*, vol. 1, nos. 2, 3.

1945 Guía arqueológica de Tula. Mexico.

1948 Exploraciones arqueológicas en Kabah y Uxmal, Yucatan. MS in Archivo Inst. Nac. Antr. Hist.

1952 Exploraciones arqueológicas en Palenque (1949). *An. Inst. Nac. Antr. Hist.*, 4: 49–60.

1952 Exploraciones en Palenque: 1950. *Ibid.*, 5: 25–46.

1952 Exploraciones en Palenque: 1951. *Ibid.*, 5: 47–66.

1952 Estudio de la cripta del Templo de las Inscripciones en Palenque. *Tlatoani*, vol. 1, no. 5.

1953 Presencia atlántica en Palenque. *In* Huastecos, Totonacos, pp. 455–62.

1955 Exploraciones en Palenque: 1952. *An. Inst. Nac. Antr. Hist.*, 6: 79–110.

1955 Uxmal-Kabah-Sayil: temporada 1953. *Inst. Nac. Antr. Hist., Dir. Monumentos Prehispánicos*, Informe 1.

1955 Uxmal: temporada de trabajos 1951–1952. *An. Inst. Nac. Antr. Hist.*, 6: 49–67.

1956 Uxmal: official guide. Inst. Nac. Antr. Hist.

1958 Exploraciones arqueológicas en Palenque: 1953–56. *An. Inst. Nac. Antr. Hist.*, 10: 69–299.

1959 Estudio preliminar de los tipos de enterramientos en el area maya. *33d Int. Cong. Amer.* (San Jose, 1958), Acta, 2: 183–99.

1962 Chichen Itza y Tula: comentarios a un ensayo. *Univ. Nac. Autónoma Mex., Estud. Cultura Maya*, 2: 205–20.

1962 Exploraciones arqueológicas en Palenque: 1957. *An. Inst. Nac. Antr. Hist.*, 14: 35–90.

RYAN, R. M.

1963 The biotic provinces of Central America as indicated by mammalian distribution. *Acta Zool. Mex.*, 6: 1–55.

SACHS, C.

1933 Eine Weltgeschichte des Tanzes. Berlin.

SÁENZ, C. A.

1956 Exploraciones en la Pirámide de la Cruz Foliada y en los Templos XVIII y XXI. *Inst. Nac. Antr. Hist., Dir. Monumentos Prehispánicos*, Informe 5.

1957 Informe sobre reconocimientos en algunos sitios de Guerrero. MS in Archivo Inst. Nac. Antr. Hist.

1961 Tres estelas en Xochicalco. *Rev. Mex. Estud. Antr.*, 17: 39–66.

1962 Exploraciones arqueológicas en Xochicalco, Morelos. *Bol. Inst. Nac. Antr. Hist.*, 7: 1–3.

1962 Xochicalco: temporada 1960. *Inst. Nac. Antr. Hist., Dir. Monumentos Prehispánicos*, Informe 11. Mexico.

1964 Últimos descubrimientos en Xochicalco. *Ibid.*, Informe 12.

1966 Cabecitas y figurillas de barro del Ixtepete, Jalisco. *Bol. Inst. Nac. Antr. Hist.*, 24: 47–49.

1966 Exploraciones en el Ixtepete, Jalisco. *Ibid.*, 23: 14–18.

1966 Exploraciones en Xochicalco. *Ibid.*, 26: 24–34.

1967 Nuevas exploraciones y hallazgos en Xochicalco, 1965–1966. *Inst. Nac. Antr. Hist., Dir. Monumentos Prehispánicos*, Informe 13. Mexico.

1968 Cuatro piedras con inscripciones en Xochicalco. *An. Antr.*, 5: 181–98.

1969 Exploraciones y restauraciones en Uxmal, Yucatan. *Bol. Inst. Nac. Antr. Hist.*, 36: 6–13.

SÁENZ, M. A.

1940 Bosquejo geo-edafalógico de Costa Rica y el Instituto Interamericano de Ciencias Agrícolas. *Inst. Defensa del Café de Costa Rica*, 17: 141–48.

SÁENZ, MOISÉS

1936 Carapan: bosquejo de una experiencia. Lima.

SÁENZ DE TEJADA, J.
1906   Hematuria.   Tesis de médico y ciru-
        jano, Facultad Cien. Méd., Univ. Nac.
        Guatemala.

SAHAGÚN, B. DE
1829   Historia general de las cosas de Nueva
        España.   3 vols.   Ed. Bustamante.
        Mexico.
1905–07 Historia general de las cosas de
        Nueva España.   F. del Paso y Tron-
        coso, ed.   Edición parcial en facsí-
        mile de los Códices Matritenses en
        lengua mexicana que se custodian en
        las bibliotecas del Palacio Real y de
        la Real Academía de la Historia, vols.
        5–8.   (Florentine Codex illustra-
        tions, prepared during same period,
        bound and distributed by Mus. Nac.
        Arqueol. Hist. Etnog., 1926, as vol.
        5 of the entire [unfinished] work.)
        Madrid.
1926   See preceding entry and Florentine
        Codex, 1926.
1927   Einige Kapitel aus dem Geschichts-
        werk des Fray Bernardino de Saha-
        gún.   E. Seler, trans.   Stuttgart.
1938   Historia general de las cosas de Nue-
        va España.   P. Robredo, ed.   5 vols.
        Mexico.
1944–46 Paralipómenos de Sahagún.   A.
        M. Garibay K., ed. and trans.   Tlalo-
        can, 1: 307–13; 2: 167–74, 235–54.
1946   Historia general de las cosas de Nue-
        va España.   M. Acosta Saignes, ed.
        3 vols.   Mexico.
1948   Relación breve de las fiestas de los
        dioses.   A. M. Garibay K., ed. and
        trans.   Tlalocan, 2: 289–320.
1949   Sterbende Götter und Christliche
        Heilsbotschaft; Wechselreden Indi-
        anischer Vornehmer und Spanischer
        Glaubensapostel in Mexiko 1524:
        "Coloquios y doctrina christiana" des
        Fray Bernardino de Sahagún aus dem
        Jahre 1564.   W. Lehmann, ed. and
        trans.   Quellenwerke zur Alten Ge-
        schichte Amerikas Aufgezeichnet in
        den Sprachen der Eingeborenen (La-
        tein-Amerikanischen Bibliothek, Ber-
        lin), III.   Stuttgart.
1950   Wahrsagerei,   Himmelskunde   und
        Kalender der Alten Azteken aus dem
        Aztekischen Urtext Bernardino de Sa-
        hagún's.   L. S. Schultze-Jena, ed.
        and trans.   Ibid., IV.
1950–69 Florentine codex: general history
        of the things of New Spain.   Tr.
        from the Aztec into English, with
        notes and illustrations, by A. J. O.
        Anderson and C. E. Dibble.   Univ.
        Utah and School of American Re-
        search.   Santa Fe.   Book 1 (1950):
        The gods.   Book 2 (1951): The cer-
        emonies.   Book 3 (1952): The ori-
        gin of the gods.   Book 4 (1957):
        The soothsayers.   Book 5 (1957):
        The omens.   Book 6 (1969): Rhet-
        oric and moral philosophy.   Book 7
        (1953): The sun, moon, and stars,
        and the binding of the years.   Book
        8 (1954): Kings and lords.   Book 9
        (1959): The merchants.   Book 10
        (1961): The people.   Book 11
        (1963): Earthly things.   Book 12
        (1955): The conquest of Mexico.
1952   Gliederung des Alt-Aztekischen Völks
        in Familie, Stand und Beruf aus dem
        Aztekischen Urtext Bernardino de Sa-
        hagún's.   L. S. Schultze-Jena, ed.
        and trans.   Quellenwerke zur Alten
        Geschichte Amerikas Aufgezeichnet
        in den Sprachen der Eingeborenen
        (Latein-Amerikanischen   Bibliothek,
        Berlin), V.   Stuttgart.
1956   Historia general de las cosas de Nue-
        va España.   A. M. Garibay K., ed.
        and trans.   4 vols.   Biblioteca Po-
        rrúa, vols. 8–11.   Mexico.
1958   Ritos, sacerdotes y atavíos de los dio-
        ses.   M. León-Portilla, ed. and trans.
        Univ. Nac. Autónoma Méx., Inst.
        Hist., Seminario de Cultura Náhuatl,
        Textos de los Informantes de Saha-
        gún, no. 1.
1958   Veinte himnos sacros de los nahuas,
        los recogío de los nativos.   A. M.
        Garibay K., ed. and trans.   Ibid., no.
        2.
1961   Vida económica de Tenochtitlan, 1:
        Pochtecayotl (Arte de Traficar).   A.
        M. Garibay K., ed. and trans.   Ibid.,
        no. 3.
1963   Náhuatl proverbs, conundrums, and
        metaphors, collected by Sahagún.   T.

D. Sullivan, ed. and trans. *Inst. Hist., Estud. Cultura Náhuatl,* 4: 73–177.

1965 A prayer to Tlaloc. T. D. Sullivan, ed. and trans. *Ibid.,* 5: 39–55.

1966 Pregnancy, childbirth, and the deification of the women who died in childbirth: texts from the Florentine Codex, book 6, folios 128v–143v. T. D. Sullivan, ed. and trans. *Ibid.,* 6: 63–95.

1969 Augurios y abusiones. A. López Austin, ed. and trans. Univ. Nac. Autónoma Méx., Inst. Hist., Seminario de Cultura Náhuatl, *Textos de los Informantes de Sahagún,* no. 4.

SAHLINS, M., AND E. R. SERVICE, eds.
1960 Evolution and culture. Ann Arbor.

SALAS, C. DE
1928 Relaciones de Tetiquipa, Rio Hondo, Tecuicuilco, Atepec, Coquipa y Xatlianguez. *Rev. Mex. Estud. Antr.,* 2: 113–20.

SALAZAR-MALLÉN, M.
1949 El aglutinogeno Lewis en la sangre de los Mexicanos. *Bol. Inst. Estud. Méd. Biol. Mex.,* 1: 25–28.

—— AND T. ARIAS
1959 Inheritance of Diego blood group in Mexican Indians. *Science,* 130: 164–65.

—— AND C. ARTEAGA
1951 Estudio de los grupos sanguíneos de los Mexicanos: consecuencias desde el punto de vista etnológica. *Rev. Mex. Estud. Antr.,* 12: 9–29.

—— AND R. HERNÁNDEZ DE LA PORTILLA
1944 Existencia del aglutinogeno Rh en los hematíes de 250 individuos mexicanos. *Rev. Soc. Mex. Hist. Natural,* 5: 183–85.

—— AND G. MARTÍNEZ
1947 Estudio sobre la frecuencia del factor Rho en diferentes grupos de habitantes de la República Mexicana. *Rev. Méd. Hospital General Méx.,* vol. 9, no. 8.

SALDÍVAR, G.
1943 Los Indios de Tamaulipas. *Inst. Panamer. Geog. Hist.,* Pub. 70. Mexico.

SALER, B.
1962 Migration and ceremonial ties among the Maya. *SW. Jour. Anthr.,* 18: 336–40.

1962 Unsuccessful practitioners in a bicultural Guatemalan community. *Psychoanalysis and the Psychoanalytic Rev.,* 49: 103–18.

1964 Nagual, witch, and sorcerer in a Quiche village. *Ethnology,* 3: 305–28.

1965 The departure of the dueño. *Jour. Folklore Inst.,* 2: 31–42.

1965 Religious conversion and self-aggrandizement: a Guatemalan case. *Practical Anthr.,* 12: 107–14.

SALES, L.
1794 Noticias de la provincia de Californias. En tres cartas de un sacerdote religioso hijo del Real Convento de Predicadores de Valencia a un amigo suyo. 3 vols. Valencia.

SALMONY, A.
1938 Carved jade in ancient China. Berkeley.

SALOMÓN, J. B., J. E. GORDON, AND N. S. SCRIMSHAW
1966 Studies of diarrheal disease in Central America. X. Associated chickenpox, diarrhea and kwashiorkor in a highland Guatemalan village. *Amer. Jour. Tropical Med. and Hygiene,* 15: 997–1002.

——, L. J. MATA, AND J. E. GORDON
1968 Malnutrition and the common communicable diseases of childhood in rural Guatemala. *Amer. Jour. Public Health,* 58: 505–16.

SALOVESH, M.
1965 Pautas de residencia y estratificación entre los Mayas: algunas perspectivas de San Bartolomé, Chiapas. *Estud. Cultura Maya,* 5: 317–38.

SALTZMAN, M., A. M. KEAY, AND J. CHRISTENSEN
1963 The identification of colorants in ancient textiles. *Dyestuffs,* vol. 44, no. 8. Allied Chemical Corp. New York.

SALVATIERRA S.
1946 Compendio de historia de Centro América. 2d ed. Managua.

SALZ, B. R.
1955 The human element in industrialization: a hypothetical case study of Ecuadorean Indians. *Amer. Anthr. Assoc.*, Mem. 85.

SALZMANN, Z.
1954 The problem of lexical acculturation. *Int. Jour. Amer. Ling.*, 20: 137–39.

SAMAYOA CHINCHILLA, C.
1934 Madre milpa. Guatemala.
1936 Cuatro suertes: cuentos y leyendas. Guatemala.
1941 La casa de la muerte: cuentos y leyendas de Guatemala. Guatemala.
1959 The emerald lizard: tales and legends of Guatemala. Indian Hills, Colo.

SAN BUENAVENTURA, G. DE
1684 Arte de la lengua maya. Mexico. (2d ed. 1888, Mexico.)

SAN FRANCISCO, DICCIONARIO DE
n.d. MS, 17th century; original missing. Copy by J. Pío Pérez. Gates reproduction. Copy by H. Berendt. *Univ. Pennsylvania Mus., Berendt Ling. Coll.*, no. 3.
n.d. Manuscript, maya-español, español-maya. Photograph in Newberry Library. 402 pp.

SÁNCHEZ, JESÚS
1887 Mapa de Tepechpan: historia sincrónica y señorial de Tepechpan y México. *An. Mus. Nac. Mex.*, ep. 1, vol. 3.
1897 Importancia de la historia natural en el estudio de la historia antigua y de la arqueología americana. *11th Int. Cong. Amer.* (Mexico, 1895), Acta, pp. 386–96.
1898–99 Historia natural médical: relaciones de la antropología y la medicina. *Gaceta Méd. Méx.*, 35: 193–206; 36: 112–22.
1899 Nota relativa al hombre prehistórico en México. *An. Acad. Mex. Cien. Exactas, Físicas y Naturales*, 3: 199–219.

SÁNCHEZ, JOSÉ MARÍA
1877 Gramática de la lengua zoque.

SÁNCHEZ, P. C.
1935 Importancia geográfica del "Eje volcánico," cordillera que atraviesa la República Mexicana. *Panamer. Inst. Geog. e Hist.*, Pub. 11.
1937 Centro America, dónde principia, dónde termina. Regiones geológicas, unidades geográficas. Su vida y desarrollo, según las enseñanzas de la geografía moderna. Sus volcanes y sismos en relación con las anomalías de la gravedad. *Ibid.*, Pub. 25.

SÁNCHEZ CASTRO, A.
1947 Los Mixes: historia, leyendas, música. Mexico.

SÁNCHEZ DE AGUILAR, P.
1937 Informe contra idolorum cultores del obispado de Yucatan. . . . Merida. (Originally published 1639, Madrid.)

SÁNCHEZ DE LA BAQUERA, J.
1747 Modo breve de aprender a ler, escrevir, pronunciar, y ablar el idioma othomi. MS in Newberry Library.

SÁNCHEZ GARCÍA, J.
1956 Calendario folklórico de fiestas en la República Mexicana: fiesta de fecha fija. Notas recopiladas y ordenadas por V. T. Mendoza. Mexico.
1958 La virgen de San Juan de los lagos en Mexico. *Anuario Soc. Folklórica Mex.*, 8: 57–79.

SÁNCHEZ GÓMEZ, J. DE J.
1891 Breve estudio sobre la pelvis. Mexico.

SANDER, D.
1959 Fluted points from Madden Lake. *Panama Archaeol.*, vol. 2, no. 1.

SANDERS, E. M.
1921 The natural regions of Mexico. *Geog. Rev.*, 11: 212–26.

SANDERS, W. T.
1953 The anthropogeography of central Veracruz. *In* Huastecos, Totonacos, pp. 27–28.
1955 An archaeological reconnaissance of northern Quintana Roo. *Carnegie Inst. Wash., Current Reports*, no. 24.
1956 The central Mexican symbiotic region: a study in prehistoric settlement patterns. *In* Willey, 1956, Prehistoric settlement patterns, pp. 115–27.
1960 Prehistoric ceramics and settlement

patterns in Quintana Roo, Mexico. *Carnegie Inst. Wash.*, Pub. 606, Contrib. 60.

1961 Ceramic stratigraphy at Santa Cruz, Chiapas, Mexico. *Papers New World Archaeol. Found.*, no. 13.

1963 Teotihuacan valley project (1960–1961), Mexico. *Katunob*, 4: 24–38.

1966 Life in a classic village. *In* Teotihuacán, pp. 123–48.

SANDOVAL, L., AND K. O. HENCKEL

1954 The ABO, MNS, and Rh-Hr blood groups of the Mapuche Indians of Cautín Province, Chile. *Human Biol.*, 11: 91–96.

SANDOVAL, R. T.

1810 Arte de la lengua mexicana. Mexico.

SANGER, R.

1955 An association between P and Jay systems of blood groups. *Nature*, 176: 1163–64. London.

——, R. R. RACE, AND J. A. JACK

1955 The Duffy blood groups of New York Negroes: the phenotype Fy (a—b—). *British Jour. Hematology*, 1: 370–74.

—— AND OTHERS (J. NOADES, P. TIPPETT, R. R. RACE, J. A. JACK, AND C. CUNNINGHAM)

1960 An Rh antibody specific for V and R's. *Nature*, 186: 171. London.

SANTAMARÍA, F. J.

1959 Diccionario de Mexicanismos. Ed. Porrúa. Mexico.

SANTA MARINA, R.

1931 Memoria de la Secretaría de Educación Pública. Mexico.

SANTIANA, A.

1956 Deformaciones del cuerpo, de carácter étnico, practicadas por los aborígenes del Ecuador. *In* Estudios antropológicos, pp. 111–29.

SANTO DOMINGO, T. DE

1693 Vocabulario en la lengua cakchiquel. MS in Bibliothèque Nationale. 286 pp.

SANTOS, J.

1716 Cronología hospitalaria . . . de San Juan de Dios. Madrid.

SANTOYO, E.

1908 La ametropsia en México. Mexico.

SAPIR, E.

1913 Southern Paiute and Nahuatl I. *Jour. Soc. Amer. Paris*, 10: 379–524.

1915 Southern Paiute and Nahuatl II. *Amer. Anthr.*, 17: 98–120, 306–28.

1915 Abnormal types of speech in Nootka. *Canada, Dept. Mines, Geol. Surv.*, Memoir 62, Anthr. Ser. 5. (Reprinted *in* Mandelbaum, 1949, pp. 179–96.)

1916 Time perspective in aboriginal American culture. *Ibid.*, Memoir 90, Anthr. Ser. 13. (Reprinted *in* Mandelbaum, 1949, pp. 389–462.)

1917 The position of Yana in the Hokan stock. *Univ. California Pub. Amer. Archaeol. Ethnol.*, 13: 1–34.

1920 The Hokan and Coahuiltecan languages. *Int. Jour. Amer. Ling.*, 1: 280–90.

1921 Language. New York. (Reprinted 1949.)

1925 The Hokan affinity of Subtiaba in Nicaragua. *Amer. Anthr.*, 27: 402–35.

1927 The unconscious patterning of behavior in society. *In* Mandelbaum, 1949.

1929 Central and North American languages. *Encyclopaedia Britannica*, 14th ed., 5: 138–41.

1929 Male and female forms of speech in Yana. *In* St. W. J. Teeuwen, ed., Donum Natalicium Schrijnen. (Reprinted *in* Mandelbaum, 1949, pp. 206–12.)

1929 A study in phonetic symbolism. *In* Mandelbaum, 1949.

1949 The status of linguistics as a science. *Ibid.*, pp. 160–66.

SAPON, S. M.

1953 A methodology for the study of socioeconomic differentials in linguistic phenomena. *Studies in Ling.*, 11: 57–68.

SAPPER, C.

1927 La lengua tapachulteca. *El Mex. Antiguo*, 2: 259–68.

SAPPER, D. E.

1925 Costumbres y creencias religiosas de los indios kekchis. *An. Soc. Geog. Hist.*, vol. 2, no. 2.

SAPPER, K.

1891 Ein Besuch bei den östlichen Lacandonen. *Ausland*, 64: 892–95.

1894 Grundzüge der physikalischen Geographie von Guatemala. *Petermanns Mitt.*, Ergänzungsheft 113.

1895 Altindianische Asiedelungen in Guatemala und Chiapas. *Veroffentlichen aus dem Königlichen Mus. Völkerkunde*, 4: 13–20.

1896 Sobre la geografía física y la geología de la península de Yucatan. *Inst. Geol. de Méx.*, Bull. 3.

1897 Die Gebraunche und religiosen Anfechaungen der Kikchi Indianer.

1897 Das nördliche Mittel-Amerika. Nebst einem Ausflug nach dem Hochland von Anahuac. Reisen und Studien aus den Jahren 1888–95. Brunswick.

1898 Die Ruinen von Mixco (Guatemala). *Inc. Archeofun Ethnog.*, 11: 1–6.

1899 Über Gebirgsbau und Boden des nördlichen Mittelamerika. *Petermanns Mitt.*, Ergänzungsheft 127.

1901 Die Alta Verapaz (Guatemala), eine landeskundliche Skizze mit 5 Karten. *Mitt. der Geographischen Gesellschaft in Hamburg*. 17: 78–224.

1901 Speise und Trank der Kekchi-Indianer. *Globus*, 80: 259–63.

1902 Mittelamerikanische Reisen und Studien aus den Jahren 1888 bis 1900. Brunswick.

1902 Beiträge zur physichen Geographie von Honduras. *Zeit. der Gesellschaft für Erdkunde zu Berlin*, 1902: 33–56, 143–64, 231–41.

1902 Die geographische Bedeutung der mittelamerikanischen Vulkane. *Ibid.*, 1902: 512–36.

1903 Der Ausbruch des Vulkans Santa Maria in Guatemala (Oktober, 1902). *Centralblatt für Mineralogie, Geol. und Palaeontol.*, 1903: 33–44, 65–70.

1904 Der gegenwärtige Stand der Ethnographischen Kenntnis von Mittelamerika. *Archiv für Anthr.*, 31: 1–38. Brunswick.

1904 Independent Indian states of Yucatan. *Smithsonian Inst., Bur. Amer. Ethnol.*, Bull. 28, pp. 623–24.

1905 Über Gebirgsbau und Boden des südlichen Mittelamerika. *Petermanns Mitt.*, Ergänzungsheft 151.

1912 Die Indianer und ihre Kultur einst und jetzt. Leipzig.

1913 Das tägliche Leben der Kekchi-Indianer. *18th Int. Cong. Amer.* (London, 1912), Acta, pp. 362–71.

1913 Die Mittelamerikanische Vulkane. *Petermanns Mitt.*, Ergänzungsheft 178.

1926 Dic vulkanische Tätigkeit in Mittelamerika im 20 Jahrhundert. *Zeit. für Vulkanologie*, 9: 156–203, 231–70.

1932 Klimakunde von Mittelamerika. *In* Koeppen and Geiger, 1932, vol. 2, pt. 2.

—— AND W. STAUB
1937 Handbuch der regionalen Geologie. *Mittelamerika*, vol. 8, no. 29.

SARKISYAN, A. S.
1960 On the determination of the steady wind currents in a baroclinic layer. *In* A collection of articles on dynamic meteorology. *Soviet research in geophysics in English translation*, 1: 58–72. Tr. from Sbornik statei po dinamicheskoi meteorologii, Trudy Geophys. Inst. Akad, Nauk, USSR, no. 37 (164), published in 1956.

SARLES, H. B.
1962 A grammar of San Bartoleño Tzotzil. MS. *In* McQuown, 1962.

SATTERTHWAITE, L.
1937 Thrones at Piedras Negras. *Bull. Univ. Pennsylvania Mus.*, 7 (1): 18–23.

1939 Evolution of a Maya temple, pt. 1. *Ibid.*, 7 (4): 3–14.

1941 Some central Peten Maya architectural traits at Piedras Negras. *In* Los Mayas antiguos, pp. 182–208.

1943 Notes on sculpture and architecture at Tonala, Chiapas. *Carnegie Inst. Wash., Notes Middle Amer. Archaeol. Ethnol.*, no. 21.

1943 Animal-head feet and a bark-beater in the middle Usumacinta region. *Ibid.*, no. 27.

1943–45 Piedras Negras archaeology: architecture. Univ. Pennsylvania Mus.

1946 *Review of* An incised Maya inscription in the Metropolitan Museum of

203

Art, New York, by H. Beyer. *Amer. Antiquity,* 12: 131.

1947 Concepts and structures of Maya calendrical arithmetics. *Joint Pub., Univ. Pennsylvania Mus., Philadelphia Anthr. Soc.,* no. 3.

1948 Further implications of Thompson's readings of Maya inscriptions at Copan. *28th Int. Cong. Amer.* (Paris, 1947), Acta, pp. 467–93.

1951 Moon ages of the Maya inscriptions: the problem of their seven-day range of deviation from calculated mean ages. *In* Tax, 1951, pp. 142–54.

1951 Reconnaissance in British Honduras. *Bull. Univ. Pennsylvania Mus.,* 16 (1): 21–36.

1952 Piedras Negras archaeology: architecture. Part 5: Sweathouses, nos. 1–4. Univ. Pennsylvania Mus.

1954 Sculptured monuments from Caracol, British Honduras. *Bull. Univ. Pennsylvania Mus.,* 18 (1, 2): 1–45.

1956 Maya dates on stelae in Tikal "enclosures." *Ibid.,* 20 (4): 25–40.

1956 Radiocarbon dates and the Maya correlation problem. *Amer. Antiquity,* 21: 416–19.

1958 The problem of abnormal stela placements at Tikal and elsewhere. *Mus. Monogr., Univ. Pennsylvania, Tikal Reports,* no. 3.

1958 Five newly discovered carved monuments at Tikal and new data on four others. *Ibid.,* no. 4.

1958 Early "uniformity" moon numbers at Tikal and elsewhere. MS of paper presented to 33d Int. Cong. Amer.

1961 Maya long count. *El Mex. Antiguo,* 9: 125–33.

1961 The mounds and monuments at Xutilha, Peten, Guatemala. *Mus. Monogr., Univ. Pennsylvania, Tikal Reports,* no. 9.

1967 Radiocarbon and Maya long count dating of "Structure 10" (Str. 5D-52, first story), Tikal. *Rev. Mex. Estud. Antr.,* 21: 225–49.

—— AND E. K. RALPH
1960 Radiocarbon dates and the Maya correlation problem. *Amer. Antiquity,* 26: 165–84.

SAUER, C. O.
1925 The morphology of landscape. *Univ. California Pub. Geog.,* 2: 19–24.

1932 The road to Cibola. *Ibero-Amer.,* no. 3.

1934 The distribution of aboriginal tribes and languages in northwestern Mexico. *Ibid.,* no. 5.

1935 Aboriginal population of northwestern Mexico. *Ibid.,* no. 10.

1936 American agricultural origins: a consideration of nature and culture. *In* Essays in Anthropology in Honor of Alfred Louis Kroeber, pp. 279–97.

1941 The personality of Mexico. *Geog. Rev.,* 31: 353–64.

1948 Colima of New Spain in the sixteenth century. *Ibero-Amer.,* no. 29.

1950 Cultivated plants of South and Central America. *In* Handbook of South American Indians, 6: 487–543.

1952 Agricultural origins and dispersals. Amer. Geog. Soc. New York.

1959 Age and area of American cultivated plants. *33d Int. Cong. Amer.* (San Jose, 1958), Acta, 1: 215–29.

—— AND D. D. BRAND
1930 Pueblo sites in southeastern Arizona. *Univ. California Pub. Geog.,* 3: 415–58.

1931 Prehistoric settlements in Sonora with special reference to Cerros de Trincheras. *Ibid.,* 5: 67–148.

1932 Aztatlan, prehistoric Mexican frontier on the Pacific coast. *Ibero-Amer.,* no. 1.

SAUSSURE, H. DE
1853 Observations sur deux individus designés comme appartenant à la race Aztèque et qu'on montre à ce moment à Londres. *Compte-rendu Séances Acad. Sci.,* 37: 192–94. Paris.

SAVILLE, M. H.
1899 Exploration of Zapotecan tombs in southern Mexico. *Amer. Anthr.,* 1: 350–62.

1900 Cruciform structures near Mitla. *Bull. Amer. Mus. Natural Hist.,* 13: 201–18.

1900 An onyx jar from Mexico in the process of manufacture. *Ibid.,* 13: 105–07.

1907 The antiquities of Manabi, Ecuador: final report. *Contrib. South Amer. Archaeol.*, vol. 1. George B. Heye Exped. New York.

1909 Archaeological researches on the coast of Esmeraldas. *16th Int. Cong. Amer.* (Vienna, 1908), Acta.

1909 The cruciform structure of Mitla and vicinity. *In* Putnam Anniversary Volume, pp. 151–90.

1910 The antiquities of Manabi, Ecuador: final report. *Contrib. South Amer. Archaeol.*, vol. 2. George B. Heye Exped. New York.

1913 Pre-Columbian decoration of the teeth in Ecuador with some account of the occurrence of the custom in other parts of North and South America. *Amer. Anthr.*, 15: 377–94.

1920 The goldsmith's art in ancient Mexico. *Mus. Amer. Indian, Heye Found., Indian Notes and Monogr.*, no. 7.

1921 Bibliographic notes on Uxmal, Yucatan. *Ibid.*, vol. 9, no. 2.

1922 Turquoise mosaic art in ancient Mexico. *Contrib. Mus. Amer. Indian, Heye Found.*, vol. 6.

1925 The wood-carver's art in ancient Mexico. *Ibid.*, vol. 9.

1928 Bibliographic notes on Xochicalco, Mexico. *Mus. Amer. Indian, Heye Found., Indian Notes and Monogr.*, vol. 6, no. 6.

1928 Bibliographic notes on Palenque, Chiapas. *Ibid.*, vol. 6, no. 5.

1929 Tizoc: great lord of the Aztecs, 1481–1486. *Contrib. Mus. Amer. Indian, Heye Found.*, vol. 7, no. 4.

1929 Votive axes from ancient Mexico. *Mus. Amer. Indian, Heye Found., Indian Notes*, 6: 266–99.

1935 The ancient Maya causeways of Yucatan. *Antiquity*, 9: 67–73.

SAYLES, E. B.
1935 An archaeological survey of Texas. *Medallion Papers*, no. 17. Gila Pueblo.

1936 Some Southwestern pottery types, Series 5. *Ibid.*, no. 21.

1936 An archaeological survey of Chihuahua, Mexico. *Ibid.*, no. 22.

—— AND E. ANTEVS
1941 The Cochise culture. *Ibid.*, no. 29.

SAYRE, A. N., AND G. C. TAYLOR, JR.
1951 Ground-water resources of the Republic of El Salvador, Central America. *U.S. Geol. Survey, Water-Supply Paper 1079-D*.

SAYRE, E. V., A. MURRENHOFF, AND C. F. WEICK
1958 The nondestructive analysis of ancient potsherds through neutron activation. Brookhaven Nat. Lab.

SCHAEFER, M. B., Y. M. BISHOP, AND G. V. HOWARD
1958 Some aspects of upwelling in the Gulf of Panama. *Bull. Inter-Amer. Tropical Tuna Comm.*, 3: 77–132.

SCHAPIRO, L., AND E. G. NAUCK
1931 Observations on hook-worm disease in Costa Rica based on postmortem findings. *Amer. Jour. Hygiene*, 14: 705–14.

SCHAPIRO, M.
1953 Style. *In* Kroeber, 1953, pp. 287–312.

SCHELLHAS, P.
1945 Die Entzifferung der Mayahieroglyphen ein unlösbares Problem? *Ethnos*, 10: 44–53.

SCHENK, A.
1910 Notes sur un crâne Otomi. *Bull. Soc. Neuchâteloise Geog.* Neuchâtel. (Tr. in *Rev. Cien. Bibliog. Soc. Antonio Alzate*, 30: 17–24 [1911].)

SCHERZER, K.
1855 Sprache der Indianer von Ixtalavacan (Quiché), von Quezaltenango, Guatemala. *Sitzungsberichte der Philos. Histor. Klasse der Kaisserl. Akad. der Wissenschaften*, 18: 227–41. Vienna.

SCHLESINGER, J.
1946 Revolución comunista. Guatemala.

SCHMIDT, J.
1872 Die Verwandschaftsverhältnisse der indo-germanischen Sprachen. Weimar.

SCHMIDT, K. P.
1943 Corollary and commentary for "Climate and Evolution." *Amer. Midl. Naturalist*, 30: 241–53.

1954 Faunal realms, regions and provinces. *Quar. Rev. Biol.*, 29: 322–31.

SCHMIDT, P. W.
1926 Die Sprachfamilien und Sprachen-kreise der Erde. Heidelberg.

SCHMIEDER, O.
1930 Oldest democracy in Mexico. *El Palacio*, 29: 292–93.
1930 The settlements of the Tzapotec and Mije Indians, state of Oaxaca, Mexico. *Univ. California Pub. Geog.*, 4: 1–184.
1931 Kulturgeographische Studien im Staate Oaxaca: summary. *El Mex. Antiguo*, 3: 73–74.
1934 Der Einfluss des Agrarsystems der Tzapoteken, Azteken und Mije auf die Kulturentwicklung dieser Völker. *24th Int. Cong. Amer.* (Hamburg, 1930), Acta, pp. 109–11.

SCHMITHÜSEN, J.
1959 Allgemeine Vegetationsgeographie. Berlin.

SCHNEIDER, R. M.
1958 Communism in Guatemala, 1944–1954. *Univ. Pennsylvania, Foreign Policy Research Inst. Ser.*, no. 7.

SCHOEMBS, J.
1949 Aztekische Schriftsprache. Heidelberg.

SCHOLES, F. V.
1937 The beginnings of Hispano-Indian society in Yucatan. *Carnegie Inst. Wash.*, Suppl. Pub. 30.

—— AND E. B. ADAMS
1938 Don Diego Quijada, alcalde mayor de Yucatan. 2 vols. *Bib. Hist. Mex.*, vols. 14, 15. Mexico.
1955 Relación de las encomiendas de Indios hechas en Nueva España a los conquistadores. *In* their 1955–61, vol. 1.
1955–61 Documentos para la historia del México colonial. 7 vols. Mexico.
1957 Información sobre los tributos que los indios pagaban a Moctezuma, año de 1554. *In* their 1955–61, vol. 4.
1958 Sobre el modo de tributar los indios de Nueva España a su majestad, 1561–1564. *In* their 1955–61, vol. 5.

——, C. R. MENÉNDEZ, J. I. RUBIO MAÑÉ, AND E. B. ADAMS, eds.

1936–38 Documentos para la historia de Yucatan. 3 vols. Merida.

—— AND R. L. ROYS
1938 Fray Diego de Landa and the problem of idolatry in Yucatan. *Carnegie Inst. Wash.*, Pub. 501, pp. 585–620.
1948 The Maya Chontal Indians of Acalan-Tixchel: a contribution to the history and ethnography of the Yucatan peninsula. *Ibid.*, Pub. 560.

SCHÖNDUBE, O.
1968 Figurillas del occidente de México. *In* Colección breve, no. 8. Mus. Nac. Antr. Mexico.

SCHOTT, A.
1866 Die Küstenbildung des nördlichen Yukatan. *Petermanns Mitt.*, 12: 127–30.

SCHOTT, G.
1935 Geographie des Indischen und Stillen Ozeans. Hamburg.

SCHREIDER, E.
1938 Une mission biotypologique au Mexique. *In* Congrès International de la Population (1937), 8: 8–13. Paris.
1953–55 Recherches anthropologiques sur les Otomis de la région d'Ixmiquilpan (Mexique). *L'Anthropologie*, 57: 453–89; 59: 253–96. Paris.
1955 Etude de quelques signes de métissage dans une population amérindienne. *Bull. et Mem. Soc. Anthr. Paris*, ser. 10, 6: 223–34.

SCHROEDER, A. H.
1952 A brief survey of the lower Colorado River from Davis Dam to the international border. Mimeographed. U.S. Dept. Interior, National Park Service.
1956 Comments on a trial survey of Mexican-Southwestern architectural parallels. *El Palacio*, 63 (9–10): 299–309.

SCHUCHARDT, H.
1900 Über die Klassifikation der romanischen Mundarten. Graz. (Presented orally 1870.)

SCHUCHERT, C.
1929 The geological history of the Antillean region. *Bull. Geol. Soc. Amer.*, 40: 337–60.

1935 Historical geology of the Antillean-Caribbean region. New York.

SCHUFELDT, P. W.
1950 Reminiscences of a chiclero. *In* Morleyana, a collection of writings in memoriam, Sylvanus Griswold Morley, 1883–1948, pp. 224–29.

SCHULLER, R.
1920 Zur sprachlichen Verwandtschaft der Maya-Qu'itše mit den Carib-Aruac. *Anthropos,* 14–15: 465–91. Vienna.
1923–24 Die ehemalige und die heutige Verbreitung der Huaxteka-Indianer. *Ibid.,* 18–19: 793–803.
1924–27 Notes on the Huaxteca Indians of San Luis Potosi. *El Mex. Antiguo,* 2: 129–40.
1924–27 La posición etnológica y lingüística de los huaxtecos. *Ibid.,* 2: 141–50.
1925 La lengua ts'ots'il. *Int. Jour. Amer. Ling.,* 3: 193–218.
1925 La única gramática conocida de la lengua pame. *Talleres gráficos del Depto. Antr.* Mexico.
1925 La patria originaria de los indios mayas. *Ethnos,* ep. 3, 1 (3–4): 52–59. Mexico.
1935 Das Popol Vuh und das Ballspiel der K'iče Indianer von Guatemala, Mittelamerika. *Int. Archiv für Ethnog.,* 33: 105–16.

SCHULTES, R. E.
1940 Plantae mexicanae V: *Desmoncus chinantlensis* and its utilization in native basketry. *Bot. Mus. Leafl., Harvard Univ.,* 8: 134–40.
1941 The meaning and usage of the Mexican place-name 'Chinantla.' *Ibid.,* 9: 101–16.
1941 Plantae mexicanae IX: *Aechmea magdalenae* and its utilization as a fibre plant. *Ibid.,* 9: 117–22.
1941 A contribution to our knowledge of *Rivea corymbosa,* the narcotic *Ololiuqui* of the Aztecs. Bot. Mus., Harvard Univ.

SCHULTZ, B. K., AND M. HESCH
1935 Rassenkundliche Bestimmungstafeln für Augen-, Haar- und Hautfarben und für Iriszeichnungen. Munich.

SCHULTZE-JENA, L. S.
1933 Leben, Glaube und Sprache der Quiche von Guatemala. Indiana, vol. 1. Jena. (Tr. into Spanish, 1945, by A. Goubaud C.)
1938 Bei den Azteken, Mixteken und Tlapaneken der Sierra Madre del Sur von Mexiko. Indiana, vol. 3.
1944 Popol Vuh: das heilige Buch der Quiche-Indianer von Guatemala. *Quellenwerke zur alten Geschichte Amerikas,* vol. 2. Stuttgart.
1590 [ed.] Wahrsagerei, Himmelskunde und Kalender der alten Azteken. Aus dem aztekischen Urtext des B. de Sahagún. *Ibid.,* vol. 4.
1952 [ed.] Gliederung des alt-aztekischen Volks in Familie, Stand und Beruf. Aus dem aztekischen Urtext des B. de Sahagún. *Ibid.,* vol. 5.
1957 [ed.] Alt-aztekische Gesänge. *Ibid.,* vol. 6.

SCHULZ, R. P. C.
1936 Beiträge zur chronologie und astronomie des alten Zentralamerika. *Anthropos,* 31. 750–88.
1942 Apuntes sobre cálculos relativos al calendario de los indígenas de Chiapas. *El Mex. Antiguo,* 6: 6–14.
1944 Los sistemas cronológicos de los libros de Chilam Balam. *Ibid.,* 6: 239–60.
1953 Nuevos datos sobre el calendario tzeltal y tzotzil de Chiapas. *Yan,* 2: 114–16.
1955 Dos variantes nuevas del calendario chinanteco. *El Mex. Antiguo,* 8: 233–46.

SCHUMANN, E. A., JR.
1936 A recent visit to southern Mexico. *Maya Research,* 3: 396–405.

SCHUSTER, C.
1951 Joint-marks: a possible index of cultural contact between America, Oceania and the Far East. *Mededeling no. 94, Afdeling Culturele en Physische Anthropologie,* 39. Koninklijk Inst. Tropen. Amsterdam.

SCHWARTZLOSE, R. A.
1952 The cultural geography of the Mormon settlements in Mexico. MS.

SCHWATKA, F.
1893   In the land of cave and cliff-dwellings.

SCLATER, P. L.
1858   On the general geographical distri-
       bution of the members of the class
       Aves. *Jour. Proc. Linn. Soc.* (Zool-
       ogy), 2: 130–45.

SCRIMSHAW, N. S.
1956   Desnutrición severa en la infancia: V,
       Epidemiología y prevención.   *Rev.*
       Colegio Méd. Guatemala, 7: 267–74.

——, M. BÉHAR, M. A. GUZMÁN, AND J. E.
GORDON
1969   Nutrition and infection field study in
       Guatemalan   villages,   1959–1964.
       IX. An evaluation of medical, social,
       and public health benefits, with sug-
       gestions for future field study. *Arch.*
       Environ. Health, 18: 51–62.

——, M. BÉHAR, C. PÉREZ, AND F. VITERI
1955   Nutritional problems of children in
       Central America and Panama. *Pedi-*
       atrics, 16: 378–97.

—— AND M. A. GUZMÁN
1953   The effect of dietary supplementation
       and the administration of vitamin B_{12}
       and aureomycin on the growth of
       school children. *In* Current Research
       on Vitamins in Trophology, Nutrition
       Symposium Series no. 7, pp. 101–17.
       National Vitamin Foundation.   New
       York.

——, M. A. GUZMÁN, M. FLORES, AND J. E.
GORDON
1968   Nutrition and infection field study in
       Guatemalan villages, 1959–1964. V.
       Disease incidence among preschool
       children under natural village condi-
       tions, with improved diet and with
       medical and public health services.
       Arch. Environ. Health, 16: 223–34.

——, J. B. SALOMÓN, H. A. BRUCH, AND J. E.
GORDON
1966   Studies of diarrheal disease in Central
       America. VIII. Measles, diarrhea, and
       nutritional deficiency in rural Guate-
       mala. *Amer. Jour. Tropical Med. and*
       Hygiene, 15: 625–31.

——, C. E. TAYLOR, AND J. E. GORDON
1959   Interactions of nutrition and infection.
       Amer. Jour. Med. Sci., 237: 367–403.

—— AND OTHERS
1956   (M. Béhar, G. Arroyave, F. Viteri,
       and C. Tejada).   Characteristics of
       kwashiorkor (síndrome pluricarencial
       de la infancia).   *Federation Proc.,*
       15: 977–85.

1957   (M. Béhar, G. Arroyave, C. Tejada,
       and F. Viteri).   Kwashiorkor in chil-
       dren and its response to protein ther-
       apy. *Jour. Amer. Med. Assoc.,* 164:
       555–61.

1957   (M. Trulson, C. Tejada, D. M. Heg-
       stead, and F. J. Stare).   Serum lipo-
       protein and cholesterol concentra-
       tions: comparison of rural Costa
       Rican,   Guatemalan   and   United
       States populations. *Circulation,* 15:
       805–13.

1961   (M. Béhar, D. Wilson, F. Viteri, G.
       Arroyave, and R. Bressani).   All-
       vegetable protein mixtures for human
       feeding: V, Clinical trials with IN-
       CAP mixtures 8 and 9 and with corn
       and beans. *Amer. Jour. Clinical Nu-*
       trition, 9: 196–205.

1966   (L. Vega Franco, R. Arellano, C.
       Sagastume, J. Ignacio Méndez, and
       R. de León).   Efecto de la yodación
       de la sal sobre la prevalencia de bo-
       cio endémico en niños escolares de
       Guatemala.   *Bol. Oficina Sanitaria*
       Panamer., 60: 222–28.

SCRIPPS INST. OCEANOGRAPHY
1957   Oceanic observations of the Pacific,
       1949.   Univ. California Press.
1960   *Idem,* 1950.
1960   *Idem,* 1955.
1963   *Idem,* 1951.
1963   *Idem,* 1956.
n.d.   *Idem,* 1952–54, 1957–59.   MS.

SEAFORD, H. W.
1953   Un breve resumen de la economía
       chocha. *Rev. Mex. Estud. Antr.,* 13:
       235–40.

1955   Observaciones preliminares de los ri-
       tos funerarios chochos. *El Mex. An-*
       tiguo, 8: 323–45.

SEARS, P. B.
1951   Pollen profiles and culture horizons
       in the basin of Mexico. *In* Tax,
       1951, pp. 57–61.
1952   Palynology in southern North Amer-

ica. Part 1: Archaeological horizons in the basin of Mexico. *Bull. Geol. Soc. Amer.*, 63: 241–54.

1955 [with others] Palynology in southern North America. *Ibid.*, 66: 471–530.

—— AND K. H. CLISBY

1955 Palynology in southern North America. Part 4: Pleistocene climate in Mexico. *Ibid.*, 66: 521–30.

SEARS, W. H.

1956 Excavations at Kolomoki: final report. Univ. Georgia Press.

—— AND J. B. GRIFFIN

1950 Fiber-tempered pottery of the southeast *and* Fabric-marked pottery in eastern United States. *In* J. B. Griffin, ed., Prehistoric pottery of the eastern United States, section 6–50. Mus. Anthr., Univ. Michigan.

SEDILLO BREWSTER, M.

1935 Mexican and New Mexican folk dances. Univ. New Mexico Press.

SEE, R.

n.d. Missionary orders in Mexico: a preliminary investigation. MS, Univ. California, Dept. Anthropology and Sociology.

SEJOURNÉ, L.

1952 Los otomís del Mezquital. *Cuad. Amer.*, 66: 17–34.

1952 Palenque, una ciudad maya. Mexico.

1952 Una interpretación de las figurillas del arcaico. *Rev. Mex. Estud. Antr.*, 13: 49–63.

1956 Estudio del material arqueológico de Atetelco, Teotihuacán. *Ibid.*, 14: 15–23.

1956 Informe sobre el material exhumado en Ahuixotla. *Ibid.*, 14: 33–35.

1956 Identificación de una diosa zapoteca. *An. Inst. Nac. Antr. Hist.*, 7: 111–16.

1957 Pensamiento y religión en el México antiguo. *Breviarios del Fondo de Cultura Económica*, no. 128. Mexico. (English trans., Burning water: thought and religion in ancient Mexico, 1957, London; 1960, New York.)

1959 Un palacio en la ciudad de los dioses, Teotihuacán. Inst. Nac. Antr. Hist. Mexico.

1961 El culto de Xochipilli y los braseros teotihuacanos. *El Mex. Antiguo*, 9: 111–24. (Homenaje al Dr. Hermann Beyer.)

1963 Exploración de Tetitla. *In* Bernal, 1963, pp. 46–49.

1965 El Quetzalcóatl en Teotihuacán. *Cuad. Amer.*, año 24, vol. 138, no. 1.

1966 El lenguaje de las formas en Teotihuacán. Mexico.

SELER, E.

n.d. The stucco façade of Acanceh in Yucatan. *In* his 1902–23, 5: 389–404.

1887 Das Konjugationssystem der Mayasprachen. Berlin. (Also in his 1902–23, 1: 65–126.)

1889–91 Altmexikanischer Schmuck und soziale und militärische Rangabzeichen. *Zeit. für Ethnol.*, 21: 69–85; 23: 114–24. (Collected Works, 2: 509–619, much charged.)

1890 Die archäologischen Ergebnisse meiner ersten mexikanischen Reise. *7th Int. Cong. Amer.* (Berlin, 1888), Acta, pp. 111–95.

1890 Die sogennanten sakralen Gefässe der Zapoteken. Altmexikanische Studien. *Veröff. Koniglichen Mus. für Völkerkunde*, 1: 181–88.

1891 Zur mexikanischen Chronologie mit besonderer Berückschtitung des zapotekischen Kalenders. *Zeit. für Ethnol.*, 23: 89–133.

1892 Notice sur les langues zapothèque et mixtèque. *8th Int. Cong. Amer.* (Paris, 1890), Acta, pp. 550–55.

1892 L'orfévrerie des anciens Mexicains et leur art de travailler la pierre et de faire des ornements en plumes. *Ibid.*, pp. 401–52. (Also in his 1902–23, 2: 620–63.)

1894 Die grossen Steinskulpturen des Museo Nacional de México. *Ethnologisches Notizblatt*, 1: 19–31.

1895 Wandmalerei von Mitla: eine mexikanische Bilderschrift in Fresko, nach eigenen, an Ort und Stelle aufgenommenen Zeichnungen herausgegeben und arläutert. Berlin.

1896 Die Ruinen auf dem Quiengola. *In* Festschrift für Adolf Bastian, pp. 419–33.

1897   Beile aus Kupfer (nicht aus Bronce) in Mexiko (Zapoteken), aus der Mixteca (Pueblo del Zapote, Distr. Jamiltepec). *10th Int. Cong. Amer.* (Stockholm, 1894), Acta, pp. 7–8.

1899   Zauberei und Zauberer im alten Mexiko. *Veröffentlichungen aus dem Königlichen Museum für Völkerkunde*, VI. Band 2/4. Heft, Altmexikanische Studien II, 1: 29–57. Berlin.

1899   Die bildlichen Darstellungen der mexikanischen Jahresfeste. *Ibid.*, 2: 58–66.

1899   Die achtzehn Jahrefeste der Mexikaner (Erste Hälfte). *Ibid.*, 3: 67–204.

1900   Das Tonalamatl der Aubin'schen Sammlung. Eine altmexikanische Bilderhandschrift der Bibliothèque Nationale in Paris (Manuscrits mexicains nrs. 18–19). Berlin. (English trans. in his 1901.)

1901   Die alten Ansiedelungen von Chacula. Berlin.

1901   Die Huichol-Indianer des Staates Jalisco in Mexiko. *Gesammelte Abhandlungen*, 3: 355–91.

1901   Die Huichol-Indianer des Staates Jalisco in Mexiko. *Mitteilungen der Anthr. Gesellschaft in Wien*, 31: 138–63.

1901   The Tonalamatl of the Aubin collection. A. H. Keane, trans. London. (English trans. of his 1900.)

1901   Codex Féjérváry-Mayer. Eine altmexikanische Bilderhandschrift der Free Public Museum in Liverpool (12014/M). Berlin. (English trans. 1901–1902, Berlin and London.)

1902   Codex Vaticanus Nr. 3773 (Codex Vaticanus B). Eine altmexikanische Bilderschrift der Vatikanischen Bibliothek. Berlin. (English trans. 1902–03, Berlin and London.)

1902   Die Tageszeichen der aztekischen und der Maya Handschriften und ihre Gottheiten. *In* his 1902–23, 1: 417.

1902–23   Gesammelte Abhandlungen zur Amerikanischen Sprach- und Alterthumskunde. 5 vols. Berlin. (2d ed. 1960–61, Graz, Austria.)

1904   Archäologisches aus Mexiko. 5: Altmexikanischer Schmuck und soziale und militärische Rangabzeichen. *In* his 1902–23, 2: 509–619. (Reprint of his 1889–91.)

1904   Alexander von Humboldt's picture manuscripts in the Royal Library at Berlin. *Smithsonian Inst., Bur. Amer. Ethnol., Bull.* 28, pp. 123–229.

1904   Wall paintings at Mitla. *Ibid.*, Bull. 28, pp. 243–324.

1904   Antiquities of Guatemala. *Ibid.*, pp. 75–122.

1904   The Mexican chronology, with special reference to the Zapotec calendar. *Ibid.*, pp. 11–56.

1904   Die alten Ansiedelungen im Gebiet der Huasteca. *In* his 1902–23, 2: 168–83. (Also in *Zeit. für Ethnol.*, 20 [1888]: 451–59.)

1904–09   Codex Borgia. Eine altmexikanische Bilderschrift der Bibliothek der Congregatio de Propaganda Fide. 3 vols. Berlin. (Spanish trans. 1963, Mexico.)

1908   Das Dorfbuch von Santiago Guevea. *In* his 1902–23, 3: 157–93.

1908   Die alten Bewohner der Landschaft Michuacan. *In* his 1902–23, 3: 33–156.

1913   Similarity of design of some Teotihuacan frescoes and certain Mexican pottery objects. *18th Int. Cong. Amer.* (London, 1912), Acta, pp. 194–202.

1915   Die Teotihuacan-Kultur des Hochlands von Mexiko. *In* his 1902–23, 5: 405–585.

1916   Mexicans [ancient]. *In* Hastings, 1916, 8: 612–17.

1916   Die Quetzalcouatl-fassaden yukatekischer Bauten. *Konigl. Akad. Wissenschaften*, no. 2.

1923   Mythus und Religion der alten Mexikaner. *Geschichte Abhandlungen*, 4: 3–156.

1927   Einige Kapitel aus dem Geschichtswerk des Fray Bernardino de Sahagún aus dem Aztekischen übersetzt. Stuttgart.

1963 Comentarios al Códice Borgia. 3 vols. Fondo de Cultura Económica. Mexico and Buenos Aires.

SELER-SACHS, C.
1900 Auf alten Wegen in Mexiko und Guatemala. Berlin.
1913 Die Reliefscherben von Cuicatlan und Teotitlan del Camino. *18th Int. Cong. Amer.* (London, 1912), Acta. (Spanish trans. 1949 in *El Mex. Antiguo*, 7: 105–18.)

SELLARDS, E. H.
1941 Stone images from Henderson County, Texas. *Amer. Antiquity*, 7: 29–38.
1952 Early man in America: a study in prehistory. Univ. Texas Press.

SELLERS, M. I., A. F. RASMUSSEN, JR., AND N.S. SCRIMSHAW
1960 Poliovirus infection in Guatemala. *Amer. Jour. Tropical Med.*, 9: 304–07.

SELTZER, C. C.
1936 Physical characteristics of the Yaqui Indians. *Texas Tech. College Bull.*, 12: 91–113.
1937 A critique of the coefficient of racial likeness. *Amer. Jour. Physical Anthr.*, 23: 101–09.

SENTENACH CABAÑAS, N.
1898 Ensayo sobre la América precolombina. Toledo.

SERGI, G.
1891 Crani africani e crani americani. *Archivio Anthr. Ethnol.*, 21: 215–68. Florence.
1911 L'uomo secondo le origini, l'antichitá, la variazioni e la distribuzione geografica. Milan.

SERNA, J. DE LA
1955 Manual de ministros de Indios para el conocimiento de sus idolatrías, y extirpación de ellas. *In* Tratados de las idolatrías, supersticiones, dioses, ritos, hechicerías y otras costumbres gentílicas de las razas aborígenes de México. *Ediciones Fuente Cultural*, 10: 41–368. Mexico. (1st ed. 1892, in *An. Mus. Nac.*, 6: 261–480. Mexico.)

SERRANO PLAJA, A.
1944 España en la edad de oro. Buenos Aires.

SERRANO Y SANZ, M., ed.
1908 Relaciones históricos y geográficos de América Central. Vol. 8. Madrid.

SERRES, P. M. DE
1955 Note sur deux microcéphales vivants, attribués à une race americaine. *Compte-rendu Séances Acad. Sci.*, 41: 43–47. Paris.

SERVICE, E.
1955 Indian-European relations in colonial Latin America. *Amer. Anthr.*, 57: 411–25.

SERVICIO METEOROLÓGICO MEXICANO
1945 Atlas climatológico de Mexico. Mexico.

SHAPIRO, M.
1956 Inheritance of the Henshaw (He) blood factor. *Jour. Forensic Med.*, 3: 152–60.
1964 Serology and genetics of a "new" blood factor: hr^H. *Ibid.*, 11: 52–66.

SHARP, A. J.
1946 Informe preliminar sobre algunos estudios fitogeográficos efectuados en Mexico y Guatemala. *Rev. Soc. Mex. Hist. Nat.*, 7: 35–40.

SHATTUCK, G. C.
1933 The peninsula of Yucatan: medical, biological, meteorological and sociological studies. *Carnegie Inst. Wash.*, Pub. 431.
1938 A medical survey of the republic of Guatemala. *Ibid.*, Pub. 499.
1951 Diseases of the tropics. New York.

—— AND F. G. BENEDICT
1931 Further studies of the basal metabolism of Maya Indians of Yucatan. *Amer. Jour. Physiol.*, 96: 518–28.

SHELFORD, V. E., ed.
1926 Naturalist's guide to the Americas. Baltimore.

SHELL, O.
1957 Cashibo II: grammemic analysis of transitive and intransitive verb patterns. *Int. Jour. Amer. Ling.*, 23: 179–218.

SHELVOCKE, G.
1814 A voyage around the world, 1719–1722. *In* Kerr, 1814.

SHEPARD, A. O.
1946 Technological notes. *In* Kidder, Jennings, and Shook, 1946, pp. 261–77.

1947 Ceramic technology. *Carnegie Inst. Wash.*, Year Book 46, pp. 190–92.

1948 Plumbate: a Mesoamerican trade ware. *Ibid.*, Pub. 573.

1956 Ceramics for the archaeologist. *Ibid.*, Pub. 609.

1965 Notas sobre la cerámica de Monte Alban. *In* Caso, Bernal, and Acosta, 1965.

SHEPARD, F. P.

1950 1940 *E. W. Scripps* cruise to the Gulf of California. Part 3: Submarine topography of the Gulf of California. *Mem. Geol. Soc. Amer.*, 43: 1–32.

SHETRONE, H. C.

1926 Exploration of the Hopewell group. *In* Certain mounds and village sites in Ohio, vol. 4, pt. 4.

SHIMKIN, D. B.

1941 The Uto-Aztecan system of kinship terminology. *Amer. Anthr.*, 43: 223–45.

SHOOK, E. M.

1940 Exploration in the ruins of Oxkintok, Yucatan. *Rev. Mex. Estud. Antr.*, 4: 165–71.

1945 Archaeological discovery at Finca Arizona, Guatemala. *Carnegie Inst. Wash., Notes Middle Amer. Archaeol. Ethnol.*, no. 57.

1947 Guatemala highlands. *Carnegie Inst. Wash.*, Year Book 46, pp. 179–84.

1948 Guatemala highlands. *Ibid.*, Year Book 47, pp. 214–18.

1949 Guatemala highlands. *Ibid.*, Year Book 48, pp. 219–24.

1949 Historia arqueológica de Puerto de San Jose, Guatemala. *Antr. Hist. Guatemala*, 1 (2): 3–22.

1949 Some recent aspects of Mayan civilization and maize culture on the Pacific coast of Guatemala. *In* Melhus, 1949, pp. 503–09.

1950 Guatemala. *Carnegie Inst. Wash.*, Year Book 49, pp. 197–98.

1950 The ruins of Sin Cabezas, Tiquisate, Dept. of Escuintla, Guatemala. *Unifruitco*, August.

1950 Tiquisate UFers scoop archaeological world. *Ibid.*

1951 The present status of research on the pre-classic horizons in Guatemala. *In* Tax, 1951, pp. 93–100.

1951 Guatemala. *Carnegie Inst. Wash.*, Year Book 50, pp. 240–41.

1951 Investigaciones arqueológicas en las ruinas de Tikal, Departamento de El Peten, Guatemala. *Antr. Hist. Guatemala*, 3 (1): 9–32.

1952 The ruins of Cotio, Department of Guatemala, Guatemala. *Carnegie Inst. Wash., Notes Middle Amer. Archaeol. Ethnol.*, no. 107.

1952 Lugares arqueológicos del altiplano meridional central de Guatemala. *Antr. Hist. Guatemala*, 4 (2): 3–40.

1952 The great wall of Mayapan. *Carnegie Inst. Wash., Current Reports*, no. 2.

1953 The X-Coton temples at Mayapan. *Ibid.*, no. 11.

1954 Three temples and their associated structures at Mayapan. *Ibid.*, no. 14.

1954 A round temple at Mayapan, Yucatan. *Ibid.*, no. 16.

1954 The temple of Kukulcan at Mayapan. *Ibid.*, no. 20.

1955 Yucatan and Chiapas. *Carnegie Inst. Wash.*, Year Book 54, pp. 289–95.

1955 Another round temple at Mayapan. *Carnegie Inst. Wash., Current Reports*, no. 27.

1956 An Olmec sculpture from Guatemala. *Archaeology*, 9: 260–62.

1956 An archaeological reconnaissance in Chiapas, Mexico. *New World Archaeol. Found.*, Pub. 1, pp. 20–37.

1957 The Tikal project. *Bull. Univ. Pennsylvania Mus.*, 21: 36–52.

1958 Field director's report: the 1956 and 1957 seasons. *Mus. Monogr., Univ. Pennsylvania, Tikal Reports*, no. 1.

1960 Tikal Stela 29. *Expedition, Bull. Univ. Pennsylvania Mus.*, 2 (2): 29–35.

—— AND W. N. IRVING

1955 Colonnaded buildings at Mayapan. *Carnegie Inst. Wash., Current Reports*, no. 22.

—— AND A. V. KIDDER

1952 Mound E-III-3, Kaminaljuyu, Guatemala. *Carnegie Inst. Wash.*, Pub. 596, Contrib. 53.

—— AND T. PROSKOURIAKOFF

1951 Yucatan. *Carnegie Inst. Wash.*, Year Book 50, pp. 239–40.

1956 Settlement patterns in Mesoamerica and the sequence in the Guatemalan highlands. *In* Willey, 1956, Prehistoric settlement patterns, pp. 93–100.

—— AND R. E. SMITH

1950 Descubrimientos arqueológicos en Poptun. *Antr. Hist. Guatemala,* 2 (2): 3–15.

SHOR, G. G., AND E. ROBERTS

1956 San Miguel, Baja California Norte, earthquakes of February 1956: a field report. *Seismological Soc. Amer. Bull.,* 48: 101–16.

SHREVE, F.

1934 Vegetation of the northwestern coast of Mexico. *Bull. Torrey Bot. Club,* 61: 373–80.

1939–40 Observations on the vegetation of Chihuahua. *Madroño,* 5: 1–13.

1951 Vegetation of the Sonoran desert. *Carnegie Inst. Wash.,* Pub. 591.

SHUMWAY, C., C. L. HUBBS, AND J. R. MORIARTY

1961 Scripps Estates site, San Diego, Calif.: a La Jolla site dated 5460–7370 years before the present. *Ann. New York Acad. Sci.,* 93: 37–131.

SIEGEL, M.

1941 Religion in western Guatemala: a product of acculturation. *Amer. Anthr.,* 43: 62–76.

1941 Resistance to culture change in western Guatemala. *Sociol. and Social Research,* 25: 414–30.

1941 Problems of education in Indian Guatemala. *Jour. Experimental Education,* 9: 285–94.

1942 Horns, tails, and Easter sport: a study of a stereotype. *Social Forces,* 20: 382–86.

1942 Effects of culture contact on the form of the family in a Guatemalan village. *Jour. Royal Anthr. Inst.,* 72: 55–68.

1943 The creation myth and acculturation in Acatan, Guatemala. *Jour. Amer. Folklore,* 56: 120–26.

1954 Culture change in San Miguel Acatan, Guatemala. *Phylon,* pp. 165–76.

1954 Perspective in Guatemala. *New Republic,* July 19.

SIGNORET, M. V.

1875 Essai sur les cochenilles ou gallinsectes (Homopteres—Coccides), 15e, 16e, et 17e parties. *Ann. Soc. Entomol. France,* vol. 44.

SILICEO PAUER, P.

1920 Distribución del índice cefálico en México. *Ethnos,* ep. 1, 1: 3–5. Mexico.

1920–21 Estudio antropométrico de la población del valle de Teotihuacán. *Ibid.,* ep. 1, 1: 186–91.

1922 El tipo físico del indio del valle de Teotihuacán. *In* Gamio, 1922, 2: 151–66.

1922–23 Conocimiento antropológico de las agrupaciones indígenas de México. *Ethnos,* ep. 2, 1: 15–35. Mexico.

1923 Los indios de Yalalag. *Mag. Geog. Nac.,* 1: 3–45.

1925 Estudio anatómico y antropométrico de los restos humanos de tipo azteca descubiertos en Coyoacán. *Ethnos,* ep. 3, 1: 67–82.

1925 Representaciones prehispánicas de dientes humanos, hecha en concha. *An. Mus. Nac. Arqueol. Hist. Etnog.,* ep. 4, 3: 220–22.

1925 Indice craniométrico de los indígenas prehispánicos y actuales de la Mesa Central de México. *Ibid.,* ep. 4, 3: 338–43.

1927 La población indígena de Yalalag, Oaxaca, con algunas otras sobre el tsapoteco-mixteco. *Anthropos,* 22: 45–65.

SILVA, M.

1907 Antropometría escolar: informe rendido a la superioridad relativo a los trabajos llevados a cabo desde julio de 1906. Mexico.

SILVA Y ACEVES, M.

1925 La colección folklórica de la Biblioteca del Museo Nacional. *An. Mus. Nac. Arqueol. Hist. Etnog.,* 3: 269–320. Mexico.

SILVERT, K. H.
1954 A study in government: Guatemala. *Tulane Univ., Middle Amer. Research Inst.*, Pub. 21.
1956 El nacionalismo: medida de su crecimiento en Guatemala. *In* Arriola, 1956, pp. 393–414.
—— AND A. R. KING
1957 Coban: 1944–53. *In* R. N. Adams, 1957, pp. 44–47.

SIMÉON, R.
1885 Dictionnaire de la langue nahuatl. Paris.
1889 Chrestomathie nahuatl, publiée pour le cours de langue mexicaine. Paris.

SIMMONS, C. S., J. M. TÁRANO, AND J. H. PINTO
1959 Clasificación de reconocimiento de los suelos de la República de Guatemala. Inst. Agropecuario Nac., Servicio Coop. Inter-Amer. de Agricultura, Ministerio de Agricultura.

SIMMONS, M. L.
1960 Pre-conquest narrative songs in Spanish America. *Jour. Amer. Folklore*, 73: 103–11.

SIMMONS, R. T.
1957 The Diego (Di^a) blood group: tests in some Pacific peoples. *Nature*, 179: 970–71. London.
——, J. J. GRAYDON, N. M. SEMPLE, AND C. N. D. TAYLOR
1951 Blood, taste and secretion: a genetical survey in Maoris. *Med. Jour. Australia*, 1: 425–31.
—— AND J. JACOBOWITZ
1951 The Lewis blood antigens and antibodies. *Ibid.*, 1: 497.

SIMONS, B. B.
1968 Los mapas de Cuauhtinchán y la Historia Tolteca-Chichimeca. Inst. Nac. Antr. Hist. Mexico.
1970 Un posible glifo de Cuauhximalpan en el mapa de Cuauhtinchan No. 2. *Rehue*, 3: 7–26. Concepcion, Chile.

SIMPSON, G. G.
1943 Turtles and the origin of the fauna of Latin America. *Amer. Jour. Sci.*, 241: 413–29.

SIMPSON, L. B.
1929 The encomienda in New Spain. *Univ. California Pub. Hist.*, vol. 19.

1934 Studies in the administration of the Indians in New Spain. 2: The civil congregation. *Ibero-Amer.*, no. 7, pp. 29–129.
1938 California in 1792: the expedition of José Longinos Martínez. San Marino.
1950 The encomienda in New Spain: the beginning of Spanish Mexico. Berkeley.
1952 Exploitation of land in central Mexico in the sixteenth century. *Ibero-Amer.*, no. 36.
1952 Many Mexicos. 3d ed. Berkeley.
1953 Unplanned effects of Mexico's planned economy. *Virginia Quar. Rev.*, 29: 514–32.
1959 Many Mexicos. Rev. 3d ed. Berkeley.

SINCLAIR, W. J.
1904 The exploration of the Potter Creek cave. *Univ. California Pub. Amer. Archaeol. and Ethnol.*, vol. 2, no. 1.

SIVERTS, H.
1955 Informe sobre Oxchuc. MS.
1958 Social and cultural changes in a Tzeltal (Mayan) municipio, Chipas, Mexico. *32d Int. Cong. Amer.* (Copenhagen, 1956), Acta, pp. 177–89.
1960 Political organization in a Tzeltal community in Chiapas, Mexico. *In* Leslie, 1960, Social anthropology, pp. 14–28.
1964 On politics and leadership in highland Chiapas, Mexico. *In* Desarrollo cultural de los Mayas, pp. 363–80.

SKINNER, A.
1920 An image of an amulet of nephrite from Costa Rica. *Mus. Amer. Indian, Heye Found., Indian Notes and Monogr.*, vol. 6, no. 4.
1926 Notes on Las Mercedes, Costa Rica Farm and Anita Grande. *In* Lothrop, 1926, app. 4.

SKINNER-KLEE, J.
1954 Legislación indigenista de Guatemala. *Inst. Indig. Interamer.*, Ed. Especiales, no. 18. Mexico.

SKUTCH, A. F.
1950 Problems in milpa agriculture. *Turrialba*, 1: 4–6.

SLOCUM, M. C.
1956 Cultural changes among the Oxchuc Tzeltals. *In* Estudios antropológicos, pp. 491–95.

SMILEY, C. H.
1960 The antiquity and precision of Maya astronomy. *Jour. Royal Astron. Soc. Canada*, 54: 222–26.

SMITH, A. L.
1937 Structure A-XVIII, Uaxactun. *Carnegie Inst. Wash.*, Pub. 483, Contrib. 20.

1940 The corbeled arch in the New World. *In* The Maya and their neighbors, pp. 202–21.

1950 Uaxactun, Guatemala: excavations of 1931–1937. *Carnegie Inst. Wash.*, Pub. 588.

1955 Archaeological reconnaissance in central Guatemala. *Ibid.*, Pub. 608.

1961 Types of ball courts in the highlands of Guatemala. *In* Lothrop and others, 1961, pp. 100–25.

1962 Residential and associated structures at Mayapan. *Carnegie Inst., Wash.*, Pub. 619, pp. 165–320.

—— AND A. V. KIDDER
1943 Explorations in the Motagua valley, Guatemala. *Ibid.*, Pub. 546, Contrib. 41.

1951 Excavations at Nebaj, Guatemala. *Ibid.*, Pub. 594.

—— AND K. RUPPERT
1953 Excavations in house mounds at Mayapan: II. *Carnegie Inst. Wash., Current Reports*, no. 10.

1954 Ceremonial or formal archway, Uxmal. *Carnegie Inst. Wash., Notes Middle Amer. Archaeol. Ethnol.*, no. 116.

1954 Excavations in house mounds at Mayapan: III. *Carnegie Inst. Wash., Current Reports*, no. 17.

1956 Excavations in house mounds at Mayapan: IV. *Ibid.*, no. 36.

—— AND G. R. WILLEY
1962 Preliminary report on excavations at Altar de Sacrificios, 1959–1960. *34th Int. Cong. Amer.* (Vienna, 1960), Acta, pp. 318–25.

SMITH, B.
1862 [ed.] *See* Anonymous, 1862.

1968 Mexico: a history in art. New York.

SMITH, C. E.
1950 Prehistoric plant remains from Bat Cave. *Bot. Mus. Leafl., Harvard Univ.*, 14: 157–80.

—— AND R. S. MACNEISH
1964 Antiquity of American polyploid cotton. *Science*, 143 (3607): 675–76.

SMITH, H. G.
1955 Archaeological significance of oriental porcelain in Florida sites. *Florida Anthr.*, 8: 111–16.

SMITH, H. M.
1939 The Mexican and Central American lizards of the genus *Sceloporus*. *Field Mus. Nat. Hist., Zool. Ser.*, no. 26.

1949 Herpetogeny in Mexico and Guatemala. *Ann. Assoc. Amer. Geog.*, 39: 219–38.

—— AND E. H. TAYLOR
1945 An annotated checklist and key to the snakes of Mexico. *Smithsonian Inst., U. S. Nat. Mus.*, Bull. 187.

1948 An annotated checklist and key to the amphibia of Mexico. *Ibid.*, Bull. 194.

1950 An annotated checklist and key to the reptiles of Mexico exclusive of the snakes. *Ibid.*, Bull. 199.

SMITH, M. E.
1963 The Codex Colombino: a document of the south coast of Oaxaca. *Tlalocan*, 4: 276–88.

1966 Las glosas del Códice Colombino. Soc. Mex. Antr. Mexico.

SMITH, P., AND R. J. WEITLANER
1957 Detalles de la fonología del idioma Proto-Chinanteco. MS.

SMITH, R. E.
1940 Ceramics of the Peten. *In* The Maya and their neighbors, pp. 242–49.

1936 Ceramics of Uaxactun: a preliminary analysis of decorative techniques and design. Mimeographed. Guatemala.

1937 A study of Structure A-I complex at Uaxactun, Peten, Guatemala. *Carnegie Inst. Wash.*, Pub. 456, Contrib. 19.

1944 Archaeological specimens from Guatemala. *Carnegie Inst. Wash., Notes*

Middle Amer. Archaeol. Ethnol., no. 37.

1949 Cerámica elaborada sin torno, Chinautla, Guatemala. *Antr. Hist. Guatemala*, 1 (2): 58–61.

1949 Guatemala highlands. *Carnegie Inst. Wash.*, Year Book 48, pp. 229–31.

1952 Pottery from Chipoc, Alta Verapaz, Guatemala. *Carnegie Inst. Wash.*, Pub. 596, Contrib. 56.

1953 Cenote X-Coton at Mayapan. *Carnegie Inst. Wash., Current Reports*, no. 5.

1954 Exploration on the outskirts of Mayapan. *Ibid.*, no. 18.

1954 Pottery specimens from Guatemala: I. *Carnegie Inst. Wash., Notes Middle Amer. Archaeol. Ethnol.*, no. 118.

1955 Early ceramic horizons at Mayapan and Santa Cruz. *Carnegie Inst. Wash., Current Reports*, no. 26.

1955 Ceramic sequence at Uaxactun, Guatemala. 2 vols. *Tulane Univ., Middle Amer. Research Inst.*, Pub. 20.

1955 A correction on "preclassic metal." *Amer. Antiquity*, 20: 379–80.

1955 Pottery specimens from Guatemala: II. *Carnegie Inst. Wash., Notes Middle Amer. Archaeol. Ethnol.*, no. 124.

1957 The Marquez collection of X fine orange and fine orange polychrome vessels. *Ibid.*, no. 131.

1958 The place of fine orange pottery in Mesoamerican archaeology. *Amer. Antiquity*, 24: 151–60.

—— AND J. C. GIFFORD

1959 A check list of prehistoric Maya pottery types and varieties. Mimeographed. Peabody Mus., Harvard Univ.

1966 Maya ceramic varieties, types, and wares at Uaxactun: supplement to "Ceramic Sequence at Uaxactun, Guatemala." *Tulane Univ., Middle Amer. Research Inst.*, Pub. 28, pp. 125–74.

——, G. R. WILLEY, AND J. C. GIFFORD

1960 The type-variety concept as a basis for the analysis of Maya pottery. *Amer. Antiquity*, 25: 330–40.

SMITH, T.

1963 The main themes of Olmec art tradition. *Papers Kroeber Anthr. Soc.*, 28: 121–213.

SMITH, V. J.

1938 Carved rock shelter. *Bull. Texas Archaeol. Paleontol. Soc.*, 10: 222–33.

SMITH, W., AND L. EWING

1952 Kiva mural decorations at Awatovi and Kawaika-a: with a survey of other wall paintings in the Pueblo Southwest. *Papers Peabody Mus., Harvard Univ.*, vol. 37.

SNOW, C. E.

1957 Adena portraiture. *In* Webb and Baby, 1957, pp. 47–60.

SNYDER, L. H.

1926 Human blood groups: their inheritance and racial significance. *Amer. Jour. Physical Anthr.*, 9: 233–63.

SO LIVE THE WORKS OF MEN

1939 So live the works of men: seventieth anniversary volume honoring Edgar Lee Hewett. D. D. Brand and F. E. Harvey, eds. Univ. New Mexico and School Amer. Research.

SOCIAL SCIENCE RESEARCH COUNCIL

1954 Acculturation: an exploratory formulation. *Amer. Anthr.*, 56: 973–1002. (Summer Seminar on Acculturation, 1953.)

SOIL SURVEY STAFF

1960 Soil classification: a comprehensive system (prepared by) soil survey staff. 7th approximation. U.S. Soil Conservation Service.

SOKOLOFF, V. P., AND J. L. LORENZO

1953 Modern and ancient soils at some archaeological sites in the valley of Mexico. *Amer. Antiquity*, 19: 50–55.

SOLÁ, M.

1936 Historia del arte precolombino. *Artes Plásticas*, nos. 391, 392. Editorial Labor, sec. 4. Barcelona.

SOLECKI, R. S.

1955 Lamellar flakes versus blades: a reappraisal. *Amer. Antiquity*, 20: 393–94.

SOLIEN, N. L.

1959 The nonunilineal descent group in

the Caribbean and Central America. *Amer. Anthr.*, 61: 578–83.

1960 Changes in Black Carib kinship terminology. *SW. Jour. Anthr.*, 16: 144–59.

SOLÍS, J. DE
1945 Estado en que se hallaba la provincia de Coatzacoalcos en el año de 1599. *Bol. Archivo General de la Nación*, 16: 195–246, 429–79. Mexico.

SOLÍS ALCALÁ, E.
1949 Códice Pérez. Tr. libre del Maya al Castellano. Merida.

1949 Diccionario español-maya. Yikal Maya Than. Merida.

SOLÍS QUIROGA, H.
1957 Industrialización y delincuencia. *Jornadas Indust.*, ep. 4, no. 52, pp. 123–60. Mexico.

SOLÓRZANO MOTA, A. W.
1963 Estudio analítico de 34 casos de esporotricosis en Guatemala. Tesis de médico y cirujano, Facultad Cien. Méd., Univ. San Carlos de Guatemala.

SORENSON, J. L.
1955 A chronological ordering of the Mesoamerican preclassic. *Tulane Univ., Middle Amer. Research Rec.*, 2: 43–68.

1956 An archaeological reconnaissance of west-central Chiapas, Mexico. *New World Archaeol. Found.*, Pub. 1, pp. 7–19.

SORIANO, J. G.
1776 Difícil tratado del arte y unión de los idiomas othomii y pamee. MS.

SOSA GALICIA, F.
1948 Estado actual de los espiroquetales (especies confirmadas hasta hoy en Guatemala). Tesis de médico y cirujano, Facultad Cien. Méd., Univ. San Carlos de Guatemala.

SOTUTA, LIBRO DE
n.d. [Medicina maya.] MS. Photograph in Newberry Library. 108 pp.

SOUSTELLE, J.
1933 Notes sur les Lacandons du Lac Peljá et du fleuve Jetjá, Chiapas. *Jour. Soc. Amer. Paris*, 25: 153–80.

1935 Deux contes otomis. *Ibid.*, 27: 1–12.

1935 Le culte des oratoires chez les otomis et les mazahuas de la region d'Ixtlahuaca. *El. Mex. Antiguo*, 3 (5–8): 97–117.

1935 Les idées religieuses des Lacandons. *La Terre et La Vie*, 5: 170–78.

1935 Le totémisme des Lacandons. *Maya Research*, 2: 325–44.

1936 Mexique: terre indienne. Paris.

1937 La culture matérielle des Indiens Lacandons. *Jour. Soc. Amer. Paris*, 29: 1–95.

1937 La famille Otomi-Pame du Mexique central. *Univ. Paris, Inst. Ethnol., Travaux et Mem.*, no. 26.

1940 La pensée cosmologique des anciens Mexicains (representation du monde et de l'espace). Paris. (Spanish trans. 1959, Puebla.)

1951 Documents sur les langues Pame et Jonaz du Mexique central. *Jour. Soc. Amer. Paris*, 60: 1–20.

1953 La religion des Aztèques. *In* Histoire des Religions, 5: 7–30. Brussels.

1955 La vie quotidienne des Aztèques à la veille de la conquête espagnole. Paris.

1956 La vida cotidiana de los aztecas en vísperas de la conquista. Fondo de Cultura Económica. Mexico. (English trans. 1961.)

1958 Tequila: un village nahuatl du Mexique oriental. *Univ. Paris, Inst. Ethnol., Travaux et Mem.*, no. 62.

1959 Observations sur la religion des Lacandons du Mexique méridional. *Jour. Soc. Amer. Paris*, 48: 141–96.

1959 Album de la vie quotidienne des Aztèques. Paris.

1961 The daily life of the Aztecs on the eve of the Spanish conquest. London. (English trans. of his 1956; 1st ed. 1955 in French.)

1966 L'Art du Mexique ancien. Paris.

1966 Terrestrial and celestial gods in Mexican antiquity. *Diogenes*, 56: 20–50.

1967 Arts of ancient Mexico. E. Carmichael, trans. Photographs by C. Arthaud and F. Herbert-Stevens. New York.

SPAULDING, A. C.

1952 The origin of the Adena culture of the Ohio valley. *SW. Jour. Anthr.*, 8: 260–68.

1955 Prehistoric cultural development in the eastern United States. *In* Meggers and Evans, 1955, pp. 12–27.

SPENCE, L.

1923 The gods of Mexico. New York.

1926 Witchcraft and sorcery in ancient Mexico. *Discovery*, 7: 47–50. London.

1930 The magic and mysteries of Mexico. London.

SPENCE, M. W.

1967 The obsidian industry of Teotihuacan. *Amer. Antiquity*, 32: 507–14.

SPENGEL, J. W.

1877 Die von Blumenbach gegruendete anthropologische Sammlung der Universitaet Gothingen aufgenommen im Jahre 1874. *Anthr. Samml. Deutsch.*, pp. 64–67. Brunswick.

SPICER, E. H.

1940 Pascua, a Yaqui village in Arizona. Univ. Chicago Press.

1943 Linguistic aspects of Yaqui acculturation. *Amer. Anthr.*, 45: 410–26.

1945 El problema yaqui. *Amer. Indig.*, 5: 273–78.

1947 Yaqui villages past and present. *Kiva*, 13: 2–11.

1954 Spanish-Indian acculturation in the southwest. *Amer. Anthr.*, 56: 663–84.

1954 Potam, a Yaqui village in Sonora. *Amer. Anthr. Assoc.*, Mem. 77.

1961 [ed.] Perspectives in American Indian culture change. Univ. Chicago Press.

1962 Cycles of conquest. Univ. Arizona Press.

SPIER, L.

1925 The distribution of kinship systems in North America. *Univ. Washington Pub. Anthr.*, no. 1.

——, A. I. HALLOWELL, AND S. S. NEWMAN

1941 Language, culture, and personality: essay in memory of Edward Sapir. Menasha.

SPINDEN, E. S.

1933 The place of Tajin in Totonac archaeology. *Amer. Anthr.*, 35: 225–70.

SPINDEN, H. J.

1911 An ancient sepulcher at Placeres del Oro, state of Guerrero, Mexico. *Amer. Anthr.*, 13: 29–55.

1913 A study of Maya art, its subject matter and historical development. *Mem. Peabody Mus., Harvard Univ.*, vol. 6.

1915 Notes on the archaeology of Salvador. *Amer. Anthr.*, 17: 446–87.

1917 Ancient civilizations of Mexico and Central America. *Amer. Mus. Natural Hist., Handbook Ser.*, no. 3. New York. (Other eds. 1922, 1928.)

1917 The origin and distribution of agriculture in America. *19th Int. Cong. Amer.* (Washington, 1915), Acta, pp. 269–76.

1924 The reduction of Maya dates. *Papers Peabody Mus., Harvard Univ.*, vol. 6, no. 4.

1930 Maya dates and what they reveal. *Brooklyn Inst. Arts Sci.*, vol. 4, no. 1.

1935 Indian manuscripts of southern Mexico. *Smithsonian Inst.*, ann. rept. for 1933, pp. 429–51.

1937 Huastec sculptures and the cult of apotheosis. *Brooklyn Mus. Quar.*, 24: 179–89.

1948 Chorotegan influences in western Mexico. *In* El Occidente de México, pp. 34–37.

1957 Art of the Maya civilization. Martin Widdifield Gallery. New York.

1957 Maya art and civilization. Revised and enlarged with added illustrations. Part 1: A study of Maya art. Part 2: The nuclear civilization of the Maya and related cultures. Indian Hills, Colo.

SPRANZ, B.

1964 Göttergestalten in den mexikanischen Bilderhandschriften der Codex Borgia-Gruppe. *Acta Humboldtiana, Ser. Geog. Ethnog.*, no. 4. Wiesbaden.

SPRATLING, W.

1932 Little Mexico. New York.

1960 More human than divine. Univ. Nac. Autónoma Mex.

SPRINGER, V. G.
1958 Systematics and zoogeography of the clinid fishes of the subtribe Labrisomini Hubbs. *Pub. Inst. Marine Sci.*, 5: 417–92.

SQUIER, E. G.
1852 Nicaragua: its people, scenery, monuments and the proposed interoceanic canal. 2 vols. New York.
1855 Notes on Central America, particularly on the states of Honduras and El Salvador. . . . New York.
1860 Collection of rare and original documents and relations concerning the discovery and conquest of America chiefly from Spanish archives. No. 1. New York.
1861 Monograph of authors who have written on the languages of Central America and collected vocabularies or composed works in the native dialects of that country. London.
1865 [ed.] The Quiches. London.
1870 Observations on a collection of chalchihuitls from Mexico and Central America. *Ann. Lyceum Natural Hist.*, 9: 246–65.

STABB, M. S.
1959 Indigenism and racism in Mexican thought: 1857–1911. *Jour. Interamer. Studies*, 1: 405–23.

STACPOOLE, H. H.
1953 Prophylaxis of endemic goitre in Mexico. *Bull. World Health Organization*, 9: 283.

STADELMAN, R.
1940 Maize cultivation in northwestern Guatemala. *Carnegie Inst. Wash.*, Pub. 523, Contrib. 33.

STADEN, H.
1928 The true history of his captivity, 1557. London.

STANDLEY, P. C.
1920–26 Trees and shrubs of Mexico. *Contrib. U.S. Nat. Herbarium*, vol. 23.
1926 The Republic of El Salvador. *In* Shelford, 1926, pp. 602–04.
1928 Flora of the Panama Canal Zone. *Contrib. U.S. Nat. Herbarium*, vol. 27.

1930 Flora of Yucatan. *Field Mus. Natural Hist., Bot. Ser.*, vol. 3, no. 3.
1936 The forests and flora of British Honduras. *Ibid.*, vol. 12.
1937 Flora of Costa Rica. *Ibid.*, vol. 18.
—— AND S. CALDERÓN
1925 Lista preliminar de las plantas de El Salvador. San Salvador.
—— AND J. A. STEYERMARK
1945 The vegetation of Guatemala, a brief review. *In* Verdoorn, 1945, pp. 275–78.
1946–62 Flora of Guatemala. *Chicago Natural Hist. Mus., Fieldiana: Botany*, vol. 24, pts. 1–7.

STANGER, F. M.
1932 National origin in Central America. *Hispanic Amer. Hist. Rev.*, 12: 18–45.

STANISLAWSKI, D.
1947 Tarascan political geography. *Amer. Anthr.*, 49: 46–55.
1950 The anatomy of eleven towns in Michoacan. *Univ. Texas, Inst. Latin Amer. Studies*, Pub. 10.

STARR, B. W.
1951 The Chorti and the problem of survival of Maya culture. *Amer. Anthr.*, 53: 355–69.
1952 Ceremonial structures in the present day Maya area. *Univ. Chicago, Micro. Coll. MSS Middle Amer. Cult. Anthr.*, no. 31.
1952 Field notes on San Andres, Tuxtla. *Ibid.*, no. 33.
1954 Levels of communal relations. *Amer. Jour. Sociol.*, 60: 125–35.
1957 Notes on Santiago Tuxtla, Veracruz. *Univ. Chicago, Micro. Coll. MSS Middle Amer. Cult. Anthr.*, no. 40.

STARR, F.
1896 Pigmy race of men. *North Amer. Rev.*, 162: 414–23.
1897 Little pottery objects from Lake Chapala, Mexico. *Dept. Anthropology, Univ. Chicago*, Bull. 2.
1898 Notched bones from Mexico. *Proc. Davenport Acad. Natural Sci.*, 7: 101–07.
1899 The Indians of southern Mexico: an ethnographic album. Chicago.
1899 Catalogue of a collection of objects

illustrating the folklore of Mexico. London.

1900–02 Notes upon the ethnography of southern Mexico. 2 parts. *Proc. Davenport Acad. Natural Sci.*, vols. 8 and 9.

1902 The physical characters of the Indians of southern Mexico. *Univ. Chicago, Decennial Pub.*, 4: 53–109.

1903 The sacral spot on Maya Indians. *Science*, 17 (428): 432–33.

1908 In Indian Mexico: a narrative of travel and labor. Chicago.

1908 The purple spot on Maya babies. *In* preceding entry.

START, L. E.
1948 The McDougall collection of Indian textiles from Guatemala and Mexico. *Pitt Rivers Mus., Occasional Papers on Technology*, no. 2. Oxford.

STAUB, W.
1919 Some data about the pre-Hispanic and the now living Huastec Indians. *El Mex. Antiguo*, 1: 1–65.

1920 Neue Funde und Ausgrabungen in der Huaxteca (Ost-Mexiko). Beiträge zum Jahresbericht über die Ethnographische Sammlung. Bern.

1923 Beiträge zur Landeskunde des nordöstlichen Mexiko. *Zeit. Gesellschaft für Erdkunde zu Berlin*, nos. 5–7, pp. 187–211.

1926 Le nord-est du Mexique et les Indiens de la Huastèque. *Jour. Soc. Amer. Paris*, 18: 279–96.

1930 Zur Kenntnis der indianischen Orstnamen in der Huaxteca (ost Mexiko). *Zeit. Gesellschaft für Erdkunde zu Berlin*, Jahrgang 1924, pp. 215–34.

1933 Zur Uebereinanderschichtung der Völker und Kulturen an der Ostküste von Mexiko. *Mitteilungen Geog.-Ethnog. Gesellschaft*. Zurich.

1939 Algunos datos acerca de los indios huastecas prehispánicos y de los contemporáneos. *Divulgación Hist.*, 1: 423–32.

—— AND C. LAGER
1922 Über eine erloschene Vulkanische Tätigkeit in der Golfregion des Nordöstlichen Mexiko. *Zeit. für Vulkanologie*, 5: 103–13.

STAVENHAGEN, R.
1960 Descendencia y nombres entre los mazatecos. *Rev. Mex. Estud. Antr.*, 16: 231–32.

STECK, F. B.
1951 Motolinía's history of the Indians of New Spain. *Pub. Acad. Amer. Franciscan Hist., Doc. Ser.*, no. 1. Washington.

STEGGERDA, I. D., M. STEGGERDA, AND M. S. LANE
1936 A racial study of palmar dermatoglyphics with special reference to the Maya Indians of Yucatan. *In* Cummins and others, 1936, pp. 129–94.

STEGGERDA, M.
1931 Physical anthropology in Yucatan. *Carnegie Inst. Wash.*, Year Book 30, pp. 124–25.

1931 Results of physiological tests given to Maya Indians in Yucatan, Mexico. *Eugenical News*, 16: 205–10.

1932 Anthropometry of adult Maya Indians: a study of their physical and physiological characteristics. *Carnegie Inst. Wash.*, Pub. 434.

1936 A physical and physiological description of adult Maya Indians from Yucatan. *In* Cummins and others, 1936, pp. 17–21.

1941 Maya Indians of Yucatan. *Carnegie Inst. Wash.*, Pub. 531.

1950 The living South American Indian: anthropometry of South American Indians. *In* Handbook of South American Indians, 6: 57–69.

—— AND F. G. BENEDICT
1932 Metabolism in Yucatan. *Amer. Jour. Physiol.*, 100: 274–84.

—— AND T. J. HILL
1936 Incidence of dental caries among Maya and Navaho Indians. *Jour. Dental Research*, 15: 233–42.

—— AND E. MACOMBER
1939 Mental and social characteristics of Maya and Navaho as evidenced by a psychological rating scale. *Jour. Social Psychol.*, 10: 51–59.

—— AND R. MILLAR
1936 Finger lengths of the Maya Indians as compared with Negroes and

Whites. *In* Cummins and others, 1936, pp. 83–100.

—— AND H. C. SEIBERT
1941 Size and shape of head hair from six racial groups. *Jour. Heredity*, 32: 315–18.

STEINBECK, J., AND E. F. RICKETTS
1941 The sea of Cortez: a leisurely journal of travel and research. New York.

STEINER, P. E.
1954 Cancer: race and geography. Baltimore.

STEININGER, G. R., AND P. VAN DE VELDE
1935 Three dollars a year: being the story of San Pablo Cuatro Venados, a typical Zapotecan Indian village. New York.

STEINMAYER, R. A.
1932 A reconnaissance of certain mounds and relics in Spanish Honduras. *Tulane Univ., Middle Amer. Research Inst.*, Pub. 4, pp. 1–22.

STENDAHL, A. E.
1952 *Foreword to* Ancient art from Costa Rica. Scripps College.
1957 *Foreword to* Art of the Maya civilization. Martin Widdifield Gallery. New York.

STEPHENS, J. L.
1841 Incidents of travel in Central America, Chiapas and Yucatan. 2 vols. New York.
1843 Incidents of travel in Yucatan. 2 vols. New York.

STEPHENS, S. G.
1947 Cytogenetics of Gossypium and the problem of the origin of New World cottons. *In* Advances in genetics, 1: 431–42.

STEPHENSON, R. L.
1950 Cultural chronology in Texas. *Amer. Antiquity*, 16: 151–57.
1951 Archaeological excavations at the Falcon Reservoir, Starr County. Smithsonian Inst., Texas report prepared by River Basin Surveys.

STERN, P.
1934 Evolution du linteau Khmer. *Rev. Arts Asiatiques*, 8: 251–56.

STERN, T.
1948 The rubber-ball games of the Americas. *Monogr. Amer. Ethnol. Soc.*, no. 17.
1954 A note on Rouse's "The circum-Caribbean theory, an archaeological test." *Amer. Anthr.*, 56: 106–07.

STEVENS, W. L.
1950 Statistical analysis of the A-B-O blood groups. *Human Biol.*, 22: 191–217.

STEVENSON, P. H.
1929 On racial differences in stature: long bone regression formulae. *Biometrika*, 21: 301–21.

STEWARD, J. H.
1936 The economic and social basis of primitive bands. *In* Essays in anthropology, presented to A. L. Kroeber, pp. 331–50.
1946–59 [ed.] Handbook of South American Indians. 7 vols. *Smithsonian Inst., Bur. Amer. Ethnol.*, Bull. 143.
1949 South American cultures: an interpretative summary. *In* Handbook of South American Indians, 5: 669–772.
1950 Area research: theory and practice. *Social Sci. Research Council*, Bull. 63.
1951 Levels of sociocultural integration: an operational concept. *SW. Jour. Anthr.*, 7: 374–90.
1955 Theory of culture change. Univ. Illinois Press.

—— AND L. C. FARON
1959 Native peoples of South America. New York.

—— AND OTHERS
1955 Irrigation civilizations: a comparative study. *Pan Amer. Union, Social Sci. Monogr.*, no. 1. Washington.

STEWART, D.
1957 Reconstrucción de tono para Otomí-Mazahua. MS.

STEWART, T. D.
1936 The cephalic (length-breadth) index. *Amer. Jour. Physical Anthr.*, 22: 97.
1939 Anthropometric observations on the Eskimos and Indians of Labrador. *Field Mus. Natural Hist., Anthr. Ser.*, 31: 1–163.
1940 The life and writings of Dr. Aleš Hrdlička (1869–1939). *Amer. Jour. Physical Anthr.*, 26: 3–40.

221

1942 Equivalent definitions of cranial measurements. *Anthr. Briefs,* no. 1, pp.
16–17. New York.

1943 Skeletal remains from Tajumulco,
Guatemala. *In* Dutton and Hobbs,
1943, app. 1.

1947 Anthropometry of the highland Maya.
Carnegie Inst. Wash., Year Book 46,
pp. 195–97.

1947 [ed.] Hrdlička's Practical Anthropometry. 3d ed. Wistar Inst. Anatomy
and Biology. Philadelphia. (4th
ed. 1952.)

1948 The true form of the cranial deformity
originally described under the name
"tête trilobée." *Jour. Washington
Acad. Sci.,* 38: 66–72.

1948 Distribution of the type of cranial
deformity originally described under
the name "tête trilobée." *In* El Occidente de México, pp. 17–20.

1949 Notas sobre esqueletos humanos prehistóricos hallados en Guatemala.
Anthr. Hist. Guatemala, 1: 23–34.

1950 Deformity, trephining, and mutilation
in South American skeletal remains.
In Handbook of South American Indians, 6: 43–48.

1952 A bibliography of physical anthropology in Latin America: 1937–48.
Wenner-Gren Found. Anthr. Research. New York.

1952 Amérique. *In* Catalogue des hom-
mes fossiles, H. V. Vallois and H. L.
Movius, Jr., eds., pp. 293–306. Ex-
tract from Fas. V, comptes-rendus,
19th session, Int. Geol. Cong. Al-
geria.

1953 Skeletal remains from Zaculeu, Guatemala. *In* Woodbury and Trik, 1953,
1: 295–311; 2: figs. 287–91.

1955 El cuerpo humano y el ambiente.
Homenaje al IV Centenario de la
Fundación de la Universidad [Na-
cional Mayor de San Marcos de
Lima], 1551–1951. *Actas y Trabajos, Conferencia de Cien Antr.,* 1:
108–16.

1956 Skeletal remains from Xochicalco,
Morelos, Mexico. *In* Estudios antropológicos, pp. 131–56.

1958 Stone Age skull surgery: a general

review, with emphasis on the New
World. *Smithsonian Inst.,* ann. rept.
1957, pp. 469–91.

—— AND M. T. NEWMAN

1950 Skeletal remains of the South American Indians. *In* Handbook of South
American Indians, 6: 19–42.

—— AND P. F. TITTERINGTON

1944 Filed Indian teeth from Illinois.
Jour. Washington Acad. Sci., vol. 34,
no. 10.

STEYERMARK, J. A.

1950 Flora of Guatemala. *Ecology,* 31:
368–72.

STILLE, H.

1955 Recent deformation of the earth's
crust in the light of those of earlier
epochs. *In* Crust of the Earth, pp.
171–92. *Geol. Soc. Amer.,* Special
Paper 62.

STIRLING, M. W.

1940 An initial series from Tres Zapotes,
Vera Cruz, Mexico. *Nat. Geog. Soc.,
Contributed Technical Papers, Mex.
Archaeol. Ser.,* vol. 1, no. 1.

1941 Expedition unearths buried masterpieces of carved jade. *Nat. Geog.
Mag.,* 80: 278–302.

1943 Stone monuments of southern Mexico. *Smithsonian Inst., Bur. Amer.
Ethnol.,* Bull. 138.

1945 Letter quoted in "News and Notes."
Amer. Antiquity, 11: 137.

1947 On the trail of La Venta man. *Nat.
Geog. Mag.,* 91: 137–72.

1955 Stone monuments of the Rio Chi-
quito, Veracruz, Mexico. *Smithsonian Inst., Bur. Amer. Ethnol.,* Bull.
157.

1957 An archaeological reconnaissance in
southeastern Mexico. *Ibid.,* Bull.
164, pp. 213–40.

1965 Monumental sculpture of southern
Veracruz and Tabasco. *In* Hand-
book of Middle American Indians, R.
Wauchope, ed., vol. 3, art. 28.

STOLL, O.

1884 Zur Ethnographie der Republik Guatemala. Zurich. Also in *An. Soc.
Geog. Hist. Guatemala,* 11: 191–216
(1934).

1887 Die Sprache der Ixil-Indianer. Leipzig.

1888 Die Sprache der Pokonchi-Indianer. Vienna.

1889 Die Ethnologie der Indianerstämme von Guatemala. *Internat. Archiv für Ethnog.*, 1: 112, supplement. Leipzig.

1894 Suggestion und Hypnotismus in der Völkerpsychologie. Leipzig.

1901 Die ethnische Stellung der Tzutijil Indianer. *Festschrift Geog.-Ethnog. Gesellschaft*, Jahresbericht für 1900–01, pp. 27–59. Zurich.

1908 Das Geschlechtsleben in der Völkerpsychologie. Leipzig.

1913 Zur Psychologie der indianischen Hochlandssprachen von Guatemala. *Ann. Geog. Ethnog. Geschichte*, 1912/13: 34–36.

1928 Das Vokabular der Sprache von Aguacatan, no. 2 (Guatemala). *Mitteilungen Geog.-Ethnog. Gesellschaft*. Zurich.

1958 Etnografía de Guatemala. Ministerio de Educación Pública. Guatemala.

STONE, D. Z.

1938 Masters in marble: a study of vase types from the Uloa Valley, Honduras. *Tulane Univ., Middle Amer. Research Inst.*, Pub. 8.

1941 Archaeology of the north coast of Honduras. *Mem. Peabody Mus., Harvard Univ.*, vol. 9, no. 1.

1943 A preliminary investigation of the flood plain of the Rio Grande de Terraba, Costa Rica. *Amer. Antiquity*, vol. 9, no. 1.

1949 Los grupos mexicanos en la América Central y su importancia. *Antr. Hist. Guatemala*, 1 (1): 43–47.

1949 The Boruca of Costa Rica. *Papers Peabody Mus., Harvard Univ.*, vol. 26, no. 2.

1951 Orfebrería pre-columbina. Mus. Nac. San Jose.

1954 Estampas de Honduras. Mexico.

1956 Breve esbozo etnológico de los pueblos indígenas costarricenses. *In* Estudios antropológicos, pp. 503–11.

1956 Date of maize in Talamanca: an hypothesis. *Jour. Soc. Amer. Paris*, 45: 189–94.

1957 The archaeology of central and southern Honduras. *Papers Peabody Mus., Harvard Univ.*, vol. 49, no. 3.

1957 Brief notes on the Matagalpa Indians of Nicaragua. *In* R. N. Adams, 1957, pp. 256–60.

1958 A living pattern of non-Maya–non-Mexican Central American aborigines. *In* Misc. Paul Rivet, 1958, pp. 669–79.

1958 Introduction to the archaeology of Costa Rica. Mus. Nac. San Jose.

1959 The eastern frontier of Mesoamerica. *Mitteilungen aus dem Mus. für Völkerkunde in Hamburg*, 25: 118–21.

1959 [ed.] Acta, 23d Int. Cong. Amer., vol. 1. San Jose, Costa Rica.

1962 The Talamancan tribes of Costa Rica. *Papers Peabody Mus., Harvard Univ.*, vol. 43, no. 2.

—— AND C. BALSER

1958 The aboriginal metalwork in the isthmian region of America. Museo Nacional, San Jose, Costa Rica.

STONOR, C. R., AND E. ANDERSON

1949 Maize among the hill peoples of Assam. *Ann. Missouri Bot. Garden*, 36: 355–404.

STORM, M.

1939 Hoofways into hot country. Mexico.

1945 Enjoying Uruapan: a book for travelers in Michoacan. Mexico.

STRANGEWAYS, T.

1822 Sketch of the Mosquito shore, including the territory of Poyais. Edinburgh.

STREBEL, H.

1885–89 Archäologische Beiträge zur Kulturgeschichte seiner Bewohner. 2 vols. Hamburg and Leipzig.

1890 Studien über Steinjoche aus Mexiko und Mittel-Amerika. *Internat. Archiv für Ethnog.*, 3: 16–28, 49–61. Leiden.

1893 Nachtrag zu Studien über Steinjoche. *Ibid.*, 6: 44–48.

STRESSER-PÉAN, G.

1944–46 La danse des barbares et la danse des démons dans la religion des Indiens huastèques. *Inst. Français Anthr., comptes rendus sommaires des séances*, 21–41: 8–9.

1948 Danse des aigles et danse des jaguars chez les Indiens huastèques de la région de Tantoyuca. *28th Int. Cong. Amer.* (Paris, 1947), Acta, pp. 335–38.

1952 Montagnes calcaires et sources vauclusiennes dans la religion des Indiens huastèques. *Rev. Hist. Religions*, 141: 84–90. Paris.

1953 Les Indiens huastèques. *In* Huastecos, Totonacos, pp. 213–34.

1953 Les Nahuas du sud de la Huasteca et l'ancienne extension méridionale des Huastèques. *Ibid.*, pp. 287–90.

1955 Mission au Mexique (1950–1955). *Jour. Soc. Amer. Paris*, 44: 245–52.

1959 Ixtab, Maximón et Judas: croyances sur la pendaison chez les Mayas de Yucatan, du Guatemala et de la Huasteca. *33d Int. Cong. Amer.* (San Jose, 1958), Acta, 2: 456–61.

1964 Première campagne de fouilles à Tamtok, près de Tamuín, Huasteca. *35th Int. Cong. Amer.* (Mexico, 1962), Acta, 1: 387–94.

———, A. Ichon, and Y. Guidon

1963 La première statue antique en bois découverte dans la Huasteca. *Jour. Soc. Amer. Paris*, 52: 315–18.

Strömberg, E.

1942 Technical analysis of textiles recovered in Burial 1. *In* Linné, 1942, pp. 157–60.

Stromsvik, G.

1931 Notes on the metates of Chichen Itza, Yucatan. *Carnegie Inst. Wash.*, Pub. 403, Contrib. 4.

1941 Honduras. *Ibid.*, Year Book 40, pp. 292–95.

1942 Honduras. *Ibid.*, Year Book 41, pp. 249–50.

1942 Substela caches and stela foundations at Copan and Quirigua. *Ibid.*, Pub. 528, Contrib. 37.

1947 Guide book to the ruins of Copan. *Ibid.*, Pub. 577.

1950 Las ruinas de Asuncion Mita, informe de su reconocimiento. *Antr. Hist. Guatemala*, 2 (1): 21–29.

1952 The ball courts at Copan, with notes on courts at La Union, Quirigua, San Pedro Pinula and Asuncion Mita. *Carnegie Inst. Wash.*, Pub. 596, Contrib. 55.

1956 Exploration of the Cave of Dzab-Na, Tecoh, Yucatan. *Ibid., Current Reports*, no. 35.

Strong, J. P., H. C. McGill, C. Tejada, and R. L. Holman

1958 The natural history of atherosclerosis: comparison of the early aortic lesions in New Orleans, Guatemala and Costa Rica. *Amer. Jour. Pathol.*, 34: 731–44.

Strong, W. D.

1925 The Uhle pottery collections from Ancon. *Univ. California Pub. Amer. Archaeol. Ethnol.*, 21: 135–90.

1934 Hunting ancient ruins in northeastern Honduras. *In* Explorations and field work of the Smithsonian Institution in 1933, pp. 44–48.

1935 Archeological investigations in the Bay Islands, Spanish Honduras. *Smithsonian Misc. Coll.*, vol. 92, no. 14.

1947 Finding the tomb of a warrior-god. *Nat. Geog. Mag.*, 91: 453–82.

1948 The archeology of Honduras. *In* Handbook of South American Indians, 4: 71–120.

——— and C. Evans, Jr.

1952 Cultural stratigraphy in the Viru valley, northern Peru. *Columbia Studies in Archaeol. Ethnol.*, vol. 4.

———, A. Kidder II, and A. J. D. Paul, Jr.

1938 Preliminary report on the Smithsonian Institution–Harvard University archeological expedition to northwestern Honduras. *Smithsonian Misc. Coll.*, vol. 97, no. 1.

Stroup, M., M. MacIlroy, R. Walker, and J. V. Aydelotte

1965 Evidence that the Sutter belongs to the Kell blood group system. *Transfusion*, 5: 309–14.

Stuart, L. C.

1943 Taxonomic and geographic comments on Guatemalan salamanders of the genus *Oedipus*. *Univ. Michigan, Mus. Zool.*, Misc. Pub. 56.

1954 A description of a subhumid corridor across northern Central America, with comments on its herpetofaunal indicators. *Contrib. Lab. Vertebrate Biol., Univ. Michigan,* no. 65.

1954 Herpetofauna of the southeastern highlands of Guatemala. *Ibid.,* no. 68.

1956 El ambiente del hombre en Guatemala. *Seminario Integración Social en Guatemala,* Pub. 3, pp. 17–30.

1958 A study of the herpetofauna of the Uaxactun-Tikal area of northern El Peten, Guatemala. *Contrib. Lab. Vertebrate Biol., Univ. Michigan,* no. 75.

1963 A checklist of the herpetofauna of Guatemala. *Univ. Michigan Mus. Zool.,* Misc. Pub. 122.

STUDHALTER, R. A.
1936 *In* Studies of the Yaqui Indians of Sonora, Mexico. *Texas Tech. College Bull.,* vol. 12, no. 1.

STUDLEY, C. A.
1884 Notes upon human remains from caves in Coahuila. *Peabody Mus., Harvard Univ.,* 16th ann. rept., pp. 233–59.

STUIVER, M., E. S. DEEVEY, AND L. J. GRALENSKI
1960 Yale natural radiocarbon measurements, V. *Amer. Jour. Sci., Radiocarbon Suppl.,* 2: 49–61.

STURTEVANT, W. C.
1960 The significance of ethnological similarities between southeastern North America and the Antilles. *Yale Univ. Pub. Anthr.,* no. 64.

SUÁREZ, L.
1960 Pellicer denuncia: las palas mecánicas destruyen en Tabasco un cementerio maya del siglo 7. "Novedades" suplemento dominical México en la cultura, no. 592.

SUÁREZ DE PERALTA, J.
1878 Noticias históricas de la Nueva España. Madrid.

SUÁREZ ISLAS, J.
1935 Estudio sobre la herencia de la individualidad de la sangre en familias mexicanas. Mexico.

SUHM, D. A.
1959 Abstracts of papers, 24th ann. meeting of Soc. Amer. Archaeol.

——, A. D. KRIEGER, AND E. B. JELKS
1954 An introductory handbook of Texas archaeology. *Bull. Texas Archaeol. Soc.,* vol. 25.

SULLIVAN, L. R.
1917 Variations in glenoid fossae. *Amer. Anthr.,* 19: 19–23.

1920 The fossa faringea in American Indian crania. *Ibid.,* 22: 237–43.

1922 The frequency and distribution of some anatomical variations in American crania. *Amer. Mus. Natural Hist., Anthr. Papers,* 23: 203–58.

—— AND M. HELLMAN
1925 The Punin calvarium. *Ibid.,* 23: 309–37.

SUMA DE VISITAS
1905–06 Suma de visitas de pueblos por orden alfabético. *In* Paso y Troncoso, 1905–06, vol. 1.

SUMMA ANTHROPOLOGICA
1966 Summa anthropologica: en homenaje a Roberto J. Weitlaner. A. Pompa y Pompa, ed. Inst. Nac. Antr. Hist. Mexico.

SUMMER INSTITUTE OF LINGUISTICS
1960 Twenty-fifth anniversary bibliography. Glendale.

1964 Bibliography, February, 1964. Santa Ana, Calif.

SUSIA, M.
1961 The Morett sequence. Mimeographed. Dept. Anthropology, Univ. California, Los Angeles.

SUTTON, H. E., G. A. MATSON, A. R. ROBINSON, AND R. W. KOUCKY
1960 Distribution of haptoglobin, transferrin, and hemoglobin types among Indians of southern Mexico and Guatemala. *Amer. Jour. Human Genetics,* 12: 338–47.

SUZUKI, H.
1940 Ueber 3 neue Funde der Zackenfeilung. *Jour. Anthr. Soc. Tokyo,* 55 (637): 489–96.

SVERDRUP, H. U.
1941 The Gulf of California: preliminary discussion of the cruise of the *E. W. Scripps* in February and March,

1939. *Proc. 6th Pacific Sci. Cong.*, 3: 161–66.

1943 Oceanography for meteorologists. New York.

——, M. W. JOHNSON, AND R. H. FLEMING

1942 The oceans: their physics, chemistry, and general biology. New York.

SWADESH, M.

n.d. Kin terms common to Tarasco and Zuni. Inst. Hist., Univ. Nac. Autónoma Mex.

1940 Orientaciones lingüísticas para maestros en zonas indígenas. Depto. Asuntos Indígenas. Mexico.

1947 The phonemic structure of Proto-Zapotec. *Int. Jour. Amer. Ling.*, 13: 220–30.

1949 El idioma de los zapotecos. *In* Mendieta y Nuñez, 1949.

1951 Lexicostatistic dating of prehistoric contacts. *Proc. Amer. Phil. Soc.*, vol. 96.

1952 Salish phonologic geography. *Language*, 28: 232–48.

1953 The language of the archaeologic Huastecs. *Carnegie Inst. Wash., Notes Middle Amer. Archaeol. Ethnol.*, no. 114.

1954 On the Penutian vocabulary survey. *Int. Jour. Amer. Ling.*, 20: 123–33.

1954 Perspectives and problems of Amerindian comparative linguistics. *Word*, 10: 306–32.

1954 Algunas fechas glotocronológicas importantes para la prehistoria nahua. *Rev. Mex. Estud. Antr.*, 14: 173–92.

1955 Towards greater accuracy in lexicostatistic dating. *Int. Jour. Amer. Ling.*, 21: 121–37.

1956 Problems of long-range comparison in Penutian. *Language*, 32: 17–41.

1958 Some new glottochronologic dates for Amerindian linguistic groups. *32d Int. Cong. Amer.* (Copenhagen, 1956), Acta, pp. 671–74.

1959 La lingüística de las regiones entre las civilizaciones mesoamericanas y andinas. *33d Int. Cong. Amer.* (San Jose, 1958), Acta, 2: 551–59.

1959 Mapas de clasificación lingüística de México y las Américas. *Univ. Nac.*

Autónoma Mex., Inst. Hist., Pub. 51, Antr. Ser. no. 8.

1959 Indian linguistic groups of Mexico. Escuela Nac. Antr. Hist. Mexico.

1959 Linguistics as an instrument of prehistory. *SW. Jour. Anthr.*, 15: 20–35.

1959 The mesh principle in comparative linguistics. *Anthr. Ling.*, 1 (2): 7–14.

1960 La lingüística como instrumento de la prehistoria. *Inst. Nac. Antr. Hist.*, Pub. 9. Mexico.

1960 The Oto-Manguean hypothesis and Macro-Mixtecan. *Int. Jour. Amer. Ling.*, 26: 79–111.

1960 Tras la huella lingüística de la prehistoria. *Univ. Nac. Autónoma Mex., Cuad. Seminario de Problemas Cien. y Filo.*, no. 26.

1960 Algunos reflejos lingüísticos de la prehistoria de Chiapas. *Rev. Mex. Estud. Antr.*, 17: 145–59 [1961].

1960 Interrelaciones de las lenguas mayas. *An. Inst. Antr.*, 11: 231–67.

1960 Estudios sobre lengua y cultura. *Acta Antr.*, ep. 2, II–2.

1961 Interrelaciones de las lenguas mayas. *An. Inst. Nac. Antr. Hist.*, 13: 231–67.

1962 Nuevo ensayo de glotocronología Yutonahua. *Ibid.*, 15: 263–302.

1962 Afinidades de las lenguas amerindias. *34th Int. Cong. Amer.* (Vienna, 1960), Acta, 2: 729–38.

1964 Interim notes on Oaxacan phonology. *SW. Jour. Anthr.*, 20: 168–89.

1964 Algunos problemas de la lingüística otomangue. *An. Sección Antr.*, 1: 91–123.

1966 Porhé y maya. *Ibid.*, 3: 173–204.

1967 Lexicostatistic classification. *In* Handbook of Middle American Indians, R. Wauchope, ed., vol. 5, art. 4.

SWANTON, J. R.

1929 A point of resemblance between the ball game of the southeastern Indians and the ball games of Mexico and Central America. *Jour. Washington Acad. Sci.*, 19: 304–07.

1952 The Indian tribes of North America. *Smithsonian Inst., Bur. Amer. Ethnol.*, Bull. 145.

SWAUGER, J. L., AND W. J. MAYER-OAKES
1952 A fluted point from Costa Rica. *Amer. Antiquity*, 17: 264–65.

SYKES, G. G.
1937 The Colorado delta. *Carnegie Inst. Wash.*, Pub. 460.

T., J. A.
1946 Documentos en los cuales se refieren los sucesos ocurridos en Bluefields, República de Nicaragua en el año de 1894. *Rev. Acad. Geog. Hist. Nicaragua*, 8 (2): 49–68. Managua.

TABLADA, J. J.
1927 Historia del arte en México. Mexico.

TABOADO, E.
1962 Desarrollo cconómico integral de la cuenca del Grijalva: planeación agrícola. MS. Sec. Recursos Hidráulicos. Mexico.

TAMAYO, J. L.
1941 Morfología de la República Mexicana y división regional de la misma. *Rev. Geog.*, 1: 221–35.
1946 Datos para la hidrología de la República Mexicana. Mexico.
1949 Geografía general de México. 2 vols. and atlas. Mexico. (Rev. ed. 1960.)
1958 El aprovechamiento del agua y del suelo. Mexico.
1959 Geografía de América. 2d ed. Mexico.
1959 México y Centro América. *Geog. Universal*, vol. 18. Barcelona.
1960 Geografía moderna de México. Mexico.
1962 Atlas geográfico general de México, con cartas físicas, biológicas, demográficas, sociales, económicas y cartogramas. 2d ed. Inst. Mex. Invest. Económicas. Mexico.

TANNENBAUM, F.
1950 Mexico: the struggle for peace and bread. New York.

TAPIA, A. DE
1866 Relación hecha por el Sr. Andrés de Tapia, sobre la conquista de México. *In* García Icazbalceta, 1858–66, 2: 554–94.

TAPIA ZENTENO, C. DE
1753 Arte novissima de lengua mexicana. Mexico. (Mexico, 1885.)
1767 Noticia de la lengua huasteca. . . . Mexico.

TARAYRE, E. GUILLEMIN
See Guillemin Tarayre, E.

TASSIN, W.
1902 The Casas Grandes meteorite. *Nat. Mus.*, 25: 69–74. Washington.

TATUM, J. L.
1931 General geology of northeast Mexico. *Amer. Assoc. Petroleum Geol.*, Bull. 15, pp. 867–93.

TAX, SOL
1937 The municipios of the midwestern highlands of Guatemala. *Amer. Anthr.*, 39: 423–44.
1941 World view and social relations in Guatemala. *Ibid.*, 43: 27–42.
1944 Information about the municipio of Zinacantan, Chiapas. *Rev. Mex. Estud. Anthr.*, 6: 181–95.
1946 The towns of Lake Atitlan. *Univ. Chicago, Micro. Coll. MSS Middle Amer. Cult. Anthr.*, no. 13.
1947 Notes on Santo Tomas Chichicastenango. *Ibid.*, no. 16.
1947 Miscellaneous notes on Guatemala. *Ibid.*, no. 18.
1949 Folk tales in Chichicastenango: an unsolved puzzle. *Jour. Amer. Folklore*, 62: 125–35.
1950 Panajachel: field notes. *Univ. Chicago, Micro. Coll. MSS Middle Amer. Cult. Anthr.*, no. 29. (Contains autobiography of Santiago Yach from Panajachel.)
1951 [ed.] The civilizations of ancient America. Selected papers of the 29th Int. Cong. Amer. Chicago.
1952 [ed.] Heritage of conquest: the ethnology of Middle America. Viking Fund seminar on Middle American ethnology. Glencoe.
1952 [ed.] Acculturation in the Americas. Selected papers of the 29th Int. Cong. Amer. Chicago.
1952 Indian tribes of aboriginal America. *Ibid.*
1952 Economy and technology. *In his* 1952, Heritage, pp. 43–75.
1953 Penny capitalism: a Guatemalan Indian economy. *Smithsonian Inst., Inst. Social Anthr.*, Pub. 16.

1957 Changing consumption in Indian Guatemala. *Econ. Development and Cult. Change*, 5: 147–58.

1957 The Indians in the economy of Guatemala. *Univ. College of the West Indies, Inst. Social and Econ. Research, Social and Econ. Studies*, pp. 413–23. Jamaica.

1958 The Fox project. *Human Organization*, 17: 17–19.

1960 [ed.] Aboriginal languages of Latin America. *Current Anthr.*, 1: 430–38.

1960 Evolution after Darwin. Chicago.

1964 Cultural differences in the Maya area: a 20th century perspective. *In* Desarrollo cultural de los mayas, pp. 279–328.

TAX, SUSAN
1964 Displacement activity in Zinacantan. *Amer. Indig.*, 24: 111–21.

TAYLOR, D. M.
1951 The Black Carib of British Honduras. *Viking Fund Pub. Anthr.*, no. 17.

TAYLOR, E. H.
1951 A brief review of the snakes of Costa Rica. *Univ. Kansas Sci. Bull.*, 34: 3–188.

1952 The salamanders and caecilians of Costa Rica. *Ibid.*, 34: 695–791.

1952 The frogs and toads of Costa Rica. *Ibid.*, 35: 577–942.

1956 A review of the lizards of Costa Rica. *Ibid.*, 38: 3–322.

TAYLOR, H. C., JR.
1948 An archaeological reconnaissance in northern Coahuila. *Bull. Texas Archaeol. and Paleontol. Soc.*, 19: 74–87.

TAYLOR, H. M.
1933 Spur-of-the-rock: hero of the Mayo Indians. *Pub. Texas Folklore Soc.*, 11: 5–47.

TAYLOR, P. S.
1933 Making cántaros at San Jose Tateposco. *Amer. Anthr.*, 35: 745–51.

1933 A Spanish-Mexican peasant community: Arandas in Jalisco, Mexico. *Ibero-Amer.*, no. 4.

TAYLOR, W. P., W. B. McDOUGALL, C. C. PRESNALL, AND K. P. SCHMIDT
n.d. Preliminary ecological survey of the northern Sierra de Carmen, Coahuila, Mexico. Mimeographed. U.S. Dept. Interior, Fish and Wildlife Service.

TAYLOR, W. W.
n.d. The occupation and utilization of arid lands: ancient and modern cultures in north Mexico. Paper presented to Sec. Anthr., Illinois Acad. Sci., 1960.

1948 A study of archeology. *Amer. Anthr. Assoc.*, Mem. 69.

1956 Some implications of the Carbon-14 dates from a cave in Coahuila, Mexico. *Bull. Texas Archaeol. Soc.*, 27: 215–34.

1961 Archaeology and language in western North America. *Amer. Antiquity*, 27: 71–81.

1964 Tethered nomadism and water territoriality: an hypothesis. *35th Int. Cong. Amer.* (Mexico, 1962), Acta, pp. 197–203.

1968 A burial bundle from Coahuila, Mexico. *Papers Archaeol. Soc. New Mexico*, 1: 23–56. Santa Fe.

—— AND W. C. BOYD
1943 Blood groups of the prehistoric Indians of Coahuila by serological tests of their mummified remains. *Year Book Amer. Phil. Soc.*, 1943, pp. 178–80.

—— AND F. GONZÁLEZ RUL
1960 Archaeological reconnaissance behind the Diablo Dam, Coahuila, Mexico. *Bull. Texas Archaeol. Soc.*, vol. 31.

TEEPLE, J. E.
1930 Maya astronomy. *Carnegie Inst. Wash.*, Pub. 403, Contrib. 2.

TEILHARD DE CHARDIN, P.
1939 On the presumable existence of a world-wide sub-Arctic sheet of human culture at the dawn of the Neolithic. *Bull. Geol. Surv. China*, 19: 333–39. Peiping.

TEJADA VALENZUELA, C.
1955 Informe preliminar sobre hallazgos patológicos en el síndrome pluricarencial de la infancia en Guatemala. *Rev. Colegio Méd. Guatemala*, 6: 1–10.

1956 Desnutrición severa en la infancia:

III, Aspectos patológicos. *Ibid.*, 7: 235–57.

——, F. J. AGUILAR, AND L. N. FIGUEROA
1958 Leishmaniasis visceral (kala azar) en Guatemala. *Ibid.*, 9: 231–35.

——, M. BÉHAR, AND E. COFIÑO
1956 Estudio clínico-patológico de las bronconeumonías del niño desnutrido. *Ibid.*, 7: 134–41.

—— AND F. CASTRO
1958 Miocarditis crónica en Guatemala: estudio de 44 casos. *Ibid.*, 10: 63–85.

——, I. GORE, J. P. STRONG, AND H. C. McGILL
1958 Comparative severity of atherosclerosis in Costa Rica, Guatemala and New Orleans. *Circulation*, 18: 92–97.

——, C. LIZAMA, J. V. ORDÓÑEZ, AND F. CASTRO
1960 Blastomicosis Sur Americana: descripción de los dos primeros casos en Guatemala. *Rev. Colegio Méd. Guatemala*, 11: 7–13.

—— AND OTHERS
1959 (M. Sánchez, M. A. Guzmán, N. S. Scrimshaw, and E. Bregni). Blood groups in Mayan populations. *Records Genetics Soc. Amer.*, 28: 542 (abstr.); *Genetics*, 44: 542 (abstr.).
1961 (M. Sánchez, M. A. Guzmán, E. Bregni, and N. S. Scrimshaw). Distribution of blood antigens among Guatemalan Indians. *Human Biol.*, 33: 319–34.

TEJEDA, A.
1947 Drawings of Tajumulco sculptures. *Carnegie Inst. Wash., Notes Middle Amer. Archaeol. Ethnol.*, no. 77.

TELETOR, C. N.
n.d. Compendio de la doctrina cristiana en lengua quiché y castellano. Guatemala.
1942 Breve manual de conversación quiché. Guatemala.
1943 Toponimia guatemalteca. *An. Soc. Geog. Hist. Guatemala*, 19 (2): 116–24.
1945 Bailes que representan los indígenas en Baja Verapaz. *Ibid.*, 20: 51–56.
1949 Algunos apuntes sobre Rabinal, Baja Verapaz, y algo sobre fonética del dialecto Quiché. *Ibid.*, 24 (3–4): 208–19.

1955 Algunos para una monografía de Rabinal (Baja Verapaz) y algo de nuestro folklore. Guatemala.
1959 Diccionario castellano-quiché y voces castellano-pokoman. Guatemala.

TELKKA, A.
1950 On the prediction of human stature from the long bones. *Acta Anatomica*, 9: 103–17.

TELLECHEA, M.
1826 Compendio gramatical para la inteligencia del idioma tarahumar. . . . Mexico.

TELLO, A.
1650 Fragmentos de una historia de la Nueva Galicia escrita hacia 1650. *In* García Icazbalceta, 1858–66.
1891 Libro segundo de la crónica miscelánea. . . . Guadalajara.

TEMPSKY, G. F. VON
1858 Mitla: a narrative of incidents and personal adventure. London.

TEN KATE, H. F. C.
1883 Mesures d'indiens Papagos: indices céphaliques. *Rev. Ethnog.*, 2: 90–91. Paris.
1883 Quelques observations ethnographiques recueillies dans la presqu'île Californienne et en Sonora. *Ibid.*, 2: 321–26.
1883 Les Indiens de la presqu'île de la Californie et de l'Arizona. *Bull. Soc. Anthr. Paris*, ser. 3, 6: 374–76.
1883 Indiens de la Sonora et de l'Arizona. *Ibid.*, ser. 3, 6: 634–37.
1884 Materiaux pour servir à l'anthropologie de la presqu'île Californienne. *Ibid.*, ser. 3, 7: 551–69. (Spanish tr. in *An. Mus. Nac. Mex.*, ep. 1, 4: 5–16.)
1884 La collection Strebel à Hamburg. *Rev. Ethnog.*, 3: 456. Paris.
1892 Somatological observations on Indians of the southwest. *Jour. Amer. Ethnol. Archaeol.*, 3: 119–44. Boston.
1905 Die blauen Geburtsflecke. *Globus*, 87: 53–58. Brunswick.
1911 Observations au sujet des "Recherches anthropologiques sur la Basse Californie" by Dr. Rivet. *L'Anthropologie*, 22: 37–40. Paris.

1911 Encore l'anthropologie de la Basse Californie. *Ibid.*, 22: 374–75.

1917 Mélanges anthropologiques: Indiens de l'Amérique du Nord. *Ibid.*, 28: 129–55, 369–401.

TENAYUCA

1935 Tenayuca: estudio arqueológico de la pirámide de este lugar. Sec. Educación Pública, Depto. Monumentos. Mexico.

TEOTIHUACÁN

1966 Teotihuacán. Onceava mesa redonda: El Valle de Teotihuacán y su contorno. Soc. Mex. Antr. Mexico.

TEPEXPAN MAN

1949 *See* De Terra, Romero, and Stewart, 1949.

TERMER, F.

1927 Observaciones geográficas en los Altos Cuchumatanes. *An. Soc. Geog. e Hist. de Guatemala*, 4: 7–13.

1930 Über die Mayasprache von Chicomucelo. *23d Int. Cong. Amer.* (New York, 1928), Acta, pp. 926–36.

1930 Los bailes de culebra entre los indios quichés en Guatemala. *Ibid.*, pp. 661–67.

1930 Zur Ethnologie und Ethnographie des nördlichen Mittel-Amerika. *Ibero-Amer. Archiv*, 4: 303–492.

1930 Archäologische Studien und Beobachtungen in Guatemala in den Jahren 1925–29. *Tagungsberichte der Gesellschaft für Völkerkunde*, pp. 85–102.

1931 Zur Archäologie von Guatemala. *Baessler Archiv*, 14: 167–91.

1931–36 Der Palo de Volador in Guatemala. *El Mex. Antiguo*, 3: 13–23.

1932 Geologie von Nordwest-Guatemala. *Zeit. Gesellschaft für Erdkunde zu Berlin*, pp. 241–48.

1933 Paisajes geográficos del norte de América Central. *Bol. Soc. Geog. Nac.*, 60: 19–34, 92–103.

1936 Zur Geographie der Republik Süd-Guatemala. *Mitt. Geog. Gesellschaft in Hamburg*, 44: 89–275.

1936 Die Bedeutung der Pipiles für die Kulturgestaltung in Guatemala. *Baessler Archiv*, 19: 108–13.

1948 Récit d'un voyage archéologique dans le sud-est de la République de Guatemala. *28th Int. Cong. Amer.* (Paris, 1947), Acta, pp. 511–28.

1950 La densidad de población en los imperios Mayas como problema arqueológico y geográfico. *Bol. Soc. Mex. Geog. y Estad.*, 70: 211–39.

1951 The density of population in the southern and northern Maya empires as an archaeological and geographical problem. *In* Tax, 1951, pp. 101–07.

1952 Die Mayaforschung. *Nova Acta Leopoldina*, 15: 93–164.

1954 Die Halbinsel Yucatan. *Petermanns Mitt.*, Ergänzungsheft 253.

1957 Etnología y etnografía de Guatemala. Seminario de Integración Social Guatemalteca. Guatemala. (Tr. of his 1930.)

TERMIER, H., AND G. TERMIER

1958 The geological drama. New York.

1960 Atlas de paléogéographie. Paris.

TERNAUX-COMPANS, H., ed.

1837–41 Voyages, relations et mémoires originaux pour servir à l'histoire de la découverte de l'Amérique: recueil de pièces relatives à la conquête du Mexique. 20 vols. Paris.

TERRES, J.

1893 Algunas consideraciones acerca de la medición. Mexico.

TERRY, R. A.

1956 A geological reconnaissance of Panama. *California Acad. Sci. Occasional Papers*, no. 23.

TESTUT, L.

1932 Tratado de anatomía humana. Vol. 1. 6th ed. Barcelona.

TEZOZOMOC, H. A.

See Alvarado Tezozomoc, H.

THAELER, A. D., JR., J. ARNOLD, AND A. S. ALVING

1953 A clinical study of primaquine in the treatment of malaria among the Miskito Indians of Nicaragua. *Amer. Jour. Tropical Med.*, 2: 989–99.

THAYER, W. H.

1916 The physiography of Mexico. *Jour. Geol.*, 24: 61–94.

THIEME, F. P.

1951 An anatomical relationship predisposing to lumbo-sacral fusion. *Amer. Jour. Physical Anthr.*, 9: 149–58.

THIEME, P.
1958   The Indo-European language. *Sci. Amer.* (October), pp. 63–74.

THOMAS, C.
1902   Provisional list of linguistic families, languages and dialects of Mexico and Central America. *Amer. Anthr.*, 4: 207–16.

—— AND J. R. SWANTON
1911   Indian languages of Mexico and Central America and their geographical distribution. *Smithsonian Inst., Bur. Amer. Ethnol.*, Bull. 44.

THOMAS, N. D.
1967   The nexus of envy, witchcraft, and ceremonial organization in a Zoque Indian pueblo. Doctoral dissertation, Univ. California, Berkeley.

THOMPSON, A. H.
1904   Ethnographic odontography: some Mexican tribes. *Dental Digest*, 10: 658–86.

1904   Ethnographic odontography: the Mound Builders and pre-Indian people of the Mississippi Valley. *Fourth Int. Dental Cong.*, no. 1.

1904   The variations of the molars among the ancient Peruvians, Mexicans and Mound Builders. *Dental Brief*, 9: 771–88.

1906   Dental lesions among the ancient Peruvians, Mexicans and Mound Builders. *Ibid.*, vol. 11.

THOMPSON, D. E.
1954   Maya paganism and Christianity: a history of the fusion of two religions. *Tulane Univ., Middle Amer. Research Inst.*, Pub. 19, pp. 1–36.

—— AND J. E. S. THOMPSON
1955   A noble's residence and its dependencies at Mayapan. *Carnegie Inst. Wash., Current Reports*, no. 25.

THOMPSON, E. H.
1892   The ancient structures of Yucatan not communal dwellings. *Proc. Amer. Antiquarian Soc.*, 8: 262–69.

1895   Ancient tombs of Palenque. *Amer. Anthr. Soc.*, 10: 418–21.

1897   Explorations in the cave of Loltun,

Yucatan. *Mem. Peabody Mus., Harvard Univ.*, vol. 1, no. 2.

1897   The chultunes of Labna, Yucatan. *Ibid.*, vol. 1, no. 3.

1898   Ruins of Xkichmook, Yucatan. *Field Columbian Mus., Anthr. Ser.*, 2: 209–29.

1904   Archaeological researches in Yucatan. *Mem. Peabody Mus., Harvard Univ.*, vol. 3, no. 1.

1938   The high priest's grave, Chichen Itza, Yucatan, Mexico. Prepared for publication, with notes and introduction, by J. E. S. Thompson. *Field Mus. Natural Hist., Anthr. Ser.*, vol. 27, no. 1.

1957   *See* Tozzer, 1957, pp. 194–96.

THOMPSON, J. E. S.
1927   The civilization of the Mayas. *Field Mus. Natural Hist., Anthr. Leafl.*, no. 25.

1928   Some new dates from Pusilha. *Man*, vol. 28, no. 70.

1929   Comunicaciones y comercio de los antiguos Mayas. *An. Soc. Geog. e Hist. de Guatemala*, 6: 40–44.

1930   Ethnology of the Mayas of southern and central British Honduras. *Field Mus. Natural Hist., Anthr. Ser.*, 17: 23–214.

1931   Archaeological investigations in the southern Cayo district, British Honduras. *Ibid.*, vol. 17, no. 3.

1932   The humming bird and the flower. *Maya Soc. Quar.*, 1: 120–22.

1932   Some jade-inlaid teeth of ancient Mayas. *Field Mus. News*, vol. 3, no. 3.

1933   Mexico before Cortez. New York.

1934   Sky bearers, colors and directions in Maya and Mexican religion. *Carnegie Inst. Wash.*, Pub. 436, Contrib. 10.

1935   Maya chronology: the correlation question. *Ibid.*, Pub. 456, Contrib. 14.

1936   The civilization of the Mayas. *Field Mus. Natural Hist., Anthr. Leafl.*, no. 25. 3d ed.

1937   A new method of deciphering Yucatecan dates, with special reference to

Chichen Itza. *Carnegie Inst. Wash.*, Pub. 483, Contrib. 22.

1938 Sixteenth and seventeenth century reports on the Chol Mayas. *Amer. Anthr.*, 40: 584–604.

1939 Excavations at San Jose, British Honduras. *Carnegie Inst. Wash.*, Pub. 506.

1939 The moon goddess in Middle America, with notes on related deities. *Ibid.*, Pub. 509, Contrib. 29.

1940 Late ceramic horizons at Benque Viejo, British Honduras. *Ibid.*, Pub. 528, Contrib. 35.

1941 Apuntes sobre las supersticiones de los Mayas de Socotz, Honduras Británica. *In* Los Mayas antiguos, pp. 101–10.

1941 Dating of certain inscriptions of non-Maya origin. *Carnegie Inst. Wash.*, *Theoretical Approaches to Problems*, no. 1.

1941 Maya arithmetic. *Ibid.*, Pub. 528, Contrib. 36.

1941 Yokes or ball game belts? *Amer. Antiquity*, 6: 320–26.

1942 Las llamadas "Fachadas de Quetzalcouatl." *27th Int. Cong. Amer.* (Mexico, 1939), Acta, 1: 391–400.

1943 A trial survey of the southern Maya area. *Amer. Antiquity*, 9: 106–34.

1943 A figurine whistle representing a ball-game player. *Carnegie Inst. Wash.*, *Notes Middle Amer. Archaeol. Ethnol.*, no. 25.

1943 Some sculptures from southeastern Quezaltenango, Guatemala. *Ibid.*, no. 17.

1943 Representations of Tlalchitonatiuh at Chichen Itza, Yucatan, and at El Baul, Escuintla. *Ibid.*, no. 19.

1943 Pitfalls and stimuli in the interpretation of history through loan words. *Tulane Univ.*, *Middle Amer. Research Inst.*, *Philol. and Documentary Studies*, vol. 1, no. 2.

1945 A survey of the northern Maya area. *Amer. Antiquity*, 11: 2–24.

1946 Tattooing and scarification among the Maya. *Carnegie Inst. Wash.*, *Notes Middle Amer. Archaeol. Ethnol.*, no. 63.

1948 An archaeological reconnaissance in the Cotzumalhuapa region, Escuintla, Guatemala. *Ibid.*, Pub. 574, Contrib. 44.

1949 Tentativa de reconocimiento en el área maya meridional. *Antr. Hist. Guatemala*, 1 (2): 23–48.

1950 Maya hieroglyphic writing: introduction. *Carnegie Inst. Wash.*, Pub. 589. (2d ed. 1960, Univ. Oklahoma Press.)

1951 Canoes and navigation of the Maya and their neighbors. *Jour. Royal Anthr. Inst.*, 79: 69–78.

1951 The Itza of Tayasal, Peten. *In* Homenaje Caso, pp. 389–400.

1952 The introduction of Puuc style of dating at Yaxchilan. *Carnegie Inst. Wash.*, *Notes Middle Amer. Archaeol. Ethnol.*, no. 110.

1952 La inscripción jeroglífica del tablero de El Palacio, Palenque. *An. Inst. Nac. Antr. Hist.*, 4: 61–68.

1953 Relaciones entre Veracruz y la región maya. *Rev. Mex. Estud. Antr.*, 13: 447–54.

1954 The rise and fall of Maya civilization. Univ. Oklahoma Press.

1954 Memoranda on some dates at Palenque, Chiapas. *Carnegie Inst. Wash.*, *Notes Middle Amer. Archaeol. Ethnol.*, no. 120.

1954 A presumed residence of the nobility at Mayapan. *Ibid.*, *Current Reports*, no. 19.

1956 Notes on the use of cacao in Middle America. *Ibid.*, *Notes Middle Amer. Archaeol. Ethnol.*, no. 128.

1957 Deities portrayed on censers at Mayapan. *Ibid.*, *Current Reports*, no. 40.

1958 Research in Maya hieroglyphic writing. *Pan Amer. Union, Social Sci. Monogr.*, no. 5, pp. 43–52.

1958 Symbols, glyphs, and divinatory almanacs for diseases in the Maya Dresden and Madrid codices. *Amer. Antiquity*, 23: 297–308.

1959 La civilización maya. Mexico.

1959 Systems of hieroglyphic writing in Middle America and methods of deciphering them. *Amer. Antiquity*, 24: 349–64.

1959 The role of caves in Maya culture. *In* Bierhenke, 1959, pp. 122–29.

1960 Maya hieroglyphic writing. 2d ed., with original pagination, new preface, and additional bibliography. Univ. Oklahoma Press. (*See* his 1950.)

1961 A blood-drawing ceremony painted on a Maya vase. *Univ. Nac. Autónoma Mex., Estud. Cultura Maya,* vol. 1.

1961 Investigaciones en la escritura jeroglífica maya. *Bol. Centro Invest. Antr. Mex.,* 11: 3–12.

1962 A catalog of Maya hieroglyphs. Univ. Oklahoma Press.

——, H. E. D. POLLOCK, AND J. CHARLOT
1932 A preliminary study of the ruins of Coba, Quintana Roo, Mexico. *Carnegie Inst. Wash.,* Pub. 424.

THOMPSON, L.
1950 Culture in crisis: a study of the Hopi Indians. New York.

THOMPSON, M. L., AND A. K. MILLER
1944 The Permian of southernmost Mexico and its fusulinid fauna. *Jour. Paleontol.,* 18: 481–504.

THOMPSON, R. H.
1958 [ed.] Migrations in New World culture history. *Univ. Arizona, Social Sci. Bull.,* no. 27.

1958 Modern Yucatecan Maya pottery making. *Soc. Amer. Archaeol.,* Mem. 15.

THORADE, H.
1909 Über die Kalifornische Meeresstromung. Oberflächentemperaturen und Strömungen an der Westküste Nordamerikas. *Ann. Hydrog. und Mar. Meteorol.,* 37: 17–34, 63–76.

THORPE, J., AND G. D. SMITH
1949 Higher categories of soil classification: order, suborder, and great soil groups. *Soil Sci.,* 67: 117–26.

THOULET, M. J.
1898 Oceanography. *Smithsonian Inst.,* ann. rept., pp. 407–25.

THWAITES, R. G.
1905 The personal narrative of James O. Pattie of Kentucky. *In* Early western travels, 1784–1846, vol. 18.

TIBÓN, G.
1960 Olinalá. Mexico.

1961 Pinotepa nacional: mixtecos, negros y triques. *Univ. Nac. Autónoma Mex.,* pp. 129–54.

TILDESLEY, M. L.
1927 Determination of the cranial capacity of the Negro from measurements of the skull or the living head. *Biometrika,* 19: 204–06.

—— AND N. DATTA-MAJUMDER
1944 Cranial capacity: comparative data on the techniques of Macdonell and Breitinger. *Amer. Jour. Physical Anthr.,* n.s., 2: 233–49.

TIPPETT, P. A., R. SANGER, I. DUNSFORD, AND M. BARBER
1961 An Rh gene complex, r^M, in some ways like r^G. *Vox Sanguinis,* 6: 21–33.

TÍTULO DE TIERRAS . . . SANTA ISABEL TOLA
1897 Título de tierras del pueblo de Santa Isabel Tola. Manuscrito americano no. 4 de la Biblioteca Real de Berlin. *In* Peñafiel, 1897–1903, vol. 1.

TÍTULOS DE LA CASA IXQUIN-NEHAIB
1957 Títulos de la casa Ixquin-Nehaib, señora del territorio de Otzoyá. *In* Recinos, 1957, pp. 71–94.

TIZIMIN, CHILAM BALAM DE
1870 Manuscript. Photograph in Newberry Library. 55 pp.

TLALOCAN
1943–57 A journal of source materials on the native cultures of Mexico. 3 vols. Sacramento, Calif., and Azcapotzalco, Mexico.

TODD, T. W.
1927 Skeletal records of mortality. *Sci. Monthly* (June), pp. 481–96.

TOKYO SCIENTIFIC EXPEDITION
1960 Andes. Rept. Univ. Tokyo Sci. Expedition to the Andes, 1958. Tokyo.

TOLSTOY, P.
1953 Some Amerasian pottery traits in north Asian prehistory. *Amer. Antiquity,* 19: 25–39.

1958 Surface survey of the northern valley of Mexico: the classic and post-classic periods. *Trans. Amer. Phil. Soc.,* vol. 48, pt. 5.

1958 The archaeology of the Lena basin and its New World relationships.

Part 1: *Amer. Antiquity*, 23: 397–418; part 2: *ibid.*, 24: 63–81.

—— AND A. GUÉNETTE
1965 Le placement de Tlatilco dans le cadre du pré-classique du bassin de Mexico. *Jour. Soc. Amer. Paris*, 54: 47–91.

—— AND L. PARADIS
1970 Early and middle preclassic cultures in the basin of Mexico. *Science*, 167: 344–51.

TONALAMATL AUBIN
1900 Tonalamatl de Aubin. Collection de M. E. E. Goupil. Loubat ed. Paris. (See Seler, 1900.)

TOOR, F.
1925 The passion play at Tzintzuntzan. *Mex. Folkways*, 1: 21–25.
1926 I am cured of fright. *Ibid.*, 2: 31–32.
1928 Gentes y escuelas de la sierra de Juárez. *Ibid.*, 4: 119–29.
1939 Mexican popular arts. Mexico.
1947 [ed.] A treasury of Mexican folkways. New York.

TOPINARD, P.
1874–75 Sur les deux microcéphales présentés à la société. *Bull. Soc. Anthr. Paris*, ser. 2, 9: 826–29; 10: 36–39.
1884 L'Anthropologie. Bibliothèque des Sciences Contemporaines. Paris.
1885 Eléments d'anthropologie générale. Paris.

TOQUERO, R.
1946 Los zapotecas, los "beniguelaza." *Ex-Alumnos*, 2 (75): 5–6.

TORO, A.
1922 Influencia de la raza negra en la formación del pueblo mexicano. *Ethnos*, ep. 1, 1: 215–18. Mexico.
1924–27 Una creencia totémica de los zapotecas. *El Mex. Antiguo*, 2: 123–28.

TORQUEMADA, J. DE
1723 Los veinte i un libros rituales i monarchía indiana. . . . 2d ed. 3 vols. Madrid. (1st ed. 1615, Seville; 3d ed. 1943–44, Mexico; 4th ed. 1964, Mexico.)

TORRE VILLAR, E. DE LA
1952 Las reducciones de los pueblos de Indios en la Nueva España. Mexico.
1960 El arte prehispánico y sus primeros críticos europeos. *In* Homenaje García Granados, pp. 259–318.

TORRESANO, E.
1754 Arte de la lengua kakchiquel. . . . MS in Bibliothèque Nationale.

TOSCANO, S.
1940 La pintura mural precolombina en México. *Bol. Bibliográfico Antr. Amer.*, 4: 37–51.
1944 Arte precolombino de México y de la América Central. Univ. Nac. Autónoma Méx., Inst. Invest. Estéticas. (2d ed. 1952.)
1945 Informe sobre la existencia de jugadores de pelota mayas en la cerámica escultórica de Jaina. *Carnegie Inst. Wash., Notes Middle Amer. Archaeol. Ethnol.*, no. 54.
1946 El arte antiguo. *In* México y la cultura, pp. 81–163.
1947 Mitos y leyendas del antiguo México. *Biblioteca Enciclopédica Popular*, no. 182. Mexico.
1951 Codices Tlapanecas de Azoyu. *Cuad. Amer.*, 10: 4.

TOTTEN, G. O.
1926 Maya architecture. Washington.

TOUSSAINT, M.
1931 Taxco: su historia, sus monumentos, características actuales y posibilidades turísticas. Mexico.
1942 Pátzcuaro. Mexico.
1948 La conquista de Pánuco. Mexico.

——, F. GÓMEZ DE OROZCO, AND J. FERNÁNDEZ
1938 Planos de la Ciudad de México, siglos XVI y XVII: estudio histórico, urbanístico y bibliográfico. Inst. Invest. Estéticas. Mexico.

TOVAR, A.
1954 Linguistics and prehistory. *Word*, 10: 333–50.

TOVAR, J. DE
1944 Códice Ramírez. Manuscrito del siglo XVI intitulado: Relación del origen de los indios que habitan esta Nueva España, según sus historias. Mexico.

TOVAR CALENDAR
1951 See Kubler and Gibson, 1951.
TOWER, D. B.
1945 The use of marine Mollusca and their value in reconstructing prehistoric trade routes in the American Southwest. *Papers Excavators Club*, vol. 2, no. 3.
TOWLE, M. A.
1952 The pre-Columbian occurrence of Lagenaria seeds in coastal Peru. *Bot. Mus. Leafl., Harvard Univ.*, 15: 171–84.
TOWNSEND, C. H.
1901 Dredging and other records of the U.S. Fish Commission steamer *Albatross*. *Rept. U.S. Comm. Fish and Fisheries* (1900), pp. 387–562.
TOZZER, A. M.
1907 A comparative study of the Mayas and the Lacandones. New York.
1911 A preliminary study of the prehistoric ruins of Tikal, Guatemala. *Mem. Peabody Mus., Harvard Univ.*, vol. 5, no. 2.
1913 A preliminary study of the ruins of Nakum, Guatemala. *Ibid.*, vol. 5, no. 3.
1913 A Spanish manuscript letter on the Lacandones in the archives of the Indies in Seville. *18th Int. Cong. Amer.* (London, 1912), Acta, 2: 497–509.
1921 A Maya grammar, with bibliography and appraisement of the works noted. *Papers Peabody Mus., Harvard Univ.*, vol. 9.
1921 Excavation of a site at Santiago Ahuitzotla, D. F., Mexico. *Smithsonian Inst., Bur. Amer. Ethnol.*, Bull. 74.
1930 Maya and Toltec figures at Chichen Itza. *23d Int. Cong. Amer.* (New York, 1928), Acta, pp. 155–64.
1941 [ed.] Landa's Relación de las cosas de Yucatan. Tr. and ed. with notes. *Papers Peabody Mus., Harvard Univ.*, vol. 18.
1941 Stephens and Prescott, Bancroft and others. *In* Los Mayas antiguos, pp. 35–60.
1957 Chichen Itza and its cenote of sacrifice: a comparative study of contemporaneous Maya and Toltec. *Mem. Peabody Mus., Harvard Univ.*, vols. 11, 12.
—— AND G. M. ALLEN
1910 Animal figures in the Maya codices. *Papers Peabody Mus., Harvard Univ.*, vol. 4, no. 3.
TREASURY OF MEXICAN FOLKWAYS, A
1947 See Toor, 1947.
TREGANZA, A. E.
1942 An archaeological reconnaissance of northeastern Baja California and southeastern California. *Amer. Antiquity*, 8: 152–63.
1947 Notes on the San Dieguito lithic industry of southern California and northern Baja California. *In* Heizer and Lemert, 1947, pp. 253–55.
TREND, J. B.
1953 The language and history of Spain. London.
TRENS, M. B.
1942 Historia de Chiapas: desde los tiempos más remotos hasta la caída del segundo imperio. Mexico. (2d ed. 1957.)
1947 Historia de Veracruz. 2 vols. Jalapa.
TREUTLEIN, T.
1949 Sonora: a description of a province. Albuquerque.
TREVOR, J. C.
1950 Anthropometry. Chambers's Encyclopaedia.
TRIK, A. S.
1939 Temple XXII at Copan. *Carnegie Inst. Wash.*, Pub. 509, Contrib. 27.
TRIMBORN, H.
1959 Das alte Amerika. Stuttgart.
TROIKE, N. P.
1962 Archaeological reconnaissance in the drainage of the Rio Verde, San Luis Potosi, Mexico. *Bull. Texas Archaeol. Soc.*, 32: 47–55.
TROLL, C.
1952 Das Pflanzenkleid der Tropen in seiner Abhängigkeit von Klima, Boden und Mensch. *Deutscher Geog. Frankfurt, 1951*, Tagungsber. und wiss. Abh., Remagen, pp. 35–56.

235

TROTTER, M.
1930 The form, size, and color of head hair in American Whites. *Amer. Jour. Physical Anthr.*, 14: 433–45.
1934 Septal apertures in the humerus of American Whites and Negroes. *Ibid.*, 19: 213–27.
1943 Hair from Paracas Indian mummies. *Ibid.*, n.s., 1: 69–75.
—— AND H. L. DAWSON
1934 The hair of French Canadians. *Ibid.*, 18: 443–56.
—— AND G. GLESER
1951 Trends in stature of American Whites and Negroes born between 1840 and 1924. *Ibid.*, n.s., 9: 427–40.
1952 Estimation of stature from long bones of American Whites and Negroes. *Ibid.*, n.s., 10: 463–514.
1958 A re-evaluation of estimation of stature based on measurements of stature taken during life and of long bones after death. *Ibid.*, n.s., 16: 79–123.

TUAN, YI-FU
1960 Coastal land forms of central Panama. Rept. field work carried out under ONR Contract 222(11) NR 388 067. Univ. California, Dept. Geography.

TUMIN, M.
1945 Culture, genuine and spurious: a re-evaluation. *Amer. Sociol. Rev.*, 10: 199–207.
1945 Some fragments from the life history of a marginal man. *Character and Personality*, 13: 261–95.
1946 San Luis Jilotepeque: a Guatemalan pueblo. *Univ. Chicago, Micro. Coll. MSS Middle Amer. Cult. Anthr.*, no. 2.
1949 Reciprocity and stability of caste in Guatemala. *Amer. Sociol. Rev.*, 14: 17–25.
1950 The dynamics of cultural discontinuity in a peasant society. *Social Forces*, 29: 135–41.
1950 The hero and the scapegoat in a peasant community. *Jour. Personality*, 19: 197–211.
1952 Caste in a peasant society: a case study in the dynamics of caste. Princeton Univ. Press.

1956 Cultura, casta y clase en Guatemala: una nueva evaluación. Seminario de Integración Social Guatemalteca. Guatemala.
1958 [ed.] Values in action: a symposium. *Human Organization*, 17: 2–26.

TUOHY, D. R., AND W. C. MASSEY
n.d. Coiled basketry from central Baja California and its affiliations. MS.

TURNER, J. K.
1911 Barbarous Mexico. Chicago.

TURNER, P. L., AND D. L. OLMSTED
1966 Tequistlatecan kinship and limitations on the choice of spouse. *Ethnology*, 5: 245–50.

TYLOR, E. B.
1861 Anahuac, or Mexico, and the Mexicans, ancient and modern. London.
1879 On the game of patolli in ancient Mexico, and its probable Asiatic origin. *Jour. Anthr. Inst. Great Britain and Ireland*, 8: 116–29.
1896 On American lot-games, as evidence of Asiatic intercourse before the time of Columbus. *Internat. Archiv für Ethnog.*, suppl. to vol. 9, pp. 55–67.

UGARTE, S.
1954 Catálogo de obras escritas en lengua indígena de México o que tratan de ella. Mexico.

UHLE, M.
1906 Bericht über die Ergebnisse meiner Südamerikanischen Reise. *14th Int. Cong. Amer.* (Stuttgart, 1904), Acta, pp. 567–79.
1922 Influencias mayas en el alto Ecuador. *Bol. Acad. Nac. Hist.*, 4: 205–40.
1923 Civilizaciones mayöides de la costa pacífica de Sudamérica. *Ibid.*, 6: 87–92.
1923 Toltecas, Mayas y civilizaciones sudamericanas. *Ibid.*, 7: 1–33.
1927 Estudios Esmeraldeños. *An. Univ. Central*, 39: 1–61. Quito.
1931 Las antiguas civilizaciones de Manta. *Bol. Acad. Nac. Hist.*, 12: 5–72.

ULLMANN, S.
1953 Descriptive semantics and linguistic typology. *Word*, 9: 225–40.

ULLOA, F.
1925 Memorial and relation . . . to isla de la Cedros (1540). *In* Wagner, 1925.

UMAÑA ARAGÓN, R.
1959 Cirrosis hepática en Guatemala. Tesis de médico y cirujano, Facultad
Cien. Méd., Univ. San Carlos de
Guatemala.

UMEHARA, S.
1936 Étude des bronzes des royaumes com-
battants. Kyoto.

UNDERHILL, R. M.
1938 A Papago calendar record. Univ.
New Mexico Press.
1939 Social organization of the Papago
Indians. *Columbia Univ., Contrib.
Anthr.*, vol. 30.
1940 The Papago Indians of Arizona and
their relatives, the Pima. Haskell
Inst. Lawrence, Kansas.
1946 Papago Indian religion. *Columbia
Univ., Contrib. Anthr.*, vol. 33.
1948 Ceremonial patterns in the greater
southwest. *Amer. Ethnol. Soc.*,
Monogr. 13.
1954 Intercultural relations in the greater
southwest. *Amer. Anthr.*, 56: 645–
62.

UNITED NATIONS
1949 Fundamental education: a description and programme. *Educational,
Scientific, and Cultural Organization,
Monogr. Fundamental Education*,
no. 1.
1954 The population of Central America
(including Mexico), 1950–1980.
*Dept. Economic and Social Affairs,
Population Studies*, no. 16.
1956 Methods for population projections
by age and sex. *Ibid.*, no. 18.

UNITED STATES BUREAU OF COMMERCIAL FISH-
ERIES, SAN DIEGO LABORATORY
1960 [Monthly] Sea-surface temperature
charts, eastern Pacific Ocean. (Continued in California Fishery Market
News Monthly Summary, part 2,
Fishing Information.)

UNITED STATES COAST AND GEODETIC SURVEY
1915 Pacific coast tide tables for western
North America, eastern Asia, and
many island groups for the year
1916. General Tide Tables.
1956 Surface water temperatures at tide
stations: Pacific coast of North and

South America and Pacific Ocean
islands. Special Pub. 280. 5th ed.
1957 Density of sea water at tide stations:
Pacific coast of North and South
America and Pacific Ocean islands.
Pub. 31–4. 5th ed.

UNITED STATES DEPARTMENT OF AGRICULTURE
1869 The ni-in of Yucatan. *In* Rept. to
40th Cong., 3d Sess. (1868–1869),
pp. 268–71.
1938 Soils and men. Yearbook.

UNITED STATES GEOLOGICAL SURVEY
1954 Compilation of records of surface
waters of the United States through
September 1950. *Water-Supply Paper 1313*.
1958 Surface water supply of the United
States, 1956. *Water-Supply Paper
1434, 1441, 1442*.

UNITED STATES HYDROGRAPHIC OFFICE
1947 Atlas of surface currents: northeastern Pacific Ocean. Pub. 570.
1951 Sailing directions: west coast of
Mexico and Central America. Pub.
84. 9th ed.

UNITED STATES WEATHER BUREAU
1930–52 Climatological data, West Indies
and Caribbean service.
1947 Weather summary, West Indies.
Hydrographic Office, Pub. 530.
1948 Weather summary, Central America.
Ibid., Pub. 531.
1949 Weather summary, Mexico. *Ibid.*,
Pub. 532.
1955–60 Climatological data. National
Summary, vols. 6–11.
1959 World weather records, 1941–50.

UPSON, J.
1956 Some Chatino riddles analyzed. *Int.
Jour. Amer. Ling.*, 22: 113–16.
1960 A preliminary structure of Chatino.
Anthr. Ling., 2: 22–29.

U'REN, M. R.
1940 From Coatzacoalcos to Salina Cruz.
Mex. Life, 16(5): 24–26, 41–42.

URIBE Y TRONCOSO, M.
1911 Antropometría escolar. *Bol. Instrucción Pública*, 16: 1031–35. Mexico.
1912 Reseña de la organización del Servicio
Higiénico Escolar en el Distrito Federal y sus resultados. *Gaceta Méd.
Méx.*, 7: 331–449.

1912 Informe de los trabajos efectuados por el Servicio Higiénico de la Escuelas, durante el años 1910 y 1911. *An. Higiene Escolar*, 2: 40–42. Mexico.

1917 Resultados de la inspección médica en las escuelas del Distrito Federal durante los últimos cinco años. *Mem. Soc. Cien. Antonio Alzate*, 34: 97–113. Mexico.

URRUTIA RUBIO, G.
1958 Estudio sobre los diferentes tipos de anemia en enfermos desnutridos. Tesis de médico y cirujano, Facultad Cien. Méd., Univ. San Carlos de Guatemala.

VAILLANT, G. C.
1927 The chronological significance of Maya ceramics. Doctoral dissertation, Harvard Univ.

1928 The native art of Middle America. *Natural Hist.*, 28: 562–76.

1930 Notes on the cultures of Middle America. *23d Int. Cong. Amer.* (New York, 1928), Acta, pp. 74–81.

1930 Excavations at Zacatenco. *Amer. Mus. Natural Hist., Anthr. Papers*, vol. 32, pt. 1.

1931 Excavations at Ticoman. *Ibid.*, vol. 32, pt. 2.

1932 A pre-Columbian jade. *Natural Hist.*, 32: 512–20, 556–58.

1932 Some resemblances in the ceramics of Central and North America. *Medallion Papers*, no. 12.

1934 The archaeological setting of the Playa de los Muertos culture. *Maya Research*, 1: 87–100.

1935 Excavations at El Arbolillo. *Amer. Mus. Natural Hist., Anthr. Papers*, vol. 35, pt. 2.

1935 Early cultures of the valley of Mexico: results of the stratigraphical project of the American Museum of Natural History in the valley of Mexico, 1928–1933. *Ibid.*, vol. 35, pt. 3.

1935 Chronology and stratigraphy in the Maya area. *Maya Research*, 2: 119–43.

1935 Artists and craftsmen in ancient Central America. *Amer. Mus. Natural Hist., Science Guide*, no. 88. (2d ed. 1949.)

1937 History and stratigraphy in the Valley of Mexico. *Sci. Monthly*, 44: 307–24.

1938 A correlation of archaeological and historical sequences in the Valley of Mexico. *Amer. Anthr.*, 40: 535–73.

1939 An early occurrence of cotton in Mexico. *Ibid.*, 41: 170.

1940 A sacred almanac of the Aztecs (tonalamatl of the Codex Borbonicus). Amer. Mus. Natural Hist.

1940 Patterns in Middle American archaeology. *In* The Maya and their neighbors, pp. 295–305.

1941 Aztecs of Mexico, New York. (Rev. eds. 1950, 1962, 1966.)

1944 La civilización azteca. Fondo de Cultura Económica. Mexico.

1949 Artists and craftsmen in ancient Central America. 2d ed. New York.

VAILLANT, S. B., AND G. C. VALLIANT
1934 Excavations at Gualupita. *Amer. Mus. Natural Hist., Anthr. Papers*, vol. 35, pt. 1.

VALDIVIESO, E. R.
1929 El matrimonio zapoteco. *Quetzalcoatl*, 1: 21–22, 89.

VALENTINI, P. J. J.
1899 Trique theogony: an alleged specimen of ancient Mexican folklore. *Jour. Amer. Folklore*, 12: 38–42.

VALENZUELA, J.
1942 Informe de la primera temporada de exploraciones en Arroyo Tlacuache, municipio de Ojitlan. MS in Archivo Inst. Nac. Antr. Hist.

1945 Las exploraciones efectuadas en Los Tuxtlas, Veracruz. *An. Mus. Nac. Arqueol. Hist. Etnog.*, 3: 83–107.

1945 La segunda temporada de exploraciones en la región de Los Tuxtlas, estado de Veracruz. *An. Inst. Nac. Antr. Hist.*, 1: 81–94.

VALLADARES, L. A.
1957 El hombre y la maíz: etnografía y etnopsicología de Colotenango, Guatemala.

VALLE, F.
n.d. Quaderno de algunas reglas y apuntes sobre el idioma pame. MS.

1925 La única gramática conocida de la lengua pame. . . . Mexico.

VALLE, R. H.
1937 Bibliografía zapoteca. *Neza*, 3 (2): 72–87.

VALLE MATHEU, J. DEL
1956 Guía sociogeográfica de Guatemala. Tipografía Nacional de Guatemala, Impreso no. 3502.

VALLOIS, H. V.
1938 Les méthodes de mensuration de la platycnèmie: étude critique. *Bull. et Mem. Soc. Anthr. Paris*, ser. 8, 9: 97–108.

VAN DE VELDE, P.
1933 Breve vocabulario comparado del idioma zapoteca. *Invest. Ling.*, pp. 251–57.

—— AND H. M. VAN DE VELDE
1939 The black pottery of Coyotepec, Oaxaca, Mexico. *SW. Mus. Papers*, no. 13.

VAN DEN BERGHE, P. L., AND B. N. COLBY
1961 Ladino-Indian relations in the highlands of Chiapas, Mexico. *Social Forces*, 40: 63–71.

VAN MARTENS, E.
1890–1901 Terrestrial and fluviates Mollusca. *In* Biologia Centrali-Americana, Zoology, vol. 9.

VAN ROSSEM, A. J.
1945 A distributional survey of the birds of Sonora, Mexico. *Louisiana State Univ., Mus. Zool., Occasional Papers*, no. 21.

VARA GÓMEZ, C.
1948 Exploración sanitaria e incidencia del bocio endémico en el municipio de Xatatlaco, Mexico. Univ. Nac. Antr. Mex.

VARELA, F. DE
17thC? Calepino en lengua cakchiquel. MS in American Philosophical Society. 477 pp.

VARGAS CATALÁN, I.
1957 Incidencia de la amebiasis en el niño menor de dos años en Puerto Barrios. Tesis de Médico y cirujano, Facultad Cien. Méd., Univ. San Carlos de Guatemala.

VAVILOV, N. I.
1951 Phytogeographic basis of plant breeding. *Chronica Botanica*, 13: 14–54.

VÁZQUEZ, F.
1937–44 Crónica de la provincia del Santísmo Nombre de Jesús de Guatemala. *Bib. Goathemala*, vols. 14–17. Guatemala.

VÁZQUEZ DE ESPINOZA, A.
1942 Compendium and description of the West Indies, 1629. Tr. by C. U. Clark. *Smithsonian Misc. Coll.*, no. 102.

VÁZQUEZ GAZTELU, D.
1726 Arte de lengua mexicana. . . . Puebla.

VÁZQUEZ RAMÍREZ, I.
1946 Estudio médico sanitario de villa de Chalco. Mexico.

VÁZQUEZ SANTANA, H.
1931 Calendario de fiestas típicas. Mexico.
1940 Fiestas y costumbres mexicanas. Mexico.

—— AND J. I. DÁVILA GARIBI
1931 El carnaval. Mexico.

VECETICH, J.
1904 Dactiloscopía comparada. Penser. La Plata.

VELASCO, A.
1929 Semblanza de la villa de Zaachila. *Bol. Soc. Mex. Geog. Estad.*, 41: 131–71.

VELASCO RAMOS, J.
1950 Informe general sobre la exploración sanitaria del municipio de Chiconcuac, estado de México. Mexico.

VELÁZQUEZ, P. F., ed.
1897–99 Colección de documentos para la historia de San Luis Potosí. 4 vols. San Luis Potosi.
1945 *See* Codex Chimalpopoca, 1945.

VELÁZQUEZ ANDRADE, M.
1912 Biometría: procedimientos estadísticos aplicados a la antropometría. Tesis. Mexico.

VELÁZQUEZ GALLARDO, P.
1948 Toponimia tarasca. *In* El Occidente de México, pp. 125–26.

VENEGAS, M., AND A. M. BURRIEL
1943 Noticia de la California y de su conquista temporal y espiritual hasta el tiempo presente. 3 vols. Mexico City. (Madrid, 1757.)

VERA, J. DE
1905 Relación de Acatlan y su partido. *In* Paso y Troncoso, 1905–06, 5: 55–80.

VERA, L.
1925 La leyenda de Tzuatzinco. *Mex. Folkways,* 1: 11–13.

VERBA . . . TLACAUEPANTZI
1946 Verba sociorum domini Petri Tlacauepantzi. G. Rosas Herrera, trans. *Tlalocan,* 2: 150–62.

VERDOORN, F., ed.
1945 Plants and plant sciences in Latin America. Chronica Botanica.

VERDUGO, A.
1896 La responsabilidad criminal y las modernas escuelas de antropología. Mexico.

VERGARA, M.
1904 Influencia del sexo en la criminalidad en el estado de Puebla: estudio de estadística criminal. *Mem. Soc. Cien. Antonio Alzate,* 21: 13–27. Mexico.

VERGARA LOPE, D.
1890 Refutación teórica y experimental de la teoría de la anoxihemia del doctor Jourdanet. Tesis. Mexico.

1893 La anoxihemia barométrica: medios fisiológicos y mesológicos que ayudan al hombre a contrarrestar la acción de la atmósfera rarificada de las altitudes. Mexico.

1895 El mal de la montañas se debe a perturbaciones circulatorias: ruina de la teoría de Jourdanet. *Mem. Soc. Cien. Antonio Alzate,* 9: 61–71. Mexico.

1896 De la tension du sang dans ses rapports avec la pression atmospherique. *Ibid.,* 10: 221–40.

1910 Una nueva e importante aplicación de la ortoradiografía. *Gaceta Méd. Méx.,* 5: 174–85.

1910 Description du toracographe. *Mem. Soc. Cien. Antonio Alzate,* 27: 217–21.

1910 Un nuevo procedimiento antropométrico. *Mem. General IV Cong. Méd. Nac.,* pp. 195–227. Mexico.

1910 Investigación de los promedios anatómicos y funcionales de los niños mexicanos, según sus diversas edades.

Bol. Instrucción Pública, 13: 541–49. Mexico.

VERMEER, D. E.
1959 The cays of British Honduras. Rept. field work carried out under ONR Contract 222(11) NR 388 067. Univ. California, Dept. Geography.

VERNEAU, R.
1875 Le bassin dans les sexes et dans les races. Paris.

1890 Les races humaines. Paris.

—— AND P. RIVET
1912 Ethnographie ancienne de l'Equateur. Vol. 6. Paris.

VERRILL, A. H.
1927 Excavations in Cocle province, Panama. *Mus. Amer. Indian, Heye Found., Indian Notes,* vol. 4, no. 1.

1929 Old civilizations of the New World. Indianapolis.

VESSBERG, B.
1937 Un bronze du style Houai, découvert à Rome. *Mus. Far Eastern Antiquities,* Bull. 9, pp. 127–31. Stockholm.

VETANCURT, A. DE
1673 Arte de la lengua mexicana. . . . Mexico.

1870 Teatro mexicano. 4 vols. *Bib. Histórica Iberia,* vols. 7, 8. Mexico. (1st ed. 1698.)

VETCH, CAPTAIN
1837 On the monuments and relics of the ancient inhabitants of New Spain. *Jour. Royal Geog. Soc. London,* 7: 1–11.

VEYTIA, M.
1907 Los calendarios mexicanos. Mexico.

1944 Historia antigua de México. 2 vols. Mexico.

VEYTIA CALENDAR WHEEL 4 (GEMELLI CARERI)
1907 *See* Veytia, 1907, pl. 4.
1944 *See* Veytia, 1944, vol. 1, pl. 4.

VEYTIA CALENDAR WHEEL 5 (SANTOS Y SALAZAR)
1907 *See* Veytia, 1907, pl. 5.
1944 *See* Veytia, 1944, vol. 1, pl. 5.

VICO, D. DE
17thC? Vocabulario quiché-cakchiquel. MS in Bibliothèque Nationale. 572 pp.

1675? Arte de la lengua quiché. . . . MS in Bibliothèque Nationale.

VIENNA, DICCIONARIO DE
n.d. Bocabulario de Mayathan por su abecedario. MS in National Library, Vienna. 199 pp.

VILAPLANA, H. DE
1763 Vida portentosa del americano septentrional apostol el V. P. Fr. Antonio Margil de Jesus. Mexico.

VILLA ROJAS, A.
1934 The Yaxuna-Coba causeway. *Carnegie Inst. Wash.*, Pub. 436, Contrib. 9.

1939 Notas sobre la etnografía de los Mayas de Quintana Roo. *Rev. Mex. Estud. Antr.*, 3: 227–41.

1941 Dioses y espíritus paganos de los Mayas de Quintana Roo. *In* Los Mayas antiguos, pp. 113–24.

1945 The Maya of east central Quintana Roo. *Carnegie Inst. Wash.*, Pub. 559.

1946 Notas sobre la etnografía de los indios tzeltales de Oxchuc. *Univ. Chicago, Micro. Coll. MSS Middle Amer. Cult. Anthr.*, no. 7.

1947 Kinship and nagualism in a Tzeltal community, southeastern Mexico. *Amer. Anthr.*, 49: 578–87.

1948 Breve noticia acerca de las investigaciones antropológicas en la cuenca del Papaloapan. *Bol. Indig.*, 8: 130–34. Mexico.

1955 Los mazatecos y el problema indígena de la cuenca del Papaloapan. *Inst. Nac. Indig.*, Mem. 7. Mexico.

1956 Notas introductorias sobre la condición cultural de los mijes. *In* W. S. Miller, 1956, pp. 13–69.

1961 Notas sobre la tenencia de la tierra entre los Mayas de la antigüedad. *Estud. Cultura Maya*, 1: 21–46.

1962 Distribución y estado cultural de los grupos mayances del México actual. *Ibid.*, 2: 45–77.

1963 El nagualismo como recurso de control social entre los grupos mayances de Chiapas, México. *Ibid.*, 3: 243–60.

1964 Barrios y calpules en las comunidades tzeltales y tzotziles del México actual. *35th Int. Cong. Amer.* (Mexico, 1962), Acta, 1: 321–34.

1967 Los Lacandones: su origen, costumbres y problemas vitales. *Amer. Indig.*, 27: 25–54.

VILLACORTA C., J. A.
1926 Monografía del departamento de Guatemala. Guatemala.

1934 Estudios sobre lingüística guatemalteca. *An. Soc. Geog. Hist. Guatemala*, 10: 41–81, 170–205, 331–73, 431–77.

1936 Memorial de Tecpan-Atitlan (Anales de los Cakchiqueles). Guatemala.

1938 Prehistoria e historia antigua de Guatemala. Guatemala.

—— AND C. A. VILLACORTA R.
1927 Arqueología guatemalteca. Guatemala.

1930 Códices mayas: Dresdensis, Peresianus, Tro-Cortesianus. Guatemala.

VILLACORTA VIDAURRE, L.
1953 Los cerros y el maíz. *Yikal Maya Than*, 14 (169): 175–76.

VILLADA, M. M.
1870 Memoria acerca de la exploración de las lomas de San Juan Ixtayopan. *Mem. Sec. Justicia e Instrucción Pública*, pp. 181–97.

1903 El hombre prehistórico en el Valle de México. *An. Mus. Nac.*, ep. 1, 7: 455–58. Mexico.

VILLAGRA CALETI, A.
1947 Los danzantes: piedras grabadas del montículo "L," Monte Alban, Oax. *27th Int. Cong. Amer.* (Mexico, 1939), Acta, 2: 143–58.

1949 Bonampak, la ciudad de los muros pintados. *An. Inst. Nac. Antr. Hist.*, suppl. to vol. 3.

1951 Las pinturas de Atetelco en Teotihuacán. *Cuad. Amer.*, 10: 153–62.

1951 Murales prehispánicos: copia, restauración y conservación. *In* Homenaje Caso, pp. 421–26.

1953 Teotihuacán y sus pinturas murales. *An. Inst. Nac. Antr. Hist.*, 5: 67–74.

1954 Pinturas rupestres: "Mateo A. Saldaña" Ixtapantongo, estado de México. *Caminos de México*, no. 9.

1956 Teotihuacán, la ciudad sagrada de Tlaloc. *Ibid.*, no. 21.

1959 La pintura mural. *In* Esplendor del México antiguo, 2: 651–70.

VILLAGUTIERRE SOTO-MAYOR, J. DE
1933 Historia de la conquista de la provincia de el Itza (1701). Guatemala.
VILLASEÑOR Y SÁNCHEZ, J. A.
1746–48 Theatro americano, descripción general de los reynos, y provincias, de la Nueva-España, y sus jurisdicciones. 2 vols. Mexico. (Facsimile ed., 1952, Mexico.)
VILLAVICENCIO, D.
1692 Luz y método de confesar idólatras y destierro de idolatrías. Puebla. (Reproduced in Gillow, 1889, pp. 77–88.)
VIÑAZA, CONDE DE LA [C. Muñoz y Manzano]
1892 Bibliografía española de lenguas indígenas de América. Madrid.
VINCENT, J. E.
1960 Some comments about Oaxaca. Katunob, 1: 40–41.
VINSON, G. L.
1960 Two important recent archaeological discoveries in Esso concessions, Guatemala. Exploration Newsl., Standard Oil Co., New Jersey.
VIQUERA, C., AND A. PALERM
1954 Alcoholismo, brujería y homicidio en dos comunidades rurales de México. Amer. Indig., 14: 7–36.
VIRCHOW, H.
1927 Ein Toltekan Schädel. Zeitschr. für Ethnol., 59: 132–39. Berlin.
VIRCHOW, R.
1887 Schaedel von Merida, Yucatan. Zeitschr. für Ethnol., 19: 451–55.
1891 Die sogennanten Azteken und die Chua. Ver. Gesellschaft für Anthr. Ethnol. Urgeschichte, pp. 370–77. Berlin.
1892 Crania ethnica americana. Berlin.
1897 Gräberschädel von Guatemala. Ver. Gesellschaft für Anthr. Ethnol. Urgeschichte, pp. 324–28.
1901 Die beiden Azteken. Zeitschr. für Ethnol., 33: 348–50.
VISITACIÓN . . . CORTÉS
1937 Visitación que se hizo en la conquista, donde fue por Capitán Francisco Cortés. In Nuño de Guzmán contra Hernán Cortés, sobre los descubrimientos y conquistas en Jalisco y Te-

pic, 1531. Bol. Archivo General de la Nación, 8: 556–72.
VIVÓ, J. A.
1941 Razas y lenguas indígenas de México, su distribución geográfica. Inst. Panamer. Geog. Hist., Pub. 52. Mexico.
1942 Geografía, lingüística y política prehispánica de Chiapas y secuencia histórica de sus pobladores. Rev. Geog., Inst. Panamer. Geog. Hist., 2:121–57.
1943 Los límites biogeográficos en América y la zona cultural mesoamérica. Ibid., 3: 109–31.
1943 Rasgos tribales y nacionales del problema indígena. Cuad. Amer., 9: 155–63.
1946 [ed.] México prehispánico: culturas, deidades, monumentos. Mexico.
1946 Culturas de Chiapas. In preceding entry.
1949 Geografía de México. Fondo de Cultura Económica. Mexico and Buenos Aires. (4th ed. 1958.)
1954 La integración de Chiapas y su agregación a la nación mexicana. Bol. Soc. Mex. Geog. Estad., 78: 389–505.
1958 La conquista de nuestro suelo. Mexico.
1959 Geografía humana de México. Estudio de la integración territorial y nacional de México. Mexico.
1961 Esbozo de geografía física humana de Chiapas. In Los Mayas del Sur, pp. 11–20.
—— AND J. C. GÓMEZ
1946 Climatología de México. Mexico.
VOEGELIN, C. F.
1945 Influence of area in American Indian linguistics. Word, 1: 54–58.
1950 A testing frame for language and culture. Amer. Anthr., 52: 432–34.
1953 [ed.] Results of the conference of anthropologists and linguists. Supplement to Int. Jour. Amer. Ling., 19: 2.
1956 Subsystems within systems in cultural and linguistic typologies. In Halle, Lunt, McLean, and Van Schooneveld, 1956, pp. 592–99.

—— AND Z. S. HARRIS

1945 Linguistics in ethnology. *SW. Jour. Anthr.*, 1: 455–65.

1950 Methods of determining intelligibility among dialects and natural languages. *Proc. Amer. Phil. Soc.*, 95: 322–29.

—— AND F. M. ROBINETT

1954 'Mother language' in Hidatsa. *Int. Jour. Amer. Ling.*, 20: 65–70.

VOGEL, J. P.

1929–30 Le makara dans la sculpture de l'Inde. *Rev. Arts Asiatiques*, 6: 133–47. Paris.

VOGLER, E. B.

1949 De monsterkop uit het omlijstings-ornament van tempeldoorgangen en-nissen in de Hindoe-Javaanse bouw-kunst. Leiden.

VOGT, E. Z.

1951 Navaho veterans: a study of chang-ing values. *Papers Peabody Mus., Harvard Univ.*, vol. 41, no. 1.

1955 Some aspects of Cora-Huichol ac-culturation. *Amer. Indig.*, 15: 249–63.

1957 Acculturation of American Indians. *Ann. Amer. Acad. Polit. Social Sci.*, 311: 137–46.

1959 Zinacantan settlement patterns and ceremonial organization. MS of pa-per presented at 58th annual meeting, Amer. Anthr. Assoc.

1960 On the concepts of structure and process in cultural anthropology. *Amer. Anthr.*, 62: 18–33.

1961 Some aspects of Zinacantan settle-ment patterns and ceremonial organi-zation. *Estud. Cultura Maya*, 1: 131–45.

1964 Ancient Maya concepts in contem-porary Zinacantan religion. *6th Int. Cong. Anthr. Ethnol. Sci., Mus. de l' Homme*, 2: 497–502.

1964 Ancient Maya and contemporary Tzotzil cosmology: a comment on some methodological problems. *Amer. Antiquity*, 30: 192–95.

1964 Cosmología maya antigua y tzotzil contemporánea: comentario sobre algunos problemas metodológicos. *Amer. Indig.*, 24: 211–19.

1964 Some implications of Zinacantan so-cial structure for the study of the ancient Maya. *35th Int. Cong. Amer.* (Mexico, 1962), Acta, 1: 307–19.

1964 The genetic model and Maya cul-tural development. *In* Desarrollo cultural de los Mayas, pp. 9–48.

1965 Ceremonial organization in Zinacan-tan. *Ethnology*, 4: 39–52.

1965 Structural and conceptual replication in Zinacantan culture. *Amer. Anthr.*, 67: 342–53.

1965 Zinacanteco 'souls.' *Man*, no. 29, pp. 33–35.

1966 [ed.] Los zinacantecos: un pueblo tzotzil de los altos de Chiapas. Inst. Nac. Indig. Mexico.

1967 Tendencia de cambio en las tierras altas de Chiapas. *Amer. Indig.*, 27: 199–222.

1968 Zinacantan: a Maya community in the highlands of Chiapas. Harvard Univ. Press.

—— AND A. RUZ LHUILLIER, eds.

1964 Desarrollo cultural de los Mayas. Wenner-Gren symposium at Burg Wartestein on the cultural develop-ment of the Maya. Univ. Nac. Au-tónoma Mex.

VOGT, H.

1954 Language contacts. *Word*, 10: 365–74.

VOORHEES, T. E.

1959 The formal analysis and comparison of Yuman kinship systems. Master's thesis, Stanford Univ.

W., M.

1752 The Mosqueto Indian and his golden river, being a familiar description of the Mosqueto kingdom in America (written about 1699). *In* A collec-tion of voyages and travels, 6: 279–312.

W., P. A.

1951 Algunas observaciones acerca de la religión de los Mixtecas guerrerenses, *Rev. Mex. Estud. Antr.*, 12: 147–64.

WADELL, H. A.

1938 Physical-geological features of Peten, Guatemala. *In* Morley, 1937–38, 4: 331–48.

WAFER, L.

1934 A new voyage and description of the

isthmus of America. *Hakluyt Soc.,* ser. 2, vol. 73.

WAGLEY, C.

1941 Economics of a Guatemalan village. *Amer. Anthr. Assoc.,* Mem. 58.

1949 The social and religious life of a Guatemalan village. *Ibid.,* Mem. 71.

1957 Santiago Chimaltenango: estudio antropológico-social de una comunidad indígena de Huehuetenango. Seminario de Integración Social Guatemalteca. Guatemala. (Tr. of his 1941 and 1949, with new preface.)

1958 On the concept of social race in the Americas. Mimeographed.

—— AND M. HARRIS

1955 A typology of Latin American subcultures. *Amer. Anthr.,* 57: 428–51.

1958 Minorities in the New World: six case studies. New York.

WAGNER, H. R.

1924 The voyage of Sebastian Rodriguez Cermenno. *California Hist. Soc. Quar.,* vol. 3, no. 1.

1925 California voyages: 1539–1541. San Francisco.

1930 Pearl fishing enterprises in the Gulf of California. *Hispanic Amer. Hist. Rev.,* 10: 188–203.

1942 [ed.] The discovery of New Spain in 1518, by Juan de Grijalva. Cortés Soc.

WAGNER, P. L.

1955 Parras: a case history in the depletion of natural resources. *Landscape,* 5: 19–28.

1958 Nicoya: a cultural geography. *Univ. California Pub. Geog.,* 12: 195–250.

1959 Precipitation in the transect area. *In* McQuown, 1959, fig. 7.

WAIBEL, L.

1933 Die Sierra Madre de Chiapas. *Mitt. Geog. Gesellschaft in Hamburg,* 43: 12–162.

1946 La Sierra Madre de Chiapas. *Soc. Mex. Geog. y Estad.,* Ser. Geog., no. 2.

WAITZ, P.

1906 Les geysers d'Ixtlan. *10th Cong. Geol. Int.* Guide Géologique du Mexique, part 12. Mexico.

1910 Excursión al Nevado de Toluca. *Bol. Soc. Geol. Mex.,* 6: 113–17.

1910 El Nevado de Toluca, uno de los dos grandes volcanes de México a que ascendió Humboldt. *Memoria de Humboldt,* pp. 59–62.

1914–15 Der gegenwärtige Stand der mexikanischen Vulkane und die letzte Eruption des Vulkans von Colima. *Zeit. für Vulkanologie,* 1: 247–74.

1943 Reseña geológica de la cuenca de Lerma. *Bol. Soc. Mex. Geog. y Estad.,* 58: 123–38.

WALDECK, F. DE

1838 Voyage pittoresque et archéologique dans la province d'Yucatan (Amérique Centrale) pendant les années 1834 et 1836. Paris. (Tr. into Spanish, 1930, Merida.)

1866 Monuments anciens du Mexique: Palenque et autres ruines de l'ancienne civilisation du Mexique. Paris.

WALFORD, L. A.

1958 Living resources of the sea. New York.

WALKER, A. R. P.

1958 Certain biochemical findings in man in relation to diet. *Ann. New York Acad. Sci.,* 69: 989.

WALKER, B. W.

1960 The biogeography of Baja California and adjacent seas. Part 2: The distribution and affinities of the marine fish fauna of the Gulf of California. *Syst. Zool.,* 9: 123–33.

WALKER, R. H., AND OTHERS (C. I. ARGALL, E. A. STEANE, T. T. SASAKI, AND T. J. GREENWALT)

1963 Anti-Js^b, the expected antithetical antibody of the Sutter blood group system. *Nature,* 197:295. London.

1963 Js^b of the Sutter blood group system. *Transfusion,* 3: 94–99.

WALLACE, A. F. C.

1960 [ed.] Men and cultures. Selected papers, 5th Int. Cong. Anthr. Ethnog. Sci.

1961 Culture and personality. New York.

WALLACE, A. R.
1876 The geographical distribution of animals. 2 vols. New York.

WALLACE, J., AND OTHERS (G. R. MILNE, J. MOHN, R. M. LAMBERT, H. G. ROSAMILA, P. MOORE, R. SANGER, AND R. R. RACE)
1957 Blood group antigens Mi^a and Vw and their relation to the MNSs system. *Nature,* 179: 478. London.

WALLÉN, C. C.
1955 Some characteristics of precipitation in Mexico. *Geografiska Annaler,* 37: 51–85.
1965 Fluctuations and variability in Mexican rainfall. *Amer. Assoc. Advanc. Sci.,* Pub. 43, pp. 141–55.

WALLIS, E.
1956 Simulfixation in aspect markers of Mesquital Otomi. *Language,* 32: 453–59.

WARDLE, H. N.
1905 Certain clay figures of Teotihuacan. *13th Int. Cong. Amer.* (New York, 1902), Acta, pp. 213–16.

WARKENTIN, M., AND J. OLIVARES
1947 The holy bells and other Huave legends. *Tlalocan,* 2: 223–34.

WARREN, B. W.
1959 New discoveries in Chiapas, southern Mexico. *Archaeology,* 12: 98–105.
1961 The archaeological sequence at Chiapa de Corzo. *In* Los Mayas del Sur, pp. 75–83.

WARREN, J. M.
1851 An account of two remarkable Indian dwarfs exhibited in Boston under the name of Aztec children. *Amer. Jour. Med. Sci.,* 20: 285–93. Philadelphia.

WARWICK, A. W.
n.d. A report of the Los Angeles mining district, state of Chihuahua, Mexico. MS prepared for Messrs. F. Stallforth, Hnos., Sucs. y Cía.

WASHINGTON, H. S.
1922 The jades of Middle America. *Proc. Nat. Acad. Sci.,* 8: 319–26.

WASLEY, W. W.
1960 A Hohokam platform mound at the Gatlin site, Gila Bend, Arizona. *Amer. Antiquity,* 26: 244–62.

——— AND J. E. OFFICER
1959 Report on the Yecora trip, June 17–22, 1959. MS. Arizona State Mus., Univ. Arizona.

WASSON, V. P., AND R. G. WASSON
1957 Mushrooms, Russia and history. 2 vols. New York.

WATERHOUSE, V.
1949 Learning a second language first. *Int. Jour. Amer. Ling.,* 15: 106–09.
1949 Oaxaca Chontal: sentence types and text analysis. *El Mex. Antiguo,* 7: 299–314.
1960 The psychological reality of linguistic structure. *In* Elson, 1960, Townsend, pp. 687–92.
1962 The grammatical structure of Oaxaca Chontal. *Int. Jour. Amer. Ling.,* vol. 28, pt. 2, 121 pp.

——— AND M. MORRISON
1950 Chontal phonemes. *Ibid.,* 16: 35–39.

WATERMAN, T. T.
1917 Bandelier's contribution to the study of ancient Mexican social organization. *Univ. California Pub. Amer. Archaeol. Ethnol.,* 12: 249–82.

WAUCHOPE, R.
1934 House mounds of Uaxactun, Guatemala. *Carnegie Inst. Wash.,* Pub. 436, Contrib. 7.
1938 Modern Maya houses: a study of their archaeological significance. *Ibid.,* Pub. 502.
1941 Effigy head supports from Zacualpa, Guatemala. *In* Los Mayas antiguos, pp. 211–31.
1942 Cremations at Zacualpa, Guatemala. *27th Int. Cong. Amer.* (Mexico, 1939), Acta, 1: 564–73.
1942 Notes on the age of the Cieneguilla cave textiles from Chiapas. *Tulane Univ., Middle Amer. Research Inst.,* Pub. 15, no. 2.
1948 Excavations at Zacualpa, Guatemala. *Tulane Univ., Middle Amer. Research Inst.,* Pub. 14.
1948 Surface collection at Chiche, Guatemala. *Tulane Univ., Middle Amer. Research Inst.,* Pub. 15, no. 10.
1949 Las edades de Utatlan e Iximche. *Antr. Hist. Guatemala,* 1 (1): 10–22.
1950 A tentative sequence of pre-classic

ceramics in Middle America. *Tulane Univ., Middle Amer. Research Inst.*, Pub. 15, no. 14.

1954 Implications of radiocarbon dates from Middle and South America. *Ibid.*, Pub. 18, no. 2.

1956 [ed.] Seminars in archaeology: 1955. *Soc. Amer. Archaeol.*, Mem. 11.

1964 Southern Mesoamerica. *In* Jennings and Norbeck, pp. 331–86.

WAVRIN, MARQUIS DE
1937 Moeurs et coutumes des Indiens sauvages de l'Amérique du Sud. Paris.

WEATHERS, K.
1946 La agricultura de los tzotzil de Nabenchuac, Chiapas, México. *Amer. Indig.*, 6: 315–19.

WEBB, C. H.
1960 A review of northeast Texas archaeology. *In* Jelks, Davis, and Sturgis, 1960, pp. 35–62.

WEBB, W. S., AND R. BABY
1957 The Adena people, no. 2. Ohio State Univ. Press.

—— AND C. E. SNOW
1945 The Adena people. *Univ. Kentucky Repts. Anthr. Archaeol.*, vol. 6.

WEBBER, B. N., AND J. OJEDA R.
1957 Investigaciones sobre lateritas fósiles en las regiones sureste de Oaxaca y sur de Chiapas. *Inst. Nac. Invest. Recursos Minerales de Mex.*, Bol. 37.

WEBER, F. VON
1922 Zur Archäologie Salvador. *In* Lehmann, 1922, pp. 619–44.

WEBER, H.
1959 Los páramos de Costa Rica y su concatenación fitogeográfica con los Andes suramericanos. Inst. Geog. Nac., San Jose, Costa Rica.

WEDEL, W. R.
1943 Archaeological investigations in Platte and Clay counties, Missouri. *Smithsonian Inst., U.S. Nat. Mus.*, Bull. 183.

WEED, W. H.
1902 Notes on a section across the Sierra Madre Occidental of Chihuahua and Sinaloa, Mexico. *Trans. Amer. Inst. Min. Eng.*, 32: 444–58.

WEEKS, L. G.
1956 Paleogeografía de América del Sur. Lima.

WEIANT, C. W.
1940 Los Tarascos. *Monogr. Hist. Etnog. Econ.* Mexico.

1943 An introduction to the ceramics of Tres Zapotes, Veracruz, Mexico. *Smithsonian Inst., Bur. Amer. Ethnol.*, Bull. 139.

1955 Notes on the ethnology of San Lorenzo, a Tarascan village of the sierra. *El Mex. Antiguo*, 8: 365–74.

WEIGAND, P. C.
1968 The mines and mining techniques of the Chalchihuites culture. *Amer. Antiquity*, 33: 45–61.

WEINREICH, U.
1953 Languages in contact: findings and problems. *Ling. Circle New York*, Pub. 1.

1954 Is a structural dialectology possible? *Word*, 10: 388–400.

1957 On the description of phonic interference. *Ibid.*, 13: 1–11.

1957 Functional aspects of Indian bilingualism. *Ibid.*, 13: 203–33.

1958 On the compatibility of genetic relationship and convergent development. *Ibid.*, 14: 374–79.

WEITLANER, I.
See Johnson, I. W.

WEITLANER, R. J.
1939 Los chinantecos. *Rev. Mex. Estud. Antr.*, 3: 195–216.

1939 Notes on the Cuitlatec language. *El Mex. Antiguo*, 4: 363–73.

1940 Notes on Chinantec ethnography. *Ibid.*, 5: 161–75.

1941 Chilacachapa y Tetelcingo. *Ibid.*, 5: 255–300.

1942 La rama olmeca del grupo Macro-Otomangue. *In* Mayas y Olmecas, pp. 33–35.

1945 Parentesco y compadrazgo coras. *Escuela Nac. Antr.*, Pub. 4, pp. 3–11.

1946 Paul Radin's "Classification of the languages of Mexico." *Tlalocan*, 2: 65–70.

1948 Lingüística de Atoyac, Guerrero. *Ibid.*, 2: 377–83.

1948 Situación lingüística del estado de

Guerrero. *In* El Occidente de México, pp. 129–33.

1948 Exploración arqueológica en Guerrero. *Ibid.*, pp. 77–85.

1948 Etnografía del estado de Guerrero. *Ibid.*, pp. 206–07.

1951 Notes on the social organization of Ojitlan, Oaxaca. *In* Homenaje Caso, pp. 441–55.

1952 El sol y la luna: versión chinanteca. *Tlalocan*, 3: 169–74.

1952 Curaciones mazatecas. *An. Inst. Nac. Antr. Hist.*, 4: 279–88.

1952 Sobre la alimentación chinanteca. *Ibid.*, 5: 177–95.

1958 Notas del campo sobre Tetzu, San Andres Jilotepec, etc. MS en Depto. Invest. Antr., Inst. Nac. Antr. Hist. Mexico.

1958 Un calendario de los zapotecos del sur. *32d Int. Cong. Amer.* (Copenhagen, 1956), Acta, pp. 296–99.

1960 Field notes on San Felipe Otlaltepec, Puebla. MS.

1961 Datos diagnósticos para la etnohistoria del norte de Oaxaca. *Inst. Nac. Antr. Hist., Dir. Invest. Antr.*, Pub. 6.

1963 Los zapotecos del sur. MS.

—— AND R. H. BARLOW

1944 Expeditions in western Guerrero: the Weitlaner party, spring, 1944. *Tlalocan*, 1: 364–75.

1955 Todos santos y otras ceremonias en Chilacachapa. *El Mex. Antiguo*, 8: 295–321.

—— AND C. A. CASTRO G.

1954 Papeles de la Chinantla: Mayultianguis y Tlacoatzintepec. *Mus. Nac. Antr., Cien. Ser.*, no. 3. Mexico.

—— AND G. DECICCO

1962 La jerarquía de los dioses zapotecos del sur. *34th Int. Cong. Amer.* (Vienna, 1960), Acta, pp. 695–710.

——, M. T. FERNÁNDEZ DE MIRANDA, AND M. SWADESH

1959 Some findings on Oaxaca language classification and culture terms. *Int. Jour. Amer. Ling.*, 25: 54–58. Abbreviated version of their 1960.

1960 El panorama etno-lingüístico de Oaxaca y el istmo. *Rev. Mex. Estud. Antr.*, 16: 137–57.

—— AND S. HOOGSHAGEN

1960 Grados de edad en Oaxaca. *Ibid.*, 16: 183–209.

—— AND I. W. JOHNSON

1943 Acatlan y Hueycantenango, Guerrero. *El Mex. Antiguo*, 6: 140–204.

1946 The Mazatec calendar. *Amer. Antiquity*, 11: 194–97.

——, P. VELÁZQUEZ, AND P. CARRASCO

1947 Huitziltepec. *Rev. Mex. Estud. Antr.*, 9: 47–77.

—— AND E. VERBITSKY

1956 Field notes of the Cuicatec. Mus. Nac. Antr., Field Notes Files. Mexico.

WEITZEL, R. B.

1949 Mean new moons. *Pop. Astron.*, 57: 283–85.

WELCKER, H.

1886 Die Kapacität und die drei Hauptdurchmesser der Schädelkapsel bei den verschiedenen Nationen. *Archiv für Anthr.*, 16: 1–159. Brunswick.

WELLHAUSEN, E. J., A. FUENTES O., AND E. HERNANDEZ X. in collaboration with P. C. MANGELSDORF

1957 Races of maize in Central America. *Nat. Acad. Sci., Nat. Research Council*, Pub. 511.

——, L. M. ROBERTS, AND E. HERNANDEZ X. in collaboration with P. C. MANGELSDORF

1952 Races of maize in Mexico. Bussey Inst., Harvard Univ.

WELLMAN, P.

1947 Death on horseback. New York.

WELLS, L. H.

1959 Estimation of stature from long bones: a reassessment. *Jour. Forensic Med.*, 6: 171–77.

WELLS, R.

1954 Archiving and language typology. *Int. Jour. Amer. Ling.*, 20: 101–07.

WELLS, W. V.

1857 Explorations and adventures in Honduras. New York.

WERCKLÉ, C.

1909 La subregión fitogeográfica costarricense. San Jose, Costa Rica.

WEST, R. C.

1948 Cultural geography of the modern Tarascan area. *Smithsonian Inst., Inst. Social Anthr.*, Pub. 7.

1961 Aboriginal sea navigation between Middle and South America. *Amer. Anthr.*, 63: 133–35.

1964 Surface configuration and associated geology of Middle America. *In* Handbook of Middle American Indians, R. Wauchope, ed., vol. 1, art. 2.

—— AND P. ARMILLAS

1950 Las chinampas de México. *Cuad. Amer.*, 2: 165–82.

WESTHEIM, P.

1948 Textilkunst in Mexiko. *Ciba Rundschau*, 78: 289.

1950 Arte antiguo de México. Mexico. (English trans. 1965, New York.)

1956 La escultura del México antiguo. *Univ. Nac. Autónoma Méx., Col. de Arte*, no. 1. (English trans. 1963, New York.)

1957 Ideas fundamentales del arte prehispánico en México. Fondo de Cultura Económica. Mexico and Buenos Aires.

1963 The sculpture of ancient Mexico. New York. (English trans. of his 1956.)

WEYERSTALL, A.

1932 Some observations on Indian mounds, idols, and pottery in the lower Papaloapan basin, state of Vera Cruz, Mexico. *Tulane Univ., Middle Amer. Research Inst.*, Pub. 4, no. 2.

WEYL, R.

1955 Geologischen Studien in der Cordillera de Talamanca von Costa Rica. *Neues Jahrbuch für Geol. und Palaeontol.*, Monatsheft, 6: 262–69.

1955 Vestigios de una glaciación del Pleistoceno en la cordillera de Talamanca, Costa Rica, A. C. *Informe Trimestral (Julio a Setiembre) del Inst. Geog. de Costa Rica*, pp. 9–32.

1955 Beiträge zur Geologie El Salvadors, VI–Die Laven der jungen Vulkane. *Neues Jahrbuch für Geol. und Palaeontol.*, Abh. 101: 12–38.

1956 Geologische Wanderungen durch Costa Rica. *Natur und Volk*, 86: 13–24, 93–102, 211–19, 380–90, 410–21.

1956 Eiszeitliche Gletscherspuren in Costa Rica (Mittelamerika). *Zeit. für Gletscherkunde und Glazialgeologie*, 3: 317–25.

1956 Costa Rica, die Schweiz Mittelamerikas. *Zeit. für Schulgeographie*, 8: 470–74.

1961 Die Geologie Mittelamerikas. Berlin.

WHEAT, J. B.

1948–49 A double-walled jar from Chihuahua. *Kiva*, 14 (1–4): 8–10.

1955 Mogollon culture prior to A.D. 1000. *Soc. Amer. Archaeol.*, Mem. 10.

WHETTEN, N. L.

1948 Rural Mexico. Univ. Chicago Press.

1961 Guatemala: the land and the people. Yale Univ. Press.

—— AND R. G. BURNIGHT

1956 Internal migration in Mexico. *In* Estudios antropológicos, pp. 537–52.

WHITAKER, T. W.

1957 Archaeological Cucurbitaceae from a cave in southern Baja California. *SW. Jour. Anthr.*, 13: 144–48.

—— AND J. B. BIRD

1949 Identification and significance of the cucurbit materials from Huaca Prieta, Peru. *Amer. Mus. Novitates*, no. 1426, pp. 1–15.

—— AND G. F. CARTER

1954 Oceanic drift of gourds—experimental observations. *Amer. Jour. Botany*, 41: 697–700.

——, H. C. CUTLER, AND R. S. MACNEISH

1957 Cucurbit materials from three caves near Ocampo, Tamaulipas. *Amer. Antiquity*, 22: 352–58.

WHITE, L. A.

1940 Pioneers in American anthropology: the Bandelier-Morgan letters, 1873–1883. 2 vols. Univ. New Mexico Press.

1944 A ceremonial vocabulary among the Pueblos. *Int. Jour. Amer. Ling.*, 10: 161–67.

1959 The evolution of culture. New York.

—— AND I. BERNAL

1960 Correspondence de Adolfo F. Bandelier. Inst. Nac. Antr. Hist. Mexico.

WHITE, S. E.

1951 Geologic investigations of the late Pleistocene history of the volcano Popocatepetl, Mexico. Doctoral dissertation, Syracuse Univ.

1956 Probable substages of glaciation on Iztaccihuatl, Mexico. *Jour. Geol.*, 64: 289–95.

1960 Late Pleistocene glacial sequence for west side of Iztaccihuatl, Mexico. Abstract. *Bull. Geol. Soc. Amer.*, 71: 2001.

WHITE, W. C.

1934 Tombs of old Lo-Yang. Shanghai.

WHITEFORD, A. A.

1960 Two cities of Latin America: a comparative description of social classes. *Logan Mus. Anthr.*, Bull. 9. Beloit.

WHITING, B. B.

1950 Paiute sorcery. *Viking Fund Pub. Anthr.*, no. 15.

WHITING, J. W. M.

1959 Sorcery, sin, and the superego. *In* Nebraska symposium on motivation [not paged]. Univ. Nebraska Press.

WHITLESEY, H. G.

1935 History and development of dentistry in Mexico. *Jour. Amer. Dental Assoc.*, 22: 989–95.

WHORF, B. L.

1933 The phonetic value of certain characters in Maya writing. *Papers Peabody Mus., Harvard Univ.*, vol. 13, no. 2.

1935 The comparative linguistics of Uto-Aztecan. *Amer. Anthr.*, 37: 600–08.

1942 Decipherment of the linguistic portion of the Maya hieroglyphs. *Smithsonian Inst.*, ann. rept. for 1941, pp. 479–502.

1943 Loan words in ancient Mexico. *Tulane Univ., Middle Amer. Research Inst.*, Pub. 11, no. 1.

1946 The Milpa Alta dialect of Aztec, with notes on the classical and Tepoztlan dialects. *In* Hoijer and others, 1946, pp. 367–97.

1950 An American Indian model of the universe. *Int. Jour. Amer. Ling.*, 16: 2.

1952 Collected papers on metalinguistics. U.S. Dept. State, Foreign Service Inst.

WICK, S. A.

1951 Phonemics of the Quiché language. Master's thesis, Univ. Chicago.

WICKE, C. R.

1956 Los murales de Tepantitla y el arte campesino. *An. Inst. Nac. Antr. Hist.*, 8: 117–22.

1957 The ball court at Yagul, Oaxaca: a comparative study. *Mesoamer. Notes*, 5: 37–78.

1966 Tomb 30 at Yagul and the Zaachila tombs. *In* Paddock, 1966, Ancient Oaxaca, pp. 336–44.

—— AND M. BULLINGTON

1960 A possible Andean influence in central Mexico. *Amer. Antiquity*, 25: 603–05.

WIELAND, G.

1913 The Liassic flora of the Mixteca Alta: its composition, age and source. *Amer. Jour. Sci. and Arts*, 4th ser., 36: 251–81.

1914 La flora Liásica de la Mixteca Alta. *Inst. Geol. de Mex.*, Bol. 31.

WIENER, A. S., J. P. ZEPEDA, E. B. SONN, AND H. R. POLIVKA

1945 Individual blood differences in Mexican Indians, with special reference to the Rh blood types and Hr factor. *Jour. Experimental Med.*, 81: 559–71.

WILDER, C. S.

1941 The Yaqui deer dancer: a study in cultural change. Master's thesis, Univ. Arizona.

WILDER, H. H.

1904 Racial differences in palm and sole configuration. *Amer. Anthr.*, 6: 244–93.

WILLARD, T. A.

1926 The city of the sacred well. London.

WILLEY, G. R.

1945 Horizon styles and pottery traditions in Peruvian archaeology. *Amer. Antiquity*, 11: 49–56.

1948 A functional analysis of "horizon styles" in Peruvian archaeology. *In* Bennett, 1948, pp. 8–15.

1955 The interrelated rise of the native cultures of Middle and South America. *In* Meggers and Evans, 1955, pp. 28–45.

1955 The prehistoric civilization of nuclear America. *Amer. Anthr.*, 57: 571–93.

1956 The structure of ancient Maya society: evidence from the southern lowlands. *Ibid.*, 58: 777–82.

1956 [ed.] Prehistoric settlement patterns in the New World. *Viking Fund Pub. Anthr.*, no. 23.

1956 Problems concerning prehistoric settlement patterns in the Maya lowlands. *Ibid.*, pp. 107–14.

1956 *Review of* Tlatilco and the pre-classic cultures of the New World, by M. N. Porter. *Amer. Antiquity*, 22: 88–89.

1958 Estimated correlations and dating of South and Central American culture sequences. *Ibid.*, 23: 353–78.

1960 New World prehistory: the main outlines of the pre-Columbian past are only beginning to emerge. *Science*, 131: 73–86.

1960 Historical patterns and evolution in native New World cultures. *In* Tax, Evolution after Darwin, 2: 111–41. Univ. Chicago Press.

1962 The early great styles and the rise of the pre-Columbian civilizations. *Amer. Anthr.*, 64: 1–14.

1964 An archaeological frame of reference for Maya culture history. *In* Desarrollo cultural de los Mayas, pp. 137–78.

1966 An introduction to American archaeology. Vol. 1: North and Middle America. Englewood Cliffs, N. J.

—— AND W. R. BULLARD, JR.

1956 The Melhado site: a house mound group in British Honduras. *Amer. Antiquity*, 22: 29–44.

1961 Altar de Sacrificios, Guatemala: mapa preliminar y resumen de las excavaciones. *Estud. Cultura Maya*, 1: 81–85.

——, ——, AND J. B. GLASS

1955 The Maya community of prehistoric times. *Archaeology*, 8: 18–25.

——, ——, ——, AND J. C. GIFFORD

1965 Prehistoric Maya settlements in the Belize Valley. *Papers Peabody Mus., Harvard Univ.*, vol. 54.

—— AND J. M. CORBETT

1954 Early Ancon and early Supe culture. *Columbia Studies in Archaeol. and Ethnol.*, vol. 3.

——, G. F. EKHOLM, AND R. MILLON

1964 The patterns of farming life and civilization. *In* Handbook of Middle American Indians, R. Wauchope, ed., vol. 1, art. 14.

—— AND J. C. GIFFORD

1961 Pottery of the Holmul I style from Barton Ramie, British Honduras. *In* Lothrop and others, 1961, pp. 152–70.

—— AND C. R. McGIMSEY

1954 The Monagrillo culture of Panama. *Papers Peabody Mus., Harvard Univ.*, vol. 49, no. 2.

—— AND P. PHILLIPS

1944 Negative-painted pottery from Crystal River, Florida. *Amer. Antiquity*, 10: 173–85.

1958 Method and theory in American archaeology. Univ. Chicago Press. (2d ed. 1962, Phoenix Books, P88.)

—— AND A. L. SMITH

1963 New discoveries at Altar de Sacrificios, Guatemala. *Archaeology*, 16: 83–89.

——, ——, W. R. BULLARD JR., AND J. A. GRAHAM

1960 Informe preliminar, Altar de Sacrificios, 1959. *Antr. Hist. Guatemala*, 12 (1): 5–24.

1960 Altar de Sacrificios, a prehistoric Maya crossroads. *Archaeology*, 13: 110–117.

—— AND T. L. STODDARD

1954 Cultural stratigraphy in Panama: a preliminary report on the Giron site. *Amer. Antiquity*, 19: 332–43.

——, E. Z. VOGT, AND A. PALERM, eds.

1958 Middle American anthropology. *Pan Amer. Union, Social Sci. Monogr.*, no. 5. Washington.

1960 Middle American anthropology. Vol. 2. *Ibid.*, no. 10.

—— AND OTHERS

1956 An archaeological classification of culture contact situations. *In* Wauc-hope, 1956, pp. 5–30.

WILLIAMS, A. F.
1946 Notes on the Popoloca Indians of San Felipe Otlaltepec, Puebla. *Amer. Anthr.*, 48: 683–86.

WILLIAMS, G. D.
1931 Maya-Spanish crosses in Yucatan. *Papers Peabody Mus., Harvard Univ.*, vol. 13, no. 1.

—— AND F. G. BENEDICT
1928 The basal metabolism of Mayas in Yucatan. *Amer. Jour. Physiol.*, 85: 634–49.

WILLIAMS, H.
1950 Volcanoes of the Paricutin region, Mexico. *U.S. Geol. Survey*, Bull. 965-B.
1952 Geologic observations on the ancient human footprints near Managua, Nicaragua. *Carnegie Inst. Wash.*, Pub. 596, Contrib. 52.
1952 Volcanic history of the Meseta Central, Costa Rica. *Univ. California Pub. Geol. Sci.*, 29: 145–80.
1952 The great eruption of Cosigüina, Nicaragua, in 1835, with notes on the Nicaraguan volcanic chain. *Ibid.*, 29: 21–46.
1960 Volcanic history of the Guatemalan highlands. *Ibid.*, 38: 1–86.

—— AND H. MEYER-ABICH
1955 Volcanism in the southern part of El Salvador, with particular reference to the collapse basins of lakes Coatepeque and Ilopango. *Ibid.*, 32: 1–64.

WILLIAMS, M. W.
1929 Secessionist diplomacy of Yucatan. *Hispanic Amer. Hist. Rev.*, 9: 132–43.

WILLIAMS GARCÍA, R.
1950 Informe preliminar sobre el municipio de Cardonal, Hidalgo. MS en Bib. Inst. Indig. Interamer. Mexico.
1950 Orizabita, etnografía y folklore de la zona árida del municipio de Ixmiquilpan, estado de Hidalgo, México. *Ibid.*
1953 Etnografía prehispánica de la zona central de Vera Cruz. *Rev. Mex. Estud. Antr.*, 13: 157–61.

1953 Un mito y los mazatecas. *Bol. Indig.*, 13: 360–64.
1955 Ichcacuatitla: vida en una comunidad indígena de Chicontepec, Veracruz. MS.
1961 Los huaxtecos: guión para la planeación e instalación del Museo Nacional de Antropología. Mexico.
1963 Los tepehuas. Univ. Veracruzana, Inst. Antr. Jalapa.

WILLOUGHBY, C. C.
1932 Notes on the history and symbolism of the Muskhogeans and the people of Etowah. *Phillips Acad., Dept. Archaeol., Etowah Papers*, no. 1.

WILSON, C.
1966 Crazy February. New York.

WILSON, D.
1857 Supposed prevalence of one cranial type throughout the American aborigines. *Canadian Jour. Sci. Lit. Hist.*, 2: 406–35. Also *Edinburgh New Philos. Jour.*, 7: 1–32 (1858).
1863 The American cranial type. *In* Prehistoric man: researches into the origin of civilization in the Old and the New World, 2: 199–288. Also *Smithsonian Inst.*, 10th ann. rept., p. 249 et seq.

WILSON, E. A.
1950 The basal metabolic rates of South American Indians. *In* Handbook of South American Indians, 6: 97–104.

WILSON, G., AND M. WILSON
1945 The analysis of social change: based on observations in central Africa. Cambridge Univ. Press.

WILSON, J. A.
1951 The burden of Egypt. Chicago.

WILSON, T.
1901 Arrow wound. *Amer. Anthr.*, n.s., 3: 521.

WILSON, W. B., AND A. COLLIER
1955 Preliminary notes on the culturing of *Gymnodinium breve* Davis. *Science*, 121 (3142): 394–95.

WINNIE, W. W., JR.
1958 The Papaloapan project: an experiment in tropical development. *Econ. Geog.*, 34: 227–48.

WINNING, H. VON
1948 The Teotihuacan owl-and-weapon

symbol and its association with "Serpent Head X" at Kaminaljuyu. *Amer. Antiquity*, 14: 129–32.

1956 Offerings from a burial mound in coastal Nayarit. *Masterkey*, 30: 157–70. Los Angeles.

1958 Figurines with movable limbs from ancient Mexico. *Ethnos*, 23: 1–60.

1959 Eine keramische Dorfgruppe aus dem alten Nayarit im westlichen Mexiko. *In* Amerikanistiche Miszellen (Festband Franz Termer). *Mitteilungen aus dem Museum für Völkerkunde in Hamburg*, 25: 138–43.

1961 Two figurines with movable limbs from Veracruz, Mexico. *Masterkey*, 35: 140–46. Los Angeles.

1961 Teotihuacan symbols: the reptile's eye glyph. *Ethnos*, 26: 121–66.

—— AND A. STENDAHL
1969 Pre-Columbian art of Mexico and Central America. New York.

WINSHIP, G. P.
1896 The Coronado expedition, 1540–1542. *Smithsonian Inst., Bur. Amer. Ethnol.*, 14th ann. rept. (1892–93), pp. 329–637. (Reprinted 1964, Chicago.)

WINTROBE, M. M.
1951 Clinical hematology. 3d ed. Philadelphia.

WISDOM, C.
1940 The Chorti Indians of Guatemala. Univ. Chicago Press.

1950 Materials on the Chorti language. *Chicago Univ., Micro. Coll. MSS Middle Amer. Cult. Anthr.*, no. 28.

1952 The supernatural world and curing. *In* Tax, 1952, Heritage, pp. 119–41.

WISSLER, C.
1931 Observations on the face and teeth of North American Indians. *Amer. Mus. Natural Hist., Anthr. Papers*, 33: 1–33.

1938 The American Indian. 3d ed. New York.

WITTE, N. DE
1913 Carta de Fray Nicolas de Witte a un ilustrísimo señor, Metztitlan 27 de Agosto de 1554. *An. Mus. Nac. Arqueol. Hist. Etnog.*, 3d ser., 5: 145–51. Mexico.

WITTFOGEL, K. A.
1957 Oriental despotism. Yale Univ. Press.

WITTICH, E. L. M. E.
1935 Bergfenster und Naturbrücken in Mexiko. *Mitt. über Höhlen u. Karstforschung*, 1935: 1–9.

1935–38 Höhlen und Karsterscheinung in Mexiko. *Ibid.*, 1935, 3: 81–87; 1936, 1: 1–16; 1937, 1: 16–30; 2–3: 74–82; 1938, 1–2: 42–44.

WOLF, E. R.
1953 La formación de la nación: un ensayo de formulación. *Cien. Sociales*, 4: 50–62, 98–111, 146–71.

1955 The Mexican Bajío in the 18th century: an analysis of cultural integration. *Tulane Univ., Middle Amer. Research Inst.*, Pub. 17, no. 3.

1955 Types of Latin American peasantry: a preliminary discussion. *Amer. Anthr.*, 57: 452–71.

1956 Aspects of group relations in a complex society: Mexico. *Ibid.*, 58: 1065–78.

1957 Closed corporate peasant communities in Mesoamerica and central Java. *SW. Jour. Anthr.*, 13: 1–18.

1958 The virgin of Guadalupe: a Mexican national symbol. *Jour. Amer. Folklore*, 71: 34–39.

1959 Sons of the shaking earth. Univ. Chicago Press. (Reprinted 1962.)

1960 The Indian in Mexican society. *In* Leslie, 1960, Social anthropology, pp. 3–6.

—— AND S. W. MINTZ
1957 Haciendas and plantations in Middle America and the Antilles. *Social and Econ. Studies*, 6: 380–412.

—— AND A. PALERM
1955 Irrigation in the old Acolhua domain, Mexico. *SW. Jour. Anthr.*, 11: 265–81.

WOLFE, R. I.
1950 The phylogeny of digital patterns in man and its bearing on racial affinities: a study in human ecology. *Human Biol.*, 22: 34–64.

WOLFF, H.
1959 Intelligibility and inter-ethnic attitudes. *Anthr. Ling.*, 1 (3): 34–41.

1959 Subsystem typologies and area linguistics. *Ibid.*, 1 (7): 1–88.

WÖLFFLIN, H.
n.d. Principles of art history, the problem of the development of style in later art. New York. (Dover ed.)

WOLFRAM, R.
1951 Die Volkstänze in Osterreich und verwandte Tänze in Europa. Salzburg.

WON, G. D., AND OTHERS (H. S. SHIN, S. W. KIM, J. SWANSON, AND G. A. MATSON)
1960 Distribution of hereditary blood factors among Koreans residing in Seoul, Korea. *Amer. Jour. Physical Anthr.*, n.s., 18: 115–24.

WONDERLY, W. L.
1946 Textos en zoque sobre el concepto del nagual. *Tlalocan*, 2: 97–105.
1946 Phonemic acculturation in Zoque. *Int. Jour. Amer. Ling.*, 12: 92–95.
1947 *Review of* Mapas lingüísticos de la República Mexicana, Departamento de Asuntos Indígenas (1944). *Ibid.*, 13: 122–25.
1947 Textos folklóricos en zoque: tradiciones acerca de los alrededores de Copainala, Chiapas. *Rev. Mex. Estud. Antr.*, 9: 135–63.
1949 Some Zoquean phonemic and morphophonemic correspondences. *Int. Jour. Amer. Ling.*, 15: 1–11.
1949 Folklore zoque: cuento del weyaweya. *Hontanar*, vol. 1, no. 5. Tuxtla Gutierrez.
1951–52 Zoque: phonemics and morphology. Reprinted from *Int. Jour. Amer. Ling.*, vol. 17, nos. 1–4; vol. 18, nos. 1 and 4.
1953 Sobre la propuesta filiación lingüística de la familia totonaca con las familias zoqueana y mayense. *In* Huastecos, Totonacos, pp. 105–13.
1960 Urbanization: the challenge of Latin America in transition. *Practical Anthr.*, 7: 205–09. Valhalla, N.Y.

WOODBURY, G., AND E. WOODBURY
1935 Prehistoric skeletal remains from the Texas coast. *Medallion Papers*, no. 18.

WOODBURY, R. B.
1961 Prehistoric agriculture at Point of Pines, Arizona. *Soc. Amer. Archaeol.*, Mem. 17.

—— AND A. S. TRIK
1953 The ruins of Zaculeu, Guatemala. 2 vols. Richmond, Va.

WOODRING, W. P., AND T. F. THOMPSON
1949 Tertiary formations of Panama Canal Zone and adjoining parts of Panama. *Bull. Amer. Assoc. Petroleum Geol.*, 33: 223–47.

WOODSON, R. E., R. W. SCHERY, AND OTHERS
1943–62 Flora of Panama. *Ann. Missouri Bot. Garden*, vols. 30–33, 35–37, 45–49.

WOODWARD, A.
1936 A shell bracelet manufactory. *Amer. Antiquity*, 2: 117–25.

WOOLLARD, G. P., AND J. MONGES CALDERA
1956 Gravedad, geología regional y estructura cortical en México. *An. Inst. Geofis.*, 2: 60–112.

WOOSTER, W. S.
1959 Oceanographic observations in the Panama Bight: *Askoy* Expedition, 1944. *Bull. Amer. Mus. Natural Hist.*, 118: 113–52.

—— AND T. CROMWELL
1958 An oceanographic description of the eastern tropical Pacific. *Bull. Scripps Inst. Oceanogr.*, 7: 169–282.

—— AND F. JENNINGS
1955 Exploratory oceanographic observations in the eastern tropical Pacific, January to March, 1953. *California Fish and Game*, 41: 79–90.

WORLD HEALTH ORGANIZATION
1948 Manual of the international statistical classification of diseases, injuries, and causes of death. Sixth revision of the international lists of diseases and causes of death. Geneva.

WORMINGTON, H. M.
1957 Ancient man in North America. 4th ed., rev. *Denver Mus. Nat. Hist.*, *Popular Ser.*, no. 4.
1962 A survey of early American prehistory. *Amer. Scientist*, 50: 230–42.

WRIGHT, H. B.
1935 Facial types and environmental factors among Mixe Indians of Mexico. *Jour. Dental Research*, 15: 164.

WYLLYS, R. K.
1716 Padre Luis Velarde's Relación of Pimeria Alta.

WYSS, J.
1953 Amebiasis cutánea. *Rev. Colegio Méd. Guatemala,* 4: 84–86.

WYSS, N.
1946 Consideraciones sobre la oxiuriasis en Guatemala. Tesis de médico y cirujano, Facultad Cien. Méd., Univ. San Carlos de Guatemala.

XEC, P., AND G. MAYNARD
1954 Diccionario quiché preliminar: quiché-español, español–quiché. Mimeographed. Quezaltenango.

XIMÉNEZ, F.
1720 Historia de la provincia de San Vicente de Chiapa y Guatemala de la Orden de Predicadores. *Bib. Goathemala,* vols. 1–3. Guatemala. (Another ed. 1929–31.)
1722? Arte de las tres lenguas cacchiquel, quiche y tzutuhil. . . . MS in Newberry Library.
1944–45 El Popul Vuh. *Yikal Maya Than,* vols. 5–7. Merida.

XIU, J. A.
1954 El árbol que llora. *Yikal Maya Than,* 15 (176): 52–53, 60–62.

XIU CHRONICLES
1608–1817 [Constitutes Ticul MS and Crónica de Oxhutzcab.] Photograph in Newberry Library of original in Peabody Museum, Harvard Univ. 164 pp.

YÁÑEZ, A.
1942 Mitos indígenas. Biblioteca Estud. Univ. Mexico. (Another ed. 1964.)

YÁÑEZ-PÉREZ, L., AND E. MOYO PORRAS
1957 Mecanización de la agricultura mexicana. Inst. Mex. Invest. Econ. Mexico.

YDE, J. M.
1932 Architectural remains along the coast of Quintana Roo: a report of the Peabody Museum expedition, 1913–1914, compiled from the field notes of R. E. Merwin. MS in Peabody Mus., Harvard Univ.
1938 An archaeological reconnaissance of northwestern Honduras. *Tulane*

Univ., *Middle Amer. Research Inst.,* Pub. 9. (Reprinted from Acta Archaeol., vol. 9, Copenhagen.)

YOSHIDA, K., AND H. L. MAO
1957 A theory of upwelling of large horizontal extent. *Jour. Marine Research,* 16: 40–54.

YOUNG, F. W., AND R. C. YOUNG
1960 Social integration and change in 24 Mexican villages. *Econ. Development and Cult. Change,* 8: 366–77.
1960 Two determinants of community reaction to industrialization in rural Mexico. *Ibid.,* 8: 257–64.

YUNCKER, T. G.
1945 The vegetation of Honduras, a brief review. *In* Verdoorn, 1945, pp. 55–56.

ZABALA CUBILLOS, M. T.
1961 Instituciones políticas y religiosas de Zinacantan. *Estud. Cultura Maya,* 1: 147–57.

ZABOROWSKI, S.
1901 Photographies d'Indiens Huichols et Coras. *Bull. et Mem. Soc. Anthr. Paris,* ser. 5, 2: 612–13.

ZALLIO, A.
1935 Curious skin anomaly. *Amer. Jour. Physical Anthr.,* 20: 494.

ZAMBRANO BONILLA, J.
1752 Arte de lengua totonaca, conforme a el arte de Antonio Nebrija. Puebla.

ZANTWIJK, R. A. M. VAN
1960 Los indígenas de Milpa Alta. *Inst. Real Trópicos, Amsterdam no. 135, Sec. Antr. Cultural y Física,* no. 64.
1963 Principios organizadores de los mexicas: una introducción al estudio del sistema interno del régimen azteca. *Inst. Hist., Estud. Cultura Náhuatl,* 4: 187–222.
1965 Introducción al estudio de la división en quince partes en la sociedad azteca y su significación en la estructura interna. *Jour. Soc. Amer. Paris,* 54: 211–22.

ZÁRRAGA, F.
1890 La pelvimetría. *Rev. Anatomía Patológica y Clínica,* 1: 447–50. Mexico.

ZAVALA, L. J.
1949 Exploraciones arqueológicas en Pa-

lenque, Chiapas, 1949. MS in Inst. Nac. Antr. Hist., Archivo Monumentos Prehispánicos.

ZAVALA, M.
1898 Gramática maya. Merida.

—— AND A. MEDINA
1898 Vocabulario español-maya. Merida.

ZAVALA, S. A.
1935 La encomienda indiana. Madrid.
1937 La "Utopia" de Tomás Moro en la Nueva España y otros estudios. Mexico.
1941 Ideario de Vasco de Quiroga. Fondo de Cultura Económica. Mexico.
1945 Contribución a la historia de las instituciones coloniales en Guatemala. Mexico.
1951 Los esclavos indios en Nueva España. *In* Homenaje Caso, pp. 427–40.

—— AND J. MIRANDA
1954 Instituciones indígenas en la colonia. *In* Caso, 1954, pp. 31–94.

ZEVALLOS MENÉNDEZ, C., AND O. HOLM
1960 Excavaciones arqueológicas en San Pablo. Ed. Casa de la Cultura Ecuatoriana, informe preliminar. Guayaquil.

ZIMMER, H.
1955 The art of Indian Asia. *Bollingen Ser.*, no. 39.

ZIMMERMAN, C.
1961 The religion of the Mayas of X-Cacal and Chunpom. MS. Detroit Univ.

ZIMMERMANN, G.
1955 Das Cotoque, die Maya-Sprache von Chicomucelo. *Zeit. für Ethnol.*, 80 (1): 59–87. Brunswick.
1956 Die Hieroglyphen der Maya-Handschriften. *Abh. Gebeit der Auslandkunde*, vol. 62. Hamburg.
1960 Das Geschichtswerke des Domingo de Muñón Chimalpahin Quauhtlehuanitzin. *Beiträge zur mittelamerikanischen Völkerkunde*, no. 5. Hamburg.

ZINGG, R. M.
1932 Tarahumara children's toys and games. *Mex. Folkways*, 7: 107–10.
1938 Christmasing with the Tarahumaras.

Pub. Texas Folklore Soc., 14: 207–24.
1938 The Huichols: primitive artists. *Univ. Denver, Contrib. Ethnog.*, no. 1.
1939 A reconstruction of Uto-Aztekan history. New York.
1940 Report on archaeology of southern Chihuahua. *Univ. Denver, Center of Latin Amer. Studies*, no. 1.
1942 Genuine and spurious values in Tarahumara culture. *Amer. Anthr.*, 44: 78–92.

ZOPPIS DE SENA, R.
1957 El volcán Masaya de Nicaragua. *Bol. Servicio Geol. Nac. de Nicaragua*, 1: 45–64.

ZORITA, A. DE
1864 Breve y sumaria relación de los señores y maneras y diferencias que había de ellos en la Nueva España. *In* Col. doc. Indias, 2: 1–126.
1891 *Idem. In* García Icazbalceta, 1886–92, 3: 71–227.
1909 Historia de la Nueva España. *In* Col. libros y documentos referentes a la historia de América, vol. 9. Madrid.
1941 Breve y sumaria relación. . . . *In* García Icazbalceta, 1941.

ZOUTENDYK, A.
1955 The blood groups of South African natives with particular reference to a recent investigation of the Hottentots. *Proc. 5th Int. Cong. Blood Transfusion*, pp. 247–49.

ZUAZO, A.
1858 Letter written to Fray Luis de Figueroa, dated November 14, 1521. *In* García Icazbalceta, 1858–66, 1: 359.

ZUÑIGA, D.
1720 Arte de la lengua pocomchi . . . y traducido en la lengua pocoman de Amatitlán. MS in Bibliothèque Nationale.

ZUÑIGA, I.
1835 Rápida ojeada al estado de Sonora. Mexico.

ZUNO, J. G.
1952 Las llamadas lacas michoacanas de Uruapan no proceden de las orientales. *Cuad. Amer.*, 11: 145–65.

Location of Artifacts Illustrated

MARJORIE S. ZENGEL

THE INTENTION of this project was to locate the present owner of each pre-Columbian American artifact illustrated in volumes 1–11 of the *Handbook of Middle American Indians*, to report the catalogue, accession, and/or inventory number, or other discrete symbol which the owner assigns to the object, and to record its size.

Initially, it was expected that the authors of the articles making up the *Handbook* could and would supply these data. With rare exceptions little came of this. It also developed that museums with substantial representation in the *Handbook* illustrations were unable to cooperate by mail. Searches of the literature were sometimes indicative but not often definitive. A number of individuals, scholars, and museum staff-members here, in Europe and in Latin America have been as helpful as they could manage to be, and for this I am unendingly grateful. But the bulk of what has been achieved here came from searches made in person.

Three lists follow. The first is of the abbreviations used for the names of owners. It includes libraries, governmental institu-

tions, museums, and one private establishment, the Museo Arqueológico Victor Emilio Estrada of Guayaquil, to visit which advance arrangements need to be made. Private collectors, galleries, and certain plazas and other places to which sculptures have been moved are omitted here, but are covered in both subsequent lists.

The second list, by owners, has been kept as brief as possible. It refers only to the appropriate *Handbook* figures and omits details which are set out in the third list. It includes private collections and locations other than museums, to which portable objects have been moved, but omits things still *in situ*. As also used in the third list, enclosure in parentheses denotes incomplete information.

The third list, arranged in the order of their appearance in the *Handbook*, is of artifacts surely identified. When an entry is enclosed in parentheses, the information is probable but not confirmed, or is the latest information in point of time. Items not found, motifs extracted at some distance from objects, illustrations too schematic to permit firm identification, hypothetical

259

restorations, and most chipped stone pieces have all been omitted. The "lost" items in this list are the things reliably reported to be gone, such as those destroyed, potsherds discarded, or things lost in shipping. Objects such as stelae and altars, which are capable of being removed, but which are still *in situ*, are recorded only in this list. Purely architectural features are not covered. In the entries, the first fact stated is the owner and his identification of the object. All abbreviations are common ones, except "inv." for inventory. A single dimension in centimeters comes next, designated as diameter (D), height (H), length (L), or width (W); where it includes a "c." it is no more than an informed guess. Corrective material sometimes follows. This occurs on the instruction of an author, where information supplied by the present owner adds to or differs from that in the figure caption, or where it contributes to identification. "Same" refers to other *Handbook* appearances of the same artifact. Assuming that partial information may be more useful than none at all, I include entries which are incomplete.

In the third list I make page citations to Deckert and to Förstemann for the Dresden Codex material. Because difficulties exist in making clear exactly how the bibliographical entries compare, I include here for convenience the forms as prepared by John B. Glass, taken from his Article 32 in volume 15 of the *Handbook*. My references to Deckert are to the separate facsimile plates of Lips and Deckert, 1962; my references to Förstemann are valid for all three editions.

FÖRSTEMANN, ERNST
1880   Die Maya Handschrift der Königlichen öffentlichen Bibliothek zu Dresden . . . mit 74 Tafeln in Chromo-Lichtdruck.   Leipzig, Verlag der A. Naumann'schen Lichtdruckerei.   18 pp., 74 individually mounted facsimiles.   In portfolio.
1882   Die Maya Handschrift der Königlichen öffentlichen Bibliothek zu Dresden . . . mit 74 Tafeln in Chromo-Lichtdruck.   Leipzig, Verlag von A. Nauman & Schroeder.   18 pp., 74 individually mounted facsimiles.   In portfolio.
1892   Die Maya Handschrift der Königlichen öffentlichen Bibliothek zu Dresden . . . zweite Auflage.   Mit 74 Tafeln in Chromo-Lichtdruck.   Dresden, R. Bertling.   14 pp., 74 individually mounted plates.

LIPS, EVA, AND HELMUT DECKERT
1962   Maya Handschrift der Sächsischen Landesbibliothek Dresden: Codex Dresden.   Berlin, Akademie Verlag, [Introduction by Lips.]   18 pp., 1 pl., Geschichte und Bibliographie [by Deckert].   86 pp., 1 pl., 74 separate facsimiles, and "Konkordanztafel," 1 f.

Special attention should be directed at what is happening in Mexico. The Sección de Máquinas Electrónicas of the Museo Nacional de Antropología has been working since 1964 toward computer programing of artifact cataloguing. Their twenty-seven analyses, published to date, include efforts to develop and fix a single descriptive vocabulary usable both verbally and mathematically. Particular bodies of objects have been studied, such as Tlatilco vessel shapes and figurine traits, ethnographic ceramics, and architectonic representations in Mixtec codices. As more groups of materials come under scrutiny, it may be anticipated that a universally applicable scheme may be developed, to permit retrieval from computer storage of data both for single artifacts and for clusters, as they may be defined by a researcher.

The scope of this project is nationwide. Under the Federal Law of Mexico, enacted April 28, 1972, and published officially on May 6, 1972, registration of all artifacts is stipulated, whether they be in private, public, or quasi-public possession. These, too, are to be included in the master computerized records. Such an achievement would make superfluous what I have tried to do here, at least as far as Mexico is concerned.

1. Abbreviations Used For Owners

Basel, MV
Museum für Völkerkunde
Berkeley, RHLMA
The Robert H. Lowie Museum of Anthropology, University of California
Berlin, MV
Museum für Völkerkunde
Boston, MFA
Museum of Fine Arts
Cambridge, PM
Peabody Museum of Archaeology and Ethnology, Harvard University
Campeche, MA
Museo Arqueológico
Carbondale, UM
University Museum, Southern Illinois University
Cempoala, MZA
Museo de la Zona Arqueológica de Zempoala
Chicago, FMNH
Field Museum of Natural History
Chichicastenango, MM
Museo Municipal de Chichicastenango, Coll. Padre Ildefonso Rossbach
Cholula, MZA
Museo de la Zona Arqueológica de Cholula
Cleveland, CMA
The Cleveland Museum of Art
Copan, MRAM
Museo Regional de Arqueología Maya de las Ruinas de Copán. The village near the archaeological site is commonly known in the region as "Las Ruinas de Copán," or simply "Las Ruinas," rather than by its formal name of "San José de Copán." Its plaza, on which the museum stands, is 1.2 km. by road from the entrance to the site, and 64.2 km. from La Entrada, on highway CA4
Costa Rica, MN
Museo Nacional de Costa Rica
Cuernavaca, PC
Palacio de Cortés
La Democracia, MRA
Museo Regional de Arqueología, La Democracia, Depto. Escuintla
Dresden, SL
Die Sächsische Landesbibliothek zu Dresden
Dzibilchaltun, MZA
Museo de la Zona Arqueológica de Dzibilchaltun

Florence, BML
Biblioteca Medicea Laurenziana
Florence, BNC
Biblioteca Nazionale Centrale di Firenze
Guadalajara, MAOM
Museo de Arqueología del Occidente de México
Guanajuato, MR
Museo Regional de Guanajuato
Guatemala, IAH
Instituto de Antropología e Historia
Guatemala, MNAE
Museo Nacional de Arqueología y Etnología de Guatemala
Guayaquil, MAVEE
Museo Arqueológico Victor Emilio Estrada
Hamburg, MV
Museum für Völkerkunde
Hermosillo, MR
Museo Regional de Sonora
Houston, MFA
The Museum of Fine Arts
Jalapa, MAUV
Museo de Antropología de la Universidad Veracruzana
Leyden, RV
Rijksmuseum voor Volkenkunde
Liverpool, CLM
City of Liverpool Museums
London, BM
The British Museum. Artifacts and manuscripts depicted in the *Handbook* are now in The Museum of Mankind in London, The Department of Ethnology of The British Museum; original catalogue numbers are retained
Los Angeles, CMNH
Los Angeles County Museum of Natural History
Los Angeles, SWM
Southwest Museum
Los Angeles, UCLA
University of California, Los Angeles, Department of Anthropology
Madrid, BPN
Biblioteca del Palacio Nacional
Madrid
Museo de América

Merida, INAH
 Instituto Nacional de Antropología e Historia, bodegas
Merida, MA
 Museo de Arqueología de Yucatán
Mexico, A
 Anahuacalli
Mexico, DP
 Departamento de Prehistoria, Instituto Nacional de Antropología e Historia
Mexico, INAH
 Instituto Nacional de Antropología e Historia
Mexico, MC
 Museo de las Culturas
Mexico, MNA
 Museo Nacional de Antropología
Morelia, MR
 Museo Regional Michoacano
New Haven, YUAG
 Yale University Art Gallery
New Orleans, MARI
 Middle American Research Institute
New York, AMNH
 The American Museum of Natural History
New York, BM
 The Brooklyn Museum
New York, MAI
 Museum of the American Indian, Heye Foundation
New York, MMA
 The Metropolitan Museum of Art
New York, MPA
 The Museum of Primitive Art
Oaxaca, MR
 Museo Regional de Oaxaca
Oaxaca, MR, Cat.T.7
 Museo Regional de Oaxaca, Catálogo de las joyas encontradas en la tumba 7 de Monte Albán
Oxford, BL
 Bodleian Library
Palenque, MZA
 Museo de la Zona Arqueológica de Palenque
Panama, MN
 Museo Nacional de Panamá
Paris, BN
 Bibliothèque Nationale
Paris, BPB
 Bibliothèque du Palais Bourbon
Paris, MH
 Musée de l'Homme

Philadelphia, UM
 The University Museum
Puebla, IPAH
 Instituto Poblano de Antropología e Historia
Rome, BAV
 La Biblioteca Apostolica Vaticana
San Diego, MM
 San Diego Museum of Man
San Salvador, MNDJG
 Museo Nacional David J. Guzmán
Santa Fe, MNM
 Museum of New Mexico
Stockholm, EM
 Etnografiska Museet
Stuttgart, WL
 Württembergisches Landesmuseum
Tajin, MZA
 Museo de la Zona Arqueológica de El Tajín
Tepic, MR
 Museo Regional de Tepic
Tikal, MSGM
 Museo Sylvanus G. Morley
Tucson, ASM
 Arizona State Museum
Tula, MZA
 Museo de la Zona Arqueológica de Tula
Tuxtla Gutierrez, MR
 Museo Regional de Chiapas
Tuxtla Gutierrez, MR, NWAF coll.
 Museo Regional de Chiapas, New World Archaeological Foundation Collection
Vienna, MV
 Museum für Völkerkunde
Vienna, NB
 Nationalbibliothek
Villahermosa, MR
 Museo Regional de Tabasco
Villahermosa, PMLV
 Parque Museo de La Venta
Washington, DO
 Dumbarton Oaks, Robert Woods Bliss Collection
Washington, NGS
 National Geographic Society
Washington, USNM
 Smithsonian Institution, Department of Anthropology, National Museum of Natural History. The former name, United States National Museum, has been retained by law for these collections
Zaculeu, MA
 Museo Arqueológico de las Ruinas de Zaculeu

2. Artifacts, by Owners

Amapa, anonymous coll.
Vol. 11, p. 718, fig. 20.
(Ann Arbor, coll. Dr. Norman Hartweg, as of 1940)
Vol. 2, p. 203, fig. 5.
Anonymous collections
Vol. 3, on loan to New York, AMNH, p. 570, fig. 30. Page 854, fig. 11,*a*.
Vol. 11, p. 565, fig. 8, on loan to New York, AMNH; p. 724, fig. 23,*a*.
Antigua, coll. Sra. Lily Cofiño Durán
Vol. 2, p. 161, fig. 11.
Antigua, coll. Sr. Juan Pellicer
Vol. 2, p. 160, fig. 8.

Basel, MV
Vol. 2, p. 482, fig. 8,*a*, all except right, upper and lower.
Vol. 3, p. 608, fig. 4; p. 637, fig. 6, top row third from left.
Belmont, Mass., coll. Mr. William H. Claflin
Vol. 4, p. 199, fig. 16,*e*.
Berkeley, coll. Dr. and Mrs. William F. Kaiser
Vol. 11, p. 724, fig. 23,*b*; p. 730, fig. 28; p. 738, fig. 31,*d*.
Berkeley, RHLMA
Vol. 4, p. 46, figs. 5, top row left, bottom row, 6; p. 48, fig. 8.
Vol. 11, p. 729, fig. 27,*d–g*; p. 762, fig. 6,*a,b, e,f*; p. 764, fig. 8,*a,b*; p. 766, fig. 10, *c,d,f–i,m,n*.
Berlin, anonymous coll.
Vol. 2, (p. 128, fig. 17,*e*).
Berlin, MV
Vol. 2, (p. 136, fig. 19,*a*); p. 543, fig. 19; p. 544, fig. 21.
Vol. 3, (p. 639, fig. 8,*h*; p. 748, fig. 18); p. 926, fig. 59, left, and next to left.
Vol. 4, p. 286, fig. 14,*d*.
Vol. 10, p. 96, fig. 6; p. 113, fig. 34.
Vol. 11, p. 568, fig. 14,*d*.
Beverly Hills, coll. Dr. and Mrs. Melvin Silverman
Vol. 11, p. 740, fig. 34,*c*.
Boston, MFA
Vol. 4, p. 195, fig. 13,*a,b*.
British Honduras
Vol. 3, on loan to London, BM, p. 564, fig. 11.

Cambridge, PM
Vol. 1, p. 448, fig. 2; p. 449, fig. 3; p. 457, fig. 19; p. 487, fig. 39.
Vol. 2, (p. 118, fig. 13,*f*); p. 388, fig. 7; p. 392, fig. 9; p. 396, fig. 11; p. 398, fig. 12; p. 404, fig. 18; p. 413, fig. 26; p. 419, fig. 31; p. 420, figs. 32, 33; p. 422, fig. 34; p. 424, fig. 36; p. 425, fig. 37; p. 426, fig. 38; p. 430, fig. 41; p. 432, fig. 42; p. 433, fig. 43; p. 435, fig. 45; p. 436, fig. 46; p. 541, fig. 12; p. 544, fig. 20.
Vol. 3, p. 562, figs. 3, 5; p. 563, fig. 8; p. 565, fig. 14; p. 568, fig. 24; p. 569, fig. 28; p. 572, figs. 35, 40; p. 573, fig. 42; p. 574, figs. 44, 45; (cast, p. 608, fig. 4; p. 767, fig. 55; p. 883, fig. 14,*f*).
Vol. 4, (p. 85, fig. 28; p. 146, fig. 9; p. 148, fig. 10,*a,c–k*); p. 160, fig. 2; p. 165, fig. 3; p. 166, fig. 4; p. 168, fig. 5; p. 170, fig. 6,(*a*),*b–g*; p. 172, fig. 7; p. 176,*a–c* are on loan, *e,f*; p. 186, fig. 4,(*d*),*f–h*; (p. 187, fig. 5,*c*; p. 188, fig. 6,*a–d*; p. 189, fig. 7, lower; p. 191, figs. 9,*a,b*, 10); p. 194, fig. 12, (*a–c*),*d*,(*e*); p. 195, fig. 13,(*f*),*g*; p. 198, fig. 15,*c.d*; p. 199, fig. 16,(*a*), *b–d*; (p. 200, fig. 17); p. 202, fig. 18,*a*,(*b*),*c*,(*d*),*e*; p. 203, fig. 19,*c,d*,(*e*); p. 204, fig. 20,*c–f*; p. 206, fig. 21,*e,f*; p. 247, fig. 3,*f–h*; p. 251, fig. 7,*k,l*; p. 279, fig. 2,*a*; p. 281, fig. 7,*a*; p. 290, fig. 18,*a*.
Cambridge, coll. Miss Tatiana Proskouriakoff
Vol. 2, p. 491, fig. 13,*b*.
Campeche, MA
Vol. 1, (p. 455, fig. 16).
Vol. 2, p. 550, fig. 39.
Carbondale, UM
Vol. 2, on loan: p. 538, fig. 7; p. 539, fig. 9; p. 541, fig. 13; p. 543, fig. 18; p. 551, fig. 40; p. 554, fig. 46.
Vol. 11, on loan: after p. 800, fig. 2, *Vesuvio red-filled engraved, Gualterio red-on-cream, exterior decorated, six sherds, Gualterio red-on-cream, interior decorated, Refugio red-on-brown, Amaro red-on-cream, Mercado red-on-*

Honduras, coll. Mrs. Whiting Willhauer
   Vol. 4,   p. 176, fig. 8,*a–c*, on loan to Cambridge, PM.
Houston, MFA
   Vol. 2,   p. 479, fig. 5.

(Jalapa, coll. Gov. Teodoro Dehesa, as of 1904)
   Vol. 4,   p. 281, figs. 6,*b*, 9,*a*.
Jalapa, MAUV
   Vol. 3,   p. 699, fig. 16; p. 703, figs. 21, 22; p. 706, figs. 25, 26; p. 718, figs. 2, 3; p. 719, fig. 4,*b*; p. 720, fig. 5; p. 724, fig. 11; p. 727, fig. 15; p. 728, figs. 16, 17,*a*; p. 730, fig. 19; p. 732, fig. 21,*b*; p. 734, fig. 24; p. 737, fig. 29, upper; p. 763, fig. 50,*b*.
   Vol. 4,   p. 289, fig. 17,*b*.
   Vol. 11,   (p. 518, fig. 12); p. 524, fig. 18,*a*, (*b*),*c*,(*d*),*e–g*,(*h–k*); p. 525, fig. 19; p. 529, figs. 21, 22; p. 530, fig. 23; p. 531, figs. 24, 25,(*a*),*c*,*d*; p. 532, fig. 26,*b–d*; p. 533, fig. 27; p. 534, fig. 29; p. 535, fig. 30; p. 536, fig. 31,*b*; p. 539, figs. 33, 34; p. 540, fig. 35.

Lausanne, Switzerland, coll. Mr. and Mrs. Samuel Josefowitz
   Vol. 10,   p. 418, fig. 21.
Leyden, RV
   Vol. 2,   p. 241, fig. 5,*d*.
   Vol. 3,   p. 575, fig. 46; p. 606, fig. 2.
Liverpool, CLM
   Vol. 2,   (p. 557, fig. 51).
   Vol. 10,   p. 334, fig. 1,*a*,*f*,*p*,*t*; p. 404, fig. 4.
   Vol. 11,   p. 599, fig. 3.
London, BM
   Vol. 2,   p. 344, fig. 9; p. 482, fig. 8,*a*, right, upper and lower,*b*; (p. 544, fig. 21, *b*; p. 548, fig. 31).
   Vol. 3,   on loan, p. 564, fig. 11; p. 568, fig. 26; (p. 587, fig. 4,*a–d*,*f–o*); p. 637, fig. 6, second row left; p. 639, fig. 8,*j*,*l*; p. 642, fig. 10,*a*; p. 749, fig. 22; p. 916, fig. 40,*a*,*c*; p. 926, fig. 59, third from left, and right; p. 953, fig. 5,*a*; p. 954, fig. 6; p. 959, fig. 10; p. 960, fig. 11.
   Vol. 10,   p. 78, fig. 31, top row next to left, middle row third from left, bottom row left and third from left; p. 101, fig. 14; p. 118, fig. 46; p. 329, fig. 3; p. 415, fig. 14.

   Vol. 11,   p. 476, fig. 1; p. 484, fig. 3; p. 488, fig. 5; p. 498, fig. 7; p. 501, fig. 9; p. 503, fig. 10.
Los Angeles, CMNH
   Vol. 10,   on loan, p. 99, fig. 11.
   Vol. 11,   p. 723, fig. 22,*a*,*b*; p. 725, fig. 25.
Los Angeles, David Stuart Galleries
   Vol. 11,   p. 740, fig. 33,*c*.
Los Angeles, coll. Dr. and Mrs. Ernest Fantel
   Vol. 11,   p. 712, fig. 14,*a*.
Los Angeles, coll. Dr. and Mrs. George C. Kennedy
   Vol. 11,   p. 712, fig. 14,*c*,*d*; p. 715, fig. 17, *b*,*c*; p. 738, fig. 31,*b*,*c*.
Los Angeles, coll. Mr. Edward Primus
   Vol. 11,   p. 740, fig. 33,*b*.
Los Angeles, SWM
   Vol. 11,   p. 701, fig. 2,*a*,*b*,(*c*),*d*,*f*; p. 702, fig. 3.
Los Angeles, coll. Mr. Proctor Stafford
   Vol. 6,   p. 198, fig. 5.
   Vol. 11,   p. 714, fig. 16,*a*; p. 726, fig. 26.
Los Angeles, coll. Mr. and Mrs. Edgar Dorsey Taylor
   Vol. 11,   p. 713, fig. 15,*a–c*.
Los Angeles, UCLA
   Vol. 11,   p. 701, fig. 2,*e*; p. 705, fig. 6,*e–j*,*k*, top left, *l*,*r*; p. 706, figs. 7,*a*,*d*,*e*,*g*, 8; p. 707, fig. 9,*a–c*,*e*; p. 708, fig. 10,*b*; p. 709, fig. 12,*a*,*c*,*d*. On loan: p. 704, fig. 5; p. 705, fig. 6,*a–d*,*k*, all except top left, *m–q*,*s*,*t*; p. 706, fig. 7,*b*,*c*,*f*, *h*,*i*; p. 707, fig. 9,*d*,*f*; p. 708, figs. 10, *a*,*c–f*, 11; p. 709, fig. 12,*b*,*e*,*f*.

Madrid, BPN
   Vol. 2,   p. 90, fig. 8,*a*.
   Vol. 6,   p. 161, fig. 5; p. 162, fig. 6.
   Vol. 10,   p. 358, fig. 6; p. 430, fig. 47; p. 438, fig. 52; p. 443, fig. 54.
Madrid, MA
   Vol. 3,   p. 590, fig. 7,*d*; p. 591, fig. 8,*e*,*i*,*j*; p 637, fig. 6, third row center; p. 639, fig. 8,*q*; p. 646, fig. 14.
   Vol. 4,   p. 286, fig. 14,*a*; p. 288, fig. 16,*a*.
   Vol. 10,   p. 406, fig. 6.
(Merida, coll. Sr. Oswaldo Cámara Peón, as of 1955)
   Vol. 2,   p. 520, fig. 10,*h*.
Merida, INAH
   Vol. 2,   p. 495, fig. 16; p. 522, fig. 11,*a*,*g*,*h*;

p. 524, fig. 12,*b,f,j*; p. 526, fig. 13;
p. 528, fig. 14,*a,b,f,g*; p. 530, fig.
15,*b–e*; p. 532, fig. 16,*a–h,l.*

(Merida, coll. Sr. Alberto Márquez, as of 1956)
Vol. 2,　p. 520, fig. 10,*f,i.*

(Merida, coll. Mr. Arthur Metcalf, as of 1955)
Vol. 2,　p. 550, fig. 39.

Merida, MA
Vol. 2,　p. 520, fig. 10,*a,c,e,j*; p. 522, fig. 11,
d; p. 524, fig. 12,*e*; p. 528, fig. 14,*d*;
p. 530, fig. 15,*a*; p. 532, fig. 16,*i–k.*

(Merida, coll. Sr. Herman D. Pérez, as of 1955)
Vol. 2,　p. 522, fig. 11,*i.*

(Merida, coll. Sr. Rafael Regil, as of 1941 or
1953)
Vol. 2,　p. 520, fig. 10,*d*; p. 522, fig. 11,*b,c,e,
f,j*; p. 524, fig. 12,*a,c,d,g–i.*

Mexico, A
Vol. 10, p. 416, fig. 17.

Mexico, anonymous collections
Vol. 3,　p. 705, fig. 24; p. 706, fig. 27; p.
760, fig. 43,*d*, top row right.
Vol. 10, p. 306, fig. 12; p. 314, fig. 16; p.
315, fig. 17.
Vol. 11, after p. 800, fig. 2, *Gualterio red-on-
cream, exterior decorated*, top row
left, *Suchil red-on-brown*, second
row next to left, third row, *Vista
paint cloisonné*; before p. 801, fig. 3,
Monochrome wares, top row center,
seventh row right, eighth row right.

Mexico, DP
Vol. 11, p. 629, fig. 6; p. 662, fig. 2,*b–l*; p.
664, fig. 4.

(Mexico, formerly coll. Sr. Guillermo Echániz)
Vol. 10, p. 115, fig. 37; p. 428, fig. 43.

Mexico, coll. Mr. Frederick V. Field
Vol. 3,　p. 760, fig. 43,*c*, left, *f*; p. 762, fig.
47.

Mexico, INAH
Vol. 2,　on loan to Carbondale, UM: p. 538,
fig. 7; p. 539, fig. 9; p. 541, fig. 13;
p. 551, fig. 40.
Vol. 3,　(p. 694, fig. 10; p. 709, fig. 28; p.
712, fig. 31; p. 760, fig. 43,*a*, third
row right).
Vol. 4,　On loan to Washington, USNM: p.
62, fig. 2; p. 65, fig. 3; p. 66, figs.
4, 5; p. 68, fig. 6; p. 69, fig. 7; p. 70,
fig. 8; p. 71, fig. 9; p. 72, figs. 10,
11; p. 73, fig. 12; p. 74, figs. 13, 14;
p. 75, figs. 15, 16; p. 76, figs. 17, 18;

p. 77, fig. 19; p. 78, fig. 20; p. 79,
figs. 21, 22; p. 80, fig. 23; p. 81,
fig. 24; p. 82, fig. 25; p. 83, fig. 26;
p. 84; fig. 27; p. 86, fig. 29. (Page
252, fig. 11,*f–h*; p. 259, fig. 19,*d,f*).

Vol. 11, On loan to Los Angeles, UCLA: p.
704, fig. 5; p. 705, fig. 6,*a–d,k*, all
except top left, *m–q,s,t*; p. 706, fig.
7,*b,c,f,h,i*; p. 707, fig. 9,*d,f*; p. 708,
figs. 10,*a,c–f,* 11; p. 709, fig. 12,*b,e,f.*
On loan to Carbondale, UM: after p.
800, fig. 2, *Vesuvio red-filled engraved, Gualterio red-on-cream, exterior decorated*, six sherds, *Gualterio
red-on-cream, interior decorated, Refugio red-on-brown, Amaro red-on-
cream, Mercado red-on-cream, Michilia red-filled engraved*, top row,
Negative A, Suchil red-on-brown,
second row left, *Canutillo red-filled
engraved, interior decorated, Canutillo red-filled engraved, exterior decorated*, five sherds; before p. 801, fig.
3, *Monochrome wares*, bottom.

Mexico, coll. Sra. Irmgard Weitlaner Johnson
Vol. 10, p. 312, fig. 13.

Mexico, MC
Vol. 10, on loan: p. 208, fig. 1,*b*; p. 209, fig.
2,*b*; p. 215, fig. 5,*d*; p. 226, fig. 18.

Mexico, MNA
Vol. 1,　p. 387, fig. 2; p. 452, fig. 9; p. 470,
fig. 32.
Vol. 2,　p. 239, fig. 2,*e–g*; p. 241, fig. 5,*b,c*;
p. 308, fig. 16; p. 476, fig. 3,*b*; p.
477, fig. 4; p. 489, fig. 12,*c*; p. 493,
fig. 14,*d*; p. 528, fig. 14,*e*; p. 540,
fig. 11; p. 541, fig. 15; p. 546, figs.
(25), 26; p. 548, figs. 32, 33; p. 549,
fig. 35; p. 550, fig. 39; p. 553, fig.
44.
Vol. 3,　p. 564, figs. 10, 12; p. 566, figs. 17,
18; p. 568, fig. 23; p. 582, fig. 1; p.
637, fig. 6, top row left; p. 690,
fig. 6; p. 695, fig. 11; p. 697,
fig. 13; p. 698, fig. 14,*a,b,(c–f),g,
(h–k)*; (p. 700, fig. 17); p. 701,
figs. 18, (19); p. 702, fig. 20; (p. 710,
fig. 29; p. 711, fig. 30); p. 719, fig.
4,*c*; p. 722, fig. 7; p. 725, fig. 12,*a*;
p. 729, fig. 18; p. 734, fig. 25,*a*; p.
735, fig. 26; p. 741, fig. 4; p. 747,
fig. 17; p. 749, fig. 20; p. 750, fig.

23; p. 754, figs. 30, 31; p. 756, figs. 34, 35; p. 757, fig. 36; p. 758; figs. 37, 38, 39, 40; p. 759, fig. 42; p. 760, fig. 43,*a*, top row, second row right, third row left, bottom row left; fig. 43,*b*, next to left, right; fig. 43,*c*, center, right; fig. 43,*d*, bottom row right; fig. 43,*e*, left column bottom, right column bottom; fig. 43,*g*, right; fig. 43,*h*, top row, second row, bottom row right; p. 761, fig. 44; p. 762, fig. 48; p. 763,*a*, middle; p. 764, figs. 51, 52; p. 854, figs. 11,*c,d,f,* 12; p. 855, fig. 13; p. 856, fig. 15; p. 857, figs. 16, 17; p. 860, fig. 22,*(c),e,(g)*; p. 863, fig. 26; p. 872, fig. 1; p. 873, fig. 4; p. 874, fig. 5,*a,(b,c),e*; p. 875, fig. 6,*(a,b),c*; p. 876, fig. 7,*a,(b)*; p. 877, fig. 8; p. 878, fig. 9,*a–c,(d,e),f, g*; p. 879, fig. 10,*a* is on loan to Oaxaca, MR, *(b),c,d,(e,f),g*; p. 880, fig. 11,*(a–c),d*; p. 881, fig. 12,*a–d, (e),f–h*; p. 882, fig. 13; p. 883, fig. 14,*a,(b–d),e*; p. 884, fig. 15,*a,(b),c, (d),e,f,(g,h),i,(j)*; p. 885, fig. 16,*a,b, (c,d),e,f,(g,h),i,j*; p. 886, fig. 17,*(a–c), d–f*; p. 887, fig. 18,*(a,b),c,(d)*; (p. 890, fig. 20); p. 891, fig. 21,*(a–g),h, (i,j)*; p. 892, fig. 22,*a,(b–e),f*; (p. 893, figs. 23, 24; p. 894, fig. 25); p. 897, figs. 1, 2, 3,*b*; p. 898, fig. 4; on loan to Oaxaca, MR, p. 899, fig. 5; p. 900, fig. 6; p. 901, figs. 7, 8,*(a),b,* 9; p. 902, figs. 10, 11, 12; p. 903, figs. 13, *a,b,c* is on loan to Oaxaca, MR, (14); p. 904, fig. 15; p. 905, figs. 16, (17); p. 906, figs. 18, 19; p. 907, fig. 20, top row left, (second and third from left), fourth from left is on loan to Oaxaca, MR, bottom row (left), second from left and extreme right; p. 908, fig. 22; p. 909, figs. 23,*a,(b), c–e,* 24; p. 910, figs. (25), 26, (27), 28; p. 911, fig. 30 all, except middle row third from left is on loan to Oaxaca, MR; p. 912, fig. 31, all except (lower row left); (p. 913, fig. 32); p. 919, fig. 47; p. 927, fig. 60; p. 928, fig. 61; p. 932, fig. 1,*b,c*; p. 934, fig. 5,B, second row right; p. 935, fig. 8,A,G,L–O,(U),Y; p. 939, fig. 15, middle row center, bot-

tom row left; p. 943, fig. 19.

Vol. 4, (p. 255, fig. 14,*a*); p. 256, fig. 16,*b*; p. 279, fig. 3,*a*; p. 289, fig. 17,*d*.

Vol. 6, p. 197, fig. 4; p. 201, fig. 11; (p. 204, fig. 15); p. 205, fig. 17.

Vol. 10, p. 48, fig. 6; p. 95, fig. 2; p. 101, figs. 13, 15; p. 102, fig. 16; p. 104, fig. 19; p. 105, fig. 20; p. 108, fig. 26; p. 111, fig. 31; p. 112, fig. 32; p. 113, fig. 33; p. 114, figs. 35, 36; p. 115, fig. 39; p. 116, figs. 40, 41; p. 117, fig. 42; p. 118, fig. 44; p. 119, figs. 47, 48; p. 120, fig. 49; p. 121, figs. 50, 51; p. 122, figs. 53, 54, 55; p. 123, fig. 56; p. 124, fig. 57; p. 125, fig. 58; p. 126, fig. 59; p. 127, fig. 61; p. 128, fig. 62; p. 129, fig. 63; p. 130, fig. 64; p. 138, fig. 6; p. 142, fig. 12; p. 147, fig. 22; p. 153, fig. 31; p. 160, figs. 1,*(a),b,(c,d), e–h,* (2); p. 161, fig. 3,*a,(b),c,d,(e), f,g*; p. 162, fig. 4; p. 163, fig. 5,*(a,b), c–e,(f,g),h,(i),j,(k–n),o,(p–s)*; p. 164, fig. 6,*a–e,(f)*; p. 165, figs. 7, 8,*a,(b),c*; p. 166, fig. 9; p. 167, fig. 10; p. 168, figs. 11, 12, (left, next to left), third from left, and right; p. 169, fig. 13, A,B,C5,(C9),D1,(D2,K), baby face; p. 170, fig. 14,*a,(b,c),d*; p. 171, figs. 15, 16,*a,b,(c),d*; p. 172, figs. 17, all except (sixth from left, and right), 18; p. 174, fig. 20; p. 175, fig. 21; p. 183, fig. 1; p. 184, fig. 2; p. 191, figs. 6,*a,(b),c,* 7; p. 194, fig. 10,*(a,b),c*; p. 195, fig. 11; p. 208, fig. 1,*b* is on loan to Mexico, MC, *c,d*; p. 209, fig. 2,*b* is on loan to Mexico, MC, *c,d*; p. 215, fig. 5,*a,b,d* is on loan to Mexico, MC; (p. 217, fig. 7); p. 221, fig. 11; p. 224, figs. 15, 16; (p. 225, fig. 17); on loan to Mexico, MC, p. 226, fig. 18, p. 239, fig. 6; p. 241, figs. (9,1), 10,7; p. 305, fig. 10; (p. 306, fig. 11; p. 313, fig. 14; p. 317, fig. 18); p. 325, fig. 1, bottom row right; p. 327, fig. 2; p. 399, fig. 2; p. 414, fig. 12; p. 415, fig. 15; p 416, fig. 18; p. 418, fig. 22; p. 419, fig. 25; p. 423, figs. 32, 33, 34; p. 428, fig. 44.

Vol. 11, (p. 532, fig. 26,*a*); p. 568, fig. 14, *(a),b*; p. 623, fig. 2; p. 668, fig. 6, all except fourth row left; p. 669, figs. 7, all except left column top, 8; p. 670, figs. 9,*a*,(*b*),*c*,(*d*),*e*,(*f*–*h*),*i*,*j*,(*k*),*l*,(*m*,*o*), 10,(*a*–*r*,*t*–*x*),*y*,(*z*,*z'*); p. 671, fig. 11, (*b*–*d*),*e*,(*f*),*g*,(*h*),*i*, (*j*),*k*,(*l*), *m*, *n*,(*o*–*w*); p. 684, fig. 20,*a*; p. 729, fig. 27,(*a*),*b*, (*c*,*h*); (p. 731, fig. 29); p. 758, fig. 3,*a*,(*e*),*h*,*i*; p. 760, fig. 4,(*b*),*d*,*f*,*j*,(*k*); p. 761, fig. 5,(*a*–*c*),*e*,(*g*); p. 762, fig. 6,*c*,(*d*,*g*); p. 763, fig. 7; (p. 764, fig. 8,*c*; p. 765, fig. 9; p. 766, fig. 10,*a*,*b*, *e*,*j*–*l*); after p. 800, fig. 2, *Michilia red-filled engraved*, bottom row (next to left), and third from left, *Suchil red-on-brown*, top row, (second row third from left), bottom row (left) and right, *Canutillo red-filled engraved, exterior decorated*, second row right, bottom row left; before p. 801, fig. 3, *Otinapa red-on-white*, bottom row center and (right), *Morcillo* molcajetes, (left), *Neveria red-on-brown*, (second row center and right), *Amaro red-on-cream*, (top row left), *Mercado red-on-cream*, left column next to top, *Refugio red-on-brown*, bottom, *Monochrome wares*, (top row left and right, second row, third row), fourth row (left), next to left, third from left and (right), fifth row right, (seventh row left, upper and lower, eighth row left).

Mexico, coll. Dr. Kurt Stavenhagen
   Vol. 11, p. 739, fig. 32.
Morelia, MR
   Vol. 11, p. 670, fig. 10,*s*; p. 671, fig. 11,*a*; p. 682, fig. 17; p. 684, fig. 20,*a*,*b*.
Mulege, Baja California, Castaldí coll., care of Sra. Cristina Huñaus
   Vol. 4, p. 46, fig. 5, top row right.

New Haven, YUAG
   Vol. 2, p. 544, fig. 22.
New Orleans, MARI
   Vol. 1, p. 451, fig. 8; p. 454, figs. 14, 15; p. 455, fig. 17.
   Vol. 2, p. 340, fig. 6; p. 545, fig. 24.
   Vol. 3, p. 590, fig. 7,*h*.
   Vol. 4, p. 278, fig. 1,*a*; on loan, p. 282, fig. 10,*g*.
   Vol. 11, p. 596, fig. 2.
New Orleans, coll. Mr. Hugh A. Smith, Jr.
   Vol. 11, p. 566, fig. 11.

New York, AMNH
   Vol. 2, p. 547, fig. 30; p. 551, fig. 41.
   Vol. 3, p. 562, fig. 4; p. 566, fig. 15; p. 570, fig. 30; p. 572, figs. 36, 39; p. 745, figs. 13, on loan, 14; p. 751, fig. 26; p. 752, fig. 27; p. 755, fig. 33; p. 760, fig. 43,*e*, right column top; on loan, p. 764, fig. 53, lower.
   Vol. 4, p. 280, fig. 5,*d*; p. 281, fig. 8,*a*; p. 289, fig. 17,*e*.
   Vol. 10, p. 96, fig. 5; (p. 190, fig. 5); p. 272, fig. 1; after p. 276, fig. 2; p. 280, fig. 3; p. 282, fig. 4; p. 286, fig. 5; p. 290, fig. 6.
   Vol. 11, p. 561, fig. 2; p. 562, fig. 3; on loan, p. 563, fig. 5; on loan, p. 565, fig. 8; p. 566, fig. 10; p. 758, fig. 3,*f*,*g*; p. 760, fig. 4,*a*,(*c*),*e*,*g*,*h*,*i*; p. 761, fig. 5,*d*,*f*,*h*.

New York, BM
   Vol. 2, p. 422, fig. 35; p. 428, fig. 39.
   Vol. 3, on loan, p. 743, fig. 7; on loan, p. 747, fig. 16; on loan, p. 749, fig. 21; p. 949, fig. 1.
New York, coll. Mr. Ernest Erickson
   Vol. 11, on loan to New York, AMNH, p. 563, fig. 5.
New York, coll. Mr. and Mrs. Alastair Bradley Martin
   Vol. 3, on loan to New York, BM, p. 743, fig. 7; on loan to New York, AMNH, p. 745, fig. 14; on loan to New York, BM, p. 747, fig. 16; on loan to New York, AMNH, p. 749, fig. 21; on loan to New York, AMNH, p. 764, fig. 53, lower.
New York, MAI
   Vol. 2, p. 132, fig. 18,*e*,*f*; p. 547, fig. 29.
   Vol. 3, p. 570, fig. 31.
   Vol. 4, p. 186, fig. 4,*i*; (p. 187, fig. 5,*b*,*d*; p. 190, fig. 8; p. 191, fig. 9,*c*,*d*; p. 192, fig. 11); p. 256, fig. 15,*a*,*b*,*d*; p. 262, fig. 25,*a*.
   Vol. 11, p. 552, fig. 4; p. 564, fig. 6; p. 565, fig. 9.
New York, MMA
   Vol. 2, p. 550, fig. 37.
   Vol. 3, p. 572, fig. 38.
New York, MPA
   Vol. 2, p. 545, fig. 23.
   Vol. 3, p. 748, fig. 19; p. 760, fig. 43,*d*,

left, and right; p. 334, fig. 1,*b,d,g,h, j,k,o*; p. 407, fig. 7.
Vol. 11, p. 500, fig. 8.

St. Louis, coll. Mr. Morton D. May
Vol. 11, p. 741, fig. 35,*a.*
(El Salvador, coll. Sr. Inocente Aguirre, as of 1944)
Vol. 4, p. 144, fig. 8,*a,c,h,i,l–n*; p. 149, fig. 11,*b,c,f–j*; p. 150, fig. 12,*b–d,m,p.*
(El Salvador, coll. Anliker, as of 1944)
Vol. 4, p. 144, fig. 8,*b,k.*
El Salvador, coll. Sra. Maria de Baratta
Vol. 4, p. 142, fig. 7,*i.*
El Salvador, coll. Sr. Francisco Dueñas
Vol. 4, p. 137, fig. 5,*d–f.*
El Salvador, coll. Sr. M. A. Gallardo
Vol. 4, p. 142, fig. 7,*d.*
(El Salvador, coll. Guerrera, as of 1944)
Vol. 4, p. 149, fig. 11,*a.*
(El Salvador, coll. Matheis, as of 1944)
Vol. 4, p. 140, fig. 6,*e,f*; p. 142, fig. 7,*c,e–g.*
(El Salvador, coll. Melara, as of 1944)
Vol. 4, p. 144, fig. 8,*j*; p. 149, fig. 11,*e*; p. 150, fig. 12,*f.*
(El Salvador, coll. Montalbo, as of 1944)
Vol. 4, p. 150, fig. 12,*o.*
El Salvador, coll. Sra. Carolina Salazar de Feller
Vol. 4, p. 142, fig. 7,*a,b.*
(El Salvador, coll. Valiente, as of 1944)
Vol. 4, p. 140, fig. 6,*g.*
San Andres Tuxtla Plaza
Vol. 3, p. 723, fig. 8,*a.*
San Diego, MM
Vol. 2, p. 381, fig. 3.
San Marino, Calif., coll. Mr. and Mrs. Donald Jones
Vol. 11, p. 740, fig. 34,*a.*
San Martin Huamelulpan
Vol. 3, p. 853, fig. 9.
(San Salvador, coll. Sr. Justo Armas, as of 1943)
Vol. 3, p. 571, fig. 34.
San Salvador, coll. Dr. José Cepeda
Vol. 4, p. 148, fig. 10,*b.*
San Salvador, coll. El Club Salvadoreño
Vol. 4, p. 137, fig. 5,*a–c.*
San Salvador, MNDJG
Vol. 4, p. 140, fig. 6,*a–d*; p. 142, fig. 7,*j,k*; p. 286, fig. 14,*c.*
San Salvador, coll. Sr. Walter Soundy

Vol. 4, p. 144, fig. 8,*d–f,(g),o*; p. 149, fig. 11,*d*; p. 150, fig. 12,*a,e,g–l,n,q.*
Santa Fe, MNM
Vol. 2, p. 132, fig. 18,*b.*
Santiago Tuxtla Plaza
Vol. 3, p. 732, fig. 22,*a*; p. 733, fig. 23; p. 737, fig. 29, lower.
Stockholm, EM
Vol. 10, p. 191, fig. 6,*a*; p. 238, fig. 5.
Stuttgart, WL
Vol. 10, p. 429, fig. 46.

Tajin, MZA
Vol. 11, p. 512, fig. 3; p. 534, fig. 28.
(Taxco, coll. Mr. William Spratling, as of 1946)
Vol. 3, p. 754, fig. 29.
Tepic, MR
Vol. 11, p. 718, fig. 19.
Tikal, MSGM
Vol. 2, p. 463, fig. 1, entire, but *a, d*, and *g* are on loan to Guatemala, MNAE; p. 472, fig. 1; p. 474, fig. 2; p. 542, fig. 17.
Vol. 3, p. 567, fig. 19; p. 633, fig. 1.
Tres Zapotes Plaza
Vol. 3, p. 726, fig. 13,*a*; p. 732, fig. 22,*b.*
Tucson, ASM
Vol. 4, p. 34, fig. 4.
Tula, MZA
Vol. 3, p. 910, fig. 29.
Vol. 10, p. 108, fig. 27; p. 110, figs. 29, 30; p. 241, figs. 9, 2–6, 10,6.
Tuxtla Gutierrez, MR
Vol. 2, p. 231, fig. 24.
Tuxtla Gutierrez, MR, NWAF coll.
Vol. 2, p. 205, fig. 6; p. 207, fig. 7; p. 209, fig. 8; p. 211, fig. 9; p. 212, fig. 10; p. 213, fig. 11, all except left side, third row; p. 214, fig. 12, top row left and next to left, second row third from left, bottom row next to left, fourth from left and right, and upper right; p. 216, fig. 13,*a*, bottom row third from left and right, *b*, bottom row, *c*, next to left and right, *d,e*; p. 220, fig. 17,*b*, top row left and third from left, bottom row right, *c*, right column; p. 224, fig. 19, all except *b*; p. 225, fig. 20; p. 226, fig. 21; p. 227, fig. 22; p. 228, fig. 23,*c*, bottom, *d*, bottom row right, upper.

271

Vol. 4,   p. 247, fig. 3,*e*.

(Unknown, Anderson coll. as of 1926)
 Vol. 4,   p. 188, fig. 6,*e–h*.
(Unknown, coll. John Wise)
 Vol. 3,   p. 760, fig. 43,*g*, center.

Vienna, MV
 Vol. 3,   p. 916, fig. 40,*b*; p. 953, fig. 5,*b*.
 Vol. 10, p. 127, fig. 60.
 Vol. 11, p. 568, fig. 14,*c*.
Vienna, NB
 Vol. 10, p. 78, fig. 31, top row left, third
       from left and right, middle row left,
       bottom row next to left and right.
Villahermosa, MR
 Vol. 3,   p. 719, fig. 4,*a*.
Villahermosa, PMLV
 Vol. 1,   p. 467, figs. 27, 28.
 Vol. 3,   p. 687, fig. 3; p. 688, fig. 4; p. 689,
       fig. 5; p. 690, fig. 7; p. 717, fig. 1; p.
       725, fig. 12,*c*; p. 726, figs. 13,*b*, 14;
       p. 731, fig. 20; p. 732, fig. 21,*a*; p.
       736, fig. 28; p. 760, fig. 43,*d*, middle
       row right, *e*, right column next to
       top, *h*, bottom row left; p. 761, fig.
       45; p. 763, fig. 49, second, third, and
       fourth from left.

Washington, DO
 Vol. 1,   p. 450, fig. 5.
 Vol. 3,   p. 742, fig. 6; p. 743, figs. 8, 9; p.
       744, fig. 11; p. 746, fig. 15; p. 750,
       fig. 24; p. 751, fig. 25; p. 754, fig.
       32; p. 760, fig. 43,*a*, bottom row
       right; p. 763, fig. 50,*a*, bottom left.
 Vol. 10, p. 95, fig. 3.
 Vol. 11, p. 564, fig. 7; p. 567, fig. 12; p. 569,
       fig. 15.
Washington, NGS
 Vol. 2,   p. 303, fig. 10.

Washington, USNM
 Vol. 2,   p. 555, fig. 49.
 Vol. 3,   p. 576, fig. 47; p. 607, fig. 3; (p.
       691, fig. 8, p. 692, fig. 9); p. 699,
       fig. 15; p. 748, fig. 18; p. 753, fig.
       28; p. 760, fig. 43,*d*, bottom row
       left, *e*, left column middle, *g*, left;
       p. 763, fig. 49, seventh and eighth
       from left; p. 854, fig. 11,*b*; p. 916,
       fig. 41.
 Vol. 4,   p. 48, fig. 9.   On loan: p. 62, fig. 2;
       p. 65, fig. 3; p. 66, figs. 4, 5; p. 68,
       fig. 6; p. 69, fig. 7; p. 70, fig. 8; p.
       71, fig. 9; p. 72, figs. 10, 11; p. 73,
       fig. 12; p. 74, figs. 13, 14; p. 75,
       figs. 15, 16; p. 76, figs. 17, 18; p.
       77, fig. 19; p. 78, fig. 20; p. 79, figs.
       21, 22; p. 80, fig. 23; p. 81, fig. 24;
       p. 82, fig. 25; p. 83, fig. 26; p. 84,
       fig. 27; p. 86, fig. 29.   Page 204, fig.
       20, *a,b*; p. 206, fig. 21,*a–d*; p. 246,
       fig. 2,*a–c*; p. 247, fig. 3,*a*; p. 249, fig.
       4,*c–f*; p. 251, figs. 6,*a–d*, 7,*a–f*, 8,
       a–c; p. 252, figs. 9,*a–c*, 10,*a,b*; p.
       254, fig. 13,*c*; p. 255, fig. 14,*b*; p.
       257, fig. 17,*c–g*; p. 259, fig. 19,*a,b*;
       p. 260, fig. 20; p. 263, fig. 26.

Zaachila Plaza
 Vol. 3,   p. 857, fig. 18; p. 860, fig. 22,*b*; (p.
       935, fig. 8,H).
Zaculeu, MA
 Vol. 2,   p. 112, fig. 10,*d–f*; p. 114, fig. 11,*f*;
       p. 116, fig. 12,*h*; p. 124, fig. 16,*c*;
       p. 138, fig. 20,*a,b*; p. 140, fig. 21,*i*;
       p. 158, figs. 4, 5; p. 159, fig. 6; p.
       164, fig. 1; p. 166, fig. 3,*b,c*; p. 173,
       fig. 13; p. 175, fig. 16.
 Vol. 3,   p. 564, fig. 13; p. 566, fig. 16; p.
       568, fig. 27; p. 577, fig. 48.

3. Location of Artifacts Illustrated, in the Order of Their Appearance

Volume 3

page *figure*

row left; v. 3, p. 854, fig. 11,*d;* v. 3, p. 932, fig. 1,*b.*

760 43,*c*, left. Mexico, coll. Mr. Frederick V. Field. Same, whole: v. 3, p. 762, fig. 47. Same: v. 3, p. 760, fig. 43,*f.*

760 43,*c*, center. Mexico, MNA, 13-240, inv. 7468. L 13.

760 43,*c*, right. Mexico, MNA, 13-426, inv. 9623. L 14. Same, whole: v. 3, p. 762, fig. 48. Same: v. 3, p. 760, fig. 43,*d*, bottom row right.

760 43,*d*, top row right. (Mexico, anonymous coll.).

760 43,*d*, bottom row left. Washington, USNM, 231,107. H 21. Same, whole: v. 3, p. 748, fig. 18. Same: v. 3, p. 760, fig. 43,*e*, left column middle, *g*, left; v. 3, p. 763, fig. 49, seventh and eighth from left.

760 43,*d*, middle row center. New York, MPA, 56.52. L 36.5. Same, whole: v. 3, p. 748, fig. 19. Same: v. 3, p. 760, fig. 43,*e*, right column next to bottom.

760 43,*d*, bottom row right. Mexico, MNA, 13-426, inv. 9623. L 14. Same, whole: v. 3, p. 762, fig. 48. Same: v. 3, p. 760, fig. 43,*c*, right.

760 43,*d*, middle row right. Villahermosa, PMLV, uncat., position 5. H 160. Same, whole: v. 3, p. 731, fig. 20,*b.* Same: v. 3, p. 760, fig. 43,*e*, right column next to top.

760 43,*e*, left column middle. Washington, USNM, 231,107. L 21. Same, whole: v. 3, p. 748, fig. 18. Same: v. 3, p. 760, fig. 43,*d*, bottom row left, *g*, left; v. 3, p. 763, fig. 48, seventh and eighth from left.

760 43,*e*, left column bottom. Mexico, MNA, 13-451, inv. 3070. L 15.

760 43,*e*, right column top. New York, AMNH, 30.1-2168. H 8.7. Same: v. 3, p. 745, fig. 13.

760 43,*e*, right column next to top. Villahermosa, PMLV, uncat., position 5. H 160. Same, whole: v. 3, p. 731, fig. 20,*b.* Same: v. 3, p. 760, fig. 43,*d*, middle row right.

760 43,*e*, right column next to bottom. New

page *figure*

York, MPA, 56.52. L 36.5. Same, whole: v. 3, p. 748, fig. 19. Same: v. 3, p. 760, fig. 43,*d*, middle row center.

760 43,*e*, right column bottom. Mexico, MNA, 13-599, inv. 6525. H 95. La Venta, Monument 19.

760 43,*f.* Mexico, coll. Mr. Frederick V. Field. H 8.2. Same, whole: v. 3, p. 762, fig. 47. Same: v. 3, p. 760, fig. 43,*c*, left.

760 43,*g*, left. Washington, USNM, 231,107. H 21. Same, whole: v. 3, p. 748, fig. 18. Same: v. 3, p. 760, fig. 43,*d*, bottom row left, *e*, left column middle; v. 3, p. 763, fig. 49, seventh and eighth from left.

760 43,*g*, center. (Location unknown, coll. John Wise). H 11. Design incised on a greenstone tubular object shaped like a femur bone.

760 43,*g*, right. Mexico, MNA, 13-406, inv. 8131. L 12. Same: v. 3, p. 758, fig. 38.

760 43,*h*, top row left. Mexico, MNA, 13-441, inv. 9674. L 30.8. Same, whole: v. 3, p. 747, fig. 17. Same: v. 3, p. 760, fig. 43,*a*, top row left, *b*, right; v. 3, p. 854, fig. 11,*d;* v. 3, p. 932, fig. 1,*b.*

760 43,*h*, top row right. Mexico, MNA, 13-787, inv. 320. H 74.5. Same: v. 3, p. 695, fig. 11; v. 3, p. 725, fig 12,*a;* v. 3, p. 759, fig. 42.

760 43,*h*, second row left. Mexico, MNA, 6-6228, inv. 9654. H 10.3. Same: v. 3, p. 897, fig. 2.

760 43,*h*, second row right. Mexico, MNA, 13-784, no inv. H 331. Same, whole: v. 3, p. 729, fig. 18,*b.* Same: v. 3, p. 854, fig. 11,*f.*

760 43,*h*, bottom row left. Villahermosa, PMLV, uncat., position 6 or 19. L 760. Same: v. 3, p. 689, fig. 5; v. 3, p. 761, fig. 45.

760 43,*h*, bottom row right. Mexico, MNA, 4-1900, inv. 327. H 182. Same: v. 3, p. 729, fig. 18,*a.*

761 44. Mexico, MNA, 13-589, inv. 3069. L 14.7.

761 45. Villahermosa, PMLV, uncat., posi-

VOLUME 4

Volume 6

Volume 10

page *figure*

106 24. *In situ.* H 460. Same: v. 10, p. 48, fig. 6; v. 10, p. 208, fig. 1,*d;* v. 10, p. 209, fig. 2,*d.*

108 25. Original *in situ.* H 54.

108 26. Mexico, MNA, 15-189, inv. 81783. L 89.

108 27. Tula, MZA, uncat. H 185.

109 28. *In situ.* H 81.

110 29. Tula, MZA, uncat. H 88.

110 30. Tula, MZA, uncat. H 93.

111 31,*a.* Mexico, MNA, 15-127, inv. 81768. H 115.

111 31,*b.* Mexico, MNA, 11-3474, inv. 48555. H 116.

112 32. Mexico, MNA, 11-3289, inv. 81556. W 40.

113 33. Mexico, MNA, 11-2917, inv. 1104. H c. 50.

113 34. Berlin, MV, IV Ca 4401. H 30.5.

114 35. Mexico, MNA, 11-3182, inv. 46614. H 31.

114 36. Mexico, MNA, 11-3511, inv. 81663. D 82.

115 37. (Mexico, formerly coll. Sr. Guillermo Echániz). Same: v. 10, p. 428, fig. 43.

115 38. Chicago, FMNH, 94902. H 23.

115 39. Mexico, MNA, 11-3225, inv. 81549. H 93.

116 40. Mexico, MNA, 24-1198, inv. 46668. H 74.

116 41. Mexico, MNA, 11-3055, inv. 1097. H 19.

117 42. Mexico, MNA, 11-3191, inv. 1137. H 40.

117 43. Paris, MH, 87.159.193. H 20. Coll. Franck.

118 44. Mexico, MNA, 11-3361, inv. 81671. L 48.

118 45. Paris, MH, 87.155.17. L 59. Coll. Latour-Allard.

118 46. London, BM, 8624. D 27.9.

119 47. Mexico, MNA, 11-2765, no inv. L 30.

119 48. Mexico, MNA, 11-2774, inv. 9681. W 22.5.

120 49. Mexico, MNA, 11-3276, inv. 81561. H 115.

121 50. Mexico, MNA, 11-3285, inv. 1143. H 215.

page *figure*

121 51. Mexico, MNA, 11-3003, inv. 1160. H 90.

121 52. *In situ.*

122 53. Mexico, MNA, 11-3331, inv. 81270. L 60.

122 54. Mexico, MNA, 11-2932, inv. 78329. L 72.

122 55. Mexico, MNA, 11-3224, inv. 81548. H 123.

123 56. Mexico, MNA, 11-3293, inv. 81562. H 58.

124 57. Mexico, MNA, 11-3202, inv. 1155. H 65.

125 58. Mexico, MNA, 11-3425, inv. 1162. D 265. Same: v. 10, p. 327, fig. 2.

126 59. Mexico, MNA, 11-3290, inv. 1123. D 360.

127 60. Vienna, MV, inv. 59896. D 15.5.

127 61. Mexico, MNA, 11-3311, inv. 1159. D 92.

128 62. Mexico, MNA, 11-3385, inv. 46699. H 72.

129 63. Mexico, MNA, 24-1243 (formerly -1359), inv. 46713. H 79.

130 64. Mexico, MNA, 11-3203, inv. 1085. H 90.

131 65. *In situ.*

138 6. Mexico, MNA, uncat., no inv. Same: v. 10, p. 215, fig. 5,*a,b.*

141 10. Same: v. 4, p. 281, fig. 9,*b.*

142 12. Mexico, MNA, uncat., no inv. Same: v. 10, p. 224, figs. 15, 16.

143 13. Same: v. 10, p. 223, fig. 14.

147 22. Mexico, MNA, uncat., no inv.

151 28. Original altars *in situ.*

153 31. Box: Mexico, MNA, 11-2909, inv. 2801. W 24.

155 34. Original mural *in situ.*

160 1,*a.* (Mexico, MNA).

160 1,*b.* Mexico, MNA, 1-2855, inv. 1633. H 10.8.

160 1,*c,d.* (Mexico, MNA).

160 1,*e.* Mexico, MNA, 1-2854, inv. 1639. H 19.3.

160 1,*f.* Mexico, MNA, 1-1209, inv. 42098. Tlapacoya.

160 1,*g.* Mexico, MNA, 1-1607, inv. 42496. H 8.7. White.

160 1,*h.* Mexico, MNA, 1-2856, inv. 1635. H 13.

314

VOLUME 11

321

page figure
after

800 2. *Michilia red-filled engraved.* Top row, 4 sherds: Carbondale, UM. On loan from INAH. Bottom row left: (Durango, coll. Sr. Federico Schroeder, as of 1969). D 11.5. Bottom row next to left: (Mexico, MNA). D 11.5. Bottom row third from left: Mexico, MNA, 12-1040, no inv. D 10.1. Bottom row right: (Durango, coll. Sr. Federico Schroeder, as of 1969). D 9.7.

after

800 2. *Negative A.* Four sherds: Carbondale, UM. On loan from INAH.

after

800 2. *Suchil red-on-brown.* Top row left: Mexico, MNA, 12-1077, no inv. D 17.3. Top row center: Mexico, MNA, 12-1043, no inv. D 19.7. Top row right: Mexico, MNA, 12-1072, no inv. D 22. Second row left: Carbondale, UM. H 8.8. On loan from INAH. Second row next to left: Mexico, anonymous coll. Second row third from left: (Mexico, MNA). D 17.8. Third row left: Mexico, anonymous coll. H 11.9. Third row center: Mexico, anonymous coll. Third row right: Mexico, anonymous coll. Bottom row left: (Mexico, MNA). D 22. Bottom row right: Mexico, MNA, 12-1085, no inv. D 21.9.

after

800 2. *Vista paint cloisonné.* Three vessels: Mexico, anonymous coll.

after

800 2. *Canutillo red-filled engraved, interior decorated.* Bottom: Carbondale, UM. D 36.1. Reconstruction from two sherds. On loan from INAH. Remainder, 6 sherds: Carbondale, UM. On loan from INAH.

after

800 2. *Canutillo red-filled engraved, exterior decorated.* Second row right: Mexico, MNA, 12-1044, no inv.

page figure

D 15.5. Now restored. Bottom row left: Mexico, MNA, 12-1042, no inv. D 15.4. Remainder, 5 sherds: Carbondale, UM. On loan from INAH.

before

801 3. *Nayar white-on-red.* Top row left: (Durango, coll. Sr. Federico Schroeder, as of 1969). H 13.5. Top row center: (Durango, coll. Sr. Frederico Schroeder, as of 1969). H 15.5. Top row right: (Durango, coll. Sr. Frederico Schroeder, as of 1969). H 12.8. Bottom row left: (Durango, coll. Sr. Federico Schroeder, as of 1969). H 16.7. Bottom row center: (Durango, coll. Sr. Federico Schroeder, as of 1969). H 15.4. Bottom row right: (Durango, coll. Sr. Federico Schroeder, as of 1969). H 10.

before

801 3. *Madero fluted ware.* Left: (Durango, coll. Sr. Federico Schroeder, as of 1969). H 9.1. Right: (Durango, coll. Sr. Federico Schroeder, as of 1969). D c. 17.5.

before

801 3. *Canatlan red band ware.* (Durango, coll. Sr. Federico Schroeder, as of 1969). H 31.6.

before

801 3. *Otinapa red-on-white.* Top row left: (Durango, coll. Sr. Federico Schroeder, as of 1969). H 13.3. Top row next to left: (Durango, coll. Sr. Federico Schroeder, as of 1969). H 14. Top row third from left: (Durango, coll. Sr. Federico Schroeder, as of 1969). H 13.5. Top row right: (Durango, coll. Sr. Federico Schroeder, as of 1969). H 10.6. Bottom row left: (Durango, coll. Sr. Federico Schroeder, as of 1969). H 18.7. Bottom row center: Mexico, MNA, 12-532, inv. 10181. D 18.5. Bottom row right: (Mexico, MNA, or Durango, coll. Sr. Federico Schroeder, as of 1969). H 23.3.

page figure

before
801 3. *Morcillo molcajetes.* Left: (Mexico, MNA). H 7.7. Right: Carbondale, UM, 54.49/169. D 20.5.

before
801 3. *Lolandis red rim ware.* (Durango, coll. Sr. Federico Schroeder, as of 1969). D 26.6.

before
801 3. *Neveria red-on-brown.* Top: (Durango, coll. Sr. Federico Schroeder, as of 1969). H 22.5. Same: this group, bottom row right. Second row left: (Durango, coll. Sr. Federico Schroeder, as of 1969). H 20.5. Second row center: (Mexico, MNA). H 12.5. Refugio red-on-brown. Second row right: (Mexico, MNA). H 8.5. Bottom row left: (Durango, coll. Sr. Federico Schroeder, as of 1969). H 20.5. Bottom row right: (Durango, coll. Sr. Federico Schroeder, as of 1969). H 22.5. Same: this group, top.

before
801 3. *Amaro red on cream.* Top left: (Mexico, MNA). D 16.3. Top right. (Durango, coll. Sr. Federico Schroeder, as of 1969). D 17. Second row left: (Durango, coll. Sr. Federico Schroeder, as of 1969). D 16.6. Second row next to left: (Durango, coll. Sr. Federico Schroeder, as of 1969). D 18.6. Bottom row left: (Durango, coll. Sr. Federico Schroeder, as of 1969). D 13. Bottom row next to left: (Durango, coll. Sr. Federico Schroeder, as of 1969). D 14. Bottom row right: (Durango, coll. Sr. Federico Schroeder, as of 1969).

before
801 3. *Mercado red-on-cream.* Top row left: (Durango, coll. Sr. Federico Schroeder, as of 1969). D 17.5. Top row center: (Durango, coll. Sr. Federico Schroeder, as of 1969). H 3.6. Top row right: (Durango, coll. Sr. Federico Schroeder, as of 1969). D 9.5. Left column next

to top: Mexico, MNA, 12-1037, no inv. D 19.8. Left column third from top: (Durango, coll. Sr. Federico Schroeder, as of 1969). H 5.6. Left column bottom: (Durango, coll. Sr. Federico Schroeder, as of 1969). H 8.2. Right column next to top: (Durango, coll. Sr. Federico Schroeder, as of 1969). H 9.2. Right column bottom: (Durango, coll. Sr. Federico Schroeder, as of 1969). H 8.5.

before
801 3. *Refugio red-on-brown.* Top row left: (Durango, coll. Sr. Federico Schroeder, as of 1969). H 10.6. Mercado red-on-cream. Top row center: (Durango, coll. Sr. Federico Schroeder, as of 1969). H 6.3. Top row right: (Durango, coll. Sr. Federico Schroeder, as of 1969). H 8.1. Bottom: Mexico, MNA, 12-531, inv. 10179. D 17.7.

before
801 3. *El Conejo red-filled engraved.* (Durango, coll. Sr. Federico Schroeder, as of 1969). H 11.

before
801 3. *Monochromo wares.* Top row left: (Mexico, MNA). H 6.5. Top row center: Mexico, anonymous coll. H 9.4. Top row right: (Mexico, MNA). H 11.2. Second row left: (Mexico, MNA). H 13.9. Second row center: (Mexico, MNA). H 10.1. Second row right: (Mexico, MNA). D c. 14.8. Polished red ware. Third row: (Mexico, MNA). D 17.2. Fourth row left: (Mexico, MNA). H 14.5. Fourth row next to left: Mexico, MNA, 12-1084, no inv. H 6.8. Fourth row third from left: Mexico, MNA, 12-1036, no inv. H 12.7. Fourth row right: (Mexico, MNA). D 14.7. Fifth row left: (Durango, coll. Sr. Federico Schroeder, as of 1969). H 10.5. Fifth row right: Mexico, MNA, 12-1088, no inv. H 21.4. Sixth row: (Durango, coll. Sr. Federico

323

page *figure*

Schroeder, as of 1969). H 10.5.
Seventh row left, upper: (Mexico,
MNA). H 7.5. Seventh row left,
lower: (Mexico, MNA). H c.
10.2. Seventh row right: Mexico,
anonymous coll. H 24.8. Eighth

page *figure*

row, left: (Mexico, MNA). H c.
16.2. Eighth row right: Mexico,
anonymous coll. D c. 13.8. Bottom: Carbondale, UM. On loan
from INAH.